Illustrated Dictionary
of Practical Pottery

Illustrated Dictionary of Practical Pottery

Robert Fournier

A & C Black • London
Krause Publications • Wisconsin

Third edition 1992
Fourth edition 2000
A & C Black (Publishers) Limited
35 Bedford Row, London WC1 R 4JH

ISBN 0 7136 4957 7

First edition 1973, Second edition (paperback) 1977
Published by Van Nostrand Reinhold Inc.

A CIP catalogue record for this book is available from the
British Library and the US Library of Congress.

Published simultaneously in the USA by
Krause Publications
700 East State Street, Iola, W1 54990–0001

ISBN 0 87341 905 7

Designed by Jo Tapper
Photographs by John Anderson, Robert Fournier and others
Diagrams by Sheila Fournier

Cover image: Pillow, by Robert Sanderson. Photograph by
John McKenzie.

Printed and bound in Great Britain by Hillman Printers Ltd.,
Frome, Somerset.

Acknowledgments

Without John Anderson's fine series of action photographs
together with other essential illustrations, and my wife Sheila's
diagrams, this book would be a shadow of its present self; my
sincerest thanks are offered to them.

Other contributors to the illustrations include: Ron Sloman, of
the St. James Gallery, Bath (including the dramatic 'porcelain'
and charming 'flute'); Reg Singh, Beaux Arts, Bath; and the
potters Jack Doherty, Jim Robison, Monica Young, Joan
Hepworth, Mike Dodd, Eric Mellon, Dave Roberts, Maggie
Berkowitz, Joanna Constantinidis, Barbara Lock, John Leach,
Rosemary Cochrane, Owen Rye, Greg Daly, John Malthy,
Kevin White, Michael Casson, and many more. William Hunt,
Editor of *Ceramics Monthly* (U.S.), and Janet Mansfield, Editor
of *Ceramic Art & Perception* (Australia) gathered welcome
examples of their country's work.

Many others have also helped; Peter Smith gave generously
from his recipes and research; Frank Hamer's 'Dictionary' has
been a valuable authority; John May put me right on computers; Leslie Savage on electrical matters, and the Editors of
Ceramic Review, Eileen Lewenstein and Emmanuel Cooper,
have contributed not only material from the magazine but also
pictures from their archives. Steve Mills, of Bath Pottery
Supplies, has given useful advice, as has John Porter.

The various suppliers listed sent catalogs and other useful
material.

Mick Casson, Alan Caiger-Smith and other potters have given
time and expertise, while valuable information has been
derived from writings by Ken Clark, Ivan England, Ben
Cooper, Jane Lord, A Lewis-Evans, Richard Behrens, and many
others. Maurice Ball meticulously corrected the revised edition
of 1977 (he is not responsible for any errors which may have
crept in since!).

My gratitude to them all.

INTRODUCTION

This dictionary collects into an easily available form much of the practical information now open to craft potters. It stays strictly within the scope of its title: aesthetics are considered only where inseparable from discussion of the entry, while historical references are kept to a minimum. Similarly industrial or archaic terms have generally been omitted, entertaining though these often are. All the material will, it is hoped, be of practical use to potters: student, amateur and professional alike.

Materials and equipment which you may encounter in merchants' catalogues have been covered together with terms used in books on ceramics. Some duplication of information has been inevitable in order to avoid constant cross-reference by readers. Charts have been compiled where necessary to make facts as accessible as possible. Sources are mentioned where appropriate and a bibliography will be found at the end of the book.

The factual nature of the book is balanced by the illustrations of completed work which help to keep the craftsman's ultimate goal in sight — the production of good and individual pots. The author's other two dictionaries (of form and decoration) deal with the historical and aesthetic aspects of ceramics and include more extensive discussions of specialized techniques than is possible in this book.

REVISED EDITION, 2000

Many entries have been updated and expanded and new ones added. Over one hundred of the illustrations have now been replaced. While the basic information is timeless there has obviously been technological progress since the last edition which needs to be incorporated in the entries. Certain health aspects have also been stressed.

The name and initials mentioned in the text (e.g. Cardew, or Rhodes CGP) are authors and abbreviated bibliographic references. The initials are given where the same author has several books listed. The full titles will be found in the Bibliography at the end of the book.

FIVE NOTES

Analyses. The analyses by weight included in this dictionary have been arranged with the various oxides in their $RO: R_2O_3: RO_2$ columns, i.e. in a similar way to glaze formulas. It is hoped that this will give potters a more immediate picture of the material than the normal listing which places the higher percentage first. It has been carefully stated in each case that the analysis is by weight, not molecular parts as would be represented in a formula.

Unless otherwise specified, gallons are given as UK gallons.

Italicization. The words printed in italics indicate a reference to another entry which may help to clarify the definition or the discussion. Minerals and oxides have not, in general, been treated in this way, it being understood that each has its own entry to which reference can be made if required.

Atomic and Molecular Weight. The number immediately following any element, oxide or mineral mentioned in the dictionary indicates the atomic or molecular weight of that material to the nearest whole number or one decimal point.

Spelling. The earlier issues of the dictionary used a mixture of British and American spellings. In this edition American spellings have been used throughout.

Temperature. Wherever possible, temperatures have been given in both °C and °F. Occasionally, however, this has not been possible. Please see *temperature degree* for Fahrenheit conversions where necessary.

Abrasive

A hard, sharp material used for cutting, grinding or polishing. The usual abrasives for pottery are *silicon carbide* and *fused alumina*, the latter avoiding carbide contamination of the surface of biscuit which can result from the use of carborundum and cause scum in the subsequent glaze firing. The Cintride range of abrasive blocks are useful although the base metal to which the tungsten fragments are attached is too soft; the file with fine and coarse faces is preferable. A small, high-speed electric grinding wheel can be used on minor glaze faults. Always wear a mask and goggles when using a grinding wheel. There is a wide range of wheel qualities and bonding materials which are listed in Dodd. See also *grinding wheel* for some details.

Dry clay or soft biscuit will respond to medium glass paper, the several grades of emery paper (or, better still, emery cloth which can be washed), a 'rubber scrubber' (Briar Wheels) for *greenware*, foam porcelain sanders (Kemper), or an abrasive pad as made for sanding machines. A biscuit file is listed by Briar Wheels and a 'greenware file' by Georgies. Washable sheet cleaners are available in grit sizes from 150 (coarse) to 600 (fine) which 'clean without leaving scratches', and flexible sanders in 150–400 grades (Kemper).

To level unstable pots, clip the abrasive sheet to a whirler or wheel-head and rotate it while holding the piece firmly in the center. Georgies list an abrasive disc with a peel-off adhesive backing which can be fastened to a circular wheel bat.

David Leach uses car engine grinding-in paste (a water-bound corundum) for setting wobbly lids into the flanges of teapots, etc. It has a high cutting power and will deal with stoneware and porcelain. It is possible to make your own abrasive blocks by wiping away the softer clay from a block of finely grogged clay leaving the grog proud. Highly fired this is not as effective as *carborundum* but does not have caborundum's disadvantages.

A pot which needs a lot of grinding is usually a 'second', anyhow. An exception must be made for *crystalline glazes* which often necessarily involve extensive grinding. Abrasive blocks of calcined alumina are available for cleaning shelves, sharpening tools, etc.

Absolute temperature

A scale on which 'absolute zero' (–273°C/–523°F) becomes 0° Kelvin, symbol K. The boiling point of water (100°C/212°F) thus equates with 373°K. It is used to determine gas expansion, essential data in kiln design, and approximate *sintering* temperatures (see also *temperature conversion table*).

Absorption

The taking up of liquid into the pores of a pot. The water absorption of a ceramic material is an indication of its degree of *vitrification*. It is expressed as a percentage of the weight of the dry material.

If a pot weighing 1 kg/2.2 lb absorbs 150 g/5.3 oz of water it has an absorption of

$$\frac{150}{1000} \times \frac{100}{1} = 15\%$$

A rough test is to weigh a pot after thoroughly drying it in an oven, then to immerse it in water (or fill with water for a rough test of body vitrification or possible glaze *crazing*) for twelve hours and reweigh it. Use the equation above to work out the absorption rate. Absorption can also refer to the taking up of gases, light, or heat. (See also *adsorption, porosity*.)

Accessory mineral

A mineral to be found in small quantities in a clay or rock, e.g. mica is usually present in china clay.

Acid, acidic oxides, acid radical

Among potters, the term 'acid' is used rather loosely. Strictly speaking an acid is a compound containing hydrogen which will combine with a base to form a *salt* releasing the hydrogen in the form of water (H_2O) and rendering each material chemically neutral.

Example: $HCl + NaOH = NaCl + H_2O$.

An acidic substance without acidic hydrogen is known as an acid radical. Where an acid contains oxygen, the abstraction of water H_2O will leave the acidic oxide, and it is this acid oxide which is referred to when 'acid' is mentioned in this book. For instance, silica SiO_2, and not the true silicic acid H_2SiO_3, is listed under the heading 'acid' in glaze formulas. Most pottery 'acids' are acid radicals.

It is useful to know to which main chemical group an oxide belongs, for this will give some indication of its behavior in the kiln. The principal acid oxides used in pottery are silica and the oxides of boron, antimony, tin, chromium, titanium and zircon. Two others of less importance are phosphorus and germanium which, together with the first three listed above, act as *glass formers*. In general, acids are refractory: *boric oxide* is an exception. (See also *chemistry of pottery*.)

The main acidic oxides (acid radicals) used in pottery.

oxide	chemical formula	main use
Antimony oxide	Sb_2O_3	Yellow pigment with lead
Boric oxide	B_2O_3	Glass former/flux. See *boron*
Chromic oxide	Cr_2O_3	Pigment (but see at *chrome*)
Germanium oxide	GeO_2	Glass former
Phosphorus pentoxide	P_2O_6	Glass former
Silicon oxide (silica)	SiO_2	Glass former
Tin oxide	SnO_2	Opacifier
Titanium oxide	TiO_2	Opacifier
Zirconium oxide	ZrO_2	Opacifier

An acid such as *vinegar* or *calcium chloride* will retard glaze settling. Acidic fumes from kilns, especially unventilated electric kilns, can attack window glass (and lungs!), see *ventilation*.

Rocks which are high in silica, such as granite and rhyolite are known as 'acidic' even though they may also have higher proportions of R_2O (the 'fluxes') than the basic basalt which is higher in calcia. Sutherland lists the mean composition of the main types of igneous rocks which well repay study. (See also *basalt*.)

Acid resistance

It is essential that glazes used on wares which will come into contact with chemically active substances should be stable and well-balanced. Vinegar, wines (especially if fermented in the vessel) and some fruits are the main sources of danger, which arise from the tendency of some glaze ingredients, especially lead, to separate and dissolve into the liquid forming a poison.

Adherence to the *Seger formula* principles in formulating glazes, especially for earthenware, will minimise the risk (e.g. a lead glaze formula 1.0 PbO: 0.3 Al_2O_3: 3.0: SiO_2) but the use of a totally leadless glaze for cooking ware has been made compulsory. All glazes containing lead (or selenium) made for table or kitchenware must be tested to the British Standard (in Great Britain) or to the US standard, see *metal release* for some international standards, *soluble lead*, *Thorpe's ratio* and the various glaze entries. Needless to say, the glazes should not be crazed.

Industrial sanitary wares, acid holders, and the like are vitrified, and sometimes salt-glazed, one of the most acid-resistant of all glazes. A stoneware glaze with a well-balanced formula is less likely to be affected by acids but some less stable recipes (my turquoise glaze is one), may be attacked by very active juices (pineapple for instance) if left in contact for a period of time.

Adhesive

Adhesives in general have little place in pottery. Dry clay can sometimes be repaired with *vinegar*. Glazes or colors may be treated with gum (see *gum arabic*) to make them less friable, for use on low-absorbency biscuit, or for glaze-over-glaze techniques. Potclays sell an adhesive called Propit for fastening props into place before firing. A range of glues which will bond ceramics up to stoneware temperatures is available from Aremco Products Inc. USA.

Adobe

A sun-dried clay-mud, with additions of straw or chaff, used in hot, dry climates for building. Very substantial buildings — some of the older, traditional houses of Cyprus for instance — demonstrate the high dry strength of some clays and clay-sand mixtures.

The adobe bricks or blocks, usually 12–18in/30–45cm square and 4in/10cm thick, are not, of course, subjected to sufficient heat to turn them into ceramic material, and they would disintegrate in persistent rain. Adobe is an excellent heat insulator. G. Woodman describes an adobe kiln for firings up to 1100°C/2012°F (PQ 23). See also *brick* for a useful press for adobe slabs.

Adsorption

The taking up of a liquid, vapor or gas onto a solid surface. Adsorption may cause expansion of a body (even a fired one) and is one of the causes of delayed crazing after a period of exposure to the atmosphere. It is, of course, more likely on low-fired porous ware.

Water adsorbed on clay particles is dependent on the attractions or resistance of electric charges on atoms, is therefore resistant to evaporation and requires a temperature of at least 120°C/248°F (figures as high even as 200°C /392°F have been mentioned) to remove it. The volume of liquid is small but nevertheless expands very quickly under heat and can break a pot. Clay cannot therefore be considered to be completely dry at room temperature. Ware which has been heated at 120°C/248°F and allowed to cool again will readsorb moisture and still be susceptible to damage.

Aeroclay

Clay which has been dried and separated by a current of air, leaving any coarse particles. Used especially for *china clay*.

Aerograph

Spray using compressed air. See *airbrush*.

Agate

One variety of *cryptocrystalline* silica (chalcedony). A banded, variegated hard stone. Polished, it is used to burnish gold (and, in South America, for burnishing pots), or for making small mortars and pestles.

Agate ware

A pottery body resembling agate stone in its marbled appearance. Produced by layering different color clays, pressing them together and using the resultant multi-sandwich for throwing or handbuilding. Care must be taken that the relative shrinkage of the layers is as nearly uniform as possible. For this reason it is advisable to use stains or oxides to derive different colors from a single body.

The technique is used by a number of modern potters and can give results which are sharp and bright or merged and subtle. A thrown agate vessel will generally need to be turned over its whole visible surface to reveal the pattern. A more controlled effect is achieved by Jack Doherty who places a thin slab of colored clay onto the surface of a half-finished pot or bowl, then continues with the throwing; a technique closer to *rolled inlay* (where it is illustrated). In yet another variation Jennifer Lee uses different colored clays (based on T-material) as flat, shaped strips in constructing a coil pot (CR95). Agate ware can also be made

A subtle use of the agate technique by Marianne de Trey.

in a mold when it is nearer to *neriage*. See also *marbling*.

It is not necessary to use a large number of layers. One or two colored slabs used between blocks of unstained clay offer more control and subtlety. Agate ware is discussed and illustrated fully in Fournier DPD.

Aggregate

The non-cement materials in a *cement* or *concrete* mixture. In concrete (which is not suitable for use in ceramics) these comprise stones and sand. Sand and crushed firebrick, grog or other refractories are used in a kiln mortar or brick mixture, (using a high-alumina high-temperature cement). Aggregates are normally used at the rate of about five times the volume of the cementing material. *Leca granules* have been used as an aggregate to build a 'mud kiln'. Stones can sometimes explode in the kiln but sand, grog, etc. have frequently been used, beaten into clay, for textural or decorative effects.

Aging of clay

Also known as 'souring'. Authorities differ on the period necessary for the attainment of full plasticity and workability in a clay (the percolation of water between the particles and layers) given variously as a generation in China; two years according to Leach and Billington; a week (Rhodes). Isaac Button's procedure of two months in a damp atmosphere followed by re-plugging yielded excellent results. Hamer gives a useful article on aging. (See also *algae, weathering*.)

Air

The gaseous envelope or atmosphere which surrounds the earth. Composed (on average) of 78% nitrogen, 21% oxygen, with very small amounts of other gases, water vapor, and dust. The oxygen is 'free', that is, available to maintain life, or to form oxides of elements. Oxidation produces heat; when the reaction is very rapid (e.g. the oxidation (burning) of carbon producing CO and CO_2) the heat can be used as a source of energy.

Airbrush, *aerograph*

A method of applying color and, occasionally, glaze by means of a spray-gun powered by compressed air, see also *spraying*. Airbrushing equipment sold for art-work is widely available using a canned propellant though, because it is intended for easel paints, the nozzle may clog with the sometimes coarser pottery pigments. A model supplied by a potter's merchant should be selected to deal with this problem—you can then complain if it doesn't work. Spraying from cans could prove expensive where much work is done but they are useful for experimental pieces. For regular use a motorized compressor is essential. (See *spraying* and illustration at *bone china*.)

Resists can be used to build up complex sprayed colors and surfaces. It is difficult to keep paper or other material stencils in place due to the power of the spray. Hanna Hombordy (CR142) suggests the use of weights and adhesives but perhaps *latex resist* is the answer. Various materials can be used as resists to provide a background texture — holes punched in paper, lace, loose-woven cloth, etc.

Air-setting   *cement, clay, mortar*

Normal clay/grog mortar hardens on firing but fire resistant mortars or cements are available which harden at air temperature. Useful for setting arches and unsupported parts of a kiln structure, but not essential. The makers of 'Sairset', a commercial air-setting cement, suggest its use as a protective coating on furnace linings, or mixed with crushed firebrick for patching kilns. See also *aluminous cement, ciment fondu, kiln wash*.

See *unfired clay* for some commercial materials which harden without firing. A recipe from Eva Thomas (CR 156) for an air-setting clay which can be thrown, modeled, biscuit fired, and glazed is: a white fireclay (parts) 5, 6, or 8 to sand 10, 9, or 7 (totalling 15), with 5 cement, and 25% water. To this can be added oxides. It hardens in 16 hours. Useful for large sculptural pieces.

Albany clay, slip

A clay found near Albany, New York. A similar material is found in Michigan.

Quoted analysis CaO 5.7, MgO 2.7, alkalis 3.1, Al_2O_3 14, Fe_2O_3 5.2, SiO_2 57.6.

The high proportion of fluxes, combined with a very fine grain, causes it to melt at around 1240°C/2264°F giving a greenish-brown *slip glaze*. Recipes for its use may be found in Rhodes CGP. Color brown to black. Behrens in CM 20/4 gives two recipes using 90% Albany clay with 10% *wollastonite* or *cryolite*, the latter producing a 'patterned' glaze, or feldspar can provide the flux. Can be used on the insides of pots (as it was originally in 19th century America). Available from Axner and others. (See also *slip-glaze, tenmoku*.)

Alberta clay

Can replace *Albany slip*. Available from Plainsman Clays Ltd, Alberta, Canada — the original source.

Albite

Soda feldspar. Ideal formula Na_2O, Al_2O_3, $6SiO_2$, mol. wt. 524. Can cause unwanted bubbles in a glaze above 1200°C/2192°F. Most commercial feldspars are mixtures of soda and potash spar (orthoclase) though usually with a preponderance of the latter and quoted 'potash feldspars' are available.

Algae

Factors in the *souring* and *aging* of clay. It was formerly believed that the activity of microscopic single-cell plants broke down the particles and increased plasticity but it now appears that the algae are a secondary but linking factor in the process of *ionic exchange*. The CO_2 released will slowly alter the *pH factor* of the clay which, in turn, affects its plasticity.

Alginate

An organic *suspender* derived from sea water.

Alkali

A subdivision of the chemical bases. Strictly speaking the term refers to soda, potash, and lithia but it is also used to cover the *alkaline earths*. Alkalis are glass *modifiers* and strong *fluxes*. Soda, especially, produces intense colors, e.g. Egyptian paste. Unfortunately many of the alkalis have high coefficients of expansion with consequent glaze crazing and, in many forms, are soluble (see *alkaline frits*).

Feldspar, china stone, lepidolite, nepheline, petalite, and spodumene are insoluble sources of the alkalis.

Alkali attack

See *enamels*.

Alkaline earths

The oxides of barium, beryllium, calcium, magnesium, and strontium (see under these headings). All operate as bases (glass modifiers) in glaze function. Normally more active at higher temperatures although they also appear as secondary fluxes in many earthenware glazes.

Alkaline glazes, frits

It is difficult to include the alkalis in significant proportions in a glaze, particularly a *soft glaze*, due to their solubility. For this reason they are normally added as *frits* and as such are widely available.

The high coefficient of expansion of the alkalis, especially soda, makes their use in any considerable quantity in glazes increasingly prone to crazing. Alkaline glazes also have a short firing range, and some are slightly soluble in even weak acids (fruit juice, etc.) which can lead to a dulling of the surface. In spite of this the 10th-century Islamic glazes, and even Ancient Egyptian high soda, low alumina glazes are still bright and undimmed. Lithia is more adaptable but the minerals which contain it (see *lepidolite* and *spodumene*) have their own problems, such as the bubbling of the fluorine in lepidolite. Adding alumina or the *alkaline earths* will steady the glaze but only with a loss of some of its character.

The frits are useful for lowering the maturing temperature of glazes, including stonewares; for affecting the color response in earthenware (the brilliant turquoise from *Egyptian Paste*, is an instance); and for use in larger proportions at the low end of the scale in *raku*, etc. The suppliers will usually tell you the make-up of any particular frit. (See also *frit, raku glazes*.)

Alligator hide

Quoted by Dodd as a glaze effect achieved by increasing the refractory oxides.

Alluvial clay

Deposits of clay left by rivers and by flood. In England, for instance, the valley clays of the Humber and Thames are alluvial. Used in brickmaking. Composition varies, but the clays are fine-grained, plastic, often iron-stained and sticky. (See also *estuarine, fluvine*.)

Alpha form

A term given to the crystalline form of quartz at temperatures below the *inversion* point.

Altered form

Today many potters use a thrown form simply as a starting point for more complicated shapes; cutting, pressing, or otherwise distorting the original shape. In extreme cases it is cut up and reassembled. See figs **1** and **2**.

Alternating current (or AC)

The normal main electricity supply which alternates or changes direction of flow at a very rapid rate. The number of changes or cycles per second is called the frequency. In England the normal frequency is 50, in the USA, it is normally 60. See *electricity*.

1 A thrown cylinder reformed into an 'envelope' shape by Joanna Constantinidis.
2 A pedestal bowl thrown and altered. By Kevin White.

For most of the electrical apparatus, light bulbs, kilns, etc. used by potters, AC current is the norm but certain pieces of equipment, especially motors, are designed either for AC or for *direct current* (DC), and these must only be used on the type of supply specified. It is possible to pass AC through a rectifier to convert it into DC.

Alumina

Oxide of aluminium. Al_2O_3, 102. m.p. 2050°C.
Supplied as the oxide, as aluminium hydrate $Al_2O_3.3HO_2$, which decomposes at around 300°C to alumina, or as *calcined* alumina. Fused alumina, which has been subjected to a very high temperature is used as an *abrasive*.

One of the essential ingredients of all clays and most glazes. Chemically *amphoteric*, it has a balancing and unifying effect between bases and acids and between glaze and body. It is rarely used as a separate mineral in glazes; instead it is introduced by adding clay or 'natural frits', e.g. china stone, feldspar, and nepheline syenite, which are the main sources; there are others. See list of *minerals*. The normal molecular equivalent in a glaze is from 10–12% of the silica content. It acts as a *network modifier* and helps to lessen recrystallization during cooling (for this reason it is kept to an absolute minimum in *crystalline glazes*). Alumina will also increase the hardness and stability of a glaze; its tensile strength; and its resistance to crazing. In excess it will produce a matt surface, pinholes, and other faults associated with too 'stiff' a glaze.

As a separate oxide it is used mainly for *placing* pottery and as a wash to prevent lids sticking in the firing. Calcined alumina is preferable to the hydrate for this purpose. It is also used in special forms as bubbles, etc. as a heat insulator, see also *bubble alumina, insulation of heat*.

High alumina clays (silliminite, some fireclays, etc.) are used for making kiln furniture and other refractories.

Alumina bubbles

See *bubble alumina, insulation of heat*.

Aluminous cement

A refractory cement. A fused mixture of limestone and bauxite. In combination with a crushed refractory material sets in 24 hours. (See *ciment fondu*.)

Aluminous refractory

Materials high in alumina will be less subject to damage from thermal shock than high-silica refractories. The best grades of *fireclay* are aluminous. (See also *bat, brick, firebrick, kiln shelf*, etc.)

Aluminum, aluminium

A metallic element, Al. 27. It occurs in a crystalline form as corundum, and as the gems, sapphire, ruby, and topaz. Manufactured as a metal by calcining alumina hydrate from *bauxite*. (See *alumina*.)

Amakusa

A Japanese *china stone*.

Ambient temperature

The temperature of the surrounding atmosphere.

Amblygonite

A lithium mineral of variable composition, high in alumina, from southern Africa. Ideal formula $Li.AlF, PO_4$, but can contain sodium and fluorine, e.g. (Li, Na) $AlPO_4$ (F,OH), LOI 17.4. Typical analyses: Li_2O, 7.8; Al_2O_3. 34.2; SiO_2 2.8; P_2O_5, 47.5. Melts to a glass at 1300°C/2372°F. Lepidolite and petalite are more commonly found and therefore less expensive. Used in small amounts in oxidized glazes for its phosphorus content, larger additions can cause blistering.

Amboy clay

An American plastic, siliceous *fireclay*. PCE 32+.

American bond

Brickwork of stretcher courses with a header course every 5th course. See also *bricklaying*.

Ammeter

An instrument for measuring electrical current flow in *amperes*. Useful for checking the correct working, and the effects of aging, of kiln elements. A low reading will suggest that the elements are wearing thinner; a reading of no current on the ammeter indicates a broken circuit.

Ammonium bichromate

See *bichromate of ammonia*.

Ammonium (meta)-vanadate

A less dangerous form of *vanadium*, NH_4VO_3. 117. 10% gives a rather weak yellow, improved by the use of an opacifier usually tin oxide. Not greatly affected by stoneware temperatures (up to 1280°C/2336°F) or, according to some authorities, by reduction. With zirconia can give turquoise, etc. (Dodd).

Amorphous

Without a structured shape. An amorphous mineral is one that does not build up regular crystals. Diatomite is an amorphous silica. Flint was once considered to be amorphous but is now classed as micro-crystalline. Glass, when cooled normally (i.e. not slowly enough to allow crystals to form), is an amorphous 'frozen' liquid, and is without a definite melting point.

Ampere

An electrical unit of current (symbol I) that one volt sends through one ohm of resistance.
Useful equations to calculate amperage:

$$I \text{ (amperage)} = \frac{P}{E}, \text{ or, } \frac{E}{R}, \text{ or, the square root of } \frac{P}{R}$$

(P in watts; E in volts; R in ohms). (See *electrical symbols*.)

Amphora

A general name for pointed or very narrow-based pots, generally with handles, typified by the Greek amphora.

They are still thrown in a few places in the Mediterranean countries. The top half is thrown first, half dried, reversed onto a chuck, and the pointed base thrown onto it from a thick coil. This method is useful for any narrow-based form. (See also *two-piece throwing*.)

Amphoteric

'Amphi'—two ways, or half. Applied to an oxide which does not exhibit strong acidic or basic characteristics. The middle column of the *Seger formula* (R_2O_3). Alumina is amphoteric; iron oxides vary in effect; ferric being amphoteric, while ferrous iron will act as a flux.

Anagama kiln

An early type of Japanese kiln, dug as a tunnel on rising ground. Clay soil was chosen and the walls slowly 'biscuited' (see Olsen in bibliography). Developed into the *chambered kiln*, or *climbing kiln*.

Analysis

The theoretical breakdown of a material into its constituent *elements*, *oxides*, or *minerals*. A laboratory can produce an elemental or 'ultimate' analysis listing the oxides as comparative or percentage weights. It is possible to regroup these into probable minerals — sometimes known as the *rational analysis*.

Example:
Tony Benham's hop ash has been analyzed as (percentages):

Soda Na_2O	0.3	Phosphate P_2O_5	2.8
Potash K_2O	10.8	Sulfate SO_3	9.0
Lime CaO	12.9	Chloride Cl	1.6
Magnesia MgO	1.5	Moisture H_2O	2.5
Alumina Al_2O	0.9	Carbon C	2.8
Iron Fe_2O_3	9.6	Undetermined	2.1
Silica SiO_2	35.3	Carbonates CO_2	7.9

These oxides can be re-grouped as probable minerals:

Fine sand	26	*The greater part of the silica*
Chalk	15	*Most of the lime and some carbonate*
Calcium silicate mineral	9	*The rest of the lime and some silica*
Potassium sulfate	20	*Potash and sulfate*
Hematite	10	*The ferric iron*
Magnesium carbonate	3	*Magnesium and the remaining carbonate*
Granite minerals	4	*Bases, alumina, the remaining silica*
Minor compounds carbon and moisture	13	

Some reasonable inferences as to the behavior of this ash in a glaze are:
1 Some of the 'fine sand' will fail to pass a 120 sieve.
2 Lack of alumina suggests instability and poor interface development if used alone.
3 The bases are adequate, but over half consist of lime.
4 The alkalis may be soluble and will be lost if the ash is washed.
With some feldspar and a little clay it should give an interesting iron glaze.

While analyses are useful in forming a general impression of a material, their value is limited especially in assessing clays. Other factors, such as grain size, are important. Practical experiment is essential. An analysis can be reformulated in terms of the Seger formula (see *analysis into formula*). Cardew, Appendix 10, gives details of a method for deriving the probable minerals from a list of oxides (calculated formula).

Potters' merchants will sometimes provide analyses of their minerals, and there are firms of analytical chemists who will quote.

What is known as the ultimate analysis in ceramics will take into account the changes which take place in the kiln, i.e. some molecules will split up and dispel one or more of their constituents as gases, marked in analyses as 'Loss' or 'Loss on ignition' — LOI. Materials can also be analyzed according to physical qualities such as grain size in clay, etc.

Analysis into formula

Where an analysis of a mineral or other material is given as parts-by-weight it is useful to be able to convert it into *molecular* parts for a truer appraisal of its behavior, especially in a glaze. It is usual to group the constituents in the general order of the *Seger formula*.

Method: Divide each of the figures by the molecular weight of that oxide. Group the RO and the R_2O oxides, R indicating any relevant element, (the *alkalis*) and total the parts. Divide each figure in the formula by this total.

Example:

A mineral with the analysis by weight:

12.40 K_2O	÷ mol.wt. 94	= 0.132
3.15 Na_2O	÷ mol.wt. 62	= 0.05
18.60 Al_2O_3	÷ mol.wt. 102	= 0.182
65.85 SiO_2	÷ mol.wt. 60	= 1.096

The total *RO group* comprises 0.132 + 0.05 = 0.182.

If we divide each of the results of the example above by this total we arrive at the formula:

Na_2O plus K_2O	1
Al_2O_3	1
SiO_2	6

which is near the ideal formula for orthoclase feldspar.

A natural mineral will be more involved than the simple example above, but the method can still be applied.

CO_2, H_2O, and other *loss on ignition* oxides, if listed separately, can be ignored. If quoted as *carbonates*, the molecular weight of the carbonate will allow for the CO_2. (See also charts at *formula into recipe*.)

Anatase

One of the ores of titanium. A crystalline form of TiO_2. The source of white titania. Converts to rutile above 700°C/1292°F.

Anchor

Given by Dodd-Murfin as pieces of metal or pins to hold ceramic fiber in place. Can also involve ceramic fittings. (See *ceramic fiber*.)

Andalusite

A mineral, $Al_2O_3SiO_2$, 162. Occurs in S Africa and America. A refractory raw material — one of the sillimanite group. Converts by firing into *mullite* $3Al_2O_3.2SiO_2$ plus silica (as *cristobalite*) with little change in volume.

Andesite

Quoted by Brickell as a hard, grey, crystalline rock inter-

mediate between *basalt* and the more acidic volcanic rocks (*diorite* and *rhyolite*) found in New Zealand and the Pacific region. Contains *plagioclase feldspar* and ferromagnesia minerals. Can form a brown stoneware glaze at 1300°C.

Anhydrous, anhydrite

Without water of *crystallization*. A natural anhydrite is $CaSO_4$, often found in close conjunction with *gypsum*. Also, among the more commonly used materials is calcined borax, $Na_2O. 2B_2O_3$.

Animal charcoal

Charcoal obtained from bones. Said to be preferable to wood charcoal as a *reduction* agent.

Anion

A negatively charged particle, i.e. with surplus *electron(s)*. A positvely charged ion is called a *canion*. (See *atomic theory*.)

Anise, aniseed oil

Used as an *enamel* medium. Potclays issue a substitute called 'Aniseed Turpens'.

Anisotropic, anisometric

Different values in different directions, applied to crystals. The *lamellar* structure of clay can lead to uneven shrinkage if some plates are aligned and others random.

Annular

A disc with a hole in it — like a doughnut! Some potters consider it an easier shape to center on the wheel, especially with large masses of clay. A bottle kiln would have an annular bag wall. (See also *centering*.)

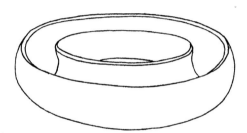

What is sometimes called a 'posy ring', an annular form which is interesting to throw.

Annular centering is especially useful for larger pieces of clay.

Anorthite, anorthosite

Anorthite is a calcium feldspar, $CaO.Al_2O_3.2SiO_2$, 278. There is a series of solid solutions known as the plagioclase feldspars between anorthite and *albite*, also called the Ab-An series. Anorthosite is a coarse-grained rock consisting almost entirely of *plagioclase* (see *feldspar*).

Anorthoclase

A soda spar, some way between *albite* and *orthoclase*. Written as $NaKO. Al_2O_3. SiO_2$. Term sometimes used for any mixed-based feldspar.

Anti-flux

A term used by Hamer to describe the temperature range below which certain RO oxides fail to act as effective glaze fluxes though this is complicated by the interaction of one on another and by the amount used. All are active at stoneware temperatures, though their effect varies. See under individual materials and at *fluxes*. The effect of red iron oxide as an 'anti-flux' is reversed under reduction.

Antimonate of lead

Approximately $3PbO, Sb_2O_3$, sometimes written $Pb_3(SbO_4)_2$. A yellow pigment for earthenware, also known as Naples Yellow. Toxic.

Although unstable above 1150°C it has a *refractory* nature and needs the addition of a soft lead frit in the proportions of 1:1 when used as a pigment. Adding 5% will give a yellow color in a lead glaze. In painting, if it is not to assume the unpleasant quality of dried mustard, dilute with the base glaze or with a soft frit. Owing to its refractory nature the color will often fail to migrate through a tin

glaze and may even cause crawling when used as an underglaze color.

It is not very satisfactory in or on a leadless glaze. Apply evenly and fairly thinly as a pigment on maiolica. (See also *antimony*.)

Antimony, oxides

A metallic element Sb (Stibium), 122.
Oxide Sb_2O_3, m.w. 291.5 m.p. 630°C, s.g. 5.5.

Holds an ambiguous position as a *metalloid*. Also listed as a *glass-former* in the *Seger formula*. **Toxic**.

A low-temperature oxide which will combine in various ways with glaze materials, modifying and opacifying. With lead oxide yields a yellow pigment (see *antimoniate of lead*). Will begin to volatilize at 1200°C/2192°F.

Apatite

A source of calcium phosphate but the fluorine and chlorine content can give trouble. *Bone ash* is preferable as a source of calcium phosphate.

Applied decoration

Three-dimensional decoration with a wide variety of character and method. It can be as simple and direct as the pressed or stroked-on pellets of clays found on English medieval jugs, or as mechanical and intricate as Wedgwood sprigs. The thumb pot illustrated shows how applied decoration can become part of the form.

The clay can be applied direct if the decorative element is small, but larger pieces must be slipped and carefully pressed on from the center outwards. Betty Woodman

There is no clear borderline between applied decoration and modeled form.

1 *Multi-rim additions to a handbuilt bowl by Sheila Fournier.*

2 Here strips and bosses have been applied to a pinch pot by Alex Watson.

3 Bold thrown spirals applied to lamp bases by Sheila Fournier.

covers her simple shapes with extruded, combed, and pressed ribbons and bosses; Irene Vonck adds wafers of clay to break otherwise severe contours. Tony Birks warns against striving after natural forms which will rarely relate to the shape on which they are applied. (See further

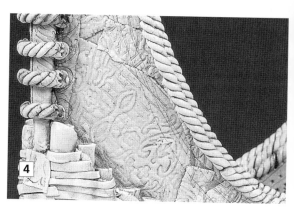

4 Detail of Lara Scobie's 'Cobalt Ship', using strips and coils.

illustrated examples under *sprig, lug*). More extensive discussions and illustrations may be found in Fournier DPD.

Arabian luster

Reduced sulfides or carbonates of copper, depositing a thin layer of metal on the surface. (See *luster*.)

Arch

See *bricklaying*.

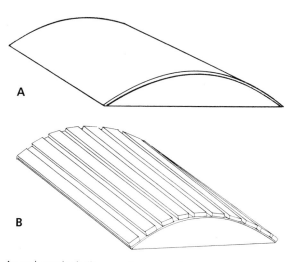

An arch can be built over a former made:
A from hardboard or
B slats nailed over arch-shaped wooden ends. These are removed when the mortar between the bricks has set.

Arenaceous

Sandy. Some arenaceous rocks however, may be quite hard, e.g. greywacke and millstone, the sands cemented by silica or limestone. Can sometimes be found as sands which may give interest to a clay body.

Argillaceous

Clayey. Materials with layered crystals, as clay, also including mica. Hamer, however, gives it as 'mudstone' which 'often contains a proportion of clay'. 'Illite is the commonest clay mineral in argillaceous rocks' Cardew PP. Clayey mud from tidal river beds can be used to modify glazes, or as an ingredient of slip glazes.

Argillite

A sedimentary rock containing clay minerals.

Ark

A quaint name for large slip and glaze containers with mechanical stirrers.

Armature

A supporting core of wood or wire used in modeling. It must, of course, be removed if the piece is to be fired. Sculptors' techniques often trap air in the clay and also develop very uneven wall thicknesses, both of which can be disastrous in the kiln. Coiling or similar building methods are advised if the piece is intended for firing.

An armature of crushed and bound paper can give some support; either pulled out piecemeal when the model is completed and dry, or burned out in the firing (with much smoke in an electric kiln!). Theoretically any combustible material could be used but may give rise to other problems.

Armenian bole

An earthy compound of iron, used as a pigment. Now seldom listed by merchants. (See *bole*.)

Arsenic oxides

As_2O_3. Very toxic. A glass-forming oxide which has been used in ceramics in the past. Very small quantities act as a decolorizer.

Asbestolux

A trade name for a steam-pressed insulating and fireproof material originally made from asbestos but now known as 'Non-asbestos Asbestolux'! Standard size 8 x 4ft (approx. 2.4 x 1.2m), thicknesses up to $\frac{1}{2}$in/approx. 12.5mm, also known as 'Superlux', it is made from calcium silicate. Reasonably strong, but liable to crush at the corners. Can be cut with an ordinary saw. It does not easily warp and 'will not crack or shatter at furnace heat' say the makers. It is useful for the outer cases of kilns, where it will prove good thermal insulation, and also for working bats and for stiffening pots after throwing. If used for throwing bats, however, its high absorbency needs quenching with a coat of polyurethane varnish. It is still essential to use a mask when cutting this or any similar material which may send dust or fibers into the air, and especially when sweeping up afterwards (preferably use a *vacuum-cleaner*).

Asbestos

A fibrous natural mineral consisting of silicates of magnesia and calcium with iron. It loses water at 400°C/752°F and rapidly weakens above about 500°C/932°F. Two types; cryolite and amphibole (blue) asbestos. Because of its carcinogenic effects this very useful material has been phased out from most of its applications. It has been replaced by ceramic and mineral wool and other materials in heatproof sheeting (though these are also dangerous if sawn or abraded without using a mask) and electric wire insulation, the last now using butyl and silicone-rubbers which have lower operating temperatures. (See *asbestos cement, asbestosis, asbestolux, ceramic fiber, electric kiln wiring, mineral wool, superlux*.)

Asbestos cement

Cement and asbestos cast into thin sheets, one side smooth, the other textured. Strong but brittle, slightly absorbent, and liable to warp unless braced with timber or metal. Will crack or shatter under heat and is therefore not recommended for kiln casing. Now generally made with mineral wool or other asbestos substitute, but check with your supplier. All dust promoting activities are dangerous to health.

Asbestosis

Inflammation of the lungs caused by breathing in blue (amphibole) asbestos. Cryolite (white) asbestos is not considered quite so dangerous but all types are best avoided.

Asbolite

An impure cobalt ore, used by Chinese potters. Yields a pleasant quenched blue which we can approach by adding red clay, ferric, manganese, etc. to the pure oxide. Has been quoted as containing 2–20% CoO with MnO_2, Fe_2O_3, etc. (See also at *cobalt*.)

Ash

A powdery residue left after the combustion of any organic material. The ashes useful in ceramics are those from trees and plants (*bone ash* is dealt with separately) where the incombustible residue is composed of the inorganic substances, mainly metal oxides and silica, which they have taken up from the soil during their lifetime. The different parts of a plant will use or store certain groups of minerals: grass stems obtain much of their brittle strength from silica, and straw ash is therefore refractory. The trunk of a tree is likely to store lime in greater quantities than the bark, and the bark may become richer in silica as it ages. Box and apple wood, for instance, yield 5–10% of silica and up to 70% or more of lime; in reed ash the proportions are reversed. Cardew suggests that the first be considered an interesting alternative to limestone, the latter an impure silica. In general the harder and more woody the plant, the softer (more fluxing) the ash is likely to be. This is a guide only, there are exceptions such as the Australian turpentine tree which has almost 90% silica content. On the other hand I have used a cedar ash which, alone, melts to a shiny liquid at 1260°C/2300°F. For painting on stoneware Eric Melton, in CR183, states that smaller bushes (low in calcium) will give a more stable glaze.

Other factors influence the behavior of an ash, the type of soil and, possibly, the time of year the plant is cut. Few ashes are high in alumina, although those from fruits may contain more than others. The alkalis are often soluble and can be lost in washing. Magnesia and phosphorus can impart a milky luster. Sometimes known as the '*jun*' effect.

Ash glaze with a vengeance! By Owen Rye (Australia). On one side of the pot ash has accumulated over five days of firing.

The very considerable variation, even in the narrowest field of study, makes the direct testing of every ash sample indispensable. A typical ash analysis is given at *analysis*. Several others are given in Leach, Cardew, and other books.

Ash is normally well burnt to a pale grey or white powder; although a black ash contains carbon which may be used as a local reducing agent, producing iron reds and blacks in an electric kiln (see *ash preparation, reduction*). It can be reburnt or calcined to about 700°C/1292°F in the kiln after washing. Reburning will also have the advantage of curing its tendency to flocculate. A great deal of vegetable material is required to produce a small amount of washed, sieved ash; the final count might be as little as 3% of the plant weight! (See *ash glaze, ash preparation*.)

Coal ash is fundamentally an aluminum silicate with iron and other impurities. It has low fluxing power and acts in a similar way to clay. See recipe under *coal ash*.

Ash glaze

Glazes which contain large proportions of plant ash are not necessarily superior to more consciously formulated ones, though the subtlety of the natural ash compounds can give unique results. There is little value in using ash in glazes to be fired below stoneware temperatures. The particular qualities of ash glaze are better exploited in reduction rather than in oxidation, although interesting results can be achieved in electric kilns. Owing to soluble constituents, ash glazes are liable to give variable results even during the use of a single glaze batch. In partially burnt ash the carbon provides local *reducing* conditions during the firing of the glaze and can give terracotta reds and blacks (occasionally with a yellowish fleck) in an electric kiln.

Few ashes will provide a satisfactory glaze used alone, and they tend to give a poor and powdery dip. Small test bowls, or *button tests*, will, however, give some idea of the fusibility or refractoriness of a sample. Normally an ash is used as an ingredient in a recipe. The 'classic' starting point is 2 ash: 2 feldspar: 1 clay. Dolomite and nepheline are also useful additions, although the former may overload the lime content. One of the most interesting constituents of many ashes is the phosphorus (pentoxide P_2O_5) which can give a pearly or opalescent quality. Jim Malone (CR140) suggests trials of ash in equal parts with one other material, while Phil Rogers (CR131) uses as much as 53% of pine or beech ash to 25–30% feldspar/stone. (See also under *ash* for more discussion of ash behavior.) Caroline Gordon (CR123 Zimbabwe) has had 'very pleasing results' from the use of tobacco ash.

Ray Silverman in CR171 turns an *empirical formula* for a wood ash into a *recipe* using the normal glaze materials.

This is made into a slip, dried, and used as ash in a full glaze recipe. Analyses of ashes, however, are difficult (or expensive) to obtain though some typical examples are quoted in Cardew and other reference books. See also *coal ash* with recipe.

Ash preparation

To prepare plant ash for use, one should ensure that it is well-burnt (but see note below on the decorative and reduction possibilities of not so thoroughly burned or washed ash). Some potters go to great trouble to obtain a clean and perfect example, burning on a swept stone slab. Ash burned in a Baxi or other domestic fire with an efficient draft will give a good white ash. Cardew recommends calcining the washed ash in a kiln to about 900°C/1652°F, packing it in a *saggar*. For practical work the ash must also be available in sufficient quantity — at least half a dustbinful, and preferably more. Ashes from various sources can be mixed though this would be frowned upon by the dedicated ash-experimenter. Ash dust is caustic and care must be taken not to inhale it. (Wear a mask when dealing with it.)

A careful initial sieving through a garden sieve will remove the rough stuff. It is then soaked in plenty of water and passed through a 30 mesh sieve or lawn. As the ash settles, the surface water will contain a considerable concentration of soluble alkalis and will be caustic (will affect sensitive skins) so it is advisable to carry out these operations wearing rubber gloves. This liquid can be poured or scooped away and replaced with clean water. The ash is well-stirred and again left to settle. The 'washing' process can be repeated two or three times, during which soluble fluxes will be removed and the ash will become progressively more *refractory*. Reasonable washing is essential for ash which is to be added to tableware glazes, but for purely decorative purposes a totally unwashed ash can give entertaining results. A certain degree of carbon (black) left in the ash can give local reduction (see also note at *ash*).

After the final settling and decanting, the sludge is spread out to dry (beware of ash on plaster slabs — the alkalis will attack the surface). When dry it is stored and weighed like any other glaze ingredient, care being taken not to raise a dust.

Atom

The unit particle of a chemical element. Often cited as the smallest particle of matter which can partake in chemical action, though certainly not the smallest particle which exists. The make-up and behavior of atoms is continually under revision but simple, basic molecular theory is normally sufficient for the potter. Hamer PDMT deals extensively with the atomic make-up of pottery materials. (See *atomic theory*.)

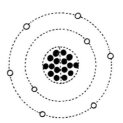

A representation of the oxygen atom. The nucleus is composed of 8 protons and 8 neutrons and is surrounded by two 'orbits' of electrons, the first of 2 electrons and an outer one of 6, a total of 8 to balance the positive charge of the protons. Oxygen occurs only as molecules of 2 atoms which share 2 electrons, to make up the 'magic' number of 8 in the outer shell.

Atomic numbers

The atomic number is derived from the number of *protons* (or *electrons*) in an atom. Thus hydrogen has a single proton and is number 1, helium has two protons and is number 2, and so on. (See *periodic table*.)

Atomic radius

The 'size' or radius of an atom will determine how it will act and which combinations it can form. Potassium and sodium have large atoms which are close enough in size to be interchangeable in feldspar, etc. Sodium and calcium are also very close and form the plagioclase series of feldspars. Silicon is a small atom and can fit within a pyramid of four (large) oxygen atoms, forming the SiO_4 group on which all ceramics are founded. The radii are measured in Ångström units, 10^{-8}cm, and vary between 0.20 Ångström units (boron) to 1.43 (barium) in common pottery elements. (See Cardew for list.)

Atomic theory

The 'classical' theory of the structure of matter is still broadly valid for potters. To quote Holderness:

1 All elements are made up of small particles called atoms. Atoms are defined as the smallest particle of an element which can take part in chemical action.
2 Atoms cannot be created or destroyed.
3 Atoms are indivisible.
4 Atoms of the same element are alike in every way.
5 Atoms combine in whole numbers.

All these have been modified in the light of later research (we know to our cost that atoms can be 'split') but insofar as we are dealing with chemical change and *inorganic materials*, Dalton's postulates above are still useful in practice. The fourth definition is complicated by the discovery of '*isotopes*', but constant isotopic mixtures occur so that, again, for practical purposes, the application of this principle will be valid. The main effect of isotopes is to complicate *atomic weights*, which are no longer convenient whole numbers but are worked out as averages of the isotopes, and can therefore run into many places of decimals. In this book atomic weights are confined to one or two decimal places.

The application of simple atomic science to pottery is dealt with under *atoms, atomic radius, atomic weights, elements, molecules*, and *valency*. Here we can discuss briefly the way in which the modern chemist views the structure of matter. For deeper insight into the theories see Hamer PDMT, and CR2. The atom, once thought to be the ultimate particle, is now considered as having some parallel with a solar system and to be made up of a number of smaller fundamental units. These are distinguished by their electrical characteristics: the neutrons, electrically neutral; the positive protons; and the much smaller negatively charged electrons, are the principal units. The first two make up the nucleus or core of the atom and account for most of its 'weight'. The electrons have 'orbits' round the nucleus and form from one to seven layers or 'shells' at various distances from it. The number of protons in the nucleus and, when the atom is electrically neutral, the number of electrons surrounding it, is called the *atomic number*. The chart of atomic numbers is called the *periodic table*.

The total weight of an atom consists of its total number of protons and neutrons as compared with hydrogen. Hydrogen is unity with one proton (no neutrons); oxygen has eight of each. Thus the atomic number of oxygen is 8 and its atomic weight 16. In the heavier atoms there are more neutrons than protons in the nucleus.

Isotopes are those atoms in which the proton number is constant but the number of neutrons varies. Since the atomic weight (a.w.) equals the sum of these particles, an element can have more than one atomic weight. Within the mass of an element, however, these variations occur in regular proportions, so that the atomic weight can be given as a mean weight. Thus chlorine has an a.w. of 35.5 — most of the atoms weighing 35, but some 37.

The electrons directly affect chemical behavior. The shells lie at various distances from the nucleus, and each contains a fixed number of electrons. The outer shell is crucial to chemical action and to the formation of molecules or linked groups of atoms (*lattices*). It may hold from one to eight electrons. An outer shell of two or eight electrons is the stable state to which all atoms 'aspire', and the atom will borrow or share another's electrons to make up eight or to lose all so that the next innermost shell becomes the

'complete' one. Atoms behaving in this way are joined one to another in chains or networks which make up the involved, infinitely various, and apparently distinct compounds which constitute the world as we experience it.

When an atom 'loses' an electron it ceases to be electrically balanced and has a spare positive 'charge' from a proton. The element symbol is altered from R to R+. If, on the other hand, two electrons are gained it is written R- -, and so on. Unbalanced atoms are known as *ions*. In many cases a number of elements enter into combination, and the sharing becomes complicated and on several planes, leading to the build-up of *crystal* structures. The bonds formed between ions are *electrovalent*.

Where sharing which does not disturb the balance takes place 'covalent' bonds are formed and *molecules* result. (See also *covalent, electron, valency*.)

Atomic weights

The 'weight' of an *atom* is derived from the total of the *protons* and *neutrons* in the nucleus. It is a comparative number based on hydrogen at one or oxygen at sixteen. Used by potters as a means of translating *molecular parts* into tangible recipes. The 1961 International Atomic Weights Table is taken to seven decimal places, but we can be content with approximation to a single decimal place (it would not greatly affect the result to use the nearest whole number considering the empirical nature of most calculations and the comparatively small amounts). Atoms, in fact, obviously occur only in whole numbers but the presence of *isotopes* complicates the 'weight' of elements. The numbers for the most useful ceramic compounds are:

Element	Symbol	Weight	Element	Symbol	Weight
Aluminum	Al	27.0	Antimony	Sb	121.8
Barium	Ba	137.3	Bismuth	Bi	209.0
Boron	B	11.8	Cadmium	Cd	112.4
Calcium	Ca	40.0	Carbon	C	12.0
Chlorine	Cl	35.5	Chromium	Cr	52.0
Cobalt	Co	59.0	Copper	Cu	63.5
Fluorine	F	19.0	Germanium	Ge	72.6
Hydrogen	H	1.0	Iron	Fe	55.8
Lead	Pb	207.0	Lithium	Li	7.0
Magnesium	Mg	24.3	Manganese	Mn	55.0
Nickel	Ni	58.7	Oxygen	O	16.0
Phosphorus	P	31.0	Potassium	K	39.0
Praseodymium	Pr	59.0	Selenium	Se	79.0
Silicon	Si	28.1	Silver	Ag	107.9
Sodium	Na	23.0	Strontium	Sr	87.6
Sulfur	S	32.0	Tin	Sn	118.7
Titanium	Ti	48.0	Vanadium	V	51.0
Zinc	Zn	65.3	Zirconium	Zr	91.2

Auger

An *extruder* in which the clay is forced through dies by means of a continuous screw, like a corkscrew.

Autoclave

An airtight chamber which can be used to test the liability of a glaze to *crazing* by heating it under steam pressure. The method is not entirely satisfactory as it confuses the effects of moisture expansion (*adsorption*) with *thermal shock*.

Automatic kiln control

Sophisticated electronic apparatus is widely available for terminating or *soaking* a firing automatically according to the program set by the potter. The rate of rise and fall of temperature, both during the firing and at its termination, is also controllable. Cromartie issue a good range as do many other suppliers. Some potters would prefer to have direct control but such equipment is useful for repeating a program of firing once it is established.

A simpler mechanical device usually makes use of mini-bars. A rod, set within the kiln, introduced through the spyhole, rests on the bar and when the bar sags, indicating that the required temperature has been reached, the rod drops and switches off the kiln. Also known as a 'kiln-sitter'. (See also *kiln-sitter, controlling pyrometer.*)

Aventurine glaze

Aventurine is a mineral, a feldspar with small shiny crystals of *hematite*. In glazes it therefore refers to a decorative surface effect produced by the formation of small, sometimes bright crystals (*devitrification*). Larger (occasionally very large and impressive) crystals can also be generated, see *crystalline glazes*. The aventurine crystals are generally of hematite and the method is similar to that described at *crystalline glazes*. High iron oxide content in lead glaze, combined with low alumina will help to develop the effect. Zinc (around 0.3 equivalents in the glaze formula), rutile, bismuth, and titania have been mentioned. Slow cooling especially in the 900–700°C/1652–1292°F range is essential.

Quoted recipe:

Lead/borax frit	75
Cornwall stone	15
Oxide of iron	6
Oxide of copper	1
Chromate of iron	3

from Billington with the usual advice for the type 'apply thickly, fire and cool slowly'.

The glazes are suitable only for decorative pieces.

Backstamp

A printed or impressed stamp beneath a pot giving information about the maker or the making of the piece. Not often used by the studio potter who generally prefers to stamp the foot-ring or outer base of the piece.

A backstamp could be useful to collectors and historians, not to mention the interested public; the average potter today is very anonymous. But see Yates-Fournier.

Bacteria in clay

It is thought that the growth of bacteria in damp clay promotes acid gels which have a beneficial effect on plasticity, see at *aging*. Rhodes CGP recommends mixing a little well-matured clay with new batches. The bacterial action will assist vegetable decomposition which is a link in the chain leading to *ionic exchange*, a factor in plasticity. (See *algae*.)

Bag wall

A wall of brickwork built between the firebox and setting-space of a kiln. It deflects the heat upwards and also serves to prevent the flame from impinging directly onto the ware or the saggars (although it is possible to build a bag wall of saggars). Cardew recommends the use of a thin brick, 9 x 4 x 1–1.5in (approx. 225 x 110 x 35mm), with 3in/75mm between the bag wall and the kiln wall, and terminating 5in/125mm or so below the springers of the dome.

These measurements, especially that of the distance between the bag wall and the kiln wall, will vary with the design of the kiln but too great a gap will waste heat. Bag walls are sometimes built with apertures to spread the flames through the ware nearest them. Lightweight or insulating brick have obviously no advantage for bag walls which, anyhow, are subject to fierce fire and require a good grade *firebrick*.

Bail handle

An overarching handle, sometimes used on teapots and more commonly on pottery 'baskets'. Bail handles can be made from a variety of mediums such as wood or metal; pottery bail handles give a firmer grip than cane ones but are more vulnerable. See Figures **1** and **2**. (See also *cane handle, handle.*)

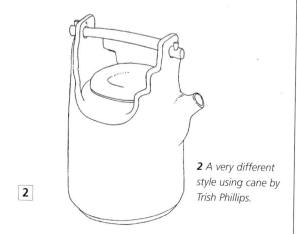

1 A ceramic over arching handle on a teapot by Sheila Fournier, attractive and easy to use but rather vulnerable.

2 A very different style using cane by Trish Phillips.

Balance

Finely suspended scales used in chemistry. Essential for weighing quantities under 10 grams. Normally only cobalt is likely to be used in such small amounts in working glaze batches.

Ball clay

Secondary, transported (*sedimentary*) clays which are very plastic and fire to a pale color. The name derives from the 30–35lb balls in which form they were originally made up for horse transport. As dug they often contain carbons which stain them blue or dark grey; these will be dispersed during firing. They have a high shrinkage rate and are difficult to handle on their own due to very fine particle size, e.g. their failure to settle as a slip or to dry easily from slurry to plastic. Other, coarser-grained clays are therefore added and the ball clay content of a body is normally restricted to about 30%. It has high dry strength which is valuable, but some contain carbon which must be carefully burned out, see *black core, carbon*.

In England the main beds are at Wareham, Dorset, and in Devon; in the USA, in Kentucky and Tennessee. New Zealand has sources of ball clay but '*halloysite* and *illite* are major components of these clays'. (Brickell)

Ball clays vary considerably in their mineral content. Sutherland quotes:

kaolinite	20–90%	
micaceous material	5–45%	(illite or hydrous mica)
quartz	1–70%	

'Free' silica is often a feature of ball clays, which are then known as siliceous ball clays. They are all too sticky and fine-grained to use alone but are an essential ingredient of most pottery bodies, increasing plasticity and dry strength, and assisting *vitrification* upon firing.

A typical analysis:

K_2O	1.8	Al_2O_3	33.0		
Na_2O	0.2	Fe_2O_3	1.0	SiO_2	49.0
CaO	0.3	TiO_2	0.9	MgO	0.3

A body recipe, by weight, for a 1290°C/2354°F firing might read:

Fireclay or stoneware clay	50
Ball clay	25
Flint	10
China stone or feldspar	5
Fine grog	10

(See also *clays, throwing, body*.)

Ball mill

A machine for grinding rocks and minerals, consisting of a horizontal cylinder, made from or lined with, an abrasion-resistant material (e.g. stoneware or porcelain), with some mechanical means of making it revolve.

The materials to be ground are put into the cylinder together with flint pebbles, porcelain or hard steel balls, and water. As it rotates, the balls, rolling continuously to the bottom of the curve, grind very efficiently. In the industry dry milling may be practiced, with a current of air taking away the finer material (*elutriation*). There is also a wet system where the mill is vertical and vibrates rather than rotates. The craftsman who buys commercial materials will

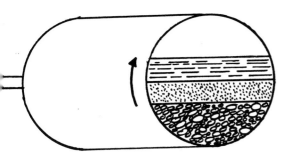

A diagrammatic section of a ball mill showing pebbles, charge, and water in their approximate proportions. These will, of course, be intimately mingled when the mill is turning.

rarely require a mill — the materials will be sufficiently ground (often too finely) — but a mill is useful for experimental and special purposes. For the pioneer potter it is indispensable. The smaller ball mills are called *jar mills* and are discussed under that entry.

Various critical factors must be taken into account when constructing a ball or jar mill. Speed of revolution varies with the size. Slightly differing equations have been put forward; the simplest is:

Maximum revolutions per minute (revs/min) = 58.18 divided by the square root of r where r is the radius of the interior of the mill in feet. Thus for a 6in (approx 150mm) diameter mill the revs/min would be 58.18 divided by the square root of 0.25ft (radius), i.e. 58.18 divided by 0.5 = 116.36. This is the maximum working speed, much faster and the balls would tend to spin round, attached by centrifugal force to the casing. One would normally grind at about 75% of this speed, i.e. 80 revs/min. Other mill sizes work out at 100 rev/mins for a 4in (approx. 100mm) mill; 70 revs/min for an 8in (approx. 200mm); 50 revs/min for a 12in (approx. 300mm).

The flint pebbles or porcelain balls, called the 'grinding medium' in merchants' catalogs. Size ½–2in (10–50mm) in diameter, and filling about 50% of the mill's capacity ('capacity' meaning two-thirds of the total space in the mill). Some authorities recommend no more than half capacity.

Water and charge (the material to be ground) are each 15–25% of capacity. The charge must already have been ground to 'sand' size. Time varies with hardness and grain size required, from two to eight hours. The mill will become warm if the charge is grinding correctly.

Cardew has an appendix on ball mills and also an ingenious system of finding the square roots of numbers below unity, useful in the speed equation above. If a ball mill is working at its optimum efficiency, Brian Sutherland romantically but evocatively suggests that it should sound 'like a breaking wave'! See *jar mill* for principle of operation. The ball mill has been largely superseded in the

industry by the *vibratory mill* (which is also coming onto the market for studio potters and has a much more rapid grinding action).

Balloon

The use of a rubber balloon as a former or support has been mentioned in CM and elsewhere. A rounded shoulder on a slab pot for instance, can be formed from a soft slab worked over a balloon, which has been sufficiently inflated just to fill the top of the pot. Not as easy as it sounds.

Banding

The spinning of pigment lines onto a pot. The brush should hold sufficient liquid to complete the band without a refill, and the hand must be held perfectly still once the brush is in contact with the pot surface. Some support which will incline the hand towards the pot, such as an

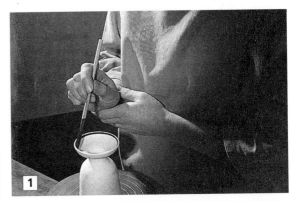

Two methods of supporting and steadying the hand for banding.
1 The left hand holds the right wrist, the potter standing to the work.
2 When seated the elbow can be used as a pivot, resting on the bench.

elbow set on a firm surface, is useful. Needless to say, the pot must be centered on a throwing wheel, or *whirler*, and a sufficient smooth turning momentum obtained. A heavy whirler is essential for technically efficient banding. Banding is somewhat mechanical in appearance but is useful as a frame and foil for more calligraphic work — and to do it well is very satisfying! The freer spinning of lines is dealt with under *spun color*.

Banding wheel

Although the term is used for any free-spinning circular turntable it is, strictly, a floor-standing wheel often with a cork inset surface. Also called a lining wheel. The term 'whirler' or 'bench whirler' is now more general for the table wheel normally used by potters. (See *whirler*.)

Bank kiln

A kiln constructed against a hill or bank, the slope, usually about 30°, providing the draft. Though crude in conception, bank kilns have probably been responsible for some fine pottery. Small bank kilns are sometimes constructed by potters today and they can be excellent teaching aids. The body of the kiln can be actually cut into the slope which will then supply efficient insulation. See Rhodes K. The oriental many-chambered *climbing kilns* are based on a similar principle.

Bar, pyrometric

See *Holdcroft bar, mini-bar*.

Barbotine

A French word for *slip* occasionally used in older books on pottery, often applied to the high-relief slip patterns of the type so brilliantly achieved by the Roman Rhenish and some Romano-British potters on beakers and other vertical surfaces, whose precise technique has never been rediscovered or equalled.

Barite

See *barytes*.

Barium, compounds

A metallic element Ba. 137.3
Oxide BaO, 153.3. Baria.
Carbonate $BaCO_3$. 197.3. See also *witherite*.
Sulfate $BaSO_4$. 233. Barytes.

An alkaline earth. Most compounds are toxic and the material should be handled with care. The carbonate is relatively insoluble and is normally used in glaze mixes (though it may react with any flocculant present). Decomposes to the oxide at 900°C/1652°F. Barium has come under suspicion of 'leaching out' (the US has now strengthened its 'release limits') and the material is not recommended for the interiors of tableware. The danger is more acute in earthenware glazes than in work fired at stoneware temperatures.

Baria acts as a *base* in glazes at high temperatures, its action similar in some respects to lime (calcia). A high proportion, 20% plus, may dull the surface of the glaze and cause pinholes unless the recipe also contains boron. Vivienne Foley (CR78) and Behrens suggest as much as 50% in a 1250°C/2282°F glaze but the average is 10–20%. Baria can give a hardness and brilliance to a glaze at 1150°C/2102°F and over.
Behrens gives a recipe:

Baria	21.5	Nepheline	24.7
Flint	31.5	Strontium	12.4
Whiting	2.8	China clay	7.1

Firing at 1225°C/2237°F.

This percentage of barium may be too high to pass the increasingly stringent 'release limits' now coming in although for non-domestic ware the only likely danger is to the potter using it in its raw state, see *poisonous materials* for sensible precautions to be taken. It will be noted that the above recipe also contains *strontium* which can replace baria to a degree but acts more like calcia. Barium also occurs in a surprising number of Japanese recipes (see Sanders). It will modify pigments sometimes in a startling way, producing blues and turquoise with copper, see *copper/turquoise glaze*. Proportions are critical and considerable experiment is necessary. Behrens mentions a red with nickel.

It is used industrially to prevent scum on bricks: the addition of 2–3% of the carbonate will do the same for red-clay biscuit ware (terracotta) which is liable to white discoloration. Wedge the carbonate into the body. The scum is caused by soluble salts, especially calcium chloride when the surface crystals are destroyed in handling. To quote Billington 'the barium effects a substitution $CaCl_2 + BaCO_3 = BaCl_2 + CaCO_3$'. The sulphate will have a similar effect.

Barytes

The natural rock of *barium sulfate* — $BaSO_4$. Associated with lead and consequently sometimes known as heavy-spar. Used to introduce baria into a glaze so long as the sulfur can be efficiently dispersed. Usually fritted with carbon into *barium carbonate*. (See also *witherite*.)

Basalt

The characteristic volcanic basic rock, smooth and black with 45–55% silica. High in iron. Ground and fired it can form a glassy material with a melting temperature variable between 1150–1250°C/2102–2282°F but is used with additional silica and feldspar to form a dark-colored glaze. Ivan England's analyses and discussion of basalts and basalt glazes appeared in PQ31, together with his glaze recipes using an 'average' basalt.

1 For a dark glaze: basalt 66; whiting 6; flint 28. This is the maximum possible proportion of basalt.

2 For a lighter color: basalt 17; feldspar 49; whiting 10; silica 16. Add bentonite 2% for suspension.

A basalt is listed by Ceramatech and others.

Basalt ware

Originated by Wedgwood as a name for a black vitreous body resembling basalt. A recipe quoted is:

Ball clay	47.0	China clay	3.0
Ironstone	40.0	Manganese	10.0

In effect basalt ware is a black slip body fired to vitrification. The recipes for *black slip* using iron, manganese and cobalt in various proportions can be adapted. A 'basalt' body is now supplied commercially. Among modern potters, Colin Pearson has used it effectively in winged cylinders.

A 'basalt body' recipe given in CM17 is:

Red clay	40	China clay	18
Ball clay	15	Ferric oxide	16
Manganese	6	Nepheline	2
Bentonite	3		

Base, basic (chemical)

One of the main chemical groupings. Inorganic materials may be classed as bases or *acids*. In general the bases cause ceramic mixtures to become *fusible*: they are *glass modifiers*. Bases and acids combine to form '*salts*'. The bases are listed under the general term RO in the *Seger formula*; they also include the R_2O oxides, usually of metals.

The principal bases in pottery are the oxides of lead, sodium, potassium, magnesium, zinc, lithium, calcium, strontium and barium. Also the pigment oxides of manganese, copper and cobalt.

The bases include the *alkalis* and the *alkaline earths*. (See also *flux*.)

Base cracks

During throwing, the base of a pot undergoes less pressure, and is worked on less, than the walls. It is thus less aligned in particle structure and liable to greater shrinkage. The compression of the base from the outside at any time in the throwing process can help to prevent base cracks. During drying, bases must always be free to contract. (See *cracking*.) Hamer PDMT has an exhaustive study of base cracks.

Basic rock

Igneous rocks comparatively high in basic minerals. They may contain 45–55% of silica but most of it is locked into silicate minerals so that there is little of the 'free' oxide. *Basalt* is the main type; generally volcanic in origin. It can decompose into clay material but, to quote Cardew, 'tends to produce montmorillonite rather than kaolinite'. The high iron content of these rocks limits their use as a glaze material.

Basic slag

A byproduct of the steel industry, rich in phosphorus and iron, with some silica and calcium. Obtainable as fertilizer. Occasionally occurs in glaze recipes. Mentioned in Green, and Cardew. The slag can be used in stoneware glazes where it will introduce an interesting, if not always predictable, well-combined batch of ingredients. *Opalescence* can result from the phosphorus. It can be used with red clay for *tenmoku* type glazes.

Basketwork

The plaiting together of strips of clay to form pots or bowls. Used by Ann Mortimer for the centres of plates and by Rita Peleg and others in the US.

Bat, batt

Applied to various types of sheet material:

1 *Kiln shelves*, or *cranks* of refractory clays.

2 A slab of plaster or low fired biscuit for drying clay.

3 Sheet material used for supporting, transporting or drying pottery. Should be slightly porous so that it releases the clay as it dries. It is easy to slide a wet pot onto a glazed surface but almost impossible to remove it when leather-hard.

4 A removable disk of wood, plaster, or other material which is fastened to the wheelhead but can be easily removed. For repetition throwing or for large pieces. See *wheel bat*.

5 A bat-shaped piece of wood (e.g. a butter pat) for beating pots or stirring glaze.

6 A short brick. In USA a broken brick — hence brickbat.

The use of a fairly stiff ring of clay to adhere a throwing bat to the wheelhead.

See also *bat printing, bat wash, ejector head, kiln shelves, wheel bat.*

Batch, *batch weight*

A proportioned mixture of materials. Batch weights are in fixed proportions to one another but have random totals. For easier comparison and calculation bring all batch weights to percentages.

Method:
Multiply each number in the recipe by 100 and then divide by the total.
An example of the same recipe as batch weights and as percentages:

Batch weight	Percentage weight	
143	44	(i.e 143 x 100 ÷ 325 = 44)
65	20	
13	4	
<u>103</u>	<u>32</u>	
325	100	

Bat printing

The transfer of designs, in oil, onto ceramics from a flexible glue or silicone pad which is then dusted with color. It has the advantage that it can accommodate a curved surface to some degree. Used by some craft potters and is included in some *photoceramic* processes.

Batwash

A *refractory* material applied to *bats, saggars* and *kiln shelves* to prevent ware sticking to them during firing. Flint or, preferably, calcined alumina and a little clay mixed with water may be brushed on. The disadvantage of coated shelves is that they cannot be reversed. A thin dust of dry alumina is usually sufficient — this can be brushed off. *Kyanite* has been mentioned as a batwash, as has the similar mineral *sillimanite*, also *bauxite*, and *zircon*. Glaze rarely sticks to *silicon carbide* shelves. Lime washes may be used for saltglaze but avoid any mixture of alumina and silica for setting or batwash. Layers of glossy paper have been suggested, relying on the lime content of the coated surface.

Bauxite

The ore of aluminium, Al_2O_3, $2H_2O$ with iron, titania and other impurities. The name derives from an early source at Beaux in France. A *sedimentary* rock with clay and iron. For a detailed discussion of 'bauxitization' see Cardew. (See also *diaspore, gibbsite*.)

Bead

Jewelry beads are often made in ceramic. The work is somewhat tedious, especially the glazing. Biscuit beads in colored or variegated bodies can be fired in bowls or on tiles. Beads need not be spherical, but may be square, cylindrical, conical, or of a flattened shape, with carved, rolled, painted, or molten glass decoration. Rolling a bead across a textured surface will transfer the pattern to the bead. The true bead will have a hole through it. This needs to be clear and without excessively sharp edges which may cut the string.

Glazed beads must either have a hole large enough to allow them to be threaded over a heat resisting nichrome, or high temperature alloy wire (Kemper), or be designed with one flat, unglazed surface on which they can rest. The wire can be supported at each end on a 'cradle' which you can make yourself. Partial or spot glazing is easier than full glaze covering, although even maiolica painting is possible if you are prepared for the rather tiresome work of ensuring that the hole in the bead and a small circle around it are free from glaze. One can apply a spot of wax to one end, impale the other on a toothpick and then dip the bead into the glaze. Threading the beads onto a fine drinking straw has been suggested, the nichrome wire being inserted through the straw, the straw burns away during firing. For higher temperatures A 'ceramic bead bar — (which) holds up to cone 10' is listed by Kemper. The use of Egyptian paste will obviate much of this work.

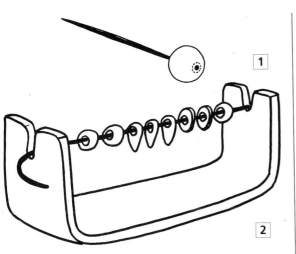

1 A bead can be glazed by impaling it on a cocktail stick or a toothpick.
2 A bead firing 'cradle' formed from a strip of clay and a length of nichrome (or Kanthal wire for higher temperatures) wire. If the wire is too long (over about 8in/20cm) or overloaded it may sag during firing. A similar 'bead tree' is listed by Axner.

Special ceramic beads are used as electrical insulators threaded onto wires which are subject to heat. Can be used for sheathing connections on electric kilns.

Beading, dotting

Lines of dots in relief, often slip-trailed, used decoratively. Hamer uses the word to describe excessive crawling of glaze into blobs. See Fournier DPF for illustration and discussion. See also at *dotting*.

Beaker

A drinking vessel with or without a handle and usually without a saucer. A very wide range of shapes is possible — the stumpy barrel being the least attractive. See Fournier DPF for a variety of forms.

Beam scale

Perhaps the most accurate and sensitive of scales, but rather expensive although, with the influx of electronic instruments, it may be possible to pick one up second hand. Can weigh from 5–10,000g (0.18oz to 32lb) and be zero adjusted to take account of containers. A 'double beam scale' which will deal with larger quantities of materials and which can be adjusted for the weight of the container is listed by Baileys.

Beaten decoration

Similar to *impressed* decoration, but more spontaneous and direct. The edge of a stick, or a textured surface such as a

1 The surface of a pot may be simply ridged with a sharp edged tool.
2 and *3* Here a circular 'sun' is beaten into a slab of clay which is then applied to the slipped surface of a pot.

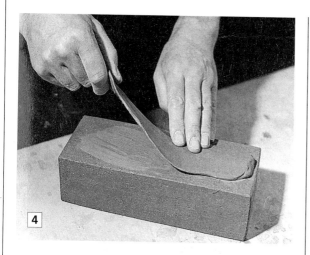

4 and *5* An irregular slab of plastic clay is luted on and the pattern then beaten in. Further subtlety can be obtained by later planing the half-dry surface.

butter pat or string wound round a bat, can be used with wide-ranging effects from subtle indented marks to deep three-dimensional impressions. The beater can be ragged or irregular although too obvious a repeat in the pattern can become rather mechanical. The edges can be left sharp, or softened with a sponge.

Beaten patterns retain more of their characteristic quality under thin spare glazes than with thicker coatings (dry ash glazes are very suitable).

The actual surface of a pot can be beaten, or an applied slab of softer (perhaps differently colored) clay can be luted on. Large decorative 'sun' forms can be beaten from circular slabs of clay. These are attractive in themselves, and the exercise can be useful in releasing pent-up tensions in the potter!

These pots were formed as rounded 'envelope' shapes and then beaten to form ridges or spines down the front and sides (more distinct on the right hand pot), the form resembling a brazil nut. By Robert Fournier.

Beaten form

Thrown or handbuilt pottery can be gently beaten to alter form, profile or emphasis, or to provide panels for decoration. It is a favorite technique among modern potters, offering a subtle contrast between curved and plane surfaces. The beating can be done as soon as the surface loses its stickiness or at any subsequent stage up to leather-hard; the different clay states yield different styles and qualities of form. The bat should be wide enough to avoid edge marks; slightly chamfered or rounded corners will help. The clay undergoes considerable strain and the blows should be just hard enough to ease it into a change of shape without forcing it. Alternatively the pot can be flattened or rocked on the bench surface.

Thrown or built pots are often distorted, more or less violently, by beating with a flat bat, a shaped piece of wood or other object, or with a sharper edged tool, at the extreme giving the almost destroyed forms favored in the USA especially during the 1970s and 1980s when iconoclasm was all.

Beater

For light work, butter pats make excellent beaters for

knocking into, or out of shape. Old pats can be found in junk shops and new ones are now available. For work requiring a heavier tool a cricket bat shape can easily be cut from a piece of 3 x ¾in (75 x 20mm) timber. Wood is the best material for beaters, nonporous surfaces such as plastic tend to stick to the clay. Edges should be rounded and faces sanded smooth.

Beaters or 'paddles' can be carved to give a simple overall pattern and many Japanese potters keep a stock of decorated paddles. Plain beaters can double up as glaze stirrers. Beaters wrapped in string or cord, or cut with groove, have been used for many centuries ('Jomon' of Japan, the earliest known ceramics, translates as 'cord impressed'). (See also illus. under *paddle*.)

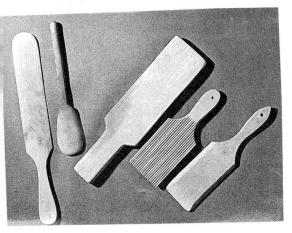

A variety of bats and beaters:
From the left: a cooking spatula, a flat-backed wooden spoon, a paddle, and two butter pats.

Bedding

See *placing*.

Beidellite

A clay mineral of the *montmorillonite* group from Beidell, Colorado. Rich in alumina.

Bell, *ceramic*

Highly decorative bells can be either handbuilt or constructed from a mixture of modeling and extruded cylinders. Nancy Hall (CR161) found that a slit with a circular hole at one end improved the sound. They are best suspended from a cord so that the resonance is not impeded.

Belly

The widest part (where this is not the *shoulder*) of a full-bodied pot form. The typical *bottle* shape.

Bentonite

There are two forms: calcium bentonite and sodium bentonite, the latter swelling as it takes up water.

A very fine-grained (*colloidal*) clay of the montmorillonite type containing bases and iron, derived from volcanic ash. The name originated from a source at Fort Benton, USA. The particle size is probably under 0.03% of the average *kaolinite* grain. It is a very sticky clay with a high shrinkage (the bonding between the unit layers allows the ingress of more water than does kaolinite) and a tendency to crack during firing and cooling. It is therefore unworkable alone or in any large quantity in a body, but its super-plasticity (at least as far as *thixotropy* is concerned) can help short bodies such as porcelains. It also assists the *suspension* of a glaze.

Calcium bentonite is the most useful type. As mentioned above, sodium bentonite will swell as it takes up water. The iron content always colors bentonite but there is a so-called white bentonite with an analysis by weight:

K_2O	5.0				
Na_2O	2.0	Al_2O_3	12.0	SiO_2	64.2
CaO	2.0	Fe_2O_3	2.0		
MgO	2.3				

This will give a better color in reduction than in oxidation, if used in a *porcelain body*. Bentonites vary widely in plasticity and purity. A few, such as *fuller's earth*, may be relatively unplastic.

Bentonite is difficult to mix into a glaze batch. Work it into a thick slurry with a little water first and add further water only very gradually. Pass the bentonite slip several times through a 120 mesh or small 200 color lawn. If it is tipped dry into a glaze it will merely float in small globules unless it is ground and very thoroughly dispersed among the rest of the ingredients. The normal maximum is 3% for addition to a body or glaze but up to 12% has been suggested. (See also *once-fired ware*).

Berkeley clay

A plastic refractory clay from South Carolina.

Beryllia

Beryllium oxide, BeO.
An alkaline earth. An expensive (and toxic) glaze flux for

high temperatures. Emerald and aquamarine are natural forms. Now seldom listed by suppliers.

Beta form

Generally applied to the crystal form of quartz at temperatures above the *inversion point*.

Bi-, or Di-

Indicating double; in chemistry the terms are used to describe a combination with two atoms or molecules, e.g. carbon-di-oxide (two oxygen atoms to one carbon); bisilicate of lead (two molecules of silica to one of lead oxide). (See also *binary compound*.)

Bib

The rounded shoulder of a pot or the side of a bowl may be dipped into a slip or glaze to form a 'bib' which will automatically reflect the vessel shape. This may be left as a block of decoration or used as a panel for subsequent sgraffito or other treatment.

Bichromate *of ammonium or potassium*

A *photosensitive* chemical (toxic) used in printing onto ceramics. Avoid skin contact. Use goggles and mask when handling. Combustible and 'explosive in dry state' (Scott).

Bin trolley, *Dolly*

A variation on the old 'sack truck'. A two-wheeled trolley with a flat base ledge, on which bins or sacks of material can be supported or moved. Also listed are 'stair climbing' bin trolleys. A bin 'dolly' is a wheeled flat platform for moving bins around which can save many a back-ache or slipped disc though, to be really efficient you would need one for each bin.

Binary compound

A compound of two elements only, denoted by suffix -ide, e.g. sulfide of lead PbS — galena.

Biotite mica

See *mica*.

Biscuit, *bisque*

Unglazed ware, usually porous. In the USA and in the pot-

tery industry the French form 'bisque' is preferred. The biscuit firing is for convenience, to render the pots less fragile and to make glazing easier. It is also reputed to produce a tougher glazed fabric. This is certainly the case in the industry, where the biscuit fire may be 150°C/302°F higher than the glaze fire. *Earthenware glazes* are less likely to craze on a high-fired biscuit (see *cristobalite*) but it is difficult to apply the raw glaze onto a body which has *vitrified* to any great degree.

Clay turns into ceramic at 500–600°C/932–1112°F so this temperature is the minimum for a biscuit fire (primitive sawdust and similar firings do not always reach this). At least one authority believes that the change is instantaneous at a certain temperature rather than progressive. Above 600°C/1112°F clays behave in different ways, i.e. approach *sintering* and *vitrification* at different temperatures. The more 'impurities' present, the lower the temperature. Biscuit firing should be oxidized except for special unglazed effects. For stoneware the biscuit need not exceed 850–900°C/1562–1652°F but for earthenware glazes a firing approaching 1100°C/2012°F will produce some *cristobalite* which will help to prevent *crazing*.

Ground-up biscuit is called *grog*. The term *terracotta* is often given to biscuit modeling or pots, especially in red clay.

Biscuit fire

A number of alterations and stresses occur during the firing of the clay into ceramic. The principal ones are:

Up to 100°C/ 212°F	'Mixed' or water of plasticity is driven off as vapor.
100–200°C/ 212–392°F	The adsorbed water is lost and organic materials begin to burn out (carbonize).
573°C/1063°F	Quartz inversion.
500–600°C/ 932–1112°F	Chemically combined water is lost and a new (ceramic) material is formed.
600°C/1112°F	Carbons, sulfur, etc. continue to burn out. There is a certain expansion in volume up to 800–850°C. Vitrification begins (at different temperatures for different clays), the particles pack more closely, and shrinkage occurs.

The greatest risk of breakage or explosion is in the 90–150°C/194–302°F range. Thick pieces are obviously more at risk than thin-walled ware. From 200°C/392°F fairly quick firing is possible, indeed the clay-ceramic conversion may be virtually instantaneous (Peter Smith). One can quote the 20-minute African brushwood firings, while industry has experimented with even shorter periods. My own biscuit, fired (after thorough drying) in four hours, has a good ring at 980°C/1796°F. However clays and kilns are so variable that no one can be dogmatic about their behavior. An average and conservative biscuit graph is shown.

With some clays it is considered useful to slow down the

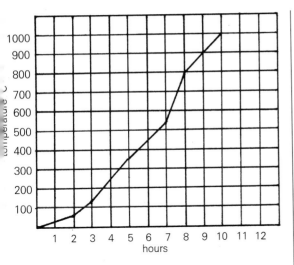

A biscuit firing graph showing three or four hours drying, including 'water smoking', a slight slowing down between 400–600°C/752–1112°F (by no means an essential refinement) then a faster rise to 1020°C/1868°F. A stoneware biscuit can be terminated earlier (900–960°C/1652–1760°F) but for earthenware a higher temperature (to c. 1090°C/1994°F if this can be reached without vitrification) will help to avoid future glaze crazing (see cristobalite). Some clays benefit from a slowdown between 900–1000°C/1652–1832°F to burn out any trapped carbon. An indication of this is shown on the graph.

rate of rise or even soak at around 900°C/1652°F in order to fully dispel impurities and to oxidize any carbon to CO_2, or *black core* and *bloating* can result in the subsequent glaze fire, caused by trapped carbon.

Biscuit stopping

Filling of cracks or repairing. See *stopping*.

Bismuth, oxide

A metallic element Bi, 209.0.
Oxide Bi_2O_3, 466, m.p. 825°C.

Can be used to produce a mother-of-pearl luster. Listed as a base in glazes, although its oxide suggests that it is *amphoteric*. Parmelee describes the preparation of bismuth luster using the resinate of bismuth, and suggests its addition to yellow and gray-brown luster. Bismuth can also be used as a carrier for other luster colors (Hamer PDMF). (See also *luster*.)

Bisque

See *biscuit*.

Bit

See *crank*.

Bivalent

A *valency* of two (will combine with two hydrogen atoms), e.g. the valency of oxygen in water (H_2O) is two. Thus it follows that the valency of calcium in calcium oxide (CaO) is also two—it is bivalent. (See diagram at *valency*.)

Black body

Similar considerations arise as in *black slips*. Only a vitrified body will approach a true black. (See also *basalt ware*, *black color*.)

Black color

The high light absorption necessary for a good black can be developed in a shiny glaze, in a vitrified body, and by reducing or carbonizing a burnished body.

A construction in partly glazed black clay — 'Firmer ground'. By Henry Pim.

When used as a painting pigment the usual iron, cobalt, manganese mixture (see *black glazes*) may separate out in some degree and may run. The industrial black pigments may contain nickel and chrome (so beware *chrome-tin-pink*). An excess of copper will fire to a cindery black. Iridium has been quoted but is difficult to obtain. Many *tenmoku* iron glazes will give a fine black.

Black core

Bricks, shards of primitive pottery, and even 17th-century slipware often show a section which is red for a few millimeters from each face, but black in the center. Caused by an inadequately oxidized or too rapid firing of a carbonaceous and, generally, high-iron clay, resulting in the formation of black iron oxide from the red. In sawdust firing the black core is inevitable (though this is more often *carbonization* than black iron), but it can be a great decorative asset where it breaks through to the surface.

A shard of Hertfordshire (England) slipware showing the black stripe in the thickest part of the section.

Black glaze

The standard black earthenware glaze has been quoted as 4% each of iron, cobalt and manganese. Many black glaze and pigment recipes approximate to this combination. Rhodes recommends 2% of each; Billington 6% manganese, 4% iron in a lead and soda glaze, or 7% manganese, 1% cobalt and 2% iron in a lead glaze.

The high pigment content necessary to produce a near-black will affect glaze fusibility. The manganese is also liable to cause bubbling. Copper blacks are possible but rather tricky: 3–5% will produce a matt surface at earthenware temperatures (see also 'gun-metal' black mentioned under *black pigments*). Copper can be combined with iron to produce a 'mirror black' (Rhodes CGP). Manganese/copper combinations, often producing a bronze color rather than black, have a very low eutectic and can cause running in glazes or pigments. Also beware of manganese with zinc.

In stoneware, especially in reduction which turns red iron oxide to the black oxide, between 5% and 12% of iron oxide in a *siliceous* glaze, and preferably on a siliceous body, should give black, although in some glazes the higher proportions may re-oxidize on the surface to produce *kaki* reds. A different quality of color can be developed with 6–8% iron and 1–2% cobalt. A high concentration of manganese in an oxidized fire can give a metallic pewter-like surface up to about 1270°C. The finest quality black wares were produced in Song China. Leach quotes the addition of 10% of medium wood ash to Hamada's 'building stone' glaze for tenmoku. Potclays 'black feldspar' could be the basis for a similar experiment. The so-called 'oil spot' or 'hare's fur' glaze markings may have derived from settled-down bubble craters. Some authorities, however, consider that these are more likely to be glass-in-glass melts. Rhodes is convinced that they are natural slip glazes, similar to *Albany clay* glazes. Manganese earthenware glazes, which are also liable to bubble, occasionally exhibit similar patterns. As well as Albany clay, ochre, burnt sienna, and spodumene have been suggested.

Black iron oxide

'Becomes a flux at temperatures over 900°C/1652°F' (Hamer PDMT) and so should be treated as such, even in earthenware glazes. Above 1200°C/2192°F its behavior is more complicated. W J Doble's black iron stoneware 'gives dramatic colors in reduction'.

Black pigment

See also *black color*. A true black pigment is difficult to mix from raw materials. The standard cobalt/manganese/iron mixture will tend to separate out, though often in a pleasant way. It will also run. In ready-made industrial colors the oxides are sintered together, with opacifiers and refractories, and are blended to maintain the hue and to minimize running and blurring. Black prepared pigments (underglaze or stains) will almost certainly contain chrome (so beware of chrome-tin reactions), and nickel will often be present (listed in many catalogs).

'Standard black' quoted by Dodd consists of 30 cobaltic oxide, 56 ferric oxide, 48 chromic oxide, 8 nickel oxide, 31 alumina. Other black mixtures quoted in Webb are for underglaze: ferric oxide 36, oxides of chrome 7, manganese 12, cobalt 32, nickel 13; and for stains — iron chromate 51, oxides of nickel 9, cobalt 21, chrome 4, iron 15. A simple mixture of 9:1 $MnO:CoO$ with perhaps a little iron oxide will give an approximate black at earthenware temperatures.

There are also iridium blacks. A gun-metal black results from equal parts of copper, manganese and cobalt. Copper and manganese can give black with a gold sheen. (See *copper/manganese gold*.)

Black slip

The traditional black slip for lead glazed slipware is red clay with up to 10% dry weight of manganese dioxide. The biscuit fire must be kept low (*c*. 1000°C/1832°F) to avoid vitrification which inhibits the glaze take-up.

Some of the manganese can be replaced with either iron and cobalt or both, but the distinctive quality of the simple slip will be lost. Manganese slip under a tin glaze will produce warm grays and even, on occasion, a gentle salmon blush, see *tin-over-slip*. The *fusible* nature of manganese is ideally suited to staining through a normally opaque glaze. Any trace of cobalt will cool the color. Black slip applied thinly (flooded over or brushed on) on a buff body will fade unevenly under a lead glaze to browns and yellowish colors. Difficult to control but very attractive at its best.

The high shrinkage of red clay-based black slip necessitates its use on clay which is slightly softer than leatherhard. Black slip, with perhaps a more sophisticated body base (see *engobes*), will be self-glazing (vitrified) at stoneware temperatures.

Blacksmith's scale

Iron spangles. Originally the blue flakes resulting from hammered iron, now produced by roasting scrap iron. (See also at *ilmenite, magnetic iron, magnetite, spangles*.)

Bleb, blebbing

An American term for small blisters on pottery caused by air pockets just below the surface. A minor form of *bloating*. Avoided by careful *wedging* and clean clay.

Bleed-through

A colloquial term for the breaking through of impurities in the body to speckle or color a glaze.

The commonest source is *pyrites* (iron sulfide) in the clay, especially fireclay. Largely an aspect of reduction at high temperatures. Attempts have been made to simulate and control the effect artificially in oxidation using iron spangles and other coarse-grained pigments. (See also *tin-over-slip*.)

Blistering

Bubbles of escaping gas, generally from carbonates, are an inevitable feature of glazes at some point in their firing. Raw material glazes are thus more liable to blister than frits. Most of the bubbles settle down as the glaze melts, but if the firing is terminated too early, or is carried on to a point where further reactions begin (often thought of as 'boiling') then unhealed craters will be left in the cooled glaze. The bubbles may be of oxygen from manganese dioxide, fluorine from some china stones, or any other gaseous material released by the firing.

Blistering may be aggravated by too thick a coating of glaze; by the slight reduction of a lead glaze; by too rapid an end-fire (1240–1280°C in stoneware); by sulfur compounds, perhaps in the body; by the use of fluorine minerals in the glaze; and, probably the commonest cause of all in earthenware, by the setting of newly glazed and inadequately dried pots in the kiln. Even a preliminary warming-up does not always help in an electric kiln and it is essential to dry the pots thoroughly **before packing**.

Bloating

The development of gas pockets in a body after it has started to vitrify and is *pyroplastic*, causing it to develop local swelling. Bad mixing or wedging, or sulfides in the clay can be causes. Gas may also be generated by carbon obtaining oxygen from the body and forming carbon dioxide, or by minute pockets of water in closed pores deep in the fabric.

Care must be taken, when firing the biscuit, to avoid vitrification by sudden or local temperature rise (see also *flashing*), especially in bodies high in carbonates. In stoneware firing Cardew recommends that oxidizing conditions be maintained to 1150°C/2102°F. My own firing schedule is a rapid one and I find that, using comparatively high iron bodies in an oxidizing fire, there is a critical temperature — about 1275°C/2327°F — where bloating may occur.

As bloating normally occurs only when the clay is sufficiently 'molten' to swell without breaking, it is thus a feature of high-fired pottery. Most bodies will bloat if they are overfired or if they have a premature glass phase, e.g. an excess of feldspathic material. Needless to say, any tiny pellets of body ingredients or 'foreign' materials will increase the risk. David Leach suggests an oxidized soaking at 1000°C/1832°F to burn out carbon, Alan Graham (CR75) half an hour of light reduction at 800°C/1472°F to produce sulfides which will decompose and disperse, though in my experience this can cause smoke staining (see *smoked ware*) which will not burn out. Hamer mentions too 'stiff' a glaze layer or a vitrifying slip as contributory causes, and Cardew an excess of $CaCO_3$ or $MgCO_3$. For once-fired ware there must be plenty of ventilation for the first 1000°C/1832°F especially when using high sulfur clays.

Good preparation, clean clay, avoidance of over-firing, the addition of some opening material such as grog or calcined china clay (*Molochite*) will all help to avoid bloating.

Potters have been known to bloat pots deliberately as a decorative feature.

Block handle

A handle cut from a clay slab with a vertical strip for fixing to the vessel.

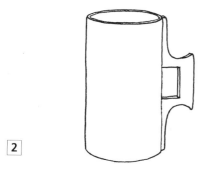

1 Example of a block handle. By Nick Homoky.

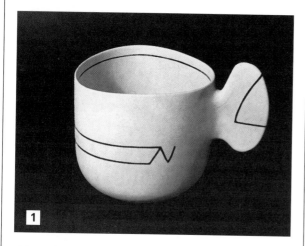

2 Another style of block handle.

Blown slip

A layered effect produced by blowing across a newly slipped surface which can then be used as a ground for further embellishment.

Blue pigment, *glaze stain*

There is a bewildering variety of blue colors listed in suppliers' catalogs. Most of them derive from cobalt, which can be mixed and fritted with other materials to give various shades of blue. Some of the shades quoted are:

Willow blue: recipe by Dodd — cobalt oxide 40, feldspar 40, flint 20. A diluted blue.

Manzarine or royal blue from cobalt with various fluxes

Matt blue: Cobalt 20, alumina 60, zinc 20. A cobalt aluminate which would need to be fritted.

Peacock blue, cobalt oxide, with china stone, *standard black* (see *black pigments*), and flint.

Early blue frits were *zaffre*, and *smalt*. Most fritted blues are for use on earthenware. At high temperatures it is difficult to prevent the formation of rather strident cobalt silicates. Even with the use of cobalt aluminates, a eutectic is formed with the silica of the glaze at around 1200°C/2192°F.

Many potters find modern cobalt oxides used as pigments too pure and stark and make additions of other materials to modify their stridency. Various combinations (up to 80% of the total pigment batch) of manganese, iron, red clay, nickel, or rutile have been suggested in an attempt to approximate to the impure *asbolite*. A simple dilution for use as a pigment on earthenware is one part of cobalt to four parts of china stone. Unless specking is required, cobalt colors need careful sieving through a 200 mesh lawn, or levigating in the way described by Cardew, who considers it a mistake to sieve pigments.

Some prepared blues will contain chrome, particularly the dark blues and slate colors. Blue is also prepared from vanadium and zircon for temperatures up to 1280°C/2336°F, e.g. 3–5% vanadium oxide; 60–70% zircon; with some silica, for a very dependable pigment. An involved formula for producing steel blue crystals from nickel 1280°C/2336°F is described in Webb CNS. Rutile in reduction is reputed to produce blue glaze, as is reduced vanadium. For discussion of *turquoise* blue from copper see under that heading, (see also *cobalt*).

For blue flushes on an alkaline glaze firing at the unusual range 1120–1140°C/2048–2084°F in oxidation, Derek Emms (CR123) quotes a recipe attributed to Heber Mathews: alkaline frit 32, feldspar 48, whiting 12, china clay 8, over iron (as pigment, in a slip, or a body).

Blue slip

The addition of 0.5–2.5% of cobalt oxide to a pale-firing clay body will produce light to dark blue slip. The higher concentrations are useful when using *tin glaze over slip*. Richard Phethean mentions 20% of cobalt oxide but this slip is used 'in thin washes' (CR169). The color can be rather hard and characterless, but may be softened by using a little red clay or any of the modifiers mentioned under *blue pigments*. Grind and sieve the colors through a 200 lawn (unless speckle is required).

Blunger

A machine for stirring and mixing ceramic materials,

usually the ingredients of a clay body, with water. The slip is then used as such, or dried to a plastic body. The machine consists of paddles revolving horizontally in a vat, usually hexagonal or octagonal in plan, the angles exerting some resistance to the circulation of the mix. A 15 gallon industrial blunger may be fairly costly but the mechanism is simple and a potter who wished to prepare his own clays could build one. The paddles are driven from above the vat at between 100–200 r.p.m. There are also impeller blungers which force the slurry through radial channels. 'Blunging' by hand can be done with a simple paddle or the old-fashioned washing 'dolly' or 'peggy stick'.

Smaller electric high-speed mixers are available for up to four gallons, and are suitable for clay which has already been broken into small pieces. Rhodes suggests an old washing machine. For small quantities clay need merely be steeped in water. The major problem in 'temperate' climes is not the mixing but the drying of the slip. The use of *dough mixers* bypasses the liquid stage. (See also *clay preparation.*)

Blush

A pink-rose colored area on a glaze usually caused by a reaction with a *volatilized* coloring oxide, usually either chrome or copper. Chrome can react with lead, lime and tin in an earthenware fire (see *chrome-tin pink*), or even in stoneware if a high-dolomite glaze with zinc is used. In reduction, copper can also stain adjacent pots. Occasionally a pleasant blush can arise using *tin glaze over slip* (black slip). Prepared colors, especially dark hues, often contain chrome and may give rise to blushing on tin glazes. Iron from the body can break through as a rosy area where it has been licked by the flames during firing, though this happy accident is rare.

Body

Any clay, mixture of clays, or admixture with other ceramic materials. Few natural clays are used alone but are blended together to produce a mixture with specific qualities. For instance, a plastic and *fusible* ball clay may be combined with a *refractory* fireclay, a little red clay and some *grog* to produce an easily workable, buff-colored, open textured stoneware body. Non-clay minerals — flint, china stone, sand, etc. may also be included. These will lessen plasticity.

Non-clay minerals: flint, sand, etc. can be added to increase silica content or to 'open' or give texture to the body. Fluxes such as china stone, nepheline syenite, feldspar or even boric oxide or calcia are sometimes added, especially to *porcelain* to increase vitrification. Those bodies with a considerable mixture of non-clays are often known as *pastes* or, when used as slips, *engobes*. All will reduce plasticity and may be balanced in some degree by the further addition of *montmorillonites* such as *bentonite*.

There are as many body recipes as there are potters. Industrial earthenware bodies are still based on Wedgwood's 18th-century experiments. The simplest recipe is equal parts of ball clay, china clay, stone, and flint. This is fired to about 1200°C/2192°F, when it becomes a tough but still porous biscuit. At 1300°C/2372°F it vitrifies into a near-porcelain, but still opaque material. For 1220°C/2228°F, firing in an electric kiln, Richard Zakin (USA) uses a fairly complicated body: stoneware clay 45%; kaolin (china clay) 35%; nepheline syenite 5%; wollastonite 5%; flint 5%; ball clay 5%. He also adds dolomite in some recipes.

A potter can modify a prepared plastic body to suit his particular purposes. I use five parts of a buff stoneware body with one of a Staffordshire red clay, wedged together, for a 1260°C/2300°F oxidized firing. It rings well, is reasonably vitrified, of a warm color, and is almost chip-proof! Simple additions to a body include sand or grog to give 'bite' and texture; ball clay to improve fusibility and plasticity (in very short bodies, e.g. porcelain, up to 3% bentonite); quartz or flint or a siliceous *fireclay* to increase refractoriness and to decrease shrinkage; red clay for fusibility and to warm the color; china clay for whiteness and to vary particle size (when in the form of *Molochite* it will also decrease shrinkage); feldspar or stone to increase fusibility. Silica, in some form, added to earthenware bodies will assist craze resistance. The effectiveness or otherwise of body mixtures or additions must always be tried and proved in the kiln. The correction of vices in clays — *warping, shattering, cracking*, etc. — can be a complicated process. Porcelain poses special problems which are discussed under that heading. Ready-blended plastic clays are often too smooth and refined and need further adjustments.

The preparation of bodies can be by simple layering and wedging. This is hard work but quite effective if done thoroughly. Cardew, however, gives a surprising warning concerning the wedging of unplastic materials (e.g. china clay) into plastic clay. The mixture, he states, will approximate to the **least** plastic of the ingredients! He recommends that china clay be added as a slip.

If a high proportion of powder or dry materials is used it is necessary to mix them together on a clean floor, work them into a slurry with water, dry to a plastic state, and wedge thoroughly. Alternatively one becomes mechanized and uses a blunger (or a large ball mill), followed by sieving, drying (see *dewatering*), and pugging. In all cases at least a week's rest is necessary for the clay to mature before use. Other body-mixing equipment includes batch mixers with rotating runners, and *dough mixers*, which have quite been the vogue among studio potters.

A special addition to a red body is barium carbonate to prevent *scumming*. Many body recipes can be found in pottery primers and magazines. (See also *ovenware, glaze-body fit, shrinkage*, etc.)

Body-glaze layer

See *interface*.

Body stain

Most of the pigment oxides and commercially prepared stains can be used to produce colored bodies (see also at *slip*, and under individual colors — *blue, green*, etc.). If metal oxides are used it is advisable to limit body color to a few simple mixtures of iron, copper, manganese, or cobalt (in larger percentages they will have an effect on the fusibility of the body).

Stoneware and porcelain glazes over stained bodies can be interesting. The swirling bands of subtle color in some of Lucie Rie's bowls and bottles are derived from *marbled* stained bodies, generally manganese bodies, in an oxidized fire. Unless speckling is required it is advisable to sieve all body stains through a 200 mesh lawn. (See also *agate ware, distinguishing stain*.)

Boiling point

Strictly speaking, the point at which the vapor pressure of a liquid is equal to the atmospheric pressure. The most familiar boiling point is that of water — 100°C/212°F — but many glaze constituents, and their mixtures, will 'boil' at some point during the maturation of a glaze, giving off a gaseous vapor and causing bubbles. These must be given time to settle although too high a temperature or excessive soaking can lead to further reactions. Fritted materials are obviously less liable to cause trouble. (See also at *blistering*.)

Bole

A friable, earthy clay, stained with iron oxide. It was the type used in Turkey for their famous underglaze red (so also called Armenian bole), and today a similar mixture of iron and clay is used for the much higher-fired red dots on David Leach's work. (See *red color and glaze*.)

Bond, atomic

Molecules and networks owe their structure to bonds or linkages between atoms. These can be of several kinds: electrovalent where electrons are transferred from one

atom to another, producing ions; covalent, where electrons are shared; and weaker bonds involving electrically neutral particles known as Van der Waals forces. Also various combinations of these types. (See also *atomic theory, valency*.)

Bone ash

Calcium phosphate, $3CaO\ P_2O_5$ [sometimes written $Ca_3(PO_4)_2$]. 310 (equivalent wt 103).

A typical analysis by weight:

MgO	1.27	Al_2O_3 0.36	P_2O_5 40.9
CaO	53.9	Fe_2O_3 0.11	TiO_2 0.01

Made by calcining bone, mainly cattle bone. A 'bone ash substitute' is listed by PSH (USA). Its principal use is in bone china bodies which may contain up to 50% of the ash. Occasionally used in a glaze (phosphorus is one of the glass-forming oxides although Hamer asserts that it does not enter the silica lattice) as an opacifier, giving a milky quality and a more matt surface, but can also lead to bubble trouble. 'Used to give texture in low fire glazes' (Axner).

Bone china

An English hybrid between soft-paste and true porcelain. The refractory and unplastic nature of English china clay inhibited the successful manufacture of porcelain. Bone china was developed during the 18th century and its ingredients fixed by Spode in 1800. It is a very translucent ware with great toughness, resembling porcelain though not in 'coldness' or structure at a fracture. The calcined bone forms about half the body. Billington gives a recipe: bone ash 40; china clay 32; china stone 28. This is obviously unplastic and must be thrown very thickly and turned to a thin wall, or, as is more usual, *slip cast*. Additions of

Slip-cast bone china 'Wing Jugs' with airbrushed decoration, h. 12cm/4 ¾in. By Sasha Wardell.

ball clay, bentonite, etc. are liable to spoil color and translucency. Shrinkage is around 10% up to 1250°C/2282°F. Industrially it is biscuit fired at 1250°C/2282°F (bedded in alumina) and glaze fired with a *soft glaze* at around 1080°C/1976°F but it is possible to reverse this schedule (see below). It is increasingly used by studio potters, notably Glenys Barton (designing for Wedgwood), Jacqueline Poncelet, and others. The work is slip cast and the walls are sometimes paper-thin. Slip-cast bone china is given a first firing to 1050°C/1922°F by Sasha Wardell in order to be able to complete the fettling without endangering the frail ware (CR111). Color and glaze are applied with a spray gun. She also recommends a one and a half hour soaking at the final 1260°C/2300°F firing.

Bonfire firing

The primitive method of bedding pots in brushwood, heaping wood and grass on top of them, and then setting the heap alight. The method can still be a valuable educational exercise and may even yield pots of a highly decorative character.

In other than tropical climes, the main danger is the *dunting* of the pots through sudden and uneven cooling. Pots must be resistant to thermal shock. This can be achieved by the addition of *grog* (preferable to sand), though the grog makes burnishing more difficult. Well rounded forms, thin-walled but with sturdy rims, are most likely to survive. Make all joins secure and keep the pots, during building, as evenly damp as possible. Pinching, coiling, and throwing are suitable techniques; slab pots are not recommended. Pots can be prefired to a low biscuit and the bonfire used as decorative treatment.

For raw clay firing the pots should be pre-heated to expel adsorbed water. The African potter inverts her large pots over a small heap of glowing embers. The pots in the bonfire are protected by shards which also probably conserve some heat.

Method: Build your bonfire on dry ground or on a brick bed. Pre-heat the pots in a kiln or over a small fire, perhaps on a grill or *grate*, and immediately bed them in dry grass and brushwood. Lay radiating rings of sticks or brushwood against the pots, topping with grass or straw. Light at several points simultaneously. The firing can be maintained for a time with fresh fuel. Protect against wind if possible. Cover with leaves and soil as the fire dies down, to minimize dunting. The use of a pit and a grill or grate (of metal, or fired pottery cylinders) will increase heat and can also be used for the initial warming.

Experiments carried out by Southampton University confirm that good results are possible only on a fairly still, warm day. Their best pots were fired in a pit dug into a pile of used stable straw, layering the pots with dry leaves and burning from the top as in *sawdust firing*, 780°C/1436°F was reached. (See also at *kiln* for a paper version.)

Bonsai bowl

Shallow bowls or trays, with drainage holes, of various decorative plans, often rectangular and slab-built, for growing dwarfed trees. The formal possibilities are wide.

A planted bonsai bowl by Peter and Dorothy Yates.

Borate

A combination with boric oxide. In glazes, boric oxide is combined with other elements. The minerals colemanite and borax are borates. Their molecular structures are diverse and involved. (See *borax*.)

Borax, borax frit

Sodium diborate, Na_2O. $2B_2O_3$. $10H_2O$, 381.5.
Calcined (anhydrous) borax, Na_2O, $2B_2O_3$. 202 m.p. 600°C.

All forms of borax are soluble to a greater or lesser degree and are normally used in a fritted form. Borax provides the base, soda, and a very fusible acid, boric oxide. It is therefore very efficient at lowering the maturing temperature of any glaze. Soft glazes must contain either lead oxide or borax — often both.

A typical borax frit, melting at 1000–1020°C/1832–1868°F. Molecular parts:

CaO 0.632	Al₂O₃ 1.15	Na₂O 0.336
SiO 2.6	K₂O 0.032	B₂O₃ 0.644

A similar frit formula is given by Hamer as

$$Na_2O.\ 2B_2O_3.\ 3SiO_2.$$

Very soft borax frits (850°C/1562°F) can be used, with the addition of 3% of bentonite, for *raku*. Borax can also be added to salt to assist *salt glazing* although it may diminish the characteristic aesthetic values of saltglaze. (See also *boron, Gerstley borate*.)

Boric acid, *boracic acid*

Given variously as $B(OH)_3$, H_3BO_3, or $B_2O_3, 3H_2O$. (See *boron*.)

Borocalite

$CaO.\ 2B_2O_3.\ 6H_2O.\ 30_4$. Also given as $2CaO.\ 3B_2O_3$ $5H_2O$, 412.

The natural mineral, with a slightly different molecular formula, is *colemanite*. Can be used in small amounts (up to 3%) to lower the maturing point of a stoneware glaze without materially affecting its character.

Boron, *boric oxide*

An element B. 10.9.
Boric oxide B_2O_3. 69.6.
Boracic acid $B_2O_3.\ 3H_2O$. 123.7.
Also occurs as soluble *borax*, and, in an insoluble form, as *colemanite*.

Boric oxide occupies an ambiguous position in the *Seger formula*. It is an acidic oxide and as such is normally listed with the silica as a glass-former. It will form glass at low temperatures, however, and its apparent effect is to soften (flux) a glaze and it replaces lead oxide in earthenware. Its formula suggests a third place, with alumina, as an amphoteric. As boric oxide in a glaze it has no melting point but a long melting range. Because of its solubility it is normally used as a frit. It can be used as colmanite up to around 10% but the results have been found to be disappointing although small amounts can add some brilliance to a glaze.

It has the great advantage over lead in that it is non-toxic—boracic acid is, of course, a mild disinfectant. However, little of the rich quality of a lead glaze is apparent in a borax glaze. With the increasingly stringent controls over lead compounds boron is becoming more generally used by craft potters, although it is still possible for lead glazes to pass all the tests. (See *metal release, soluble lead*.) Earthenware leadless glazes are all boron glazes. They are confusingly marked 'L' in catalogs, as distinct from 'LS', or low solubility lead glazes. A typical soft L *frit* is given under *borax*.

Soft borax frits (boric oxide is usually added in the form of borax) can be used as a fusible foundation for subsequent additions by the potter. The frit formulas now more frequently supplied by merchants are invaluable when modifying them with raw materials. Some clay in the batch will help the physical behavior of a boron frit, improving its suspension in water. Boric oxide tends to brighten colors in a rather unsubtle way. Copper may tend towards turquoise, and manganese towards purple.

The usual *molecular proportion* of boric oxide to silica in a glaze formula is around 1 to 4. In larger amounts it develops milkiness and surface peculiarities such as glitter and shiny patches in a duller glaze.

For the use of boron in the form of colemanite, see under *colemanite*. A curious property of boric oxide, which makes it very useful in earthenware glazes, is that, in amounts less than 10%, it has a 'negative' *coefficient of expansion* which helps craze resistance.

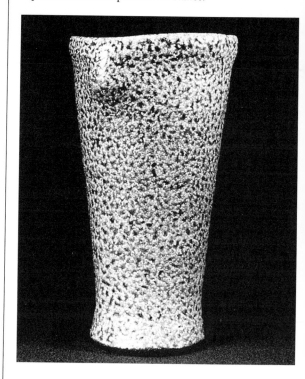

Boss *A saltglazed pot with a nicely placed boss — amusing overtones of a Roman face-pot — 'created by throwing wads of clay at the internal surface while still on the potter's wheel, creating very fluid changes in form'. By William Hunt, USA.*

Boron phosphate

BPO₄. 'Has been used in low-firing porcelain bodies '— translucent porcelain at 1000°C/1832°F — related structurally to high-cristobalite' (Dodd/Dodd-Murfin).

Borosilicate of lead

See *lead*.

Boss

An age-old decorative feature; a spherical hump traditionally formed by pressing from the inside of a pot but today more frequently applied to the outside. See illustration on opposite page.

Bossing

The use of a silk bag of cotton-wool for removing the brush-marks in the process of *ground-laying*.

Bottle form

Any pot form with a narrow neck tends to be called a bottle. It allows the maximum exploitation of contour and is favored by potters who wish to show glaze quality or other decoration to the full, the upper curve or *shoulder* being the most positive and eye-catching area of any pot. The neck is often too small to allow any 'useful' function. Those with a wider neck would still be called a 'bottle' in England but would often be referred to as a 'jug' in the United States. The word 'jar' is also used for the general form, as in 'wine jar'.

Genuine bottles such as cider jars, bellarmines and the like include some of the most noble shapes in ceramics. It is not, however, easy to attain the generous sweep of shoulder when throwing a large bottle; it poses considerable problems of clay control. When throwing the initial cylinder, concentrate on the lower half and do not overwork the top; it will need all the strength and freshness it can be given. After opening out the belly throw the shoulder inwards rather than simply compressing it, and increase the wheel speed as the circumference decreases. Avoid soaking in water. Hold a finger inside when collaring to avoid buckling. Isaac Button, the Yorkshire potter, threw large bottles with very little collaring, but eased the shoulder over with the same movement as the rest of the throwing, using a steel rib outside. He may be seen working 28lbs of clay in the film — 'Isaac Button, country potter'.

Another method is to throw an open ovoid onto which, when it has stiffened a little, a thrown ring is luted and

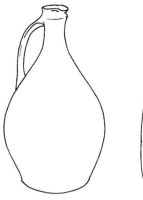

Contrasting bottle forms.

the neck is then thrown from this. (See also *two-piece throwing*.)

Bottles can be made by coiling, with multiple *pinchpots*, or with slabs. Bernard Leach has made some very handsome large rectangular *pressmolded* bottles with thrown necks. Bottles with more than one neck (see *bridge handle*), or with tube necks as in pre-Columbian American pottery, are entertaining variations.

Bottle or tank gas

A conventional term for liquified petroleum gas — LPG — which is either supplied in cylinders or delivered to special storage tanks. It is an efficient but fairly expensive alternative to town or natural gas, and needs slightly different types of burners.

Bottled gas involves very little in the way of a chimney and can be useful for the occasional reduction firing. It is clean enough for earthenware glazes.

Three-quarters of a 47kg/105lb cylinder of propane may be used in a stoneware firing of a 12cu ft (0.4cu m) kiln. Pressure drops as the gas is used, due to a lowering of temperature. At a constant temperature it will stay at a constant pressure until almost empty, but a stand-by cylinder to boost the end of the firing is essential. Supply can revert to the partly empty cylinder at the beginning of the next firing.

A changeover valve can be fitted, or two or three cylinders can be connected to a manifold and a pressure regulator and gauge. Other hazards are pressure fall in cold weather through freezing caused by the rapid evaporation of the gas liquid, and the collection of any escaping gas at ground level (the gas is heavier than air). With regard to the freezing of tanks and cylinders in icy weather Phil Rogers suggests spraying with tap water, using smaller or fewer burners, and always to keep the tank more than one third full. A 'no freeze' raku burner is listed by Axner in which 'the propane vaporizes in the burner rather than in the propane tank — thus eliminating frozen tanks'.

With tank installations, usually what is known as a 1 ton tank, pressure is more easily maintained, though not wholly free of the cold weather 'freezing up', but a guarantee of a fairly large yearly consumption must be given to the installing company.

Bottled gas may be supplied as Butane, Propane, Calorgas, etc. Butane has been quoted at 3200 Btu per cu ft and propane at 93,000 Btu per gallon (20,700 kjoules per liter). These figures compare very favorably with natural gas. (See also *gas fuel*.)

Bottle oven

As late as the 1950s every street in Stoke-on-Trent, England, seemed to have its cluster of kilns. The kiln or oven itself was surrounded by a bottle-shaped casing or 'hovel'. They were coal-fired. The splendid skyline disappeared in a few years (together, it must be admitted, with a lot of smoke and grime) with the rapid introduction of *continuous kilns*.

Stoke-on-Trent in the 1950s with bottle ovens of many sizes and shapes plus what, today, would be an unacceptable pall of smoke, dirt, and fumes.

Boulder clay

Clay which together with an assortment of stones and rocks has been transported by glacial action and then dumped as the glacier has melted. Common to large areas of North America and Europe. Used for brickmaking in the north of England. The clay itself is fusible and of an even particle size which makes the removal of impurities difficult. It has been suggested as the basis for a fusible slip.

Bourry firebox

A type of wood-burning firebox with semi-automatic firing, the lengths of wood being suspended across each side of the hearth. The downdraft flames consume the lower lengths and the upper ones sink to be burnt in their turn. (See diagram in Brickell).

Bow

A single clay-cutting wire held taut by a curved strip of bamboo or metal. In a looser way the term is applied to the more elaborate *harp*.

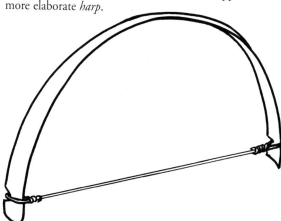

A bow made from a strip of metal or bamboo. The cutting wire may be of metal or nylon. Bows with movable wires to accommodate various clay thicknesses are available from many suppliers.

Bowl form

At once the easiest shape to throw and one of the most difficult to succeed with. The subtleties of a really lively bowl are not easy to analyze. To some potters a bowl should have a sense of enclosure, of cupped hands, but this excludes a great family of flaring forms. If the bowl has a well defined practical purpose its shape must, of course, be suited to its use, as seen in the Peter Dick mixing bowl illustrated. A sense of growth and spring from the base is essential and this involves a careful proportioning of the foot ring. The rim needs consideration, as its style will fundamentally affect the character of the bowl. A sturdy rim is more likely to maintain a circular plan but is not always aesthetically desirable.

When throwing a bowl perhaps the commonest fault is caused by the sudden lessening of support as the inner hand leaves the base clay and begins to exert pressure on the walls. Unless a finger or a knuckle of the outer hand is tucked right against the base to take the pressure, the all

1 The Peter Dick bowl referred to in the text. A basic container form with a powerful rim.

2 A highly modeled bowl by Carlos Van Reigersberg-Versluys.

3 A characteristically uncompromising bowl by Peter Smith.

reflected inside the bowl if a thick wedge is not to be left at the outer edge of the foot. Most bowls, however, will need turning, and sufficient clay must be left to form the foot ring. Cardew, some Japanese potters, and others throw a foot ring onto a reversed leather-hard bowl.

A number of bowls can be thrown from a large block of clay. This method is useful for test bowls. The mass of clay is roughly centered, the top part fully centered and the bowl thrown from this. Cutting off can be done Japanese-fashion with a loose thread which is allowed to wind itself into the clay and is then whipped sharply out, or a fine needle awl can be held sloping slightly upwards and cut in towards the center of the base.

Bowls may be *beaten* or cut (see *facet*). Other illustrations may be found under *foot-ring*. Handbuilt bowls are less common, but for details see under *handbuilding*.

Box

Pottery boxes rarely have a definite functional purpose, but are often very attractive objects and present the potter with interesting technical and aesthetic problems. The lids, especially of flattened forms, beg for decoration, even if this is simply the turning spiral of some of Richard Batterham's best boxes, or the speckled salt glaze of Gwyn Piggott Hanssen. A smooth curve will burnish well for *sawdust firing*. There are also unexploited possibilities for modeled knobs on lids. Many of Bernard Leach's earlier boxes had attractive, lively modeled knobs.

The method of holding the lid in place (the style and placing of the flange or slope) is open to many interpretations as in the Sheila Fournier box illustrated. The proportions between base and lid can be a recurring challenge and delight.

Boxes can be made by any technique. Rosemary Wren has shown how lively little boxes with excellently fitting

too common ridge and valley is formed. This becomes weaker as throwing proceeds and may finally collapse. In the earlier stages of throwing keep the wall more upright and with less curve than will finally be required, even to the extent of reversing the form — i.e. slightly convex instead of concave. The full curve is the last operation of all. The rim will benefit from being kept slightly thicker than the walls both throughout the throwing and in the finished piece. A generous rim can be an important feature and will help to maintain the bowl's circular plan.

For all sizes of bowl the wheel speed should be progressively lessened as work proceeds, in order to balance the centrifugal force exerted on the everwidening wall. Do not over-wet the clay, and complete the throwing with as few movements as possible. Large bowls are more easily controlled on a kickwheel. The centering and initial throwing can be done on a power wheel, and then the wheelhead transferred.

One can complete the bowl on the wheel, trimming the base with a bamboo or metal tool. The flat base must be

1 A three-tier box by Sheila Fournier; the wave-like junctions (shown here slightly separated) ensuring that the sections will stay in place when closed.

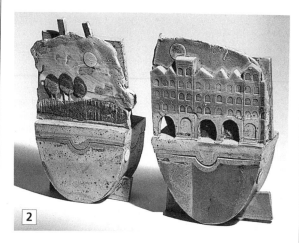

2 Two lively modeled boxes by Peter Phillips. Note his method of holding the lid in place.

lids can be made from pinch pots. Boxes may be thrown as two shallow bowls or short cylinders. Slab boxes pose their own problems; the flange can look heavy, and the sides are liable to warp inwards. They should be fairly flat in profile and put together from quite stiff clay, the joints pressed home with a wooden tool.

A good fit between lid and base will be best maintained during firing if they are fired in place. This necessitates care and thought when glazing. Sticking is less likely if the rims are waxed where they are to be left unglazed. A very thin wash of china clay and flint or alumina can be spun onto the rim before waxing.

Boxing

The packing of pottery, especially bowls and cups, rim to rim, and foot to foot. They must be of similar size with level rims. The method is most often used for biscuit firing but can also be used in the glaze fire where the rim and foot are free of glaze. The method is more wasteful of space than sitting bowls one in another but helps to lessen warpage. Boxing bowls and plates during drying can also help in retaining shape.

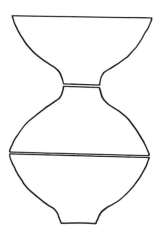

Bowls boxed for a biscuit fire. The pile or 'bung' can be extended to six or eight bowls depending on their sturdiness. It is also possible to fire glazed pieces if their rims are unglazed and there is no danger of the glaze running. See also stacking, warping.

Brass

A zinc-copper alloy occasionally used as filings to speckle bodies and glazes. It will dissociate in an oxidizing fire to a flux and copper oxide giving speckles, sometimes with a green halo. Clay will not stick to smooth brass (Brickell).

Brazier kiln

A very simple type of coke kiln used for raku. First developed in England by David Ballantyne. It can be built in half an hour from common bricks—Flettons or any open-textured house brick, between 50 and 80 are needed. Also a saggar of approximately 12in/300mm diameter, which can be purchased, or coiled from a well grogged body. Diagram **A** shows the plan, including the three half bricks on which the saggar stands; diagram **B** is a section through a completed kiln. A dry site is needed, or a foundation of bricks laid down. The interior diameter will depend on the size of the saggar which

A

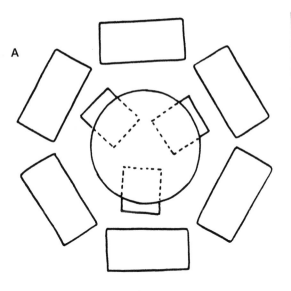

Plan of a brazier kiln (see text)

B

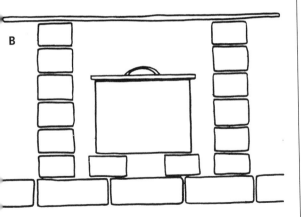

Section through a brazier kiln

should preferably be about 9in/225mm high. Allow 3in/75mm between saggar and walls all round. The space between the three supporting half bricks is filled with coke or a smokeless fuel before the saggar is positioned, and paper or firelighters placed near the bottom gaps between the bricks so that they can be lit from the outside. A layer of sticks is laid on top.

Walls are built up dry to a height of 6 in/150mm or so above the saggar, leaving 1–1.5in/30mm gaps between the bricks. The top row may be placed close together. A saggar lid must be provided, together with some means of removing it when hot. If your tongs will open wide, then the lid can be a simple kiln bat, otherwise a handle should be built onto it. The space between saggar and bricks is now filled with coke, or smokeless fuel if coke is unobtainable. The fire is lit at the base holes. See *raku* for details of firing. The

film 'Raku, English style' shows the building and firing of a brazier kiln; also the book by Riegger contains useful information.

Bread crock, bin

These fairly large, wide-mouthed, lidded pots, historically of earthenware, glazed inside only, are rarely made by studio potters, largely because of the kiln space they take up. Also, where they are purely 'useful' commodities the cost of producing them is rarely recooped in the sale price. They are, therefore, prized more for their decorative apects than their function. Despite this Mick Casson, David Lloyd Jones and others have made noble stoneware bread bins.

Brick

A clay or ceramic unit of building construction, the commonest shape being a rectangle of around 9 x 4 x 2in/225 x 100 x 50mm. Bricks have changed little over the centuries, though they are now made in an everwidening range of materials from red surface clays to bauxite and chrome ore.

The three main types of brick used by potters are easily distinguishable. They are:
1 Open-textured red clay building bricks, the cheapest being called 'flettons' in England.
2 Hard, heavy, close-grained refractory bricks.
3 Lightweight insulating bricks (See *insulation of heat*).

Group 1: Apart from their obvious building purposes, they can be used for the outer skins of kilns where they

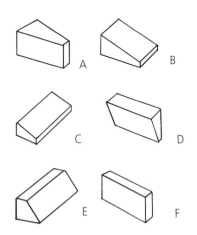

Some of the special shapes of bricks available. A an End Arch brick; B a Feather End; C a Feather Side; D a Side Arch; E a Side Scew; F a Split.
All are useful in arch building and a Split is almost impossible to cut from a whole brick.

will provide better insulation than heavy bricks. Also for low temperature and 'primitive' kilns such as the brazier type.

Group 2: Includes all grades of *firebricks* from Superduty, PCE 33, for working temperatures up to 1550°C/2822°F, to Low Heat Duty, PCE 15, which soften at 1400°C/2552°F and must be used at well below that. Grading in England is by alumina content — 45% downwards.

Group 3: These are easily abraded, very porous, light in weight, and superb *insulators*. They are made in many qualities and degrees of heat resistance. Those made from *diatomaceous earth* are either quarried and cut to shape or fired into blocks with a little clay. These are weak in structure and are comparatively fusible. The more *refractory* types are made from very pure and iron-free ceramic materials and have an open, sponge-like appearance achieved by physical means (mixing the raw material with sawdust, for instance) or chemical processes. These are graded by a K factor, the number denoting the degrees Fahrenheit which they will endure without failing, e.g. K26 = 2600°F or 1430°C. The higher numbers are stronger but marginally less effective as insulators. They are all more expensive than firebricks.

The choice of bricks will depend on a balance being struck between the extra initial cost of high insulation qualities and the extra fuel costs due to the *heat storage* and *heat loss* of hard firebrick. (See *insulation, conduction of heat.*) The care needed to avoid abrading or breaking the softer bricks may also weigh in your decision. For electric kilns, group 3 is the obvious choice.

The standard insulating brick size is 9 x 4 x 3in/225 x 100 x 75mm but there is a wide range of special shapes and sizes designed for arches, bevels, domes, etc. Insulating-brick is also available in blocks up to 18 x 9 x 4.5in/450 x 225 x 115mm. Kiln bricks can be molded by the potter either as fireclay and grog mixtures (see details in Cardew, Appendix 3), or cast from special bodies made from heat-proof calcia/alumina *cement* (not ordinary Portland cement) with an *aggregate* of crushed firebrick, insulating brick, *grog*, or expanded *perlite*. Use one part cement to four or five of aggregate. See *insulation of heat* for a home-made insulating brick recipe. A useful piece of equipment for making large unfired slab bricks, (*adobe*), even from any 'handy local dirt'! (Parks) mixed with some clay and perhaps 5–10% cement, is the Cinva-Ram press which both exerts great compressive power (by hand through a long lever) and also eases the completed 'brick' out of the mold. The blocks need a considerable time to dry out thoroughly (after a few days in the damp state if they contain cement). Illustrations can be seen in Parks' excellent book, and the address is given at the end of this dictionary. It was found that a kiln cased in this type of blocks needed a coating of stucco (Portland cement,

sand, and a litttle lime) to prevent damage in bad weather.

The use of bricks both for *hot-face* situations and especially for backing insulation has been superseded in many instances by *ceramic fiber* but clay bricks of one sort or another still have a role to play in kiln construction. High insulation hot-faced bricks and slabs have become very expensive (an increase of 2000% since the first edition of this book was published) but are still essential for wire element electric kilns and some other applications.

The term 'brick' is also used in another sense to denote a holder or container. (See *chicken brick, fish brick, flower brick.*)

Brick clay

A general name for a variety of clays, mostly red-firing and fusible and containing lime and other impurities. Fired at 900–1100°C/1652–2012°F. Bricks can be made from many surface or near-surface clays so long as their shrinkage is not too great and they are not contaminated with lime nodules. Some 'brick earths' such as those of the Thames valley in England, are of recent origin, geologically speaking (Pleistocene, two to six million years ago!), but others are from much older carboniferous times. Their quality depends partly on the underlying rock.

Sawdust, chopped grass, or brickdust can be added to brick clays to lessen the wet-dry shrinkage. Refractory bricks are made from the purer *fireclays*. (See also *marls.*)

Bricklaying

Most of the potter's work in this field will be in the building of kilns. Here bricks are laid almost in contact with one another — merely a 'buttering' of mortar between them. The mortar must be a high-temperature clay slurry or a special heat-proof cement such as Ciment Fondu or other commercial aluminous cement, and is used as a fairly sloppy mix. The bricks themselves are either soaked or, at least, well wetted on the surface. Some constructions, electric kilns in particular, can be dry built. Andrew Holden (CR87) suggests the use of ceramic paper (made from ceramic fiber) between Sayvit bricks (USA) in a dry-built gas kiln.

Long horizontal joints in brickwork are inevitable, but vertical joints are avoided by overlapping. There are several systems, but the principle is similar in each case: that each brick should, as often as possible, span the join between the two below it. In 9in/225mm walls, courses can be laid across the width (called 'header' courses because the head or end of the brick shows on the face), as well as along its length ('stretcher' courses). Bricks will often be needed in half-lengths and can be

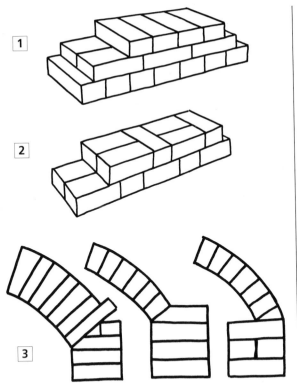

Two common brick-laying bonds.

1 *The English bond, which may consist of alternate header and stretcher courses (the short and long face of the brick), or one header to two or three stretchers.*

2 *The Flemish bond, bricks laid in alternate direction within each course. See also American bond.*

3 *Three ways of 'springing' an arch of bricks.*

cut with a brick hammer which has a chisel end, or with a 'cold' chisel or bolster. The brick may be chipped or scored along the line of the break and then tapped sharply across a hard edge.

Accurate bricklaying depends on a level and firm foundation and the frequent use of a good spirit level at least 18in/500mm long. Stretched lines or board can guide straight walls, wooden templates are often constructed over which to build arches and domes. Rhodes gives advice on bricklaying in Chapter 4 of Rhodes K. See also Cardew. A brick structure will expand on heating; it is therefore advisable to leave open (unmortared) joints, about 0.25in/6mm wide, every four bricks. W. J. Doble supply a non-setting jointing cement which allows brickwork to expand and contract without cracking. (See *expansion*.)

Bridge handle

A strap handle spanning two spouts or necks. The form has a long history. Originally probably used for carrying but now a design element.

A coiled pot with a bridge handle.

Bright gold

See *gold*.

Bristol glaze

A medium temperature glaze containing zinc oxide, originally developed in an attempt to avoid the use of lead. It is a difficult glaze to control and is subject to crawling and pinholes, especially if applied thickly. The zinc-alumina-silica eutectic is fairly high — 1360°C/2480°F — but can be brought down to below 1200°C/2192°F by the addition of feldspar and whiting. The use of clay in the recipe makes it suitable for use on green (unbiscuited) ware. Zinc glazes are not suitable for reduction.

Typical recipes (in percentages):

Feldspar	56.6	
Whiting	9.5	
Nepheline		40.0
Lithia		5.0
Zinc oxide	6.5	12.0
Clay	13.0	8.0
Flint	14.5	35.0

And from PQ13 (Merritt):

		%
Calcined zinc oxide	24.3	8.0
Feldspar	113.2	38.0
Colemanite	51.5	17.0
Barium carbonate	19.7	7.0
Talc	18.9	6.0
Flint	66.0	22.0
Calcium nitrate	2.9	1.0

Firing at 1140°C/2084°F.

The zinc is sometimes used in a calcined form to lessen drying shrinkage (see *zinc*.) The zinc will affect colors (not often to their advantage), though copper is reputed to produce turquoise (Rhodes CGP), and uranium a bright yellow in zinc glazes. The average firing temperature for Bristol glaze is around 1180°C/2156°F.

British thermal unit, Btu

A measure of heat quantity. The heat required to raise 1lb of water through 1° Fahrenheit. Equal to 252 calories. 100,000 Btu = 1 therm. The heat value of various fuels can be stated in Btu for comparison.

The unit joule is now superseding the Btu. One Btu is equivalent to 1055J or 1.055kJ (kilojoules).

Broken pottery

Broken, torn and reassembled pots, fired and unfired is an extreme technique practiced by Peter Voulkos and other potters. The pieces can be stuck together with glaze, or glazed pieces have even been glued together.

Brokes

Term used for a type of English ball clay which will not 'cut into balls' (Dodd). Generally of low plasticity. Fires greyish.

Brongniart's formula

A method of determining the weight, on a pint basis, of suspended solids in a slip or glaze, devised by 'the father of ceramic chemistry' who was Director at Sèvres in the first half of the 19th century.

Method: First weigh the container empty, then with one pint of the slip to be tested. The liquid weight is arrived at by subtraction. We then use the formula

$$P - 20 \text{ x } \frac{\text{s.g.}}{\text{s.g.} - 1}$$

in which s.g. stands for *specific gravity* of the solid material and P for the pint weight arrived at as above. The 1 stands for the s.g. of the water.

Example: The average s.g. of plastic clay is 2.6. If the pint weight was 27oz then:

$$(27 \text{ [oz]} - 20) \text{ x } \frac{2.6}{2.6 - 1} = 7 \text{ x } 1.62\text{oz}$$

i.e. 11.34oz of dry clay.

The calculation is complicated for glazes by the fact that materials with different specific gravities are mixed together. However, most common glaze minerals are in the range 2.5–3.0. Where the s.g. is much above this figure it has generally been noted in this book (e.g. lead oxide). A good approximation to the pint weight can therefore be arrived at.

Jennifer Lee uses the formula to ensure color duplication in her stained clays.

Bronze luster

Obtained by firing chromium and lead compounds in reduction, but the system is too complicated for the studio potter who can buy prepared bronze lusters. A bronze-like finish can also result from copper/manganese mixtures at most temperatures from low earthenware to porcelain. The color is brushed onto the biscuit. (See *copper-manganese gold*.)

Brookite

One of the oxide ores of titanium. The source of white titanium.

Brown mouth

A term applied to the effect of glaze running thinner from the rims of stonewares. This can even occur with buff body under a pale glaze, especially in reduction. The glaze can also be wiped from the rim and a fusible pigment (e.g. manganese) applied and, although this lacks the subtlety of the genuine article, it is useful where the glaze tends to crawl on rims as sometimes happens.

Brown pigment,   glaze

Iron oxide is the commonest brown pigment: 4–8% in most glazes, but will tend to bleach if calcium is present. Rutile gives broken cream-browns and ilmenite darker colors. *Albany slip* and some other fusible red clays including Fremington give a dark brown glaze.

Small amounts of zinc (0.5–1.5%) can develop browns from chrome. Manganese as a pigment tends towards the purple-browns. Nickel can be brownish in a barium glaze and will alter the behavior of iron and manganese. Rutile gives broken browns. Unglazed iron and copper will give blacks and browns. A recipe for a brown pigment given by Pleydell-Bouverie is:

1 measure of cobalt oxide, 10 iron, 5 manganese, 10 china clay. Grind together in a mortar.

Brucite

$Mg(OH)_2$.
A source of magnesium found in Canada and the USA.

Brush

The painting brush traditionally used in the industry is the 'liner', very long-haired and square-ended. The high absorption of pigment by biscuit or glaze makes it essential that any brush should hold a great deal of it. It is a wonder that no-one has come up with a 'fountain brush' for pottery, although something similar is available from various suppliers for underglaze colors, etc.

For the more calligraphic style of painting, liners have limited value. The *cut liners* are more lively. Goat-hair *mops* are useful for background washes, e.g. in preparation for sgraffito or wax resist. Japanese brushes, of sheep, goat, badger, and horse hair, are more responsive but, being originally designed for inks, are, in general, rather soft; a quality which can, however, give great sensitivity to a stroke. There is an attractive soft-haired flat brush on the market which is called a 'hake' brush available in widths between 90mm and 25mm (approx. 3.5in and 1in) for laying on large areas of color sometimes made as a single brush but also as multiple brushes bound together.

1 A 'spatter brush' (see text). The brush is dipped in the pigment, glaze, or slip, then drawn up through the holder so that the peg engages with the bristles and spatters the color on to the piece when the circular handle is turned.

2 A Chinese multi-brush with pegs to hold the individual brushes together, which can take the place of the wash or hakeme brush.

'Maiolica pencils' are of sable, are slightly wider than paintbrushes and give a good point. Three basic brushes will fulfill most requirements: a large sable watercolor brush, a square shader (about 0.75in/15mm wide), and a liner, or a medium Japanese brush. Experimental potters can try any sort of brush-like object with which to apply their slip or color: shaving brushes, cheap paste brushes (which give a useful dry, striated line), dabbing and working the surface to provide fresh textures. The 'throw-away' plastic sponge brushes may also have possibilities for backgrounds. Brushes for wax need to be resilient and have a good body. The modern potter uses a great variety of materials apart from the traditional brush to transfer slip or pigment to ceramic surfaces, as have peasant potters through the ages, using frayed plant stems, cloth, feathers, etc. Nylon is replacing hair in some traditional brushes. 'Spatter brushes' are available, see diagram. Coastal Ceramics (NZ) list a hog hair 'fan brush' with splayed hairs 'for dry brushing'.

Brushes must be cared for. Wash and stroke to a point after use, store preferably hanging hair-downwards (Georgies list a useful brush holder, the brush being clipped into a spiral over a container and allowed to hang and dry). If kept heads-up in a jar, dry well or the hairs may rot at the base. Do not use brushes to mix colors. One cannot easily clean wax brushes unless water-soluble emulsions are used: smooth the hairs to a point and leave them to set. A brush will be destroyed if dipped into hot wax when wet. There are quirky exceptions to all these 'rules' such as potters who prefer their brushes curved to a quarter circle through being left in the wax pot! Thus it is for each to find his or her pet tool — 'brushes are like musical instruments; they play in certain ways' (Caiger-Smith).

Lawn brushes should be easily cleanable or they will contaminate the next batch of glaze. It is advisable to keep a brush, clearly labeled, for each group of glazes and slips that you use: one for clear glaze, one for each group of glazes and slips that you use, e.g. one for pale slips, one for dark colors, and so on. The large bristle brushes often listed in merchants' catalogs are not easy to clean and they retain a lot of sludge during sieving. I consider the common nylon washing-up brush to be one of the most suitable. Unfortunately they often do not have very strong handles.

Brush-applied glaze

There is little evidence that glaze was applied to pottery with a brush in past times, and today the method is normally used only where glaze is in too short supply for dipping or pouring. However the method has possibilities for particular effects and is used by Otto Natzler among others. Without experience the result can be thin and sketchy and if one glaze is brushed onto another the first is liable to be lifted off (the addition of a siccative might help here) but with practice individual results can be obtained. A thin initial poured or dipped coat can ensure that bare patches are avoided.

Pottery suppliers now list special brush-on glazes, often needing two or three coats. Although the method is useful where only a small quantity of glaze is available the technique is normally used for special decorative effects rather than as a standard glaze coating. A brush can be used to flick the glazes on with somewhat haphazard results. (See also *brush*.)

Brushed slip

If slip is used like a pigment it must be applied very liberally if it is not to vanish in the glaze fire. This is especially true with earthenware lead glazes which use a layer of the surface clay to fulfill their glass-forming functions. As well as clay slips used in the manner of *hakeme*, slips heavily loaded with pigment oxides are used for painting on or under stonewares; either a natural iron-rich red clay, ball clay alone or stained, e.g. 98 parts of clay to one of cobalt oxide and one of iron chromate. Also cobalt with ochre. The slip is laid on generously. (See also *engobe*.) Henry

The bold impasto laying on of slip on a handbuilt form by Irene Vonck.

Hammond used a series of slips for painting his famous fish and other designs using 50% each of iron oxide and a local red clay, plus those mixtures mentioned above.

Pâte-sur-pâte was a typically painstaking Victorian method of building up a variable slip layer but the technique could be adapted to modern use.

Brushwork

A serious gap in the potter's library is an expert and wide ranging discussion of brushwork. Once the most widely practiced technique for decorating ceramics, it has been overshadowed by textural and glaze surfaces and by less consciously designed applications of slips and colors. The reputation of Eastern calligraphy which is, at its best, as taut as a spring and as individual as hand-writing, has suffered through the careless and flabby copying of historical work. A few potters continue with *maiolica* and *luster* in skillful Moresque-type patterns. Kenneth Clark and others made an impact with brush decoration in the 1950s in England but he has little to say in his books except to try using brushes other than the traditional ones to achieve fresh and exciting marks. With the inevitable reaction against the more muted and mannered work on stoneware, splashes and dabs of bright color have become fashionable, the brush used simply to transfer pigment rather than to make its own mark. At the same time, pleasant and sometimes gifted if (on the whole) unspectacular brushwork continues the world over on pots and dishes of all kinds combined with sgraffito, resist, and other techniques. Alan Caiger-Smith continues a rather lonely but successful trail, keeping the tradition of vigorous luster and tin-glaze alive. As has been said of Leach, apparent casualness combined with subtlety of form and color can inspire his brushwork with a lyrical sensibility combined with strength.

There is no quick route to good brushwork, but a start can be made by familiarizing oneself with the sorts of marks that each brush most naturally makes. Paint freely and you may spoil a number of pieces, but control will come and liveliness is essential. Many potters confine themselves to a relatively narrow range of designs, which they repeat with variations until it becomes second nature. As Hamada said of his broken reed pattern: 'I paint it thousands of times but it is not the same — never the same.' Working from detailed drawings from nature is advocated by some teachers, but this approach must be treated with caution. If you start from copying natural objects, put your drawings aside quite soon and develop the pattern in relation to the pot form. It is the nature of the pot itself which is of primary importance. Many potters limit themselves to a narrow range of designs.

The term 'brushwork' is usually associated with Oriental

1 Still the benchmark for the economical and expressive use of the brush is the best work of Bernard Leach. Here, basically, a mere couple of strokes delineate a leaping fish, combined with equally fresh sgraffito.

3 Delicate brushwork by Vic Greenaway (Australia).

2 Lively brushwork by a Spanish country potter (1989) showing a familiar farmyard occurrence!

styles or with Hispano-Moresque and other Western wares deriving from calligraphy, but it can also include the more individual work exemplified by modern American and other innovative, less reflective and stylized pottery decoration, sometimes wild and chaotic, the brush often used more like weapon than a tool, but striving for new approaches.

For the more traditional application of brushwork a few rules quickly become obvious. Use as fully loaded a brush as is consistent with maintaining a point, and do not habitually drain it on the edge of the pigment vessel.

Keep the hand 'floating' and free move the arm as much as the wrist. Let the brush do as much of the work as possible by varying the pressure upon it. Do not retouch. The great advantage of the older style of brushwork is that it accommodates the semi-transparent nature of pottery oxides. Unless special techniques are used, (see *ground-lay*) strokes of color will almost always show up after glazing. *Engobes* can help in this respect.

Try all sorts of brushes, including homemade ones; the marks may not have the fluidity of Orient-inspired work but can develop into an individual style along other lines. Some advice on types of brushes and their care is given under *brush*. There are always deviations from the norm; some potters only happy with a brush that is permanently bent through leaving it, hairs down, in the wax or pigment!

Wax resist has attracted as much significant work as brushed pigment. It lends itself to strong blocks of color and to *glaze-over-glaze* techniques. It cannot be fussed over but must be completed quickly and firmly and has those elements of 'accidents and incidents', to quote Leach, which still find great favor. (See also *calligraphy, decoration, latex, resist method*, etc.)

BSI

British Standards Institution, Linford Wood, Milton Keynes. Responsible for national standards, including ceramics, in Britain.

Brussels nomenclature

An attempt made in 1955 to agree on an International

Tariff Nomenclature of terms and meanings. Chapter 69 includes ceramics, listing china, earthenware, etc. The definitions are occasionally mentioned in this dictionary, but are more applicable to industrial work.

Btu

See *British thermal unit.*

Bubble alumina

Alumina bubbles made 'by blowing air or steam into the molten slag' (Dodd/Murfin). See *Insulation of heat.*

Bubbles in glaze

Most glazes go through a bubbling (gas releasing) stage. It is very marked in lead glazes. The bubbles must be given time to break and to settle down. If a glaze is fired beyond its optimum melting temperature, decomposition is likely to take place with the emission of further gases. The firing should therefore be terminated between these two phases.

Craters, pinholes, blisters, and milkiness in a clear glaze are evidence of bubbles. (See under *pinholes* and *blistering* for discussion of cause and cure.) Precautions that can be taken are the full oxidation of earthenware glazes and the careful drying of glazed pots **before** they are packed in an electric kiln. An even and adequate but not too thick glaze coating followed by accurate firing and possibly some soaking, especially of earthenwares, will minimize bubbling.

Some celadons owe their quality to myriads of minute bubbles possibly due to the breakdown of whiting and the release of CO_2. Its replacement by *wollastonite* gives a more transparent color.

High manganese glazes are liable to gas release: $3MnO_2 = Mn_3O_4 + O_2$. Bubbles trapped in a stoneware glaze but not evident on the surface are often an attractive characteristic; they are less welcome in a too thickly applied earthenware glaze. Deliberate '*cratering*' of the surface is used as a decorative finish — barium sulfate has been mentioned. (See also *crater glaze, volcanic glazes.*)

Buff clay

Few plastic clays fire white. Those containing 2–4% of iron fire cream in earthenware (the color depending on the degree of *calcia* content), buff or greyish at high temperatures. The term 'buff body' is often applied. The clay may be darker in the raw state, due to carbon stained ball clay or fireclay in the recipe. Many buff bodies have a long firing-range: that from Potclays (UK) ranges from 1000–1280°C/1832– 2336°F.

Some local river clays will fire to a deep buff, but local surface clays which may be yellow-buff in the raw state are most likely to fire to a red-brown. Buff clays are very suitable for slips, taking some of the brashness from cobalt and giving a slight greyness to green slips.

Buffer layer

See *interface.*

Bulldog

An impure *iron silicate*, giving browns and blacks. Used in reduction to produce blue bricks. It has now disappeared, at least under this name, from the catalogs.

Buller's ring

Annular rings, like large washers 2.5in/65mm in diameter and made from ceramic materials introduced by Bullers, Stoke-on-Trent, around 1900. They are placed in a kiln near a spyhole or at a point where they can be hooked out during firing. Their contraction in diameter is measured in a special triangular gauge, a reading indicating the heat it has reached.

They are normally used only in fairly large kilns but could be a post-firing guide to the temperature in various parts of any kiln. Their advantage over cones is that they do not melt and stick. They are made in four temperature ranges covering 960–1400°C/1760–2552°F.

Bulley, *clay bulley*

A hand-operated clay extruder (Dragon Ceramex). Can be used to form solid, hollow, square, circular, and more complicated forms.

Bull's head kneading

See *wedging and kneading.*

Bung

May refer either to the stopper in a kiln inspection hole or to a pile of pots, bowls, or *saggars* (see also *boxing*). See illustration on opposite page.

Burners, *kiln*

See *coal, drain oil, gas burner, oil fuel.*

Burning out of carbon

See *black core, blistering, bloating, carbon.*

Bungs of pots, a mixture of boxing, and bowls set one in another. The lower ones have decorative bosses which rest on the rim of the bowl below. Garden containers by Mike Bailey.

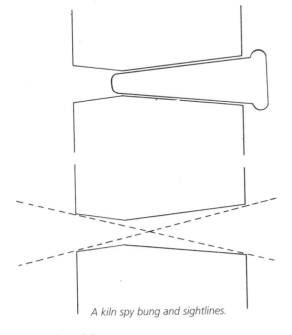

A kiln spy bung and sightlines.

Burnish gold

Also known as 'best gold', a suspension of powder in volatile oils, with a ceramic flux, and a mercury salt. The gold is dull after firing and needs burnishing with a hard smooth stone or tool. Fire to 750–760°C/1382–1400°F with ventilation especially at the early stages. More subtle than 'bright gold'. (See also *gold*.)

Burnishing

The compacting and polishing of the surface of the clay by rubbing with smooth tools. A burnished pot can give considerable visual and tactile pleasure. It is developed from the clay itself, with a consequent sense of unity between body and surface. A burnished pot will rarely be watertight, although Siddig El'nigoumi burnished coffee-pots and similar household vessels which he declared to be quite impervious.

Most bodies, even grogged ones, will burnish; the finer grained smooth secondary clays are the easiest to work on. Some micaceous material probably helps (see *mica*). The technique involves some restriction on form. Concavities, as well as lugs or other applied decoration, make work difficult. An unbroken rounded profile is the most satisfactory. Thrown boxes burnish well and show off the color variations of *sawdust firings*. The main polishing is done at the firm leather-hard stage of drying. The clay's response to burnishing can be tested at intervals during drying until

1 Burnishing with a wooden tool.
2 Finishing with the flat of the palm.

An elegant, if fragile, handbuilt burnished pot by Tina Vlassopulos.

the best results are obtained. Thrown pieces can be polished on the wheel immediately after turning, although this gives a somewhat more mechanical appearance. A final rub with the hands (so long as these are not calloused or rough) is given at the near-dry stage. Cardew mentions beating the surface in order to consolidate it; this may be useful with coarser bodies.

Although *hematite* is the classic surface coating, I have found that pigments, such as ferric oxide, or high iron slips, can be disappointing both in surface and color. A fine grain red clay is perhaps preferable. John Ablitt (now, sadly, no longer working in this field), and others, have developed a stronger and more varied palette than the more subdued colors previously used.

A fine levigated slip was reputed to have been used for Roman Samian ware and a similar material helps the development of burnish. Ben Cooper mixes clay with a water softener and a small amount of organic acid (oxgall, wine lees), a couple of tablespoons to 35lbs of clay. A thin slip is made and only the top finest particles used, after a fortnight's resting, and passed through a 200 mesh sieve. With much less hassle, as mentioned above, the leather-hard

body of a pot can be burnished with a spoon to a virtually watertight finish, using a similar slip of Fremington Clay (from the West of England) with 10% or more of precipitated iron oxide. Magdalene Odundo's splendid large pots are burnished to a black mirror finish. Burnishing is combined by Martin Smith with sophisticated arrangements of metal and epoxy resin.

Variations on an all-over sheen may be to leave certain areas matt for decorative purposes, or to comb or scratch through the shiny surface and through the slip, if used, to give contrasts of color and texture. The 'unka' or cloud-flower effect is achieved by Gen Asao (Japan) by touching the hot surface with vegetable oil. Siddig El'nigoumi obtained variations by smoke-staining the fired pot over a twist of burning newspaper. Clamp firing, of course, will also vary the surface color, sometimes subtly, sometimes strikingly.

The burnishing tool can be any conveniently shaped smooth object: a water-worn pebble, a metal spoon, bone, plastic, metal, or hardwood are all possible materials. The only essential is a firm, perfectly smooth surface, preferably slightly convex and without sharp corners or edges. Work with a steady, even pressure in small circular movements. Glass burnishers are supplied for gold burnishing, and these may be used too.

The shine will diminish as the pot dries and should be further treated: often it suffices to work it in the hands or on a piece of cloth. The leg of one's trousers can often be used! Burnish may be lost if the firing is too high – 850°C/1562°F is sufficient. Loss of shine can sometimes be remedied by re-rubbing with the hands or a soft cloth. The carbon saturation associated with sawdust firing assists the polish. A high burnish can be achieved even with a porcelain body. (See also *polishing clay, sawdust firing*.)

Burnt sienna

Calcined *ochre* or ochrous earth. A reddish-brown pigment. (See also *sienna*.)

Butane

$CH_3 (CH_2)_2 CH_3$ or C_4H_{10}. See *bottled gas, gas fuel*.

Butter pats

See *beater*.

Button

Lucie Rie, amongst others has made ceramic buttons. Buttons are best made in stoneware or porcelain but those

Incised buttons (tin over slip), by Sheila Fournier.

illustrated were in hard earthenware.

Button test

A test of the behavior of ceramic materials in the kiln. Many materials and minerals can be formed in a damp state into small balls or buttons. If these are fired on a biscuit tile one can obtain some idea of their fusibility and other qualities from the state of collapse or flow at a given temperature. An excellent educational exercise. The results of this test, however, can be slightly misleading. It is the reaction of one material with another which is of prime interest when compounding bodies or glazes. (See *chemistry of glazes*.)

The simple, individual materials could, of course, be replaced with mixtures, which would be even more illuminating but need more careful recording. Possibilities are 50% each of feldspar and clay; clay and an alkaline frit; or whiting and flint.

A tile with six depressions, in each of which a ball of pottery material — a mineral, a frit, or a mixture of several consituents — has been placed. The 'buttons' can be made by moistening and rolling the material. These are fired (the hollow retaining any fusible melt) and the results studied.

CAD

Computer aided design.

Cadmium, compounds

A metallic element Cd. 112.4.
Used as cadmium sulfide CdS and calcium selenide CdSe in low temperature (up to 850°C/1562°F) red pigments (enamels). Cadmium sulfide and barium sulfate for yellow.

Produces yellow and orange. Often combined with selenium which will withstand higher temperatures. Easily volatilized. Obtainable only as a prepared pigment. May blacken in the presence of lead. Hamer recommends fast firing in reduction. Cadmium released into food acids is a health hazard and it should not be used on tableware or storage vessels. (See *metal release*.)

Calcerous clay

Clays containing lime and thus liable to 'blowing' if the lime is in the form of even very small nodules. (See *marls, lime blowing*.)

Calcine, calcination

To disintegrate by heat: the strong heating of a material resulting in physical or chemical alteration, often to a *friable* state without fusing. Originally the term referred to the roasting of lime into quicklime.

Flints, very hard in the raw state, become a friable white powder at around 900°C but retain the same chemical composition. Bone, when calcined, loses its carbon and

A flint pebble and calcined flint powder. The chemical makeup is not altered though the physical state is very different.

only the inorganic residue of calcium and phosphorus remain, see *bone ash*. Some metal oxides can be calcined: manganese will give a more powerful pigment; cobalt oxides are prepared by calcining, the grey oxide CoO to 1050°C/1922°F, the black oxide to 750°C/1382°F. The grey oxide is thus slightly more concentrated in use, and will not change its form or lose oxygen in firing. Some wood ashes can be usefully calcined at about 750°C/1382°F. Calcining is also practiced to eliminate *water of hydration*, e.g. calcined borax. China clay is fired into *Molochite*. Calcined alumina has replaced flint for *placing*. Dry clay can be crushed and calcined (fired) into grog.

The combination of two or more pottery materials to form a new compound or glass by heating is known as *fritting*.

Calcined alumina

See *alumina, bubble alumina, placing*.

Calcite, calcspar

A natural crystalline calcium carbonate, $CaCO_3$. Also, confusingly, known as Iceland spar.

It is the mineral constituent of limestone, chalk and marble. Many natural rocks are almost pure calcite, laid down by countless sea creatures over the millenia, as also are oyster and some other shells. A method of determining the purity of a calcite rock sample is described in Cardew.

Calcium, oxide, compounds

A metallic element Ca, 40.8.
Oxide CaO. 57 (quicklime), m.p. 2570°C. Calcia.
Carbonate $CaCO_3$. 100, (lime). LOI 44%.

The carbonate decomposes into the oxide at about 850°C/1562°F. Although the melting point is very high its reaction with other ceramic compounds causes a lower melting point. A *eutectic* is: CaO1.0. Al_2O; 0.35. SiO_2 2.48, represented by 33.6% whiting, 30.39% china clay, 35.95% quartz.

$CaCO_3$ is almost pure in limestone and chalk, which are prepared as *whiting*. Because it is a pure material its proportions in a glaze must be carefully calculated. Its effect in glazes can be to shorten the solid to liquid phase. Either too much or too little can reduce the brightness of a glaze.

Lime is usually placed low in the table listing the fusible properties of bases. This is true for soft glazes, but somewhat misleading when considering stonewares, where it can be a major flux rendering the glazes more 'watery' or less *viscous*. In a series of experiments carried out some years ago it was found that 40% could be added to a stoneware glaze (at 1285°C/2345°F) before a scum began

to form. In most glazes, however, the maximum fluidity may be developed with the additions of around 15%. Hamer lists it among his 'anti-fluxes' up to 1100°C/2012°F but it appears to have beneficial effects in combination with lead and soda at a little below this temperature.

The coefficient of expansion of calcium is only half that of the alkalis. It is reputed to assist iron reduction for celadons, and has no bleaching effect on black (reduced) iron oxide. It gives hardness and durability and is responsible for the great strength of bone china. It tends to bleach color from red clays at lower temperatures. Lime in red clays will therefore yield yellowish colors as in some bricks which are fired at 1000°C/1832°F or less. In the Netherlands up to 25% of a limey clay (marl) or lime was added to the body of maiolica (Delft) tiles. According to Berendsen, this helped to stick the glaze to the clay and to prevent crazing, although it also lowered its resistance to chipping.
Other calcium minerals are:

Anorthite	CaO	Al_2O_3	$2SiO_2$
Bone Ash	3CaO	P_2O_5	
Calcium chloride	$CaCl_2$		
Colemanite	2CaO	$3B_2O_3$	
Dolomite	$CaCO_3$	$MgCO_3$ (approx.)	
Fluorspar	CaFl		
Plaster of Paris	$CaSO_4$	H_2O	
(Gypsum)	$CaSO_4$	$2H_2O$	
Wollastonite	$CaSiO_3$		
Wood ashes	Variable		

(See also *efflorescence on clay, lime, lime blowing*.)

Calcium borate

A frit of similar composition to colemanite obtainable from W.G. Ball and other suppliers.

Jane Lord (CR107) suggests a 'base' glaze of 1 clay: 2 calcium borate for around 1080°C/1976°F earthenware glazes.

Calcium chloride

$CaCl_2$. 111.

Occasionally used for the flocculation of glazes — 0.05%, and can be used in combination with bentonite. Soluble and *deliquescent*. Also accelerates the setting of *Portland cement*.

Calcium phosphate

3CaO. P_2O_5. (Tri-calcium phosphate).

Main ceramic source is bone ash. Also found in small quantities in some vegetable ashes. 'Can give texture in low-fired glazes and opaque essence in high fired glazes' (Georgies). See also *apatite, bone china, phosphorus*.

Calcium silicate

Four compounds including *wollastonite*. Can be bought in sheet form, as a substitute for asbestos or for the insulation of kilns, up to about 700°C/1292°F. (See *mineral wool block*.)

Calcium sulfate

An *anhydrous* gypsum. Can be used as a *deflocculant*.

Calcium zirconium silicate

$CaZr SiO_2$.
Used as an opacifier in high fired glazes.

Calcspar

An old name for *calcite* and has been listed as such in suppliers' catalogs.

Calculator

A specialist manual calculator is the 'Rapid Glaze Calculator' which speeds up the arithmetic involved in converting recipes to formulas, shrinkage percentages, and the like. It would be better if a little larger and correspondingly more accurate, but even so it is very useful. Available from Ceramic Calculations, Marston Magna, Yeovil, Somerset, England. The 'Dial a glaze' calculator, available in the USA, was reviewed in PQ 38.

Modern electronic calculators and computers have rendered most of the manual types virtually redundant. They are not in general, of course, particularized to ceramic problems but a number of specialized programs have been worked out. Conversion of batch weights or analysis into formula are, however, greatly eased by the use of even the cheapest calculator. (See also *computer, computer programs*.)

Calgon

A proprietary *sodium hexa-metaphosphate* used as a *deflocculant*.

Caliper

A compass of wood, metal, or plastic, usually with curved

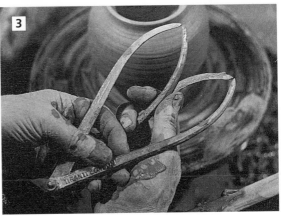

Using calipers to fit a lid.
1 The inside measurement of the flange is taken with the points outwards.
2 The lid diameter is recorded.
3 Using two calipers to transfer the measurement.

arms or arms curved at the ends. Used for measuring the inner or outer diameters of bowls, pots, lids, lid seatings, etc. Metal calipers are the most accurate but can corrode in pottery conditions. A caliper arm length of 8–9in is the most useful; one does not often need to repeat pots or bowls above 14in/350mm wide but 10-in and 12-in models are available. Cromartie (Kemper Tools) offer a handsome hardwood caliper.

Their most frequent use is for the fitting of lids. It is useful to have two calipers in order to transfer an inner to outer measurement, or vice-versa. In Fournier PT is shown an ingenious if rather cumbersome double caliper for determining the thickness of the wall of a pot, and 'lid master calipers' are available (Axner, Tucker, and others) which simultaneously measure the inside and outside dimensions. See also at *lid*. Almost any strips of metal, wood, etc. can be made into simple straight calipers but a long curve as shown has great advantages.

Calligraphic

In pottery the term is used rather loosely to indicate a free style of brushwork which uses the movement and shape of the brush itself from which to derive the design. It comes more from Oriental brush-script than from Western broad-nib writing, though there are parallels here too. (See also *brushwork, lettering.*)

Calorie, *calorific value*

A unit of heat: that required to raise 1 gram of water through 1°C. The 'large' or food calorie substitutes a kilogram for a gram and is sometimes written Kc. The *British thermal unit*, (Btu) equal to 252 calories, is a more useful scale for potters. (See also *joule.*)

Calorite

A cylindrical *pyrometric cone.*

Cancer causing materials

See *carcinogens.*

Candle, *resist*

Household candles vary in composition — wax, tallow, spermaceti, etc. — but most are suitable for *wax resist* work if melted with an equal volume of thin oil — sewing machine, or 3-in-1 type. Sharpened into a 'pencil', a candle can be used directly on biscuit or fired glaze as a resist.

Candlestick, *candelabrum*

A form (whose simple function is keeping a candle upright!) which has almost infinite possibilities; from the simple architectural bowls made by Hans Coper for Coventry Cathedral, to the decorative tree and landscape holders of Jill Main, and the massive candelabrum by Ruth Duckworth. Candle bottles, and bowls for floating candles, afford still more inventive scope.

Cane clay, *ware*

Cane marl is a low-quality fireclay from Staffordshire though Hamer described cane clay as 'a refined fireclay'. Cane ware was a light brown to straw color, fine in texture, and fired to stoneware temperatures.

Cane handle

A semi-circular hoop of cane or bamboo used for teapot handles, or occasionally for storage jars. Each end is split, one section cut away, and the remaining strip looped back round a lug on the pot.

The cane must be soaked or steamed, the ends slowly drawn together until they form rather more than a semi-circle (the curve will always spring out a little). (See *lugs* for fitting to teapot.) Cane handles are available from the Craft

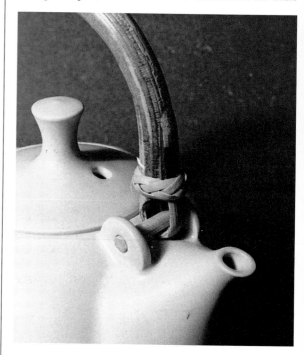

An original method of attaching the handle to a teapot by Roger Perkins.

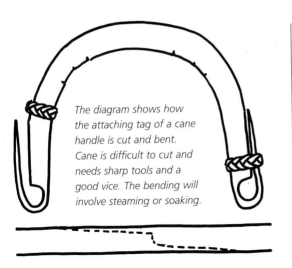

The diagram shows how the attaching tag of a cane handle is cut and bent. Cane is difficult to cut and needs sharp tools and a good vice. The bending will involve steaming or soaking.

Potters' Shop and several suppliers including Axner in the USA who list sizes 3in–7in wide.

Vine roots have been used in a similar way, giving a more variable form with sharp angles.

Cane marl

A low-quality fireclay from North Staffordshire. See also *cane clay.*

Canion

A positively charged particle (*ion*), i.e. lacking balancing *electron(s).* (See also *anion.*)

Cantilever

An area projecting beyond its support. Can be dangerous

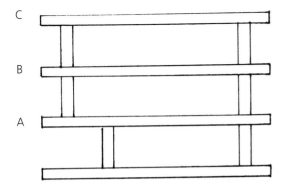

A cantilevered kiln pack where the whole weight of shelves B and C are unsupported on the left hand side and shelf A is liable to warp or even break if the pack is a heavy one. Sometimes, over large dishes, some cantilevering is necessary and this is best done higher in the pack to minimize stress.

in kiln packs, leading to warped or even broken shelves. The diagram illustrates such a situation.

Canton blue

A barium carbonate/cobalt with feldspar and flint. A violet blue pigment.

Carbon, *oxides, compounds*

A non-metallic element C. 12.
Monoxide CO. 28.
Dioxide CO_2, 44.

Carbon occurs in all organic compounds and also in a pure state as graphite, charcoal and diamond. In pottery materials it is represented by the carbonates, where a *basic* element is in combination with carbon and oxygen as CO_2, an '*acidic*' gas. In the carbonate form the bases are chemically stable, though often toxic, and usually in a convenient physical form for use in bodies and glazes, e.g. lime (calcium carbonate). The CO_2 is released as a gas during firing, leaving the oxide, RO. Carbonates are therefore always $RO+CO_2$ or RCO_3, where R is the basic element.

Carbon has a melting point of 3500°C/6364°F and is therefore one of the most refractory materials known and is also a good insulator (see caption at *saggar firing*), but this is only true in the absence of oxygen. With a plentiful supply of oxygen, i.e. in air, the gas CO_2 is produced in great quantities when burning carbonaceous fuels in kilns. Insufficient air (oxygen) will cause this to be reduced (see *reduction*) to CO, carbon monoxide, an unstable and very poisonous gas. This, in turn, will extract oxygen from the glaze pigments in order to regain its stable CO_2 form. Carbon itself, as smoke, can also act as a reducing agent, see *reduction*, but beware too early reduction when the carbon as smoke may stain a glaze which cannot be eradicated by further firing. The carbon in incompletely burnt ash used in a glaze can act as a 'local' reducing agent in an electric kiln. Carbon can be dissolved to a small extent in a melting glaze. A speck of carbon falling onto a melting glaze will reduce it locally.

In clay carbon can lead to bloating and other troubles and must be burnt out by slowing down the biscuit firing at 850–1000°C/1562–1832°F if present in any quantity.

The commonest carbon compound, apart from the carbonates, used in pottery is *silicon carbide*, SiC, a highly conductive material both of heat and electricity.

Some coloring metals can be used as carbonates: copper carbonate is green which helps to distinguish it from other oxides when painting, similarly cobalt carbonate is a purplish blue in the raw state. Unfortunately these advantages are balanced by the toxicity of many carbonates. This does not preclude their use but suggests that care should be taken.

Carbon dioxide

CO_2. The stable oxide of carbon. The product of combustion. Now in disrepute as causing harm to the environment via the ozone layer. The gas is, however, taken up by vegetation and it is the balance between its production and assimilation that is under threat. Potters, therefore, plant trees!

Carbonization, carbonized ware

Often confused with *reduction*, this is the staining of clay or glaze with unburnt *carbon* (see also *black core, smoked ware*) causing grey or black areas.

In raku and sawdust firing the body may be partly reduced but is more likely to be saturated with unburnt carbon which will turn it grey or black, often with dramatic and pleasurable results. Partial carbonization can be achieved by simply holding low-fired biscuit over a piece of burning newspaper or other material which can be made permanent by polishing immediately afterwards. Cut

Typically intricate and attractive carbonization markings on a bottle by Naomi Ogilvie-Browne.

paper shapes can be laid on dishes or held in place by clay pads on pots, for special effects in raku firing. Joan Campbell burns away unwanted or too-dark smoke stains with a gas torch.

Smoke carbon, introduced too early in the kiln can cause grey stains in glazes which may not subsequently burn out, sometimes known as 'sooting'.

Carbon monoxide

CO. A poisonous oxide of carbon; a heavier-than-air gas which will normally collect at ground level and so is less of an immediate danger than some lighter gases but can be fatal if inhaled, rapidly replacing the oxygen in the blood. An early symptom is drowsiness - if this is experienced take deep breaths in the open air. Unstable in the atmosphere, converting to the dioxide. It is the major *reducing* agent.

Can be generated even in an electric kiln so keep well ventilated and avoid firing in cellars or ill-ventilated basements. Georgies advertise a 'dosimeter' detection tube for air sampling of carbon monoxide.

Carborundum

A trade name, now become a household word, for *silicon carbide*. Used for grinding-stones. Biscuit which has been rubbed with carborundum must be well cleaned or it may cause scum on the glaze. (See also *abrasive*.)

Carboxy-methyl-cellulose

See *CMC*.

Carcinogens

Cancer-causing materials. These include, particularly, free silica (flint, etc.), asbestos, ceramic fiber, in fact any inorganic material which can be inhaled in quantity as dust. (See also at *dust, health hazard, poisonous materials*, etc.)

Card measure

A piece of card cut in such a way that it can indicate the 'vital statistics' of a pot for repetition throwing and for future reference. Other details such as clay weight and a diagram of the shape with handle position, etc. can be recorded on it.

The card can be sprayed with varnish to prevent water saturation and to retain the information written on it. Linoleum or thin plywood are also excellent materials. The illustration overleaf shows one type but there are other styles, see Fournier PT. See illustration on opposite page.

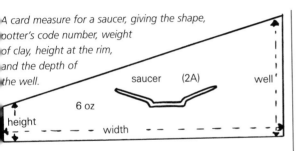

A card measure for a saucer, giving the shape, potter's code number, weight of clay, height at the rim, and the depth of the well.

saucer (2A) well

6 oz

height

width

Carination

From 'keel' or 'keel-shaped', this indicates a sharp alteration in the curve or direction of a profile forming an angle or ridge. Not commonly developed in studio pot forms it, nevertheless, can give a strong accent to a profile. Robin Welch, Dan Arbeid, Derek Davis, and others have produced carinated forms.

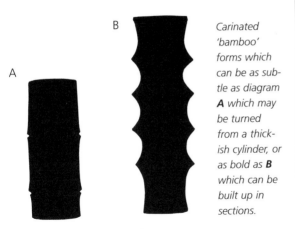

B

A

*Carinated 'bamboo' forms which can be as subtle as diagram **A** which may be turned from a thickish cylinder, or as bold as **B** which can be built up in sections.*

Carolina stone

An American *china stone*.

Carpal tunnel syndrome (CTS)

See *repetitive strain injury*.

Carved mold

Since early times biscuit and plaster molds have had designs cut into them for repeat relief designs. For clay molds one obviously inscribes the leather-hard body before firing. This will give a relief design. If the more usual intaglio style is required a second reverse mold must be cast from the first. Thus, if the original was cut into a bowl shape, the final mold will be in the form of a bowl via a hump mold: If a *hump mold* (drape mold) is wanted the original design must be cut into a 'hump' of clay.

Using the mold presents certain technical problems. Especially with slip-casting, one is faced with the problem of damage to the design through the shrinkage of the clay before the cast can be removed and it is no accident that ancient Roman molds, with the decoration in fairly high relief, restricted it to the upright top half of a bowl, the curve being plain. Press molds are more flexible as the cast can be removed almost immediately after pressing and this must have been the method for the often delicate Song plates and dishes.

Carved molds may not necessarily, of course, be made only for a whole piece but may be used like a large stamp or for *sprigging*.

Carving

As distinct from incising and fluting, carving suggests a more radical cutting away of the surface. It is popular today in porcelain, often penetrating the pot wall, producing decorative pieces of rare fragility. Fine-bladed penknives or renewable-blade surgical scalpels are favorite tools, though there is also the school of hacking away at the surface with any sharp instrument. In general, the more gradual removal of material is likely to be more successful than fierce cuts, liberating to the spirit though the latter may be! Cut edges and corners left sharp can break through dryish glazes in a pleasant manner though they may be somewhat damaging to the hands.

The walls of porcelain pieces can be partially cut away to vary the transmission of light, or the rims or upper sections cut through into 'tree' and other shapes, see *pierced decoration*. Those of thickly thrown cylinders and pots can be cut or sliced with a wire into *facets*.

Casserole

A deep lidded bowl for cooking in the oven, it should be of generous form with a well-fitting lid and an adequate knob, or a strap handle (see *handle*). The casserole usually has two *lug* handles or a short thrown one. The height of the average oven should be considered when designing pot and lid. (See also *ovenware* for discussion of body, glaze, etc.) The usual precautions associated with *thermal shock* and heat resistance must be considered.

Cast

Three associated general usages:
1 Made in a mold.
2 The method of molding, e.g. slip cast.
3 The molded object itself.

Casting

If a hollow plaster shape is filled with slip, water will be absorbed and a coating of clay will be deposited on the inner surface of the plaster. The level of the slip is kept topped-up as it is absorbed, and when the coating has become thick enough the remaining slip is poured out. The clay shape will slowly shrink away from the plaster mold and can be removed.

Casting is an industrial technique intended to produce a large number of identical objects, the initial shape often having been carved in plaster. It has less relevance to the work of the individual potter, though it is often used for bone china and sometimes for porcelain. Casting calls for its own skills, and professional results demand practice and experience. (See also *mold*.)

There are many points at which slip casting can go awry. What is known as casting spot, for instance, a vitrified mark on the bottom of a piece, caused by the first strike of the slip as it is poured into the mold. The mold will, of course, become saturated after several casts have been taken and need careful drying. (See *plaster of Paris, casting slip*.) Sasha Wardell has written a comprehensive guide to the technique (see bibliography). See chart for common problems with casting.

Casting-slip

A normal potter's slip has too high a proportion of water to solid material to be effective as a casting slip. A slip which is too thick to pour can be made fluid by the addition of a *defloculant* (*electrolyte*) which weakens the bonds between particles. Sodium silicate and soda ash are defloculants. Hamer recommends use of two defloculants to avoid thixotropic setting of slip in the mold. The slip itself can be made less viscous by using only small amounts of plastic clay. The normal industrial slip is composed of ball clay, china clay feldspar or stone and flint (see *body*). The high proportion of non-clay materials ensures that the wall of the pot will dry and stiffen rapidly and evenly.

The percentage of defloculant will vary with the type of slip from 0.5–1.5% of the dry weight. Most merchants list casting slips and recipes. Some clays will not defloculate. As a batch of casting-slip is used and re-used, plaster from the molds will reverse the action so that more alkali will be needed to maintain fluidity. Eventually the slip must be discarded. Non-electrolyte defloculants are being developed.

Catalysis

Some chemical substances have the ability to influence change in others without themselves being fundamentally

FAULTS IN CASTING

FAULT	DESCRIPTION	CAUSE	REMEDY
Pinholing	Small holes just beneath the surface on the mold side of the article	Fluidity too low	Increase water addition
Wreathing	Small uneven ridges on the slip side of the article		
Brittleness	Difficult to fettle or cut	*Thixotropy* too low	Decrease alkali content
Casting spot	Discolored patch appearing on the mold side after firing		
Cracking	Small cracks where handles join the body of the article		
Flabbiness	Soft casts difficult to handle without distortion	Thixotropy too high	Increase *alkali* addition
Slow casting	Casting time too long	Fluidity too high or thixotropy too low	Decrease water or decrease alkali addition
Bad draining	Slip failing to drain from narrow sections	Fluidity too low or thixotropy too high	Increase water or increase alkali addition

By kind permission of the British Research Association

altered by that change. The presence of alkalis and alumina for instance assist the quartz/cristobalite conversion.

Catenary arch

If a length of chain or rope is allowed to hang free between two level points it assumes a catenary curve. This curve, reversed can be used as the basis for a very stable arched kiln in which the bricks which compose it do not tend to move relative one to another. Rhodes K recommends that the height and width be nearly equal — 'it is a beautiful structure'.

Cation

If an atom loses an electron it is left with a positive charge and is then called a cation. See *ion, oxygen formula*.

Caustic

The burning or eroding effect of certain substances, notably, in potting, the alkalis. Water in which plant ash has been steeped for cleaning and sieving will feel soft and slippery (which means that it is dissolving a layer of your epidermis!). It will be caustic and obviously may damage sensitive skin. Use gloves. Caustic soda is sodium hydroxide, $NaOH$.

Celadon, celedon

The general name given to a solution color range of subtle green to blue-gray stoneware and porcelain glazes, deriving from iron in reduction. The name is said to originate, somewhat inconsequentially, from a character in French classic drama who wore green clothes.

The Yueh wares of China, dating back to early Han, were the forebears of the later and very fine Song celadons (AD 960–1260) which were likened to jade. The color is shown to greatest advantage on porcelain or pale bodied stonewares, although it can also produce a rich olive on darker bodies.

From 0.5 to 2.0% of ferric oxide is added to a transparent glaze, which should be applied fairly generously to obtain the depth and richness of color and to maintain the iron in the ferrous state during cooling, although sudden temperature reductions during firing should be avoided (Hamer). (See *reduction*.) A particular quality of slight opacity in a celadon is due to minute bubbles in the glaze. Cardew suggests a viscous glaze with an RO of 0.25–0.45 KNaO, and 0.55–0.75 CaO, with very little magnesia. This may eliminate some wood ashes from which the early celadons are thought to derive although Brickell suggests that the ash from tough grasses, high in silica, is said to be good material for inclusion in celadon glaze recipes. Rhodes CGP mentions a little bone ash to provide *opalescence*. A series of recipes is given in Leach PB which include ochre (up to 9%) as all or part of the iron content, also Fe_3O_4 (black iron) instead of ferric.

In PQ17 A. Lewis-Evans quotes the (now obsolete) Seger cone 3 formula:

K_2O	0.3	Al_2O_3	0.45		
CaO	0.7	Fe_2O_3	0.05	SiO_2	4.0

which he translates into:

China clay	7.5	Potash feldspar	45.0
Whiting	17.5	Quartz	27.5
Ferric oxide	2.5		

Celsian

A barium feldspar. Rare.

Celsius

The internationally approved name for the Centigrade scale. Luckily the sign °C can stand for either.

Cement

Any adhesive material which hardens as it dries, and particularly the large family of heat-treated mixtures of limestone, clay, bauxite, etc. These provide various grades of semi-dehydrated cements which set and gain strength when mixed with water. True refractory cements harden only as a result of ceramic alteration at high temperatures.

The ubiquitous Portland cement will explode or melt if strongly heated, but high-alumina cements such as ciment fondu and lumnite can be cast with suitable aggregates into kiln blocks, element wire holders, etc. for firing up to 1320°C/2408°F. W. J. Doble supply a non-setting jointing cement which allows brickwork to expand and contract without cracking.

Keene's cement is a hard setting *gypsum* plaster. (See also *air-setting cement*, and *mortar*.)

Centering

Pressure applied to a ball of clay on the wheel as it spins, to persuade the whole mass to run true. Potters develop their own methods, but a steady pressure in one horizontal direction, either thrusting or pulling, is the basis of the action, with a secondary downwards thrust to maintain a roughly semi-spherical mass. See also the third and fourth illustrations and *annular* for another possible approach.

Coning is an associated but separate action. Pots are also centered on a throwing wheel or on a *whirler* for turning,

1 *Centering by a sideways pressure with the left hand, the right palm holding the mass down.*
2 *The block may also be centered by a pull with the right hand towards the potter's body. (See also coning)*
3 *and* **4** *Isaac Button at work where centering and the commencement of throwing so merge that it is difficult to decide where one finishes and the other begins. See film 'Isaac Button, Country Potter'. (Also at annular.)*

banding and other work. Wheelheads are usually marked with concentric rings to simplify centering, but it can also be accomplished by a series of rapid taps on one side of the pot as it spins, a knack requiring practice.

In CPA News 28 there was the astonishing announcement of the supply of 'self-centering clay' centered in the factory and vacuum packed in its centered state! From The Saki Suyado Corporation Japan, it received an enthusiastic reception from a few distinguished potters. It was available in Britain to potters for a trial period in 1993. Nothing has been noted about it since. Axner list a centering tool, fastened to the wheel tray, in which 'a sheet of metal comes into the clay at an angle that will quickly and easily center it'.

Centigrade scale

A temperature recording scale in which the interval between the freezing and boiling points of water is divided into 100 degrees. The symbol °C, which also refers to the Celsius scale now the approved international scale and increasingly used outside the laboratory, is for most practical purposes parallel to Centigrade. To convert degrees Centigrade to the other commonly used scale, Fahrenheit, divide by five, multiply by nine, and add thirty-two. (See also *temperature conversion, temperature degrees*.)

Ceramic

Derived from the Greek keramos, 'burnt stuff', or 'an earthen vessel'. This suggests pronunciation with a hard 'c', but the soft 's' is popular, especially in the USA.

The term has now so wide an application as to have lost much of its meaning. Not only is it applied to the silicate industries but also to 'articles or coatings from essentially inorganic and non-metallic materials made permanent by heat — at temperatures sufficient to cause sintering — or conversion wholly or partly to the glassy state' (from the USA definition, 1963). The net is now cast even wider to include cements and enameling on metal.

Ceramic fiber

A mass of thread-like crystals, known as 'filaments' or 'whiskers', produced by very hot air being driven across the surface of a melt of fused silica, alumina, potassium titanate and other ceramic compounds. Used as a lightweight insulating material resembling felt. More refractory than glass-wool (*glass fiber*, or fiberglass) and can be used as a hot-face as well as a backing material, the best quality graded up to 1500°C/2732°F.

Colson 1975 discusses its use in fuel-burning kilns; Fournier EKBP in electric kilns. There are a number of trade names: Ceafibre, Fiberfrax, etc.

Because of its light weight, its efficiency as an insulator, and its ease of handling, ceramic fiber in the form of blocks, modules, blanket, wool or paper, is now more widely used in fast-firing kilns for raku, etc. (see *top hat kiln*) and is replacing brick in many others where there is little mechanical stress, e.g. gas kilns. Fordham Thermal Systems make useful 18 x 12 x 6in modules, W. J. Doble and others supply blanket and board for temperatures up to 1400°C/2552°F. The blanket or board can be fastened to the casing with the special 'cups' as in diagram but a similar system is that used by Steve Mills of Bath Pottery Supplies for both low and high temperatures. He makes stoneware clay buttons, about 2 inches across, with a lug or loop on the back. Nichrome or other heat resistant wire is taken from this loop and through the casing, held in place either by a twist in the wire on the outside of the kiln or another button. The fiber may also be 'glued' into place with a special cement. Off-cuts have been recommended for clamming-up; and even introduced into bodies for dry strength and to prevent dunting, being ground wet in a mortar and wedged into the clay. Simple, lightweight top hat lift-off raku kilns can be constructed from a 40-gallon oil drum and ceramic fiber blanket cemented to the inner surface. (See *top hat kiln.*) The paper form can be used in dry-built kilns, (see *bricklaying*). There is also a sprayed-on

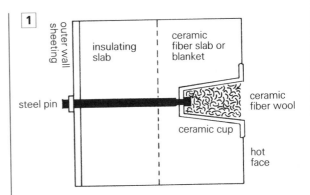

1 One method of fixing ceramic fiber sheeting (or 'blanket') on a kiln wall. The (black) metal pin holds a ceramic 'cup' with a flanged rim which is pressed into the fiber and tightened by means of a nut on the outside of the kiln wall. See also text for a simpler method.

2 Ceramic fiber in the form of felt, blanket, string, and paper. Photograph reproduced by kind permission of the Carborundum Company Ltd.

ceramic fiber available but this appears to be used on too large and technically involved a scale to be of practical use to studio potters at present.

Like all inorganic fibrous materials it is now regarded as

3 The simple attachment for the ceramic blanket in the kiln illustrated at top-hat kiln. See information in the text and also the caption at reduction. Note the use of square shelves in a round kiln which Steve Mills finds useful in maintaining an even temperature through the pack.

a category 2 carcinogen and care must be taken not to inhale fragments into the lungs; a mask should be worn when cutting or being exposed to fiber blanket especially when it has become more brittle with firing. It is forbidden in exposed areas in Germany and must be covered with brick. The Bruce Chivers kiln uses a 'vacuum formed' fiber which is 'dust free if alumina washed'. On the other hand Axner offers a raku kiln insulated with 'amorphous . . . ceramic fibers which are soluble in the lung'.

There are shrinkage problems associated with the continued use of ceramic fiber but Rath's Denka mullite fiber has, in trials, shown little evidence of this trouble.

Its comparatively low mechanical strength limits its use in some situations, for instance, earlier electric kiln element holders were not very successful, but especially hardened and machined shapes and rigidizers are now available.

Ceramic pencil

See *pencil.*

Ceramic sculpture

A term generally applied to those ceramics which are not used as pots, or where form, invention, and decoration are the sole consideration. It occupies the attention of an increasing number of potters today but detailed discussion is outside the scope of this dictionary.

Ceramist

Applied generally to potters making non-functional pieces, most commonly in the USA.

Cerium

Oxide, ceria, CeO_2.
A *rare earth* derived from monazite. Has a high melting point (specialized crucibles have been made from it). Used as a stabilizer for yellow vanadium and antimony stains. Dissolves in a glaze above about 1000°C/1832°F.

Cerlite

A vitrifiable body of clay, grog, and feldspars suitable for making large objects. Originated in Italy.

Cermet

Material containing both ceramic and metals. Can replace silica for thermocouple sheaths.

Chaledonic

Applied to flint or any cryptocrystalline form of quartz.

Chalk

A white earthy limestone, $CaCO_3$; ground and levigated into *whiting.* Formed from the shells of minute marine organisms. Deposits in England up to 2000ft/*c*. 600m thick. French chalk is a soapstone or steatite used for marking on cloth.

Blackboard chalk is made from calcium sulfate, $CaSO_4$. Sticks of chalk (or cylinders or other shapes cut from larger pieces) can be used like stamps, or as *roulettes* to roll repeat relief patterns into clay. (See also at *plaster of Paris.*)

Chambered kiln

Generally applied to the climbing kilns of the Orient, e.g. Hamada's at Mashiko (see Rhodes K). In the West,

A two-chambered kiln of the type used by craft potters. Sometimes a bag wall is built of packed saggars at each setting. Occasionally a large chimney is utilized for biscuit.

semi-continuous brick kilns have twelve or more chambers (see also *reverbatory*). Two-chambered kilns are quite common in studio potters' workshops, the second sometimes used for biscuit, or for oxidation. (See also *climbing kilns*.)

Chamois

A very soft and pliable leather, unrivalled for smoothing the rims of pots on the wheel. Unfortunately it soon becomes clay colored and not infrequently it is lost in the slurry to turn up later in a pot! An attached tab will help to avoid this.

Chamotte

A term found in Scandinavian and European books on pottery to denote a heavily grogged stoneware, often unglazed. It can also refer to the refractory grog (often fireclay) itself. Term also used in the USA. Listed in some suppliers' catalogs.

Change over switch

See *electric wiring to kiln*.

Charcoal

Vegetable or animal substance heated with the exclusion of air. Impure carbons. (See also *reduction*.) Useful for preliminary drawing on raw clay or biscuit. Could be adapted for raku firing (and for cooking the sausages at raku parties!).

Charge

In ceramics refers to the material put into a *ball mill* to be ground.

Chatter

Corrugations of the surface of clay which can develop quite suddeny during turning. The turning tool will begin to vibrate. A slack hold on the tool, clay which is too hard (or occasionally, too soft), too sharp a tool, and uneven texture or hardness of the clay, can all contribute to chatter.

To cure, continue turning with the long edge of tool or a *steel palette* held at an acute angle to the corrugations so that it rides across the tops and cannot fall into the dips. As soon as the surface is smooth again, revert to the normal tool position.

Chatter has been used as a decorative texture since Roman times and is codified as 'kasurmon' in Japan where

Showing the position of the turning tool to cure chatter (the corrugated surface).

it cuts segments from a slip coating in the manner of sgraffito — though deliberately to develop chatter in a controlled way is even more difficult than avoiding it when it is not wanted!

Cheese hard

Term sometimes used as a synonym for *leather-hard*.

Chemical analysis

One can analyze a pottery material in more than one way. The commonest is a list of parts by weight of all the separate elements, oxides, carbonates, sulphides, etc. which can be isolated from it by various physical or chemical means.

A good supplier will give analyses of the materials he sells and is useful in warning us against variations from the ideal formula which is used in glaze calculations. (See also *analysis*.)

Chemical compounds

Theoretically unvarying qualities of minerals, etc. as predicted by their *ideal formulas*: *melting points, conversion factors, specific gravities, hardness*, etc. In practice only a *chemical analysis* can tell us how near any sample is to the pure form, though from a good supplier, it will be near enough for practical purposes.

Chemical symbol

The letters (or pairs of letters) which denote the chemical elements, either singly or as combined *molecules*, are international. The symbol is either a single upper-case letter: e.g. C for carbon, or O for oxygen; or a capital and lower-case such as Si for silicon but, because the symbols are often based on Latin names, they are not always as straightforward and recognizable. Tin, for instance, uses the Latin 'stannum' and its symbol is Sn; sodium is 'natrum', Na. Because there is no element with the symbol R this letter is used to denote any element in compound; e.g RO_2 indicates any compound in which one atom will 'naturally' combine with two atoms of oxygen. See *element (chemical)* for an alphabetical list of symbols of specific interest to potters, and see *periodic table* for a complete chart.

But we need only be able to recognize about a third of the hundred odd total. When two or more elements are combined in a molecule the symbol also indicates the relative number of atoms of each of them; e.g. SiO_2 — one silicon to two oxygen. Where more than one molecule is concerned the number is placed before the symbol, e.g. gypsum is $CaSO_4 . 2H_2O$ (one calcium sulphide to two water). See also at *atom, atomic theory, compound, element, periodic table.*

Chemically-combined water

The water of *hydration*. Specifically, in clay, the H_2O which is expelled at 500–600°C/932–1112°F, altering the molecular pattern and forming a new material. The process cannot be reversed. Distinct from absorbed and adsorbed water. Leach refers to it as 'hygroscopic water'.

Chemistry of pottery

The early potters worked miracles of clay and glaze compounding and firing without true chemical knowledge, but their time scale was in generations while ours is in years. An ability to think in terms other than those of pure day-to-day experience has become essential. Simple chemistry and an outline of the current explanation of the behavior of atomic particles can short-cut many a tedious trial series and will help to explain and control results. On the other hand it is always what happens to your glaze in your kiln that matters.

One problem in presenting the subject of chemistry is that extreme simplicity can be misleading, the actual changes and reactions being complex. However, since the whole story is not known even to the specialist scientist, a general framework will be valid for most practical purposes. 'A complete chart of information . . . would probably be out of date before we had learned to read it' — Cardew. Chemistry should be seen as one of the many valuable sources of information.

The raw materials of our world are legion. Their names

tell us little about their make-up or properties. This endless diversity can be greatly simplified in chemical terms. All physical materials are combinations of a mere 100 or so unique and separate parts called the elements. Potters use some 20 of these regularly, and another 20 occasionally. The field is thus dramatically reduced. The elements sometimes exist alone, e.g. as the metal 'iron' or the element carbon as 'charcoal', but more often in combinations of two or more. These compounds are more than mere mixtures; they will rarely resemble in appearance or in general behavior any of the constituent elements. To take an extreme instance the dangerously unstable metal sodium, in combination with chlorine, a poisonous gas, forms the harmless and useful sodium chloride—table salt.

It is possible, therefore, to describe materials by listing the elements which make them up. These can be written out in full but are generally noted as abbreviations or symbols. A list of the elements relevant to ceramics will be found under *elements (chemical)* and *atomic weights.* The element symbols are international.

The commonest simple compound in *inorganic* chemistry is between an element and oxygen (another element). The result is called the *oxide* of the element, e.g. iron oxide, silica (oxide of silicon). Elements form oxides under the influence of heat, the science of ceramics is, therefore, the study of reactions between oxides at high temperatures. Once compounds have been formed they can be separated only by other chemical reactions or by the application of energy such as heat. Firing is essentially the rearranging of existing compounds, e.g. clay, and the formation of new compounds from mixed materials, e.g. glaze.

Oxides can be listed in three groups: the *bases*, the *acids*, and the *amphoterics*. In ceramics, the first group has a fluxing action, i.e. it lowers melting points; the second comprises the *glass formers* and is usually considered as refractory — it raises melting points; the third group has an intermediate balancing and uniting role. This rather crude view of the three groups is open to criticism, but will be found generally valid in practice. To decide the proportional amounts which enter into combination to produce a desired result, e.g. an earthenware glaze or a porcelain body, we must enter at least the fringe of atomic and molecular science. (See also *atomic theory.*)

Atoms combine into *compounds* in certain fixed proportions. This proportion is indicated in the symbol by a number written after and below the element. For example, in silica the silicon, symbol Si, and the oxygen, symbol O, combine in the proportion of one to two. This is written SiO_2. The reverse is true when sodium, Na, combines with oxygen, giving Na_2O. Ferric oxide combines 2:3, i.e. Fe_2O_3. These proportions can be taken to apply to the atoms (the smallest particle of an element), the actual material being a repeat pattern in infinite extension of connected atoms known as molecules. (See also *crystal, network, valency*.)

A *mineral* will often contain several oxides. Its chemical symbol will always be made up of the constituent elements and their atomic parts, but these can be arranged in several ways. The most obvious is to note each element and its proportion, for instance, potash feldspar, $K_2Al_2Si_6O_{16}$. This is, however, of little practical use for obtaining a general picture of the mineral or guessing its probable behavior in the kiln. A more helpful grouping, and that normally used by potters, would be $K_2O. Al_2O_3. 6SiO_2$. It will be seen that, instead of writing SiO_2 six times, the number 6 has been placed before it. This grouping corresponds to the *Seger formula* and the base, amphoteric, acid divisions mentioned above. The mineral (feldspar) has six times as many molecules of acidic oxide as it has of basic: we can therefore guess that it would make a glaze but only at stoneware temperatures — 1250°C/2282°F and above, and this in fact is the case. (See *Seger formula, base, acid*, etc. for further discussion.)

The letter R does not occur in the list of element symbols and so it can be used to indicate any element in combination with oxygen. Thus R_2O_3 includes any compound which unites in a 2:3 ratio with oxygen. The whole of the bases in a glaze formula may be denoted by RO in order to compare them with the amount of acid. All these symbols denote molecular parts and must be multiplied by their molecular weight to translate them into weighable materials. (See *formula-into-recipe*.)

For convenience, *minerals* are symbolized by their 'ideal' formula, i.e. as if they were quite pure, unadulterated materials. This seldom occurs in nature but rocks are selected which have the nearest approximation. The perfect mineral may be given a separate name. For instance, pure clay material — $Al_2O_3. 2SiO_2. 2H_2O$ — is 'kaolinite'. For practical computation, china clay may be considered as kaolinite although it has some 2% or more of impurities. Similarly potash feldspar has the ideal formula as listed above, but the base is nearly always a mixture of potash and soda with very small amounts of other materials, and is sometimes denoted as NaKO. Luckily the two alkalis act in a fairly similar way. A *chemical analysis* will show how far the sample strays from the pure mineral. *Secondary clays*, on the other hand, may stray a long way from kaolin and be composed of associated minerals such as illite and other micaceous substances. These variations, while necessitating practical trials, do not invalidate an understanding of the fundamental make-up of the materials a potter uses.

Chert

A very hard siliceous rock used, in ceramics, for grinding materials and as a lining for ball mills.

Chess set, board

A time-consuming but rewarding design challenge with very wide possibilities. Bernard Leach and others have produced chess sets. The pieces can be thrown, modeled, or cast, using any distinctive attribute of the various characters, and in earthenware, stoneware, or porcelain, the last two being preferable for the strength of the material, as they are often subject to somewhat rough handling. The tiles for a chess-board are traditionally black and white, not difficult for the potter to produce.

Chicken brick, fish brick

A casserole, usually thrown as a closed-top straight-sided bottle. It is laid on its side and cut through to form a base and lid. It must be large enough to take a whole chicken. A fish brick is similar in style but has wider formal and decorative possibilities.

A chicken brick by C. and M. Hemstock, the neck is solid and serves as a handle.

Chimney

A vertical shaft of brick or metal. A warm, rising column of air exerts a 'pull', drawing air and gases in from the base of the shaft. Different types of kiln require widely differing sizes of chimney. An electric kiln needs none at all; gas kilns often require only minimal chimneys, or may be quite efficient with the near horizontal 'balanced flue' taken straight through a wall. Oil, wood and coal, respectively, need increasing size and height. An updraft kiln forms its own chimney, and little if any extension is required at the top. The downdraft type obviously needs sufficient pull to force the hot gases to travel downwards through the chamber against their natural inclinations. As a rough guide, for solid fuel kilns, every 1ft/30cm of downward draft and every 4ft/120cm of horizontal movement needs 3ft/1m of chimney height.

A tall narrow chimney is generally considered to exert more 'pull' than a short wide one but Harry Davis disputes this and states that they are equally effective. The expansion of gases is very considerable (in the range of 1–5) and must be taken into account in any design, see *gas expansion*. However the movement of gases through the kiln can be maintained by forced draft at the firemouth or a fan in the chimney, thereby cutting the chimney height to a minimum though increasing the setting-up and running costs.

China

In England the term officially refers to *bone china*. Its wider use in the USA and common usage elsewhere, covers any domestic vitreous whiteware. The Brussels Nomenclature equates it with porcelain.

China clay, *kaolin*

A general name for an almost pure clay material containing, on average, 98% kaolinite — $Al_2O_3. 2SiO_2. 2H_2O$. mol.wt. 258. A *primary clay*. Found in comparatively few areas though in great quantities in Cornwall, England, in the USA (Florida, Carolina), Central Europe, and elsewhere. Usually very white, though iron-stained kaolins are found. Of the thousands of tons used annually only one fifth or less is absorbed by ceramics.

It is usually 'won' by washing from the rock face with high-pressure hoses, the resultant slurry carried along channels to settling troughs. The *micaceous* matter is separated out — this eventually forms the 'white mountains' of the St Austell district of England. Newer methods of separation have been developed.

Because of its large particle (crystal) size its plasticity is poor. Some samples are more workable than others; Chinese kaolin being probably the most plastic and the Cornish clay one of the least. China clay is used in many bodies to increase the whiteness and refractoriness and to vary the particle size of secondary clays. Industrial bodies may contain 30% or more; porcelains, 50%. In glazes it represents pure *kaolinite*. The term kaolin is often used as a synonym for china clay, but this is deprecated by some authorities. Calcined china clay is used as an 'opener' in bodies and to minimize wet-dry shrinkage. (See also *clay*, *kaolinite*, *Molochite*.)

China stone

A feldspathic mineral from partly decomposed granite; with the general formula of $NaK_2O. Al_2O_3. 8SiO_2$, 644, but variable with an RO which may also include 0.30 equivalents of lime. Also known as pegmatite, Cornwall stone, Cornish stone, Manx stone, or, simply, stone. Godfrey spar from the USA is a similar material.

An analysis by weight:

Na_2O	4.0				
K_2O	3.81	Al_2O_3	14.93	SiO_2	72.9
CaO	2.06	Fe_2O_3	0.13	TiO_2	0.02
MgO	0.09				

This is an analysis of a *defluorinated* china stone. Raw stone often contains fluorine and is purple colored; Manx stone is virtually free of fluorine. There are 'hard' and 'soft' white grades (referring to *fusibility*) in which the alteration to kaolin or secondary mica is more or less advanced (Dodd).

Stone will form a glaze between 1300–1400°C/2372–2552°F. It is used in bodies and glazes to provide some soda. 'Used in engobes for its adhesive power during and after firing' (Georgies). Also used as a dilutant for cobalt.

Chittering

Glaze flaking, especially on rims. See *shivering*.

Chromate of iron

See *iron chromate*.

Chrome

Often used to denote pigments or glazes containing chromatic oxide (see *chromium*) e.g. 'chrome green', and sometimes, loosely, for the oxide itself.

Chromel

A proprietory name for an alloy used principally in thermocouples.

Chrome-tin pink

A pottery pigment, normally used on earthenware, for underglaze painting, in enamels and as a *stain*. Used in the 18th century and originally called English Pink, it is derived from a reaction between chrome, tin oxide, and lime (calcia). 'The precipitation of fine particles of chromic oxide on the surface of tin oxide in an opaque glaze' (Dodd). It has a long firing range but becomes volatile at high temperatures. The color does not often blend happily with craft pottery. For use in glaze, Stephanie Kalan (CR 47) states that fluxes should be 'mostly lime and lead with a minimum of alkalis'. Lime stabilizes the color. There is also a chrome-zircon pink and a high-firing aluminous chrome-zinc pink for use under a leadless glaze.

Accidental blushes can occur in a firing where the necessary ingredients are present, usually in lead glazes but has also been known in stoneware if commercially prepared color is used, or sometimes with nickel-chrome (*Nichrome*) wire elements in an electric kiln.

Chromite

A chromium ore used as iron chromate.

Chromium, oxide, compounds

A metallic element Cr. 52.
Chromic oxide Cr_2O_3, 152, m.p. 2270°C.
Chromate of potash $K_2Cr_2O_7$, 294.

A relatively modern addition to the potter's palette. Can be toxic and carcinogenic, so take care not to inhale as dust. The green oxide of chrome is the form most used. Although refractory it is also *volatile* over 1000°C/1832°F and can cause pink reaction (see *chrome-tin pink*). 'The potassium form is used in glazes and frits' (Billington).

The oxide is a very versatile coloring agent, especially at low temperatures. In a high-lead, low-alumina glaze red, orange and yellow can be obtained. 1–2% can give red or orange at 900°C/1652°F or below, using the dichromate of potash (toxic). Lead/silica frits are good starting points for recipes. As the firing temperature is increased the color turns through orange to yellow (*c.*1050°C/1922°F). Hamer suggests the addition of red iron and zinc oxides at higher temperatures but the results hardly sound worth the trouble. Yellow is also reputed to be possible with lead and soda.

At more practical temperatures chrome yields dullish greens in a lead glaze and browns with zinc oxide. Colors are apt to be rather heavy and flat and are always opaque. Cardew suggests the addition of *fluorspar* for a clearer color in reduction up to 1320°C/2408°F. The green may be spoiled by the presence of tin oxide. A brighter, lighter green can result from a high lime glaze. Lithium carbonate (6–8%), in a soft lead glaze with chromium has also been mentioned. A small quantity (0.25–1.0%) with cobalt is reputed to give good colors in reduction. Chromium, with tin and calcium, and especially in *lead glazes*, can develop pinks and browns which are not always attractive. This reaction is the basis for many prepared pinks—known as *chrome-tin pinks*, also chrome-alumina-zinc pink, normally stable up to 1300°C/2372°F, and chrome-zircon pink replacing up to three-quarters of the tin oxide. Chromium is a favorite addition to many prepared stains and colors, especially dark ones; its opacity, refractoriness and low solubility make it valuable as a stabilizer. Chrome-magnesium ores are made into specialist refractories.

Chuck

As applied to throwing, a chuck is a ring or block of clay for supporting a pot or bowl on the wheelhead while turning, or for secondary throwing.

A chuck of stiff clay inside an inverted bowl or pot is preferable to dabs of clay round the outside. The piece can be removed to check thickness, etc, and is held true during the work. A chuck can be cut for the largest piece to be turned and pared down progressively smaller for the rest, or a stock of leather-hard chucks can be made and kept in condition in polythene.

Method: Stiff clay is beaten out to a flat block on a dampened wheelhead and the piece to be turned pressed gently on to it, making a mark which will indicate its width. The block is then cut to fit with a pointed turning tool. Billington (TP) illus. 71 shows bowls supported

1 A beaten-out slab of stiffish clay has been cut on the revolving wheelhead to receive the bowl for turning.
2 A circular plastic box used as a turning chuck by Jack Doherty.

above the wheelhead, but it is easier to maintain the same plane between rim and foot ring if the former is hard down, though this necessitates a precisely fitting chuck.

A hollow chuck for supporting tall pots is usually in the form of a diabolo. It may be thrown and wrapped in polythene when leather-hard, or else biscuited prior to use. Biscuit chucks should be soaked in water before use. Cup heads can also be utilized. In CR58 David Lloyd Jones illustrates a chuck for large plates: a wide annular ring thrown on a wheelhead, cut to a bevel and scored. The plate rim sits on the bevelled surface and the scoring prevents movement in relation to the chuck. (See also *turning.*)

Chun glaze

See new spelling at *jun.*

Ciment fondu

An aluminous cement (proprietary name) see *high aluminous cement.*

Circuit, *electrical*

The complete path traveled by an electric current. An unbroken length of conductor between two terminals.

The wiring in a kiln will usually be split into several circuits, each one carrying a certain current (in *amperes*) and exerting a certain resistance (in *ohms*).

If a circuit does not embody apparatus which exerts

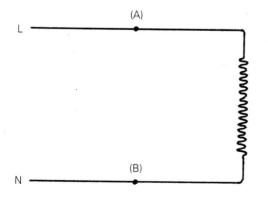

A single electric circuit, the current flowing between L (line, or, in common parlance, 'live') and N (neutral) through the length of resistance wire which limits the current. The resistance may be a light bulb, or may represent a series of elements in an electric kiln but each circuit must stem separately from the mains input at A and B. See also parallel wiring and diagram at series wiring.

resistance, unlimited current will flow — it will be short-circuited or 'shorted'. A weak link of easily melted wire — a fuse — is put into all circuits to guard against this eventuality. (See also *ELCB.*)

Circuit breaker

See *fuse, ELCB.*

Clamming

The sealing of a kiln door (and after firing, the hearths) with coarse slurry.

Clamp

A heap of bricks or, in primitive firings, pots, either covered with brushwood or other fuel, or built to allow fires within the clamp. In a simple brick clamp only about 50% of the bricks are adequately fired, but see *clamp kiln.* (See Cardew Appendix 3.)

Clamp kiln

A firing method similar to bonfire. A shallow pit is dug and lined with wood or brushwood which is set alight. On to the glowing embers bone dry pots are set and more fuel is laid over them. Turves are finally laid over the whole area and the kiln left for several hours before being unpacked. Pre-heating of the pots to the *water-smoking* stage is advisable.

Clay

The 'ideal' clay material is *kaolinite*, $Al_2O_3. 2SiO. H_2O$. 158. This never occurs pure in nature. *China clay* averages 95% or more kaolinite, but this is not the case in *secondary clays.* It has been stated that in most fine, very plastic clays kaolinite is frequently absent and the main constituents may be *illite* ('London clay is thought to be 90% illite' Cardew), montmorillonite, and muscovite mica. We must therefore be wary of equating many clays, apart from primary 'china clays', with the usual formula for kaolinite. In practice, of course, it is the physical behavior of clays which is important but a theoretical background is useful in assessing their behavior, especially when things go wrong.

For more exhaustive studies of the science of clay materials see Worrall and Hamer C. Clay is the result of the decomposition of *granite* and *igneous* rocks. The alkalis are leached out; quartz, mica and clay remain. *Primary clay* is found on the site of its formation and is therefore purer, whiter, but less weathered and plastic than are *secondary*

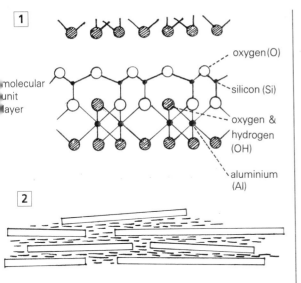

Two representations of clay 'scales'.

1 Shows the presumed molecular formation, the top and bottom rows representing repeats of the center group. The forces of attraction between each layer are weak. (Diagram based on Worrall.)

2 Perhaps a more comprehensible but still diagrammatic suggestion of plates of clay (each consisting of a grouping of the above 'scales') with a very thin layer of water between. The plates slide over one another but there is enough attraction betwen the layers to maintain their formation once pressure has been removed. The amount of water is obviously important; too little and the plates would break apart rather than slide, too much and they would cease to have sufficient cohesion and would result in a slip rather than a workable body. See thixotropy.

clays. The latter have been moved by glacial and rock-folding action (*boulder clays*), by water (*alluvial, estuarine, fluvine, lacustrine*), or by wind. The weathering and general battering they have received, together with natural levigation, have reduced the particle size with a corresponding increase in plasticity. Secondary clays have also picked up 'impurities' which lower their melting point, increase drying and firing shrinkage, and darken color. They occur very widely and are infinitely variable, but can be grouped, broadly, in order of refractoriness:

1 Fireclays: up to 1500°C/2732°F.
Associated with coal seams. Often black and compressed (see *shale*). Some free silica. Often high in alumina and low in alkalis. Fire cream to gray. Often excellent plasticity.

2 Stoneware clays: to 1350°C/2462°F.
Any plastic and reasonably refractory pale firing clay.

3 Siliceous ball clay: to 1300°C/2372°F. Ball clay: to 1250°C/2282°F.

The landscape of Cornwall (England) with the 'white mountains' of china clay waste, mostly micaceous material, on the horizon.

Sedimentary clays: of very fine grain which is an important factor in their *fusibility*, high plasticity, and comparatively high shrinkage: They fire ivory. Used in association with other clays.

4 Red clays: to 1100°C/2012°F (occasionally to 1250°C).
Plastic, very fusible, fire brown. Earthenware, slipware, terracotta, bricks, etc. A few stand the lower stoneware temperatures. Very variable. High in iron. Some so fusible that they will form a glaze at 1280°C/2336°F, e.g. *Albany clay*.

5 Other: Various minor deposits such as *pipeclay*. Also the widely distributed *marls* and loams. Very contaminated surface clays have too high a shrinkage to be useful, though they can sometimes serve as an iron pigment. *Halloysite* is a form of clay mineral as is *montmorillinite*.

Between the types listed there are many graduations. There are untypical examples within the categories, such as the Yorkshire potter Isaac Button's red clay, the melting point of which was reputed to be above 1400°C/2552°F. Brickell gives an illuminating chart of the constituents of some New Zealand clays in which we see surprising variations in the proportions.

While most clays are derived from *granite*, similar minerals have formed from *diorite, volcanic ash, basalt* and other rocks. These include *montmorillonite* which is often added to less plastic bodies. As mentioned above, some clays are considered to be largely composed of illitic minerals. (See *illite*.)

The structure of plastic clay is lamellar (flat scales). In simplified terms, the electrical cohesion between the 'sheets' is sufficient to maintain the mass of a clay in any given shape, but can be momentarily disturbed by pressure. The scales, in effect, can slide over one another, lubricated by the molecular-thin layer of water between them. On the release of the pressure the form-holding qualities are restored. The lamellar hypothesis assumes that other rock minerals, no matter how finely ground, do not exhibit plasticity and this proves true in practice. This unique quality is known as *thixotropy*. Other virtues we look for in a good potters' clay are a low water absorption, and standing strength. In montmorillonites the link or bond between plates is weaker and up to four 'thicknesses' of water molecules can penetrate. Substitution can also take place, iron and alkalis for alumina, for instance (*base exchange*), lowering refractoriness, darkening the color, and resulting in very variable compositions. Some *bentonites* swell when wetted.

For workable clay mixtures, known as 'bodies', not only are different clays blended together for their individual properties (plasticity, color, refractoriness, etc.) but non-clay minerals are frequently added, the commonest being sand, grog, or quartz, but also including china stone, nepheline syenite, feldspar, mica, iron compounds, molochite (in porcelain), and talc. See Ceramic Review CG for examples.

Two typical clay analyses*:*

SiO_2	Al_2O_3	Fe_2O_3	TiO_2	MgO	Impurities	Alakalis
Albany Clay						
57.64	14.60	5.20	0.40	2.68	3.25	00.80 (Na_2O)
Kaolin						
*c.*55.00	40.00	0.40				

For optimum plasticity the following water content of various clays is given in Salmang (this is useful when mixing dry clay and water, e.g. in a *dough mixer*). These, however, seem to be rather wide margins!

Refractory clays	15–25%
Potters' clays (natural bodies)	15–50%
Kaolins	18–40%

(See also *drying of clay and glazes*.)

Clay gun

A hand-held metal cylinder and plunger used to extrude clay through dies. Useful for fine work. Available from several suppliers.

Clay memory

A slightly fanciful term coined by Cardew for the fact that a pot which, for instance, has been 'out of shape' and subsequently corrected, will return in some degree to the original distortion, possibly in the firing.

Clay testing

Any new clay, whether purchased or 'found' (see *clay winning*) will have its own distinctive qualities and vices. 'You

cannot know too much about your subtle and elusive raw material; any clay must be deemed guilty until it is proved innocent' (Cardew).

Some simple tests can be made which will build up an overall picture of the clay you are dealing with:

1 Free lime. A pellet of clay dropped into dilute hydrochloric acid will effervesce if lime is present.

2 Soluble alkalis, or lime. Will cause staining or a whitish scumming on the surface of a dried or fired example.

3 Plasticity. A $^1\!/_2$in/12 mm coil rolled out and bent round a 1in/25mm rod (a broomstick) should not crack unduly. A pinchpot is a fairly stern test. Try throwing. Newly prepared clay should be given at least a week's rest in a damp atmosphere (wrapped in polythene) before plasticity tests are made.

4 Shrinkage. Roll out and cut a strip of plastic clay, to 10in/250mm long. An engraved ruler can be pressed into the clay to leave an accurate mark of length. Measure again when dry (keep the strip flat), if it has shrunk to less than 9in/225mm the clay is not likely to be very useful. Test also for dry strength at this stage.

5 Inspect dried samples for cracks or other faults.

6 Fire samples of pots and measured strips, preferably, at first, to about 900°C/1652°F.

If this biscuit is free from faults, try again at higher temperatures until it shows signs of vitrification and/or collapse. If a strip is supported at the ends only, the sag during firing will be an indication of pyroplastic deformation and refractoriness. Check the measured strip for firing shrinkage and compare with a known clay at the same temperature.

7 If you now have a biscuit sample of 'won' clay which is neither too dark nor faulted (cracks, bloats etc.) at 1000°C/1832°F, then you are lucky and can go on to try the clay on the wheel for standing-strength and water absorption.

8 Finally, try the clay with slip and glaze.

More elaborate trials establishing particles size, etc. are described in Cardew. (See also *shrinkage, porosity, water of plasticity*.)

A clay may fail on its own but still be a useful addition to other bodies, or its vices may be minimized by additions of flint, china clay, sand or grog. (See also *body*.) A cure for lime scumming is 2% of barium carbonate. A clay which does not pass these trials may, nevertheless, be useful as a slip (a slip-glaze if you are lucky), as a pigment, or for other decorative purposes.

Clay winning

Or clay getting. The practical work of finding and extracting clays. Books on geology are generally disappointing in their references to clay. Details of the younger sedimentary rocks, where useful materials may be found, are sparse. Layers and deposits of clay may be revealed by deep-cut river-beds or roads. Records of old potteries are valuable, as is local soil knowledge and 'folk memory'. In some regions geological surveys have been made which are available on application to the appropriate authority. White clays found outside the recognized areas are usually in small pockets, are often unplastic and sandy, and may be contaminated with lime ('pipeclays', etc.). Surface clay topped by soil will be stained with organic matter to a depth of 1–2ft/0.3–0.6m. Hill clays which may once have been buried much deeper may be more rewarding. Soil Hill Pottery, on the Yorkshire moors, England (see films), had a fine red clay topped by a buff slip clay further up the hill, and a refractory clay at the top — all on a single slope of about 400 yards. What you are least likely to find is a workable pale stoneware clay, and that is what most of us want.

Commercially, clay is dug from a pit, mined or washed from the surface with high-pressure hoses. Seams and deposits are under continuous scrutiny and analysis.

Clay getting is exciting, if not always rewarding. Sticky garden clay is usually too contaminated for practical use other than as a pigment where it can be considered as an impure iron oxide. Local brickworks may guide you to clay. Few 'local' clays will take a glaze and many will slag above 1000°C/1832°F, but for educational purposes (your own education as well as children's) the work is of value and the material can be used in sawdust or other simple firings.

Method: Dig a pound or two of clay from various parts of your 'seam'. Immerse it in buckets of water and leave to soak. The way that it breaks in the water will give some idea as to whether it is sandy and short, or sticky and cohesive. Stir and skim off any floating matter. Heavy, coarse materials will sink and the clay slip can then be poured off. Pass through a cooking sieve and then a 60 lawn. One can see how much is left in the sieves and whether enough slip has gone through to make worthwhile the work of extracting it. Dry the slip to a plastic state. The sample can then be subjected to the tests listed under *clay tests*. A very pure-looking sample could be tried in the dug state. Try the slip also for slipware and as a pigment especially on stoneware.

A useful book on finding and dealing with clays and other pottery minerals is by Sutherland (see book list).

Cleanliness

Cleanliness in working practice is anathema to some potters but the continuous dust raised by disturbing deposits of clay, glaze, and colors can seriously injure your health and potters so exposed have suffered. Tidiness is more subjective but can save the one commodity which is finite — time — which may otherwise be spent searching for tools and materials. Lack of labeling can also cause waste and spoiled work. (See also *health hazard, poisonous materials, spraying, sweeping compounds*.)

Climbing kilns

Many-chambered Oriental semi-downdraft kilns built on a hillside or on an artificial slope. The heat is drawn from one chamber to the next which is, in turn, sidestoked with wood until the required temperature is reached. Rhodes calls it 'a near perfect design'. Kilns may be 200ft/60m long and 10ft/3m high and the average slope of some 18%. (See also *chambered kilns* and *bank kilns*.) Rhodes K. contains many illustrations. In CR165 Frome Community College describe and illustrate what they call a 'snake kiln' on a slope of only 13%.

Cloth pattern

Soft clay will readily take an impression of the weave of cloth pressed onto it. The fabric can be beaten into the surface all over or in strips and other shapes. If the cloth texture itself is irregular — knotted, very open, coarse,

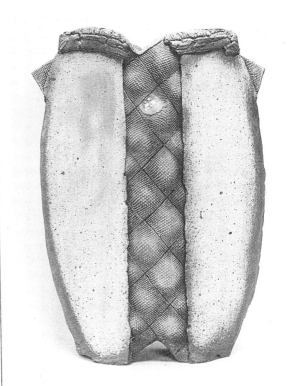

A cloth pattern with a slip overlay on a stoneware pot by Jim Robison. The pattern was created by rolling over a strip of strongly textured cloth laid on a slab of soft clay.

seamed, torn — a great variety of decorative effects are possible as has been shown by the work of Otto Heino, Stig Lindberg, Ruth Duckworth and others. There are many other variations of the technique: an open weave pressed firmly onto the surface, covered with slip (or glaze) and then peeled or burnt away; setting one thread texture against another; rubbing color or glaze into the texture; using a fine pattern as a basis for further embellishment. Holes in the cloth offer a point of rest. (See also *lace decoration*.)

CMC *Sodium Carboxy-methyl-cellulose*

'An organic cellulose gum which acts as a thickener, binder, and suspension agent' (Georgies). For use with glazes with a low clay content.

Coal

Ancient underground carbon deposits formed by the decomposition of vegetable matter over many millions of years. Peat, lignite, household bituminous coal, and anthracite are the main types. Most of the bottle kilns in Stoke-on-Trent, England, were fired with coal up to the late 1950s. High quality coal was required and was available nearby. A 9 x 9ft/3 x 3m setting space would take about 4 tons/4000kg. Peter Smith (CR130) deals in detail with coal as a kiln fuel for craft potters. He considers that, weight for weight, coal can be twice as efficient as wood, though wood has a longer flame length. Stoking should be 'little and often'.

Coal is not very suitable for small kilns. It needs a generous grate and a high chimney. Nevertheless Geoffrey Whiting (England) fired a coal kiln until 1970. It had two chambers. The final temperature of around 1300°C/2372°F, however, was achieved with wood. (See the film Geoffrey Whiting, craftsman potter). Coal lies between oil and wood for optimum efficiency per lb. of fuel at around 12,000 Btu or 12.6 kJ.

Coal ash

Has been used in glazes. Coal ash has been described by Peter Smith as fundamentally an aluminum silicate with iron and other impurities. It has low fluxing power and acts in a similar way to clay.

An unusual coal-ash glaze, firing at 1250°C/2282°F, suggested by Peter Smith:

Coal ash	20.5	S. Devon ball clay	8.3
Whiting	21.5	Feldspar	31.8
Red clay	3.1	Ochre	1.6
Quartz	13.2		

Coal gas

Now almost extinct in England — but see *gas*.

Cobalt, *oxides*

A metallic element Co, 59.
Black oxide Co_3O_4, 241. Equivalent weight 80.3.
Grey prepared oxide CoO, 75.
Carbonate $CoCO_3$, 119.

The oxide of cobalt combines with silicates and borates to produce a variety of blue colors. The carbonate is pink in its unfired state (and has finer particle size and is less liable to speckle) and so is sometimes used when painting for identification, the oxide is black. All oxide forms give stable blues at all pottery temperatures. The hue can be modified by the alumina/silica balance of the glaze and by other additions. (See also *blue pigments and stains*). A cobalt aluminate is also quoted by Dodd as a stable color. The additon of zinc oxide will soften the usual strong blue (Dodd), as will magnesia introduced as talc. Cobalt reactions are very complicated.

The blue from cobalt is strong and insistent. 'A few of the blues were overdone and the cobalt, in its horrible purple intensity, had triumphed over the iron' (Leach). This intensity can be subdued by using red clay, iron oxides and manganese as dilutants. Dilution is especially important for painting on stoneware. Leach used 98 raw ochre to 2 cobalt. Boiled green tea is used as a vehicle for cobalt in Japan; the tannin is reputed to prevent spread under the glaze. Sheila Fournier has used a mixture of cobalt, manganese and red clay in electric stoneware firings at around 1250°C/2282°F to produce a subdued blue with gold-brown streaks, based on suggestions in Cardew.

Its stability has made cobalt a favorite pigment on maiolica where it was often used to outline more fugitive colors, and on porcelain—the ubiquitous 'blue and white'. It can be diluted with china stone when used thinly as a wash. Talc will also diminish its stridency. Alkalis in a glaze will brighten and give depth, sometimes a purplish hue. Excess cobalt will separate out during firing, causing 'ironing', a rusty surface which is, however, not always unpleasant on stoneware (see *ironing of cobalt*). In soft glazes cobalt can be fritted with alumina, etc. to produce various tones (see *blue pigment*), but in stoneware it tends to revert to the purplish-blue silicate.

Owing to its high melting point cobalt is difficult to 'fix' on biscuit. China stone, a frit, or a little clay can be mixed with the pigment. In zinc glazes cobalt can produce a purple-blue or a green; with magnesia pink. In a glaze it acts as a weak flux. (See also *asbolite* (the ore of cobalt), *zaffre*, and *smalt*.)

Coefficients of expansion, c.o.e.

Materials expand upon heating at a steady and progressive rate. There is a similar contraction on cooling. The rate varies between materials, and the various degrees of expansion have been worked out as a figure (coefficient) based upon expansion per unit length per degree Centigrade and conversely, its contraction during cooling. It is the latter which is of primary interest to potters because it affects glaze-fit. Knowledge of the coefficients is also essential in preparing bodies of ovenware and fireproof ware.

There is some disagreement in the figures usually quoted for reversible linear thermal expansions of the various oxides and compounds. Also, since the expansion is a continuing process, it is usually given as a figure for a certain range, e.g. 100–1000°C/212–1832°F. This is a useful range for glazes which all harden on cooling between 800–500°C/1472–932°F. As mentioned above, there is need for more expert research on the coefficients. The tables generally available are those of English and Turner, and Winkelmann and Scott. The marked disagreements are for the values of alumina, silica, and boric oxide. We can strike a balance, but the figures should be considered as qualitative rather than literal. The progression from high to low values is borne out in practice and can be considered reliable.

It will be seen that body constituents have lower coefficients than have the glaze bases. Hence one of the causes of crazing, as the glaze contracts more than the clay. In CR 113 Potclays Ltd list the c.o.e. of all their clays and they show, in general, lower figures for raku and stoneware bodies; the highest for red clays and bone china. The negative

expansion (i.e. expansion on cooling) of boric oxide is one reason for its wide use on earthenware. The physical meaning of the figures is that they indicate the expansion multiplied by 10^6, i.e. to six places of decimals. Potash thus expands 0.000033 of its length for each degree centigrade of temperature rise.

The final computation is always complicated by quartz 'inversion' which, in effect, puts silica higher in the list and so eases matters for the potter. Also the reversible expansion considered here should not be confused with the changes in size which occur in ceramic materials, clay especially, due to sintering and vitrification, and which are non-reversible. (See *shrinkage*.) These do not greatly affect glaze-fit.

Coefficients are additive and one can get an overall value of a glaze by the following computation:
1 Multiply the analysis figure of each oxide by the coefficient.
2 Total the answers.
3 Divide the total by 100.
(For expansion of gases see *absolute temperature scale, gas expansion*.)

While there are obvious discrepancies in the readings, the order of expansion from the high figure of soda to the low or negative figure for boron is still valid and useful. The temperature range is also significant (Hamer quotes soda at only 5.8 to 600°C/1112°F). He also gives alumina and calcia at a similar reading of 2.9.

Coffee cup

Normally taller than it is wide and often straight-sided.

Coefficients of expansion for some pottery materials				
All figures to power of 10^6	*Oxide*	*English and Turner*	*Winkelmann and Scott*	*Whole number average*
Highest expansion and contraction	Soda	41.6	33.3	37
	Potash	39.0	28.3	33
Medium	Calcia (lime)	16.3	16.6	16
	Baria	14.0	10.0	12
	Titania			
	Lead oxide	10.6	10.0	10
	Antimony oxide			
	Alumina	1.4	17.0	9
Lowest	Lithia			
	Magnesia	4.5	0.4	2
	Zirconia	2.3		2
	Tin oxide			
	Silica	0.5	2.7	1
(Negative expansion up to 10% of glaze material only)	Boric oxide	–6.5	0.33	–3

A jug-type coffee pot by Danny Killick. It has a strainer behind the spout.

Coffee pot

A coffee pot form, favored by craft potters, consists of a simple lidded jug or pitcher. The spout of a traditional coffee pot, however, is longer than for a teapot and springs from nearer the base.

Coggle

A wooden or metal roulette wheel which was reputedly used to compact the rims of cooking dishes and some pots, decorating them with notches or other patterns at the same time, and which might be a useful tip for today. In a looser sense the word is used to describe any *roulette*.

Cog wheel

Increasingly difficult to obtain since the electronic revolution but have been used to impress a variety of patterns into clay.

Coil cutter

Hollow, circular, steel ribbon tools (available from most

A typical coil cutter, the ring sharpened on both sides.

potters' merchants) which can be drawn through a block of clay to cut coils for pot building, handles, or decoration. Quite a long flattish slab of clay would be necessary if used for coil pots, or a coil could be re-rolled after cutting.

Coil-form decoration

As well as being used to build ceramic forms, coils or ropes of clay are increasingly used as decorative elements: on the edges of dishes or rims of pots, or over the surface, building up sculptural details on casseroles, etc. of great effectiveness; sometimes even rolled in. It is also possible to make patterns of coils on a flat surface — lines, spirals, etc. — and then to flatten them with a rolling pin to join them into a solid sheet. The design will be sharpest if the coils are applied, lightly adhered, and the slab turned over before the final rolling-in. This method can be used for making dishes, wrap-round pots, etc.

A variation of the pressed coil is to lay patterns in a hollow mold and then to press a soft, preformed bowl over them. The coils will flatten somewhat and become inlaid by pressure. (See also *rolled inlay*.)

Coiling

An age-old technique of building pots by laying coils or ropes of clay one upon another and working them together. Until recently pots in which two or three people could stand were coiled in Cyprus. Built to hold wine they were affectionately known as 'honeymoon pots'.

Pots can be coiled, after a little practice, to a size which it would take many years to learn how to throw. Coiled pots have their own character and should not be looked upon as a stage on the way to throwing. Large models and asymmetric forms intended for firing can best be made by coiling.

Rosemary Wren uses a special coil for her large models. It resembles a stubby inverted T in section and speeds up the building, while the wide base gives plenty of clay to work downwards, maintaining a wall of even thickness. The coil is first rolled and then worked into shape with the finger and thumb.

Rolling the coil is perhaps the most difficult part of the operation. I have found the following advice useful in teaching:

1 Use reasonably soft clay.

2 Give yourself plenty of room to work in.

3 Cut your clay from a block with wire and work it into a rough thick coil before starting to roll.

4 Use long, even movements from the shoulders.

5 Use the whole length of your hand.

6 Start with the hands close together and move them apart as the coil lengthens. Inspect the ends of the coil occasionally to see that you are not forming macaroni!

7 Needless to say, the working surface must be clean, smooth, dry, and slightly absorbent.

The lazier potter will extrude coils from a *wad mill* or use a *coil cutter*. Some use flattened coils or even strips cut from rolled-out slabs which I cannot imagine being very easy to join. There are also simple coil-cutting tools (see *coil cutter*), a circle of metal on a handle which is drawn

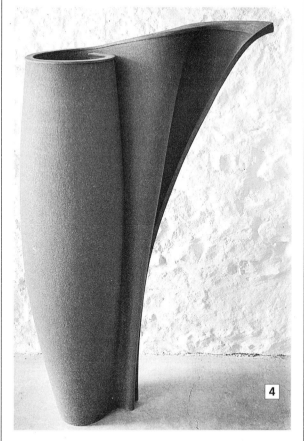

Starting a coil pot

1 The cut base with the first coil in process of being rubbed in.

2 The pot is built by stroking each coil into the wall beneath.

3 Monica Young rolling a fine, long coil.

4 An example of the strong, elegant result of her work, showing the smooth and sophisticated form which betrays no sign of the method of its construction.

5 Dave Roberts moistening the rim of a large coiled pot preparatory to adding the next coil.

6 A Cypriot village potter rolling coils vertically, with a large cone of clay beside her from which she scoops the material for each coil.

7 Unloading fine coiled pottery from a wood-fired kiln in the same village.

8 A corner of the storeroom (mass-produced coiled pots!).

through a long block or slab of clay. Some comb and slip each surface (especially for the flat strip type) but I have never found this essential and it results in slippery surfaces which are difficult to join by the stroking down method. However, it is not wise to be dogmatic as all systems can obviously be made to work. In most countries where coiling is a traditional craft, coils are rolled vertically between the two palms (and they don't use slip to join them!). See film Ladi Kwali (Films for Potters).

Method: There is no point in coiling the base of a pot. This can be a flat, beaten-out circular slab of clay. Cut a piece of paper to stick underneath so that the base will not adhere to the working surface. When building the coils, make a complete ring for each layer, it is much more diffi-cult to control the form if the coils are spiraled. Cut or nip the ends to a wedge shape so that they can be overlapped. Do not wet or slip the surfaces. Coiling, with a relatively soft clay, is one exception to the rule that joins must necessarily be moistened. The first few coils will take all the weight, so make them fairly sturdy and work the base coil well into the base slab. Always join downwards from the latest coil to the wall already built, using the ball of the thumb to drag a little of the coil clay downwards, inside and out. If the form is widened too soon or too suddenly the whole thing is likely to keel over or collapse.

Coiling can be treated as a preliminary to pinching or even throwing, and can be added to molded dishes. Various illustrations in this book show coiling as an auxiliary technique. *Saggars* can be coiled. (See *formers, handbuilding*.)

Coke

Now almost extinct, in England at any rate, since it is a by-product of burning coal for gas. Some processed coal blocks are useable in its place. As a fuel it gives a glowing radiant heat rather than a long flame, and is therefore more efficient as a contact fuel. (See *brazier kiln*.) Less air is needed for combustion than with coal or wood. Producer-gas kilns have been designed which drip water onto hot coke (a rather dangerous undertaking).

Colcothar

A name for a very finely ground red iron oxide, mentioned by Leach as used in overglaze enamel for red colors.

Cold clay

Proprietary (Fulham Pottery, London, England) self-hardening clay. (See also *unfired clay*.)

Cold color

Unfired pigment in the form of enamel paint, etc. In America especially, non-ceramic finishes have been widely used including poster colors and oil paints. Perhaps, with the easing of the threat of nuclear doom, these short-term finishes will diminish! Unfired pigments, however, have been applied to pottery throughout its history.

Some pottery suppliers list 'cold colors' for use in schools, a form of enamel paints rather than ceramic finishes.

Colemanite, colmanite

A naturally occurring calcium borate, $2CaO:3B_2O_3:5H_2O$. 412. Convenient formula weight 206, giving $CaO:1.5B_2O_3$ in the melt. Found in Nevada and California.

Gerstley borate is a colemanite. Only slightly soluble. The actual composition of colemanite is variable, that from the USA being nearest to a pure borocalcite, while Turkish colemanite contains a number of other materials in small proportions: alumina, soda, potash, and magnesia.

A powerful flux for most glazes. In earthenware it can be used to introduce boric oxide in a relatively insoluble form (though it can cause a glaze to thicken or flocculate). More than 10% is likely to cause crawling due to an unfortunate effect known as 'dusting' which can even detach the glaze from the pot just before red heat. The boron content can give opalescence in a glaze and, according to Rhodes, a broken mottled color, especially with rutile. It 'intensifies the effect of coloring oxides and increases craze resistance' (Potterycrafts).

Collaring

Reducing the size of the neck of a pot on the wheel by encircling it with the thumb, index finger, and crooked second finger of each hand spread out, and exerting an inward and upward pressure.

Another position, which helps to prevent buckling, is to hold the index finger of one hand inside the rim. Increase the wheel speed as the circumference gets shorter. (See also *egote, throwing stick*.)

Isaac Button collaring the neck of a large cider jar. From the film/video 'Isaac Button, country potter'.

Colloid, colloidal colors

Particles of matter which are ultra-fine to a degree where some are smaller than the wavelengths of visible light. The colloidal content of secondary clays is often as high as

25–30% and is thought to be associated with their plasticity. The word derives from the Greek 'Kolla' — glue. Colloidal particles dispersed in a liquid will remain in suspension for a long time but, once settled, are difficult to remix. Red copper glaze gets its color from colloidal particles, as does the bluish opalescence of *Jun*. In slips they assist burnishing and are probably responsible for the non-glaze shine on Roman and other ware, which has been successfully imitated today, using very finely levigated colloidal clays. (See *glossed ware, terra sigillata*.)

Colmanite

See *colemanite*.

Color

The physicists' explanation of color — the absorption, reflection, and refraction of different light wavelengths — may seem largely irrelevant when we are mixing oxides or reducing iron glaze, but it is useful to know the various ways in which color can develop.

The simplest and commonest is the solution color. All wavelengths other than those we see are absorbed. The hue is similar by transmitted (seen through) or by reflected light. Many of our pottery colors are in this category. 'The color is influenced by the abundance or scarcity of oxygen in the atomic environment' (John Dunn PQ17), which is a way of saying that the type and condition (i.e. reduced or not) of the glaze will affect the color derived from any one *pigment oxide*.

More difficult to comprehend is the effect of particles or fine films of matter so tenuous as to approximate to the light wavelengths. Examples are the *iridescence* of oil on water or the *devitrifying* surfaces of ancient lead glazes. Here there are no coloring pigments, but what might be called an optical effect, the cause of the color being in itself colorless. The blues of Jun glazes and the very subtle Imperial wares, Kuan and Ju from Song China, are said to derive from ultra-fine particles in suspension. There is also an elusive *opalescence* on the surface of some white raku glazes. Cardew refers to optical colors as glass suspended in glass. In practice, a thick coating of glaze is necessary and, probably, a fairly dark slip or body. Billington mentions oxide of bismuth to produce mother-of-pearl luster. Slightly larger particles — the colloids — are responsible for many red-purple colors, e.g. reduced copper in which comparatively few particles of sub-wavelength copper will produce red.

Lastly, there are the very thin films of metal, usually copper or silver, sometimes so fine as to show iridescence which we call 'lusters'.

Color terminology is imprecise and somewhat chaotic. Various attempts, such as in the British Standard Colors, and the Dictionary of Color by Maertz and Rea Paul, have been made to standardize names.

Color-affecting minerals

Some glaze ingredients can alter the tone or the hue of pigment oxides. Magnesia and baria tend to influence copper towards blue, and cobalt to purple. Baria can turn even iron to a bluish hue. Zinc will deaden some colors, but nickel and zinc are reputed to give pinks and mauves in a barium glaze. Dolomite in a glaze can result in considerable variation.

The lists of colors derived from metal oxides often given in textbooks, though accurate in general, may not always work out in practice and variations can be assessed only by testing. Copper is particularly susceptible to the foundation glaze and is an exciting and valuable pigment for this reason, especially in non-reduction stoneware firings. Different wood ashes will affect iron, as will the efficiency with which they were originally burnt. (See *carbon, Jun, turquoise*, and the *pigment oxides*.)

Color wash

The transparent water-color nature of most ceramic pigments leads naturally to their use as a background onto which stronger strokes are laid. The *hake* brush can be used, also the *mop*. Copper is rather weak and fugitive when used as a pigment and is thus more suitable as a wash. David Leach uses a weak cobalt laid onto a spinning plate or pot as a ground for stronger blue or iron pigments, his father used a mixture of 2 parts cobalt to 98 ochre for similar pale washes.

Colored body

Most clays contain some coloring material, commonly iron oxide. For agate and similar wares the clay body can be artifically colored with pigment oxides or prepared body stains.

A colored slip can be dried to the plastic state and used as a body. A cruder alternative is to damp a finely ground oxide to a thick sludge, spread it onto thin layers of plastic clay, and then to wedge them all together. This is something of a hit or miss method as regards final hue, but one can consider the plastic clay as two-thirds (0.66) solid material and weigh the oxide accordingly. Coarser pigment oxides — ilmenite, etc. — or colored grog can be added to a body to give mottled and textural effects. Red clay is, in effect, a colored body.

Colored bodies are used industrially for colored tableware, sometimes with a skin of white clay inside cups. For the craft potter they can be useful in modeling, giving a decorative result without resorting to colored glazes. (See also *agate, basalt, coil-form decoration, inlay, marbling, neriage.*)

Colored glaze

Color can be added to an otherwise clear glaze in the form of pigment oxides (the metal oxides) or prepared stains (*fritted* mixtures of oxides). If iron is required it is available in various subtle forms as red clay, ochre, etc. Many of the coloring oxides are dissolved and therefore transparent in a clear glaze, forming 'stained glass'. The hue will be stronger where the glaze is thicker, an effect which can be exploited by engraving the clay. Celadon glazes are often used in this way. The body color will have a direct influence as it is visible through the glaze. Optical color and iridescent glazes are not stained. (See *color.*)

A completely different effect is obtained by the use of opacifiers, most of the light then being reflected back at or near the surface. The body still has some influence, but it is not so marked. Maiolica painting is the local staining of an opaque glaze. Color will also diffuse upwards through an opaque glaze, but the effect will be more subdued and outlines less sharp. (See *underglaze, tin over slip.*)

The ingredients of a glaze will control the particular hue derived from any pigment. Nickel and zinc, for instance, are reputed to give pinks and mauves in a barium glaze. A glaze will have its own saturation point which varies with each oxide; an excess will render it opaque or be precipitated onto the surface. Remarkable effects will arise from the saturation of glazes, especially in stoneware, but beware *metal release* in kitchen or cooking ware. *Tenmoku* and *tessha* are iron saturated. (See also *glaze trials* and under *black glaze, red glaze* and so on. Also *line blends, color trials,* etc.)

Color-streak glazing

An approximate translation of the Japanese 'hidasuki' (Bizen) ware which utilized the pigments and chemicals contained in plants in contact with the surface of pots during firing. Cord soaked in seawater, for instance, and wrapped round a pot 'can produce red colors' (Stan Romer in CR165), but images of leaves and plants can also be imprinted during firing. The intensity of the image depends largely on the amount of natural 'pigment' in the plant.

Color trials

The color of a glaze does not necessarily proceed by simple stages from light to dark as pigment oxides are added to it.

Nor can one very accurately guess the effect of a certain proportion of oxide in a glaze. The variables — type of bases, base-acid relationship, opacity, etc. — all contribute to an infinite variety. Statements such as 'copper gives green colors', while broadly true, must always be tested in your particular glaze in your kiln.

Random tests can be made and are sometimes successful, but the most attractive combination is likely to be missed or a whole range condemned on insufficient evidence. More methodical trials, though by no means infallible, are more likely to be useful. The obvious method is to weigh and add progressively larger amounts of an oxide to a glaze, testing at each addition. This has its disadvantages: it involves a great deal of work weighing and sieving each time; cumulative error is likely; and one cannot easily return to a promising range.

An alternative is known as line blending. First determine the limits between which you wish to explore. A simple example would be a clear glaze as one limit and the accepted maximum proportion of the oxide in a similar glaze as the other. Make up these two samples in equal quantities and, as far as you can judge, of equal consistencies. They are then combined in certain proportions, a test-piece being glazed at each stage. The series can consist of as many steps as you consider useful or practicable. Ten combinations will tell you quite a lot. The measures are by volume, using any spoon or small container as a standard unit.

A line blend is usually given as:

| A | 100 | 90 | 80 | 70 | 60 | 50 | 40 | 30 | 20 | 10 | 0 |
| B | 0 | 10 | 20 | 30 | 40 | 50 | 60 | 70 | 80 | 90 | 100 |

This does not represent ideally equal steps, however, and it is not immediately obvious how to use it in practice. I suggest the following method which fulfills the same function. We will call the glazes to be blended C and D — clear and dark, if you like.

Test		Total additions
1	To 10 measures of C add 1 measure of D	1
2	To above mixture add 1 measure of D	2
3	To above mixture add 2 measures of D	4
4	To above mixture add 2 measures of D	6
5	To above mixture add 4 measures of D	10

In test 5 you have equal parts. It is extravagant in glaze to go on from here: we would need to add 50 measures of C to achieve a ratio of 1D:5C. We therefore start again from D, adding C in similar proportions.

Test		Total additions
6	To 10 measures of D add 1 measure of C	1
7	To above mixture add 1 measure of C	2
8	To above mixture add 2 measures of C	4
9	To above mixture add 2 measures of C	6
10	To above mixture add 4 measures of C	10

This brings us again to equal parts. You will in fact find that test 5 is not identical to test 10, due to slight differences in the consistencies of the glazes.

The series can be translated into percentages of oxide; if glaze C has no pigment oxide and glaze D has 4%, then in test 1 the proportion of D in the batch is 1 part in 11 and the percentage of oxide is $\frac{1}{11}$ x 4 = 0.36%. Test 2 is 2 parts in 12 and the percentage of oxide $\frac{2}{12}$ x 4 = 0.66% and so on through the series. When we reach the changeover point the proportion of D becomes 10 in 11 in test 6; 10 in 12 in test 7 and so on.

The whole range works out as follows:

Test 1: 0.36%;   2: 0.66%;   3: 1.14%;   4: 1.5%;   5: 2.0%.
Test 6: 3.64%;   7: 3.33%;   8: 2.86%;   9: 2.5%;   10: 2.0%.

Dual blending can be practiced with any two glazes, with two pigments, or with glaze ingredients. One can make a diagram for three variables (see *triaxial diagrams*). But for more than three the calculations become very involved.

All this work is useless if the actual firing tests are not fully valid. Brushing a large number of test glazes onto a single tile or shard may be just adequate for pigment trials, but it gives little or no indication of a glaze potential. Make test-pieces of each of the bodies you are likely to use; dip the glaze carefully and try different thicknesses of glaze coating. Keep an accurate record. (See also *glaze trials, records*.)

Comb, *combing*

Decoration by scoring with a multi-toothed or pronged instrument. The technique has a long history. The more

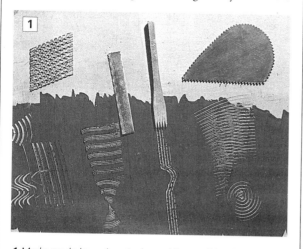
2 Some delicate combing combined with colored slips on a porcelain dish by John Glick.

traditional combs may be of wood, metal, stiff leather, rubber or felt, each of which will give its own character to the line. Broken saw blades, hacksaw blades and Surform tools are useful. Simple pieces of broken wood or twigs can be utilized. Various sizes of combs can be used in one design.

The teeth of pottery combs are usually quite broad and well spaced. Hair combs often have too sharp a point and plow up a rather unpleasant furrow. Illustration **1** shows a few types of comb and the marks they cut through pigment. Flexible or convex combs are needed for the inside of bowls, etc. Hacksaw blades can also be used. Flexible prongs are useful for curved surfaces.

The addition of grog or sand in the body will give a rougher line and a more broken edge. Rough edges to the cuts can be removed with a stiff brush when quite dry. This work must be carried out with discretion, or the sharp quality of the decoration will be smudged.

In its wider sense, the term also applies to sgraffito-like decoration through slips or glazes. The simplest 'combs' are always with us, in the form of fingers. *Finger-combing* must be done very rapidly with the slip or glaze in an almost liquid condition. Old English Devonshire slipware was sometimes finger-combed; Leach, Cardew and Whiting have used it extensively. A unique tool used by the Fishleys of Fremington consisted of four whalebone prongs set in a handle, each topped by a baby-bottle nipple! Mixed color wet slips may also be gently combed to give marbled effects. (See illustrations at *finger combing*.)

1 Marks made by various tools used for combing through pigment to leather-hard clay. From left to right: a broken piece of Surform blade, a hacksaw blade fragment and two metal sculptor's tools.

Combined water

See *chemically-combined water.*

Combustion

The oxidation of organic materials, producing CO_2 (with H_2O, SO_2 etc.) and heat.

Combustion is the source of heat in all kilns except those fired with electricity. It needs a free air supply in a continuous draft, and hence a chimney. Fuels vary in their readiness to oxidize (burn). Gas is instantaneous, wood has a low ignition point, but oil must be vaporized by a jet of air, or evaporated by dripping onto a red-hot metal plate. Coal and coke need 'starters' — wood, firelighters, etc. — to bring them to a temperature at which they will ignite. All fuels burn more readily the hotter the kiln becomes: heated *secondary air* therefore increases efficiency. Kilns are designed to provide a steady supply of oxygen (air) to carbonaceous fuels, to convert them into carbon dioxide, and then to trap and utilize as much as possible of the heat-energy which is released in the process.

When combustion takes place a good deal of water is produced, a pint of paraffin (kerosine), for instance, will liberate 1.5 pints of water. The formation of water vapor helps *reduction.*

Compass

A length of wood with two spikes or nails driven through it can be used to cut circles from a clay slab. Georgies list a double compass with variable circumference circles obtained by sliding the cutters along the length.

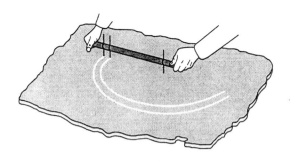

A double compass, see text.

Compound

A material of uniform composition containing two or more *elements* in a state of chemical combination. A compound possesses characteristics different from either of the elements which compose it. Iron (a blue-gray metal) plus oxygen (an invisible gas) produce the compound ferric oxide (a red powder). All pottery materials are oxides and, therefore, compounds.

Elements combine in fixed whole-number proportions. These are indicated by numbers following and slightly below the symbols for the elements. The compound mentioned above combines as two parts of iron to three of oxygen and it is written Fe_2O_3. Fe being the symbol for iron. Chemical combinations are now interpreted in electrical terms (see *atomic theory*), but for practical purposes a simplified view is generally sufficient. A glaze itself is not a compound, but is made up of a number of compounds.

Two elements may combine in a variety of proportions, although one is generally the more stable (inert). More than two elements can enter into a compound. Carbonates are made up of the oxide plus carbon dioxide, e.g. CaO + CO_2 gives $CaCO_3$ — calcium carbonate. The formula for complex minerals may include the compound symbol with a prefix figure. This is a convenient way of indicating the comparative number of whole molecules of an oxide in the make-up of the mineral. Clay, for instance, contains the oxides of aluminium (alumina), silicon (silica), and hydrogen (water) in the proportions 1:2:2 and is written Al_2O_3. $2SiO_3$. $2H_2O$. (See also *valency*.)

Compressed natural gas — CNG

Mentioned by Brickell as consisting mainly of methane and with a good deal lower calorific value than LPG (liquid petoleum gas — see *bottled gas*).

Compression

Squeezing. Fired glazes should be in a state of slight compression, that is the body should shrink a little more than its overlaying glaze. A glaze can stand more compression than tension but, in excess, it will *shiver*. Cristobalite formation in the body is useful. (See also at *crazing, shattering, shivering*.)

Computer

Although many potters are uninterested in ceramic science or are perhaps wary of computers, these machines will undoubtedly play an increasing role in ceramics. As well as its well-known use as a word processor the computer can help with many of the business tasks of the potter: stock control, accounts, forecasts, etc. in a compact, space-saving and easily accessible way. It can store, sort, and retrieve data (formulas, analyses, information, etc.), repeat procedures to manipulate figures and, of course, calculate quickly and accurately, and it can store and print out results.

A spreadsheet program will store and sort any data, but there are also specialized programs which can be purchased which avoid having to learn complicated procedures or having to find out and enter every item of basic information and calculation oneself. They are designed to do tasks specific to ceramic chemistry such as calculating from recipe to a Seger formula, thermal expansion, displaying limits, and so on. Such programs are now commonly on the market and names and addresses of some people who may be able to help are given under Suppliers at the end of the book. As an instance of their possible use, in CR116 Tony Hansen (of IMC who issue 'Insight', a chemistry computer program) suggests a system for altering glazes to fire at higher or lower temperatures while retaining similar basic qualities.

While programs are not necessarily limited to any given make and model of computer, their portability between makes can be restricted by any number of differences in specification of hardware or operating systems. Thus the choice of program is likely to influence or be influenced by the choice of computer. IBM (International Business Machines), with MS-DOS or Windows (operating systems), dominates the computer market, but for the average potter a good program on a comparatively cheap machine will cope with any task he or she is likely to require. Apple Macintosh computers and programs are easier to use and are preferred by some potters but their backup facilities, in Great Britain at least, leave something to be desired.

Any specific advice on computers and their use is likely to be out of date almost as soon as it is given, so rapidly is computer science developing, but for the potter's practical purposes he does not need to be in the 'front line' and can consider his modest machine as a rapid and flexible aid to the storage and manipulation of the information he most needs in his day to day business. Attendance at a school or short course on basic computing will dispel much of the mystique which many consider still surrounds computers, especially in the explanation of the strange language which has developed round them and is sometimes a bar to an appreciation of their usefulness but, personally, I prefer to find my own way about the machine and programs. (See also *internet, world wide web*.)

Computer programs

These are now legion and various. Most are suitable for DOS or Windows on IBM computers, or on Macintosh. They feature oxides, compounds, recipes, etc. and methods of using them. Most are quite expensive and need more memory and disc space than many potters have on their machines although today's chips offer greatly increased capacity. Typical programs are — Foresight, Tribase, Hyperglaze 11X, Program GL, and Cerama which also offers a viscosity index from but there are many others, more or less extensive. See suppliers list for stockist details. (See also *internet, world wide web*.)

Concrete

The normal Portland cement/sand/stones mixture is not suitable for use in ceramics as it will explode and disintegrate under heat. 'Concrete foundations (when building a kiln) are — the first serious mistake to be avoided' Cardew. Heatproof cements are available (see *cement*).

Conduction of electricity

Electricity will 'travel' through some materials more readily than others. Metals are usually good conductors. Most dry-clay materials are non-conductors; although they contain a metal, aluminum, this does not conduct in its oxide form. Silicon carbide is a conductor but in the form it is used in kiln shelves it is not dangerous in an electric kiln. Wet materials are better conductors than dry ones. A person standing on a wet concrete floor will conduct current (to earth) if he is in contact with 'live' or faulty equipment and the result could be fatal.

Copper metal is an almost perfect conductor and is used to carry current in wires. Other materials may conduct in some degree but at the same time put up some resistance to the flow of current, developing heat in the process. Electric kiln elements are especially designed to control conduction/resistance ratios.

Conductors: Metals, especially copper, iron, aluminium, and tin. Impure water and wet materials in general. Silicon carbide (in the form of kiln elements).

Poor or non-conductors: Dry or fired clay, hence bricks, and most clay materials. Rubber, plastic, distilled water.

Conduction of heat

The rate at which heat is transferred through a material. An important consideration in kilns (and the walls of your pottery on a cold day). In general, the denser the material the more quickly it will conduct heat. In metal this is very rapid; *silicon carbide* is also a good conductor of heat and is thus useful, if expensive, for kiln shelves. A porous brick has more resistance to the passage of heat than a non-porous one. The inner parts of a kiln — the shelves, saggars, kiln furniture, etc. — should be reasonably good conductors, the walls poor conductors. (See also *insulation, heat loss, heat storage*.)

Cone

More accurately 'pyrometric cone'. Made from mixtures of ceramic materials formed into triangular elongated pyramids, and designed to melt and bend over or 'squat' at a given temperature. The standard size is 2½in/65mm high, miniatures 1in/25mm high. They are numbered to indicate the temperature at which the point will have dropped level with the base if placed in the kiln at a slight angle (8°C/14.4°F for Orton). Because cones are composed of similar materials to the ware in the kiln, they are considered by some potters to be better indicators of *heat-work* than *pyrometers*, which measure temperature only. The speed of firing will affect the behavior of a cone, a fast firing needing a slightly higher temperature to bend the cone. Quoted firing rates of optimum cone performance vary widely. Rhodes' 10°C/50°F an hour is impracticably slow: Orton cones are quoted for 60°C/140°F and 150°C/302°F per hour. In practice one can accept the nominal temperature equivalent and work from there according to practical experience of one's own kiln and glazes. It is often recommended that three cones of successive numbers be used, the first as a warning, the second being of the temperature required. The third should remain standing at the end of the firing. A personal system of one-cone firing may be of interest. I placed the cone and socket on a piece of flat shelf so that the moment can be ascertained when the point of the cone just touches down onto the shelf as it melts. This is the point of reference, and the firing is continued for a certain number of minutes after this according to the pack and contents of the kiln. A potter need stock only one cone number for a 20–30° range of firing. A kitchen timer (or an alarm wrist-watch) is an essential aid to firing (with cones or any other method!).

At high temperature, cones may be difficult to see in a kiln. They can be brought momentarily into relief by blowing gently into the spyhole. Beware singed hair!

There are several makes of cones. Numbers begin at about 022, diminish to 01, and then increase again to 42. Staffordshire and German Seger cones have a close similarity in temperature equivalents, but the American Orton cones do not often correspond with them. This leads to confusion when glaze maturing points are quoted as cone numbers, e.g. a cone 6 glaze which would indicate 1200°C/2192°F for a Staffordshire cone but nearer 1225°C/2237°F at the same firing speed for Orton. There is some disparity between official lists of end points for cones, probably due to different rates of firing. Your particular kiln, firing rate, degree of temperature control, and type of pack will all be involved and only experience of results can finally ascertain the cone number and degree of bend which is ideal for your work.

The squatting temperature is called the 'end point'. Always leave enough room in the kiln setting to place the cone accurately and visibly. An error in reading the cone can ruin all the rest. The programmed electronic pyrometer has largely overtaken the cone for temperature guidance but they are cheap and reliable and are still preferred by some potters. (See also *PCE, Holdcroft bars, Orton cones,* and *cone socket* for self-supporting cones.)

No.	Seger (°C)	Staffs (°C)	Orton (°C)
022	600	600	600
020	670	670	635
018	710	710	717
017	730	730	747
016	750	750	792
015		790	804
015a	790		
014		815	838
014a	815		
012		855	875
012a	860	860	
011			880
011a	880	880	
010		910	890
010a	900		
09		920	923
09a	920		
08		940	955
08a	940	950	
07		960	984
07a	960	970	
06		980	999
06a	980	990	
05		1000	1046
05a	1000	1010	
04		1020	1060
04a	1020	1030	
03		1040	1101
03a	1040	1050	
02		1060	1120
02a	1060	1070	
01		1080	1137
01a	1080	1090	
1		1100	1154
1a	1100	1100	
2		1120	1162
2a	1120	1130	
3		1140	1168
3a	1140	1150	
4		1160	1186
4a	1160	1170	
5		1180	1196
5a	1180	1190	
6		1200	1222

No.	Seger (°C)	Staffs (°C)	Orton (°C)
6a	1200	1215	
7	1230	1230	1240
7a		1240	
8	1250	1250	1263
8a		1260	
8b		1270	
9	1280	1280	1280
9a		1290	
10	1300	1300	1305
10a		1310	
11	1320	1320	1315
12	1350	1350	1326
13	1380	1380	1346
14	1410	1410	1366
15	1435	1435	1431

Cone sockets

These can be purchased as singles or in groups of three or four. Considering the fact that they can often be used only once, they are expensive and it is easy enough to press a cone into a small block of grogged clay, see below.

Self-supporting Orton cones are made which stand at the correct angle and do not need a socket. They are, as may be expected, half again the price of a normal cone and might stick to the shelf if melted too far, e.g. if used as a warning cone. If you make your own socket each time from clay, a small bowl shape can be pinched into it to receive the melting cone.

Cone wheel

See *power wheel*.

Congruent meeting

See *melting point*.

Coning

A movement preliminary to throwing and associated with *centering*. The clay is allowed to rise into a column on the rotating wheel under horizontal pressure between the palms of the hands. The hands rise with the column, which is then forced down again with the right hand (for right-handers) while the left controls the spread of clay. At the end of the movement the hands will regain the centering position.

Consistency of glaze and slip

The assessment and control of the relative consistencies, or

1 Coning by evenly maintained side pressure from both palms.
2 The position of the hands for depressing the cone to a centering position.

thicknesses, of glazes and slips is a continuing problem for the potter. Industrial potters, even with their great experience, still use a number of scientific checks while most craft potters rely on guesswork.

Dipping a finger into glaze and assessing the coverage is a crude check. The relative amounts of water and solid matter are an important guide, and this can be established, approximately, by a hydrometer. Other factors to be taken into account are:

1 *Flocculation* and *thixotropy*. Ash glazes and those containing colemanite are liable to thicken as they stand.
2 *Frit* glazes should be used thinner than raw ones. They are more concentrated and their glassy nature renders them more transparent when wet.
3 A clear soft glaze needs to be applied more thinly than an opaque one.
4 When trying a new glaze, check its hydrometer reading. After inspection of the fired result you will then know which way to alter the reading.

hot zone

5 Glazes and slips will not maintain their consistency unless closely covered. Evaporation at room temperature is considerable.
6 Consistency is only one factor: biscuit porosity and speed of glazing are others. The more porous the biscuit or, for slips, the drier the clay, the thinner the mixture needs to be.

One cannot over-stress the necessity of repeated stirring before testing or during the use of the glaze or slip, especially lead or frit glazes. (See also *Brongniart's formula, casting slip, glazing, porosity, slip*.)

Continuous kiln, firing

Most industrial ware is now fired in long tunnels (see illustration above, see also *tunnel kiln*), the center of the tunnel being maintained at the peak temperature. Pottery travels through on special trucks, heating and cooling in a slow continuous motion.

There is also a type of multichamber brick-kiln where the heat is transferred from one chamber to the next, using it efficiently to pre-heat, fire, and control the cooling of the loads, known as a reverbratory kiln. The craft potter normally fires in an *intermittent kiln* but the many chambered Oriental *climbing kilns* were, in effect, similar to the brick kiln.

Contraction

See *shrinkage*.

Controlling pyrometer

A *pyrometer* equipped with mechanism which can partially or completely control the firing according to a prearranged schedule worked out by the potter. The simplest type merely switches off the current at a given temperature, others will supply intermittent current to maintain top temperature (soaking) for a given period, or alter the speed of rise and fall of temperature throughout the firing. A useful simple controller (Briar Wheels) will control the temperature up to 600°C/1112°F. The microprocessor has largely taken over from mechanical control, fully programmable for firing and cooling: time, rate, soak, etc. and to hold certain firing programs in a 'memory'. The Orton Autofire Controller, for instance, allows a cone number to be set, and some will even convert Fahrenheit into Centigrade. There are

Continuous kiln
The standard type of kiln used in the industry with the ware moved very slowly through a tunnel, the central area of which is maintained at an optimum temperature.

many models between the fully automated type, which will set you back $800/£500 or more, and the simple *pyrometer*. (See also *kiln-sitter*). There are controllers designed for gas kilns, for both oxidizing and reducing firings (Laser Kilns and others), and multi-zone controllers.

Their use depends on your individual approach to firing (and your purse).

In schools especially, these controllers can be of great benefit—if they work. But we have all heard of burnt-out kilns which have been left on 'control' over a weekend. If they are to be used in this way a 'fail-safe' device such as a *heat-fuse* should be fitted. (See at *fail-safe*.)

However, the warning above still holds: the instrument may be reliable; the setter is human and can make mistakes. Check and double-check, the cost may be a ruined kiln if it is left entirely to its own devices.

Convection of heat

All fuel-burning kilns are built on convection principles. Hot air or gas, being lighter (more expanded), will rise (e.g. in a chimney) so long as there is a supply of cooler air to take its place.

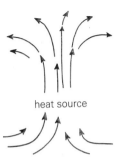

heat source

Heated air becomes expanded and therefore lighter than the surrounding air, rising and drawing cooler air in from below. As the warm air cools again and upward movement ceases a circular motion may be set up as in a room with a radiator. See also heat.

Effective convection is negligible in an electric kiln, where the top is often the coolest spot. If top and bottom bungs are removed at the same time, however, then convection will take place into the outside atmosphere, so beware of this when peering at the cone if you value your eyebrows (or eyes). Heat is transmitted by convection, *conduction* and *radiation*.

Conversion

A change in structure of a material by heating which is not reversible. Quartz is converted into *cristobalite* and *tridymite* at high temperatures (1100°C/2012°F and above).

Conversion factor

A figure used to convert one scale or type of measurement into its equivalent in another scale with which it has a regular co-relationship. For instance the factor turning inches into centimeters (both regular scales of linear measurement) is 2.54. Any number of inches multiplied by 2.54 will equal the same length in centimeters.

To convert any list of figures to percentages, divide each figure by the total of all of them and multiply by 100. In this case the total is the conversion factor. Useful lists of conversion factors are given in Hamer, the better suppliers' catalogs and other manuals. Full conversion tables are, of course, even more valuable, although modern electronic calculators make the work comparatively simple. The table for temperatures is given at *temperature conversion*. (See also at *centigrade* and *Fahrenheit*.) Another aspect of conversion concerns the amount, compared with the recipe weight, of any raw oxide which will be present in a fired glaze which will enter fusion (see at *fuse*) after carbon dioxide, fluorine, and other molecules have been driven off as gases. Other oxides might take up more oxygen and have a higher figure for the fired state.

As most glaze recipes have been tested empirically this becomes of less importance but the knowledge is useful when trying new formulations based on molecular parts and weights. Some conversion factors are mentioned under the relevant headings and there is an exhaustive table in Hamer.

See the chart for some physical factors a potter might need.

to change	into	multiply by	to obtain converse multiply by
inches	cm	2.54	0.394
feet	meters	0.305	3.281
UK gallons	liters	4.546	0.22
imperial gallons	US gallons	1.201	0.833
pints	liters	0.568	1.760
ounces	grams	28.35	0.035
pounds	kilograms	0.454	2.205
cwt	kilograms	50.8	0.02
oz/pt	g/cm^3	0.05	20.0
Btu	watt/hours	0.29	3.41
Btu	joules	1050.0	

Cooling of glaze and biscuit

The effort and expense of firing go into the heating up of pots, but changes important to the finished article occur also on cooling.

For the majority of glazes, cooling to 1000°C/1832°F can be quite rapid and is essential for high-fired stonewares to minimize the development of crystal formation. A famous potter clammed up his oil and wood-fired kiln too soon, slowing down the cooling from the top temperature with the result that the entire kiln-load started to break up within a few minutes of unloading! Inhibiting the growth of crystals also helps to keep the glaze surface 'bright'. David Leach cools rapidly to 750°C/1382°F in a two-chamber kiln: the second chamber being brought up to temperature while the first is cooled by the incoming draft. Slow cooling while the glaze is still fluid will develop *matt* qualities in certain glazes and is essential for *aventurine* and *crystalline* glazes. Below 900°C/1652°F the glaze becomes increasingly rigid, but subsequent changes occur (see 2 below) which put either the glaze or the body into a state of stress. If this is excessive *crazing, shivering,* or *shattering* can occur. The main factors at work are:

1 The comparative *coefficients of expansion.*

2 Inversions of quartz and cristobalite, at 573°C/1063°F and 220°C/428°F respectively.

The ideal is, therefore, reasonably slow cooling from red-heat almost to touch-heat. For many potters the cooling rate is built into the kiln design. Hearths and all vents in a fuel burning kiln must be clammed (but allow for fast cooling at the top temperature, see note above). An electric kiln could be covered with a ceramic fiber blanket. The particular qualities and vices of a glaze or body will be affected by the heating and cooling behavior of the kiln — no two of which are likely to be identical. This fact lessens the value of *test kilns*. (See also *dunting*.)

Copper, oxides, compounds

A metallic element Cu. 63.5.
Black cupric oxide CuO, 79.5. m.p. 1149°C.
Red cuprous oxide Cu$_2$O. 143.0.
Carbonate CuCO$_3$. 123.5 [strictly CuCO$_3$. Cu(OH)$_2$].
The cuprous oxide in the 'reduced' or lower oxide state, is

A rosebowl by Robert Fournier thrown in coarsely grogged clay. The wide rim has been turned to bring up the texture and then spun with copper oxide. Only the center well is glazed. A thicker application of a copper/manganese mixture on the edge of the rim has given a gloss — coppery-gold in places.

red but will revert to green CuO in a glaze unless the reduction is maintained. (See *copper red*.) The green carbonate will decompose in hot water and is more toxic than the oxide.

A basic, versatile pigment, slightly fluxing in a glaze. Liable to *volatilize*. In earthenware a great variety of transparent green colors derive from 1–3% of copper oxide: apple green in lead glazes; turquoise in low alumina alkaline glazes; and various shades in leadless glazes. Produces a rather watery color in slip and is usually combined with chrome.

In oxidized stoneware copper will usually give a rather characterless green-brown, but will sometimes surprise with buff to black in a high base matt, or rich turquoise and blues with barium. An excess of copper — 3% and upwards — in any glaze will generally produce a rather cindery black. With careful experiment and control this can be made quite attractive in an earthenware glaze.

Copper increases *lead solubility* to a signficant extent and must not be used in this combination on tablewares or kitchenware. As a pigment, copper is used for green colors on glazes, or for browns and blacks on unglazed biscuit. It will tend to separate out if mixed with other pigments. Copper/manganese mixtures can give a definite gold color on biscuit at any temperature, but the low eutectic can cause running if thickly applied. It will give a variety of colors in raku firings, even back to the metal which, however, is liable to be fugitive over time, see *raku*. Copper chloride is used in lusters. (See also *copper/manganese gold, luster, red colors*.)

An interesting if rather tedious method of preparing your own copper oxide for painting is given in Sanders WJC. Soak copper filings in salt water for a week, then stir and wash with water, and finally with strong tea. Dry and

remove the top layer which will contain the tannin. Carefully separate the middle from the bottom layer (which will be metallic) and use this as a pigment.

Copper luster

A metallic, ruby-red luster can be achieved by painting copper/clay (usually, ochre) mixture onto a soft (1000–1050°C/1832–1922°F), fired glaze which has been opacified with tin or titanium, refiring to about 780°C/1436°F and reducing at the top temperature and during cooling. The clay is cleaned away when the piece is cold. In-glaze luster is fired to glaze maturity and reduced during cooling, intermittently but fairly heavily. All luster firing is very tricky. Prepared lusters are available. (See also *luster*.)

Copper/manganese gold

Mixtures of black copper oxide and manganese dioxide with a greater proportion of the latter, can produce bronze-gold on biscuit over a wide range of temperatures. The biscuit can be first brushed over with manganese and the copper (or a copper/manganese mixture) then applied with a brush, sponge, or spray where the gold color is required, all over if necessary. Too heavy an application of copper will, as ever with this oxide, burn an ashy black.

Temperatures may be from high earthenware to porcelain. Around 1220°C/2228°F is optimum to avoid running which is always a problem. If crinkled or immature in appearance it can be refired. The shine can be attacked by sulfur gases, which some clays give off during firing. If this happens the piece can be refired to brightness. Lucie Rie is reputed to have used copper carbonate in place of the oxide, or even manganese alone although I have not had success with these — which only goes to show!

The color is preferable, over any large area, to gold metal

A hand-built split-rimmed bowl form by Sheila Fournier in copper-manganese gold.

on most studio ceramics, especially on handbuilt or sculptural pieces. A gold-bronze will sometimes appear on raku but this is more difficult to control.

Copper red

Copper oxide, in reduction, will yield *colloidal* particles of cuprous oxide to produce red glazes. This can be achieved at any temperature from 800–1400°C(1472–2552°F) but is fugitive and difficult to retain in the cooling glaze. The color can range from blood red through purple to a rather muddy khaki. Billington recommends a little borax, and even lead, at slightly sub-stoneware temperatures — 1150–1200°C (2102–2192°F). At any temperature the glaze needs to be fairly fluid. Small amounts of tin oxide or zinc in glazes low in alumina and magnesia have been recommended. Finely ground silicon carbide in the same proportions as the copper carbonate can give a streaked red. In CR126 Nigel Wood deals with the fine Chinese copper reds and finds that, for modern equivalents, nepheline syenite is necessary in the later (Qing) bodies and glazes though the earlier Ming glazes were quite simple potash/stone and whiting with 0.5 iron and 0.8 copper (carbonate). The bodies were all micaceous which may or may not have influenced the color. James Walford (CR124) recommends a more stable underglaze with a top glaze containing the copper sprayed onto it.

One can buy red cuprous oxide which some potters believe should be used for reduced copper glazes. It will quickly revert to cupric green in oxidation.

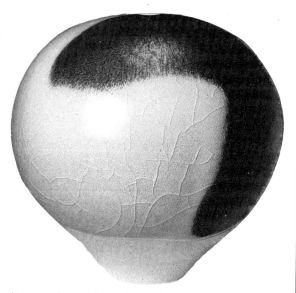

A copper glaze which local reduction has turned blood-red on one side while the left-hand area has remained a pale apple-green on a thrown pot by Greg Daly.

Use 0.5–1.0% of the oxide or carbonate. Maintain at least a non-oxidizing atmosphere during cooling, i.e. keep the kiln as airtight as possible. The typical sang de boeuf Chinese reds occur on a blue *Jun* glaze. (See also *color.*) A small amount of iron is reputed to help the red hue. It is difficult to duplicate copper red effects in detail. The colors, even at their best, are rather strident and need handling with discretion if they are to be anything more than technical achievements.

Copperas

A ferrous sulfate $FeSO_4$.
Calcined for enamels, giving nasturtium reds at 600°C/1112°F and violet at 1000°C/1832°F (Shaw).

Cord impression

The impressing or rolling of cords (string or rope) into the surface of wet clay was practiced for millennia in the Jomon period of Japan and is still a valid method of decoration. Normal, thickly woven, knotted, plaited, or bound cords can all give their distinctive impressions. The cord can be used as it is, or wound round a length of wood or dowel and rolled or beaten onto the slab or pot. Japanese 'nawame' cords of this type are widely used. The resultant pattern can be inlaid, wiped over with pigment or glaze before or after biscuit firing, or treated in other ways.

Cordierite

Magnesium-aluminium-silicate. $2MgO. 2Al_2O_3. 5SiO_2$.
It exists as a mineral—there are deposits in Wyoming, USA — but is usually synthesized at a very high temperature from clay, talc and alumina. It has a low and uniform thermal expansion (*coefficient* 1–2.5) and attempts have been made to incorporate it in fireproof bodies. Serious difficulties, however, arise when it is combined with plastic clays.

Cordon

A strap or raised continuous band round a pot, formed during throwing or turning, or applied. It can give vigor and interest to the profile and, on beakers and the like, can form a springing-off point for a handle. A cordon which has been impressed with the fingers up and down into a wavy shape is called a 'frilled cordon'. Delicate 'cordons' have even been achieved by working the throwing slip into rings with a rib.

Cornwall stone,   Cornish stone

See *china stone.*

Corundum

A natural crystalline alumina, nearly as hard as diamond. Used as an *abrasive*. Also derived from high-fired bauxite. Commonly used as *carborundum* (a trade name).

Cost of setting up

The individual potter is obviously restricted by limits of time and skill as to the number of pieces of work that can be turned out. His or her returns can only be enhanced by keeping the cost of production as low as possible. It is easy to spend many thousands of pounds or dollars on elaborate equipment; pug-mills, slab-rollers, blungers, extruders, vibratory sieves, electronic kiln controllers, etc. which would be unlikely to be recouped by the average potter for many years when, fundamentally, all that is needed is some clay, a few minerals, a kiln, and skillful fingers! Resist the temptation to order by leafing through suppliers' catalogs, and buy equipment only when it becomes essential for a line or type of work which you have experimented with and decided upon. Look through Harry Davis' 'The potter's alternative' and other manuals before embarking on purchases. The total money spent on setting up, including any interest on borrowed money, should be set against returns for a true appraisal of the financial success of a pottery venture.

On the other hand it is economical in the long run to buy materials in as large quantities as you can afford and house. This will not only be cheaper pro rata and save the aggravation of waiting for supplies, but has the great advantage that you can become familiar with a particular batch of clay or mineral. We are lucky that the materials of pottery do not deteriorate with age, may even improve — like the potter!

Costing and pricing

It is said that an object is worth whatever someone will pay for it. Up to a point, this is true of pottery. Pots, even of the highest order, do not in the West often command the prices paid for even second-rate paintings though the gap is narrowing.

The pricing of an individual piece is not, however, the main problem, which is how to arrive at a fair price for the run of tableware and 'useful' pieces which may constitute many a professional potter's bread and butter. A balance must be struck between the estimated production costs and the average price range for similar wares. A comparative beginner will use more time and materials than an experienced potter, but cost cannot be expected to cover lack of skill!

One system is to keep a kiln log of the number and description of pieces produced. Over several months an average figure will emerge. If an approximate wholesale price, based on those prevailing in the shops, is given to each piece, an estimate of one's likely gross income per week or per month can be arrived at. The wholesale price is normally the shop price minus 40–60%. The retail price should be approached even if you sell a number of pots from your own showroom; remember that it may take ten minutes or more to sell a few pounds — or dollars — worth of pots (longer if the customer is an interesting one!). Halve the gross figure of the total sales and if the final sum is not sufficient as a private income you must work harder, or more efficiently, or persuade customers that your pots are worth more. The method is rough and ready but better than none. A more logical system, though often as arbitrary, is to try to calculate the actual cost of production. To arrive at the precise cost of each article is impossible, but again, averages can be struck. Some recording and 'office work' will be involved however you arrange your accounts and the various tax people have to be satisfied. Cost is made up of materials, time and 'overheads', plus a sum to cover future development, taxes, travel and 'profit'.

1 Materials. Assess all materials used over a given period (not less than six months). Clay, glaze, minor materials such as cones, sponges, wax, fuel for kiln, etc. which are 'consumed' or used up.

2 Time. Your wages and those of any assistants. Make an assessment of hours worked and an hourly rate which would be acceptable.

3 Overheads. The proportion of rent, mortgage, telephone, building repairs, lighting, heating, which are attributable to the pottery. Exhibition and professional society charges.

4 Equipment. Capital costs, wear and tear, and depreciation. See note below.

5 Development. You should build up some capital for the future. The equipment figure is a guide to possible requirements.

6 Taxes. Value Added Tax if applicable, (or its equivalent outside the European Economic Community). National Insurance, other insurances, other taxes, bank loan or overdraft charges.

7 Other. Traveling: allow mileage costs as estimated by motoring organizations. Costs of post/mailing and carriage. Boxes and other packing, office materials, and sundries (laundry, etc.).

Items 1, 2, & 3 must be calculated on the basis of six months or a year's total cost. No. 4 is more difficult. The following example may help. The figures are arbitrary: If your kiln and kiln furniture cost $5000 with an estimated $250 a year to cover repairs and replacements, then the charge to be added to a year's costs will be 5000+250/the estimated life of the kiln (say 7 years) = $750.

Add at least the same amount and preferably double the figure arrived at in No. 4, to cover No. 5. The higher figure will help to take inflation into account. The calculations for 6 and 7 are based on one year's expenses.

The figure for each category can be reduced to a monthly rate by simple division. Add 10% for 'profit'.

A

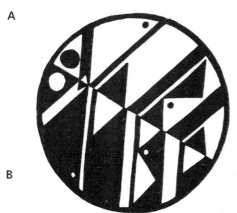

B

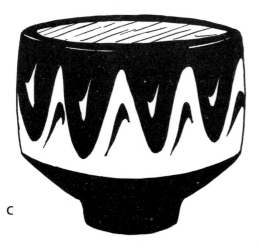

C

This final figure is the sum you should be getting for [ ] month's gross output, as arrived at by the first system men [ ] tioned above.

This need not be a continuing process. One calculation can serve as a basis for several years, balancing price against inflation.

Counter change

A design in which one half of a pattern is a mirror image of the other but in reverse colors; e.g. one part black on white, the other white on black. The diagrams illustrate the principle of the method. The style is useful as an exercise for students since it makes clear that the spaces between elements of a pattern have as much 'shape' as the elements themselves. It is particularly suited to sgraffito and paper resist, and slip trailing. Sometimes the reversals can be in panels on each side of a wavy line as often practiced by Leach (see illustrations in Fournier DPD) or, in a less formal way, by painting pigment strokes on a plain panel with resist on an adjacent one.

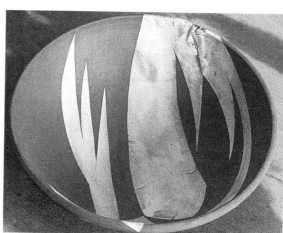

A cut-paper counter change design, in this case one element has been cut from another.

Three examples of counter change.
These diagrams are necessarily in the extremes of black and white but the use of slips and engobes can add variety, while Leach and others have used brushwork in more subtly contrasting colors.
A A stylized leaf, one side of the center stem reflecting a 'negative' image of the other.
B A more involved pattern using the same system and presenting a striking design.
C The counter change principle applied to a bowl, the lighter and darker elements reflecting one another.

Covalent bond

The sharing by two atoms of a pair of electrons, one provided by each atom. (See *atomic theory, valency*.)

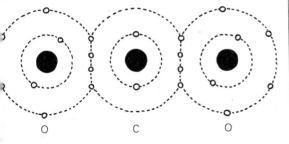

Covalent bonds between atoms of oxygen (O) which has 6 electrons and carbon (C) with 4. Two electrons from each atom are shared, making up 8 in each orbit and forming the carbon dioxide molecule.

Covercoat

A clear layer covering a *transfer (decal)* design. With warm water the covercoat slides off the decal paper taking the design with it. This is then applied to the surface of the ceramic and will burn away during firing (good ventilation is necessary during this phase). Paul Scott's excellent book deals with transfers in detail.

Commercial Decal Inc. USA incorporated a low melting glass into the covercoat (which) – served to reduce *metal release* – from lead and cadmium (Dodd/Murfin).

Cracking, cracked ware

Cracks often result from the mishandling of clay at the leather-hard stage, e.g. careless correcting of deformed pot or bowl rims. The strain may not show until the pot is bone dry or biscuit. Cooling too quickly through the *inversions* of quartz and cristobalite may cause cracks or dunting. This would be aggravated by an excess of silica in the body. A cooling crack is usually curved and sharp. Other causes of cracking:

1 Over-wetting parts of a pot, e.g. water left in the base during throwing.
2 Stretching the clay when making.
3 Uneven or forced drying — the last part to dry may crack.
4 Applying slip to a dish which is either too dry, or, conversely, has only just been pressed into a mold.
5 Very uneven wall thicknesses, especially the bases of pots.
6 Wet clay joined to drier clay.
7 High shrinkage-rate of clay.
8 Pieces of lime or stone.

9 Excessive weight on a pot or 'bung' of pots in the kiln, including piles of six or more tiles in plastic clay.
10 Slabs bent when too stiff, e.g. pots made around cylinders.
11 Over-wedging, giving a very short body.
12 Thick glaze on one side of a dish only.
13 The working of clay after it has dried beyond the plastic stage.
14 'Free' silica too fine-grained.

This is a formidable list, but in fact clean, well-prepared clay made into reasonably even-walled pots which are allowed to dry naturally will rarely suffer. (See *base cracks*). Hamer gives a remarkably detailed analysis of many types of cracks and their possible causes.

The filling of dry clay or biscuit cracks in pottery is not recommended (in modeling or 'sculptural' work it is more acceptable), although preparations are sold for this purpose. (See *mending, repairing pottery, stopping*.)

However the deliberate cracking of surfaces and of the walls of pieces has become accepted as a formal or decorative element. Surface cracking in a semi-controlled manner can be induced by laying softer clay or one with a greater shrinkage over a firmer base. The continued rolling of clay slabs will also result in a fissured splitting of the surface. (See also *texture*.)

Crackle, craquele

A term applied to the intentional *crazing* of stoneware or porcelain glazes. Vitrification of the body prevents excessive absorption of moisture.

On porcelain, crackle is used decoratively and can be stained with manganese or other color while still hot from the kiln. Nitrates of the pigment oxides are suggested by Behrens. If pottery color is used it can be fixed in a second lower firing. Non-ceramic materials such as tea, water-based paint, and black Indian ink have been used to stain crackle. Brian Beaven (CR73) warns against handling the ware before staining — finger marks will show up — and to hold the warm pot with a clean rag. Rapid cooling of raku, etc. will induce crackle and Martin Smith wipes wet strips of cloth over the areas he wants affected. In this case, of course, the result should more accurately be called crazing. A second and wider crackle may form long after firing, an effect which can be speeded up by dipping the piece into almost boiling water. Crackle is best avoided on tableware. In Hamer's 'melt-crackle' the cracks in an underfired glaze are stained with pigment oxides the piece then refired (Hamer PDMT).

Thick glaze with a high *coefficient of expansion* is needed for the development of crackle. Behrens (CM17/8) suggests a body of:

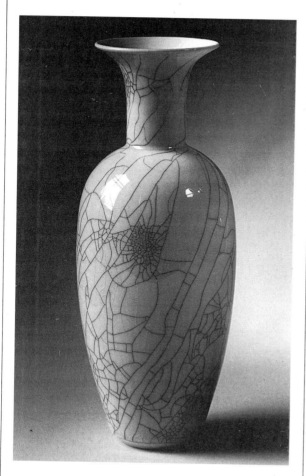

An interesting spider-web crackle on a porcelain bottle by Christine-Ann Richards. (Photograph from St. James Gallery, Bath, England)

58 ball clay   39 talc   3 bentonite
with a glaze of volcanic ash, china clay, and frit, fired to 1220°C/2228°F.

The formula for a talc crackle glaze by Victor Margrie, given in CR2, reads:

K_2O 0.20
CaO 0.29 Al_2O_3 0.20 SiO_2 2.0
MgO 0.51

firing to 1260°C/2300°F on David Leach porcelain body. (See also *crazing*.)

In general a high felspathic content is recommended for crackle glazes with whiting as a second flux, and two glazes, one as a base glaze the second sprayed on, are often used, see David White in CR169 for more details.

Crank, bit

A thin refractory kiln shelf up to about 12in/300mm long.

May be rectangular or triangular, and have bent-over tab for spacing. Used mainly for tiles. Small blocks to hold th cranks apart are called 'bits' or 'dots'.

A crank can also be a vertical structure with a series o 'pins' to hold plates or tiles of identical size. Maximum kil temperature 1200°C/2192°F. More supportive cranks hav three turned-down feet which span the tile or plate (se *plate setter, tile setter*).

Thirdly, the term may be used to cover all kiln shelves.

Crank mixture

Originally a coarse, grogged body of refractory clays used for making 'cranks' or kiln shelves. Used as a trade name for a somewhat variable mixture by Potclays, Stoke-on-Trent but has since been quoted world-wide as a hand-building material with various grades of grog down to 'smooth-textured' (Scarva Pottery Supplies).

Useful for mixing with other clays to impart a more open texture, allowing thicker walls in models, coiled pots, etc. Low shrinkage if used alone. Can be made into saggars for raku.

Craquele

An alternative term for *crackle*.

Crater glaze

A rather tricky decorative finish derived from burst bubbles in a glaze. The use of sulfates such as barium sulfate has been suggested. The 'craters' should be sufficiently melted to lose their dangerous sharpness. A light colored 'stiff' (refractory) glaze over a darker more fusible one can trap escaping bubbles which will finally break through to

1 *Teabowl with a 'cratered' glaze by Ewen Henderson.*

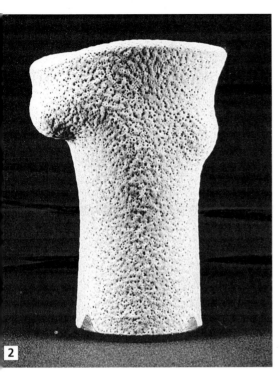

2

'A crater glaze — using outgassing from a decomposing
clay body as a source of the cratered surface, rather than
anything special about the glaze itself'. By Wiliam Hunt, USA.

form a 'crater'. Any material which will liberate gases —
the fluorides, etc. — will help to form the required effect.
Hamer gives the optimum temperature range as 1000–
1200°C/1832–2192°F.

Coarse-grained silicon carbide in the body has been suggested — a recipe from the American potter James Lovera,
using American materials, is given as (brought down to
percentages): china clay 11, silica 11, potash feldspar 42,
calcium carbonate 21, titanium dioxide 9, silicon carbide
(100 mesh) 6.

Another type of recipe from Behrens quoted in CM17/3
reads: talc 43.5, lepidolite 54.4, bentonite 2.

Crawling

A glaze fault, the glaze bunching up in places leaving other
parts bare. Some likely causes are:

In general, glazes with too high a *surface tension*.

Too thick a coating of glaze or repeated coatings. If the
glaze shows signs of cracking as it dries then it will almost
certainly crawl.

Glaze which has flocculated in the batch, due to soluble
alkalis (e.g. ash) or colemanite.

Greasy or dusty biscuit.

*Deliberate crawling achieved by pouring a thick glaze over a
rough, sand and grit beaten surface. Handbuilt stoneware by
Robert Fournier.*

5 Overloading with opacifying materials, or with feldspar,
making the glaze too viscous.

6 Underfiring.

7 Glaze materials too finely ground.

8 An exceptionally smooth body can aggravate crawling.

9 Thick underglaze pigments, especially barely sintered
oxides which have the same effect as dust.

10 Double glazing with the first glaze too dry.

11 Very 'hard' calcareous water used in throwing or sponging has been given as a cause.

12 The commencement of firing before the glaze water has
fully dried from the body. This is one of the commonest
causes. Do not dry off the glaze water in the kiln.

13 Loose materials such as sand on the surface.

Crawling on the rim of a pot is difficult to cure. I have
had to abandon otherwise excellent glazes because of this
fault. Cardew suggests a higher biscuit fire, or altering the
body by the addition of quartz or a hard, fine grog.
Crawling has been exploited as a decorative finish — for
instance Hamada's white crawled glaze on the necks of
pots. Sheila Fournier's handbuilt bowls where the crawling
is made to 'heal over' in a second fire; Lucie Rie's very controlled all-over crawling, etc. The New Zealand potter in
CR170 using glazes containing Gerstley borate and magnesium carbonate for a crawled glaze, sometimes over
another glaze. He brushes on several layers of glaze. He
warns that they might fall off the pot before melting. In
general a thick glaze containing any of the *refractory* or
opacifying materials in more than optimum amounts is
likely to crawl.

Crayon

Joan Hepworth's detailed and crisp decoration using ceramic crayons. She warns that their use is not quite as simple as it may appear to be; they need continual sharpening and tend to be soft and brittle and easily broken. They are, nevertheless, an interesting and valuable addition to the potter's palette.

Underglaze colors in the form of pencils or crayons are available from several suppliers. Use like an ordinary crayon, blow away loose dust, and fire. The effect is generally paler than when using a brush, more allied to drawing, and often resulting in a new freely drawn graphic style. A home-made crayon may be made by mixing a pigment with clay and a little glue or binder into a stiff paste and then rolling it into a cylinder, perhaps covering it in a strip of thin paper to make it more rigid.

Crazing

A network of fractures in a glaze caused by differences in contraction between body and glaze during cooling, or by subsequent expansion of the body. Term generally applied to earthenware; a similar effect on high-fired ware is often called *crackle*. It should be avoided on all pottery made for table or kitchen use. If a glaze regularly crazes despite efforts to cure it, dispense with it. One may also have to abandon a body on which crazing regularly occurs.

Crazing is most apparent in clear glazes; it can be difficult to detect in *tin* or opaque glazes — until you wash up after that delicious bowl of raspberries. *Slip* can craze.

In general, the whiter, prepared bodies may be most liable to crazing under craft conditions since they are designed for a much higher biscuit fire. Industrial frits are often applied too thickly by the student potter. Too thick a coating of any glaze will increase its susceptibility to crazing.

The perfect glaze is in slight compression after firing: it has contracted a little less than the body during the final 600°C/1112°F of cooling. The main factor working against this ideal state is the high *coefficient of expansion* of many of the bases used to *flux* a glaze. Soda and potash are the worst offenders, while silica and alumina have comparatively low coefficients. This means, in practice, using less feldspar or stone and a little more flint or clay, or a little boric oxide (as borax frit). (See *negative expansion*.) Lead is reputed to have more elasticity than the other bases; some bisilicate or a low-solubility frit may therefore be advantageous. *Colemanite* is reputed to help craze resistance. A more fundamental approach is to tackle the body increasing its contraction to put the glaze into *compression*. Silica, in a glaze, does not *crystallize* on cooling, and so contracts evenly throughout the temperature range. Crystals of silica in the body, however, undergo a very sudden change in molecular shape at 573°C/1063°F (*inversion*) accompanied by a contraction of around 1%. This helps to balance the glaze contraction and we get the apparently anomalous situation where the addition of silica to either glaze or body will help to minimize crazing.

If the silica in the body is fired high enough to form *cristobalite* then another and proportionally greater contraction occurs at 250–220°C/482–428°F, further aiding glaze compression, and at a critical temperature when the glaze is quite rigid. Cristobalite forms only very slowly at 1060°C/1940°F and above. A 1080–1100°C/1976–2012°F firing, with soaking, is therefore necessary to achieve significant results. Very finely ground flint or quartz will form cristobalite more rapidly. Prepared cristobalite can be purchased and added to a body. Remedies for crazing must be used with discretion.

Free silica in the body must be kept below 20%. To go too far in the alteration of glaze and body can build up too great a compression with subsequent *shattering*. Also a fired body with expansions in the cooking temperature range will suffer thermal shock, which may cause the crazing, during normal household use, of a glaze which came whole from the kiln.

Ordinary precautions include careful temperature control, neither under- nor over-firing; the soaking of soft glazes for 20 minutes or so; refraining from opening the kiln too early (above 100°C/212°F); avoidance of sudden drafts of cold air at dull red heat and cooler.

An indication of glaze-body fit (Seger's crazing test) can be obtained from the degree of deformation of a thin bar of clay coated fairly thickly with glaze on one face only, and fired on its side on a bed of alumina. Ideally it should urve slightly with the glaze side convex. (See also *Seger's rules, Harkort test.*)

Slips can craze due to excess shrinkage. It becomes apparent during glazing when the cracks show up as thicker deposits. To cure, apply slip on slightly damper clay or stiffen the slip with a refractory material such as china clay or fireclay. Slip-cracking is more often due to wet/dry shrinkage than to firing reactions.

A quite distinct cause of crazing is water adsorption which slightly increases the volume of the body. This may show weeks or months after firing. A pot which is fully covered with a good glaze will not be at great risk.

Cristobalite, *squeeze*

A crystalline form of silica with an *inversion* which is greater than that of quartz (3% linear expansion as compared with around 1%), and taking place at a lower temperature, 220°C/428°F. Added to or developed in a clay body, beta quartz will slowly convert to cristobalite from 1050°C/1922°F. Conversion continues to 1550°C/2822°F and is therefore never complete in a pottery body. Lime is said to accelerate its formation. Even small amounts of cristobalite, however, can be valuable in the prevention of crazing, known as the 'cristobalite squeeze'. *Soaking* during the biscuit fire at around 1070°C/1958°F will help earthenware. It can be obtained in a synthesized form, often in conjunction with *tridymite*.

Crockery

A general term used mainly for tableware and often restricted to earthenware.

Crocus martis

A natural ferric oxide, Fe_2O_3, 'with some nitrate' (Billington); 'an anhydrous ferrous sulfate' (Hamer). Soluble, but partially decomposes at around 900°C/1652°F, rendering it insoluble. The insoluble form is commercially obtainable. May turn greenish in boric glazes, using 3-6%. Can give darker browns than red ferric, and black with cobalt. May speckle in stonewares.

Cross-draft kiln

A semi-downdraft kiln usually with a single firemouth. (See diagrams under *bag wall* and *chambered kiln*.)

Cruet

See salt and pepper pots.

Crushing rock, *crusher mill*

Small experimental quantities of rock can be crushed with a 2lb/1kg hammer on a steel slab and then ground in a mortar and pestle, a teaspoonful at a time, or in a *jar mill* or *ball mill*. Larger quantities require a jaw crusher and a plate mill, normally beyond the resources of the craft potter. A rare exception was Harry Davis who crushed and compounded local Cornish rocks into glazes. Rocks vary greatly in hardness (see *Mohs' scale*).

Calcining to around 900°C/1652°F will loosen the bonds between molecules and render the rock easier to crush. A hammer (with the rock well covered under thick cloth, e.g. a strong sack) may then be sufficient to break it up. The easier way is to collect rock dust from granite and other workings. Read Sutherland, Cardew, and Davis, for practical details.

Harry Davis describes a rock crusher made by West Shore Machine Works (see Suppliers list) which is hand operated and is reputed to crush 1kg (2.2lb) of rock to mesh size in a few minutes. (See also *vibratory mill*.)

Crusilite

A proprietary (Morganite Electroheat Ltd) *silicon carbide* kiln *element*.

Cryolite

A sodium-aluminium fluoride Na_3AlF_6, 210 (convenient formula weight 420).
Fires to $3Na_3O.\ Al_2O_3$. m.p. 980°C/1796°F.

Can be used as a source of insoluble soda, but the accompanying fluorine will bubble through the glaze on escaping during the firing, and will leave pinholes unless the glaze is very fluid. The alumina is likely to give a matt surface. Used in the vitreous enamels. Obtainable from Coastal Ceramics (NZ).

Cryptocrystalline

With a crystalline structure visible only under a microscope.

Crystal, *crypto-crystalline, crystalline, crystallization*

Molecules or *lattices* which have built up into a three-dimensional repeat pattern. The solid substance assumes an individual and geometric form with plane faces. Most pure materials can be found in crystalline form, the large crystals often used as gemstones, e.g. crystallized carbon as

The regular shapes built up by crystal formation in a tin/lead alloy.

Bottle showing crystal halos by Derek Clarkson.

diamond or aluminum silicate as topaz. Crystals can be very large or micro-crystalline and invisible to the naked eye (sub-microscopic), as in clay or flint when they are known as crypto-crystalline. They form either in the melted, fluid state, or in solution. Their study is a wide-ranging and fundamental science. Perfect crystals may be transparent, hence the use of terms crystal-clear, or crystal glass (the latter very much a misnomer). Noncrystalline materials are *amorphous.*

Crystals need time in which to form from a fluid compound. Glaze is normally cooled too quickly and remains largely amorphous, though some crystals can form to show as a matt surface if very small, or as sparkling or *aventurine* glazes if larger. A bright, clear glaze is wholly noncrystalline: it is a supercooled or frozen liquid.

High alumina or calcium glazes are apt to form crystalline matt glazes 'thought to be anorthite' (Cardew PP). Zinc and titanium promote crystallization. (See also *devitrification.*) Soluble material and very soft frits will recrystallize from a solution, e.g. a frit raku glaze. See further discussion in next entry.

Crystalline glaze

Glazes which have been subject to partial devitrification are dealt with to some degree under *aventurine glaze.* The main difference between crystalline and aventurine glazes is that, in the latter, the crystals are embedded in the glaze and are usually smaller.

The crystals can vary from a slight all-over sparkle to large, striking, crystalline patterns. They are formed principally in the 900–700°C/1652–1292°F range during cooling which should take place very slowly. Suitable glazes can be refired. Many of the glazes become very fluid and can run badly. Some potters accept this; use drip bowls beneath the pieces; and spend a long time grinding off. Derek Clarkson (CR137) suggests using a pedestal, which has been covered with a wash of china clay and flint to stand the pot on, scratching with a tungsten cutter round

the glaze join after firing, tapping with a *sorting tool* until the pedestal breaks away. Finish with a carborundum block.

Alumina in the glaze should be kept at a minimum. Stephen Booth in CR80 goes as far as leaving out alumina altogether and using only zinc oxide, soda, and silica — a very fluid glaze. He gives a four hour soak at 1080°C/ 1976°F after cooling rapidly from 1290°C/2354°F. Titanium, zinc, calcium, magnesium, and ilmenite (some form of iron oxide is mentioned in most recipes) are quoted as useful in initiating or 'seeding' (Hamer) the process. Parmalee recommends using elements with low atomic weights: calcium, magnesium, iron, lithium, and, to a lesser degree, titanium, uranium, phosphorus, and bismuth. Kenneth Clark gives some percentage limits: alkaline or borax frit 45–62, flint 5–21, zinc oxide 22–27, titanium dioxide 5–9, fired to 1260°C/ 2300°F, cooled rapidly to around 1140°C/2084°F then very slowly for the next 60–140 degrees. Rada mentions up to 25% of rutile with 5% each of copper and manganese. Kate Malone in CR164 illustrates some very remarkable crystalline formations using a high alkaline frit with zinc oxide, flint, and bentonite. Ferro frit 3110 is used by a number of potters using up to 50% frit with zinc, flint, and titanium.

Cuenca

A Spanish decorating method used on countless thousands

A striking copper-luster tile decorated in the cuenca style from Granada.

of tiles and other pottery in which the areas within raised outlines of a design are filled with glaze or color, similar in technique to cloisonné enamel. The depressed areas can be formed by stamping, casting, slip-trailing, or can be cut away from a flat surface. Glazes or colors are poured, trailed, or brushed on. (See also *tube lining*).

Cuerda seca

A Spanish technique similar to cuenca but with the separating lines painted on with a thick mixture of manganese in a fatty medium. Wire has also been glued to tiles (by Storr-Britz), treated like cuerda seca, the wire melting during the firing.

Cull

American equivalent of a '*waster*', a kiln-spoiled pot.

Cullet

Pieces of colored glass used in pottery decoration. Also supplied, finely ground, as a cheap but variable glaze flux. (See *melted glass decoration*.)

Cup, *cup and saucer*

Although Rhodes dismisses the cup form — 'its functional aspects are few' — there is more to a fine cup than this. Balance, handle placing, foot, and rim have many

solutions. The height and width are normally about equal. The handle itself should be easily gripped without the fingers contacting the hot cup surface. The rim should not turn inwards nor flare excessively. A heavy handle will deform a thin rim in the firing, if not before. The design of a cup should always be considered in relation to the saucer on which it is set. There should be enough room under the handle to accommodate a spoon and to allow the cup to be lifted without tipping it. (See also *saucer*.)

In common with the teapot and the jug the cup form has been taken over as an art object or what is fashionably known as an 'icon' by various potters, notably Ron Nagle; 'not cups but about cups', Garth Clark.

Cup head

A hollow wheelhead. Can be used for supporting circular molds, e.g. for *jigger and jolley*, or for turning narrow-necked pots. (See also *molds, turning*.)

Cup lawn

A small conical or cup-shaped sieve, usually of metal, and 2–3in/50–75mm wide.

Cuprum, *cupric, cuprous*

Copper Cu. The cupric is the higher oxide CuO, cuprous the lower or reduced red oxide Cu_2O. (See *copper*.)

Current, *electric*

The flow of electricity as measured in *amperes*. (See *electricity*.)

Custer feldspar

An American potash feldspar (Pottery Supply House and others).

Cut brick

Soft insulating bricks can be cut into relief or intaglio patterns for stamping onto soft clay to produce three-dimensional textures or more controlled designs. Can also be used as a stamp for printing. Bricks have also been used as elements in a ceramic piece.

Cut-corner dish

A slab technique for making dishes. Allows variations in size and shape which the mold denies. It has its limitations, and some practice is necessary. The dishes look their best in a fairly chunky style. They can be stoneware fired.

The photographs show the principal stages. The template, cut in stiff paper, is laid on a slab or fairly soft plastic clay, and the clay cut to shape. The corners must be cut at a slant so that they can be overlapped to give a strong joint. The surfaces are slipped, the sides raised up until the corner can be luted together. Overlap the faces by about

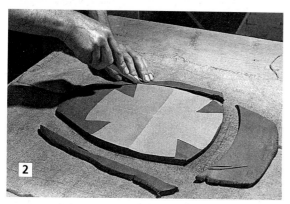

4 With the segment removed the faces are slipped and brought up together.

5 Clay supports in position to hold the dish in shape while it stiffens.

6 The joins must be gently smoothed over and the inside of the dish shaped by stroking with a rubber kidney tool. When leather-hard the inside can be further smoothed and the outside finished with a steel palette or plane.

Constructing a cut-corner dish.

1 A template is cut from a sheet of paper folded in four.

2 A clay slab is cut to the template shape.

3 The corner cut at a 45° slope.

⅛in/2mm to avoid any thinness when the joint is worked together. Supports must be prepared.

The inside face can be smoothed with a kidney rubber and, later on, with a steel palette. The top edge will need trimming flat and the back must be scraped or planed when stiff. Any style of decoration can be used on these dishes. A fairly fine grog in the clay helps, especially for stoneware.

Cut liner

Also called a 'sword liner'. A soft squirrel-hair brush cut at an angle and pointed at the end.

Cut-off needle

See *needle awl, pricker*.

Cut paper resist

See *paper resist*.

Cut rims

See *rims*.

Cut-sided pots

A rounded form, thrown or built, pot or bowl can be cut or sliced down to produce flat panels. This is an alternative to beating the sides (see *beaten-sided pots*) but has the disadvantage that the walls of the piece must be fairly thick.

The choice of tool — wire, knife, or plane — will affect the result as will the directness of the cut.

Cut sponge

Originally patterns were cut from the dense root of a sponge for printing pigment onto pottery. More open and free-formed designs can be 'printed' with foam sponges which can be cut, or burnt away with a hot metal rod into a broad pattern (but see warning at *sponge decoration*). See also *printing*, and *sponge decoration* for more information and the use of polyurethane foam.

Cutting clay

The choice of tools for cutting clay will depend on its state of dryness. For plastic clay a wire can be used for trimming the rims of molded dishes and the like, a wooden spatula tool or a very fine metal tool such as a needle awl. If wide metal tools are used on soft clay they will tend to stick and

tear. For leather-hard clay, use a slender knife with a good handle. When cutting clay for slab pots take care to hold the knife vertical and always draw it towards you. For a new cut turn the clay; do not turn the knife to an awkward angle.

Cutting through a block of clay with shaped wires or tools can also provide interesting and dramatic surface patterns, textures, or bold, three-dimensional results.

Cutting off

After throwing, pots are normally cut from the wheel with a twisted wire or thread. This may be drawn through the base, holding the stretched wire hard down on the wheel head with the index fingers and cutting away from the

1 Cutting through the base of a thrown bowl, holding the wire close to the wheelhead with the forefingers while drawing it under the base.
2 The typical shell pattern from a twisted wire used just before the wheelhead comes to a halt.

body. The Japanese method is to hold a thread at one end only, allowing the free end to wind round the base of the pot, then to give it a sharp horizontal pull. This involves throwing the pot on a mound of clay an inch or two above the wheelhead.

The two-handed technique will give various patterns beneath your pot according to whether you pull the wire through straight, allow it to curve as you cut, or cut as the wheel is coming to a halt. If water is pulled through with the wire the piece should slide off the wheel head, onto a bat (with a slightly absorbent surface, not a glazed tile from which it will need to be cut away again). A '*pot lift*' for removing pots from the wheel is listed by Pottery Supply House and by Kemper.

Cutting wire

A wire for cutting pots from the wheel should be strong, fine and flexible. It is hard to find a material which combines these qualities and which will also twist into the stranded form which acts like the 'set' of a saw, thus making the cutting both easier, more efficient, and also decorative. Steel wire is too springy for comfort; copper is too weak. A brass wire with a steel strand, as sold for picture hanging, is a compromise. Nylon is strong but will not remain twisted. A fine nylon can be plaited. The degree of twist is important. It should not be too tight; the normal twisted steel wire is too finely wound.

The gauge of wire used should be heavier for wedging and cutting blocks of clay. Coarse nylon can be useful here. Treat cutting wires with care and avoid pulling a loop which may result in an eradicable kink. Bends can be smoothed out by pulling the wire tightly back and forth across a piece of wood or table-edge. Wires for harps and multiple cutters can be of steel, sometimes known as 'piano wire'.

Handles are essential (it is painful to use a wire loop). They can be of wood dowelling, or made from clay and fired. Wires of varying lengths are required: a long wire shortened by twisting it round the fingers will not last long.

Fastening the wire to the handles or toggles is a perennial problem. If the ends are simply twisted round to fasten them they can present danger to the fingers. Soldering is one answer: the use of a sheath such as the rubber covering of electric cable, is another. Some potters bypass the difficulty by using fishing line and other types of thread. For more ideas see Fournier PT.

Cyanite

See *kyanite*.

D

Damp-cupboard, *damp-room, damp box*

A cool, airtight cupboard with non-absorbent walls. A saturated atmosphere is built up which ceases to absorb further moisture from the pots. There has often been some confusion, especially on the part of school architects, on the subject of damp-cupboards. Various measures, such as trays of wet plaster — even felt walls in one new building — have been tried. But every time the door is opened (in a school read 'left open') the built-up humidity is dispersed. The damp-cupboard is now virtually obsolete (although Potterycrafts list a galvanized 'damp storage cabinet' with rubber door seal), having been replaced by the widespread use of polythene. A suggestion from Bill Jones is to use an old freezer cabinet (disconnected from the power source, of course!).

A cool cupboard with well-fitting doors by all means, but polythene as well as soon as the piece has stiffened up sufficiently.

A clay cellar or damp-room as described by Cardew is a major construction and suitable only for the large-scale professional potter. For the amateur, the polythene box or well-sealed plastic bag has happily replaced the rusting biscuit tins and wet, rotting rags of a few years ago.

Damper

A sliding plate which can close or decrease the chimney opening and thus the draft through the kiln. Must be of stout iron or of refractory ceramic. The removal of a chimney brick will have a similar effect, bypassing the pull through the kiln chamber.

Dangerous materials *gases etc.*

See *dust, health hazards, poisonous materials, ventilation.*

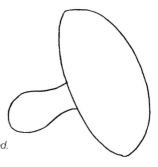

Darning head
A curved-top 'darning head', in my experience one of the most useful tools that a handbuilding or press-molding potter can have but one which suppliers have largely ignored.

Darning head

A wooden mushroom shape on a handle once used widely for darning, but useful to potters for pressing clay into molds and formers. See diagram on opposite page. Very useful if you can find one (but does anyone darn these days!) or you can make one.

De-airing clay

The removal of air from clay by passing it through a partial vacuum, usually in a special pug mill. The clay must be shredded prior to de-airing. De-aired clay is denser and, reputedly, more plastic. For the enthusiast Harry Davis invented a splendid de-airing pug. Though he is, alas, with us no more he has left plans for this and a multitude of other machinery and tools in his book (Davis).

Decal, Decalomania

Lithographic transfers (USA). The term 'decalomania' has been traced to the craze among amateur potters and pottery decorators for paper transfers at the end of the 19th century in America. Appear in some supplier's catalogs, usually of deplorable design though their old-fashioned 'bad taste' gives them a certain cachet today. A number of firms have set up offering to make decals from a potter's own artwork. (See also *covercoat, lithography, photoceramics processes, slide-off transfers, transfers.*)

Decomposition

The breaking up of chemical compounds. During firing carbonates decompose into the oxide and CO_2 which is given off as a gas, red lead breaks down, $(2Pb_3O_4) = 6PbO + O_2$, and so on. Vegetable and other organic matter present in clay will decompose at about 200°C/392°F, but the residual carbon will not burn away until the temperature has reached 800–1000°C/1472–1832°F.

In a slightly different sense fired glazes can decompose with age. (See at *devitrification.*)

Decoration

Two voices from the past, discussing the decoration of pottery, still have valid points to make for today:
Dora Billington:
'Design freely, do what and only what pleases you, and only apply principles as an aid to criticism if something goes wrong'.
Bernard Leach:
'Subordinate to form but intimately connected with it is

the problem of decoration and whether the increased orchestration adds to the total effect or not'.

Dora Billington goes on 'diffidently' to give advice on the fundamental basis of design and discusses scale, balance, variety, contrast and tension; the last conspicuously absent from much modern work. Her remarks are based on a lifetime of experience and are well worth assimilating. The potter Kenneth Clark also gives advice from a painter's point of view. His 'range of visual contrasts' is useful (Clark PPC).

It is difficult to disassociate decoration from some of the discredited 19th-century ideas of 'applied art'. For a time, especially during the 1960s, many potters followed the rule: 'if in doubt, don't!'. 'Texture' and 'glaze quality' were paramount.

Recent times, however, have seen a much more uninhibited approach, with bright colors both in underglaze and enamels. A glance at the pottery of the past from Suza slip to Spanish luster will indicate a perennial preoccupation with over-all decorated ceramics with as much brilliance of color as the craft will allow. Much of the work has been in earthenware but the white ground of porcelain, too, invites and aids brilliance of tone. Our palette has also been enlarged with chrome colors, selenium, and the like.

The techniques of pottery decoration are discussed under *applied decoration, beaten decoration, brushwork, sgraffito, resist techniques* and *slip-trailing.*

Deflocculation

The dispersion of particles especially in a clay slip leading to increased fluidity. Its prime use is in *casting slip.* It assists particle suspension and reduces comparative shrinkage, as less water is needed, in a body mixture. It is achieved by the use of an *electrolyte* (usually sodium) in silicate or carbonate (*soda ash*) form. The electrolyte alters charges on the molecules, causing them to hold away from one another (disperse). Potassium carbonate will have the same effect. Sodium tannate, pyrophosphate, and other compounds are used in special cases. If a clay already contains free alkali it will not deflocculate. Excess deflocculant will reverse the effect, the slip thickening again, while coarse grained materials such as flint will not deflocculate at all.

Recipes and instructions for using electrolytes appear in most suppliers' catalogs (see also Rhodes CGP). For maximum effect the balance is a delicate one and will vary from body to body. Add electrolyte drop by drop if you are working with liquid slip, or weigh dry against dry powdered body according to the advice of the suppliers of the body. 'One half per cent dry weight will turn soft plastic clay into slip' (Billington). Potclays and others market a polymer type deflocculant called Dispex for which they claim 'improved stability amd mold life'. Sodium silicate is sold in *Twaddle degrees*.

Defluorinated stone

China stone from which fluorine has been extracted, now often listed by merchants. May help to prevent pinholes in glaze.

Deformation

Pyroplastic deformation occurs at the temperature at which a ceramic body can no longer hold its shape due to the formation of molten compounds within the fabric. It is normally a slow and continuing process, but can be quite sudden in high-calcium bodies and artificial low-temperature porcelains. Deformation usually leads to slumping. Warping may have other causes (see *plastic memory*).

Kiln shelves are tested for 'deformation under load'. The softening effect occurs at each firing so that a curved or sagged shelf can be reversed in the next firing. (See *kiln shelves*.)

Dehydration

The removal of water. In pottery generally confined to the loss of the chemically-combined water in clay at 600–700°C/1112–1292°F.

Deliquescent

A material which will absorb moisture from the air to such a degree that it will itself become liquid. The commonest deliquescent pottery material is potassium carbonate. (See also *hygroscopic*.)

Delta wiring

See *star and delta, three phase*.

Demi-hydrate, semi-hydrate

Materials from which part of the chemically-combined water has been taken. *Plaster of Paris* is a partially dehydrated *gypsum*.

Devitrification

The change from a glassy to crystalline state. Glaze may partially devitrify during a slow cooling (see *aventurine, crystalline, matt*) giving a frosty look 'common in high clay or silica glazes' (Rhodes), or, in the case of glazes designed to crystallize readily, larger, often striking colored crystal formations.

Soft glazes, especially the early high-soda glazes from the Near East, will devitrify with great age, often developing a silvery or iridescent sheen which may obliterate the decoration. The effect is similar to that on very old glass and is most marked on early Islamic alkaline glazes. If melted glass, especially colored or stained-glass, is used in the embellishment of pots it can sometimes devitrify on cooling. (See *melted glass decoration*.)

A much magnified view of the remarkable crystalline pattern, resembling frost, developed by glass which has started to devitrify during cooling. To the naked eye it appears as a whitish rough patch about 1/2in/12mm across.

Dewatering clay

The drying of *slip* to plastic clay. It is the practice in the pottery industry to render all bodies to slips, which are then *filter-pressed* to a plastic state. A craft potter can easily rig up a *blunger* but, in temperate climes at any rate, the dewatering of the slip is a major problem. The slip will settle and the surplus water can be poured, scooped, or siphoned off but we are still left with a runny slurry. If space is available this can be poured into cloth bags (a fine one inside a stronger coarser one) which can be hung up to drip and stiffen, like cheeses for three or four days. Dave White recommends old corduroy trousers with the leg bottoms sewn up, and Mrs. S. Hardwick an old leaky wheelbarrow lined with denim! (See Fournier PT.)

Plaster or biscuit molds, raised on blocks are useful for small quantities but soon saturate. Shallow troughs such as those used at St. Ives need roofing over if they are not to flood in winter, and they entail space and time. In hot weather the simplest method is that practiced by Harry Davis: the slip is poured into a large sheet spread in a depression in the ground, the corners of the sheet being brought together and knotted. The knot acts as a wick, the water is drawn up and evaporates in the sun. Davis has also designed a piece of homemade dewatering equipment which is an ingenious reversal of the industrial filter-press. In it the water is extracted by suction in a semi-vacuum. (See Davis.)

At Soil Hill Pottery the hot gases from the kiln were drawn under a long brick trough before they reached the chimney. Cardew shows plans for brick dewatering-troughs in Pioneer Pottery. Most potters bypass the problem by buying plastic clay or by mixing clay powder and water in a *dough mixer* or in one of the various types of mechanical mixers on the market.

Diaspore, diaspore clay

Diaspore is a hydrated alumina, found in massive form. The term diaspore clay is used for one rich in alumina, valuable for making *refractories*.

Diatomite

Sometimes called 'infusorial earth' or 'Kieselguhr'. Formed from the accumulation of the siliceous remains of minute aquatic vegetable organisms (diatoms). It has very high porosity and heat resistance up to about 800°C/1472°F making it a useful, if limited, kiln insulation material. It can be used as granules, or as bricks cut from reefs, the granules are also used as a concrete aggregate for insulation. *Ceramic fiber* and other synthetic insulators with greater refractoriness have all but replaced diatomite.

Die, die press

A pug or wad box attachment which fastens over the mouth of the machine. The clay is forced through holes to form coils and other shapes. Some very large forms can be made in this way, see *extrusion*.

A 'die-press' is a damp-clay tile press.

Dielectric

Capable of withstanding electrical stresses, e.g. porcelain insulators. An iron-free *vitrified* body is essential.

Diesel oil

An easily obtained but rather smelly fuel which needs an efficient blower to burn, and a tank some two and a half feet above the jets. The kiln must be preheated to the vaporization point of the oil. (See *oil fuel, oil fired kiln*.)

Digital

The indication of temperature, time, etc. in actual numbers instead of by a marker on a dial as on the older style of pyrometer. For firing, digital readings are obviously more precise—so long as the instrument is accurate. (See *controlling pyrometer, pyrometer* for comments.)

Dilatancy

The opposite of *thixotropy*, i.e. becoming less fluid when stirred or under pressure. Wet sand 'dilates'. Dodd mentions ceramic bodies which are deficient in fine particles, the coarser ones dilating, which is the opposite effect to that required by the potter.

Diopside

A calcium/magnesium mineral, free of alumina, $CaO.MgO.2SiO_2$. Occurs as a crystal and in basalt, and can be precipitated from glazes high in dolomite, giving a matt surface.

Dioxide

A combination of one atom of an element with two of oxygen — RO_2.

Dipping

See *glazing*.

Direct current

Or DC. Electric current flowing in one direction only. Batteries and most home generators will develop direct current. The normal mains supply is *alternating current* (AC).

Direct firing

Given by Dodd as synonymous with open firing, i.e. firing without saggars.

Disappearing filament pyrometer

See *optical pyrometer*.

Dish

A shallow container which may be thrown, molded or built. The Concise Oxford Dictionary defines it as a 'flat-bottomed, usually oval or oblong vessel'. Both of these shapes can be developed from thrown dishes by cutting the base (see *oval shapes*) or by beating. Molded dishes benefit from good craftsmanship and a tidy finish. It is because the technique seems simple that those made by students and in schools are often poor.

For dishes made over, rather than in, a plaster or biscuit mold, see *hump mold*. For cutting circular molded dishes a wheel is needed. The mold is dropped into a cup-head or centered and fixed to the wheelhead. The clay slab is eased into or over it (hollow or hump mold) and roughly trimmed. The final cutting of the rim is done on the spinning wheel with a wooden spatula tool. Hold the tool with both hands, approach the surface of the clay slowly, and hold the tool firmly as it cuts into it. The method for non-circular molded dishes is shown in the figures under *pressed dishes*.

Andrew and Joanna Young make large dishes by throwing the rim or wall and luting it to a separately made base with a coil pressed into the join. By this method any plan (shape of dish) can be accommodated and the rim given crispness and character on square, oblong, or oval forms. For circular flat-bottomed dishes and plates, a coil can be attached to a thrown base and the rim formed from it on the wheel. A variation on the simple method of making a shallow rectangular dish shown at *former* is demonstrated in CR72; a flat wooden block is placed on a slab of clay and the whole reversed, the block underneath. Wooden edge pieces are then used to press the clay over the edge of the block. The whole is reversed again, the top surfaces of the edge pieces (2–3in wide) forming a wide rim. The clay is trimmed and the blocks removed as soon as it is stiff enough to stand its own weight (David Morris).

Molded dishes do not develop that parallel-plated structure in the clay fabric which gives thrown ware its strength and stability (see *clay, lamellar, plasticity*) and they are thus more liable to warp if not well supported during drying and firing. With the exception, perhaps, of flat-based pie dishes they are rarely suitable for stoneware firings. The method of making *cut corner dishes* is described under its heading. See also *oval dishes*. Slab and coil dishes are possible though perhaps less suitable for kitchen use.

Disintegration of glaze

See *devitrification*.

Disordered clays

Clays whose makeup has been subject to *substitution*. They have a fine particle size, high plasticity, and *green strength*, e.g. *ball clays* as opposed to 'ordered' *china clays*.

Dissociation

The reversible decomposition or alteration of the *molecules*

of a compound. In pottery dissociation is usually brought about by heat, the products recombining on cooling, e.g. the reoxidation of ferrous iron to ferric where it can come into contact with the oxygen in the air.

Distinguishing stain

An organic dye which will burn away on firing and is used to identify otherwise similarly colored bodies, glazes, etc. At Bullers Electrical Porcelain factory the bright pink and blue large-scale electrical porcelains were quite striking!

Distortion

See *deformation, clay memory, pyroplastic, warping*.

Division of a circle

The method of dividing the circumference of a bowl into two, four, or eight sections is obvious. There is a simple trick for making divisions of three or six. Set calipers to the radius (measure diameter and divide by two) and this length will mark off six divisions around the edge.

Five is more difficult, requiring a protractor. The easiest way with a pot is to encircle it with a strip of paper, remove the paper and divide its length by the appropriate number, marking the divisions with a pencil. Then replace the paper and transfer the marks to the pot.

Docking

See *lime-blowing*.

Dod box

See *wad mill*.

Dod handle

A strip or coil of clay can be extruded from a *dodbox* or *extruder* and formed into a handle. Dies are available, or can be cut, to give parallel grooves or other surface variations. It will lack the gradation in width of a pulled *handle* although it can be further worked on to produce a more subtle form.

Dog's teeth, dragon's teeth

Irregular tears in an extruded length of clay from the pug. Caused by friction against the mouth of the pug or the edge of a die. Clay which is too dry, short, or unevenly mixed is liable to this fault, but a badly cleaned pug mill is most often to blame.

Dolomite

A mineral $CaCO_3.MgCO_3$, 184. The double carbonate of calcium and magnesium.
Typical analysis: CaO 31%. MgO 20%. Loss (CO_2) 43%, minor impurities: silica 1.5%, with other bases and alumina 4.5%. The calcia content is sometimes greater than these figures suggest. The high 'loss' (LOI.) figure is, of course, due to the dispersal of the CO_2.

Dolomite is used mainly in stoneware glazes (temperatures above about 1175°C/2147°F). Although of worldwide occurrence it only became generally available to the craft potter in the 1960s but has enjoyed a considerable vogue since. A buff dolomite is mined in the UK but a finer white grade comes from Spain. Dodd mentions that 'because of the free lime present dolomite rapidly "perishes" in contact with the air'. There are other suitable sources of calcia but insoluble magnesia is less common. (See *talc*.)

Dolomite acts as a flux but, if used to replace whiting, it will raise the maturing temperature of a glaze. (See *magnesium*.) Average proportion in a glaze is 3–6% but up to 20% can be used for special effects. About 2% or so may be added to a porcelain body. The typical magnesia effect derived from the use of dolomite is a smooth, buttery surface. With higher concentrations and slower cooling, however, it tends to form crystals of calcium and magnesium silicates with a consequent matt surface.

Dominos

One of the many board games which can be made in ceramic, earthenware, stoneware, or porcelain. Lacking some of the possible variations of chess men dominos, and the board to play on, nevertheless present interesting design possibilities for potters.

Dosimeter

Georgies advertise a 'dosimeter' detection tube for air sampling of *carbon monoxide*.

Dot

A separating piece for *cranks*.

Dotting

Part of the attraction of the large slip dishes of the 17th and 18th century in England lies in the jewel-like dotting or spotting of a contrasting slip along the main trailed lines of the design. This is often overlooked and does not often occur on modern trailing. The decoration of pots and bowls, usually in porcelain with tiny dots of color to build up line and mass and often using the halo-like effect of copper, is practiced by Mary Rogers and others with original and delicate effect. Sometimes known as 'jeweling'.

A slip-trailed plate in the Toft style by Geoffrey and Olive Barfoot with extensive dotting.

Double calipers

An automatic method of measuring the inside and outside of a lid fitting, see *calipers*. Called a 'lid master' (Axner, Bailey, etc.).

Double eutectic

See *eutectic*.

Double glazing

See *glaze-over-glaze*.

Dough mixers

These machines, until recently used in small bakeries, have found a new lease of life in craft potteries for mixing powdered clay and bodies with water into a plastic state, thus bypassing the *blunger*, drier, etc.

Large mixers can deal with 330lb/150kg of dry powder and water in 30 minutes; smaller ones 220lb/100kg an hour. There are two types: the one illustrated in which the arm moves forward, down and up, turning and mashing

A large dough mixer from an old bakery used to ease the labor of mixing clays and water into a condition suitable for pugging or wedging. The revolving pronged arm alternately turns and mashes the mixture. About 3cwt/150kg/330lb can be prepared in 30 minutes from dry clay (here being emptied into it by Mick Casson) and water.

the mixture; and the revolving arm type. The former needs some attention but the latter can be quite automatic in its action.

Downdraft kiln

A kiln in which the hot gases from the fireboxes rise first to the roof and are then drawn down through the setting and out into the chimney through flues in the kiln floor. The heat is better distributed and more efficiently used than in an *updraft kiln*. The hot gases can be subsequently channelled under a brick floor for drying clay or pots. Rhodes K shows several types of downdraft kilns, while Cardew discusses the general principles. A good chimney is needed to exert the necessary 'pull' which forces the heat downwards against its inclination. A starting-fan or small chimney fire may be used to create the initial draft. A different sort of 'down draft' for use in electric kilns is illustrated at *ventilation*.

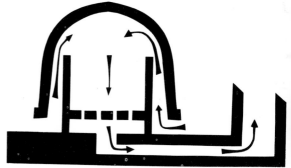

A downdraft kiln with more than one firemouth.

Climbing kilns and the Western two or three *chambered kilns* utilize a diagonal downdraft.

Draft

The upward movement of hot gases as a result of their expansion, and their replacement by further air from the atmosphere. This process is controlled in a fuel-burning kiln by the concentrated rising column in the chimney, the replacement air being drawn through the firebox or through secondary air vents. A slide or check put across the *chimney*, or a vent in the *chimney* (withdrawal of a brick) will both decrease draft.

Forced-draft may be introduced either by the use of a fan to speed the exit of gas in the chimney, or by pumping compressed air or gas into the kiln at the firemouth.

Draft is dependent on the diameter and height of the chimney and on the sizes of inlet and outlet apertures relative to the *expansion of gas*. (See also Cardew.)

Drainoil

Dennis Parks deals extensively with the use of waste oil for firing. The main disadvantage (apart from the smell and mess of dealing with it and removing any unwanted solids) is the high flashpoint which is around 245°C/473°F, against 40°C/104°F for kerosene. An efficient starter fuel such as propane or wood is therefore essential. On the other hand the fuel is obtainable without charge and has a high heat value per gallon. (See *Btu*, and *fuels*.) Good kiln design and efficient burning can minimize the smoke produced though this can be considerable and is now frowned upon. Such kilns should, therefore, be sited in open country.

Parks gives a number of suggestions for burners: both *drip-feed* (diagram), and pressure types. He reverts to diesel during reduction. Oil/water mixtures have also been used.

Drape mold

An American term for a mold or former over which a slab of clay is pressed or 'draped'. (See *hump molds, formers*.)

Drawing a kiln

Unpacking a kiln.

Draw trial

A test piece withdrawn from the kiln during firing. Only practical with a large spyhole or when a brick can easily be withdrawn. *Buller's rings*, glazed rings or small pots can be quickly cooled and inspected. They will show shrinkage and the degree to which the glaze has melted, but color and other characteristics will be falsified to some extent by the rapid cooling. (See also *glaze melt indicator*.)

Dresden green

A green pigment — 24% cobalt oxide, 52% chrome, 24% zinc oxide (Dodd).

Drip-feed, oil

A simple type of burner in which the oil is dripped onto a heated metal plate or plates. The heat volatilizes the oil, which will then ignite. An ingenious horizontal box burner is illustrated in Rhodes K. There must be some method of supplying initial heat to the pan to start the process. This could be by the use of a more volatile material such as paraffin (kerosene), or with a gas jet (perhaps *bottled gas*). Cotton waste to soak up oil and act as a wick has also been suggested. An oil and water mixture, dripped simultaneously from separate jets, has been found to be more efficient than oil alone. The plate must be protected from too direct an inrush of cold air. It has a relatively short life, but the whole burner is so simple that this is no great drawback. An attractive looking design using a small coke fire to heat the drip pan, and utilizing a reverbatory design, was

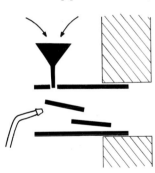

An oil-drip pan based on a design in Rhodes K. Oil and water are dripped onto it from above. A removable gas jet is shown which can heat the plates in order to start the process. Oil will burn only as a vapor.

published in PQ7 by John Dan.

The firing is liable to be smoky and, with today's sensitivity to the emission of smoke and gases, it is advisable to be as efficient as possible in the burning of all fuels. They have other limitations and are not suitable for large kilns. On the other hand crude or sump oil can be used for cheapness.

Drilling

See *pierced decoration*.

Drums

In CR123 Erik Mandaville discusses and illustrates a variety of percussion instruments. They are difficult to 'tune'. Most of them have basic deep bowl structures onto which fabric is stretched for the normal type of drum, but also as bars set over one or more hollow forms or 'resonating chambers' which are played like a xylophone with small soft-tipped mallets.

Dry glazes

Matt or 'dry' glazes are very useful for slab and other sculptural ceramics. Often these are ash stoneware glazes and often contain appreciable percentages of barium. Wood ash mixed with china clay (65 ash — 35 china clay) will usually give rather dry-surfaced yellow to orange sintered glaze which can be used decoratively on slab pots and other handbuilt ceramics, varying in effect with differences of thickness. Pour thinly with overlaps or sponge on. A wide-ranging recipe from Janet de Boos (New Zealand) was given in CR154 which can be fired from 980–1150°C/ 1796–2102°F: barium carbonate 60, china clay 25, nepheline syenite 20, alkaline frit 5, copper carbonate 6, with similar advice to apply thinly and double pour to get color variations.

Another typical recipe from Lesley McShea (CR145) is: barium carbonate 34, nepheline syenite 50, china clay 16. (See also *matt glazes*.)

Dry strength

Clays vary greatly in their dry strength. A porcelain body will be very weak, a *secondary clay* may be nearly as hard as *biscuit*. Dry strength is probably increased by a well-graded particle size from medium to very fine, allowing a close 'pack'. It is associated with plasticity. Ball clays have a high dry strength, partly due to their fine grain, but also to the lignin humus (organic wood tissue) content of 'black' ball clays. Coarser-grained bodies such as porcelain will be easily shattered.

The form of a pot and the technique used in making it will have some effect on its dry strength. A bottle or other well-rounded thrown shape has greater resistance to knocks and stresses than, for instance, a slab trough or a molded dish.

Resinous and fibrous bodies have been developed to obviate the firing of clay models in schools, e.g. *Newclay*. They can be useful in the wider field of modeling or hand-building for dry strength, and can be thrown, though there is little advantage in the latter case.

Drying of clay and glaze

Drying from slip to plastic state is dealt with under *dewatering*.

When plastic clay dries, water evaporates from the surface which becomes porous, further moisture being drawn by capillary action from the body of the clay. This action is sufficient to bring a thin-walled piece of pottery into balance with the humidity of the surrounding air. Further evaporation requires artificial heat or a drier atmosphere, and is assisted by the movement of air. The dryness of the air explains why clay may dry more rapidly on a cold night when most of the water in the air has been precipitated than on a humid day in summer.

Drying is accompanied by shrinkage. A thick wall of close-texture clay will tend to enclose a core of moisture which will have difficulty in getting away. This slows down the capillary effect and is the reason why a pot seems to stay *leather-hard* for quite a time and then change color quite quickly. The inclusion of grog or other coarse-grained material is necessary to maintain open pores in thick pots or models.

Shrinkage is caused by the particles of clay packing closer together as the layers of water between them disappear; the greatest shrinkage is therefore from plastic to leather-hard. At leather-hard the lubrication between particles is poor and they can be moved relative to one another only by careful beating. When dry this lubrication is nil. Rapid drying is not dangerous in itself, but any unevenness in the drying will cause one part of a pot to shrink, putting the fabric into tension which can be relieved only by warping or cracking.

The precise state of dryness is not easy to establish. As mentioned above, *ambient* air humidity will control natural drying. A pot, even though thoroughly dried over heat, will reabsorb moisture if left long before firing. There are various ways of testing for dryness: David Leach places the rim or other surface of a warm pot against a pane of glass; any steam will soon be precipitated onto the glass. A thick-walled piece may be too hot to touch and yet still show steam if a piece of glass or plastic is held over the mouth of the pot.

Apart from the water mixed with the clay, which is driven off at 100°C/212°F, there remains the more stubborn *adsorbed* water which may need 200°C/392°F to disperse fully. (See *adsorbed water, water-smoke*.)

The technique of *wet-firing* (described in CR1) seems to contradict these statements, but other factors are at work here (e.g. the cooling effect of very rapid evaporation) and the system is hedged about with special provisions.

Not only the clay but also glazes, especially *soft glazes* although it is equally recommended for stonewares, should be fully dried **before** packing in an electric kiln for firing, in order to avoid blistering and other faults.

Drying shrinkage

The shrinkage of a clay or body from plastic to dry is usually expressed as a linear percentage. Dodd quotes 6–10% for china clay; 9–12% for ball clay. Most of this occurs up to the leather-hard stage. Drying shrinkage is one indication of the value of a clay sample (see *clay tests*). It is useful to work out the factor for your particular clay body; it will allow you to calculate the size of a lid, for instance, which is needed for a dried pot.

The equation is $\dfrac{X \times 100}{Y \quad 1}$

where X is the percentage shrinkage of your test-piece and Y is the dry length of the test piece.

Example:

$$\frac{15 \ (\% \ \text{shrinkage})}{85 \ (\text{dry length})} \times \frac{100}{1} = 17\%$$

The lid, therefore, needs to be 17% larger than the dried pot. For replacement lids of fired pots the calculations are more difficult but could still be based on a wet clay to fired ceramic test strip, (though there are other factors involved here so don't be too hopeful!). Hamer (PDMT) has an extensive analysis of the science and mechanics of drying. (See also *shrinkage*.)

Dunting

The cracking of pottery in the kiln due to drafts of cold air striking it when firing or cooling, causing one area to contract more than the rest. *Free quartz* will increase the risk of dunting at dull red heat, and *cristobalite* at lower temperatures. A more rapid rate of cooling from top temperature to about 1100°C/2012°F will lessen the chances of this happening by keeping the silica in flux. A more vitrified body:

one containing more fluxes or fired to greater maturity will lessen the chances of dunting from silica *inversions*.

Thermal shock can cause cracking during the use of a piece after firing. A poor glaze fit, especially one in excessive compression, can crack a piece during firing or afterwards; and at the other extreme high shrinkage of thick glaze can also tear a pot apart as sometimes happens when *melted glass* is used decoratively. Tensions can be set up during uneven drying of the clay, or even before that through excessive moisture or insufficient working on the base of a pot; too great a discrepancy between the thicknesses of various parts of the piece; or, of course, by a blow or pressure. Variations in cooling between pot and kiln shelf can cause dunting of the base wall; large flat dishes or tall pots especially should be raised on rings, clay wads, or setters. Rapid all-over cooling will not necessarily cause dunting (if it did, there would be no raku). *Sawdust firing* is very prone to severe dunting if not protected from draft. Ray Finch once-fires his large plates to minimize dunting, while others set large flat plates on clay wads so that they will not be affected by the different cooling rate of the kiln shelf. (See also *cooling, cracking, shattering.*)

Dust

All excessive dust from pottery activities is a danger; there is no way out once inorganic materials settle in your lungs. The cheapest way to lay dust is to sprinkle water on it. There are also *sweeping compounds*. In particular danger are potters who habitually abrade dry clay or biscuit, as are those who regularly use sprays for glazing. A light mask, costing very little, will help; a full respirator even more, though these are cumbersome and necessary only when spraying or otherwise coming into contact with very dusty, vaporous, or hazardous materials. One of the major 'villains' is free crystalline silica — (flint, quartz, etc.). See *poisonous materials* for specific dangerous minerals.

In CR171 Clive Davies suggests the use of a *vacuum cleaner* under cover outside the studio with a long extended hose through the wall to the inside. Extra fine dust which may permeate the bag is blown away and the noise level reduced.

Duster, flat duster

An unlikely name, used in the industry for a soft flat brush, $^1/_4$–1in/6–25mm wide, for laying on background color.

Earth leakage circuit breaker

See *ELCB.*

Earthenware

The dictionary definition is 'vessels of baked clay'; in general usage it indicates pottery ware with a porous body which may or may not be covered with glaze. The Brussels Nomenclature agrees with this definition but excludes 'pottery made from common clay' — we are not told what this is to be called! The bulk of all ceramics has been earthenware, ranging from the soft, red 'earthen platter' from Portugal to the 1200°C/2192°F fine-grained 'Queen's ware' of Wedgwood, and including maiolica, delft, faience, and most slipwares. Many of the Near Eastern pots are in an anomalous position – see *frit body* – as is *soft paste.*

The same clay body can sometimes be used to produce earthenware or stoneware, according to whether it has been taken to vitrification temperature or not, but, in general, mixtures of various clays, and sometimes other minerals, are blended specifically for a given range of firing temperatures. The dividing line between earthenware and stoneware is normally in the region of 1200°C/2192°F but the craft potter's earthenware is rarely taken above 1150°C/2102°F and more often 50°C/122°F or so below this figure. Because of its innate porosity the body of earthenware is usually entirely covered with glaze unless the porosity is utilized for keeping water cool or other particular purposes (see also *flameproof ware*).

Earthenware glaze

Also known as 'soft' glazes. Broadly speaking, they are those glazes which mature below 1150°C/2102°F and are used to cover a porous body. The typical earthenware glaze is shiny and smooth; it can be brilliant and transparent, or white and fully opaque, the latter providing a background for bright clear colors. Its qualities have been exploited through the ages giving us splendid slipwares, painted tin glazes, lusters, intense turquoise colors, raku, underglaze decoration, and enamels, from all parts of the world.

The formulas for earthenware glazes differ from those of stoneware and porcelain mainly in their choice of bases, and in the ratio of base to silica. A soft glaze can be prepared with soda as the only flux (the basis of Egyptian turquoise), but these are unstable, difficult to handle, and they always craze. More commonly, lead oxide has been used as the sole or major base. This type is now called into question (see *soluble lead*), but a well-balanced and adequately fired lead glaze will be safe for the majority of tableware purposes. Lead gives a richness of quality which other fluxes cannot imitate. If a soft glaze does not contain lead oxide in significant amounts (at least 0.5 equivalents in the RO group) then it will need to contain boric oxide. This is generally added in the form of borax which is a soluble material and requires *fritting*. (See also *colemanite*.)

Soda, potash and lime are the usual secondary fluxes, with zinc oxide, lithia, strontia and magnesia sometimes playing a minor role. Boric oxide, though technically an acid and a *glass former*, nevertheless lowers the melting point of a glaze and to this extent can be thought of as a fluxing agent. Lead and boron are used in the form of silica frits, the first because of its toxic nature; the second because it is soluble in water. Recipes are legion and we cannot explore them in detail, several are quoted in Rhodes, Billington, and a host of other manuals. It is more important to have some understanding of the principles, and to be able to use the *Seger formula*.

The RO/RO₂ ratio of the majority of soft glazes is between 1:2 and 1:3. The R₂O₃/RO₂ ratio is between 1:8 and 1:12. (R stands for any appropriate element.) A typical formula might therefore read:

$$1 \text{ RO. } 0.25 \text{ Al}_2\text{O}_3. \text{ } 2.5 \text{ SiO}_2$$ where the RO group includes at least 0.5 PbO.

If lead is absent, then boric oxide must comprise about 0.2 of the total RO₂ group (a little confusing as boric oxide is both a strong flux and chemically an acid). (See *base*, *formula into recipe*, *glaze*, and under all the glaze oxides.) A variety of bases will help to give a more transparent and fully matured glaze.

The choice of bases will also influence the color reaction of any *pigment oxides*. An increase in the alumina content will take the shine from the surface, opacifying agents will tend to harden and so raise the firing temperature; manganese will act as a flux. Oxides, minerals and frits can be combined in one batch — a mixture is, in fact, advisable. It makes the physical process of glazing easier. Earthenware glaze is generally applied as a somewhat thinner coating than are the stonewares; this is especially true if frits are used. A soaking fire of about 20 minutes will improve the quality of soft glazes and also the *glaze-body fit*. (See also *crazing*, *glazing*.)

Easy-fire

Firing terminated below the maturing temperature of a body. Soft biscuit.

Efflorescence on clay

A white surface scum which forms during firing, or occurs later, usually on red clays. It cannot be easily removed, even with abrasives. It is caused by soluble salts, mainly calcium, but occasionally other bases, sulfur, or chlorine, migrating to the surface during drying as crystals, and being crushed in handling (the efflorescence is often recognizable as fingerprints). Modeling or any pottery subject to a lot of handling is especially prone. The addition of 1–2% of barium carbonate to the body will help; Billington mentions a teaspoonful to a pint of red clay slip. In CR123 Bo Ratcliffe finds (in connection with Egyptian paste) that the efflorescence may continue after firing (as happens in some bricks) which she prevents by steeping the raw paste in vinegar for 24 hours (a smelly remedy!). See *Egyptian paste* for deliberate efflorescence and also at *lime blowing*.

Egote

Japanese name for a throwing stick.

Three Japanese egote or throwing sticks. They are of wood with one rounded or beveled edge.

Egyptian paste

The body of the original Egyptian turquoise pieces (almost certainly the first glazed ceramics) is reputed to be about 90% quartz with some soda. The glaze has been given as 75% silica, 20% alkalis and calcium, 1.8% copper oxide, by analysis. The body is very open and therefore short. Glaze was either 'migratory' (see below) or applied in the usual way and was derived from natron, an indigenous copper/alkali ore.

An approximation in modern materials may be made as a paste or body from which soluble glaze materials will 'migrate' or effloresce onto the surface during drying. It follows that the drying should be slow and that the piece should be handled as little as possible. Place it on stilts ready for the kiln as soon as it is completed. Firing temperature 950–990°C/1742–1814°F.

No glaze is applied to the modern style of Egyptian paste (although as mentioned above, the ware was often glaze dipped in early times).

The usual coloring material is copper carbonate which gives the characteristic turquoise, but other carbonates can be used for other colors: cobalt, manganese, antimony, and compounds of chromium and uranium. It has been noted that copper oxide can give a darker and greener color than the carbonate.

Typical recipes:

A measure recipe (Behrens CM):-

Flint or quartz	16 parts by volume (spoonsful)
Bentonite	4 parts
Sodium bicarbonate	2 parts
Copper carbonate	$\frac{1}{2}$ part

By percentage weights:

Feldspar	35	Flint	35
China clay	12	Bentonite	2
Sodium bicarbonate	6	Sodium carbonate	6
Copper carbonate	2–3		

A more plastic version given in CM16/2:

Ball clay	25	Nepheline syenite	25
Frit ferro 3134	15	Flint	20
Fine sand	5	Anhydrous (calcined) borax	3
Soda ash	4	Bentonite	3
Copper carbonate	2–3		

Dextrin or other *siccative* can be added for dry strength. Also note that copper carbonate is toxic. Variations may be made in the feldspar/flint ratio between 20% and 40%; some ball clay can replace china clay. Up to 5% of whiting is sometimes recommended, while borax can be used to supply soda. Soluble varieties of the coloring oxide, e.g. copper chloride, may help.

More recipes are given in Fournier PT, Rhodes CGP, and others.

The material has little plasticity when moist, and is friable when dry. It is generally restricted to jewelry and other small pieces, although the Ancient Egyptians achieved some very large objects. Bo Ratcliffe (CR123) found that the salts continued to migrate to the surface of her fired beads which she cured by soaking them in vinegar for a couple of days, rinsing, and airing them until the smell of vinegar had disappeared. Sylvia Hyman (CR39) smokes beads raku-fashion to vary the color and adds copper luster to some.

Ejector head

A wheel head in the form of a shallow dish, the base of which can be raised to eject a plaster or wooden throwing-bat. Useful for large pots or for *repetition throwing*. (See also *wheel bats*.) When casting plaster bats in ejector heads the inner surface must be lightly wiped over with Vaseline, petroleum jelly or similar grease.

A pot on a plaster bat being lifted from an ejector head by upward pressure on the metal ring underneath.

Elasticity

Strictly the word implies the resumption by a material to its original shape and size when forces acting on it are removed. In pottery it is used more loosely to suggest the ability of materials to withstand stress and in this sense is a valuable quality. It is said that lead glazes are more 'elastic' than others.

ELCB

An acronym for Earth Leakage Circuit Breaker; a type of electric *trip switch* which automatically isolates the demand from the supply if a fault occurs. It is usually fitted between the meter and the fused switch box, and is activated by any slight leak between line and earth. It can be manually reset by pushing the switch button upwards but if it fails to hold then the fault must be traced and corrected. It may sometimes 'trip' off during a thunderstorm and can even be affected by a neighbor's electrical fault if exterior leads to earth are not far enough apart.

A type of tripswitch is now often attached to individual pieces of equipment which, like the ELCB, both protects the user from electric shock and lessens the chance of having to perform the often tedious business of repairing fuses.

Electric kiln

A pottery kiln heated by *resistance wire* or rods. It is, fundamentally, a simple piece of equipment. No provision need be made for the disposal of gases (chimney), for ash waste, or for vast supplies of air. All that has been done at the power-station, and energy is derived at 'second hand'. Like other 'canned' products it lacks 'incidentals', and variety must be attained through the ingenuity of the potter.

The kiln can be of any type: front loader; *top loader*, *top-hat*, etc. The hexagonal or circular top loader (not the easiest shape to pack pot shapes into) is popular in America and increasingly in Great Britain. There are models which consist of horizontal sections which can be added or subtracted according to the amount of pieces to be fired. The advantage of the electric kiln is ease of construction and compactness (narrow walls, small stress). The development of *ceramic fiber* has revolutionized the building of small kilns of all types.

Whatever its shape the electric kiln is fundamentally a box, constructed of insulating material, and housing a length of resistance wire. The heat is 'radiant', and this limits its size to about 24cu ft (slightly less than 1cu m). The proportions of the box will affect its efficiency (see *heat loss*). Insulation is of prime importance. A comparatively high initial outlay will soon be repaid in lower fuel bills. (See *insulation of heat.*) The inner brickwork must be very refractory and the element slots must be of an iron-free ceramic. The slots can be cut from HT insulating bricks (from Whitfield Ceramics UK and PSH, Canada) or they can be cast as larger units from alumina cements. The outer insulation may be of lower heat resistance bricks or slabs (around 850°C/1562°F for stoneware firing), or of ceramic fiber. The casing should be of *Asbestolux* or similar (not a cement bonded material), or sheet metal (though beware electrical connections when using metal). The skeleton structure is of angle iron or a similar material (Dexion, etc.).

The fact that an electric kiln has no chimney means that sulfurous and other gases liberated by some clays pollute the atmosphere of the pottery. Ventilation of the kiln room is essential. Experiments in venting the actual kiln atmosphere through an outside wall have, in the past, seriously retarded the temperature rise rate but there are systems today which draw air and gases down through the pack and expel them through a duct at the base and out into the open air (though in my experience the top is rarely the hottest area). This is especially true of top loaders. The more obvious venting through the top is also available. Both methods are controllable and are reputed to obviate

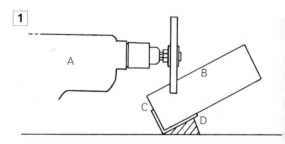

1 A system of cutting slots with a grinding wheel developed by Mike Harris. The method produces considerable dust and so a mask is essential.

2 The ideal shape for an element slot.

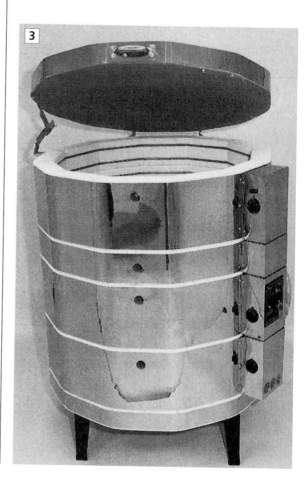

3 (Right) A typical commercial top-loading kiln. Not so easy to pack as a rectangular plan but perhaps more evenly heated.

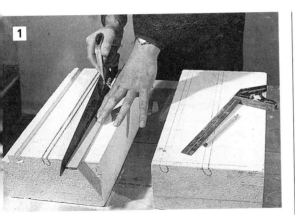

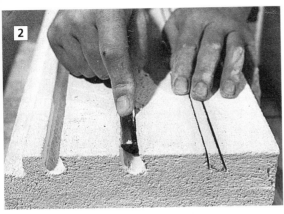

Cutting slots in insulating brick.

1 The slots are marked and sawn, using a hard fine-toothed saw with replaceable blades. A sideways pressure on the saw blade at the completion of the cut will usually snap the section but a third central cut may be necessary.

2–4 The grooves are routed out by the use of a turning tool as shown or with a short length of wound element wire.

heat loss and to produce 'brighter glaze firings' (Skutt Kilns). The weight of a kiln should also be considered when planning an installation; at one time the weight could be up to one hundredweight for every kilowatt in smaller kilns but modern materials have drastically reduced this figure. For detailed instructions on building kilns see Fournier EKP. (See also *electric wiring to kiln, element, element winding, fail-safe, Kanthal, silicon carbide, top-loading kiln, reduction in electric kilns, ventilation*, etc.)

Electric wiring to kiln

Apart from the computations involved in the resistance wiring of a kiln, the current must be conducted to it. The wire used for this purpose must be able to take the full load for long periods without getting hot. The same rules hold as for resistance wire: less resistance in thicker, shorter wires; more in longer or thinner ones. Short runs between supply and kiln are therefore preferable where possible.

A composite cable holding the line (live), neutral and earth wires can be used to conduct single-phase current, but three phases and neutral are carried on wires which are then housed separately in protective metal or plastic tubes or 'conduits'.

Switch gear, etc. must all be rated at or above the load your kiln will need. Three-phase switches are rated at amperes per phase, e.g. a 30 amp fused switch will carry a total of 30 x 3 = 90 amps.

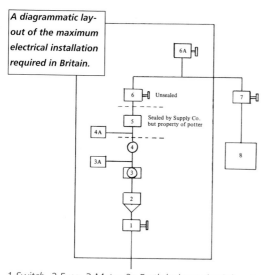

A diagrammatic layout of the maximum electrical installation required in Britain.

1 Switch. 2 Fuse. 3 Meter. 3a Earth leakage circuit breaker (ELCB). 4 Time switch clock. 4a Contactor isolating switch. 5 Contactor. 6 Fused switch. 6a Change-over switch.
7 Kiln isolating switch. 8 Kiln Numbers 1, 3a, 4, and 5 are at the discretion of the Supply Company and depend on the conditions of supply, e.g. cheap rate arrangements. 6a — change-over switches allow two or more kilns to be connected to one system of supply, firing alternately.

A two-way change-over switch with cover removed. This piece of equipment allows two kilns to be powered alternately from one system of supply. In the photograph the blades are standing out horizontally and the power is off. With the handle pressed downwards the blades connect three circuits; when pressed upwards three different circuits.

A USA plug socket guide in amperes is shown at *NEMA*.
The following is a guide to the wire gauges for conducting various loads. The heavier wires are stranded. The first figure denotes the number of strands, the second the diameter of each strand in millimeters. The table is for pvc insulated cables.

Size	Nominal cross-section area in mm²	Current rating (amps) In conduit	On surface
1/1.13	1.0	11	13
1/1.38	1.5	13	16
1/1.78	2.5	18	23
7/0.85	4.0	24	30
7/1.04	6.0	31	38
7/1.35	10.0	42	51
7/1.70	16.0	56	68

Electrical bond

The electrical charge which binds atoms into molecules (see *atomic theory, lattice, network*).

Electrical insulation

See *insulation, electric*.

Electrical porcelain

A very hard 'proto'-porcelain with high *dielectric* strength but little or no *translucency*, from which electrical insulators, switches, etc. are made.
A recipe quoted is similar to that for industrial earthenware, but fired to vitrification: ball clay 28: china clay 22: quartz 25: feldspar 25. (See also *porcelain*.)

Electrical symbol

The principle shorthand symbols used in electrical computations are:
1 Electromotive force E, measured in volts, V.
2 Current I, measured in amperes, A.
3 Power P, measured in watts, W.
4 Resistance R, measured in ohms, Ω.
(See at *electricity* for further information, and at *ampere, ohm, volt, watt*.)

Electricity

Electricity is a form of energy generated by the movements of electrons. The concept of electrical charge is the basis of *atomic science*, and enters into all chemical changes.

The term is commonly applied to the energy supplied as electric current either through metal cables from a generating-station or across the terminals of a battery. If a conducting material is placed across the terminals of an electric supply between that marked L, (which popularly is thought to stand for 'live' but actually stands for 'line'), and neutral (N), current will flow. It will flow to an excessive and dangerous degree if there is nothing to stop it, a state known as a *short circuit*. However all materials exhibit a greater or lesser *resistance* to this flow, and it is in overcoming resistance that electrical energy is converted into heat.

The heat produced is proportional to the square of the current flowing. Where resistance is total no current flows, and the material is known as an insulator; where current flows with negligible resistance the material is a conductor. Many materials, especially in the presence of water, fall between these extremes. Even the best conductors will get hot and eventually melt if too much current is passed through them. A conducting wire must therefore be stout enough to withstand the current it is expected to pass. As explained below, the thicker the wire the less resistance it will exert. *Kiln element* wire has a controlled resistance in-built to produce heat according to certain equations.

Electricity is supplied at a given 'pressure' (to use an understandable but not quite accurate term) called the *voltage*; the amount of current is measured in *amperes*; the total power in *watts*. The resistance mentioned above is calculated in units called *ohms*. These four factors — voltage, symbol E (electromotive force) is measured in Volts (V); current, symbol I, is measured in Amperes (A); power, P, is measured in Watts (W); and resistance R is measured in Ohms (Ω), are all interdependent. It is not necessary to understand the exact nature of these units to use them in simple electrical calculations.

Basic arithmetic:
If you have figures for any two unit values it is easy to arrive at a third by means of simple equations:

$$E = I \times R \quad \text{or} \quad \frac{P}{I} \quad \text{or} \quad \text{the square root of } P \times R$$

$$E = \frac{P}{E} \quad \text{or} \quad \frac{E}{R} \quad \text{or} \quad \text{the square root of } \frac{P}{R}$$

$$R = \frac{E}{I} \quad \text{or} \quad \frac{E^2}{P} \quad \text{or} \quad \frac{P}{I^2}$$

$$P = E \times I \quad \text{or} \quad \frac{E^2}{R} \quad \text{or} \quad I^2 \times R$$

To turn the equations into a specific example: If our supply is at 240 volts (but see at *volt* for changes in Great Britain from 1995) and we want to design a 10,000 watt (10 kilowatts or kWs) kiln then we need to pass:

$$\frac{10,000}{240} = 41.6 \text{ amperes of current}$$

If the kiln is wired in a single circuit, the resistance of the total wire (all the elements in series) will be:

$$\frac{240}{41.6} = 5.76 \text{ ohms}$$

If it is to be wired in two circuits then each must pass:

$$\frac{41.6}{2} = 20.8 \text{ amperes}$$

and the resistance in each circuit should be

$$\frac{240}{20.8} = 11.53 \text{ ohms}$$

There are two laws concerning resistance in a wire which have, in fact, some parallel with the way water flows through a pipe. The first is that the thicker the wire (the greater the cross-sectional area) the less resistance it will offer and the greater amount of current will flow; and the second law states that the longer the wire the more resistance it will offer, and this will reduce the current which will flow. Thus a long thin wire will pass less current than a short thick one of the same type. These considerations must be borne in mind when conducting current to a kiln as well as in the kiln itself. (See under *element, electric kiln, electric wiring to kiln*.)

The third connection which you will find on all appliances is the E (earth) terminal. This is a safety measure. Normally the flow of current will be through the apparatus connected between live and neutral and will be under control. If, however, a 'live' conductor accidentally comes into contact with another conductor not in the circuit, current will start to flow through it and it will become 'live'. A direct line to the ground, especially under damp conditions, will conduct a very high current, heating up rapidly in the process. This sudden surge can cause electric shock (burning) in human beings, or fire in a building. The earth terminal is literally what it says it is — a connection direct to the ground which will help to siphon off current which has strayed out of the circuit, and out of control. A long continuation of the flow is prevented by the insertion of a weak link in every circuit (the fuse) which will melt and break the line before much damage is done. An *ELCB* will fulfill a similar function. (See also *heat fuse*.)

Electrolyte

A compound which, when dissolved in water, partially *dissociates* into *ions* (electrically charged atoms and molecules). Added to clay slips to control flow properties (Dodd). Electrolytes in common use in ceramics are sodium silicate, soda ash and sodium tannate. (See *deflocculation.*)

Electron

An elementary particle or basic unit constituent of an atom. Electrons make up the outer 'shells' and determine *valency.* An electron bears a 'negative' electrical charge. They can be freed from their atomic orbits and taken up by other atoms which then become electrically unbalanced—a negative ion. The atom which 'loses' an electron becomes positively charged.

Atoms are most stable when their outer shells contain two or eight electrons. To achieve this state, sharing and transfers occur between atoms of elements forming 'bonds' and building up molecules and networks — i.e. crystals and all the materials of the physical world. (See also *atomic theory, valency, ion, lattice,* etc.)

The number of electrons in the successive orbits of 'shells' of atoms in the commonly used pottery elements:

Element		1st	2nd	3rd	4th	5th	6th	7th
Hydrogen	H	1						
Lithium	Li	2	1					
Boron	B	2	3					
Carbon	C	2	4					
Oxygen	O	2	6					
Flourine	F	2	7					
Sodium	Na	2	8	1				
Magnesium	Mg	2	8	2				
Aluminum	Al	2	8	3				
Silicon	Si	2	8	3				
Phosphorus	P	2	8	5				
Potassium	K	2	8	8	1			
Calcium	Ca	2	8	8	2			
Titanium	Ti	2	8	10	2			
Chromium	Cr	2	8	13	1			
Manganese	Mn	2	8	13	2			
Iron	Fe	2	8	14	2			
Cobalt	Co	2	8	15	2			
Nickel	Ni	2	8	16	2			
Copper	Cu	2	8	18	1			
Zinc	Zn	2	8	18	2			
Selenium	Se	2	8	18	6			
Zirconium	Zr	2	8	18	10	2		
Cadmium	Cd	2	8	18	18	2		
Tin	Sn	2	8	18	18	4		
Barium	Ba	2	8	18	18	8	2	
Praseodymium	Pr	2	8	18	21	8	2	
Lead	Pb	2	8	18	32	18	4	
Uranium	U	2	8	18	32	21	9	2

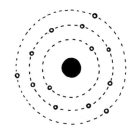

An aluminum atom, showing 'orbits' of 2, 8, and 3 electrons round a nucleus which consists of a similar number, i.e. 13 protons and 13 neutrons.

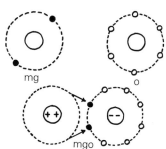

Electrovalent bonding of magnesium with 2 electrons in its outer shell and oxygen with 6. The oxygen makes up an orbit of 8 by annexing 2 from magnesium thus becoming a negatively charged ion, known as an O - - ion. The magnesium loses the whole of its outer (third) shell leaving a complete second shell of 8 electrons. The loss leaves two unbalanced positive protons and it becomes a Mg ++ion.

Electrovalent

Bonds formed between atoms through the transfer of electrons, forming positive and negative *ions.* (See *atomic theory, bond, valency.*)

Element, chemical

'A substance which, so far as we know, contains only one kind of matter' (Mellor). There are about one hundred elements and all creation is built up from these simple materials.

Elements are denoted by internationally agreed symbols. These may correspond to the English name or may be derived from the Latin, e.g. tin from stannum. Elements seldom exist alone in nature, but are found as compounds of two or more. Those elements of specific interest to potters are listed with their symbol and atomic weight under their English name in the entry for *atomic weight.* Here they re listed alphabetically according to their symbol. This will be a convenient reference when deciphering formulas.

Al	Alumina	Mg	Magnesium
Ag	Silver (argentum)	Mn	Manganese
B	Boron	Na	Sodium (natrum)
Ba	Barium	Ni	Nickel
Bi	Bismuth	O	Oxygen
C	Carbon	P	Phosphorus
Ca	Calcium	Pr	Praseodymium
Cd	Cadmium	S	Sulfur
Cl	Chlorine	Sb	Stibium
Co	Cobalt	Se	Selenium
Cr	Chromium	Sn	Tin (stannum)
Cu	Copper (cuprum)	Sr	Strontium
F	Fluorine	Ti	Titanium
Fe	Iron (ferrum)	U	Uranium
Ge	Germanium	V	Vanadium
H	Hydrogen	Zn	Zinc
K	Potassium (kalium)	Zr	Zirconium
Li	Lithium		

Element, *electric kiln*

A convenient section of a *circuit* which can be housed in an electric kiln, sometimes in a single slot, but often in two slots when it is known as a 'hairpin'. Fitting into more than two slots presents physical problems but is possible. The elements which go to make up one circuit are connected one to the other on the outside of the kiln wall (properly and fully shielded, of course) by *line taps* and heat-resistant covered wire, or by other means (solid brass connectors are sometimes used). An element is, therefore, a suitable length of wire wound into a spiral, with a 'tail' or connecting length at each end long enough to go right through the kiln wall. Occasionally an entire circuit is wound as a single element (as in circular kilns) but very long or multi-length elements are difficult to manipulate with wire thicker than 15 swg (1.8mm).

Note. swg stands for 'standard wire gauge', the wire thickness.

The following sample calculations for circuit lengths should be read in conjunction with the information given at *electricity*.

The wiring for a kiln is first broken down into suitable circuits. A convenient maximum load is around 5 kilowatts per circuit. Each circuit is then considered separately in calculating the length of wire needed. There are factors limiting the rating (wattage) of a circuit. If too much current is passed through too short or too thin a wire, the wire will be unable to disperse the heat produced and will burn out.

Nichrome wire is suitable only for low temperature kilns. *Kanthal* or a similar wire is needed for regular firings above 1000°C/1832°F. Each gauge or thickness of wire is given a rating of so many ohms of resistance per foot or meter length. It is a simple matter to divide the total ohms required by this figure to arrive at the length of a circuit. The gauge recommended for stoneware is 13 swg or thicker. (See *Kanthal*.) The ohm rating (for Kanthal A1) is roughly 0.1 per ft/0.33 per m. For instance the wire needed for a 5 kilowatt circuit on a 240 volt supply is therefore:

$$\frac{5000}{240} = 20.8 \text{ amperes}$$

$$\frac{240}{20.8} = 11.5 \text{ ohms}$$

$$\frac{11.5}{0.1} = 115 \text{ feet of 13 swg A1 Kanthal}$$

or

$$\frac{11.5}{0.332} = 34.6 \text{ meters}$$

Replacing the above with symbols so that the equations become general:

$$\frac{W}{E} = A$$

$$\frac{E}{A} = R$$

$$\frac{R}{R \text{ per foot}} = \text{circuit length of wire}$$

The individual element length can be varied so long as the total wire length over the whole circuit is not altered. Elements can also be in the form of resistance tapes or rods. (See *silicon carbide elements*.)

It is possible, for stoneware firing, to use one gauge thinner than that quoted above, i.e. 14 swg (2.03mm), and down to 18 swg (1.219mm) for earthenware. It is difficult for a potter to wind wire thicker than 13 swg. (See *element winding*.)

As mentioned above there is a minimum practical length for a circuit. As a very rough guide, reject any computation arrived at by means of the above equations which results in less than 100ft/30m of wire to produce 4 kilowatts of current.

The diameter and spacing of the coils will affect the efficiency and useful life of an element. There are two rules to be observed:

1 The diameter of the coil should measure 6–8 diameters of the wire. In practice this means winding 13 and 14 swg wire on a 9mm/³⁄₈in mandrel. This gives a coil of approximately 15mm/½in diameter. Applying the above criterion; the diameter of 13 swg is 2.33mm; multiplied by 7 gives 16.3mm for the average coil diameter — near enough. For thinner wires — 15 to 17 swg — a 6mm/¼in winding rod gives 12 and 11mm coils respectively.

2 The space between one coil and the next must equal at least one wire diameter, and preferably 1.5 diameters. A close-wound coil must therefore be stretched to two to three times its original length. It must be possible to insert a piece of the same wire between every coil and its neighbor. On the other hand, there is a limit to the degree to which one can stretch coiled wire. For 13 swg this is about a foot of wire to 5in/125mm of slot — about 7 diameters between coils.

Never attempt to lay a straight length of wire in a slot. Although this may seem a simple method of taking all connections to one end, it will expand during heating and the arc of wire will fall from its slot and may easily short circuit to the element above or below. Attempts have been made to fit elements into the roof of frontloaders; these pose obvious difficulties which are, however, not insurmountable. The main disadvantage is the narrowness of the gap left open for radiation.

There are conflicting reports as to the damage caused to wire elements by reduction. The generally accepted theory is that reduction destroys the protective oxidized layer which the element builds up in normal firings and the advice is to arrange at least two oxidized firings to each reducing one. Stephen Coulston, however, (CR88), does not experience any detriment to his Kilns & Furnaces AB40HT even though he fires at over 1300°C/2372°F (though he does not reduce (with gas) at much above 1220°C/2228°F). Element life may be reduced by allowing glaze to splash onto the coils, preventing oxidation at that point. ITC 213 refractory coating is specialized for metal coating and is reputed to protect elements against deterioration from a reducing atmosphere.

Elements sometimes tend, due to expansion and contraction during firing, to sag out of their slots. They can be heated up by switching on the kiln for a few minutes (and off again!) or with a blow lamp and gently eased back with pliers. Alternatively there are 'element pins' now on the market. (See also *element winding, ITC, Kanthal, silicon carbide elements.*) Fuller information in Fournier EKP.

Where a continuous element is used in an oblong kiln some system must be devised to stop it pulling out at the corners as it expands and contracts during firing. Even in a circular or hexagonal muffle this is a danger. If an element does ease out of its slot it can only be pushed back in when it is hot; it will be too brittle when cold. It can be heated with a gas torch or the kiln can be switched on for a period (switching off, of course, before attempting a repair!).

An obvious limitation on possible wiring schedules is the length of wire which can be physically accommodated in a kiln. As a guide, 17ft/5m of 13 swg wound on a $^3/_8$in/10mm mandrel will give 30in/750mm of stretched element. The arrangement of elements is important. They

should be housed in the floor, rear wall and two side walls of a front-opening kiln; in the floor and all four walls of a top-opener. There is always loss of heat through the roof especially in top loaders, which can be minimized by placing the upper elements closer together. The floor needs about one-fifth of the total circuitry.

Connections: the length of the element 'tails' must be the width of your kiln wall plus an extra 1in/25mm. It is a good idea to allow twice this length so that the tail can be doubled back on itself and twisted together. This effectively doubles its cross-sectional area, lowering its resistance and preventing heat being generated where it will do no good. The connectors known as *line taps* are the best type for securing the element to the connecting wires. At one time the wires would have been asbestos covered but now substitute and somewhat less heat-resistant materials are used. These wires join the elements which make up a single circuit into a continuous run, the ends of which are connected to a live and neutral of the electrical supply. (See also *circuit*). All connections must, of course, be shielded from any possibility of being accidentally touched, or of touching one another apart from the required junctions. See also *silicon carbide elements* for their particular requirements.

Resistance wire tends to be more brittle in cold weather even before being fired. After a few firings it becomes almost as brittle as glass and it is difficult to extract a fired element whole.

The power input to a kiln averages 3–3.5kW per cubic foot for stoneware. With the increasing efficiency of modern insulators (*ceramic fiber*, etc.) it may be possible to reduce these figures but a reserve of power is always useful. (See also *heat loss.*)

Element pins

High temperature wire pins and staples are available from most suppliers. These are inserted into the kiln wall to support sagging or loose elements. Or you can buy high-temperature wire (Baileys and others) and make your own.

Element-winding

Electric kiln resistance-wire up to 13 swg (2.34mm) can easily be wound into elements by hand. The winder is simply a length of iron rod bent into a handle at one end and set in two bearings (holes in a piece of $^3/_4$in/20mm) timber are sufficient (see figs **2–4**). The length of the frame depends upon your element length when tightly wound (i.e. not the stretched length). The bearings will need to be about 6in/150mm further apart than this. As a guide: 17ft/5m of 13 swg will wind into about 14in/350mm of

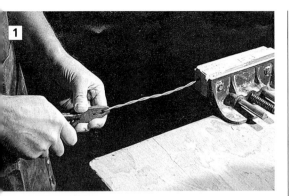

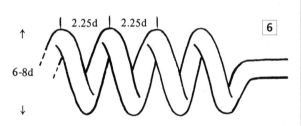

A simple system of winding electric kiln elements.

1 After measuring the length of wire needed (see text, and Fournier 1976) allow a further 18in/45cm and bend half of this extra length back at each end. With the last inch or so secured between the wooden jaws of a vice twist the double wire into a spiral as shown. This is the 'tail' which pierces the wall of the kiln. Doubling the thickness reduces the resistance of this section by three-quarters with the result that it will produce less heat.

2 and 3 A general view of a primitive but practical element winder which is within the competence of any potter, and a closeup of a double (hairpin) element in the process of being wound.

4 Showing how the bar can be removed from the bearing (a simple hole in the wood!) and the wound element slid over the handle.

5 The final stage: pulling out the close-wound element to the length required for fitting into the wall slot. Always use wooden clamp jaws in order not to damage the wire. (See also electric kiln.)

6 The spacing must be at least 1.25 diameters between the faces of the coils, or 2.25 diameters from the topmost point of one coil to the topmost point of the next, to avoid each overheating its neighbor.

close coils. An element must always be pulled out to at least twice its wound length, so this example will span a 30in/750mm kiln slot. 18–22in/450–550mm is therefore a reasonable distance between bearings. Some means of gripping one end of the wire must be provided, and it must be possible to slide the completed coil from the rod. The illustrations show one system, but others will occur to you. An old wallpaper trimmer has been utilized but these are probably extinct.

During the winding, the wire must be kept taut by feeding it through a V-slot in a wooden block which runs along a second shaft. Single and hairpin elements can be wound on this simple contraption at the rate of a dozen or so an hour.

Method: Cut the wire to the appropriate length, leaving enough for twisted tails at each end. The tails can be twisted in a vice before you start winding. Always use wooden jaws in the vice, and take extreme care never to nip, score, or damage the wire with metal tools during any process—it will only be as strong as its weakest part. Wind at a regular speed and keep the coils touching one another. Perfect elements will come with a little practice. Remove the coil from the rod, grip one end in a vice and the other with pliers or both hands, and pull it steadily apart until it has reached the length of the slot in which it is to be housed. You should be able to slot a piece of the same wire between the stretched coils which is the minimum distance apart to avoid overheating. For further details see Fournier EKP.

Elutriation

The separation of particles according to their *specific gravity* by a controlled jet of air or water. Can also be used as a method for determining particle size.

Embossing

Three-dimensional decoration applied to clay. Strictly speaking it should be in the form of a 'boss' or circular motif as has been used to embellish pots through the centuries, but the term is also used in a more general way. Lively single or repeat patterns can be achieved with deft strokes of the finger on pellets of clay applied to the dampened surface, as on some splendid Medieval jugs. A potter's seal can form a significant embossed break on a smooth surface. One can model or incise added clay to emphasize or isolate it, or to build up three-dimensional patterns. (See also *applied decoration, boss, seal, sprigging*.)

Emery

An impure *corundum*. Used as an *abrasive*.

Empirical formula

The simplest type of formula, merely listing the proportions of the elements which make up the material. Example: potash feldspar: $K_2. Al_2. Si_6. O_{16}$ which can more informatively be written as the rational formula: $K_2O. Al_2O_3. 6SiO_2$, giving an indication (using the *Seger formula*) of its behavior in the kiln.

Enamel

Enamels, or enamel colors, are on-glaze pigments with a firing range of 690-850°C/1274-1562°F. They are applied to already fired glazed ware, which is then given a third firing to melt and fix the enamels. They are, in effect, very soft colored frits. They may contain slightly toxic materials.

The term 'enamel' (like 'maiolica' when applied to a glaze) is sometimes used in a confusing way, to indicate opaque, stained earthenware glazes, but we will confine discussion here to the low-firing pigments.

The advantages of enamels are: the brilliance of color which is attainable, and the possibility of having several shots at a design without spoiling a pot. The color range is wide, with many strong reds which do not feature in the higher-fired pigments. The general tone is bright and clean, however the ease with which they can be used and the detail possible may lead to fussy work. They do not always fully integrate with the glaze and may be damaged by detergents, scourers, and dishwashers. Applying this to transfer work in enamel, I have a completely plain bowl that once boasted a ship in full sail! Enamels have more the appearance of 'applied art' than other pottery techniques.

Enamels are mixed rather like oil paints, working and grinding the pigment with a palette knife on a glazed tile or a glass muller. The traditional medium is fat oil of turpentine, not substitute turpentine but plant extracts from lavender, cloves, etc. can be used. 'Fat oil' can be prepared by leaving turpentine in a cup to evaporate for a few days until a gummy residue remains, or a prepared medium can be bought with the colors. A cheaper and more readily available medium was proposed by Hannah Arnup (CR150) — the 7Up drink allowed to go flat! The object is to make it possible to apply the color with a brush and to ensure that it will stay where it is put (one can use plain water, but the color can then be easily disturbed). Brushes are washed in turpentine. Colors cannot be reused if allowed to dry on the slab. The addition of a little olive oil is said to prolong the useful life of mixed colors. Many potters buy their enamels ready-made, but some have formulated their own. They are fundamentally composed of a soft frit, an opacifier (generally white tin oxide), a little clay, and a fairly high proportion of coloring oxide. The modern descendants of the Kakiemon family still mix their own enamels, particularly the 'kaki' (persimmon red), for which iron oxide is mixed with bark and leaf ash and 'porcelain stone', probably a form of china stone. For a base glaze Tomimoto suggests a shiny one with not too much lime. This, he says, helps to prevent the peeling of enamels. He also recommends that the glaze be covered with a thin coat of glue (or saliva!) before applying the enamel. These remarks refer mainly to porcelain. A system of dusting

A combination of resist glaze techniques with a charming ship in crimson enamel. Stoneware by John Maltby.

powdered enamel onto lacquered glaze parallels the Western industrial *ground-lay* method. Sanders quotes a number of Japanese recipes, a typical example of which is 50 parts powdered lead glaze (soft frit), 5 white lead, and 12 red iron oxide for a red color. The lead, of course, is a very toxic material and not recommended unless used in the form of a low-solubility frit. For *gold* and *silver* enamels see under those headings. Most commercial colors are intermixable except for the selenium reds. Some enamels can be obtained as sprays.

The styles of enamel painting vary widely; Tomimoto with his brilliantly if precisely painted designs and Hamada's bold strokes, are modern examples of the great range possible which are exploited by a number of Western potters in vivid and spontaneous sweeps of the brush. John Maltby uses small flecks of gold and bright enamel to set off and highlight his very direct poured glazes. The red spots on David Leach's porcelain look like enamel in their bright colors but are fired at full temperature. (See *red colors*.)

Enamels should be fired fairly slowly up to 500°C/932°F with plenty of ventilation to allow organic materials to burn away before fluxing begins. The final temperature will vary with the color, and the advice of the supplier should be followed. Wengers used to recommend firing according to the refractoriness of the glaze: 740°C/1364°F for earthenware, 780°C/1436°F for bone china, 790°C/1454°F for stoneware, and 800°C/1472°F for porcelain for the generality of their colors. A 30-minute soak at top temperature can assist in fixing the colors. For spraying, enamel can be mixed with 1% of starch and enough water to bring it to a thin creamy consistency. If enamel is applied too thickly it may peel and, where a solid color is required, two thinner coats, with the first coat fired on before applying the second, are preferable.

The surfaces to be decorated must be free from grease and can be rubbed over with whiting to ensure a clean surface.

The kiln must be well-ventilated during the early burning-off stage of the firing, and accurate temperature control established. Frequently more than one firing is required, the higher temperature range of colors being painted and fixed first, with subsequent lower temperature firings of the more fugitive reds and golds. Enamels may be combined with underglaze pigments and even be used on stoneware glaze, though they may be difficult to 'fix' and will require a fairly smooth glaze — see Tomimoto's advice above. Cleanliness during the process is essential and this includes the kiln furniture and kiln wall surface: dust or particles floating about during firing will adhere to the surface of the enamel and mar it visually and tactually.

Apart from painting, enamels can be applied by lithography from a gelatinous coated paper or by decals (transfers), increasingly used by studio potters. *Photoceramic processes* are also used. Enamel will concentrate in hairline cracks in a glaze and show up any crazing or crackle, developing a colored network. This can be utilized as a particular decorative effect. The industry has a method of applying an even coating called *ground lay*. *Silk screen* printing can give interesting and bold effects and, though it will generally lack fine detail, this can help in broadening one's approach to the material.

A special type of enamel is commonly used on metal.

Encaustic

Meaning, strictly, 'burnt in' this is a somewhat misleading term used by antiquarians for inlaid pottery decoration, especially on tiles. (See *inlay*.)

End point

The squatting temperature of a cone.

Endothermic

Heat absorbent. Clay has an endothermic peak during firing at 580°C/1076°F, when it releases its combined water, slowing down the rate of temperature rise. The converse of *exothermic*.

Engineering brick

A highly vitrified brick which may be red, gray, or black according to kiln atmosphere. Of low *porosity* and great strength. A poor heat *insulator* and not suitable for most kiln building. Used where high mechanical strength is the prime consideration. Made of Etruria *marl* or clay with a fairly high flux content.

Colored engobe painting by Barbara Lock. The engobe (slip) is unglazed (but lightly burnished) on a body of $^2/_3$ red earthenware to $^1/_3$ T material. The basic recipe for the engobes, which Barbara has kindly allowed me to reproduce, is: borax frit 15%; nepheline syenite 30%; ball clay 30%; china clay 15%; tin oxide 5%; zircon 5%. Pigment oxides and underglaze colors are added. This is a fairly involved 'slip' but one which obviously repays the labor of making it up. It has the advantage that a single batch is suitable for all the colors.

Engobe

Originally a French term for slip but which also now covers a wider field than traditional slipware. In general use in America and applied to any clay-containing coating.

Engobes may contain very little plastic clay, being largely composed of materials more usually associated with glazes — feldspars, flint, opacifiers and fluxes. As distinct from the earthy qualities of European slipware, engobes are sophisticated and often white or near-white, providing a base for coloring oxides. Engobe recipes may appear involved and artificial but they are more adaptable to stonewares and can even be used on biscuit.

The six groups of materials listed by Rhodes are:

1 The clays, including china clay for its whiteness and to control shrinkage.

2 Fluxes — the various basic fluxes used in glazes and, occasionally, *frits*.

3 Fillers — mainly flint.

4 Hardeners — borax and gums.

5 Opacifiers — zircon, etc.

6 Colorants — the *pigment oxides*.

Rhodes also lists a number of recipes. It is possible to use a commercial white casting body on most conditions of clay or on biscuit (which should be dampened). Wally Keeler, in CR112, quotes a very simple engobe for a slip on biscuit as 40 china clay: 60 feldspar. *Sintered* engobes can be made by the addition of borax, colemanite, boric

frits, etc. to clay. A porcelain body base can enhance colors, especially when used for brushwork.

Too great a shrinkage of the engobe will cause cracking or crazing; too little, scaling and flaking. Materials should not be too finely ground. A recipe is given at *brushed slip*. A vitreous engobe can replace a glaze (see also at *slip*). Parmelee discusses engobes at length in CG, and Bente Hansen (CR140) includes nepheline syenite, titanium, petalite, Molochite, and feldspar in her engobe recipes.

Engraving

See *incising*.

Envelope kiln

Sometimes used in the USA to describe a lift-off or *top-hat kiln*.

Epoxy resin

A modern material that can be used to strengthen plaster of Paris. A number of proprietary brands are on the market. A curing oven is sometimes necessary, and care must be taken to disperse the toxic fumes that may result from its use. The resin supplier will give advice. Epoxy resin as a solid material has also been used by Martin Smith as an intermediate bedding between his ceramic forms and a metal casing.

Epsom salts

Magnesium sulfate $MgSO_4.7H_2O$. 246.5.

It has been mentioned as a glaze suspender or flocculant: 3 parts of water to 1 part salts giving a concentrated solution of which 2 teaspoonfuls to a pint is an average addition. 'Thickens glaze without becoming lumpy, so that they adhere better to a non-porous surface' (Georgies). See also its use to improve the plasticity of porcelain body at *pH factor*.

Equilibrium diagram

See *phase diagram*.

Equivalent materials

While there are unlikely to be direct equivalents between the minerals mined in different countries there are rough alternatives. Always test for their effect in a body or glaze. Some examples: UK potash feldspar roughly equates with Canada Kona F-4 feldspar; SD Hymod/Tennessee ball clay; china clay/No.6 Tile clay (CR125).

Equivalent weight

A term used in connection with glaze formulas to indicate the amount, or unit, of an oxide which enters into a glaze. This is usually but not always the same as the molecular weight of the raw compound or mineral.

Bone ash, for instance is $3CaO.P_2O_3$ while the unit entering into the body or glaze composition (that at the head of the column when translating formula-into-recipe) is $CaO.0.33P_2O_3$. To keep the arithmetic correct we divide the molecular weight of bone ash by three — 310 divided by 3 = an 'equivalent' weight of 103.

Such modifications are noted against the compounds concerned in the appropriate entry in this book. Colemanite is the most common example in glaze computation.

Estuarine clay

Clays which have settled in a river estuary 'one of the better clays' — Cardew. Often deposited in thin layers with considerable variations. The ball clays of Wareham, Dorset, England, are valuable estuarine clays. Similar to *fluvial* clays.

Etching

Storr-Britz describes a rather dangerous technique involving covering a porcelain piece with wax, cutting a design through the wax, and then etching the uncovered surface with hydrochloric acid. A somewhat similar system was used in the pottery industry to produce shiny and matt surfaces on gold enamel.

Etruria marl

An ancient clay laid down in the carboniferous period — three hundred million years ago — and used for bricks, tiles and for engineering bricks. High iron content. Occurs on sites in addition to those at Stoke-on-Trent, from which it derives its name, though the term 'marl' is misleading since the clay is low in lime.

Eutectic point

That mixture of two or more substances which has the lowest melting point of the whole series. Some mixtures have more than one low or eutectic point.

It will be seen from the eutectic diagram that even though one material may have a much lower melting point than the other, the eutectic is lower still. It follows that an increase in the amount of either material — i.e. a move-ment to one side or the other of the low point — will raise the melting point of the mixture. This must be remembered when compounding glazes, an increase of the nominally fluxing material not necessarily continuing to 'soften' the glaze.

Glaze formulas for clear glazes aim at the eutectic. For expressing eutectics of three materials a biaxial diagram is needed; for more than three the problem becomes, mathematically speaking, very involved. Eutectic combinations form from materials within a pottery body, forming fluid glasses and lowering their *refractoriness* and *deformation* point. Glazes also go through liquid-in-solid phases.

The alumina-silica eutectic of 1595°C/2903°F occurs at 5.5 alumina: 94.5 silica.

Near equal mixtures of calcite, kaolinite and quartz have a low eutectic below 1200°C/2192°F. This is equivalent to the formula 1.0 CaO. 0.35 Al_2O_3. 2.49 SiO_2. (Cardew). The eutectic of potash, at 770°C/1418°F, is 1.0 K_2O. 0.5Al_2O_3. 5.5 SiO_2.

As mentioned above, the matter is further complicated by the fact that some mixtures have two or more eutectic points although one proportion usually predominates.

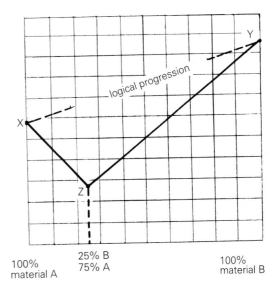

It would be reasonable to suppose that the mixtures of two materials with different melting points would melt as indicated by the line marked 'logical progression' in the diagram. This is not the case, however and there is a eutectic point (Z) which represents the most easily fusible mixture. (X) represents the melting point of material A (e.g. if each division on the scale represents 200°C/392°F this would be around 1075°C/1967°F); (Y) is the melting point of material (B). For further explanation see text.

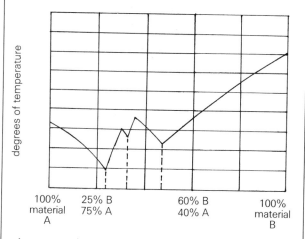

A more complicated graph which shows how two materials may have more than one eutectic. Although the most effective mixture is given as 75/25 there is a broken progression from there on, the least useful combination being 65/35 until 60/40 is reached. The diagram is purely illustrative and does not refer to any specific materials, but in practice (B) could be silica (flint, quartz) and (A) an RO (flux). Multiple eutectics are more likely to occur when one of the materials in a recipe (there are generally more than two) is itself a complicated compound such as feldspar. Eutectics are therefore very difficult to establish but these sort of reactions can throw some light on otherwise inexplicable behavior in a glaze; e.g. adding more flux or silica does not automatically lower or raise the melting point. It also suggests that precise control of temperature can be as important as a precise recipe for economical firing. Another aspect is that two of the materials may develop their eutectic (become melted and glassy) before others present, giving a milky or speckled glaze or a variable surface. (See text at calcium.)

Everted form

Turned outwards, or inside out — e.g. a rim which turns over to show the inside.

Exfoliation

Some hydrous silicates expand under heat, notably *vermiculite* which can then be used as a low-temperature (up to c. 1000°C/1832°F) heat insulator.

Exothermic

Releasing or creating heat by chemical reaction. Occurs in the firing of most clays at 900–1000°C/1652–1832°F through the burning of carbon in the body (see *brick clay*), causing a more rapid rise in temperature for the the same heat input.

Expanding pulley

A pulley wheel in which the flanges are separate. They are held together by a spring, but can be forced apart by the strong pull of an A-shaped belt. As the belt approaches the center of the pulley, the speed ratio will be altered. The system has been utilized for varying the speed of a *power wheel*. See PQ34 for building details (Bill Read).

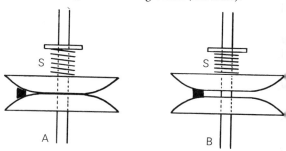

The principle of the expanding pulley. Figure A shows the belt (black section) near the perimeter of the pulley when under minimum tension, the spring (S) holding the faces of the pulley together. B If the tension or pull on the belt is increased it forces the halves apart and the comparative speed of the pulley is increased.

Expansion

Expansion takes place when a material is heated. In pottery materials there are three types of thermal expansion:
1 The reversible expansion common to most materials, which occurs steadily and progressively upon heating, with contraction upon cooling. Oxides have different rates of expansion which have been worked out as coefficients. An understanding of these is of great help in compounding glazes, especially with reference to crazing.
2 The expansion associated with quartz and *cristobalite inversion* which takes place very suddenly at 573°C/1063°F and 220°C/428°F respectively. These are reversible.

A diagrammatic illustration of an expansion joint in the corner of a kiln which can be packed with ceramic fiber for insulation. A straight run of bricks may also need provision for expansion.

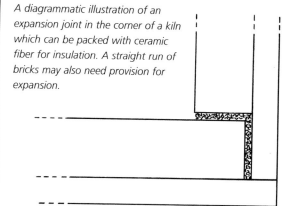

The expansion which occurs in a clay body up to about 50°C (when it will have been altered to ceramic) and is not reversed on cooling. A low-fired biscuit pot will be slightly larger than the dry clay pot. As soon as *vitrification* begins it involves a non-reversible shrinkage. At Crowan Pottery, Harry Davis fired very soft biscuit and then packed his glazed pots actually touching one another in the saggars, the shrinkage being sufficient to part them before the glaze melted.

A fourth, very slight, expansion can result from moisture *adsorption* by the fired pot. It will be enough to cause delayed *crazing* if the glaze is already in slight tension.

Extruder, extruded clay, form

Clay pressed or pugged through dies or even simply through a coarse sieve can be used for applied decoration of many kinds. The *dod box* or *clay gun* is a simple piece of equipment for this purpose. A cake-icing type of extruder can also be utilized to produce soft coils for applying directly to a clay surface, a technique called 'sprigging' by Shafer, though this is the wrong term for it. The strands of clay can be beaten flat and then stamped or otherwise decorated. Dies can be used on a pug-mill or dod box to produce ribbing or other three-dimensional surface decoration. Coils and more elaborate shapes can be extruded and are used by potters for the coiling method of building (mass-produced coiled pots!), for making handles, and for decorative additions to pots. Sculptural constructions are also made using larger extruded shapes. A machine known as a clay 'bulley', made by Dragon Ceramex, will extrude square, circular and many other forms up to 12in/300mm across. Less ambitious extruders with variable dies to give solid or tube shapes. Bricks, pipes, and other articles are formed by extrusion in industry. (See also *bulley, clay gun, wad box*.)

Fabric

See *cloth patterns* and *lace*.

Facet

Thrown pots and bowls can be beaten or cut to produce facets or panels. Cut bowls are thrown thickly and cut with a wire while still soft, or may be roughly beaten prior to cutting; the resultant circle within a polygon is an attractive contrast. There is no need to restrict them to vertical stripes. Short cuts part way down the form can also be tried using a knife or plane.

The facets are often used as a frame for further decoration; sgraffito, brushwork, alternate color slip or glaze dips, etc. Beating may be done up to the leather-hard stage and will give a softer effect than cutting which can have a crisp directness as exemplified in the work of John Reeve and others. See also illustration at *Salt-glaze*.

A soda-glazed teapot by Ruthanne Tudball, the body lightly faceted all round.

Boldly cut facets on a thrown bowl, by John Reeve.

Factor

See *conversion factor*.

Fahrenheit scale

A temperature recording scale in which the interval between the freezing and boiling points of water is divided into 180 degrees (degrees designated with a small °), with the freezing point put at 32°F and the boiling point at 212°F. To convert a given temperature to the celsius or centigrade scale, subtract 32; multiply by 5; divide by 9.
Example: $2300°F - 32 = 2268 \times 5 = \dfrac{11340}{9} = 1260°C$

Faience

As well as an inappropiate name for Egyptian paste the term is also applied to the once-fired tin-glazed wares of 18th-century France, the name derived from Faenza where tin-glazed maiolica was extensively made. Later used to denote any glazed earthenware. The French call the fine-bodied English earthenwares 'faience-fine'. In the USA it indicates a clear-glazed decorated pottery, a definition still further from its origins. Even more surprisingly it is applied to any large ceramics used on buildings.

Fail-safe devices

When mechanical or electronic (or human!) systems fail to shut off a kiln the results can obviously be disastrous. A clock-switch or a heat fuse can be fitted which will mitigate the worst effects and are advertised in suppliers' catalogs. However, by their nature, they must operate at a temperature above the optimum and are designed to protect the shelving and the kiln itself rather than the wares. A heat-fuse is used like a thermocouple and is connected to the electrical supply through a contactor. See also *kiln-sitter*. A simple alarm clock or, better still, an alarm wrist watch, can save many a heartache.

Fan brush

A brush with splayed hog bristle 'for dry brushing' supplied by Coastal Ceramics (NZ).

Fat clay

Any highly plastic, workable, fine-grained clay.

Fat oil

The thick, varnish-like residue resulting from the exposure of turpentine to the air for a period of time. It can be prepared by leaving pure turpentine (not turpentine substitute) in a cup for a few days until only a gummy residue remains. Take care that there is no turpentine on the inner sides of the cup or it will flow over by capillary action and down the outside (Billington). Fresh turpentine can be added periodically. It is the traditional vehicle for underglaze and, especially, on-glaze colors — *enamels*. A similar substance, in which turpentine has been heated to 145°C/293°F and then steam distilled, can be bought ready-prepared from Suppliers. (See also *anise*).

Feathering

A type of decoration in which trailed lines and dots of slip are drawn out by means of a thin and preferably pliable tool, such as the center rib of a feather. If the tool is drawn in alternate directions an overall pattern develops. The technique should be used with discretion — design values can be lost in an excess of random feathering. With skill, a number of variations can be developed — curved lines, or

A close-up of a 19th-century trailed dish whch has been feathered back and forth in parallel lines.

quick flick at the end of a stroke, for instance. The technique is often combined with design trailing, e.g. for delineating a bird's beak or for fish scales.

Because both the base slip and the trailed line must be wet and fluid the work is sometimes done on a flat slab of clay that is rather softer than for other slip techniques. One should avoid cutting into the clay beneath. Use the feather fairly upright; if its length is dragged through the slip, a dead and muddy line will result. Turn the dish to reverse the line direction. After trailing but before feathering lift and drop a corner of the board on which the clay rests; this will flatten the trailed line and give a more integrated effect. The dish is formed, when the surface has lost its shine, over a hump mold or, very carefully, in a hollow one.

Apart from the traditional style there are a number of possible variations: radial feathering from the center of a bowl through circles which have been trailed on a wheel; dots of slip on or between trailed lines; restricting the feathering to bands, areas, or panels. Large blobs and dots — black on a red or white ground, for instance, can be feathered outwards from the center or used in the familiar 'wheat ear' pattern.

Multiple feathers, mounted on a batten, have been used. A distinct type of feathering involves a more random pulling of dots and lines to give a marbled appearance. Feathering on upright or convex surfaces, as done on 17th-century beakers, for instance, needs considerable skill.

Feldspar, felspar, minerals

Feldspar is now the internationally agreed spelling. A large group of minerals which have decomposed from granite and *igneous* rocks and are thus allied to clay. Of world-wide occurrence.

The main group consists of the alumino-silicates of potassium, sodium, calcium, and, more rarely, barium. The ideal formulas, never quite achieved in nature, are:

Potash feldspar	Orthoclase	$K_2O.Al_2O_3.6SiO_2$	556
Microline	Similar chemical make-up but with a different crystalline structure.		
Soda spar	Albite	$Na_2O.Al_2O_3.6SiO_2$	524
Lime spar	Anorthite	$CaO.Al_2O_3.2SiO_2$	278

Most feldspars are mixtures and are selected according to the predominance of one or other base. A typical analysis of an orthoclase spar by weight:

K_2O	10.3				
Na_2O	2.5	Al_2O_3	17.5	SiO_2	68.2
CaO	0.25	Fe_2O_3	0.2		
MgO	0.12				

There is a series of mixtures between soda and lime spars known as the *plagioclase*. There is no potash-lime series. In the USA 'Minspar' (Georgies) is a soda feldspar, 'Custer' is a potash spar (Pottery Supply House and others).

Feldspars are the most useful minerals in ceramics, apart from clays. Used as a primary flux above 1200°C/2192°F and as a secondary flux in earthenware. Also in bodies and engobes. Soda spars are reputed to give brighter colors from pigments. Many spars begin to melt at 1180°C/2156°F and continue to form complex fluids up to 1500°C/2732°F. They are natural *frits*. Molten feldspar has a high *viscosity* which assists the standing-strength of porcelains and helps prevent glazes running during firing.

China stone is a slightly more refractory spar containing all three bases. *Nepheline syenite* is a fusible feldspathoid, high in alumina. (See also *feldspathic, feldspathoid, petalite, spodumene*, etc.)

Feldspar convention

The normal analysis of clays will list the oxides present. A rational analysis, listing the assumed minerals present, is more useful as a guide to its behavior and in calculating its *Seger formula*.

Under the feldspar convention, it was assumed that the minerals in clay were kaolinite, feldspar and quartz. Recent research suggests that mica rather than feldspar more accurately fulfills the theoretical grouping of oxides. Hence the *mica convention*. Both however are arbitrary, and the practical value of considering feldspar as a mineral in the rational formula is not significantly diminished.

Cardew points out that the mineral *illite* may have to be considered, and that some kaolinite may be replaceable by *montmorillonite*. Recent research on the subject stresses the importance of illite and the comparative dearth of kaolinite in many clays, even to the latter's virtual exclusion. None of this alters the observed behavior of clay but can illuminate certain aspects of it.

Feldspathic, glazes, minerals

Containing feldspar. Generally used in connection with stoneware or porcelain glaze where the mineral is used to provide the primary flux. Characteristically a smooth clean glaze if sufficiently thickly applied, but without a strong character.

The feldspathic minerals constitute a large family: as well as those discussed under *feldspar*, there is also *leucite* which, with *nepheline*, is sometimes called a *feldspathoid*.

Feldspathoid

A term sometimes applied to the more distant members of the feldspar family: principally leucite, nepheline and china stone. Also mentioned as feldspathoids are lepidolite, petalite, and spodumene. For details see under respective materials.

Felspar

Alternative spelling, see *feldspar*.

Ferric chromite

See *iron chromate*.

Ferric oxide

The stable red oxide of iron, Fe_2O_3.

The source mineral is *hematite*. Ferric oxide has a high melting point (1565°C/2849°F) and does not act as a flux. The *ferrous* oxide, however, behaves very differently.

Iron compounds revert to the ferric form in an oxidized fire, though Dodd states that, it loses oxygen to form Fe_3O_4. Many types will be listed in merchants' catalogs, all with the formula Fe_2O_3. A 'synthetic' ferric is produced, very fine and pure, but I have not found that it noticeably improves color. Crocus martis is a natural ferric: ochre, sienna and umber are earthy oxides. Ferric is the coloring matter in red clay. Hematite produces the sparkle in *aventurine glazes*.

Ferric iron can be used as a pigment in all glazes, with a normal maximum addition of 12%. The red quality is lost in most glazes where ferric produces yellow-brown to black. Iron precipitated onto the surface in kaki glaze holds nearest to the original color (See *red glazes*.) Results are more interesting and variable if red clay is used to supply ferric. (See also *iron*.)

In ash glazes, in an oxidizing (or neutral electric kiln) fire, quite good terracotta reds can be achieved. (See recipe at *oxidized stoneware*.)

Ferroso-ferric oxide

Fe_3O_4, ($FeO.Fe_2O_3$) see *iron, magnetite*.

Ferrous oxide

The 'lower', black oxide of iron FeO. 72. m.p. 1370°C/2498°F. 'Soluble in [fired] glazes up to saturation point (about 8%)' (Hamer). Will revert to ferric in an oxidized fire. Ferrous (reduced) iron in a body will act as a flux, causing it to melt, slump, or slag if present in quantity. In high-temperature glazes it also acts as a flux. It is considered to be ferrous iron which produces the typical reduced greens and blues of celadons. (See also *ilmenite*.)

Ferruginous

Impregnated with iron. An iron oxide-bearing mineral *Ochre* for instance is a ferruginous earth.

Fettling

Term used more often in the industry than by craft potters. It signifies the trimming and smoothing of a leather-hard pot, especially the sharp edges left by molds. Cardew uses the term to cover the removal of glaze from foot rings, lids and so on, but this is unusual. Fettling is best done with a fine-bladed knife.

Fiber, Ceramic

See *Ceramic fiber*.

Fiber clay

Clay mixed with various fibers — rice husk, fiberglass (even cow dung in India!) have been used world-wide. Fiber clay has a certain strength when dry and used in schools for modeling which is then painted, or for large scale modeling for firing. Nylon fibers are listed by several suppliers. Normal usage 1.5–2% by weight. (See also *newclay, unfired clay*.)

However in the late 1990s, what is generally referred to as 'paper clay' began to be widely used by studio potters and great claims have been made for it, especially for hand-building, modeling, and large pieces. When fired, of course, the fiber or paper is burnt away. (See *paper clay* for details.)

Fiberglass, fibreglass

Trade names, see *glass fiber*.

Fictile

Capable of being molded (as applied to potter's clays), or simply 'having to do with pottery' (SOED).

Filler

A silica or other refractory non-plastic addition to a clay body: to open or texture with sand, grog, flint; to control shrinkage; or to control or alter its behavior in the kiln. Hamer warns that silica of too fine a grain size (200 mesh or finer) may not behave as a refractory. 'Fillers' also often feature in *engobe* recipes. Rhodes mentions *pyrophyllite*.

Filter press

Equipment for *dewatering* clay, consisting of a concertina-like set of canvas bags which are filled with body slip. These are squeezed from either end, forcing out the water. Filter presses involve major engineering work, occupy a lot of space, and are expensive. Almost £6000/$8940, in England, for a hand operated studio press. They are of limited effectiveness with very plastic clays, which quickly coat the canvas and render it almost waterproof. For a more promising approach for studios see *vacuum filter*.

Filter presses are available in smaller sizes but are expensive and not often used by studio potters. They are more suitable for porcelain and other *pastes* than for plastic clays.

Finger combing, finger sgraffito, finger wipe

Decoration in wet slip on the surface of a dish or pot. Two or three fingers are drawn steadily and rapidly through the slip, either in straight across or, as is more often the case, in wavy lines. The work is done a few minutes after slipping. The slip coat should not be too thick.

A similar effect can be achieved with glaze and glaze-over-glaze. A 'finger wipe' utilizes a single stroke of the finger.

2 A finger wipe softened by thick running hawthorn ash glaze, by Mike Dodd.

1 A direct and clean finger-combing on beaten pots by Phil Rogers.

3 A swift and sure movement is essential in finger-combing. The technique can also be used with glaze.

Fire extinguisher

Few cases have been reported of fires started by kilns (a bag of weed-killer may prove a greater danger as Mick Casson discovered), but precautions should be taken. Have a fire extinguisher handy (if you employ assistants it is a statutory necessity). The solid (powder) extinguishers are recommended for electrical fires.

Firebox

See *grate*.

Firebrick

A refractory brick, generally made from fireclay and grog. Industrial firebricks are given PCE (pyrometric cone equivalent) ratings. In America these are:

1 Superduty   PCE 33
2 High-duty   PCE 31.5
3 Medium heat duty   PCE 29
4 Low heat duty   PCE 15

Grade 2 is recommended for kilns. The PCE refers to the deformation point. In England the grading is according to alumina content: those with more than 38% alumina are called aluminous fireclay refractories — (1650–1750°C/3002–3182°F).

The refractoriness of firebricks increases with their alumina content. They are strong and resist spalling, but their high density reduces insulation value. Conduction loss is five or six times that of the same thickness of a No. 23 grade insulating brick, with four times the heat storage. Against this, firebrick has greater strength and abrasion resistance than insulating brick. Firebricks are never used in electric kilns, but are more common in oil or solid-fuel fired kilns. See *bricks* for some available shapes of firebricks.

Super-quality firebricks are made from 'soaked' refractory minerals producing mullite and silliminite in the body. (See also *silliminite.*)

Fireclay

A general name for *sedimentary clays* usually associated with coal measures — they are very ancient deposits. Many are black and shaley, compressed to a coal-like consistency, and must be pulverized before use. The 'underclays' immediately beneath the coal seams break down more readily in water. In the best fireclays the impurities, i.e. minerals or oxides other than kaolinite, alumina and silica, should not exceed 5%. Not all fireclays are especially refractory, however, and may contain carbonates of iron and calcium. Particle size averages 0.1–5.0 microns. Reasonable plasticity and dry strength. Fired color is buff to light-brown. Used by potters in refractory mixtures and as a body component. If used in large proportions, however, its carbon content can cause trouble such as *black core* and *bloating*.

Grading of the refractory clays is by alumina content. Those with 38% Al_2O_3 or more are called aluminous fireclays. The common fireclays have 35–37% alumina — the

A raku pot with a body mainly of fireclay, reduced with gum leaves, by Joan Campbell (Australia).

high-duty clays 45% or more. (See also *PCE.*)

Rich glaze quality and color in celadons and other reduced iron glazes is reputed to derive from the use of fireclay in bodies. Mr Noakes of Potclays called it 'sweated color'. The *pyrites* in fireclays can also add interest.

Firecord

A type of Japanese pot decoration known as Hidasuki. Straw rope is soaked in salt water and wound round a pot; the whole is then fired, giving semi-glazed lines occasionally bright red.

Firecrack

May be due to the opening up of an incipient crack caused by mishandling in the leather-hard state, bad joins, uneven thicknesses in the pot wall (particularly the base), over-wetting, or joining soft clay to hard. In all these cases the crack will be rather ragged. If due to *dunting*, the crack is likely to be curved and sharp. Dodd mentions too rapid a fire, but this is not confirmed in practice, although the termination of a biscuit fire at 500–600°C/932–1112°F (dull red heat) is likely to result in extensive cracking. (See also *shattering.*)

Bad packing in the kiln; too great a weight in a bung of pots or bowls; and the sitting of one pot in the neck of another can lead to cracking during firing.

Firing

The heat treatment of ceramic materials at least to the *sintering* stage, (in practice to a minimum of red heat 600°C/1112°F). It is the indispensable factor in pottery. A kiln should therefore be the first consideration when setting up a pottery or school department. Neither sun heat nor a cooking-oven will 'fire' pottery. *Sawdust kilns* frequently fail to develop the minimum temperature.

Firing involves two cycles: heating and cooling. The following chart shows the principal changes and alterations. Involved chemical and physical changes take place during firing: firstly sintering, then a series of melts in the fabric as *eutectics* are reached. Clay expands slightly up to about 800°C/1472°F then begins to shrink as particles come closer together, either taking part in the glassmaking activity or packing in a glassy matrix. When a certain proportion of glass is formed, the ceramic will begin to flow. This is

Firing chart

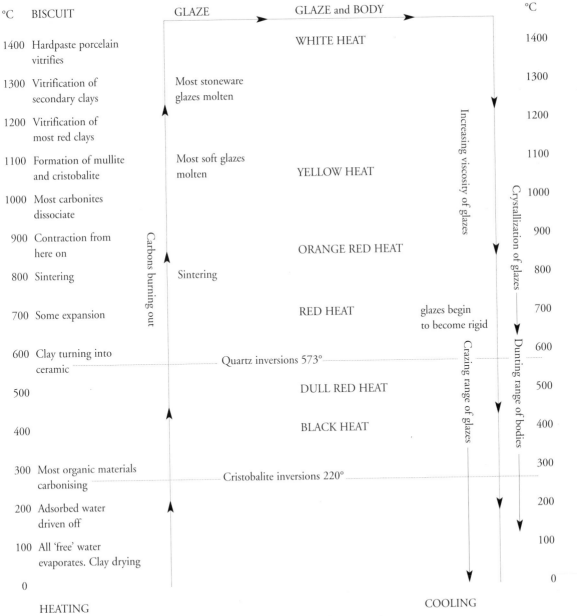

°C	BISCUIT		GLAZE	GLAZE and BODY		°C
1400	Hardpaste porcelain vitrifies			WHITE HEAT		1400
1300	Vitrification of secondary clays		Most stoneware glazes molten			1300
1200	Vitrification of most red clays					1200
1100	Formation of mullite and cristobalite		Most soft glazes molten	YELLOW HEAT		1100
1000	Most carbonites dissociate					1000
900	Contraction from here on			ORANGE RED HEAT		900
800	Sintering		Sintering			800
700	Some expansion			RED HEAT	glazes begin to become rigid	700
600	Clay turning into ceramic		Quartz inversions 573°			600
500				DULL RED HEAT		500
400				BLACK HEAT		400
300	Most organic materials carbonising		Cristobalite inversions 220°			300
200	Adsorbed water driven off					200
100	All 'free' water evaporates. Clay drying					100
0						0

Carbons burning out — Increasing viscosity of glazes — Crystallization of glazes — Crazing range of glazes — Dunting range of bodies

HEATING   COOLING

See *temperature degree* for Fahrenheit conversions

the deformation point of a body. The normal reversible expansions and inversions also cause molecular changes in volume. (See *crazing, thermal shock,* etc.) The speed as well as the temperature reached will affect the result of a firing.

It will be seen that the most significant changes take place early in a biscuit fire and late in a glaze fire. Firing schedules should take this into consideration. While science and logic both suggest slow firing and cooling the tolerances are, in fact, very wide. The Japanese kilns at Tamba were raised from 700°C/1292°F to 1300°C/2372°F in two and a half hours, and cooled nearly as quickly. Biscuit, in a bonfire, develops almost instantaneously, while raku shows what stresses an open body will stand without serious damage. *Bone china* has been fired to 1250°C/2282°F in seven minutes!

In test kilns glazes are fired very quickly. All one can say for certain is that the quality of a glaze will vary considerably with the firing schedule, but only experience can show whether fast or slow firing gives the more desirable results.

See also *nitrogen* for an essential aspect of firing efficiency.

Firing graph

A kiln graph is the most economical and most easily inter-

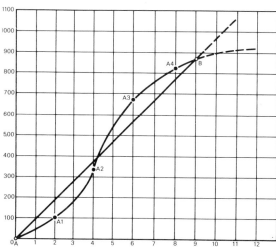

A firing graph with projections (dotted lines) of a kiln's possible further performance had the firing continued at a steady rate. It will be seen that, if only two readings are taken, (A) and (B) (the commencement and finish of the firing) the speed of the further temperature rise will be falsified. The line A-A1-A4-B shows intermediate readings on a pyrometer and these help in plotting a very different path which indicates that, in this case, the temperature rise will probably level out for the same input of energy, (the kiln failing to get hotter from around 1000°C).

preted method of recording a firing, but it must be based on a minimum of three readings, either from cones or a pyrometer. The graph shows how a single end-point can be misleading.

The progressive heat loss which occurs as the gap between the ambient temperature and the temperature inside the kiln increases always produces a slowly flattening curve, and explains why the last few degrees are sometimes so difficult to attain. Graph lines can start at intervals along the base line for successive firings, to facilitate direct comparison. (See *graphs, kiln log.*)

Firing speed

The rate of rise (and fall) of temperature during a firing will always affect the result. Rapid firing in a test kiln can therefore often be misleading. Obviously, in a biscuit firing, the thickness of the clay walls is crucial in avoiding bursts. A 1-inch thick wall would need a very slow 50°C/122°F an hour, at least for the first 700°C/1292°F, whereas a $\frac{1}{4}$in could be taken at 150°C/302°F an hour, always with the proviso of a slower first 200°C/392°F. (See *adsorbed water.*)

It is possible to fire most glazes very rapidly without harm though, as mentioned above, this will alter their fired character. The industry has, experimentally, successfully fired bone china in well under half an hour!

Fish brick

See *chicken brick.*

Flaking

Usually applied to a fault in the raw glaze rather than in the fired glaze. It is due to the surface coat shrinking less or much more than the body. *Flocculated* glazes (ash, colemanite) are prone to flaking, as are glazes too thickly or unevenly applied. Flaking of fired ware is called *shivering.*

Flambé

A glaze, generally on porcelain, streaked with reduced copper reds and purples, i.e. flame-like. Less than 0.5% of copper oxide in the glaze is recommended. Some crude modern copies are produced by an *on-glaze* method.

Flame-proof ware

Flameproof pottery, as distinct from ovenware, is difficult to achieve. The very considerable thermal shock due to expansion and the inversion of cristobalite in a high-fired body, combined with the comparatively low conductivity

A Portuguese flameproof dish in soft earthenware, showing the curved base (only the interior is glazed).

of ceramics (relative to metal, for instance) present almost insoluble problems.

The solution among primitive and less sophisticated communities is to use a body so soft and open that the shock can be accommodated within the structure. This involves a comparatively coarse body and presents glazing difficulties. A soft lead glaze is traditional, but this is frowned on today. The body needs to have a range of particle sizes and a minimum of 'free' silica. Porous red dishes up to 20in/500mm diameter from Portugal and elsewhere, with vertical sides and a curved base are miraculously flame-proof (and can be put onto a gas-ring) if soaked in water for 24 hours before being used for the first time. There is no obvious explanation, although the low firing to sintering without the formation of any glassy phases has been suggested. The effect of the water is even less obvious: perhaps adsorbed water helps to balance thermal shock?

Shape is a factor; for instance a shallow but continuously curved base which can expand without putting excessive strain on the wall. This may also be a reason for the predominance of rounded bases found in primitive pottery throughout the ages. There is no intermediate ceramic material between this type and a high-fired body of very low thermal expansion, e.g. true porcelain (1400°C/2552°F).

Cardew discusses the use of petalite and spodumene, i.e. lithium bodies. Zircon, also, has a low *coefficient of expansion*. See also *ovenware*.

Flange

A flat narrow projection, usually at right angles, in the form of a collar or rim. Most commonly used by potters in connection with the seating of lids. (See under *lids* for several diagrams.)

Flash wall

See *bag wall*.

Flashing

Accidental and partial reduction or over-firing, usually on biscuit. Also applied to the effect, on a part of a glaze surface, of a tongue of flame or hot gas which smokestains or alters the degree of *reduction*. Wood ash settling on the surface can be a cause, also volatiles from a number of minerals and pigment oxides. See *chrome-tin-pink, copper*, etc. Deliberate flashing can be achieved by confining a piece of pottery in a saggar together with salt and/or other volatiles in open bowls. Copper and lusters will sometimes develop a halo round the painted line which is a form of local flashing. (See *fuming, kiln gloss, smear glaze, volatilization*.)

Flat liner

A long, slender, square-cut flat brush.

Flatware

An industrial term for plates, saucers, etc. Flatware presents problems in throwing, drying and firing, especially when using highly plastic clay. This is evidenced by the dearth of handmade plates. (See *plates*.)

Fletton

An English building brick. Named after the original center of manufacture near Peterborough, but now made in vast quantities from a deeper and harder clay seam which stretches from Yorkshire to Dorset, known as Oxford (Jurassic) clay. It is shaley and contains organic matter which assists firing. Flettons are made by a semi-dry method. Suitable for *raku* and similar firings and for the outer skins of higher temperature kilns. Flettons are more porous and better insulators than firebricks, but are not for hot-face use except for low heat (less than 950°C/1742°F) situations such as *sawdust firing*.

Flexmould

A proprietary (Flexmould Inc. USA) flexible mold-making material which allows for some undercuts in the form.

Flicked-on color

Slip, glaze, or pigment thrown or flicked onto a surface can complement the form as it flows naturally over the curve of the pot. Very fine application, using a hog's hair or other stiff brushes can provide a background for further decoration. (See also *brush* and illustration.)

Flint

A dark blue-gray boulder pebble found in chalk seams. It is a form of micro- (or crypto-) crystalline silica, SiO_2, of considerable purity. A typical analysis by weight:

CaO	0.68		
Na_2O	0.05	Al_2O_3 0.29	SiO_2 97.9
MgO	0.01	Fe_2O_3 0.07	TiO_2 0.01

It is used to provide silica in glazes and bodies, and to whiten the latter. It is less pure but finer-grained than quartz, and thus more readily converted into *cristobalite*. It is available in 140–325 mesh (Pottery Supply House and others). The finer the grain of the flint the more effectively it will be involved in the glassy state. Hamer warns, however, that a very fine-grained silica cannot, therefore, be considered as a refractory. In the USA the term is often given to any fine-ground silica rocks used in ceramics.

Flint, like any form of silica, is a health hazard if inhaled and partly for this reason its use as a setting material has largely given way to alumina. In America 'flint' refers to any form of ground silica including quartz.

Floatatives, floatation

An American term for additions to slips and glazes which prevent them settling in water. See at the English equivalent — *suspender*.

Flocculation, flocculant

The aggregation or coming together of particles in suspension. A flocculant is a material (an *electrolyte*) which causes this flocking. The effect of salt from the sea on river-borne clays is responsible for *estuarine* deposits. While a flocculant will hasten the settling of fine clay particles its immediate effect is to thicken (useful when glazing a low-porosity biscuit), and to keep larger particles of glaze, etc. in suspension. The converse is *deflocculation*.

Gelatine and polymer adhesives will act temporarily, but this is a physical suspension rather than flocculation. Vinegar is also used but is unpleasant and its effect is not permanent. The commonest inorganic material is bentonite. Calcium chloride, magnesium chloride (epsom salts) in very small proportions (a few drops of concentrated solutions) together with bentonite have been recommended in glazes. I have found ochre in a glaze to have a similar effect, as can also wood ash and colemanite. An unwanted result can be the increased shrinkage if the mixture gets too thick and water is added, causing glaze or slip to craze or peel as it dries.

Flower brick

An oblong box, usually about the size of a standard house brick, with holes in the top to take flower stems. A simple form but capable of many variations and nuances, from the carefully constructed slab pot to the rough-hewn finishes typified by Otto Natzler and Peter Smith among others.

A rough-hewn 'flower brick' by Peter Smith.

Fluid, fluidity

A substance that takes the shape of the containing vessel. A liquid (or a gas).

The degree to which a material (glaze, slip, etc.) approaches a liquid is its fluidity. The reciprocal of *viscosity*. Glazes are less fluid than glass, which does not contain alumina. Alkalis increase the fluidity of glazes. (See *poise, viscosity*.)

Fluorine

A gaseous element. F. 19. The fumes are a health hazard. Known as a halogen or salt-producer; it reacts with alkalis to form a lattice similar to that of common salt. It also reacts with other pottery oxides. Can cause blisters on release from a glaze (see *fluorspar*). China stone is sometimes *defluorinated*. Cryolite, sodium fluoride and lepidolite will also provide fluorine. In CM 19/7 Behrens discusses fluorine and gives some simple recipes, e.g.

Lepidolite	52.0	Sodium fluoride	2.8
Fluorspar	12.4	Flint	32.8
Firing to cone	4.0		

He mentions that the glazes may be smooth or 'cratered' (bubbled), but does not give further advice. 'Considerable color variation from the norm' may be expected from the pigment oxides.

Fluorspar

'Derbyshire spar'. CaF_2, 78.
Decomposes in the presence of silica, forming a gas SiF_4, leaving CaO in the glaze. Toxic.

'It perhaps has a catalytic effect on the calcium and other elements in the batch'. (Cardew). Not widely used in pottery glazes, where over 5% may cause blistering through the release of fluorine. Can help to give a more transparent green stoneware glaze from chrome. Acts as a flux in a multi-base glaze but the release of harmful gases must be catered for with good ventilation. (See *fluorine*.) 'Can be destructive of kiln furniture after long-term use' (Georgies).

Flute

See *ocarina, whistle*.

A charming double flute or pipe by Neil Ions.

Fluting

The cutting of grooves into the surface of a pot. Leach PB illustrates a fluting tool: a thin strip of metal with a short cross-cut about $\frac{1}{2}$in/12.5mm from one end, beaten down

A lively, swirling fluting on a tenmoku glazed bottle by Leo F. Matthews.

to form a tooth which gives a controlled, curved cut (very like one of the individual cutting edges on a *Surform* tool). A fine wire-ended tool, perhaps with a 'stop' on it to prevent too deep a cut, is more easily available. Less 'accurate' but livelier cutting is done with a bamboo tool sharpened to a chisel edge towards the outer, harder skin of a large-diameter bamboo. When fluting round a large bowl or pot, the corners of the bamboo tool may wear away, altering the appearance and crispness of the cut and for this reason a steel tool is sometimes used.

The state of dryness of the clay will affect the character of the cuts. Fluting on softer clay is more fluid — or 'fluky', to quote Cardew. David Leach works on leather-hard clay and cuts with a sweep of the arm from a supported elbow, 'locking' the wrist to a fixed position.

The flutes can be fine and regular or wide and free, and are sometimes combined with combing.

Fluvial clay

Clays which have been deposited in rivers, similar to *estuarine* clays.

Flux, fluxing, fusible

In ceramics the term indicates an oxide, generally a *base*, which lowers the melting point of an *acidic oxide*, especially silica. *Boric oxide* has an ambiguous position. The fluxes are *network modifiers*.

Individual oxides may have a low or high melting point (e.g. Sb_2O_3 656°C, CaO 2570°C/4658°F) but it is the reaction between the oxide and silica which is of interest to potters. Lime can be a very fluid flux at stoneware temperatures. From the *eutectic* it will be seen that a 'fluxing' oxide will be increasingly effective up to a certain proportion; beyond that it will begin to reverse the effect and lead to *crystallization* of the cooling glaze. Basic matt glazes can be achieved in this way, but care must be taken not to develop an unstable formula with resultant *metal release*.

Oxides vary in their effectiveness as fluxes — i.e. the temperature at which they become active. With certain exceptions, a variety of bases will be more efficient than a single one. The following list is a general guide, starting with the most active fluxes; the later ones are used in stonewares.

Lead oxide PbO *Soft glazes* only. Can be used as sole flux.
Boric oxide B_2O_3 Essential in soft *leadless glazes*. The only *acidic* oxide in the list.
Potassium oxide K_2O Features in all types of glazes. A primary flux in stoneware and porcelain, secondary in earthenware. Efficient at lower temperatures.
Sodium oxide Na_2O All glazes. Can be a primary flux in soft glazes.
Lithium oxide Li_2O Efficient at low temperatures.
Strontium oxide SrO Some similarities to calcium but more effective at low temperatures though in this case it should be introduced as a frit (the carbonate will not start to be effective below about 1100°C/2012°F).
Zinc oxide ZnO Up to 3% is effective in earthenware. The major flux in Bristol glazes (1180°C/2156°F).
Calcium oxide CaO Secondary flux in small amounts in earthenware. Can develop very fluid glazes above 1250°C/2282°F.
Magnesium oxide MgO Used in small amounts. Most effective from 1150°C/2102°F upwards.
Barium oxide BaO Fairly refractory. Stonewares.

Of the pigment oxides, manganese is very fusible, copper and cobalt are weak fluxes. Iron is fusible only in reduction. Fluxes in a body will also, of course, form glassy melts leading to *vitrification*. The type of flux will affect the color from pigments, see individual entries.

Fly ash

Ash carried by draft through a kiln. Can be responsible for 'kiln-gloss' or *flashing*. May also spoil the appearance of a lid or any horizontal pot surface in a kiln, especially when salt glazing.

Foamed clay

Insulating bricks made by generating bubbles, physically or chemically, in thick slip. These are trapped as it dries.

Folded form

Pots and bowls can be folded or deformed in very different styles. Pots can be pressed inwards in the style of the New Forest pots of Roman times or given the more subtle indentation of Eileen Lewenstein's cylinders. The rims of bowls and dishes have been manipulated into the elaborate frills of Mary Rogers or the simple lifted rim of Sheila Fournier's sawdust-fired dishes.

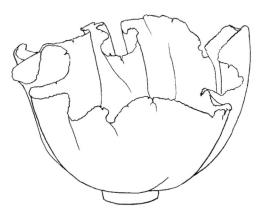

A folded form by Mary Rogers.

Foot, foot-ring

The foot, as distinct from the base, is the termination of the form; it is that part of the piece on which the main shape stands. This may hardly exist but for a bevel at the base, or may turn outwards or subtlely change direction. It is an important part of the form and can alter its character.

Most bowls need a foot-ring, sometimes referred to as a 'foot-rim'. It is, in effect, a low pedestal which can be thrown onto the turned, inverted bowl, or cut from the surplus clay left at the base when it was thrown. The bowl section should not vary in thickness to any great extent throughout its whole curve. The proportions of a foot-ring — its height, width and splay — can make or mar a bowl form. It must be in tune with, and emphasize, the character of the bowl: its sturdiness, lightness, roundness, etc. Physically it must support the curve: a small foot on a flat bowl can result in slumping or warping. The foot should be visible from an oblique viewpoint.

Three bowls showing how the slope of the foot-ring can affect the form. The bowls are identical with only the foot-ring varied.

A foot-ring being turned on a bowl. (For more detail see under turning).

The ring width will appear to be smaller (narrower) when you are turning it than it will when the bowl is set right way up. Cut a somewhat smaller ring, therefore, than you think the bowl will need or, better still, use an inside chuck so that it can be removed and checked during the turning. Cut your initial ring quite wide so that it can be corrected later. Most foot-rings are vertical but variations are possible, even the slightest of which can alter the general character of the bowl. (See *turning.*)

Forced draft

A mechanical augmentation of the normal chimney draft through a kiln. Air is either blown into the firing chamber, or movement in the chimney is speeded up with a fan. A fan can be used to blow air into the combustion chamber of a wood kiln which needs a great deal of ventilation. A forced draft kiln may need only a minimal chimney (see also *oil burners*).

Formaldehyde, *formalin*

Chemical formula HCHO. Suggested as an additive to prevent the decomposition of gums used in glazes. Formalin is the liquid form. (See *suspender.*)

Former

A rather wider term than 'mold' which suggests a predetermined shape, and used to cover any constructed or 'natural' form which can be utilized in the process of shaping.

In addition to a biscuited bowl or other pottery shape into which clay can be pressed, many common objects — a pebble, a balloon, a bag of sand, a roll of paper or card — have been used as formers. Clay release is easier if the

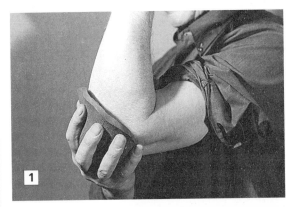

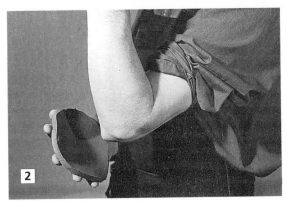

1 and *2* Making a small dish over one's elbow!
3 A joined up group of small dishes formed over stones.

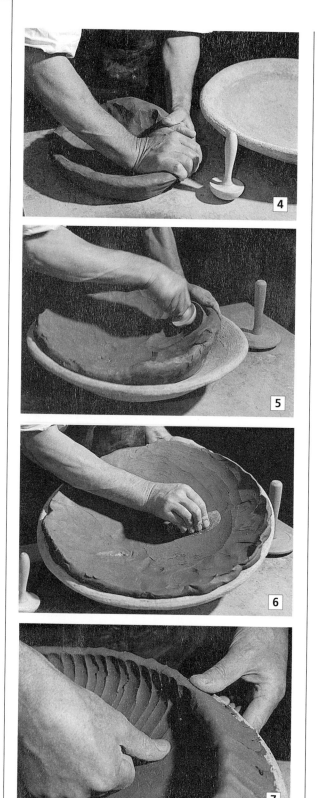

4–7. Stages in pressing a large dish or unit of construction in a biscuit former or mold. First a block of fairly soft, usually grogged clay is pressed with the palm of the hand, or rolled out, and then eased into the shape, thinning the wall with a darning head. Finally the surface is scraped and smoothed with a steel palette. Extensions to the form can be coiled on. *8–10* A simple former made from four strips of leather-hard clay, a slab of clay eased into the central space.

material of the former is slightly absorbent. In Japan, small pots and bowls have been formed over the elbow, the knee, or the hand. Carlton Ball deals with many variations as do many primers (basic text books). (See also *handbuilding*.)

A raku dish made in this way by Sheila Fournier.

Formula

A chemical or *molecular* description of a material. A glaze may be written as a formula or as a recipe. A formula is written as a list of the *elements* or *oxides* which enter into the fired glaze; a recipe is a proportional list of the *minerals* and other materials which will most nearly approximate to the formula.

The *element symbols* are used in the formula. A small figure following and slightly below the symbol (e.g. Pb_2) indicates the number of atoms in the *molecule*. A figure preceding an oxide formula indicates the number of molecules of the whole oxide. Thus $3Al_2O_3$ represents three molecules of alumina, which is itself made up of two atoms of aluminum to every three of oxygen.

The ultimate or *empirical formula* merely lists the relationship between the atoms of the material, e.g. $Al_2Si_2H_4O_9$, or it might read $Al_2Si_2O_3(OH)_4$. These tell a potter little about the material, except that the second formula suggests that it is a *hydrated* mineral. If the same elements are grouped into oxides as $Al_2O_3. 2SiO_2. 2H_2O$, we can recognize kaolinite. This is the *rational formula*.

The symbols are, of course, relative ones, and do not refer to any practical amounts or weights. They can, however, be translated into weighable minerals and oxides. (See *analysis, formula-into-recipe.*)

Formula from percentage weights

To turn a weight percentage list of oxides (analysis) into a molecular formula, divide each number by its molecular weight.

Example:
46.5 SiO_2, 39.5 Al_2O_3, 14 H_2O

$$\frac{46.5}{60} = 0.775$$

$$\frac{39.5}{102} = 0.387$$

$$\frac{14}{18} = 0.777$$

If each is divided by the smallest number a molecular ratio is arrived at — $2SiO_2. Al_2O_3. 2H_2O$ or the formula for *kaolinite*.

The figures derived from an analysis can also be used in *Seger formula* terms by adding the bases together and dividing all the figures by the total.

Formula-into-recipe

The fundamental equation is:
Molecular parts x molecular weight = parts by weight. 'Parts by weight' refers to physical comparative weights: grams, ounces, or what you will. It is rarely possible, however, to use simple oxides in a recipe. They will more often be one constituent of more elaborate minerals. To simplify the arithmetic, two charts have been suggested. The molecular make-up or formula of a glaze or mineral is tabulated according to the Seger formula, i.e. in the proportions of the bases, amphoterics and acids, the sum of the bases being kept at unity. This can be transcribed into a list of physical materials with their proportional weights, as follows.

A chart is made up of as many columns as there are oxides in the formula, plus five more, and as many horizontal spaces as there will be raw materials in the recipe, plus two.

It will be seen that the 'molecular parts' figure is that represented by unity in the formula for the mineral. For instance, the clay is $Al_2O_3.2SiO_2.2H_2O$. The H_2O (water) is lost in the firing and is ignored (although allowed for in the total molecular weight of clay); of the rest, the alumina is at unity so the figure of 0.3 is used. The molecular weight for oxides and minerals is given under each entry. The bottom line gives the totals for the oxides, which must correspond with the formula.

The recipe is always approximate, as the minerals are considered to be in exact accordance with the *ideal formula*, which is rarely the case. It is possible to have each mineral analyzed into its actual oxide proportions, but for the average craft potter this is impractical. Results of these computations can be taken as a reference-point and guide. The proof is always in the firing.

Decisions as to which materials to use to translate the formula are a matter of trial and error. Start with materials which will satisfy the *RO (base)* requirements. These may be oxides or carbonates such as litharge or whiting, in which case the decision is a simple one. In many cases this will not be so. Lead oxide is forbidden in schools, and a frit must be used. This will automatically introduce silica into the glaze batch. In the example shown in chart A below, sesquisilicate is listed; this has the formula PbO. $1.5SiO_2$. For every one molecule of lead, one and a half molecules of silica are introduced. We could use the monosilicate, proportions 1:1, or the bisilicate, 1:2, entering the appropriate proportions of silica in its column. Working from left to right, alumina is the next oxide to be considered. It would be possible to use calcined alumina, but it is too coarse and, as a general rule, natural minerals are preferable to synthetic ones. We need a mineral which does not include unwanted oxides. China clay fulfills the requirements, introducing one alumina molecule to two silica. The 0.3 alumina is therefore entered in the appropriate

column and the accompanying 0.6 of silica in its column.

In satisfying the lead and alumina requirements we have, willy-nilly, put 1.5 + 0.6 silica into the batch, a total of 2.1. This falls 0.9 short of the required 3.0 parts and, luckily, there are two minerals which are nearly pure SiO_2: flint and quartz. This completes the formula. If we had used bisilicate of lead, only 0.4 parts of flint would have been required.

One more example with a longer formula: a hypothetical stoneware glaze.

Example:

K_2O 0.3	Al_2O_3 0.32	SiO_2 3.3
CaO 0.6		TiO_2 0.2
MgO 0.1		

Working from left to right as before:

1 K_2O. The most convenient material is potash feldspar

Formula into recipe–chart A

PbO	Al_2O_3	SiO_2	Material	Molecular parts x weight		Parts by weight		%
1.0		1.5	Lead sesquilicate	1.0 x 313	=	313	=	70.5
	0.3	0.6	China clay	0.3 x 258	=	77.4	=	17.4
		0.9	Flint	0.9 x 60	=	54	=	12.1
1.0	0.3	3.0	TOTALS			444.4	=	100.0

Formula into recipe–chart B

K_2O	CaO	MgO	Al_2O_3	SiO_2	TiO_2	Material	Molecular parts x weight		Parts by weight		%
0.3			0.3	1.8		Feldspar	0.3 x 556	=	166.8	=	48.47
	0.5					Whiting	0.5 x 100	=	50.0	=	14.53
	0.1	0.1				Dolomite	0.1 x 184	=	18.4	=	5.34
			0.02	0.04		China clay	0.02 x 258	=	5.2	=	1.50
				1.46		Quartz	1.46 x 60	=	87.6	=	25.52
					0.2	Titania	0.2 x 80	=	16.0	=	4.64
0.3	0.6	0.1	0.32	3.3	0.2	TOTALS			344.0	=	100.0

which will also bring in, for one part of potash, one part of alumina, and six silica, e.g. for 0.3 K₂O, 0.3 alumina and 0.3 x 6 = 1.8 silica. See that these proportions are not more than are required.

2 CaO. This can be used as the carbonate, whiting, 0.6 parts. Nothing else is added in the process.

3 MgO. The most readily available source of magnesia is dolomite where it occurs in equal parts with calcium. If we use 0.1 part of dolomite to provide magnesia we also add 0.1 parts of CaO. We must therefore reconsider the whiting and alter the 0.6 parts to 0.5, so that the total introduced by whiting plus dolomite does not exceed the formula requirements.

4 Al₂O₃. The feldspar has already provided 0.3 parts, leaving only 0.02 to be accounted for. Using clay we can add this amount, with the appropriate 0.04 entry under silica.

5 SiO₂. Feldspar has given 1.8 and clay 0.04. We require 3.3, or 1.46 more and can use flint or quartz.

6 TiO₂. Titanium oxide can be used, 0.2 parts. (See Chart B)

In both cases dealt with above it has been possible to satisfy the formula with common minerals. If, however, formula B had required 0.45 parts of potash, this would have given similar parts of alumina — more than required — and so feldspar could not have been used. In fact there is no common mineral which would have been suitable, and you would have had to resort to a frit. Where this situation arises it may be better to reconsider your formula, especially where a stoneware glaze is being formulated.

Formula weight, *Molecular weight*

Also known as the *molecular weight*. The total of the atomic weights of all the elements which make up the formula. **Example**: clay, Al₂O₃.2SiO₂.2H₂O = 2 x 27 (Al) + 2 x 28 (Si) + 4 x 1 (H) + 9 x 16 (O) = 258. The figure following the formula for each of the minerals in this book is the molecular or formula weight. (See also *equivalent weight*.)

Fountain, *waterfall*

Forms in which water runs from one level to another has a great fascination. An ingenious potter can devise many variations on this theme. The flow can be made continuous by means of a small pump.

Free silica

That proportion of silica in a raw or fired body which is not combined with other oxides, i.e. remains as crystals.

Quartz or flint added to the body may remain 'free'. During heating and cooling the free silica undergoes *inversions* with consequent strain on the body. At temperatures above 1070°C/1958°F it is slowly converted into another SiO₂ form — *cristobalite*. Siliceous ball clay contains quartz grains. (See also *crazing*).

Fremington clay

A fine-grain, very clean, fusible red clay from Devon (UK) comparatively low in lime and high in alkalis. Probably *glacial*. Very clean and can generally be used as dug. It is famous for its throwing qualities; has been used as a *burnishing* slip; and as a *slip glaze* with some extra fluxes and silica, at temperatures above 1250°C/2282°F.

French chalk

A preparation from *steatite (talc)*.

Friable

Crumbly, easily reduced to small pieces or to a powder.

Frilled cordon

A band or clay strap round a pot or bowl which is pressed with the finger alternately up and down to form a 'frill'.

Frit

A ground glass or glaze. The potter utilizes naturally occurring minerals as far as possible, but sometimes it is difficult to find an insoluble and non-toxic source for a required oxide. Borax, for instance, the main source of boric oxide, is soluble even after *calcining*. Litharge, white and red lead are all poisonous and are usually used as *silicate* glasses or frits.

Frits are always used on industrial pottery in order to ensure uniformity of color and other qualities, and to avoid uneven settling in the glaze batch. Frits have lost any combined water and carbon dioxide, which may have been present in the raw materials. They are therefore concentrated and must be applied more thinly. The transparency of the glaze immediately after dipping can be misleading — one feels the coating is too thin. Frits settle rapidly in water. Common salt is reputed to assist *floatation*.

They are best used as a basis for further additions of raw minerals, i.e. treated as one item in a recipe. To use frits scientifically one must know their formula, which should be treated like any other multi-oxide material. The lead silicates and the softer borax and alkaline frits are useful to the earthenware potter. With few exceptions (one being David Leach's stoneware glaze) all commercially prepared glazes are frits. Fritting can alter and control colors.

The potter can prepare his own frits in small quantities, but they are normally made by the industry and sold in a finely powdered state. Glaze materials, soluble and otherwise, are mixed and melted together in a special oven, often in the form of a revolving cylinder. When quite fluid the molten glaze is let out in a stream into a tank of cold water. It will break into fragments under the thermal shock, resembling granulated sugar. The grain size is further reduced in a *ball mill* or a *vibratory mill*.

The craft potter has to melt his materials in a bowl in the kiln, break the bowl away and pulverize the frit, or else heat them in a crucible and continue as above. If ground in a mortar and pestle, a teaspoonful must be dealt with at a time. A ball mill or *jar mill* is a virtual necessity. David Eeles makes large quantities of an alkaline frit for use in his fine celadon glazes, melting china clay, quartz, and soda ash in biscuited pots which have been washed over with quartz, then crushing and milling the frit. Several suppliers list the contents of their frits.

Frit body

Clay bodies are not often combined with frit by studio potters unless the *feldspathoids* are considered as frits, see *porcelain*. Exceptions are *bone china* and *Egyptian paste*. (See also *soft paste*.) Frits are, however sometimes used in engobes or *slip glazes*.

Frost, frozen pots

A rain-saturated garden pot is always liable to frost damage although most of the danger results when a pot is allowed to become partly filled with water or very wet soil. It is not advisable, therefore, to plant directly into a garden pot but into a plastic container which can be housed (on bricks if necessary) within it, or suspended from the neck of the pot. Holes in the base, cut during making or drilled after firing, to prevent the build-up of water, are essential for open-air pots. Stoneware is obviously less susceptible to frost damage than earthenware although the fine large porous pots from Crete and elsewhere can stand quite a severe frost without damage. See for more information John Huggins' 'Pots for gardens'.

A potter is always likely to be caught by a sudden intense frost within his or her studio, if this is unheated at night, with usually disastrous results on wet clay or even on ware at the soft-leather stage. I well remember a damp-cupboard-full of teapots which suffered in this way and were consigned to the bin. However when Alan Ashpool

(CR 11/59) who slip-casts ware, found his work cracked with frost, instead of immediately disposing of them he found that the breaks slowly disappeared and the clay knitted together as it warmed. The ware was fired without mishap. This may be a feature of his particular slip-cast pieces but it seems as well to wait a while in case the miracle happens to you!

Fude

The standard Far Eastern brush, around 1in long and ³⁄₈in wide (25mm x 11mm) or wider, made of badger, dog, deer, or goat hair. Softer than a sable brush, they are intended to be used vertically held well away from the point. (See *brush*.)

Fuel

Material used to produce heat by *rapid oxidation*. (See *coke, gas, oil, paraffin, wood*.) Electricity is not, in this sense, a fuel: it is energy supplied at one remove. Fuels vary in their flame temperatures. The maximum attainable heat has been given as around 1370°C/2498°F for wood, 1500°C/2732°F for coal, 1650°C/3002°F for oil. *Drainoil* is reputed to have a higher Btu rating per gallon than any other fuel. Coal varies from 10–14 thousand, and wood 6–9 thousand *btus* (see *British Thermal Units*) per pound; *natural gas* 1000 btus per cubic foot; liquid petroleum gas 2500 btus per cubic foot.

Fuller's earth

A calcium *montmorillonite* type mineral with impurities sometimes including iron oxide. Originally used for the 'fulling' or cleaning of wool. There are contrary opinions as to its plasticity. Cardew dismisses it as 'nonplastic'; James Walford (CR60) 'highly plastic'. It is possible that different sources for the 'earth' give different results, Walford's coming from North Africa, though the mineral is widely distributed in England and elsewhere.

Walford suggests that it can be used in clay bodies in small quantities and also, after calcinating at around 850°C/1562°F in celadon glazes (10–15%), the fuller's earth itself supplying the necessary iron oxide. He sprays the glaze onto the pot to avoid crawling.

Fumes

The fumes from burning materials can be dangerous to health as can the products of *reduction*, especially *carbon monoxide*. The problem is most acute in electric kilns which are often unvented. Well-ventilated kiln areas

hould be ensured. Some attempts to discharge the sul-
urous and other fumes from electric kilns which often
occur in the firing of clays and glazes have resulted in unac-
ceptably low rates of temperature rise, but many suppliers
advertise kiln ventilation equipment which must have been
tested in this regard. Others (Georgies, etc.) list the more
traditional counterweighted hood ventilator system (see
ventilation).

Fuming

Surface effects on bodies and glazes, generally at stoneware
temperatures, obtained by firing pots in enclosed saggars
with volatiles; the chlorides, sulfates, or nitrates of metals.
Keep a good standard of ventilation in the kiln room. The
fuming materials can be put into a small biscuit bowl in
the bottom of the saggar; some potters layer them with
sawdust or charcoal, some with sand to slow down the
decomposition. (See *volatilization*.)

Salt-glaze is itself a form of fuming. Parks introduces
copper fuming into his kiln by the use of old plumbing
items of copper or brass in the hearth at the end of the firing, giving somewhat unpredictably placed red blushes on
the ware. He also suggests two teaspoonful of stannous
chloride at red to black heat for mother-of-pearl effects.
Using stannous chloride, strontium nitrate, and barium
chloride, John Conrad, quoted in CR153, gives a bluish
blush.

It must be stressed that these materials are **very toxic** as
are the fumes given off during firing, and every precaution
must be taken — efficient ventilation, the wearing of a
mask, and so on.

Fuse, electric

A 'weak link' of easily melted wire put into a circuit to
avoid the over-heating which would develop from the flow
of more *current* than the *conducting* wires will take, i.e.
from what is known as a *short-circuit*. Fuses are graded
according to the current in amperes which they will conduct without failing, e.g. a 15 amp fuse will begin to over-
heat at 16 amps, and will melt at approximately 20–25
amps. Fuses may be of wire or a wire enclosed in a capsule.
An *ELCB* fulfills a similar function. (See also *heat-fuse, fail-
safe*.)

Fuse, fusion, fusible

To melt together. Fusible materials are those which melt
easily or lower the melting point of a mixture such as a
glaze. Some oxides are *refractory* in themselves but act as
fusible agents (see *flux*) in a glaze.

Fused alumina

Used for *abrasives*.

Fused silica

A translucent or transparent vitreous silica made by fusing
quartz sand in an open furnace.

Fusion

In ceramics it indicates the melting of one or a number of
appropriate materials into a liquid mass. (See *glaze*.)

Fusion flow test

See *button test*.

Gabbro

A basic granite, usually high in iron oxides (usually around 10%). Widely distributed (found in Cornwall, England and elsewhere). 'The *plutonic* equivalent of *basalt*.' Macmillan Encyclopedia.

Average analysis: MgCaO, 20%; Na₂K₂O, 2%; FeO/Fe₂O₃, 5% (but variable; no iron in Saxony gabbro, for instance); Al₂O₃, 20%; SiO₂, 48%. (See also at *glazes from natural sources*.)

Galena

A lead ore, lead sulfide PbS, 239, s.g. 7.5. *Conversion factor* 0.93.

Widely distributed. Used on medieval pottery and 17th-century slipware. Toxic but less so than litharge or white lead. Contains copper and other impurities (some silver is extracted) which enhances its value for slipware but not for more sophisticated glazes. Needs plenty of ventilation during firing to disperse the sulfur and to form PbO. Not, therefore, very suitable for electric kilns. Galena-glazed pots are often once-fired (as in the film 'Isaac Button, country potter'). Other types of glaze in the same kiln may be spoiled. 'Updraft kilns are best for galena glazes' (Leach).

Example of raw-clay galena glaze recipe:

Galena	66
Plastic clay	16
Flint	18

Weights can be transposed from litharge recipes.

A lead glaze will use part of the body surface to assist its maturity during firing; it will thus eat away thin slip.

Ganister

A fine-grain silica rock found in lower coal measures (e.g. in Yorkshire, England, and in the USA). It is ground, mixed with clay, and used in *silica refractories*.

Garnet

A group of crystalline minerals used as abrasives and gemstones. The *RO* constituents vary, the general formula being RO.R₂O₃.3SiO₂.

Gas

Any substance in the gaseous state, scientifically defined as 'occupying the whole of the space in which it is contained' (Uvarov). Its molecules are in a free state and not connected to one another in any pattern. Air is the most common gas. In everyday use 'gas' is usually taken to mean *gas fuel*.

Gas burner

Gas fuel must be mixed with air for combustion. This is normally done at the point where the gas escapes from the pipe. The burners may be divided into three groups:

1 Atmospheric or inspiratory burners where the forward movement of gas under pressure draws in the air needed for combustion.

2 Burners in which a current of air draws in gas, itself under small or nil pressure.

3 Where gas and air are mixed in a chamber behind the burner.

The first of these is the simplest and the most commonly used. Gas is easily ignited and the burners are more simple in construction and principle than those used for oil. See also Rhodes K for other useful information. Axner lists a 'raku burner' in which the propane vaporizes in the burner itself rather than in the tank, 'eliminating frozen tanks even when only small amounts of propane exist'.

Gas expansion

The expansion for a given temperature rise of any gas will be the ratio in Kelvin degrees. Example: air at 10°C/50°F is at 283°K; at 1100°C/2012°F its equivalent in K is 1373°K. The expansion (based on °C) will be 1373/283 = 4.68.

Thus the atmospheric pressure of a cubic meter of air at 10°C/50°F will have increased in volume to 4.68cu m at 1100°C/2012°F. Kilns must be designed to accommodate such volume differences between cold air inlets and hot air outlets.

Gas fuel

'Town' or coal gas has a high proportion of free hydrogen; 'natural' or well-gas is largely methane.

The Office of Gas Supply (UK) arrives at therms for costing purposes by multiplying the volume of gas (or the weight) by its calorific value and dividing the result by 100,000.

Example: 7.500 cu. ft. of natural gas =

$$\frac{7500 \times 1000}{100,000} = 75 \text{ therms}$$

or 350lb of propane   =

$$\frac{350 \times 21,500}{100,000} = 75 \text{ therms}$$

(In Great Britain the therm is likely to be replaced by a European Community system.) The proportions of ingredients will vary a little but it will be seen that *natural* gas has none of the very poisonous CO while its high methane content gives it greater efficiency and, reputedly, a 'cleaner' and better firing in the kiln.

Cylinder or *bottled gas* (LPG) produces nearly three times as many Btu per cubic foot as natural gas. Supply gas is lighter than air and will rise, whereas LPG is heavier than air and will collect at a low level making it dangerous in enclosed spaces or basements.

See chart.

Gas kiln

If gas supply is available in sufficient quantity (a 2in/50mm mains is the minimum requirement), a gas kiln can provide clean, versatile, and comparatively trouble-free firing.

Design can be of the open-chamber or *semimuffle* type, and there are several ways of burning the gas. Most kilns mix the fuel and air at the primary air or burner point.

For smaller kilns, a pressure of around 8oz is required (somewhat higher than those of 15cu ft/0.5cu m or more). Your local gas supplier should be consulted.

The design of gas kilns, both for supply and *bottled gas,* allows wide variations and can be very simple. 'Strict rules for (proportions of parts) should be viewed with some reserve' (Casson). There are normally several burners or jets. No chimney is normally required but poisonous gases are released and, at a minimum, a ventilation hood and extractor piping must be provided.

Mick Casson has found that natural gas has a lazier flame than had town gas and that the burners are easily extinguished when burning low. Ideally the burners should be within the kiln wall. Good *secondary air* control is essential. Natural gas takes more air for combustion than did town gas and larger flues are needed. Great heat and strong reduction are possible. There is some tendency for spalling and disintegration to occur in refractories.

As with other types, gas kiln design has been revolutionized by ceramic fiber and other new materials. Andrew Holden, in CR87, describes the building, in a few hours, of a gas kiln using *Sayvit bricks* and *ceramic fiber.* Fordham Thermal Systems supply a kit for building your own 5cu ft LPG model. (See also *gas burner, inspirating burner.*)

Gault clay

A brick clay with a high calcium content and consequent short *vitrification* range (maximum firing temperature around 1100°C/2012°F) used for brick-making. The iron content is bleached by the calcia to yellow or buff in a clay body, but when used as a *slip glaze* at high temperatures some samples will behave more like *Albany clay.*

Breakdown of Gas Fuels					
% volume of	Coal gas	Reformed gas	Natural gas	Propane	Butane
Methane CH_4	15	25	94.5		
Higher hydrocarbons	5	2	4	C_3H_8	C_2H_{10}
Carbon monoxide CO	14	2	nil	known as LPG liquid petroleum gases	
Carbon dioxide CO_2	4	14	nil		
Hydrogen H	55	57	nil		
Nitrogen N	7	nil	1.5		
Calorific value (gross)					
Btu/cu ft	500	500	1000	2500	3000
Btu/lb				21500	21200
Specific gravity	0.49	0.49	0.59	1.5	2.0
Air required for combustion given as cu ft per cu ft of gas	4.5	4.5	9.5	24.0	31.0

Geology

Geology is the study of the whole physical earth. The study of the rocks which form the earth's crust, and which is more important to the potter, is known as *petrology*.

Geranium, oxide

A metallic element Ge, 72.5. Oxide GeO_2 104.5.
    Sometimes listed as a *glass-former*, i.e. with silica.

Gerstley borate

An impure *colemanite* or borate of sodium and calcium with some magnesium, from the Gerstley Mine, Death Valley, California. The ore is a mixture of colemanite and ulexite (Harry Fraser). It has proved to be a particularly 'well-behaved' form of colemanite, only very slowly soluble in water. 'Helps to prevent crazing and acts somewhat as an opacifier' (Georgies).

Gerstley borate appears in a number of American glaze recipes in proportions averaging 10–12%, especially for the lower stoneware range 1210–1230°C. Typical analysis (USA Borax Corp): 28% B_2O_3; 20.6% CaO; 5.3% Na_2O; the rest water and shale. Imported in the UK by Potclays Ltd and available in the USA from Georgies, etc.

Gibbsite

A hydrated alumina mineral, $Al(OH)_2$, or, Al_2O_3 $3H_2O$. Calcined at a high temperature to eliminate high shrinkage. The alumina in kaolin is in the form of a 'modified gibbsite sheet' (Worrall). Can be used, with a little china clay, as a *bat wash*.

Gilding

Dodd defines gilding as 'the painting of pottery with liquid gold to be fired on at 700°C/1292°F' but as a general term 'gilding' usually indicates the application of gold leaf with an adhesive or as a paint. (See *gold*.)

Glacial clays

Clays which have been transported by glaciers are deposited more or less as they are picked up; they are not separated into particles sizes as are river-borne clays. They are therefore often mixed with non-clay matter and with boulders — hence boulder-clay. Cardew cites the *Fremington clay* of North Devon in England as a possible glacial clay.

Glass

A 'melt' of *inorganic* materials cooled sufficiently quickly to prevent crystallization, and so retaining its amorphous structure. A super-cooled liquid. It has a three-dimensional network structure, but without the symmetry of crystals. Glaze is a special form of glass, containing alumina, and with a comparatively low thermal expansion.

Foremost of the materials which can form glass is silica. It will 'fuse' alone at 1713°C/3115°F but in combination with larger atoms of lower valencies it will melt at lower temperatures. These elements, generally the *bases*, weaken the *network* bond. Glass can be so soft as actually to dissolve in water (sodium silicate), or hard enough to withstand great abrasion or chemical reaction (salt-glaze, which is also a soda-silicate but of different formation). Window glass will lie somewhere between these extremes and is produced with little or no alumina. (See also *glaze, glass-formers, network modifiers, Seger formula*, etc.)

Glass cullet

Pieces or powder of transparent or colored glass. (See *cullet*.)

Glass decoration

Pieces of glass or, especially, mirror glass have been used decoratively, set into pottery after firing. Delan Cookson uses molded glass in some of his enigmatic 'screw' forms, as in 'Jelly Press' where the jelly is of transparent glass. (See also *melted glass decoration*.)

Glass fiber

Fine threads of glass woven into a matted form for use in comparatively low-temperature insulation situations. Not recommended for kilns. A good electrical insulator.

Glass former

Or *network former*. Only a few materials, all acidic oxides, can form glass. The most useful to potters are silica and boric oxide, the former being the prime essential in all glazes and in the great majority of ceramic bodies. Antimony oxide and phosphorus pentoxide are of some interest (the latter retaining much of its crystalline structure and giving the particular effects seen in Jun glaze), though it has no place in the glass *network* (Hamer).

The silica tetrahedrons form a random network of linked molecules in the liquid state which can be 'opened' or modified by *bases* to become fluid at a lower temperature. Quick ooling 'freezes' the random network, which cannot then rrange itself into crystals.

Germanium oxide and arsenous oxide are also listed. Under some conditions alumina can also assist in glass-forming.

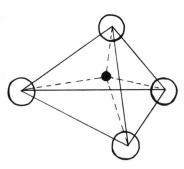

A representation of the silica molecule. A configuration of a small silicon atom (black) and four larger oxygen atoms set in a pyramid formation which is the basis of the silica glass-forming network. It does not exist as a separate entity but is extended in every direction, another Si atom sharing each face with a further O atom. In the whole complex there are therefore twice as many oxygen as silicon atoms and it is written as SiO_2 in glaze formulas.

Glass modifier

See *network modifier*.

Glass muller

A sort of flat-ended *pestle* for grinding and mixing color, especially enamels, with medium. Used on a glass slab or glazed tile.

Glass paper

A wet-and-dry glass paper will last much longer than sand-paper or emery cloth for rubbing down dry clay forms. It is advisable to use a mask for this kind of work.

Glass phase

A stage in the heating of ceramics when glass begins to form in the fabric. If excessive the piece may collapse or deform. (*See vitrification, phase diagrams, clay, porcelain,* etc.)

Glauconite

An hydrous mineral containing iron, potassium, and other minerals, greenish — hence the name—and sometimes contaminating sand present in some pale-colored clays from S. England.

Glaze

A ceramic glaze is a special sort of glass, differing from window glass and glassware in its lower thermal expansion and higher alumina content, which increase its viscosity and help it to adhere to the clay body. The general principles are discussed under *glass, glass formers, network modifier, Seger formula*, etc.

All glazes start as mixtures of a number of oxides and minerals with water. The craft potter may use these as raw materials even *once-firing* them on a clay pot, but an industrial pottery will use them as ground glass or frit. Industrially prepared glazes are usually in the form of *frits* though Potterycrafts and others now list 'powder glazes' in great variety.

One can arrive at a glaze either by the empirical trial-and-error method, or by the application of the principles of simple chemistry. Neither, alone, is sufficient. Science is one valuable aid among others, which include careful observation and intuition. Glazes are discussed in this book under *earthenware, stoneware* and *porcelain*, but the differences are not fundamental. They lie mainly in the choice of bases, some of which are not active at the lower temperatures (see *flux*).

The most useful guide to glaze computation, and the easiest to handle, is the *Seger formula*. This discusses glazes in terms of molecular equivalents rather than physical weights, but the translation from one to the other is not difficult to make (see *formula-into-recipe*).

The main factors governing the overall behavior of a glaze are:

1 The *base: silica* ratio (see also *Seger formula*). The normal practical limits of this ratio are 1:2 and 1:4.5. An average soft glaze will be in the region of 1:2.8, a stoneware 1:3.8. Above 1300°C/2372°F the proportion of silica rises sharply and in hard-paste porcelains may be as high as 1:10.

2 Choice of bases. These vary in their effectiveness as fluxes (see list under *flux*). Multi-base formulas are generally preferred to single-base ones.

3 The use of boric oxide. Although a glass former, boron operates at a very low temperature and its visible effect is that of a flux. It must be used where lead is not present in a soft glaze. It is usually listed as part of the acidic oxide RO_2, and this can lead to some untypical formulas, e.g. 1 RO: 4.8 RO_2 — the acid made up of 4.0 of silica and 0.8 B_2O_3 — for a soft frit.

4 The alumina ratio. Alumina is essential for a stable, well-adhered glaze. The ratio for a clear, bright glaze is alumina:silica from 1:8 to 1:10. An excess is liable to produce a matt surface.

5 Pigment oxides. These will behave like other glaze ingredients, the acids rendering the glaze more refractory, the

A simple glaze recipe of equal parts feldspar, china clay, and dolomite on a porcelain body giving a textured surface resembling saltglaze. Handbuilt by Sheila Fournier.

A striking pattern on a hand-formed burnished terracotta dish with 'carved glaze'. By Louise Gilbert Scott.

bases tending to soften the glaze.

Some materials such as iron oxide are influenced by the kiln atmosphere, and many stoneware glazes appear to achieve greater maturity in *reduction*.

For advice on the formation of glazes see *chemistry of pottery, Seger formula*, and under special glaze headings such as *earthenware glazes, aventurine, Bristol, celadon*, etc. The influence of the various minerals is discussed under their entries.

Glaze-body fit

Glazes and bodies undergo a number of expansions, contractions and shrinkages which affect the final state of the cooled ceramic. If the glaze has contracted more than the body after it has become rigid (700°C/1292°F and below) it will be in a state of *tension*, which can be relieved only by the glaze crazing. If the reverse is true and the glaze is

in slight *compression*, then it will be stable and can also accommodate some thermal shock or expansion through absorption. Excessive compression of the glaze will have a similar effect on the body as that of tension in the glaze, shattering being the result in extreme cases, or the glaze may *shiver* away on rims, etc. Large dishes which are glazed on one side are vulnerable.

Glaze-body fit is arrived at by sensible application of the principles of thermal expansion and inversions (and by the careful observation and evaluation of results from the kiln). (See especially *coefficients of expansion, crazing, quartz inversion, shattering, silica*.)

Glaze decoration

Glazes are, in themselves, obviously decorative but there are techniques for their use apart from the coverage of a ceramic piece. These are dealt with under *crawling, cuenca, cuerda seca, flashing, glaze inlay, glaze over glaze, glaze sgraffito (cut glaze), glaze trailing, painted glaze, poured glaze, run glaze, tin glaze over slip, wax resist*, etc. A single glaze can produce a variety of colors and textures according to its thickness.

Glaze disposal

For notes on the disposal of waste glazes, see *waste glaze disposal*.

Glaze flashing

See *flashing*.

Glaze from natural sources

All glaze materials, apart from frits and prepared colors, are, of course, 'natural' materials but some hardy souls wish to bypass the commercial suppliers and look for their own locally or sometimes much farther afield. Searching for and dealing with rocks and deposits suitable for glaze-making involves some prior geological knowledge and subsequent hard and noisy work rendering them fine enough to use. Harry Davis was so keen he went to New Zealand to work on the basaltic (volcanic) rocks which abound there after he had exhausted his interest in *igneous* Cornwall! Cardew and, especially, Brian Sutherland's book of the same title as this short article, together with various issues of CR (for instance the color plate of rock fragments in No.118 and a series of diagrams by David Green in No. 84) will give a good start to a potter interested in this activity. Green analyzes such common materials as fuller's earth, slate, and various ashes including *coal ash*. (See also *clay winning*, *rushing rocks, granite, grinding of rocks,* etc. and under the *various mineral headings.*)

Glaze inlay

Treated like slip inlay, glaze can be brushed across incised lines and then wiped off the surface areas. A rarely used technique but one that could be interesting to explore. A second glaze could be applied over the inlaid lines.

Glaze melt indicator

If a sufficiently large aperture is available, pieces can be extracted from the kiln during firing as indications of its progress. These can be pieces of the actual body and ware in the setting. If the pieces are in the form of a ring or hoop they will be easier to withdraw with a simple iron rod. (See *Buller's ring, cone, draw trial.*)

Glaze mixing

See advice at *weighing glaze ingredients,* and when you are sure that you have them all accurately weighed up they can then be sprinkled by hand into a large bowl or bin of water, taking care that you do not raise dust from the materials in doing so (alternatively wear a mask). They will then soak more quickly without aggravating lumps.

The exceptions to this method are *talc* and *bentonite.* The first needs mixing with other ingredients and should then be worked into a paste with a little water before soaking, otherwise it will float on the surface and refuse to mix. Bentonite should be similarly treated, adding water very gradually to form first a thick paste and preferably put through a 200 sieve before being added to the batch.

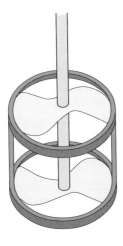

The glaze mixer mentioned in the text.

The soaked ingredients can usefully be first brushed through a coarse nylon sieve (such as a cook's sieve), preferably not a wire one as the metal may stain the glaze, before the appropriate lawn is used — usually 60 or 100 mesh for stoneware, 100–120 for earthenware — though special materials may have their own demands. Sieve twice if the glaze is to be used immediately and stir very thoroughly; the efficient melting of the glaze depends on the close association of each ingredient with the others.

There are a variety of mechanical glaze mixers on the market. A reasonably priced 'Jiffy mixer' is listed by Georgies, with outer rings to prevent damage to container walls (a danger when using plastic buckets), which is powered by an electric drill. An ingenious potter can construct his or her own.

Glaze over glaze

A technique of decoration where one glaze is poured over another in part, as a complete re-coating, or in conjunction with a *resist* material or *sgraffito.*

In earthenware attractive results can be obtained by covering a saturated glaze, on which a bold, simple wax design has been painted, with a clear glaze. This is most successful on tiles, bowls and dishes, i.e. on semi-horizontal surfaces. The second coating should be poured or dipped while the first is still damp but not shiny. Practice is required, as with all glaze over glaze techniques, to assess correctly the comparative consistencies of the glaze batches used, and to avoid too thick a final layer. There will always be a degree of flow from one glaze to another, softening and altering the shape of the resist line. Fire experiments

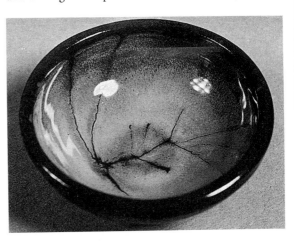

An earthenware bowl with a saturated manganese glaze which has been painted with a wax design and then covered with a second (tin) glaze. The original waxed line has become finer and narrower with the running of the glaze.

Stoneware (reduced, 1280°C/2336°F) with a black glaze poured over a clear glaze. Underglaze cobalt blue brushwork plus, in a second firing at 780°C/1436°F, further decoration with onglaze enamels. By Kevin White (Australia).

on a bat with plenty of alumina in case of running. A thinner top coat will give a crisper design but less contrast. It is advisable to wax the rim after the first coat. Stoneware glazes, being more viscous, run and merge less than *soft glazes*. Experiments can be carried out using a more *refractory* glaze.

Panels can be dipped, or the pouring action itself be used to provide a pattern. A number of modern potters pour glaze as sweeps of contrasting color from the center line outwards to give a variety of patterns. Glazes may also be treated like slip and trailed one onto another. A *flocculant* can give some *viscosity* in the trailer, but a sure and rapid motion is called for. Glazes can be sprayed, either in the open air or with an efficient extractor.

The comparative thicknesses of the glazes, the types of glaze (*refractory, matt, opaque,* etc.), the colors, the *soaking* time in the kiln and other factors will all influence and vary the results.

A second glaze can be poured over a fired glaze. This will give a less contrasting effect. *Crazing* will sometimes absorb glaze when dipped, or a *crawled* glaze can be filled with another color by sponging a thick glaze into the cracks.

A remarkably decorative glaze-on-glaze method was developed by Alan Wallwork, though on the simplest of ceramic forms, the commercial glazed tile. Drops of colored glaze, singly or imposed one on another, were laid until the tile was more or less covered. During firing the glazes spread and settled into patterns. David Eeles paints pale and colored glazes onto unfired glazed pots.

Glaze sgraffito, *cut glaze*

Cutting away glaze to the biscuit, either as a line or mass, has been practiced since the introduction of stonewares. The cutting should be done when the glaze shine has gone but it is still damp — a *fixative* could be a useful addition.

Earthenwares would be too fluid and the revealed body porous and liable to staining though, with care one glaze could be cut away to an underglaze (which should be more viscous than the top coating). (See *glaze over glaze.*)

Glaze stain

The term 'stain' is generally applied to the *fritted* colors in suppliers' catalogs, as distinct from the *pigment oxides* used raw. Variations in hue, apart from the combining of various oxides, are obtained by *sintering* with such non-coloring additions as alumina, soda, flint, etc. which alter the hue. When redissolved in a glaze, the stain may revert to the typical oxide color, and care must be taken to use only the glaze recommended for the color. Stains are more dilute than oxides and are added in proportions of around 10%, or as directed by the makers.

Glaze thickness

The thickness of a glaze coating is a critical factor in its behavior and fired appearance. Too thick, and it is liable to *peel, crawl* or *craze*; too thin, and it will fail to develop its true character (though see note below). There is no one ideal consistency; each recipe has its optimum thickness which can be decided only by trial and experience. A reading with a *hydrometer* is useful, while tight-fitting bin lids will help to control the inevitable evaporation between firings.

Factors controlling glaze coating are:

1 Biscuit porosity. The glaze take-up depends on water being absorbed, leaving a solid coat of glaze material on the surface. Keep biscuit firings as standard as possible. The thickness of the pot wall is allied to porosity. A thin wall will saturate quickly and cease to develop further coatings — in fact the glaze already solidified can be re-saturated from the water in the batch and may wash off again. If this happens the pot must be cleaned, dried over a strong heat, and another attempt made. A thick wall will absorb more moisture and thus retain a thicker coating. Good glazing therefore depends on even-walled throwing and making. An open, grogged body will obviously be more porous than a close one. The more porous the pot, the more water is required in the glaze batch in relation to solid matter. (See *tongue test.*)

2 The batch consistency. It follows from the previous

Decoration derived from varying the glaze thickness of an oxidized dolomite/copper glaze which goes black where it is thicker. The bowl was dipped first one side and then the other; the center swathe being the overlapped portion. Pouring the glaze from the dish resulted in the lower darker area. By Robert Fournier. The technique can give subtle and integral designs.

remarks that a thicker mixture will result in a thicker coating. Test with a *hydrometer*, or more roughly by dipping in a dry finger or test-strip; note the reading for future occasions. A glaze may appear to thicken as it stands; this is a result of flocculation caused by soluble alkalis or colemanite. This glaze will have a jelly-like consistency. If further water is added, it may lead to excessive contraction of the glaze-coating followed by peeling. Ash glazes are liable to *flocculation*; more careful washing of the ash will help to minimize the trouble.

3 Speed of work. Quick dipping will give less time for absorption than a slow one, and thus cause a thinner coat to develop. Very slow dipping may saturate a pot wall so that the glaze will fail to dry. A steady but unhesitating action is called for. Do not shake violently after dipping; a short circular or twisting movement will cast off the drips.

4 Type of glazes. Glazes vary in their optimum thickness; and you may actually want to vary it for different effects. Raw material glazes need a thicker coat than do frits which have already lost their volatile components. Also, frits, being powdered glass, will look very thin when the pot is lifted from the glaze but the coating will become opaque as it dries. In general a transparent glaze will need a slightly thinner coating than an opaque or colored one.

5 Double-dipping needs careful preparation, the first coat can become very absorbent if allowed to get too dry, and may bubble. (See *glaze over glaze*.)

To summarize, as a general guide:
A thinner glaze mixture for:
    Frits
    Porous biscuit
    Thick-walled pots
    Slow glazing (difficult pots)
    Clear glazes (earthenware)

A thicker glaze mixture for:
    Higher-fired, low-porosity biscuit
    Thin-walled pots
    '*Skimming*' of tiles
    Opaque glazes (generally)

A single glaze can often give a variety of tone and color simply by varying the thickness. This is more pronounced in stonewares. Copper glazes are especially useful in this regard (see *turquoise glaze*) but many others will behave in a similar way.

A glaze thickness tester is listed by Axner in which 'a needle penetrates the glaze which you have applied to your pot — measured accurately to within $^2/_{1000}$s of an inch'!

Glaze trailing

Glazes as well as slips can be *trailed*. The decoration is necessarily fairly broad in style. The addition of feldspar can

Typically rapid and emphatic black trailing onto a flattened bottle by Shoji Hamada. (See also photo at tube lining.)

assist definition by making the glaze more viscous. Trailing can be done on the biscuit, or on a glaze coating. A certain spread and softening of the line are inevitable when two glazes are used, but trailing can be quite crisp on biscuit or on a refractory glaze. Maggie Berkowitz trails, pours, and cuts glazes to build up her tile pictures.

Glaze trial log

The records which a potter needs to keep will vary with particular kinds of work. The closer one gets to the final recipe, the more information one needs to keep. A possible log book is shown in the chart. The information on the actual glaze trial can be tied in with kiln logs or records; this is especially important in reduction firings.

Glaze trials

One is always faced with the necessity to compromise in the making up of test glaze batches. Large quantities will be wasteful, but small samples are liable to error during

weighing, in the relative dampness of the ingredients, and in preparation losses: 10 oz/300gm must be considered a minimum batch. *Line blends* or *triaxial blending* allow larger initial batch weights.

The object of a series of glaze trials is to arrive at a useful recipe. Haphazard, unrepeatable mixtures are merely tantalizing. It is necessary to record at least the weights, subsequent alterations and the firing temperature. Never rely on memory. (See also *records, glaze trial log*.) The recipe is, of course, only one factor: others include the size of the kiln, speed of firing and cooling, kiln atmosphere and glaze thickness.

Glaze trials merely brushed onto tiles or shards are insufficient. Small bowls can be thrown very rapidly from cones of clay, cylinders can be cut into sections, or curved tiles about 2ft x 1ft x ¼in (600 x 300 x 5mm) can be stood on end, or formed over a rolling-pin. Circular disks with a hole may be glazed and filed, or hung on a board or on the actual glaze-bin. For the ultimate trials, full-sized production pieces are used.

The golden rule for glaze trials or any other trial is: alter

Glaze Trial Log				
Test no		*1*		*2*
RECIPE	Lead sesquisilicate China clay Flint Tin oxide (500 gms)	70 20 10 12		
TEST PIECE	Curved tile			
BODY	Red			
TEST SURFACE	Impressed			
GLAZE THICKNESS	Thin and medium			
KILN AND FIRING	1080°C/1976°F Soaked Small kiln 10 minutes			
POSITION IN KILN	Middle			
NOTES	Biscuit low fired			
TYPE	Opaque			
COLOR	White			
SURFACE	Shiny			
NOTES	Breaking well to red-brown at sharp edges Poor where thin			
ASSESSMENT	Good			
ALTERATIONS	None needed			
NAME	Soft tin glaze			

nly one ingredient at a time. If two variables are operat-
ng together, it is difficult to decide which of them is pri-
narily responsible for the result. This is admittedly a coun-
el of perfection and is not followed in all the permutations
f the second series discussed below.

It is useful to test materials on their own (see *button test*),
ut, unless they are natural or artificial frits (e.g. feldspar
r lead silicate) the essential reaction between the material
r oxide and silica will not be shown. (See *calcium* for an
xtreme example.)

Trials with three simple materials such as a lead frit, clay,
nd flint can be of great education value with students. A
imple series may run as follows:

Trial no	1	2	3	4	5	6	7
Frit	100			33	70	15	15
Clay		100		33	15	70	15
Flint			100	33	15	15	70

Nos. 1, 2 and 3 are for testing the materials alone, No.
4 tests them in equal quantities; and 5, 6 and 7 are tests
involving an excess of one ingredient over the other two.
The use of red clay would further differentiate the results.
For stonewares, almost any three minerals can be tried in
similar proportions.

An interesting series of glaze trials (see chart) were
achieved by a mixture of line blending and more intuitive
experiment. The series may be taken as one model (among
many) for a trial sequence. It by no means covered the field
but it did give a useful general picture. The variables were:
five similar batches of glaze, each with the accepted maximum proportion of a coloring oxide (i.e. 'saturated glazes');
a similar opaque glaze with 10% tin oxide which was
added in various quantities to dilute the colors; and a softer
frit which tested the effect of both dilution and a more
fluid melt.

The series, which was repeated for each color and for
eight permutations of two colors, was as follows:

Group A – single color

	colored glaze	tin glaze	soft frit	
No 1	2	1		parts
No 2	2	1	1	parts
No 3	1	4		parts
No 4	1	4	2	parts

Group B – two colors

	color (1)	color (2)	Tin	Frit	
No 5	1	1			parts
No 6	1	1	1		parts
No 7	1	1	3	1	parts
No 8	1	4			parts
No 9	1	4	3		parts
No 10	1	4	5	2	parts
No 11	4	1			parts
No 12	4	1	3		parts
No 13	4	1	5	2	parts

The standard 'part' is often a dessertspoonful but any
small receptacle could be used. All tests were fired at the
same temperature and on buff and red trial pieces.

To work back from any mixture to a recipe, multiply
each of the ingredients of the constituent glazes in the mixture by the 'parts'; list them in a chart, find the totals and
divided each figure by the total number of 'parts' as shown
in the chart below. The same type of chart can be used for
any mixtures or blends.

Example. In Group B, Test No. 10 in the above series has
been worked back to a recipe assuming that:

C (1) was	Lead sesquisilicate	60
	China clay	15
	Whiting	5
	Flint	20
	Copper oxide	2.5

and C (2) was a similar glaze with 10% manganese dioxide and T was a similar glaze with 10% tin oxide. S being
a soft frit.

Recipes for glaze trials									
Glaze	Parts	Lead ses.	Clay	Whiting	Flint	MnO₂	Tin	Frit	CuO
C1	1	60	15	5	20				2.5
C2	4	240	60	20	80	40			
T	5	300	75	25	100		50		
S	2							200	
Totals	12	600	150	50	200	40	50	200	2.5
Recipe	1	50	12.5	4.1	16.5	3.3	4.1	16.7	0.2

The same type of chart can be used for any mixtures or blends

Glazing

It is probable that more pots are spoiled during glazing than at any other stage. That 'it will all smooth out in the firing' is a common delusion. Certainly some glazes are more accommodating than others. Opaque and colored glazes will show differences in thickness more clearly than transparent ones.

Bubbling, *crazing* and other ills can often be traced to faulty glaze application. In all cases, the tidier a pot looks when it goes into the kiln the better it is likely to look when it comes out. Consistency of the batch is discussed under *glaze thickness*. Pots can be dipped, rolled, poured or sprayed. Speed and smoothness of movement are the keys to good glazing. Think carefully before starting each piece, and work out the best procedure for it.

Where there is plenty of glaze, the quickest and easiest method is immersing. Hold a pot by the rim and base, or a dish each side of the rim, using as few fingers as possible or, better still, a wire gripper. After a quick sweep through the glaze — with dishes the edge farthest from the potter enters the glaze first — hold the piece vertically to drain it for a few moments and then stand it down on a stilt.

Pots, beakers, etc. in a shallow glaze should be held with two fingers on the base and two on the rim 'walked' round the pot so that the piece revolves in the glaze. Tip it the right way up for an instant to ensure that the base is covered inside, and then invert to drain.

Tiles can be held across the back with fingers and thumb and skimmed across the glaze surface, the leading edge entering first. With practice, a neat glaze line along the edges can be achieved.

For stoneware and other pieces which are not to be glazed over the base there are three possibilities. They can be filled, emptied and dipped in quick succession. Large pots may need to have glaze poured over them. If it is possible to grip the base, turn the pot as far round in one direction as possible, so that a smooth and complete revolution can be made as the glaze is poured. Use a big enough jug and a large bowl to catch the surplus. If the pot is too heavy

or awkward it can be supported on a central stick, across two supports on the bowl, or on a turntable.

The 'water spout' dip takes some practice (try it when washing-up!), but it is ideal for the rapid glazing of beakers, wide-mouthed pots, bowls, etc. particularly for stonewares.

1

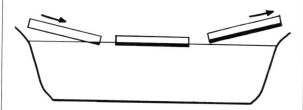

2

1–4 Glazing by filling and dipping. The pot is filled to the brim with glaze, or partly filled and revolved as it is emptied, reversed, dipped immediately to the required depth, lifted out and given a slight sideways twist to shake off drips. The whole process is a continuous movement. For pouring glaze over a tall pot which can be gripped at the foot, it is first held (upside down) with the wrist turned as far round towards the body as possible. As the glaze is poured steadily from a large jug into a large bowl, the pot is given a complete revolution. 5–13 A teapot poses special problems in glazing. The series shown here embodies some of Geoffrey Whiting's methods. The flange and base are waxed in order to resist the glaze at these points, and the pot filled with glaze and emptied by pouring steadily from the spout (see text). The shoulder and end of the spout are glazed by inverting and dipping. The teapot is then turned right way up, gripped by the inside of the lid flange, and again dipped until the glaze levels overlap but being careful that none runs into the spout. The lid is dipped upside down just to the top edge of the rim.

Glazing tiles by skimming them across the surface of a well-stirred glaze. The tile can be held with the thumb and finger, or with a glazing gripper.

The piece is gripped by the foot or base, dipped to the desired level outside, then sharply lifted straight up until it barely leaves the glaze, the suction causing a 'water spout' to rise. Very quickly the pot is pushed downwards onto the rising column of glaze which will coat the interior even of tall jugs. After trying it, you will probably add 'sometimes', but with practice it is a very reliable method. A foot-operated mechanical 'fountain glazer', which does much the same thing more easily, is listed by Axner, and others.

Spraying. Blowing glaze through a spray is dangerous. A bulb or mechanical pump should be used, together with an

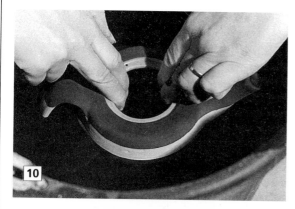

extractor-fan. It takes a good deal of spraying to achieve thick enough glaze coating, but for slip glazes, thin laye and special effects it can be useful, though it always resul in a somewhat mechanical finish.

Some general notes:

1 Pour some of the clear water from the top of a glaz before stirring. Keep this water handy in a jug and ad again if necessary. Stir your glaze very thoroughly and kee it stirred during use.

2 Label permanent containers clearly. Beware changin containers when re-sieving a glaze, which will be necessar from time to time. Use a container of a suitable size an shape for the piece to be glazed.

3 Touch up holding marks with finger or brush immedi ately after glazing. Smooth the repair over as it dries, an carefully scrape down blotches or runs with a sharp knif (e.g. a photographic re-touching knife). Although fo tableware and much other pottery a smooth, even coatin of glaze is desirable, it is obviously possible to use differen thicknesses of glaze in a free and exciting way on more dec orative or sculptural pieces. Even on tableware, the mark left by the gripping fingers of a skillful potter can add to the attractions of a pot. Other glaze faults such as *crawling* or even *peeling* can be used positively.

4 It is easier to protect a surface from glaze than to scrape it off afterwards. This can be done by brushing with wax. (See *wax*.)

Teapots present special problems, especially the clogging of strainer holes. One can fill the teapot with glaze and pour it all out of the spout. This saturates the strainer and a sharp jerk will free the holes, or you can blow sharply down the spout (don't eat the glaze!). Alternatively a pad of clay can be pressed over the holes prior to glazing, or they can be thickly waxed. (See also *poured glaze*.)

Glazing gripper

Metal grippers are especially useful when glazing flatware or bowls. They can be cut from sheet aluminum or brass, or made from thick galvanized wire. It is possible to work with

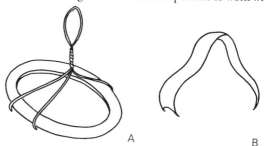

A   B

A glazing gripper of galvanized or kiln element wire, and B of sheet metal aluminum or brass.

single strand on each arm, but two claws on one arm give firmer hold. Two or three sizes will be necessary to cover the likely range of pots and bowls with 3–6in/75–150mm, –10in/150–250mm, and 10–14in/250–350mm spans.

Interior grippers which exert pressure outwards have a limited but occasionally essential use. (See at *raku*.)

Globar

A trade name (Carborundum Company, UK and USA) for *silicon carbide* kiln elements.

Gloss ware

Somewhere between a slip and a glaze, gloss can be achieved either by *burnishing* or (since Greek and Roman times) by the application of a very finely levigated slip (see *terra sigillata*).

Glost fire

Term used for the glaze-firing of ceramics, especially in the industry and in America. More rarely applied as 'glost ware'.

Gloves

Fireproof, heat-insulating gloves or mittens are essential for raku and are sometimes useful for normal firings. If a pot is liable to burn your hand, however, it means that it is still too hot to take it from the kiln. There are special heat-proof gloves available though these may be expensive and leather gardening gloves or kitchen oven gloves are alternatives, though less efficient.

Gold

Gold *enamel* is fired onto glazed pottery at about 700°C/1292°F. It is used as a prepared liquid and painted on with a brush. Before firing it is brown and sticky. It is prepared as either a gold chloride, or as a gold sulforesinate, and a flux, perhaps bismuth (for 'bright' gold), or as gold powder in essential oils for 'burnish' or 'best' gold.

Bright gold comes from the kiln shiny; burnish gold is dull from the firing and must be rubbed with a stone (traditionally a 'blood-stone' or agate) or with a glass burnisher to bring up the surface glint.

Leach mentions the admixture of gold dust with red enamel in Japan, which softens the crudity of the color. Experiment on these lines might be rewarding. Curious colors result from the use of gold in raku firing. Painting with prepared gold will reveal any hidden crazing. Gold and tin oxide give *purple of cassius*. Pinks and reds in enamels may also be obtained from gold.

The firing must be very precise, especially if the painting is done in thin strokes. A few degrees over and a purple may develop. On some glazes, however, the gold cannot be subdued even at 1000°C/1832°F.

Gold enamel felt-pens are available for fine drawing. (See also *copper-manganese gold*.)

Gold eraser

Erasing liquids for removing unwanted gold marks on fired pieces are available (Georgies).

Gosu

A Japanese name for *asbolite*, an impure cobalt.

Grain size

Apart from the obvious textural effects of differences in grain size of grog, sand, etc. in a clay body, too fine a material will have ill effects on plasticity and can cause over-vitrification and deformation in the firing, especially in reduction. The grain size of the clay will affect its behavior. China clay particles have a surface area 1500 times that of ball clay and therefore take much longer to melt (Hamer). He also quotes a minimum of 200 mesh for flint in earthenware bodies and 80 for sand in stonewares.

Granite

Most intrusive rocks are in the form of granite, which is classified as an *acidic* rock, i.e. with a high silica content. A feldspathoid (Hamer). An analysis of a typical granite shows some 70% of silica; 14.5% alumina; various bases in percentages from 4.5 potash to 0.05 baria; 3% or less of iron compounds with some phosphorus and titanium.

In decomposition, therefore, granite contains the ingredients of the pottery minerals — feldspar, stone, quartz, etc. — and, at one remove, clay. The range of rocks of which granite is one is known as igneous (from fire). Ivan Englund discusses the 'average' granite, which he calls 'avgran', for use in glazes, (CR various issues, especially No. 87). Because it is such a hard rock, he recommends using dust from granite workings, or else heating it in a fire or kiln to weaken the molecular bonds. His final recipe suggestion as a 'starter' is: granite 73; whiting 18; silica 9; bentonite 2 while Jim Malone CR140 suggests blends of granite, ash, and clay as trials. It will inevitably contain some iron oxide. (See also *crushing rocks*.)

Graph

A graph is a pictorial or diagrammatic representation of the relationship between two variables. The information it contains would take many sentences to describe; it can estimate intermediates between known points and can sometimes be extended to indicate probabilities.

A graph consists of a vertical measured line and a horizontal one, joined at their lower left-hand terminations. Each line is divided into regular units appropriate to the data. A familiar example will explain how to set out a graph.

The vertical numbers represent intervals of 100°C/212°F, the horizontal ones hours. At any point in your firing you can consult the pyrometer and draw a horizontal line from the temperature and a vertical one from the time which has elapsed since commencement. Readings every two hours are shown. The points of conjunction can be joined by straight lines or drawn as an estimated curve. If the slowly increasing curve is continued beyond the last reading it will give a rough indication of the maximum temperature the kiln may reach, or at what time it would reach a given higher figure.

Graphs can be drawn for any two sets of variables. A particularly ingenious one is described in Cardew 1969, Appendix 8, to produce approximations to square roots below unity. Graphs do not have to show a steady progression, but can show broken lines and sharp angles, frequently caricatured as profit and loss graphs. The principle remains the same.

A graph may be misleading if based on insufficient or inaccurate information.

The use of squared paper facilitates graph-making.

Graphite

A natural form of carbon which, although it has a melting point of some 3300°C/6004°F in an oxygen-less (reducing) atmosphere, at much lower temperatures it has been used to obtain an intensely black, high polish on clamp and bonfire firings. Also called 'blacklead' and 'plumbago' and is the 'lead' in lead pencils. (See also *reduction*.)

Grate, firebox

The bars which support burning fuel and allow the passage of air through it. The development of the fire grate (grating) marked a significant step forward from the flat surface with its heaped-up fuel and ash mixture. The earliest grates were composed of ceramic cylinders laid horizontally across stones. The grate made a hotter and more controllable flame possible, with the ash falling away and more

Graph for variable time and temperature during a firing

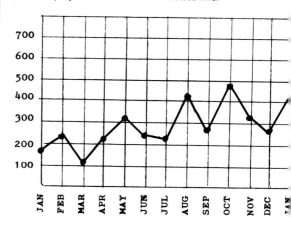

1 A typical firing graph with readings taken every two hours (horizontal (figures). The broken lines connect the vertical (°C figures) scale with the time divisions. The points of intersection are marked. The slowly flattening curve is typical of firing graphs (the increasing heat loss slowly balancing output). A possible 'projection' is shown as a dotted line.

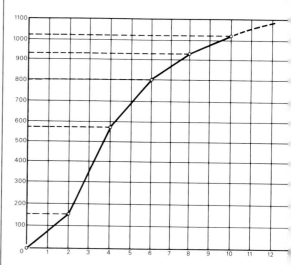

2 Another typical graph. The numbers could represent monthly pot production and the sequence of months. This graph suggests a somewhat erratic output but does show an overall improvement over the period. The number of pots could be related to their value and a second graph superimposed which will give a more accurate idea of the financial health of the workshop.

easily disposed of. The modern type of grate was used by Bottger to achieve his remarkable 1300°C/2372°F plus for porcelain. The heat can either travel direct into the kiln from the fuel surface, or be drawn through the bars.

The development of refractory steels and casting has reduced grates with a long life, but care must be taken that the ash never comes into contact with the underside of the metal or the bars will twist and fail. Oil or gas burners, of course, do not require grates. Parks recommends that the hearth or grate size should be one-third of the loading area.

Green glazes

There are two families of green colors in glazes: those derived directly from pigment oxides, usually copper or chrome; and those from reduced iron.

We will deal here mainly with the first group. Chrome is a hard, dense opaque coloring agent, and it is advisable to keep the proportions in a glaze to 1% or less. It will give green in a zinc-free multibase lead glaze at 1050–1150°C/1922–2102°F, and in stoneware glazes. At lower temperatures it may give very different colors. Combined with cobalt the color is brighter and somewhat less dense, though still liable to give a rather lifeless surface. Although *refractory* it will *volatilize* and can be a danger in the presence of tin oxide. (See *chrome-tin pink*.)

Copper, in proportions of 1–3 in an oxidizing atmosphere, will give a variety of greens in soft glazes: apple green in a lead glaze, a brighter color in a lead-lime-potash or leadless glaze, progressing towards turquoise as the alkalis are increased and the alumina content diminished.

Greens from copper or chrome (see *Dresden green*) can be modified or assisted by additions of other oxides. Cobalt has been mentioned (use only about 0.2% in the batch): iron, nickel, rutile, vanadium and antimony can be experimented with. Prepared stains have been derived from zirconium/vanadium, and praseodymium phosphate. Iron and cobalt mixtures tend to give gray rather than green, but antimoniate/cobalt mixtures will give better results when used as a pigment, see below. Nickel oxide can give gray-green in a lead borax glaze. Some magnesium in the formula can improve the color. Most of these mixtures and stains are more suitable for soft glazes, but Fulham Pottery lists a zircon/vanadium/praseodymium green stain which will hold for temperatures up to 1280°C/2336°F. Cobalt in a zinc glaze can give a bright green.

True turquoise in a soft glaze demands a soda-silica glass, which is somewhat unstable as a glaze. See also *Egyptian paste*. For stoneware, a *turquoise* to blue-green recipe is given at that entry. In fluid glazes copper will volatilize and is apt to be uncertain in its effect above 1200°C/2192°F.

Kathleen Pleydell-Bouverie gives a sea-green or olive-green mixture for addition to oxidized stonewares:

| Iron | 1% | Manganese | 0.3–0.5% |
| Copper | 0.3–0.5% | Cobalt | 0.5% |

Copper is dangerous in lead glazes, see *metal release, soluble lead*. For a discussion of reduced greens see *reduction* and *celadon*.

Green glazing

A term sometimes applied to once-fired ware, i.e. glazed on the raw or 'green' clay. (See *once-fired ware*.)

Green pigment

Copper, either as the oxide or carbonate (slightly toxic), is commonly used on earthenware glazes to produce various hues of a rather watery kind. It is normally used as a wash or filler for a design, and needs applying with care, since any excess will fire black and cindery.

Chrome is also difficult to use alone, being refractory and having a heavy opacity. Beware pink reactions from chrome. Prepared colors are generally mixtures of these oxides fritted with zinc, whiting, borax, etc. to induce variety of hue. The coloring agent for Victoria green is stated to be $3CaO.Cr_2O_3.3SiO_2$. Cobalt can be added to chrome with advantage. Simple mixtures of cobalt and iron, or cobalt and antimoniate of lead (or yellow stain), can give subtle greenish colors in a tin glaze, sometimes partly separating out in a pleasant way. Green pigment is less often used on stoneware. Cobalt in a zinc glaze can produce a rather strident green. See also at *green glazes* for some less familiar compounds which are also utilized in green pottery pigments.

There are dangers in using copper in lead glazes (see *metal release, soluble lead*).

Green slips

Chrome and copper in equal parts will provide a reasonably pleasant and stable green in slip. The first is too hard and opaque alone, the second too watery. 1.25% of each, in a pale buff slip, is adequate. Iron or a darker slip will gray the tone. John Solly (CR166) suggests 2.5% of copper and 0.5% iron in a ball clay for green slip. Blue slip under a *honey* (iron) glaze will tend towards green. Chrome can also be used, see *slip recipes* (always with the danger of the development of chrome-tin-pinks in the presence of tin), as can mixtures of rutile, titanium, and cobalt.

Green strength

A term used to indicate the strength of unfired, dry clay.

Greenware

Unfired pottery. Leach uses the term for leather-hard clay suitable for turning and cutting, but it is also used for dry clay. Green strength is an important virtue in a body (see *dry strength*).

Greywacke

A dark-colored sedimentary rock which can be used in stoneware glaze recipes but which '(weathers down to) earthenware and terracotta clays' in New Zealand — Brickell.

Grinding of rocks

Most commercially supplied materials are in a finely ground form — sometimes too fine. For breaking down experimental quantities of rock, etc. a *mortar and pestle* can be used, or a *ball* or *jar mill*. A primitive but effective grinding pan used until recently at Soil Hill Pottery, Yorkshire was simply a circular metal container with a revolving central shaft which dragged flat stones round on chains. (See also *crushing rock, pan mill, vibratory mill*.)

Grinding wheel

An abrasive disc which revolves on a central axis. The old, large wheels were turned quite slowly with a treadle; the modern wheel is spun at high speed by an electric motor. It needs to be true on the center or considerable and dangerous vibration will be set up. The disk can be of bonded *silicon carbide* or *alumina* (marked 'C' and 'A' on British standard wheels); (see *abrasive*). There are many grades and grain-sizes. A hard grade of medium grain with a vitrified bond (marked 'V') would be of general use, but finer wheels may be necessary for glaze grinding. In the USA Axner lists a 'green wheel' for which it claims advantages over the normal grinding wheel.

Always wear a mask and goggles when using a grinding wheel.

Grog

Ground, fired biscuit (sometimes even ground up glazed ware in porcelain factories). Incorporated into clay bodies to give texture, to impart 'bite' when throwing, to assist drying, or to increase firing strength. It will reduce the rate of clay shrinkage during drying and, in the firing, up to the temperature at which the grog itself was fired. (See also *chamotte*.)

Standard grog is made from a refractory *fireclay* and is relatively inert at potters' temperatures. It is graded according to the size of grain, e.g. a '30 to dust' grog would be composed of all the grades which would pass a 30 mesh sieve. '30–60' will pass a 30 mesh but be retained by a 60. Some suppliers grade still more carefully, e.g. all through 40, 25% retained in 60, 25% by 100, 50% through 100 mesh — this last would be a very fine grog, almost too small even for throwing clay. A grog which is too fine may be a hazard, causing the clay to absorb water rapidly. For normal body up to 10% of grog may be added, but much more for large pieces and special work.

As a rough guide to grog size: that which passes a 50 sieve is no more than a calcined clay dust, through 30 would be a fine grog; through 14 a medium one; and through 8 mesh a coarse sample.

Grog can be made in small quantities by crushing dry clay to a suitable size, or plastic clay can be used on an ordinary kitchen grater, and firing it in an unglazed bowl. Colored grog can be tried for particular effects, e.g. red clay grog beaten into the surface of stonewares. Grog for raku can be crushed soft brick. (See also *ilmenite*.) An interesting grog recipe for coloring with chrome and other pigments is given in CR102 by Mark Stanczyk; 80 china clay; 16 frit; 4 bone ash.

A coarse grog, as clay or colored, can be used to produce a textured surface, either lightly beaten in, incorporated into or sprinkled onto wet slip, or brought to the surface by working the clay with a wet sponge.

Ground-hog kiln

A semi-updraft kiln partially buried in a bank of earth. The earth acts as a heat insulator and building the kiln in a sloping bank helps to create draft. The idea has parallels in the Eastern sloping kilns and could be utilized for 'primitive' firings such as raku. Rhodes quotes their use by country potters of the Southern Highlands of the USA (illustration in Rhodes K). As a type, however, it was widespread. Sometimes adapted today for temporary outdoor kilns at ceramic festivals and tutorials.

Ground-lay

A method of applying an even layer of pottery color by first coating the biscuit or glaze with a tacky oil, onto which the pigment is then dusted. Mainly used in the industry on bone china, but the principle, in a more flexible form, could be adapted to craft ceramics and modeling.

Grouting

Filling the joins between tiles or tessarae after they have

een set in cement, glued, or otherwise fastened down. The grouting material should be of the same kind as the backing if set as described under *mosaic*. For tiles there are a number of proprietary grouting materials, but most are white and could well be stained to make the grouting less conspicuous. *Portland cement* can be used if dried very slowly under polythene (2–3 days).

Growan stone

A Cornish *china stone*.

Gum Arabic, tragacanth

Vegetable gum can be purchased as liquid or as powder. Powders are dissolved in water or denatured alcohol by soaking overnight, boiling for a few minutes and straining through a 40 mesh. A dessertspoonful of tragacanth dissolved in a pint of water is sufficient for around six gallons of glaze. 'Gummed glaze forms a surface (which) takes painted decoration better', (Sutherland). Sometimes added to glazes (e.g. raku), or colors, to give a harder coating when dry, avoiding rubbing and smudging. All gums will decay in time and spoil the glaze. A little *formalin* has been suggested to counteract decomposition.

Gum arabic has some *deflocculant* effect. Tragacanth promotes *suspension* or *floatation*. Dextrin is an alternative. Cardew mentions a gum and quartz mixture for painting lid flanges, etc. to prevent sticking during firing. Fine alumina might he preferable in place of the quartz.

Gumbo

A very sticky surface clay (Rhodes).

Gypsum

A widely distributed evaporate rock (from evaporation of salt water). A hydrated calcium sulfate $CaSO_4$: $2H_2O$. Shells embedded in clay and attacked by sulfuric acids from metallic sulfides form transparent gypsum crystals. Most gypsum is derived from the *anhydrite*. The pure micro-crystalline form is alabaster.

When crushed and heated in a revolving cylinder to 120°C/248°F, gypsum loses more than half of its water of crystallization and becomes an unstable demi-*hydrate* powder. Upon the addition of water it re-assumes something of its original hard state. This is *plaster of Paris*. If the powder or plaster is heated above 120°C/248°F it becomes 'dead-burnt' and will not reset. So do not dry molds on a hot kiln. Hamer suggests using small quantities of gypsum in or under the first glaze of a double layer to promote oilspot in a fluid glaze.

Haematite

The accepted English dictionary spelling but see under the simplified *hematite*.

Hake

A soft, flat handmade Japanese *brush*, 1–3in/35–90mm wide.

Hakeme

A form of decoration using a white slip and a coarse brush often as a ground for iron painting, Early examples can be found on the rough pots and bowls of the Korean Yi period. Leach has a drawing of a hakeme brush described as 'a miniature garden broom made of the grain ends of the rice straw'. The technique has been used by Bill Marshall of St Ives and, of course, by Hamada, amongst others. The slip, which must be fairly thick or it may vanish under the glaze, (though this is not such a danger in stoneware), is normally spun onto the surface of the pot or bowl on a slow-turning wheel or banding-wheel. The effect is a subtle contrast between body and slip, the slip being a little lighter in color than the body. Leach recommends Pike's siliceous ball clay GFC. but other light colored clays will do, perhaps with the addition of some china clay and

A type of hakeme achieved by a rapid dabbing of a slip loaded brush onto the slip-coated surface of a bowl as it slowly revolves on the wheel.

feldspar, though to go too far with additions to the natural clay will destroy the quality of the result which, to quote Honey 'implies a principle fundamental in all the arts — it speaks clearly of a process'. In the Far East some potters use a technique of dabbing a very wide brush rapidly up and down on a flattish bowl as it turns giving a regular broken pattern of slip — it needs a lot of practice!

Halloysite

A kaolinite (clay) mineral in which the plate-like structure is rolled into tubes, causing high and uneven shrinkage due to their sudden collapse on drying. The mineral may be present in various clays. Found in New Zealand, Japan, North Africa, and Mississippi, USA.

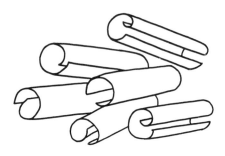

The possible structure of halloysite showing curled 'plates' which collapse during firing, leading to excessive and uneven shrinkage.

Handbuilding

A convenient term for the forming of ceramics without a wheel. Can include *coiling, pinching, slab building, molding*, or combinations of these. Bowls and other rounded forms can be stroked and beaten out of a ball of clay as in many primitive and traditional techniques. The illustrations show a bowl made by a combination of pinching, stroking and coiling, using rubber and steel palettes. (See also *formers, cut-corner dishes,* etc.)

Stages in the handbuilding of a bowl.
1–3 A sufficiently large ball of fine-grogged clay is pinched into a hollow form, using both hands. This is further thinned and shaped by holding the curve in the palm and stroking the surface with the fingers of the other hand, finally smoothing with a kidney rubber.
4 It is dropped into a biscuited bowl to stiffen.
5 At the soft-leather stage the inside and the outside are further smoothed and shaped with a steel palette.
6–7 The bowl is reversed onto a whirler, an area brushed with slip, and a foot coiled on.

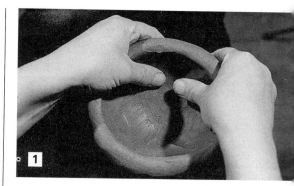

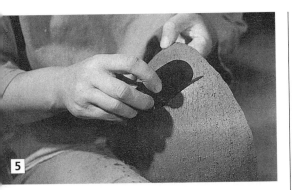

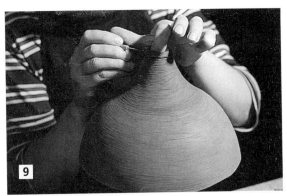

8–10 The base is carefully leveled with a needle awl and finally worked into the curve of the form with a palette.
11 The finished bowl.

Hand cream

In addition to the many commercial hand creams on the market, Judith Rivers (New Zealand) suggests granulated sugar with about the same amount, or slightly more, of any vegetable oil.

Massage into the hands and wash off under a warm tap.

Handle

The forerunner of the handle was the pierced lug, one on either side of the pot. These can be found in the Shang Yin pots from Central China and in ceramics from the near tropical countries from Africa to Peru. They are still used by potters, sometimes decoratively, sometimes when the pot is designed to be suspended, which was their original use. From the lug to the true side handle intended for grasping with the hand was a considerable step but intermediate stages appear to be few.

There are many contrasting forms of handles: those applied to commercial pottery differ in some fundamental ways from those found on the craftsman-potter's work. In industry the handles may be carefully considered in relation to the pot, but it is always made, in a press or slip-mold, as a separate entity. A distinct point of junction is thus apparent. A 'stop' or thumb-hold at the top may be worked into the design to prevent the hand from slipping. These handles need not have a smooth, arched flow of the pulled handle but may be angled or built up from broken curves. It is the clean articulation of parts which is

The placing of a handle is crucial to the overall effect. Each of these positions alters the character of an identical basic form.

distinctive of the best industrial ceramics.

At the other end of the scale, an English Medieval jug handle springs like a branch from the main form, to which it is firmly secured by strokes of the thumb. This apparently natural growth gives satisfaction from all angles, not merely from a profile view. The strong 'pulling lines' and bold wipe of the clay each side of the juncture are delights in themselves. The thumb movement at once fastens the handle and decorates the pot. Since this is a practical dictionary we will ignore quirky 'handles' which are designed as decorative or symbolic aspects of non-functional ceramics, an entertaining enough game which has been practiced since the earliest examples, and mention only a few aspects of those handles designed for use.

The placing, shape, and size of a handle is dictated by its use. 'Size' also includes thickness or degree of sturdiness compatible with the material; earthenware, porcelain, etc. and the general character of the vessel. A handle which looks as if it might break when grasped will never give comfort or pleasure to the user.

Placing — the placing of a handle is governed by three main considerations: the curves of the main form; the number of fingers required to lift the vessel when full of liquid (the thickness and width of the handle must also be in direct relation to this weight); physical and formal balance.

Between the curve of the pot and that of the handle there is a space. Not only must this be sufficient to accommodate the finger or fingers comfortably, but the shape of the space is of great aesthetic importance. On a more or less cylindrical jug or beaker it may be no more than the simple letter D — the one-finger handle is an example — but on the inward curve between the belly and neck of a well-designed jug it will be very subtle. These related curves should merge into a whole.

It is usually advisable to spring the handle across a concave section of the pot form. If it straddles a bulge a rather ugly crescent is formed and the handle may become awkwardly long, or difficult to hold, or both.

When dealing with the question of placing, one can say generally that a handle which springs higher than the rim

A classic jug form by John Lomas, illustrating how the inward curve of the body and the spring of the handle can result in a satisfying leaf-shaped space which may be as important as the actual form of the pot.

of the pot will make it awkward to invert for draining, while one that is too near the base will not allow a firm grip when picking up or setting down.

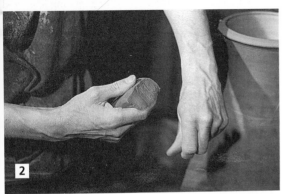

Michael Casson forming a handle on a large jug.
1 After being well-wedged it is slapped into a wedge shape.
2–3 The end is broken away with a flick of the thumb to leave a curved face which is then applied to a slip-coated area of the jug just below the rim.
4–6 The block of clay is well pressed on and fastened all round the joint, the jug then being tipped over onto its back, supported by one palm while the other hand begins to 'pull' the handle form with a gentle stroking and squeezing motion.

7

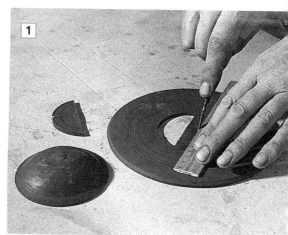

1

7 When the handle has reached the required length and slightly tapering thickness the jug is stood down and the handle curved over, the upper section supported by the hand.
8 With one hand supporting the wall inside, the lower junction is pressed home and 'wiped' off with firm strokes of the thumb.

Within these limits, however, a case can be made for both high and low positions. For instance, the center of gravity of a beaker may be said to be below the halfway mark as it is rarely quite full of liquid. A low handle should, therefore, give a better balance. On the other hand, the leverage resulting from a low placing gives less control when drinking from the beaker. This is a matter for

8

Two stages in making a 'strap' handle for a casserole.
1 The lid, which can be flat as shown or in the form of a shallow inverted bowl, has two semicircles cut from the center leaving a 'bridge' between them.
2 A separately thrown small bowl is then luted on beneath the lid.

An exuberant teapot bail handle by Bill Brown.

individual discretion. A small 'bud' of clay about an inch from the top joint (see illustration at *handle stop*) will help to give a firm grip when pouring, especially from large jugs.

The recessed type of strap handle illustrated (see fig **2**) is

Handles put to original use by Jitka Palmer.

really an alternative to a knob which, though it can be an aesthetic crowning glory to a lid, in the case of the casserole can be a nuisance in practical use. The strap handle will allow for a larger vessel in a small oven and will also ensure that the lid won't get damaged when withdrawing the casserole. (See also *bail handle, block handle, lug.*)

Handle cutter

A shaped wire ring attached to a wire or wooden handle and used for cutting strips of clay for forming pot handles. An alternative to pulling or extruding but, like the latter, the cut handle results in an even thickness from top to bottom which is not always desirable. Widely available or can be made by the potter. (See illustration at *coil cutter.*)

Handle stop

A projection near the top of a handle designed to give the thumb a better grip. This simple form has attained a very wide variety of variations and inventions since the earliest times.

The simplest is a small roll of clay fastened about an inch from the upper termination of the handle, perhaps wiped into the handle form to resemble a bud on a branch, but modeled stops of some complexity have been used.

A spirited handle stop on a modern pitcher.

Hanging planter

Fundamentally a deep bowl, the hanging planter is capable of many variations in form and needs no base on which to stand, releasing the potter to invent modeled terminals. Unglazed earthenware has the advantage that the plants can 'breath' but they soon dry out in hot situations. Stoneware, on the other hand, does not suffer *scumming* from soluble salts, though some form of drainage is advisable.

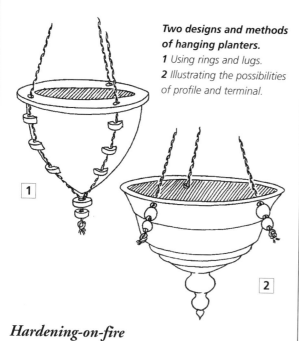

Two designs and methods of hanging planters.
1 *Using rings and lugs.*
2 *Illustrating the possibilities of profile and terminal.*

Hardening-on-fire

A separate firing, usually up to about 800°C/1472°F, which fixes underglaze pottery pigments onto the biscuit in order to prevent smudging or washing off during glazing. The process is common in the industry, but for craft potters it can be avoided by painting onto the raw clay, or by adding a little clay to the pigment if it is to be used on biscuit, as practiced by Geoffrey Whiting. If neat oxides are used, some will still be loose on the surface at 1020°C/1868°F, and must be rinsed off before glazing. A little flux may be added — china stone will help with cobalt. Gum can be used when painting on biscuit or when glazing directly over the unfired color but this will affect the glaze take-up.

Hard-leather

Used in this book to indicate clay on the dry side of *leather-hard*.

Hardness scale

Also known as Mohs' scale. Based on a series of minerals in order of hardness: each mineral can be scratched by the one below it.

1 Talc	6 Feldspar (orthoclase rock)
2 Gypsum	7 Quartz
3 Calcite	8 Topaz
4 Fluorspar (fluorite)	9 Corundum
5 Apatite	10 Diamond

The scale is used as a convenient reference, e.g. a mineral or rock might be rated 5–6, between apatite and feldspar.

Hard paste porcelain rates 6–7.

For practical purposes the following has been suggested: No. 2 can be scratched with the fingernail; No. 3 with a copper wire; Nos. 4–5 equate with window glass; Nos. 5–6 with a pocket knife; Nos. 6–7 can be abraded with a file; Nos. 7–8 will themselves scratch a steel knife blade. The main use of *Moh's scale* is as a preliminary clue to the identification of rocks.

Hard paste

The name given to 'true' porcelain of European type firing at 1350–1450°C/2462–2642°F and composed of china clay (kaolin) with china stone or feldspar. Craft potters rarely fire to this range and it is difficult to find a pure clay which can also be thrown on the wheel. The theoretical ideal composition of hard paste is 25% quartz, 25% feldspar, 50% kaolin. CR3 gives a recipe (Richard Parkinson) for a throwable 1320°C/2408°F porcelain. (See under *Limoges porcelain, porcelain*.)

Hare's fur glaze

A name given to a range of mottled or streaked dark brown Chinese glazes. Rhodes asserts that these are *slip glazes*. Fairly fluid, and subject to blistering—the healed over blisters causing the darker marks. The temperature is critical and varies with the glaze. (See also *tenmoku*). I have found that manganese as well as iron, if heavily loaded into an oxidized glaze, will give something of the same effect. Yellow spots, which also occur in early examples, can appear on iron/ash glazes in oxidation.

Harkort test

A method of testing glaze for its liability to craze. The piece is heated repeatedly and at successively higher temperatures from 120°C/248°F to 190°C/374°F, and plunged into cold water (quenched) between each stage. A note is made of the temperature at which crazing becomes apparent. The higher the temperature stage, the longer its probable craze-free life (from 3 months after quenching at 150°C /302°F to 2½ years at 170°C/338°F). There are other factors in crazing besides *thermal shock*, (see *moisture crazing*) but a simple form of this test gives an indication of the strength of your glaze and of *glaze-body fit*. In professional equipment the pieces are heated under steam pressure.

Harp, bow

A clay-cutter in the form of a semi-circular hoop of metal or bamboo with a wire or wires stretched across it. The

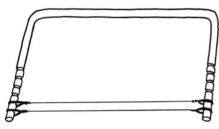

A 'harp' with two wires on a metal frame for cutting multiple slabs.

harp can be used for trimming clay—e.g. rims on the wheel or the edges of *molded dishes*—or it can be dragged through a block of clay to cut slabs. In the latter case it needs to be sturdily constructed with the wire fixed at a given distance from the ends, so that, when the cut is made and the ends pressed tightly to the bench surface, an even thickness slab results. A number of notches can be provided to control the cut, or several wires used at once. For slab cutting, very strong steel piano wire is used (some ingenious ideas are suggested by potters in Fournier PT). There is always a slight tendency for the wire to rise in the middle. Considerable strength is needed to cut a large block into several slabs.

Harrison pyrometric cones

See *Seger cones*.

Haydite

A trade name for a US expanded clay aggregate.

Health hazard

The inhaling of the dust from clay, glazes, and other powdery materials is the main hazard in the general run of studios. Those who use abrasives to smooth dry clay or biscuit are especially vulnerable and more than one potter has suffered. Some materials are more dangerous than others, lead compounds, flint, and quartz for example but inhaling or ingesting any of them is a bad thing. Use all materials wet where possible and be especially careful when sweeping or brushing. There are a number of sweeping compounds on the market; in England Dusmo Farinol, Miller Road, Bedford and Sweeping Component, Unit 4, Prospect Way, Royal Oak Industrial Estate, Daventry are two suppliers. The outlay may seem unnecessary until you begin to get short of breath! Remember that clothing can hold (and release) amounts of dust from materials so a wipeable apron is advised, see *overall*. The really dangerous materials are marked 'toxic' under their headings but see also

poisonous materials for further discussion which includes my set of rules for a long potting life.

For more advice, Vol. 16 No. 1 of *Art Hazards News* has comprehensive advice on clay, glaze, and kiln dangers: while the Center of Safety in Arts, 5 Beekman Street, Suite 1030, New York, NY 10038, USA; and HMSO in Britain are sources of advice concerning the Approved Code of Practice in relation to ceramic processes. (See also *carbon monoxide, ventilation.*)

Hearth

See *grate*.

Heat

Heat is the result of the translation, rotation or vibration of molecules. It is energy which can be put to work by potters to rearrange the molecular structure of matter, e.g. forming ceramic from clay. In a fuel-burning kiln it is the result of the chemical combination of carbon with hydrogen and oxygen; in an electric kiln it is the result of electronic and molecular movement. It can be transmitted by conduction, convection and radiation. Heat is not gauged merely in terms of temperature. In the firing of pottery, time is also a factor. (See *Heat work.*)

Diagrams **2** and **3** show how simple heat control in an electric kiln can be acheived by switching between circuits.

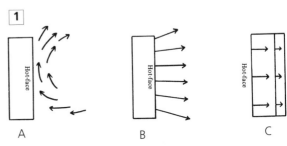

Three ways in which heat can be distributed.

A Convection. Air (or any gas), when heated, will rise and cooler air flow in to take its place. Convection occurs only to a small extent inside an electric kiln (unless top and bottom spyholes are open together, a dangerous proceeding), but it is the basic mechanism in a fueled kiln, creating the draft in the chimney. In all kilns it is a factor in heat loss from the outside.
B Radiation. Heat given off from a hot body (kiln elements, burning fuel, etc..) to pots, kiln furniture and walls in a kiln and, as the temperature rises, from hot wall to pack and from pot to pot. Air is not involved in radiation which spreads out in straight lines like light rays.
C Conduction. Heat is transferred through all materials in a kiln, though at different rates according to their composition.

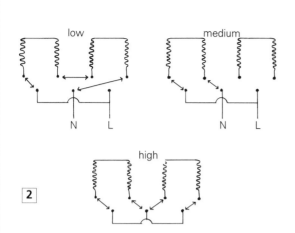

2

Connections for a multi-position electric switch heat control.

Low heat. *The current passes through two circuits in series. For drying.*

Medium. *One circuit only. Burning off wax, etc.*

High. *Two circuits in parallel. Full power.*

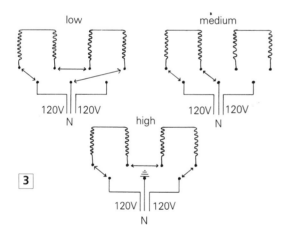

3

Results from two 120v circuits with neutral (USA).

Low. *120v through two circuits.*

Medium. *One circuit at 120v.*

High. *Two circuits in series (no neutral) at 240v. Full power. (Courtesy Wikey).*

Heat control

Solenoid connectors to gas burners can be used with a controlling pyrometer to vary the heat input and thus the firing speed automatically. A somewhat expensive luxury. For general kiln control see *controlling pyrometer, heat fuse, kiln sitter, pyrometer.*

The diagrams show how simple heat control in an electric kiln can be achieved by switching between circuits.

Heat-fuse

Electric current can be conducted through a short length of metal inside the kiln which will melt at a given temperature, break the circuit, and cut off the supply to the kiln elements. Similar in appearance to a *pyrometer*. The fuse must be rated somewhat above the optimum firing temperature and its object is to prevent a total burn-out of the kiln. It is not an automatic cut-off for normal firing.

As well as the melting heat fuse which has only one 'life', resettable and electronic fuses are available from Potterycrafts and others with 20–50°C/68–122°F increments of control up to 1350°C/2462°F.

Heat insulation

See *insulation of heat.*

Heat loss

Heat can escape from a kiln in various ways. With combustible fuels the chimney takes away probably a third or more of the heat produced at the hearth. Hence the attempts by downdraft, multi-chamber kilns, and other designs, to utilize as much heat energy as possible before the chimney is reached. Simple updraft kilns are the most expensive; the ancient Eastern climbing kiln or the modern electric kiln probably the most economical. In the industry, the tunnel kiln wastes very little heat.

Heat loss through walls can be controlled by the use of special *insulating bricks, ceramic fiber, mineral wool block,* etc. though only the first two are suitable for hotface use and all are easily abraded or broken. Heat loss increases as the difference between the ambient and chamber temperature increases. It is also proportional to wall area (rather than to the volume of the firing chamber). A perfect cube is ideal in this respect, a long narrow rectangle the least efficient. The total area can easily be worked out and compared with volume. A 2 x 2 x 2ft/0.6 x 0.6 x 0.6m chamber will have a volume of 8cu ft/0.216cu m; a 4 x 2 x 1ft /1.2 x 0.6 x 0.3m chamber will also contain 8cu ft/0.216cu m. The first, however, has 24sq ft/2.23sq m of wall area (four sides, floor and roof) while the latter has 28sq ft/2.6sq m or 16% more. Wall loss will obviously vary with the type of bricks or other insulation used but it has been estimated at up to 20% at higher temperatures.

Bricks will also store heat, i.e. use up energy in getting hot themselves. This will vary dramatically between a close, heavy *firebrick* and an open, insulating brick (See *heat storage.*) If, for reasons of strength and heat resistance, the hotface must be of firebrick, this should be as thin as possible and backed by more insulating material. (See *insulation*.) When other heat expenders such as the production of steam and poor combustion are taken into account, not much more than 20% of the actual hearth heat is available to fire the pots. (See also *thermal conductivity*.)

Too little attempt is made to utilize chimney and other heat losses in a kiln for space heating, clay drying, etc. While there are problems with fumes from electric kilns, they certainly warm the studio and a gas kiln could also be utilized for space heating as well as firing. I have even cut ducts, fitted with fans, through walls to distribute kiln heat through the house.

Heat resistance

The power of resisting change (to the molten state) when heated. (See *eutectic, refractories*, etc.)

Heat shock

Taking pots from too hot a kiln can cause crazing or dunting which may not occur during slower final cooling. (See *thermal shock*.)

Heat storage

The amount of heat that kiln bricks, kiln furniture, saggars, etc. will 'hold', i.e. that amount required to heat them to the point where they radiate as much energy as they take in. This storage represents wasted fuel; bricks should be chosen with as low a heat storage as is compatible with abrasion resistance, etc. (See also *heat loss*). The denser the brick, the more heat it will absorb. The average firebrick will store some 30,000 *Btu* (30.6 mJ) per sq ft 9in/230 mm thick; a high quality insulating brick 6–8000 Btu (6–8 mJ). The familiar household storage heater utilizes the heat storing properties of heavy brick.

Heat-treatment

The control of temperature during cooling to create special effects, especially *crystal* formation. The temperature may be held at various stages, or a degree of reheating may be practiced. Changes can also be made in the glaze by means of subsequent refiring at submaturing temperatures. Many of the interesting glazes from Scandinavia and Germany are 'heat-treated'.

Heat-work

In the firing of pottery there are two factors, temperature and time, which taken in conjunction will represent the energy input or heat-work. Thus soaking will alter glaze qualities although the temperature remains constant. *Pyrometric cones* respond to heat-work in a similar way to glazes, and this is their principal advantage over *pyrometers*.

Heatproof ware

See *ovenware* and *flameproof ware*.

Hematite, haematite

The mineral of ferric *iron* Fe_2O_3. Described by Billington as 'an iron-earth ... found in a stone-like form'. Has been recommended for coating pots prior to burnishing to give a good color, but the type of hematite generally offered by merchants is too pure and the burnish tends to fade. The inclusion of some fine-grain red clay could help. (See *burnish*.) Red *ochres* are impure hematites, used for *burnishing* and in *crystalline* glazes.

Hidasuki

See *firecord*.

High alumina cement

See *aluminous cement*.

High temperature colors

The oxides of cobalt, iron, and manganese will all stand stoneware or porcelain temperatures, the first of these being the most stable, with copper, chromium, and antimony to a lesser degree. Vanadium as ammonium metavanate will also survive fairly high temperatures. Kiln atmosphere, of course, affects the colors in some degree; copper oxide, in reduction, for instance, can be fired as high as 1340°C/2444°F.

Holdcroft bar

Holdcroft Thermoscope. Special ceramic bars 2¼in/57mm long, supported at each end, and used like pyrometric cones. A bar will sag at the temperature indicated by its number. Numbers are from 1–360. Temperatures are in °C.

No. 40 – 700	No. 230 – 1100	No. 270 – 1250
No. 120 – 905	No. 250 – 1140	No. 280 – 1280
No. 190 – 1000	No. 260 – 1200	No. 290 – 1300
No. 210 – 1060	No. 265 – 1230	No. 360 – 1490

See *temperature degree* for Fahrenheit conversions.

Similar bars, now more widely available are *Pyro minibars* (used in *kiln sitter*).

Hole cutter

Double-edged, semi-cylindrical knives for cutting holes for teapot strainers and other purposes are available from many suppliers and perform a quick, neat job if the clay condition is just right (on the soft side of leather-hard). There are several sizes from around ⅛in to ½in wide. Some are tapered, allowing for variable sized holes from one tool.

Hollow dish mold

A concave mold of plaster or biscuit in which a dish is

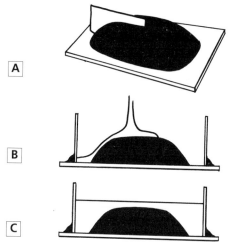

Making a hollow dish mold.
A *shows a block of clay which has been cut to the desired shape. Start with a flat-topped block, cut the plan shape with the aid of a card template, then steadily pare the curve away with a wooden spatula tool. Finish with a template of metal, stiff card or wood as in diagram. The template is scraped round the form until it touches at all points. Build up any area which has been cut too low. Ensure a sharp, clean angle between the clay and the base board. The slope of the sides should not be too steep or, in use, it will be difficult to ease a slab of clay into the finished mold. There should be a flat or even slighty dipped area on the top of the former so that the dishes made from it will sit firmly.*
B *A wall of lino, corrugated card, or similar material is built round the completed former and made water-tight as shown in the section. A smooth mixture of plaster (see plaster of Paris for mixing) is poured steadily over the former, giving it time to flow into the surrounding wall without cavities, and continue until the level is about an 1in/25mm above the clay, as in diagram.*
C *When the plaster is set the wall is removed, the clay former peeled out and the outer corners of the mold bevelled. Keep the inner corners sharp. (See also pressed dishes.)*

formed. It is the easiest type of mold to make. Hump molds can be made from it.
Method. The illustration shows a block of clay which has been cut with a tool and finally shaped with a template to an inverted version of the required dish shape. Make sure that there is a sharp and clean angle between the clay and the board and ensure that this is not undercut at any point. A watertight wall of clay, corrugated card, metal or leather is built round the clay shape and about an inch from it. This is then filled with *plaster of Paris* poured steadily onto the middle of the clay form until it rises to a level ½in/12mm above the highest point. This is left to set, the wall removed, the whole reversed, and the clay-former peeled out. The surfaces of the mold can be scraped smooth and clean and the top inner edge cut to a sharp corner. The outside corners are bevelled with a plane. (For use see *dishes*.)

A hollow dish mold in use, of the type shown in the diagrams. The clay is first beaten flat with the palm, rolled to the required thickness, lifted by the cloth or, if it is firm enough, directly by the hands as in the photograph and lowered into the mold. (See also pressed dish, rolling clay.)

Honey glaze

A general name for a high-lead glaze with some iron oxide, generally introduced by the use of red clay in the recipe. The natural impurities in the old slipware glazes gave a slightly yellowish or honey colored tinge which had a unifying effect on the design. A small amount of manganese can also help.
A typical modern 'honey' glaze recipe is:

Lead sesquisilicate	70	Feldspar	10
Red clay	12	China clay	6
Whiting	2		

fired at around 1070°C/1958°F. (See also *lead frits* and at *trailing* for another recipe).

Horneblend

An intermediate igneous rock. Complex silicates of calcium, magnesium, iron and sodium.

Hot-face

The inner surface of a kiln wall.

Hot-face bricks

Bricks capable of standing great heat and, in a solid fuel kiln, abrasion and *spalling*. The various qualities of high-alumina *firebrick* are generally used, except in electric kilns where the more efficient but softer insulating (HTI) brick composes the hot-face and often the entire wall. (See *insulation*, *heat loss*, etc.)

Used with care, the more efficient *ceramic fiber blanket* or *block* can replace hot-face bricks in some situations.

HTI bricks

High temperature insulating bricks. See *bricks*, *electric kiln*, *heat loss*, *hot-face bricks*, *insulation*, *heat*.

Hump-mold, mushroom-mold, drape-mold

Dish molds with a convex surface. Useful for *trailed* and *feathered* dishes. The disadvantage of the type is that the dish may crack across it when drying. A hump-mold without a foot can be used as a 'master' from which to reproduce hollow molds. If a hump-mold is cast from a hollow one, the expansion of the plaster can cause trouble and it is advisable to line the hollow mold with a thin sheet of clay to accommodate this expansion. Hump-molds can also be made from metal pie-dishes (thinly greased before casting). If other concave shapes are used, always bear the expansion factor in mind — it is powerful enough to split glass or pottery.

See diagrams for the method of making a mold from a pie-dish.

Hydrate, hydration

A compound containing *chemically combined water*. Clay is a hydrated aluminum-silicate. Firing drives off the water leaving alumina silicate. In this case the operation is irreversible, but this is not always so. With gypsum it is partially reversible under certain conditions. Hamer recommends that any glaze containing a hydrate, e.g. colemanite, be fired slowly to 800–900°C/1472–1652°F to avoid damage to the glaze layer during dehydration.

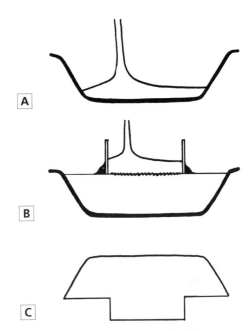

A hump-mold made in a metal pie dish.

A The dish is lightly greased with warm Vaseline, petroleum jelly or similar and filled with an even mix of plaster of Paris until the level is just below the point where the dish wall begins to turn outwards towards the rim.
B The central area of the set plaster is scored or roughened, and a wall of card, lino, or similar sheet material is set on it, made water-tight with clay, and filled to a depth of about 2in/50mm with plaster.
C The completed (reversed) mold.

Hydrocarbon gases

Gases of carbon and hydrogen compounds, e.g. methane CH_4. The paraffin series are hydrocarbons, also *natural gas*. Mentioned in connection with *reducing atmospheres*.

Hydrogen

A gaseous element H, 1. Lightest substance known. Inflammable (see *gas fuel*). Combines with oxygen to form water, H_2O. True acids will contain hydrogen in their formula but the acidic oxides used in pottery do not. Originally used (as unity) to calculate *atomic weights*, but now superseded by oxygen for this purpose. Hydrogen is the unit of *valency*.

Hydrometer

Or 'slip-gauge' (Leach). An instrument for determining the density (specific gravity) of a liquid/solid mixture, i.e. the consistency or thickness of a slip or glaze. A hollow glass

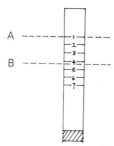

A simple hydrometer, cross-hatching indicating the weighted end which holds it upright in the liquid. The dotted line (A) indicates its level in pure water. In a glaze it would float higher, as at line (B), giving a reading of 4 to 5 on the scale marked on the hydrometer. The divisions on the scale are arbitrary and used for comparative reference. If wood or a permeable material is used it must be protected with paint; it will sink lower if it absorbs water and falsify the reading.

cylinder (a test-tube, for instance) or a wooden rod about 1in/25mm x 6in/150mm is weighted at one end so that it floats upright. The more solid matter present in the mixture, the greater the length of hydrometer which will show above the surface. A scale can be marked on it, using its position in clear water as a base line. Its value lies in its ability to compare one glaze with another or to maintain a standard for any one glaze. Approximate readings for true weight and volume can be noted by testing the hydrometer in a batch of known dry weight and water content.

Pottery supply merchants list hydrometers, but they are not difficult to make.

Hydroxyl, *hydroxide*

An ionic combination of one oxygen atom and one hydrogen atom forming part of a *compound*. Known as the OH group and shown as (OH) in formulas. The alkalis, boron and phosphorus can form hydroxides, as can aluminum, see *bauxite*.

Hygroscopic water, *substance*

Term occasionally used to indicate the *chemically combined water* in clay. A hygroscopic material, however, is one capable of absorbing water from the surrounding air. Exceptionally hygroscopic substances are *deliquescent*, e.g. potassium carbonate.

Hymod ball clay

A high iron content — up to 2.5% — Devon (UK) ball clay, typically 55% SiO_2. See also *Hyplas*.

Hyplas ball clay

A high-silica (over 70%), low iron, white firing clay, from Devon (UK). See also *Hymod*.

Ideal formula

The theoretical formula for a mineral, to which natural materials approximate: the simple ones, such as flint or whiting, very closely; more complex formulas, such as the feldspars, less so. The ideal formulas are used to represent natural minerals in simple glaze computations. For greater accuracy, in the industry for instance, a true formula derived from analysis would be used. Because of possible divergencies, it is advisable for potters to buy their raw materials in as large quantities as they can house (they are much cheaper pro rata, too) so that they can become familiar with their actual properties as distinct from those expected from an 'ideal formula'.

Identification of materials

Every so often a potter loses the label from a bag of material. If the material is near black it is likely to be a pigment oxide (cobalt, copper, black iron, nickel, ilmenite, or manganese) and can be checked by firing a brushstroke on a glaze. Chromium oxide will be green, as will copper carbonate, iron oxide, of course, red-brown.

The rest—the great majority of pottery materials—are white or off-white. Feldspar is often pinkish, Cornish stone (not defluorinated) pale blue. The remainder need more sophisticated methods of indentification. The *button test* is one such, another is *specific gravity* but these are so close for many materials that very precise measurements are required and difficult to obtain. A detailed chart was published in CR166.

Identifying stain

See *distinguishing stain*.

Igneous rock

From 'fire' (Greek). Rock which has been molten and has formed during the cooling of the earth, or by intrusions from a molten core into the earth's crust in more recent times. In some cases the cooling has been slow and the rocks have had time to crystallize into individual minerals. Granite is the prime example. These old rocks are generally acidic, i.e. they have a high silica content of 70% or more.

The molten material which has been forced through the crust—volcanic or extrusive rock—has solidified rapidly as lava and has a very fine crystalline grain. This material tends to be basic with 50% or less of silica, *Basalt* is the commonest. One might say that the granite system represents the body and the volcanic rocks the glaze of a ceramic.

Feldspars and *kaolinite* clays have decomposed from granitic rocks: *montmorillonite* more probably from extrusive ones. In England many igneous rocks are often used as roadstones, and could be used as a foundation for a stoneware glaze. It is worth trying any hard rock dust that you can get. 'Chemical Analyses of Igneous Rocks' was published in 1931 (South West England) and 1956 (Northern England) by Her Majesty's Stationery Office, and similar sources of information elsewhere. A useful table of the mean compositions of igneous rocks is given in Sutherland. The USA and Canadian Departments of Mines also issue geological surveys on clays and other deposits in the various regions.

Illite

Described variously as a hydrous mica or a clay mineral. 'In London clay the mineral is thought to be 90% illite' (Cardew). Worrall doubts its separate existence: 'It seems likely that (illite, etc.) are mixtures rather than pure minerals.' Thought to be altered from *kaolinite* by the action of ancient seas.

Illite has less potash and more OH groupings (see *hydrogen*) than mica and may have been converted by seawater from kaolinite. Secondary clays often contain a proportion of illite, even, some believe, to the exclusion of kaolinite. '— responsible for the vitrification of clay —' (Hamer). It is reputed to aid in *burnishing*, and in *gloss ware*.

The name originates from Illinois, where it was first isolated (as late as the 1930s).

Ilmenite

An ore, ferrous titanate, $FeO.TiO_2$, 152, m.p. 1365°C/2489°F s.g. 4.7.

An ore of titanium. A similar combination to rutile, but with more iron. Found as beach-sand in Australia, South-West India, America and Scandinavia. Grinds to grog-like granules and can be used in bodies or glazes to provide speckle—'a peppery appearance' (Rhodes). The iron will dissolve at the perimeter of the granule to give an amber 'halo'. 1–3% is the normal addition. Can be bought in various grades. Can assist crystalline development in glazes, and will give a yellowish color when used as a pigment.

Impervious, impermeable

Will not absorb water or allow water to pass through. In pottery the degree of vitrification controls permeability. There are strict industrial tests, floor and wall tiles, for instance should not exceed an absorption of 0.5%. (See also *porosity*.)

Impressing

Impressed decoration has been one of the most popular techniques of the mid and late 20th century. The ideal of a close integration between pot and decoration is combined with direct and spontaneous 'instant' action and an enhanced glaze interest.

The *roulette* or *stamp* are less favored than the chance patterns developed by 'found' objects: a broken edge of wood, a cog-wheel, rolled string, etc. This can result in freedom and freshness, or incoherence and muddle, according to the degree of skill and sensitivity employed.

Order and design are more easily obtained by restricting one's impressing tools to two, or even to a single one, building up a pattern by repetition and variation of placing. If several sheets of clay are rolled out, experiments can be made before working on a pot. Impressing is very suitable for slab pots and can be done before the piece is assembled. The state of the clay will dictate the character of the impression: too dry will obviously give a shallow or partial image; too soft will give a cushioned effect, riding up at the edges. *Beaten decoration* is a related technique.

Any relief materials, woven or uneven surfaces, can be utilized to obtain an impressed pattern on clay: anaglypta paper, wood, leaves, trellis, plastic mats of all sorts, the list is endless. The design needs to be reasonably 'abstract' and used with sensibility if it is to become integrated with the form of the ceramic and not merely used for its own sake.

A wide variety of impressed marks made into a slab of soft clay by common, everyday objects.

Stamps can be cut from chalk sticks, wood, plaster (which can be made more durable by the addition of epoxy resin), etc. and can be cast one from another to form positive and negative images. Old-fashioned metal printer's type (if you can find any in this electronic age) can be used purely decoratively or to spell out a name or a quotation. Small combustible items such as rice grains can be impressed into or through the surface, but the kiln will then need to be ventilated. (See *printing, rice-grain pattern,* and *roulette.*)

Tiles will tend to distort if impressed. This can be minimized by using a tile frame, see *tile*, or a design in relief can be set in the bottom of a frame and the clay pressed on to it.

Impurities

In a mineral, any oxide or material not included in the formula. 'Purity' is the prime object of the industrial potter, since it ensures uniformity. The careful extraction of iron traces from clay by electromagnets is an instance.

Commercial suppliers are industrially orientated and the craft potter has to accept a greater degree of purity than he sometimes wants. The alternative is to go and find materials for himself (see *glazes from natural materials*). The subtlety and quality of the older ceramics — early Chinese blues, slipware glazes, etc. — arose partly from impurities which it was beyond the technology of the time to remove. There is no genuine way of returning to unrefined materials except by pioneering in the way that Cardew and Harry Davis have done, and more recently Brian Sutherland and others.

We can still use some composite natural materials, e.g. red clay to introduce iron; colemanite instead of borax frit, etc. David Green suggests trials with everyday materials such as scouring powder, fertilizers, etc. Copper metal can be oxidized in a kiln or in salt water, iron oxide can be scraped and ground as rust and so on. (See *button test.*)

Leach tells of Hamada's 'building stone' used neat as a glaze. Potclays once listed an interesting 'black feldspar' and suppliers should be encouraged to include the less common minerals. Some are, in fact, widening the range with basalt and similar materials. In the West, generally, we put a premium on time and take the quickest way out.

Incidentals

The term incidental is defined by Webster as 'being likely to ensue as a chance or minor consequence' and, less complimentarily in the Little Oxford Dictionary, as merely 'casual, non-essential'. Unplanned happenings, however, are often integral to modern studio pottery — and the bane of the industry. We make allowance for them or even partly plan them, but they fuel the impatience that makes one open a kiln too soon, even a lifetime of such events. Leach's famous paragraph in *A Potter's Book* distinguishes incidental from the accidental in the ceramic process. The second may be due to luck or carelessness, but the former — as manifested in fire-flash, bleed-through, degrees of reduction, glaze variation in different parts of the kiln, the running of colors, even the crawling of glaze in some instances — can be considered as peculiar to the process of firing natural materials and is often happy evidence of it.

Their acceptance is due in degree to contact with Japan, but they are sometimes taken to absurd lengths. Mishaps such as shattering and cracking are added to acceptable decorative/formal effects.

Shock rather than pleasure is often the aim, arising from the fear of complacency. As ever, the best work, usually that of the originators, surmounts apparent chaos with brilliance and aplomb. Incidentals have come a long way in 50 years!

Incising, *engraving*

A design cut into clay, usually with a wooden or bamboo tool cut to an angle or to a rounded point. This is preferable to a sharp metal point, which will give a weak and furrowed line. Experiment on various conditions of clay, up to leather-hard: the drier the clay the tighter and sharper will be the cut line. Incising can also be done on soft biscuit.

The decoration can be enhanced by an overlay of slip or a dry, usually ash, glaze. The traditional glaze for use over engraving is, however, a semi-transparent colored stoneware such as celadon on a fairly pale body. The increased depth of glaze in the cut line deepens the color and delineates the design. (See also *fluting.*)

Incising is often better and cleaner without glaze. Fluting may be considered a form of incising, especially the triangular cut as used by David Leach, but it is often nearer to carving. Generally an incised pattern is a line pattern, though it may vary in character from the blunt and vigorous to the fine and nervous, and be graduated in breadth and depth. It is possible to cut soft biscuit with a sharp, hard tool, useful on delicate pieces and occasionally practiced today.

Many potters use incising either as the main or as a peripheral aid in decoration. Hans Coper's pots have cut lines that gently emphasize forms or give movement to them. Work by Michael Casson shows the free sweep of sharply cut lines, which are given mystery and sensitivity by the overlay of slip and dry ash glaze. On Ladi Kwali's fine jars are blocks of pattern so closely crosshatched as to give a feeling of being in relief.

As has been suggested, the work should be done with a sharp, hard tool: metal, bamboo, or, as Leach mentions, pine with the bark removed. Clay needs to be stiff if a clean cut is required. Such is the variety, skill, and simple perverseness of potters, however, that all rules are often broken to good and original effect. (See also *Combing*.)

Incongruent melting

Pottery materials may dissociate during firing into compounds with varying melting points, i.e. into liquids within a solid. The whole structure melts incongruently. This is especially true of bodies, although it also occurs in glazes, during the firing. (See *eutectic, melting point*.)

In bodies it helps vitrification without deformation and, in glazes, renders them sufficiently *viscous* not to run from the pot.

Indentation

An impressed mark normally leaves the identity of the tool or object, but indentation can also distort the formal character of a pot and so becomes more of a shaping than a decorative process.

A rounded pot can be indented with vertical strokes of a finger or blunt, rounded edge tool to form lobes or rounded or other shaped indentations made in the wall of a pot or cylinder. A number of modern pots, by Eileen Lewenstein and others are deeply and effectively indented. Repeated indentations have been used since the beginning of ceramics to decorate or enhance the form.

A stoneware bottle by John Tuska (Rhodes SP) has deep vertical furrows down which a very thick glaze has run.

Infusorial earth

An old name for *diatomite*.

Inlay

A technique of decoration used in medieval floor tiles, Korean Koryu wares, etc. The clay is inlaid with another of a contrasting color to a depth of up to about $1/16$in/2mm. The typical pattern is fairly bold and broad, although the Korean wares mentioned were often very fine in line.

Early potters used wooden stamps with which to impress the pattern, but the usual method today is to cut with a wooden or bent-wire tool into leather-hard clay. The impressions can also be stabbed, combed, or textured by repeated marks. The cavities are then filled either with slip

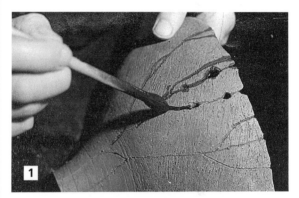

Tile inlay. *The design has been cut into a leather-hard tile and slip brushed or trailed into it. When stiff, the surface can be cleaned level with a knife or scraper. (See also mishima.)*

A finer type of inlay on a handbuilt bowl.
1 and 2 A manganese/cobalt/clay mixture is brushed into engraved lines and the surface gently scraped clean.

or with soft clay. When the slip has stiffened, scrape the surface with a straight-edge to remove excess inlay clay and to leave the design sharply defined. A finer line can be filled with thin slip or pigment. (See also *mishima*.)

Potters also inlay more involved 'sculptural' clay forms in contrasting colors, not to mention non-ceramics

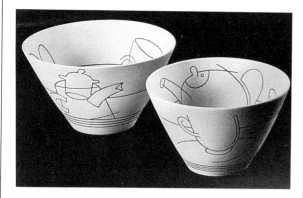

Sharp, precise line inlay on porcelain by Nicholas Homoky.

Jutka Fischer constructs her pots from patchwork sheets of various colored clays and then inlays with further colored bodies to a depth of about half the thickness of the wall. Underglaze additions of small details (such as polka dots on a handle) complete the scheme. When quite dry the pot is sanded with a fine grade wire wool. Sprayed alumina matt glaze, earthenware.

such as silver, plastics, and other materials. (See also *neriage, rolled inlay.*)

Insoluble

Will not dissolve in water. Clay, for instance, will mix intimately with water but will not dissolve and disappear as sugar does. Glaze materials must be insoluble for the following reasons: solutions are likely to crystallize out: if surplus water is poured from a settled glaze, then the

dissolved material will go too; the solution will be carried into the pores of the biscuit; the solution is likely to separate out onto the surface of the biscuit; it may cause flocculation; if the solution is caustic (as is the water from washing ash) it may affect your skin.

Ash contains soluble alkalis, hence the need for washing. Borax can be rendered insoluble only by fritting with silica. *Lead* is used as a *silicate*: although insoluble in the water of the glaze it can enter the human system as a solution if the glaze formula is not a stable one. (See *metal release.*) *Colemanite* is slightly soluble. Luckily 90% of the potter's minerals are insoluble. (See also *ash, ash preparation, washing ash.*)

Inspirating burner

A gas-burner in which the gas pressure draws the air of combustion into the mixture. The converse is the aspirating principle where air pressure draws gas in. (See *gas burner, Venturi burner.*)

Instrumentation

See *controlling pyrometer, pyrometer.*

Insulating brick

See *insulation of heat.*

Insulation of electricity

Electricity is a good servant when under complete control. All electric kilns (and other equipment) must be protected against current-carrying wires making contact with each other or with any other conductor—including the potter!

It is not practicable to insulate the actual connections between the ends of the elements and the wires connecting them, though the wires themselves can be covered with woven asbestos (or see below), and the whole system must be shielded from the possibility of being touched. This type of heatproof wire is not always available and the alternatives are butyl-rubber and silicone-rubber insulating-material. The latter has a rating of 140°C/284°F maximum. They are both expensive. Porcelain beads strung on wire were once widely used, and a potter could make his own in the form of short tubes. All connections to the kiln should be housed in flexible metal tube, or in a metal or, preferably, plastic conduit.

The main insulating materials are, air, rubber, most dry ceramics, dry wood, dry thick cloth, insulating tape and plastic.

Insulation of heat

The prevention of heat loss or thermal conductivity, especially, for potters, through the fabric of a kiln. A major consideration in design, and the choice of materials. Air is an excellent insulator, and is utilized by trapping it in small pockets in a brick or other rigid heatproof material. Thus the insulating properties of a brick will decrease as its density increases.

A *hot-face* may need strength at the expense of insulation (in electric kilns, however, the softer but still strong insulating bricks (HTIs) are sufficient) but all backing should conserve heat. These can be of low temperature insulating ceramic, such as Molers (now Alpha Insulations) red slabs, *diatomite* brick, or at least an open textured house brick (Flettons). Clay and ash or even coke mixtures are possible in situations protected from the air. Aluminum foil will reflect heat back from its surface. Newer insulators,

suitable particularly for electric kilns now include *ceramic fiber* (now widely used for many kilns, especially gas and oil firings), *micropore* (expensive but several times more efficient than the best brick), *bubble alumina, kipsulate* and proprietary brands of *non-asbestos heatproof sheeting* (see *asbestolux*, see also *vermiculite*). 75–150mm/3–6in of ceramic fiber can replace some 18in of firebrick as an insulator but the more rapid rise and, especially, the fall in temperature will alter the character of a glaze. Super-efficient insulators are therefore subject to the law of diminishing returns. Laser kilns use 25mm/1in of hot-face ceramic fiber, 25mm/1in of 'super-efficient middle isulation', and 50mm/2 in of 'high density back up' for their downdraft gas kilns. (See also *heat storage*.)

For making your own insulating bricks Pete Brown (CR 58) suggests: 4 parts (by volume) fireclay or a mixture with china clay; 1 part coarsely crushed firebrick; 5 parts fine sawdust, and Dez Johnson (CR150); 20% each of china clay, ball clay, and sawdust, with 40% crushed firebrick or stoneware grog. Fire slowly at first then fast as soon as the sawdust carbon has burnt away.

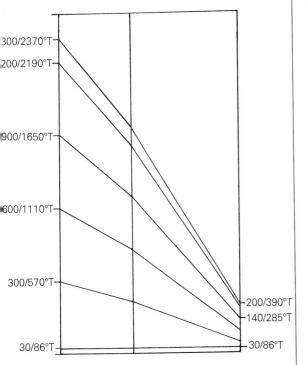

A section through brickwork showing the hot face tempertures, probable values at the junction with an insulating brick, and at the outside surface. The heat does not, of course, penetrate instantly and this sort of diagram is based on a given period of time that the hot face is subjected to a particular temperature. As the whole wall becomes hotter its heat storage capacity decreases; and the outer temperature, and consequently radiation and convection, will rise. A very slow firing is therefore less fuel efficient in this respect and the top temperature becomes more difficult to attain.

Insurance

As well as the normal fire, burglary, and damage risks a potter should take out at least a Third Person Accident insurance to cover any mishap by customers or others in the pottery or its immediate surroundings. Product failure is, hopefully, a rare occurrence but insurance against the possibility is also available if large-scale kitchenware is produced, especially pots for cooking in (see *oven ware*).

Intaglio

A term, used especially by ceramic historians, to indicate an engraved incised design as opposed to 'cameo', which is in relief.

Interface

The area, in a section through a pot, where glaze and body merge into one another. When a glaze melts on the surface of clay it 'uses' or reacts with it in fulfilling its glass-making function. The interface is at its most diffuse in stoneware, porcelain and in once-fired earthenware. A well-developed reaction is responsible for the tight grip a glaze has on a body. Its development aids craze resistance. Alumina is an important factor in its formation. Calcium in body and glaze is reputed to increase the development of interface, and may have been added to Delft bodies for this purpose.

Intermittent kiln

Kilns which are filled, heated, cooled and emptied. All studio kilns are of the intermittent type, while most industrial ones are now continuous. The nearest we get to a continuous kiln is in raku-firing. Intermittent firings are inevitably more wasteful of fuel, but they involve a certain rhythm which gives satisfaction and which the industry, feeding an unending production line, has lost.

Internet

If you own a computer then you can, at some expense, connect with the Internet, a source of information and communication. You will need a modem, a telephone connection, an arrangement with an Internet Service Provider, and an Internet or Web 'address'. There are millions of subscribers, any one of whom can 'correspond', exchange information, order goods and materials, advertise text or images via e-mail, and newsgroups, access the World Wide Web or any other subscriber. In practice it can take quite a lot of time. See Pogue and other manuals. (See also *World Wide Web*.)

Inversion-point

The temperature at which an alteration in crystalline form takes place, involving a change in volume. (See *quartz inversion, cristobalite*.)

Ion, ionic exchange, bonding

An electrically charged element or bonded group of elements. Atoms with 'incomplete' electron shells (other than two or eight) may gain or lose electrons to other atoms. They become electrically bonded and build up into a lattice or crystalline structure. Single molecules are seldom formed by this type of bond, which is known as electrovalent. Most silicates are formed by ionic bonding.

If an atom loses an electron it is left with a positive charge, and vice-versa if it gains one. Electro-positive ions are written R^+; if they lose more than one they may be R^{++} or R^{2+}. Silicon shares four electrons with oxygen atoms and becomes Si^{4+} in what is known as the SiO_4 grouping. Electro-negative ions — the gainers of electrons — are shown as R^-. The *alkali* metals form electrovalent compounds.

These theories provide explanations of the observable habits of inorganic compounds, and do not destroy the usefulness of the hypothesis of a single *molecule* or unit. Although mentioned as an SiO_4 grouping above, the quartz lattice in fact is a three-dimensional structure in which, overall, there are twice as many oxygen as silicon atoms, each O_4 group being linked above and below with two atoms of silicon. In a formula we therefore refer to the proportion of atoms in a complex or lattice as SiO_2.

Ionic exchange can take place on the surface or edges of crystals in order to stabilize the electrical charge. In clays the bentonites have a greater capacity for exchange than kaolinites and are therefore more variable in their composition.

Ionic radius

The comparative size of an atom which controls its powers of combination with others. (See *atomic radius*.)

Iridescence

A prismatic, opalescent effect often seen on soap bubbles, petrol, etc. and occurring principally in tin/bismuth lusters, and occasionally, in high concentrations of manganese in glazes. Raku pieces sometimes exhibit iridescence.

Iridium

A metallic element, Ir.192, of the platinum group. Mentioned by Billington as a source of fine stable blacks and greys, but its rarity and expense preclude its use at present.

Iron

A metallic element. Fe. 56.

Oxides: Ferric, Fe_2O_3, (hematite)	160	m.p.	1550
Ferrous (reduced) FeO	72	m.p.	1360
Ferroso-ferric Fe_3O_4 (magnetite)	232	m.p.	1538

(For other iron compounds see under *copperas, crocus martis, ilmenite, iron chromate/chromite, ochre, red clay, rutile, sienna, synthetic iron oxide.* Also *Albany clay*.)

The average percentage of iron in magnetite is 72%; in hematite, 70%; in limonite, 60%; in pyrites, 46.6%; in ilmenite 36.8% (Peter Smith CR96). He also finds pronounced differences in the analyses of similarly described iron oxides; empirical trials are therefore essential when following a given recipe. The color will be bleached by lime in a body or glaze.

In earthenware, iron gives buffs and browns (1–8%) and more reddish colors in a high alkali, lime-free glaze. It can be combined with other oxides for black, or to modify cobalt (see *below*), etc. Red clay is the most subtle source of iron for many colors and glazes; in *honey* glazes and in many stonewares where it also has a fluxing action in reduction. It can be used in high proportions in a glaze

15–20% and more). In an ash glaze, in oxidation, depending on the degree of washing of the ash (residual carbon acts as a local reducing agent) it can give red to an almost 'mirror' black. High iron glazes (or brushstrokes) can give near-reds through saturation. As a pigment iron oxide gives a variable result from yellow to black according to the strength of the brushstroke. There are a number of types of the oxide: red, black, and ochre, but the fired result is similar. The mineral known as '*bole*' is a little more reliable when applied thickly. A very small addition of titania is reputed to maintain somewhat brighter colors. Mixed with manganese and cobalt, e.g. 30% cobalt carbonate; 35% manganese dioxide; 25% ferric oxide; and 10% red clay, it approximates to *asbolite* for brush painting on stoneware though it may separate to some degree giving golden flecks in oxidation. Crystalline glazes are produced from hematite. Avoid zinc with iron, it will kill the color. In coarse particles, such as ilmenite, iron produces specking.

Chemically an *amphoteric*, it will have little effect in an oxidizing fire but will behave as a flux in reduction. The most stable iron form is the *spinel*—$FeO.Fe_2O_3$, or Fe_3O_4. Its role in glazes is complex (see Hamer's PDMT, for a long article on the subject).

Iron leads the field as a coloring agent in reduced glazes with a range from black through brick-red to blue. (See *celadons, reduction, tenmoku*, etc.)

Iron chromate, chromite

Chromate of iron, ferric chromate, $FeCrO_4$. By analysis Fe_2O_3 34.6. Cr_2O_3 49.8.

In a glaze 0.5–2.0% will produce grays. Also used in bodies as a stain, to produce dark colors in engobes, and to a lesser extent as an opacifier. Yields brown with zinc. Used in crystalline glazes. May be used to modify other pigment oxides. If used for brushwork 'the edges can variously bleed with different colors' (Hamer).

An iron chromite (a chrome iron ore $FeO.Cr_2O_3$) is listed by Potters Supply House.

Iron earths

A series of impure, clayey, high-iron compounds, sometimes with manganese. They are generally more stable to 1400°C/2552°F than iron oxides, and are preferred by some potters for introducing iron into glazes, slips and pigments. (See *ochre, umber, sienna*.)

Iron spangles

See at *spangles*.

Iron spot

A speckled effect on some high-fired glazes caused, generally, by iron pyrites in the body, usually a 'natural' presence but sometimes deliberately added in the form of iron spangles or crushed granite. Coarsely ground, hard-dried red clay in the glaze has also been suggested. (See also *bleedthrough*.)

Ironing of cobalt

Reddish to black patches on cobalt caused by too high a concentration. Due to crystallization of cobalt silicate (Dodd). Generally considered a fault, but can sometimes be pleasant on a brushstroke. To avoid ironing, cobalt can be diluted with china stone or a frit. When modified with other oxides, e.g. red clay and/or manganese the effect can be very decorative. (See *cobalt*.)

Ironstone, ironstone ware

A hard iron ore. Known as 'ironstone ware', with a dark colored vitrified body.

Isotope

It has been found that, though the proton number of an element is constant, the number of neutrons varies. Since the atomic weight is the sum of these fundamental particles, an element can have more than one 'weight'. The deviations from the formerly accepted weight are called isotopes. Luckily the ratio of the number of isotopes is constant in a mass of material, so that an atomic weight can be worked out which is an average or mean number. Thus if two-thirds of an element has a weight of 14, and one-third a weight of 15, the atomic weight of a mass of that element would be 14.33 recurring (a hypothetical case). As a result, the convenient whole numbers have given way to several places of decimals. (See also *atomic theory, atomic weights, atomic numbers*.)

ITC 100

A spray-on refractory coating made by the ITC (International Technical Ceramics, Florida. Available from Scarva). Also an ITC 213 metal coating for use on elements and kiln grates.

Jar mill

A small ball mill, usually turned by friction on revolving horizontal rods about 2in/50mm in diameter. The jars range from 2 pints/1 liter to a gallon/5 liters. The advantage of the jar mill mechanism is that various sizes of jars can be used, and more than one jar at a time. The critical factors are those given under *ball mill*.

The jar can be of a hard ceramic. The lid must be quite watertight, and capable of firm closure. Size from 4in/100mm internal diameter upwards. The mechanism is shown in the diagram. Only one roller is driven, the other(s) run free. One might compromise by constructing the drive and purchasing the jars from a merchant.

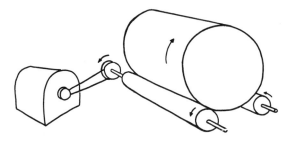

Diagram of a jar mill showing the drive from the motor to one of the rollers, the second running free. In practice some gearing or speed reduction system, would be needed between motor and roller, and a computation made for the roller and jar revolution speeds by a comparison of their relative cirumferences, as detailed at ball mill.

Jasper ware

The name given by Wedgwood to a fine-grain, unglazed, vitreous stoneware, often stained with oxides. A quoted recipe:

Ball clay	26	China clay	18
Barytes	45	Flint	11

Jersey stone

An American equivalent to china stone.

Jeweling

The application of dots of colored slip onto a trailed line. Adds enrichment to slip trailing. (See *dotting, trailing* for illustrations.)

Jigger

The pivotted arm of a *jigger and jolley*.

Jigger and jolley

A machine for molding hollow ware and flatware. The clay is squeezed between a profiled metal tool (the template or 'die') and a revolving plaster mold. The face of a plate or saucer is formed by throwing a slab of clay onto a revolving mold, while the shape of the back and the thickness are controlled by the die, which is brought down by means of a pivoted arm onto the spinning clay, squeezing and cutting away the surplus. For hollow shapes the outside is formed by the mold, and the inside by the die.

It is essentially an industrial operation for large-scale production of identical pieces. It needs some skill (although automated systems have largely taken over in industry) but is obviously a mechanical technique. To say that the method destroys the 'plastic feeling' is to ignore the fact that the industrial bodies used have little plasticity anyhow. Plastic clays such as the craft potter uses are rather sticky to operate. 'Jiggering' usually refers to hollow ware, and 'jolleying' to flatware.

Hollow forms are limited to those which will lift directly from the mold — fundamentally cylinders or forms approaching inverted cones, and without 'return' angles

Robin Welch using a jigger and jolley machine for forming a plate. (Photo Eileen Lewenstein.)

see diagram at *mold*). Foot-rings are minimal on most shapes.

Several hundred molds may be used for one service, each piece being left to stiffen before it can be removed from its mold.

Amateur jolleys can be rigged up for special purposes—cutting the clay former and the plaster foot of a circular dish mold, for example. Jolley arms can be purchased. The template or die can be sheet brass or wood.

A simple cylinder jolley mold and some of the variations derived from the basic shape. Robin Welch workshop.

Jolley

See *jigger and jolley*.

Jordon clay

A light-burning stoneware clay from New Jersey, USA.

Joule

The standard international unit of heat quantity (work or energy). Symbol J.

1 Btu	=	1050 J
	=	1.05kJ
1 Therm	=	100,000 Btu
	=	105,000,000 joules
	=	105,000 kJ
	=	105 mJ
kJ	=	one thousand Joules (10^3)
mJ	=	one million Joules (10^6)

Jug shape

A satisfactory jug shape combines a generous and well-defined form with utility. Cardew suggests a combination of beaker and sphere and gives advice on throwing this basic pottery form. The 'inverted beaker' shape has, however, been much favored. Medieval English pottery provides a patternbook of splendid jugs in a wide variety of

Three fine, strongly formed salt-glaze jugs by Sarah Walton. Note thumb stops on the larger pieces.

'Jug with Birds' in earthenware by Alison Britton.

A sophisticated and finely proportioned version of the Medieval style by Bernard Leach. Subtly scored and with a strong rim and apt handle.

shape and finish. The jug handle is crucial to its form and should be balanced by the lip.

Points of utility to be remembered are that a jug must be easily cleanable, though with modern kitchen tools it is not essential to be able to get one's hand inside, and that it should withstand moderate thermal shock.

When full, its weight will be more than doubled and the handle should be **seen** to have sufficient strength to lift it without danger. The handle should not rise above the rim of the jug. (See *handle*.)

Today, in common with the cup, teapot, and other humble ceramics, the jug has been subjected to many variations, deformations, and indignities. These are aesthetic matters and outside the scope of this book.

Jun glaze

The new spelling of 'Chun'. A type of opalescent Chinese glaze which has fascinated many craft potters. It has a milky bluish tinge but does not contain pigment oxides, the color arising from suspended globules of 'glass in glass'

(Cardew) known as 'optical color' (see *color*), or 'scattered light from suspended particles of colloidal size' (Hamer) which are difficult to control. If overfired the result will be transparent; if underfired dull and semi-matt. Chinese Jun was often associated with colloidal copper reds.

Phosphorus, usually derived from wood ashes, is probably a necessary ingredient. The glaze is unaffected by kiln atmosphere except that the body color will show through to a degree and will influence that of the glaze. Cardew deals at some length with 'jun' glazes. He recommends a thick application over a darkish body or even a tenmoku glaze. Talc is a useful addition. The 'Jun' effect can also result from suspended particles (dicalcium silicate which may precipitate in the molten glaze has been suggested to aid suspension), or from minute bubbles of gas.

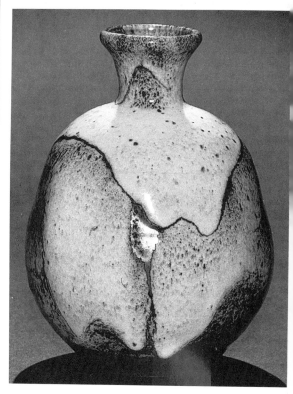

Rich, overlapping, fluid Jun glazes on a pot by Peter Rushforth (Australia).

K factor

See *absolute temperature, Kelvin scale.*

Kaki

Japanese for 'persimmon', applied to a series of red-brown, broken-color, *reduced*-iron glazes. In Mashiko the use of a local building-stone, crushed, gave kaki glaze without additions. Leach mentions glazes with a high feldspathic content, some limestone and about 5% iron oxide. Several recipes are given in Leach pp170–1. They have a higher iron content — up to 20–30% of ochre — and also suggest that the color can be obtained in oxidation which is, anyhow, necessary during cooling to allow the formation of red iron crystals on the surface. Rhodes includes kaki under *slip glazes,* and there is some parallel here with the ochre recipes. Certainly the iron needs to be in sufficient quantity for some to be precipitated onto the surface where it will react with oxygen and crystallize on cooling. (See also *red glazes.*)

A translation from Japanese to American materials of a kaki recipe gives:

Nepheline syenite	38.7
Colemanite	20.0
Zinc	8.1
Barium	9.85
China clay	25.8
Flint	33.3
Iron	2.0–6.0% addition

Kalium

See *potassium,* atomic symbol K.

Kandite

'A group name for kaolinic minerals' (Dodd).

Kanthal

Suppliers of a wide range of electrical resistance materials for use in kilns and furnaces. Originating in Sweden, they are now supplied under licence in other countries: in England by Kanthal Ltd, Stoke-on-Trent; in the USA by Kanthal of Bethel, Connecticut. Alloys are made into wires, strips, rods, tubes, ribbons, etc.

Kanthal A is suitable for temperatures up to 1400°C/2552°F; Kanthal 'Super' is a special molybdenum/silica alloy rated at 1850°C/3362°F. Wires are supplied in 37 different diameters in two series or gauges called swg (standard wire gauge), and B & S (Brown & Sharpe). Diameters between 1.6mm/approx. $^{1}/_{16}$in, and 2.35mm/approx. $^{3}/_{16}$in are the most useful to potters. These are in the ranges 16–13 swg and 14–11 B & S. The higher the gauge number, the thinner the wire. The thicker wires are recommended for stoneware firing. For potters' kilns the A quality wire is the most widely used element material. Although it will run at a maximum of 1400°C/2552°F there is always a lag between element temperature and that of the kiln, the working maximum firing temperature is nearer 1350°C/2462°F. The wire will last longer at 1300°C/2372°F. In my experience well-designed and carefully wound elements should last up to 200 stoneware firings in oxidation. They become thinner and slower with use, and the coils tend to collapse sideways but they are economical, if not abused. (See also *electricity, electric kilns, electric wiring to kiln, element, element-winding.*)

Some data on Kanthal A1 resistance wire					
Wire gauge		Diameter		resistance in	
		in.	mm	ohms per foot	ft/lb
swg	18	0.048	1.219	0.3786	179.4
B & S	16	0.0508	1.290	0.3376	160.3
swg	17	0.056	1.422	0.2781	131.9
B & S	15	0.0571	1.450	0.2677	127.1
swg	16	0.064	1.626	0.2129	101.0
swg	15	0.072	1.829	0.168	79.85
B & S	13				
swg	14	0.08	2.032	0.136	64.6
B & S	11	0.0907	2.304	0.1059	50.3
swg	13	0.092	2.337	0.1031	48.87

Kaolin

The name derives from the Chinese Kao — high, and Ling—hill, a ridge or mountain where it was discovered. It is synonymous with *china clay*, this name being preferable to avoid confusion with *kaolinite*, the pure, theoretical clay substance or mineral.

Kaolinite

The 'ideal' clay mineral $Al_2O_3.2SiO_2.2H_2O$, 258, to which china clay approaches most closely. The true kaolinite crystal consists of alternate layers of SiO_4 groups and $Al(OH_6)$ groups (see *gibbsite*), arranged in the lamellar structure which gives clay its quality of plasticity. In most natural clays this 'stacking' has been disorganized to some degree, allowing the intrusion of alkalis, iron, etc. and varying the plasticity and 'other ceramic properties' (Dodd/Murfin). For a molecular stacking diagram see Worrall, Hamer PDMT, and diagram at *clay*. *Mullite* is formed at temperatures over $1100°C/2012°F$.

The mineral is the result of the decomposition of alumina-silicate rocks, e.g. feldspar. Non-kaolinite clays include the *montmorillonites* and it is now widely believed that many secondary clays may contain only small percentages of kaolinite, if any. (See *clay*, *illite*, etc.)

Kaolinization

The action of hot gases, mainly CO_2 and H_2O, have in geological time acted on *feldspathic* minerals to leach out the alkalis and to form kaolinite. A very simplified notation for the process is: Feldspar + steam + carbon dioxide, rearranged as potassium carbonate + quartz + clay. In chemical terms:

$$K_2O.Al_2O_4.6SiO_2 + (2)H_2O + CO_2 = K_2CO_3 + (4)Si_2 + Al_2O_3.2SiO_2.2H_2O$$

There are doubts as to whether kaolinization, by weathering, is still proceeding.

Kaowool

A proprietary name (Morganite Ceramic Fibers) for a form of ceramic fiber.

Kelvin

Symbol K. A temperature scale allied to Celsius but beginning at 'absolute zero' (minus 273°C). (See also *absolute temperature*, *centigrade*, *conversion factors*, *gas expansion*, *sintering*.)

Keramiton

A proprietary name (Faber-Castell) for an air drying modeling clay which can also be fired.

Keuper marl

A 'marl of variegated color' — name derived from German 'Koper' a spotted fabric (Dodd). Also known as Mercia mudstone. A source is given in Sutherland: Keuper Marl (Brickworks) Hartlebury, Hereford, UK but it is widely distributed and Potclays sell a 'Keuper Red' clay. Mentioned in connection with *oil spot* and *slip glazes*.

Kickwheel

A foot-operated potter's wheel. There are two main types:
1 On the genuine 'kicked' wheel, the potter sits over a large stone flywheel which he rotates by direct friction with the sole of his foot. This is the traditional wheel of the Mediterranean and other countries, and is occasionally used by the modern craft potter. There is often no tray, so throwing must be fairly dry. Axner list a wheel of this type with concrete flywheel.
2 The crankshaft wheel, where the 'kick' is transmitted to the shaft via a bar or connector. The potter may stand on one leg and swing a frontally suspended bar with the other. This type is not recommended for serious potters; one's stance is unstable and the strain on the standing leg is considerable. It is however found in many schools and colleges. The seated type is better-designed, affording greater control with the minimum exertion. The direct drive to the shaft imposes a limited speed but recent refinements include a geared wheel giving a ratio of about 1:1.5 between kick-bar and wheelhead speeds.

The kickwheel is especially useful for turning. Many potters prefer its direct and instinctive control to the one-remove of the power wheel. A well-made seated kickwheel with a good flywheel can be worked for hours without unduly tiring the potter.

There are many wheels on the market. Sturdy construction, good bearings, quietness and comfort are points to check. Wheels are not difficult to build if one has minimal carpentry and/or metalwork skill. Use a hard wood for the frame — beech is excellent. The frame is triangular in plan, each side about 36in/1m long. Height depends on the stance you like to adopt when throwing but the average is 30in/750mm. Joints should be short mortise and tenon, not glued but pulled in tight with studding threaded ½in/12mm rods with a nut at either end. The bar is supported in some designs by a

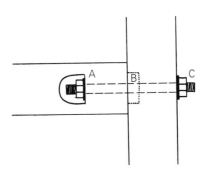

The jointing system used in the kickwheel illustrated. A short mortise and tenon is made between the horizontal and upright timbers which should fit adequately but not be glued. A hole is drilled straight through the upright, the mortise (B), and horizontal bar as shown, and a slot cut large enough to take a washer and a nut at (A). A length of $^1/_2$in/12mm studding (threaded metal rod) is inserted, screwed into a nut in the slot, and the whole joint drawn up tight with a second washer and nut at (C). As the wood contracts or compresses the nut can be tightened while, conversely, the whole structure can easily be dismantled. A touch of grease will prevent the nuts rusting on.

vertical chain and, as a result, swings in an arc. This is comfortable for the leg, but is a difficult movement to transmit to the crankshaft. A flexible leather connector may be used, but a better system mechanically is shown in the photographs, where the support is taken back diagonally to the same pivot line as the kick-bar itself, ensuring a true horizontal drive. David Ballantyne developed a geared wheel in which the arc and horizontal drive are ingeniously combined. The actual wheel shaft is normally made of 1in/25mm steel, but an increase to $1^1/_8$in/28mm will reduce 'whip' very considerably. Any wheel which has an uncomfortable action or involves too bent a back must be avoided.

Two views of one type of kickwheel (with tray removed). It was constructed, in oak, in 1947 and has been in continuous use ever since. The timbers are 3 x 2in (75 x 50mm). The connecting rod is from an old car, the flywheel from a lathe. A thrust bearing (the clutch bearing from a car) is set at the base of the crankshaft with a ballbearing at the top, protected from the water by a disk of ply and plastic. The kick-bar support is taken back to the axis of the bar, giving a smoother motion than does a chain-supported action.

Kidney tool

The kidney-shaped tool, embodying several curves, is a favorite one with potters. It may be of hard or soft rubber, or of thin, pliable sheet-steel. Sheet-steel kidney tools are called 'steel *palettes*'. They are also made in aluminum (from Cromartie) and rubber, the latter useful for smoothing surfaces and even for burnishing. Other uses for the tools are scraping, smoothing, turning and pressing. The hand-builder will find them invaluable.

Kieselguhr

A German name for *diatomite.*

Kiln

Called an 'oven' in the industry. Essentially a box of refractory bricks, into or around which heat is introduced either by combustion or by radiant heat. A kiln must be capable of reaching at least 600°C/1112°F. A cooking oven, therefore, cannot be used as a kiln. In smaller kilns the ware is packed straight into the box, in large ones it may be protected and supported by saggars.

The very primitive, but nevertheless often effective, brushwood bonfires cannot be said to have used a kiln at all. In some cases the pots were covered with a layer of shards as protection and to retain heat, and this represented the first step towards a kiln. Cultures which aimed at a finer type of pottery soon began to enclose their wares in brick or stone boxes which allowed a greater control and higher temperatures. In the simplest kilns, a fire is lit under the floor, the heat rises through the pots and out at the top. The whole kiln acts as a chimney. Though more economical and reliable than a bonfire, its heat utilization is low. The final step was to direct the heat against its inclination across the kiln setting and, eventually, downwards through it. A strong draft or pull is essential; this is provided by a tall chimney (a straight-up kiln needs no separate chimney) as in most Western kilns, or by a stepped series of firing chambers as in the East. All intermittent kilns are variations or improvements on these types. An *electric kiln* has no combustion or draught and is thus a simple fireproof box.

Rhodes gives an excellent account of the history, types, and designs of kilns: kilns come in countless sizes, shapes, and degrees of complexity and it is impossible to deal with them in a dictionary. Just one piece of advice if you are considering building your own is to start from a module of the size of available kiln shelves plus an inch or so to get your fingers round the edges when deciding on the plan of the chamber. David Miller (CB85) has designed an original *cross-draft* for salting with the front wall lifted by pulleys for packing and removing pots.

Bruce Chivers (see Suppliers) has designed a raku-type *ceramic fiber*-lined kiln, fired with propane gas, which, he states, will attain 1300–1450°C/2372–2642°F, 1000°C/1832°F in 20 minutes. But perhaps the most startling of all appeared in CR115 (Sebastian Blackie) — a paper kiln! The pots, surrounded by wood blocks, are piled onto a cone shape on a steel grid and the whole covered with layers of glossy paper brushed with slip. The structure is lifted by the grid and dried out over smouldering embers. Eventually the wood blocks turn to charcoal in the absence of air which burns in its turn to produce temperatures of anything between 950–1250°C/1742–2282°F before the paper finally collapses.

(See also *brazier kiln, chambered kiln, chimney, climbing*

A trolley kiln (see also illustration at truck kiln) for wood-fired salt-glaze at the workshop of Janet Mansfield (Australia). Note catenary form.

kilns, clamp kiln, continuous kiln, controllers, downdraft, electric kiln, gas kiln, grate, groundhog kiln, insulation of heat, intermittent kiln, kiln furniture, oil kiln, raku, sawdust firing, truck kiln, updraft, etc.)

Kiln furniture

Term applied to pieces of *refractory* material used to support pots during firing, including *shelves* and *props*. More particularly, the term refers to the small equipment designed to prevent glazed ware sticking to kiln shelves.

The commonest piece of kiln furniture is the *stilt* which has three radial arms ending in upright conical points. Spurs have one point up and three down; three or more can replace a stilt when supporting larger dishes or irregular shaped pieces. Triangular sectioned *saddles* will hold tiles or flat-based models. There are ingenious constructions called *cranks*, which hold similar sized plates or tiles apart from one another in a pile or *bung*. Tile bats may also be called cranks and can be built up on their own 'cranked' or turned-over edges, or with spacing cubes (bits).

It is important to bear in mind that all clays become *pyroplastic* during firing. When placing 'furniture', try to imagine that the piece of pottery (especially flat plates and dishes) is still plastic and can sag under its own weight. A plate will warp on a small out-of-center stilt or on spurs placed too far apart. (See *warping*.)

Kiln furniture, in the sense of stilts and similar articles, is intended for oxidized earthenware only, it will fail at temperatures over 1200°C/2192°F. Even shelf props, if cast, may collapse in stoneware *reduction* firings unless specifically made for this purpose (check with the supplier). Stoneware pots, therefore, are normally left with unglazed bases.

See also *bats, kiln shelves, prop,* and under the individual items mentioned.

Kiln gloss

A, usually accidental, partial shine on a pot caused by local vitrification or by the deposit of ash or other fluxing material onto the surface. *Soda firing* and *salt-glaze* may be considered as kiln gloss in its widest sense. Some red clays, e.g. *Albany clay*, will self-glaze at stoneware temperatures. (See also *flashing, fuming, smear glaze.*)

Kiln log

A record of firings is always useful, especially with a new kiln or during the first year of work in a new pottery. A kiln log will materially assist pricing and costing.

The record can be a very full one, or merely a list of pieces with length of firing and top temperature noted. It is advisable to keep the same sort of record each time so that the data is comparable. Priorities will vary with type of kiln and work fired. If your kiln has a chimney it will be sensitive to the weather. Leach always recorded not only weather but also oil pressure, temperature of kiln at various stages, atmosphere, and damper positions, for all of which he developed a private code. Cardew suggests recording the weight of clay used in the kiln setting which will also give density of packing, an important factor affecting firing. A broader indication of density such as 'loosely packed', 'large pots', 'very full', or the number of shelves used, is more practicable. In electric firing the

No	1sts	Value	
15	Plates	20	Cobalt too strong
12	Saucers	3	
16	Cups	6	
	Tall pot	5	
	"	3	Ash 1 glaze
	"	7	Ash 2 glaze
30	Egg cups	7	
7	Various Small pots	10	Blue slightly overfired on middle shelves
	2nds		
2	Plates	1	Underfired
2	Saucers	30	Spinners
1	Tall pot	2	50 Crawled (floor left)
		64 80	

A possible simple layout for a kiln log. In more sophisticated reduction firings more information (the weather, etc.) would be useful.

weather is not of direct consequence unless the kiln is in a very cold or draughty place. *Voltage drop* can occur in winter.

A firing-*graph* will replace many words and may be used as a basis of the kiln log. A possible layout is shown.

A reduction *graph* will show 'steps' in the line. A deliberate stepped firing known as 'fire-change' is used in Japan. Geoffrey Whiting used a '*stepped graph*' in an electric kiln to obtain special colors (see also *heat treatment*).

Kiln shelves

Kiln shelves (often referred to as 'bats' or 'cranks') are made of compacted high-alumina clays (see *fireclay*), with cordierite, mullite, sillimanite, silicon carbide, or zirconium silicate additions. It is difficult to make one's own shelves. The underlying science which controls the behavior of shelves under load is a complicated one. Some of the problems are discussed in Cardew. Silicon carbide shelves are more conductive of heat than clay, but are expensive.

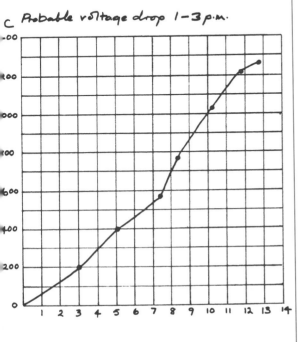

A firing graph.

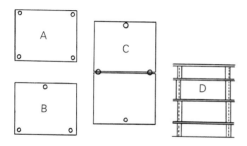

The propping system for kiln bats.

A *Shows a logical but unsatisfactory position for supports: it is difficult to get a firm seating on four columns and the stresses are along edges or across long diagonals.*

B *Using three props, gives an automatically firm seating and shortens the diagonal spans. Two closely adjacent shelves can be supported as in plan* **C**.

D *In the elevation the props are not immediately under one another, as is the ideal state, but the dotted lines show that the shelves are nowhere cantilevered, i.e. the weight is all taken by the columns and not by the shelves, so some degree of variation of position is acceptable. (See cantilever.)*

Circular shelves are available which would be useful in the normal commercial hexagonal top-loader (though they need either to be smaller in circumference than the kiln or to have two chips taken out to allow the fingers to hold the shelf when placing). Also hexagonal shelves and half shelves are listed by Georgies. One of the major manufacturers in England, Acme Marls, who supply a great variety of shelves, including perforated and 'extruded' shelves which 'give the same performance as solid batts of the same thickness (but) are only half the weight (and) less energy is needed to heat each batt'. They have provided the following data on shelf performance in the kiln:

1 Cracks may be due to fast heating or cooling—the ho[t] load cooling slowly while the shelf cools more rapidly. Als[o] to gross overloading, usually because of a badly place[d] prop.

2 An overloaded bat will normally bend and will ulti[-] mately tear.

3 The life of a shelf is dependent on how much it bend[s] in the firing; this is governed by the load, the unsupport[-] ed span, the temperature and the thickness.

4 The bending rate will also depend on the time that an[y] given temperature is maintained.

5 It is quite in order to turn shelves over to correc[t] bending.

6 A bat bends more rapidly at the beginning of its life tha[n] at the end.

7 Concentrated loads will have the effect of reducing th[e] life afterwards.

8 A good test for a cracked bat is to support it on a pad i[n] the center, cover it with fine, dry alumina, and tap i[t] sharply to make it resonate. The alumina parts where ther[e] is a crack.

The table gives a rough idea of the normal distribute[d] loads which bats will stand at different temperatures. There is no smooth graduation in the series for differen[t] thicknesses. A bat must carry its own weight as well as the load and this must be subtracted from the gross loading.

Kiln-sitter

A gadget for shutting off your kiln while you are out enjoying yourself! It does not measure temperature direct but uses a metal arm which rests on a *Pyro minibar* or similar, and which drops as the minibar bends and switches off the kiln. Fairly widely available from suppliers and kiln merchants. A back-up system based on time should the sitter

Specimen deformation data on kiln bats											
Temperature in °C	900–1050°C 1652–1922°F			1050–1200°C 1922–2192°F			1200–1250°C 2192–2282°F			1250–1280°C 2282–2336°F		
Thickness in mm	12.5	17.5	25	12.5	17.5	25	12.5	17.5	25	12.5	17.5	25
Size of bat												
47.5 x 41.5	14	40	77	6.5	22	45	0	7	19	0	0	6
44.5 x 42	16	42.5	81	7.7	23.5	47	0.6	6.5	21	0	0	8
40.0 x 28	14	35	60	7.4	21	36	2.2	9	17	0.25	3.5	7.5
35.5 x 21	12	32	59	6.5	19.5	37	2.5	9.5	20	0.5	4.5	10

These figures represent loads in lb which the shelf will take without deformation. The load to be spread reasonably evenly over the surface. Calculations made for alumina shelves and reproduced by kind permission of Mr H Gautby of Acme Marls, Hanley, Stoke-on-Trent.

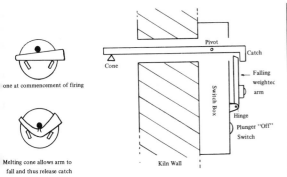

one at commencement of firing

Melting cone allows arm to
fall and thus release catch

Pivot
Catch
Cone
Falling
weighted
arm
Switch Box
Hinge
Plunger "Off"
Switch
Kiln Wall

The action of a mechanical electric kiln switch. Other systems may be more sophisticated but the principle remains similar.

fail to operate is listed by Georgies and others. Today more reliance is placed on the *controlling pyrometer*.

Kiln wash

A thin layer of *refractory* material spread over the *hot-face* of the kiln. *Air-setting* cements have been suggested for this, washed over with a brush or sprayed on (see *Sairset*). 'Pebesil' is another commercial surface cement which can be applied to soft insulating brick to make it more abrasion resistant. It has high heat retention. (See also *bat wash*, *ITC*.)

Kilowatt

Symbol kW. 1000 watts.

Kimmeridge clay

A Dorset brick clay, often contaminated with lime or bituminous substances.

Kneading clay

See *wedging*.

Knife

A really sensitive knife which will also be strong enough for use on clay is very difficult to find. The ideal is a blade $\frac{1}{2}$in/12mm wide and tapering, about 1in/25mm long with a fairly fine back edge, and with a comfortable handle. 'Stanley' knives are too short and clumsy; scalpels with renewable blades are too delicate and too sharp for safety: penknives do not always have a good grip. Photographic touching-up knives are useful. A local cutler will generally grind a knife to your specification. Some merchants now offer more attractive knives than the usual *fettler*, while Kemper list a useful-looking, pointed heavy duty knife.

Reward Supplies sell a good range of potters' knives. Cromartie's and Kemper's are long and slim (and look a little dangerous), made with a soft or hard blade. Kemper Tools 'commercial trim knife' looks more manageable and has a 'file hard' blade — capable of extended usage on highly abrasive clay products. Tucker's do a small, short-bladed knife.

Knob

The knob of a *lid* is no trivial object. A quick survey of ceramics will reveal not only rich variety but also show that the lid and its knob or handle can be the crowning glory of a pot. Modeled knobs of considerable size and intricacy, such as the splendid teams of stylized horses, are found on

A bold coiled knob by Jane Hampton.

Six varieties of thrown knob.

187

Three ways of forming a knob.
1 Turning the shape from the stem of a thrown lid (see lids).
2 Throwing a knob on a flat casserole-type lid.
3 Throwing a hollow knob on a recessed lid.

early Greek pots. Those from the Far East may be more subdued, but are carefully considered in relation to the overall form of the pot and sometimes have a touch of fantasy. Michael Casson's early knobs and Ian Godfrey's often crowded and dominant lids are modern examples.

The principle underlying good design is to provide stem of length adequate to accommodate finger and thumb, spreading out to a wider top. No matter how elegant or aesthetically suited to the main form, a knob which cannot easily be gripped and held must be accounted as failure. But within these limitations there is a multitude of possible forms. The knob should not be too high on oven ware. See recessed type at *handle*.

The illustrations show various ways of forming a knob. It can be modeled and luted on; turned from the thick base of a thrown lid; thrown onto the leather-hard turned lid inset into a cut lid; or made in the form of a pulled handle or a simple thumbed-down coil.

Kryolite

See *Cryolite*.

kW

The symbol for a kilowatt or 1000 watts. A kilowatt hour (kWh) is the electricity consumed by a one kW piece of apparatus in one hour. (See also *electricity, units of electricity*.)

Kyanite

A mineral $Al_2O_3.2SiO_2$, similar to *sillimanite* but with different physical properties. Considerable volume increase at 1300°C/2372°F, when it breaks down into *mullite* and *cristobalite* (Dodd). Has been mentioned as a *bat wash*. Obtainable from Kyanite Mining Corporation, Dillwyn, Virginia, USA and other suppliers. Tucker's list two grades 100 and 35 mesh, PSH calls it kyanite grog and includes 48 mesh. Tom Buck (CR143) includes 30% kyanite in his suggested raku body.

Labradorite

A soda-lime feldspar. See *plagioclase*.

Lace decoration

Open-weave cloth or lace can be soaked in slip and laid on a clay surface or used in modeling. The fibers burn away in the kiln to leave a clay skeleton of the fabric. Early porcelain figures often used the technique, sometimes even as 'free' items of modeling, i.e. not laid on a surface.

Lacustrine clay

Clays which have been deposited, in geological time, on the bed of a lake. Similar to *estuarine* clays.

Lamellar

In the form of sheets or scales. Clay is considered to be lamellar in structure and this is the general explanation of its plastic qualities. (See *clay*, *plasticity*.)

Laminated clay

Sheets of different colors or types of clay pressed together and then used in various ways to construct pots or other ceramic forms. Ewen Henderson builds up his rugged pots from a variety of clays, mixing stoneware and porcelain.

A powerfully designed laminated-clay dish by Michael Bayley.

A laminated-clay pot by Mal Magson.

(See *agate*, *marbling*, *neriage*.)

Lanthanoids

See *rare earths*.

Laterite

A hydrated aluminous material, see also *bauxite*.

Latex resist

A preparation used in the manner of *wax resist*. Its main advantages over wax is that it can be used cold, but more especially, that it can be peeled off, leaving a clear, sharp image similar to that gained from *paper resist* but with the possibility of a much freer and more spontaneous use of line and mass. The resisted areas can be repainted or treated in any other way. It is suitable for work with pigment, slip and glaze, especially *glaze-over-glaze* techniques. The treatment

A film of rubber laid on as a resist can be lifted off and further detail then added to the resisted areas.

A detail of a dish by John Maltby showing the resisted area from which the latex has been peeled away, glaze trailing being subsequently applied in some of the spaces.

is necessarily fairly broad. John Maltby uses latex to produce remarkable designs which could not be achieved by any other technique. Another attractive feature is that brushes can be cleaned in water (before the latex sets). Its transparency is a disadvantage but it may be stained with a vegetable dye such as 'Coldron'. See also illustration by Chris Speyer at *resist method*.

If left on a piece the fumes during firing are rather noxious and the kiln room should be well ventilated.

Lattice

A regular three-dimensional pattern or network of linked atoms building up into a crystalline substance. Quartz, for instance, has a lattice unit of one silicon atom and four

oxygen atoms in a pyramid or tetrahedron. Further S atoms share half the electron charge with each of the O atoms, the pattern being repeated in every direction. This is known as the SiO_4 lattice. This crystalline lattice has tight structure but it can be altered and weakened by the intrusion of other atoms (see *network modifiers*, and diagram of SiO_4 under *glass former*.)

Lava, glazes

Volcanic rocks of variable composition equivalent to around 50% feldspar and 50% ferro-magnesium mineral (Frazer, CR17). The iron content is high and the rock yields dark-colored tenmoku-type glazes. See *basalt*. For 'lava glazes' see *volcanic glazes*.

Lawn, lawn mesh

A fine-meshed *sieve* originally of woven silk or fine linen (hence the name) but now usually of phosphor-bronze wire. The mesh (the tiny holes where the wires cross each other) is graded according to the wires per linear in/25.5mm: 80 wires per inch for a number 80 lawn, etc. Some quoted apertures for comparison are:

No.		
	30 (USA 35)	0.50 mm
	60	0.25 mm
	80	0.18 mm
	120	0.125 mm
	200	0.075 mm

It will be seen that the aperture halves as the number doubles. Lawns are seldom made larger than 40 mesh, the coarser wire or nylon sieves taking over for wide apertures. Hamer quotes a 2:1 relationship, e.g. a 100 mesh with a hole $\frac{1}{200}$in wide. Luckily the numbers for lawns are reasonably comparable in Britain and the USA. In Europe, however, the system is quite different. The potter soon comes to know which sieve number best suits his purpose.

Lawns are mounted on ash-wood, plastic or metal rims. (See also *sieve*). A phosphor-bronze lawn carefully used will last a lifetime. Useful rim sizes are 6in/150mm for glaze trials, 10in/250mm for slips, 8–12in/200–300mm for glaze batches. Color sieves or 'cup' sieves about 3 in/75mm across are made for pigments. Lawn mesh sizes in general use are: 60–80 for slips and many stoneware glazes; 100–120 for earthenware glazes; 200 for pigments and stains.

If you have unmounted lawns or a piece of lawn from a broken frame, a fairly easy do-it-yourself sieve can be made by cutting the base from a circular plastic box or bucket or cutting a section from a plastic drainpipe, laying a piece of lawn on the top and fastening it by carefully melting the plastic rim beneath it with a soldering iron or, as Lynn Carter suggests for smaller sieves, heating the lawn on a

...otplate and pressing the plastic onto it. Other useful ideas may be found in Fournier PT (and see also *sieve*).

Lawn prover

A small glass magnifier, set above a one inch square aperture through which one can count the wires in a lawn to determine its gauge or number. Could be of use to check the mesh of unmounted lawns.

Layering clay

See *agate, marbling, neriage, wedging*.

Lead, oxides, compounds

A metallic element Pb, 207.
Litharge PbO, 223. Toxic.
Peroxide, red lead Pb_2O_3, 686 (useful equivalent weight 228.5). Toxic.
White lead (basic) $2PbOCO_3:Pb(OH)_2$, 775 (equivalent wt. 258). Toxic.
Galena (sulfide) PbS, 239.
Lead chromate $PbCrO_4$. 323

A *base*, and a powerful *flux* in the 750–1150°C/ 1382–2102°F range. It is the principal base in most soft glazes which do not contain boric oxide. The rich quality of many early glazes owes much to the use of lead. Its *coefficient of expansion* is in the middle range and lead glazes are reputed to adapt to tension better than others. Litharge was the traditional oxide for slipware glazes. Galena has been widely used in the past but needs a very well-ventilated kiln. Lead is now used as a frit (see *lead frits, lead glazes*).

Lead oxide is toxic both as a raw material and in an unbalanced or ill-fired glaze from which it may be dissolved by food acids. The addition of copper oxide will greatly increase this danger (see *soluble lead*). Its use as raw lead oxides was forbidden in factories in 1949 and *any* lead compound is now banned or severely restricted under any conditions. In 1974 individual potters were included in the legislation for the first time. Use a lead frit, preferably *lead bisilicate* and maintain the greatest care when handling it. A 'lead test kit' which colors in the presence of lead is listed by Baileys.

Lead antimonate

A compound of lead and antimony, quoted as $Pb_2(SbO)_4$. Composition variable. Toxic. Used as a yellow pigment—'Naples' yellow. Dilute with a lead frit for painting. Up to 8% can be added to a soft lead glaze. Not suitable for use in stoneware. (See also *antimony, yellow*.)

Lead bisilicate

See *lead frits*.

Lead borosilicate

A low-solubility frit containing oxides of lead, boron and silicon, with other trace compounds as stabilizers. Available from W G Ball Ltd.

Lead chromate

$PbCrO_4$. 323 Toxic.
Has been suggested (Emmanuel Cooper CR160) for producing flecks in slips under many glazes. Handle with care.

Lead frit

The sole use of lead in the form of *silicates* is now compulsory in schools and factories in most countries (if lead is not banned altogether as it is in some countries).

The commonest frits in use are:
1 Lead monosilicate $PbO.SiO_2$, 283, m.p. 670–750°C/ 1238–1382°F
2 Lead sesquisilicate $2PbO.3SiO_2$, 627. ($PLO. 1.5SiO_2$, 313) m.p. 690–850°C/1274–1562°F
3 Lead bisilicate $PbO.2SiO_2$, 343, m.p. 710–800°C/ 1310–1472°F

The actual frit batch can include small amounts of alumina (up to 3%), or titania. Some suppliers quote a 'coated' frit, reputed to be less liable to *metal release*.

Sesquisilicate is perhaps the most useful for potters but the bisilicate is safer in use while monosilicate does not comply with British regulations governing lead in glazes. The melting points given above are derived from quotes by various suppliers. Apart from simple silicates, many lead frits are available for temperatures up to 1150°C/2102°F. The simplest basis for bisilicate/clay proportions is 3:1. Use iron oxide or red clay for a *honey glaze*. A simple recipe by Sophie MacCarthy (CR156) reads: lead bisilicate 80, china clay 10, flint 10, firing at 1100°C/2012°F with a 1 hour soak. (See *low solubility glaze*.)

Lead glaze

Lead can be used as the only flux in an earthenware glaze. The formula limits are:
1 PbO. $0.23–0.35Al_2O_3$. $2.0–3.5SiO_2$ with an average 1:0.3:3.0 firing at 1100°C/2012°F with a recipe:

Lead sesquisilicate	70.5
China clay	17.4
Flint	12.1

See also '*honey glaze*' for the use of red clay in the recipe. This is useful for *slipware*, especially slip-trailing.

Lead can be combined with other bases but must represent at least 0.5 of the RO group, e.g.

$$0.6 \; PbO$$
$$0.2 \; K_2O$$
$$0.2 \; CaO$$

If the lead equivalent is less than 0.5, boric acid must appear in the RO_2 column, unless it is a high soda glaze. A glaze recipe, embodying frit, by Anthony Phillips (CR123) is given as:

Lead bisilicate	57
Boric frit	25.6
China clay	10.3
Flint	7.1
Bentonite	2.0
Firing at 1105°C/2021°F	

If there is any significant lead content in a glaze it is generally labeled as 'low sol'. The mixed base glazes are more purely transparent and viscous than simple ones, and are therefore chosen for underglaze painting and for tin glazes (see *maiolica*).

Once-fired earthenware often utilizes lead oxide as the main or only base. Higher proportions of the oxide are used — although not the 100% litharge mentioned by Billington! A typical recipe: 75% lead bisilicate, 10% china stone, 15% plastic clay.

Most pigment oxides readily dissolve in lead glazes giving yellow-brown from iron, apple-green from copper (but beware, see *soluble lead*); blue from cobalt; purple-brown from manganese. Lead and soda glazes produce brighter colors and have been suggested for soft-glaze black. Lead oxide is toxic and if the formula is not balanced can constitute a health hazard even when fired in a glaze. (See discussion under *soluble lead*.)

Average recipes using lead silicates:

Recipe A		Recipe B	
Lead bisilicate	72.8	Lead sesquisilicate	52.8
China clay	12.1	Feldspar	31.1
China stone	13.5	Whiting	5.6
Flint	1.6	China clay	7.2
		Flint	3.3

Firing at 1060–1110°C/1940–2030°F

Some potters add 2–5% of zinc oxide, or a borax frit. Strontium is used in some countries as a substitute for lead oxide in glazes.

The laws on lead glazes have been tightened recently and it is now used much less as a flux. Any new lead glaze, if it is to be used on tableware or pottery which may come into contact with edibles, or is used by an employed person, must be laboratory tested for *metal release*. Some pottery merchants (e.g. Potclays) offer this service. In the UK

(1997) the compliance was for flatware 20ppm (ppm parts per million), hollow ware 7ppm, storage vessel 2ppm (Hamer 1975–97). In the USA the revised compliance guide is more stringent and has been quoted (Georgies) as 3ppm for flatware, 2ppm for small hollow ware, 1ppm for hollow ware larger than 1.1 liters, 0.5 ppm for pitchers (jugs), cups and mugs.

(See at *metal release* for a lead test swab.)

Lead solubility, *lead poisoning*

See *metal release, soluble lead*.

Leadless glaze

A glaze with not more than 1% of its dry weight of PbO (British regulations). Most leadless glazes (rather confusingly marked 'L' in suppliers' lists) have no lead content at all. It is replaced, in effect, by boric oxide, although this is listed with the RO_2 in the *Seger formula*. The bases can include soda, potash, strontium, lime, magnesia, and zinc oxide.

There is no form of insoluble boric oxide which can be used in a soft leadless glaze. Calcined borax is the nearest approach, but it will crystallize in a comparatively short time (as will very soft leadless frits). Colemanite can help, but introduces lime. A leadless frit which melts at 1000°C/1832°F or lower can be mixed with raw materials such as clay to aid suspension and strengthen the dry coating. Many suppliers quote the formulas for their frits; these can be entered in the glaze formula computation (see *formula-into-recipe*).

High soda frits, e.g. Na_2O; 3.5 SiO_2; 2.0 B_2O_3 will produce a turquoise from copper, but the lack of alumina renders it unstable. A more regular L frit might read:

0.27 Na_2O		
0 59 CaO	0.42 Al_2O_3	4.7 SiO_2
0.01 MgO		0.96 B_2O_3
firing at 1040°C/1904°F		

It will be seen that the silica and alumina ratio is much higher than one would expect from the normal Seger ratios. This is caused by the anomalous position of boron which, in practice, acts as a flux and could quite logically be listed with the bases. In the above formula this would bring the silica equivalent down to 2.5. Leadless earthenware glazes have been compounded from strontium and zinc additions. (See *Bristol glaze*.)

Leadless fritted glazes need to be applied more thinly than lead or raw glazes. Colors from manganese, copper and cobalt are apt to be unsubtle and strident. They should not be fired with high lead glazes which can coat them with a thin skin of lead oxide and make them dangerous in use.

The term has little meaning in connection with

stoneware and porcelain glazes, which are outside the lead range.

Leaf resist

The use of leaves, petals, etc. as *resist* materials has a long history but an interesting variation was used by George Martin. A leaf was first adhered to the clay, the whole background waxed, and the leaf removed. The whole was then covered with a black slip, veins and holes later marked out by sgraffito. This technique can be used with wax or latex, the latter allowing further variations and embellishments.

The resist leaf as decribed in the text.

Lean clay

A clay or body of low *plasticity. Aging* will help some lean clays.

Leather-hard

A stage in the drying of clay when it has become almost rigid but is still damp. One might elaborate by using the terms 'soft-leather' and 'hard-leather' to indicate stages either side of leather-hard, and these are occasionally used in discussions in this book. Work done at leather-hard includes *turning, engraving, sgraffito, planing,* and techniques involving the use of metal tools.

At this stage most of the drying shrinkage will already have occurred — the particles are just touching one another. The size difference between leather-hard clay and soft biscuit is small. There is just enough plasticity in leather-hard clay to allow gentle beating to change its form. Clay can still be joined, but it is advisable to score and slip, or to work up a slip with a little moisture by rubbing the two

parts together. For absorbent clays (which include most of those made up by merchants) raw clay glazing (*once-fired* ware) is best done at leather-hard dryness.

Leca granules

Expanded red clay granules. Used by Ian Byers (CR155), mixed with clay to build a 'mud kiln' (looking like a beehive). The mixture has good insulating properties. Obtainable from Alpha Aggregates Ltd.

Lepidolite

A feldspathoid mineral with the ideal formula $(LiNaK)_2,(F.OH)_2, Al_2O_3, 3SiO_2$, 472, m.p. 1170°C/2138°F. A typical analysis by weight:

K$_2$O 8.3, CaO 0.4, MgO 0.08, Li$_2$O 3.6, Al$_2$O$_3$ 25.5,
FeO 0.16, MnO 0.06,
F 5.33, SiO$_2$ 54.0.

A *lithium* mica, with a lower melting point than feldspar, beginning its fluxing action at around 1150°C/ 2102°F. Difficult to grind. A source of lithium for bodies and glazes, but its use is complicated by the release of *fluorine* as a gas during firing which can cause bloating in a body and bubbles in a glaze (see also *crater glazes*). Has been suggested for inclusion in *turquoise glazes*, up to 45%, firing to 1280°C/2336°F. Obtainable from Coastal Ceramics (NZ).

Lettering

Lettering has been *stamped, impressed, printed, transferred, painted, resisted, trailed* and *sgraffitoed* onto pots and dishes. The last four techniques need some calligraphic training and skill. (See illustration at *trailing.*)

Gordon Whittle offers the following advice on lettering in sgraffito. 'The pot, preferably made from a fine-textured

Sgraffito lettering through a blue slip under a white glaze by Gordon Whittle.

body, is coated when leather-hard with high clay engobe plus oxide/body stain. When this is on the dry side of leather-hard the lettering is cut through using a bamboo "pen" (cut as a reed without the ink-slit). Size and spacing of the inscription can be roughed out using food coloring or a soft wax crayon.

The combination of slip and glaze needs to be carefully controlled to minimize any flow or bleeding of the color'.

Leucite

A mineral $K_2O.Al_2O_3.4SiO_2$.

A potash feldspar which melts incongruently into a liquid plus leucite, which is an explanation of its high viscosity. Leucite can be formed when alkalis attack fireclay. Known as a *feldspathoid*. It is found in *lavas* (Australia, USA, etc).

Levigation

Defined in the Oxford Dictionary as to 'reduce to a fine powder', but in pottery it is taken to mean the separation of particles in a flowing stream (of slip), the finer ones remaining in suspension, the coarser sinking to the floor of the vessel or channel. China clay is levigated to remove the relatively coarse *micas*, the dumping of which produces the 'white mountains' of St Austell. Cardew illustrates a levigating trough 12ft/3.5m long, with 1 inch in 14 slope and a 2in/50mm high check-gate at one end. Slip is fed in at the higher end, heavy particles sinking below the 'gate' level while the fine ones flow over it. Hamer PDMT illustrates a stepped type of trough. The natural levigating action of rivers has led to the accumulation of fine clay particles in their estuaries (*estuarine clay*).

A long, shallow trough with a sloping floor. The liquid mixture flows in at A and out at B. During the slow passage through the trough coarser particles will sink and the finer ones remain in suspension to flow out at B.

Lias clay

A calcium-contaminated brick clay.

Lid, lid seating

The covered pot is a comparatively sophisticated object,

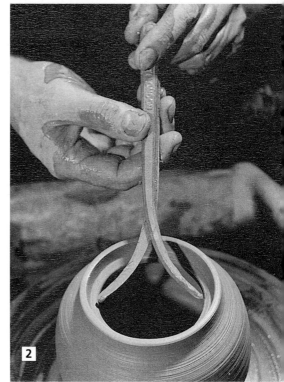

Two types of thrown lid.
1 The clay is brought up into a cone from the top of which an inverted lid is thrown.
2 The required diameter of the outside of the flange is measured with a caliper (an ingenious double caliper which will simultaneously give the inside and outside measurements is available).
3 and 4 Forming an inset lid. The required diameter is similarly measured with calipers, a short upright wall thrown with a mound of clay left in the center of the lid. The top half of the wall is then eased over and outwards and the knob thrown from the central mound. (See at knob for an intermediate action).

3

4

5

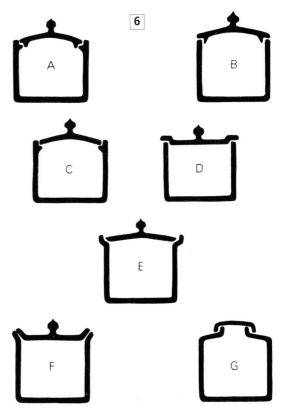

6

Seven types of lid seating.
A with a flange on both lid and vessel, typical of teapots and jars.
B has a flange on the lid only, useful where a large aperture is needed at the mouth of the container, but it must be a good fit. The edge of the lid overhangs the sides of the pot so that it can be lifted without a knob, (lid should be width of a handspan).
C A flange on the pot only. Typical of casseroles.
D An inset lid (see photograph of throwing method).
E The flange formed from an outward slope of the rim.
F A tapered lid and flange, self-adjusting to a degree but necessitating true circles for a snug fit.
G A lid for a small-mouthed jar or bottle.

5 *The use of an irregular junction between lid and base by Eileen Lewenstein.*

and we do not find ceramic lids in general use until after the craft had graduated from coiling to throwing. Those who have tried to make a well-fitting lid on a coiled pot will appreciate the difficulties.

The design of a lid depends as much on the method used to stop it falling off as on its formal relationship with the pot. The diagrams (see fig 6) show several ways of securing a lid. Apart from F, each involves a horizontal surface for the lid to sit on, and an upright wall or flange to prevent sideways movement. The tapered lid will automatically accommodate a tighter or looser fit but its success depends on the maintenance of two perfect circles — not always achieved in pottery!

The simplest way of throwing a lid is flat on the wheel-head as in photos 3 and 4. A domed lid is thrown upside-down either as a simple curve or with a flange. The knob may be turned from the stem of clay left at the base. (See also *box, calipers, knob.*)

Lift-off kiln

See *top-hat kiln.*

Lifting-off

For advice on lifting a pot or bowl from the wheelhead after throwing see *cutting off, pot lift*.

Lime

Lime, strictly speaking, is a burnt limestone CaO, an unstable *anhydrous* material (quicklime) which may be slaked with water to produce Ca(OH)$_2$. In ceramics the word is used, imprecisely, to indicate whiting, CaCO$_3$, or a calcium material which will be converted into CaO in the glaze or body melt. Used to produce lime matt glazes, which need careful firing, avoiding over-firing, and giving time for the crystals to form during cooling. These glazes are not usually suitable for tableware, but will give good colors with pigment oxides. (See also *calcium*.)

Lime-blowing

Pellets of lime (as CaO) in clay will be turned into quicklime in the firing. Moisture will subsequently slake the lime which expands and breaks pieces of pot away. If lime is suspected in a pot, dip it into water and put aside for checking in a day or two. Philip Stanbridge, in British Ceramic Review, Summer 91, discusses and enlarges on some interesting research by Harry Fraser and Derek Basnett. They have concluded that it is possible for dispersed lime in a clay or glaze to coagulate into nodules under the influence of damp and warmth, even though the original slip may have been passed through a fine lawn. Blunged bodies are said to be less prone but are not immune. If, therefore, you find spit-outs in fired bodies due to lime fragments soon after receiving the clay then it is probably a supplier problem, but clay which has been kept moist and warm for a longer period may possibly develop its own nodules spontaneously.

Stanbridge suggests that acid rain may be leaching more lime into our water supply, aggravating the problem. The only treatment at present available is to add barium carbonate (toxic, but not a great danger in the small quantities of 2–3% required, see at *efflorescence*), or a biocide chemical which might have its own hazards and prevents the natural and useful 'souring' of clay. Bricks soaked in water immediately after firing (known as 'docking' — Dodd) has been suggested as a cure for lime blowing and this might be tried with pots made from suspect clay though Dodd/Murfin also says that this is 'a cure that is more of an expedient'. Clay suppliers continue to work on the problem.

Limestone

The sedimentary rock of calcium carbonate or calcite. Formed from lime in solution or from organic deposits (fossil shells), and sometimes as pure as 98% calcite. There are mixtures of calcite and clay (marls), and sandy (quartz) limestones. Chalk is an earthy variety. Marble is an 'altered' limestone.

Limit formula

A term used by Rhodes CGP to indicate the minimum and maximum amounts of any oxide which can be used in a particular formula. The silica limits are given as 1–5 (compared with the RO of 1, see *Seger formula*); alumina 0.05–0.5; KNaO maximum 0.4; CaO–up to 0.7 (at 1250–1300°C/2282–2372°F); B$_2$O$_3$–0.15–0.6. The limits, of course, varying with the temperature at which the glaze is to be fired. (See also *glaze, saturated glaze*, and under the individual minerals and oxides.)

Limoges porcelain

A hardpaste porcelain from France now available from Potterycrafts. 'Fires to a radiant, clear, soft white in reduction (but) a difficult clay to work with' Prue Venables in CR171, though Edmund de Waal says (CR158) that it is 'highly plastic and easy to throw softly'. Needs slow drying. Can be slightly translucent as low as 1220°C/2228°F when thin but can be fired higher.

Limonite

An hydrated iron oxide; a 'bog ore'. Crumbly and often fairly pure. The mineral of *ochres*. See also *yellow ochre*. Recommended for mixing with cobalt; 'very nice for brush decoration' (Harry Davis).

Line blend

A method of working out intervals in a series of mixtures of two different colors, glazes, etc.
The simplest blend is:

| A— | 100 | 75 | 50 | 25 | 0 | —A |
| B— | 0 | 25 | 50 | 75 | 100 | —B |

each vertical pair being tested.

The principle can be extended to any number of intervals. For a slightly different approach discussed in practical detail see *color trials*, also *glaze trials* for working blends back to a recipe.

Line tap

A form of connector for thick electric wires, especially useful to potters for joining kiln elements to their connecting

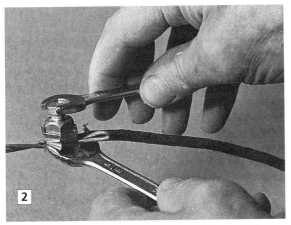

1 *A line tap, showing the parts separate and assembled. These are, of course, not insulated and are used only in fully guarded situations. (See Fournier EKP).*
2 *The great advantage of the line tap is that two spanners can be used as shown here. This not only ensures a tight connection but it also makes it easy to undo, even if corroded, without breaking a brittle element tail.*

wires, and for joining the neutrals in a three-phase star system. The Sherardized finish inhibits corrosion. If difficult to buy, ask your electricity company.

Lino cut

In CR162 Juliette Goddard describes her methods of transferring lino-cut images to biscuit and fired glaze using flat slabs which are cut and assembled into pots and dishes. The 'ink' was made to a similar consistency to oil-based printing ink and used in the same manner. Alternatively a lino-cut can be printed onto paper which is applied to biscuit. The lino cut can also be pressed onto the plastic clay and the resultant raised image used in various ways.

Lip

There is some overlapping and confusion over the use of this term to describe a part of a pot. It is sometimes applied to the upper termination of a pot or bowl, also variously called the 'edge' or the 'rim'. For the purposes of this entry 'lip' is taken to mean the pouring lip of a jug, mixing bowl, etc.

The lip can be formed immediately after throwing by a steady out-and-over pull or a side-to-side stroking motion with one finger, while the finger and thumb of the other hand support the rim at each side. Alternatively a somewhat crisper type of lip can be beaten out with the side of a rigid finger, after the pot has been turned or at soft-leather stage. Moisten the clay and give full support with a crooked finger under the lip as it is formed. Finish with smooth sweeps round the curve. A lip which curves slightly downwards at the very edge is more likely to pour well than one which finishes with an upward slope. The last drop of liquid will fall from the end of the lip rather than round it (to dribble down the side of the jug). Similarly a sharper edge will cut the flow more efficiently than a rounded one, though there are obvious limits.

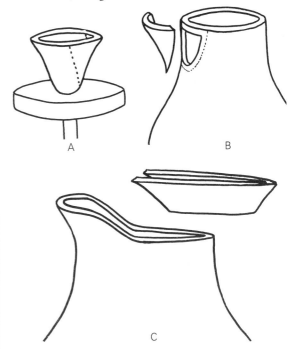

Two types of lip
A *A small flaring cup shape is thrown and a segment cut from it with a wire. An equivalent area of the neck of the jug is either cut right away, left with a bridge across the top, or pierced with holes.*
B *The segment of the thrown shape is then luted onto the jug.*
C *A section cut away from a jug rim to form a raised lip.*

A standard, fully rounded lip on a mixing bowl by Robert Fournier, its form emphasized by the glaze.

1 Tapping or beating a lip from soft-leather clay. The under-side of the lip must be supported so that the clay is pressed between the two surfaces and not stretched or it will split. A wipe of water on the rim before starting will help. Finish with a side to side movement.

2 The supporting and forming positions of the fingers when pulling a lip from a newly thrown pitcher. Other potters may vary these positions but the principle of two supports and side to side stroking followed by an outwards and downwards fin-ish to form the edge of the lip is common to most methods.

Two other forms are:

1 The ewer type in which a flared rim is cut down for the greater part of its circumference, the section of the original rim acting as a raised lip.

2 Lips made separately, either thrown as a small inverted cone which is cut in two, or molded, and luted onto the rim. The rim behind the lip can be cut away entirely: a bridge can be left across the top; or it can be perforated.

Whichever method is used, make the lip generous and well-defined. It will then be aesthetically attractive as well as efficient in directing the flow of liquid. A somewhat involved type of 'non-drip' lip is described in Fournier PT.

A fine large pitcher by Doyle Long (USA) the upstanding spout/lip luted onto the form.

Liparite

A *rhyolite* type rock, mainly of feldspars and quartz (from the Lipari Islands, Sicily).

Liquid petroleum gas

LPG. (See *bottled gas*.)

Liquidus

The line on a temperature equilibrium or phase diagram above which the components become a liquid or, conversely, below which a liquid begins to precipitate solids.

Litharge

Lead monoxide PbO. 223.

A yellow or orange powder which like all lead compounds is **toxic** if taken into the body. Forbidden for use in most countries. The use of lead frits (silicates) is now essential for all potters. (See *lead, metal release.*)

Lithify

To turn to a stone-like state, generally by natural pressure and heat, e.g. *shale* is lithified clay.

Lithium

An alkaline metallic element. Li, 7. Oxide Li_2O, 30. Lithia, soluble. Carbonate Li_2CO_3, 74. An insoluble ('slightly soluble' Hamer) form.

See also *amblygonite, lepidolite, petalite* (sometimes referred to as lithium feldspar), and *spodumene.*

Acts in a glaze like soda or potash, i.e. with a strong fluxing action, and has the added advantage of a low *thermal expansion*. Will brighten colors.

Lithium compounds have been expensive and are still around six times the price of feldspar. Lithia, however, is light in weight (the lightest of the metals) and the addition of only 0.5–2.0% markedly affects glaze fusion. Its use is frequently suggested by Behrens in all types of glaze and in amounts up to 20% of the batch. Even *raku* recipes may contain up to 20% lithia (with a very soft frit, clay and flint), 3% lithia in a stoneware glaze can bring its melting point down 2 or 3 cones. Around 2% of other fluxes, e.g. calcium borate, can be replaced with lithium.

Lithium has been tried in porcelain bodies. The common lithium minerals have certain disadvantages, e.g. the fluorine content of *lepidolite*.

Martin Rees in 'Before the Beginning' says of lithium in the universe — 'a rare element which, like helium, is believed to be primordial — a fossil of the big bang'!

Lithography

In ceramics, a method of making transfers printed in lithographic oil, the color being dusted onto the oil. They are applied to ware coated with a tacky varnish. Now generally replaced by slide-off transfers, called *decals* in the USA. (See also *photoceramic processes.*)

Paul Astbury 'incorporates litho images with pre-fired reduction glazes. The lithos are underfired to give the correct quality at 750°C/1382°F. This gives a broken, dry texture.' The 'correct quality', of course, refers to his particular and personal use of the medium. Lithography in general is of limited and specialized use to the potter. Ceramic transfers can be made by printing in lithographic oil, dusting with pottery color, and applying to ware coated with a tacky varnish. The paper is soaked away with water. See Scott (booklist) for details.

Lithophane

A term given to 19th-century porcelain pieces, mainly tiles, in which the light transmitted through a translucent body is controlled by the thickness of the material. By varying the depth of carving into the wall of a pot, bowl, or tile, designs can be made to appear in shades of gray when the article is held up to the light.

Today, potters use variations of the same technique. Victor Margrie and others cut the walls of their pots to thinner sections or even pierce them. Alan Whittaker casts and *sandblasts* patterns to a wafer thinness over whole areas of tall bowls. Some of the most remarkable pieces with the same general effect are those of Rudolf Staffel, where clay is lapped and folded to build up his aptly named 'Light Gatherers'. The technique can also be very effective for light shades. (See also *translucency.*)

Loam

A clayey earth with sand and gravel.

Local clay

It is fun, and always instructive, to dig clay from the ground but you are not very likely to find good, workable deposits in regions where they are not already known. The study of local industries of the past may reveal clay workings, also the names of fields, etc. Few geological books deal specifically with clays. In America the State Geological Departments may be able to help; in England the British Geological Survey. If you have access to any local rock-formation studies take note of Cardew's dictum that 'it is broadly true that the younger geological systems and strata are more likely to yield workable clays than the older ones'. Brick clays will seldom take a glaze satisfactorily. Details on the testing of clays may be found under *clay testing*, (see also *clay, body, clay-winning*). 'Glazes from Natural Sources' by Brian Sutherland also discusses finding and digging your own clay.

LOI

See *loss on ignition*.

London clay

A brick clay (Oligocene period, *c.* 25 million years ago) from the Home Counties (those counties around London). *Vitreous* at about 1000°C/1832°F. 'Possibly 90% *illite*' (Cardew).

Loss on ignition

The loss in weight when strongly heated (of a clay or mineral) through the dispersal of carbonates, etc. For clays the figure quoted in catalogs is the percentage of its dry weight lost at 1000–1100°C/1832–2012°F. With frits the temperature quoted will be below the fusion point.

To ascertain the LOI of a mineral or rock, weigh it very carefully; fire it and weigh it again. The percentage figure will be: dry weight minus fired weight; divided by dry weight; multiplied by 100. The loss can be very considerable, up to 50% for dolomite which means that a fired glaze will have only half the amount listed in the recipe. Ash, on the other hand loses hardly anything at all since it has already been 'fired', and frits, of course, nothing. The loss from feldspars is negligible; from *colemanite* and *talc* around 20% and 40% respectively.

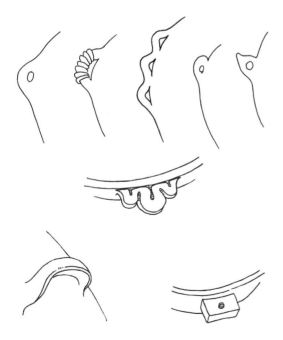

Eight variations on the lug handle.

LPG *Liquid petroleum gas*

See *bottled, tank gas*.

Low solubility glaze

Frits which comply with the Pottery Health Regulations not to 'release more than 5% of its dry weight of soluble lead when subjected to specific tests in hydrochloric acid'. Often marked LS in catalogs.

Lug

A small handle or pierced piece of clay on the side of a pot. Originally for suspending a pot on a rope, lugs are now

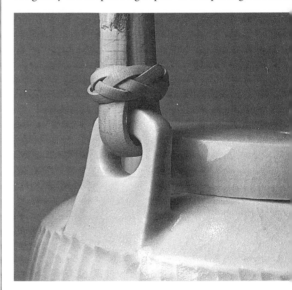

A sturdy lug on a porcelain teapot by David Leach.

Shell-shaped lug handles on a painted earthenware dish by Bennett Cooper.

Something between a lug and a handle on a jar by David Morris.

often used purely decoratively (see also *cane handles*). They can be modeled, made from a section of a pulled handle, or cut from a slab.

Lump ware

In the industry 'defective ware of the lowest saleable quality'. The grades are: best, seconds, lump. Rather too much 'lump' appears as 'seconds' in some studio potteries!

Luster, *lustre*

The deposition of thin metallic coatings on a glaze, producing *iridescence*, using the precious metals gold, silver, and platinum, as well as tin, *bismuth*, and copper, is fairly easy to comprehend in theory but more difficult to carry out successfully.

The metal is obtained by *reduction* either in a reducing atmosphere or by the addition of a reducing agent to metal *salts*. The luster is applied to an already-fired glaze, preferably an *alkaline* one (sodium is important and Alan Caiger-Smith has learned that biscuit firing at 1050°C/1922°F and glaze at 1030–1040°C/1886–1904°F helps to minimize the crazing due to the high alkalinity of the glaze), and refiring just hot enough to adhere the metal to the glaze surface —650–800°C/1202–1472°F. Lusters can be bought ready to fire, or reduced in the kiln from a paste of red ochre with silver sulfide or copper carbonate and a little gum. The Fe_2O_3 in the red ochre is reduced to FeO and, together with the clay constituent, inhibits the re-oxidation of the underlying luster metal during cooling. Care must be taken, when using an ochre paste not to take the temperature above the softening point of the glaze. Ochre reduced luster will need cleaning with a mild abrasive when taken from the kiln. An overall luster glaze can be obtained by silver nitrate, bismuth sub-nitrate, or copper sulfate in concentrations of 1–3%. The pots must be reduced during cooling until the color has gone from the kiln. Soft 900–1000°C/1652–1832°F glazes are used. Parmelee also mentions iron chloride dissolved in sodium resinate, or manganese and copper sulfates treated in the same way. Silver color is derived from platinum. Luster is a tricky technique and the result may not always be as expected; repeated experiment will be necessary.

Copper and *manganese* can be used up to stoneware temperatures without resorting to reducing atmospheres (see 5 below). Lusters may be incorporated to become an aspect of the glaze itself applied to the surface of an already fired glaze and developed at a lower temperature. There appear to be as many ways of compounding lusters as there are potters using them.

The Arabian lusters were made from silver sulfide, cinnabar (HgS), iron oxide, and alum in vinegar; fired in a smoky kiln. The lusters from 16th-century Spain must have been fired in a comparatively simple way and without sophisticated chemicals. Rhodes K shows a simple updraft 'Spanish luster kiln'. Lusters can be produced in reduction in an electric kiln with wood, mothballs, gas, etc. Raku frequently exhibits luster from alkali/copper glazes. See Fournier DPD and Hamer for more detailed discussion and Caiger-Smith LP for a lifetime of experience and an answer to most queries. He also features in John Anderson's film/video 'Lustre firing' (Films for Potters).

Frank Hamer helps to sort out the main types in his 'Potter's Dictionary'. The first three are on-glaze or painted pigments; the fourth deals briefly with in-glaze effects; and the fifth is painted or sprayed directly onto the biscuit.
1 Precious metals are dissolved in acid and made up with a medium for painting. The medium burns out in firing, reducing the chloride back to a film of metal. (See *gold*.)
2 Copper oxide, painted onto the raw glaze, can be fired in reduction to the melting point of the glaze and then given a second, lower temperature reduction. (See also *copper luster*.)
3 Copper may be mixed with clay that has previously been calcined to at least 200°C/392°F above the luster temperature. Ochre is often quoted as a suitable material. The luster is produced in reduction during cooling, and the coating of clay and washed off when cold. An added silver

nitrate will help if a more golden color is required. This system is called by Hamer 'transmutation luster'. Bismuth nitrate dissolved in resin and oil will fire to a mother-of-pearl surface (disparaged as 'slimy' by some commentators). The usual firing temperature is around 700°C/1292°F.

4 Tin or copper in-glaze lusters. The iridescent tin effect has become familiar on raku reductions. In a glaze 2–8% of copper may be used to give a reduced layer of luster on the surface of the glaze. Reduction is during cooling and must be in fairly intense bursts. The glaze is normally a soft one, maturing at below 1000°C/1832°F.

5 Subdued bronze-gold to black colors can be obtained from copper at almost any pottery temperature up to 1270°C/2318°F in oxidation. It is used in combination with manganese (some assert that manganese alone will do it) and is painted onto the biscuit. (See *Copper-manganese gold*.)

This theoretical background, however, masks a multitude of problems. For example in 5 the reaction at 1200°C/2192°F is often wrinkled and somewhat immature in appearance while at some 50°C/122°F higher it is smooth — but it runs like water. After a number of fairly calamitous kilns, a double firing at about 1215°C/2219°F proved the best solution. Another unexpected effect arose out of the difficulty of laying the 'luster' on. A pot was sprayed using copper carbonate because the black oxide clogged the jet. Result — unrelieved black! Simply replacing the oxide with the carbonate totally inhibited the effect. According to the caption on one of Val Barry's porcelain bowls in Lane's 'Studio Porcelain', a crinkled gold can result from the use of a heavy application of manganese alone. Lucie Rie uses the same bronze-gold on her bowls strikingly combined with blue and black, or even pink.

Commercially prepared lusters are generally of type 1 and, while fairly reliable, they lack subtlety. They are available in many colors including black, which may be covered with a mother-of-pearl luster for special effects. Caiger-Smith use types 2 and 3 and has spent years in experiment, building up his experience, as he says, from nowhere. His success rate from four kilns a year was 15–80%. In an exhaustive series of experiments Clive Fiddis, in articles in Ceramic Review 61 and 62 called 'The Lure of Luster', quotes a very wide range of recipes. Discussing type 2 he suggests that lead in the glaze inhibits luster and that a high-alkali recipe is preferable (see also above). The pigment, applied to the raw glaze, is subjected to 15 minutes or so of reduction during cooling at around 725°C/1337°F. Too heavy a reduction will blacken, and partial reduction can give a turquoise center and lustered edges to a brushstroke. A tendency to the 'bleeding' of copper red from the edges is common, and a number of Caiger Smith's pieces show this effect. The pigment can vary from 100% copper to 10% copper/90% bismuth. He suggests

using the carbonate of copper. High bismuth mixtures give a pale gold. He found no totally successful method for the oxide and clay type.

Other advice for special or particular applications include: shiny glazes accept lusters better than matt ones; salts for use in luster include silver sulfide, silver carbonate and cupric sulfate, a suitable base for which is 85% alkaline frit, 10% china clay, and 5% whiting. Silver is liable to tarnish so platinum is usually used. Piepenburg lists two parts silver nitrate to one of tin for a color in raku. For a 'copper penny' color the following is suggested: 2% black copper oxide, and 1% cobalt oxide. Raku lusters may be impermanent. Bismuth can be used for a 'mother-of-pearl' effect.

Conrad divides luster types into 'hard' or 'Persian' and 'Arabian' the latter composed of metal salts, ochre, and a binder, the former fired to glaze temperature and reduced during cooling through 900–550°C/1652–1022°F. Salts of copper, chrome, silver, uranium, and manganese may be used for hard luster, which is more durable and becomes an integral part of the glaze, which is normally a glossy one and which may mature at Orton cone 02 or higher. The thickness of application is important: too thick may flake; too thin may disappear. As with all luster work, surfaces must be kept absolutely clean. A wipe over a glazed surface with whiting can help. Brushes should be washed in benzol. Mather, in Ceramic Review 33, discusses a mother-of-pearl luster obtained by adding a few teaspoonfuls of stannous chloride into the kiln chamber as the glow fades on cooling. A very interesting variation is that by Geoffrey Swindell, who sprays his brushed-on lusters with detergent or paraffin (kerosene) to break the surface tension and cause a honeycomb-like texture. Further applications can blend this into a mysterious and decorative surface. Subtle and lustrous surfaces are obtained by Joanna Constantinidis, who fires in sealed saggars containing mustard seed, salt, and other materials for 'flashed' effects. The pots are previously sprayed with copper or iron oxides. A crackled glaze can be wiped over gold luster and cleaned off with thinners. The crackle will generally fire to a pinkish line. Oldrich Asenbryl prints blocks of luster by silkscreen onto a transluscent glaze. Robin Welch enhances the richness of gold by painting it over a glaze saturated with black copper oxide.

'Burgos luster' is quoted in Dodd as a red for porcelain made by diluting a gold luster with bismuth and tin, both iridescent. 'Cantharides' was a yellow luster from silver, so called from its surface appearance of beetles' wings. Oil sprayed through a tube covered with muslin was used by the Wedgwood factory to give a mottled effect, a technique similar to that used today by Geoffrey Swindell. Manganese was used with platinum for a 'polished steel' surface. Luster was sometimes dusted onto a tacky oil medium transferred from copper plates. Similar effects

The powerful but integrated effect of an amber luster on a grayish glaze by Alan Caiger-Smith.

The seductively varied surface (which needs the subtle color to show its real quality) of a luster-glazed vase by Greg Daly (Australia). An 'alkaline glaze with copper, bismuth and silver' fired in an electric kiln to 1000°C/1832°F followed by a third firing to 800°C/1472°F with heavy reduction down to 620°C/1148°F.

could be obtained today using lino cuts.

Luster painting demands a book in itself. The brushes are important and those supplied for sign-writers by A.S. Handover, Highgate, London, UK have been recommended. Susan Bennett (CR127) recommends painting the luster on a warm pot to hasten drying.

Today there is a limited but quite intense interest, and some potters expend a large part of their effort to it. A specialist is Caiger-Smith, and his 'Lustre Pottery' is an exciting story of discovery and struggle by potters over the centuries. He treats his own work in a fairly traditional way. Luster is a tricky technique and the result may not always be as expected; repeated experiment will be necessary.

Avoid skin contact and always ensure good ventilation when firing.

The modern users of lusters are exploring many byways, which are by no means exhausted. An occasional meditation on the sublime work of the 12th-century Spanish potters will, however, help to retain a perspective.

Luting

The joining of plastic or leather-hard clay with slip or water. Called 'sticking-up' in the industry. Clay models, especially children's work, often disappointingly fall to pieces as they dry due to poorly joined or insufficiently moist junctions. Clay surfaces at any stage will adhere more firmly with a thin layer of water or slip between them. Only the soft clay used on coil pots built by the fingering down method seems not to require slipping. Scoring the joint is an extra precaution but a little liquid will usually suffice at the plastic or soft-leather stages. One can rub up a slip with one's finger between the surfaces to be joined.

Lynn sand

Or Llyn sand. Given by Billington as a ground quartz, and by Leach as a pure form of quartoze sand. Does not now appear in suppliers' lists.

Macaloid

A superior form of bentonite. 'An excellent *suspender*'. Listed by Reward Products, Georgies, and others.

Caroline Whyman, in her book 'Porcelain', suggests the use of macaloid in place of the more usual bentonite for aiding plasticity, and firing whiter, but warns that it may 'gradually break down in the presence of mold and bacteria' if the clay is aged while normal bentonite does not.

Mafic minerals

Silicates containing iron, magnesium, and often calcium. Biotite *mica*, *basalt*, olivine, and pyroxene are mafic minerals. Most are difficult to grind. 'Cheap minerals sometimes substituted for feldspars', Dodd. (See also *oil-spot glaze*.)

Magnesite

The natural mineral of magnesium carbonate $MgCO_3$ with some $FeCO_3$. Widely distributed. Is the chief ore of magnesium. It can be substituted for talc in *ovenproof* bodies. Used also for basic *refractories*.

A listed calcined magnesite has an analysis MgO 88.2, Al_2O_3 1.0, SiO_2 4.3. Potclays list a pure form with 94% MgO.

Magnesium, oxide, compounds

An unstable metallic element Mg, 24.
Oxide MgO, 40, magnesia, m.p. 2800°C/5104°F.
Carbonate $MgCO_3$, 84. Decomposes to oxide at 350°C/662°F.
Sulfate $MgSO_4$, $7H_2O$, 246.5. *Epsom salts*.

The ore of the mineral is magnesite. It is also derived from seawater. Steatite (soapstone) is an hydrated silicate of magnesia.

Although a refractory oxide it is *basic* and will, like calcium, act as a flux in higher temperature glazes. It is classed as one of the *alkaline earths*. The normal formula equivalent is around 0.3 parts of the RO. *Talc* and *dolomite* are most generally used by potters as a source of magnesia. They also, of course, introduce silica and lime respectively. An average amount is 5% in a recipe but it can be exceeded. Magnesia can give a pleasant 'buttery' surface to a glaze. The carbonate, either precipitated or as ground magnesite, is slightly soluble. 'In glazes imparts strength and color with little shrinkage.

In large quantites it gives an opaque, dry appearance (Georgies). Its effect on cobalt can vary: giving purple or even red (Rhodes), or, used as talc can 'quench' the blue to a blue-gray (Cardew). It is considered by many to be an essential ingredient in Jun-type glazes, but it may turn celadons brownish. Used in *flame-proof bodies* (*cordierite*) and as magnesia refractories.
A calcined magnesia is listed by Reward Products.

Magnesium zirconium silicate

'A zircon opacifier, produces high opacity, strong color softness of texture and excellent matt finishes. Introduces MgO without serious devitrification' (Georgies).

Magnetite, magnetic iron

The *spinel* oxide of iron Fe_3O_4 ($FeO.F_2O_3$). Also in the form of magnetic iron ore (loadstone, will respond to a magnet), or black iron oxide. It may be prepared by roasting scrap iron in the kiln at about 1100°C/2012°F, see also 'Blacksmith's scale'. Tends to be coarse-grained due to its great hardness and can therefore produce speckle in glazes, bodies, and pigments. Brushstrokes may be fluxed by the glaze to produce a broken color.

Maiolica, majolica

In the pottery industry and in merchants' catalogs, a 'majolica' glaze indicates a *soft*, *opaque*, colored glaze firing of 980–1080°C/1796–1976°F. However maiolica (spelt with an 'i' as is the original Italian word) is the painting with metal *oxides* on a white, generally tin-opacified earthenware glaze. In Holland the style was known as delftware, after the main production town, and as faience in France and elsewhere, from Faenza (Florence). It used a highly calcerous or dolomitic body (Cardew).

The art of maiolica painting has suffered an eclipse but it still has unexplored potential and great satisfaction can be derived from its practice. It is very flexible and can be treated as broadly or as finely as you wish. The basic technique is simple. A pot or plate is evenly coated with an opaque glaze such as a lead-lime-potash glaze (see *lead glaze*) with 10% tin oxide. The use of a light *terracotta* body will give warmth to the glaze. The design is painted straight onto the raw glaze. One may start work as soon as the wetness has gone from the surface, which then accepts the color like a dampened watercolor paper. Alan Caiger-Smith, however, works on the dry glaze. The timing depends partly on the physical strength of the dried coating (which will usually be rather powdery if frits are used). *Gums* or other binders can be added to the glaze.

The oxides are ground with water, either in a mortar or with a palette knife on a glazed tile. See also *pigment oxides.* The depth of color will depend on the amount of water used. Most oxides will become transparent and each stroke will be revealed after firing even though they appear as a solid block of color when raw. Many of the unfired oxides are black and this can lead to confusion. It will help to use those *carbonates* which have distinctive hues, though these will change in the firing. The carbonates are slightly toxic. Cobalt and manganese are the most stable colors: copper is rather watery with blurred edges; lead antimoniate is refractory and needs softening with lead oxide or frit and careful application; iron is rather fugitive, varying from a pale amber to dark brown within a single stroke. Prepared stains are available. *Chrome* is rarely used because of possible tin-pink reactions.

With practice one can work with these particular properties and turn them to advantage. Oxides can be mixed. Rather firmer greens can be obtained with antimony/cobalt mixtures. Much of the older maiolica painting uses a thin outline of cobalt or manganese to give definition to the washes of copper and antimony.

A long-haired *brush* is traditional but all kinds may be used, care being taken not to abrade the glaze coating or to saturate it. Painting should be rapid and direct — it has more affinity with Eastern calligraphic styles than is often realized. The Italian maiolica glazes were compounded of tin-ash with a lead-clay-sand frit and after painting, a thin coat of clear glaze was applied. The clear glaze would also have been mixed with the oxides to help them to flux. Colors will vary with the type of glaze and opacifier. Tin oxide is kinder to the pigments than zirconium: leadless glazes will develop more brash hues than lead ones. The glaze must be applied with care, runs or thick areas pared down with a sharp knife, and the firing carefully controlled. The high degree of opacity may cause some *crawling.* As mentioned the body may be a mixture of red and buff clays.

Painted maiolica pots are difficult to handle when packing the kiln. One may use siccatives to fix the glaze or color, but if the painting is designed with this problem in mind, and if the piece is held firmly, the difficulty can be minimized. With top-loading kilns the pot can be held by the inside.

The spelling 'majolica' is also used for large industrial sculptural ceramics, probably infuenced by the Della Robbia plaques and figures.

Malm

A natural high-calcia brick clay. Will melt to a glass at 1200–1250°C/2192–2282°F.

Manganese, *oxides, compounds*

A metallic element Mn, 55. Oxide MnO, 71.
Dioxide MnO_2, 87 (pyrolusite) loses oxygen at 535°C/995°F.
Tetraoxide Mn_3O_4, 229.
Carbonate $MnCO_3$, 115.

Toxic in large quantites in the raw form (Georgies). A coloring oxide, typically brown or purple-brown in a glaze but capable of variation. Used in concentrations of 2–10% in soft glazes and even higher in stonewares. Essentially an oxidizing pigment.

The question of manganese poisoning has been aired — it has even been given as a cause of Parkinson's disease but the cause of this disease is unknown and there is no evidence that potters are more prone to it than any other profession. However the usual care must be taken as with any other chemical (see *poisonous materials*).

In a lower oxide state it is basic in effect, i.e. softens or fluxes a glaze. On heating, however, it alters to Mn_2O_3 and to Mn_3O_4. As the valency rises it acts as an amphoteric and then as an acidic oxide. In earthenware glazes, therefore, and especially in lead recipes it can be considered as quite a powerful flux: in oxidized stoneware it will behave more like alumina. The alteration or decomposition results in the release of gas which can lead to *bubbles* or *craters* in the glaze at around 1070°C/1958°F. This bubbling in soft glazes can be avoided by using prepared glaze stains but this is expensive.

A stoneware casserole on a candle heater. The glaze is heavily loaded with manganese dioxide (15%), giving a lustrous surface effect. By Robert Fournier. (See also saturated glaze, super-saturated glaze).

Fraser recommends replacing whiting with *wollastonite*. A soak near top temperature may allow the bubbles to settle down, or firing a little lower plus soak. In high temperature reduction it should, theoretically, revert to its basic state; 2% has given a gray in reduction. Fully reduced MnO gives a green similar to chrome.

As well as a variety of purple-browns (often lurid in a leadless glaze), manganese can produce pink. I have occasionally achieved a salmon blush on tin glaze over black (manganese) slip. A pink *stain* is prepared from manganese, alumina, and borax. It is used with other oxides for black; and 10% and over will cause metallic surface deposits giving *iridescence* and other effects. Manganese and zinc have a low eutectic and the mixture is best avoided. Manganese and copper can give a muted gold surface on biscuit, but the mixture has a tendency to run. Manganese is sensitive to the presence of sulfur gases, which may explain why it bubbles in a glaze on some bodies and not on others. Painted onto raw clay or biscuit it will fire to a dull gloss at 1090°C/1994°F and can also be used on stoneware. A granular manganese is listed by Potters Supply House. (See also *copper/manganese gold*.)

Marbling

Marbled or variegated slip patterns can be achieved in three ways:
1 Tiles, small pots, pottery figures, etc. can be dipped into a bowl of slip onto the surface of which contrasting colored slips have been dribbled or *trailed*. The traditional Sussex 'Pig-bank' is decorated in this way.
2 Slip may be trailed directly onto a dish or pot which is then either shaken sideways or given a sharp twist. Use a minimum of movement—if the effect is not immediately attractive, continued shaking will only make it more muddy. A variation is to trail blobs of contrasting slip onto

A well-controlled slip-marbled dish by Jane Smith.

Dipping a pinch-pot pig money-box into a bowl of black slip into which white and red slips have been trailed, giving a very fluid marbling effect.

the edge of a dish or plate and allow them to run to the center and then give a twist to the piece. The colors tend to become less defined after glaze firing, due to overlapping slip becoming slightly transparent and showing the color beneath. This effect can also be turned to your advantage.
3 Slips of one or more colors trailed or poured onto the surface and combed or feathered into the typical veined effect of marble.

Marbled bodies result from layered clays of different colors. The clays should be of similar shrinkage — it is advisable to use a single clay variously stained. The layers are sharply smacked together, pressed into a convenient shape, sliced through, and then used for making pottery in the normal way but with a maximum economy of movement. The surface of thrown pots will be smudged but the design can be sharpened by turning or by scraping, when leather hard, with a steel palette. (See also *agate ware*).

Mark

See *seal, stamp*.

Marl

An imprecise term given to some iron-bearing secondary clays, generally with calcium impurities. Examples: Keuper marl, of variegated color and containing magnesium carbonate and gypsum. Etruria marl, however, is almost lime free marl. Cambridge marl contains some 40% CaO. The term is applied to a low grade fireclay (e.g. saggar marl). Leach mentions the use of a marl with a finely dispersed

me content for slipware. Its contraction during cooling
[a]ids craze-resistance. Much traditional slipware must have
[b]een made with this type of clay, which is common all over
[E]ngland.

Marquetry

A term sometimes used to describe a variety of *agate* or
meriage wares.

Mask

The danger of breathing unhealthy dusty materials by pot-
[t]ers varies with their working habits (see *dust, poisonous
materials* and *safety in the workshop*). The simplest mask,
obtainable from pharmacies, is a light metal shape into
which filter pads are fitted, and which is held in place with
[e]lastic round the back of the head. The Standard EN mark
(European Standard) specifies minimum requirements for
[f]iltering half-masks. A very reasonably priced 'respirator

mask (to ceramic industry standards)' is quoted by The
Potters Connection. More elaborate and more effective
models (resembling gas-masks) are now often provided
with two filters to make breathing easier.

Wearing this clumsy equipment is anathema to many
people but some effective filter should always be used
when spraying, sanding dry clay for any length of time,
and for any work which results in a prolonged dusty
atmosphere (or the air holding fine droplets in suspension,
as with spraying).

Minimize dust production in the first place; respirators
should be considered a last line of defense.

Masking tape

Ordinary adhesive masking tape has been used by potters
as a *resist* material on clay or biscuit. The simplest but
often striking effect is of broad stripes, though the tape can
be cut and manipulated to produce other designs. Can be
used as resist between slips (see *terra sigillata)* and on raku.

*Masking tape resist decoration on a raku bowl. By David
Roberts.*

Massive form of rock

The rocky, solid, or block form of a mineral, e.g. *steatite.*

Master mold

Or block mold. A high quality copy taken from a hollow
mold and from which 'case molds' can be made. In the case
of simple dish molds, the 'block' would be in the form
of a solid inverted dish (which can be used as a *drape* or
hump mold).

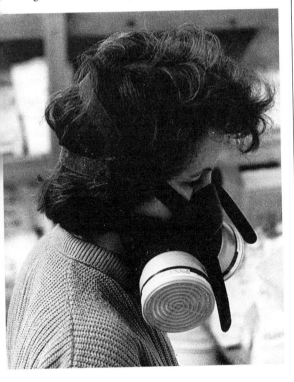

*The double filter mask in use. Easier for breathing but large
and clumsy. Essential, however, for assistants to potters or
suppliers (this picture was taken at Bath Pottery Supplies, UK),
where dry pottery materials are handled or spraying done.
Simpler, cheaper pad masks are available for occasional use but
this more efficient type is recommended if regular spraying,
sanding, or other dust-producing processes are practiced.*

Matrix

The 'ground mass' of a mineral or ceramic material in which larger crystals are embedded.

Matt, mat

A non-shiny or 'dry' surface. Term sometimes confused with *opaque*. Opacity is, in fact, involved, since a fully transparent glass does not have *crystalline* structure and does have a bright surface. The matt effect is due to the breakup of reflected light by minute variations in the surface level. A matt glaze will, therefore, tend to stain or mark more easily than a shiny one.

Matt glazes can result from underfiring but these are less satisfactory than those due to the development of very small surface crystals. Slow cooling in the upper temperature range (maturity down to 800°C/1472°F) will assist crystallization. Alumina in slight excess of the optimum balance with silica; high base glazes; titanium; barium in low boron glazes; zinc oxides; hematite; lime (below 1200°C/2192°F); will all tend to make a glaze matt. 3% of copper oxide may produce a rather ashy matt black. Lime mats are a result of the formation of *wollastonite*. (See also *dry glazes*.)

Matt blue

A cobalt-aluminate pigment usually with zinc.

Maturing of glaze

The optimum condition of a glaze when it has fully melted or otherwise achieved its potential. Most potters believe that the involved physical and chemical changes need time fully to 'mature'. This is not always proved in practice. In the older kilns it was not possible to fire quickly and the idea of a long, *soaking* fire may be linked with this fact. The same glaze will give quite different results in different kilns and firing schedules, and I have found that some of the most attractive and apparently 'mature' glazes have come from fast test firings. The question is an open one, but the subtleties of a well-developed *interface* and other considerations will for many potters swing the balance in favor of longer firings. A twenty-minute soaking certainly helps *earthenware* glazes to settle down.

MDF, medex

A hard material used for *throwing bats*. Bath Pottery Supplies list a throwing bat made of 'exterior type MDF (known as Medex)'.

Measuring spoon

These can be bought in various sizes from a teaspoon to tablespoon. Scrape the surface of the material flat for accurate measurement. Useful for small tests and especially for *line blends* of glazes, etc. Attempts have been made to translate weight recipes into spoonsful by taking density into account, but it is much easier to weigh larger amounts of glaze and slip materials. The measuring spoon, however, could find a use in schools where scales are not always available.

Medium

The oily or watery liquid which is mixed with enamels and other forms of pigments and which burn away in the firing. Traditionally this is *fat oil* of turpentine but a prepared medium can be purchased. (See *enamel*.)

Melted glass decoration

Ordinary commercial window glass will melt at around 1060°C/1940°F — above or below this figure according to its type. It will also stand heating up to 1270°C/2318°F or more without trouble. On cooling it has the very high contraction natural to soda glass. This may be powerful enough to tear stonewares apart.

Molten glass is very fluid and, if not contained in a well or cavity, will flow like water. This quality can be turned to advantage in certain freely modeled dishes or other pieces giving a 'frozen fall'. Too thin a coating will *devitrify* to dull powdery surface: this can also occur on any melted glass surface — forming a white powder (with the glass beneath it dull and faulted), which may even appear weeks after the glass has been fired. Refiring is more likely to scum the surface with bubbles than to cure the fault unless further glass is laid on top. Colored glass is more liable to this fault than clear glass. (See illustration under *devitrification*.)

The glass will always be very 'shattered' in appearance through excessive *crazing* but, as the surface usually heals over the effect is decorative and mysterious. Glass can be colored by laying it over glaze or pigment and firing them together. It is best used in a well-broken but not powdered form — the latter may involve too much trapped air. Wrap the glass to be broken in thick newspaper, thick plastic (for flat sheets), or a cardboard box, and hammer it from the outside. You can usually get a supply of broken pieces from a local builder's glass cutter. Window glass is easier to handle and more reliable in melting than bottle-glass. (See also under *box*.)

without collapse and assisting the *viscosity* of glazes. Reference books will often quote the melting points of the metals and oxides we use, but the knowledge is of limited use. To take magnesium, for instance: the m.p. of the metal is 651°C/1203°F, that of the oxide 2800°C/5104°F. Apart from the startling difference between these two figures, neither of them tells us much about their behavior in a glaze or body. It is more important to know where it stands in relation to the *Seger formula*, and its habits and effects in conjunction with silica.

Melting points in reaction with other materials will always differ from those of the oxide or mineral on its own—this is the limitation of the button test for individual materials, instructive though that can be. The study of ceramics is the study of *eutectics* rather than of individual melting points.

Mending clay and biscuit

'Mending' is used in the industry to mean the luting or joining of clay, as in the assembly of porcelain figures. Leach mentions the mending, in the more usual sense, of kiln props, etc. with powdered fireclay and *water-glass*. Repairs to unfired clay, can be made with slip up to the hard-leather stage but joins in dry clay or biscuit are unreliable. One may sometimes get away with the use of vinegar with a little clay to repair dry clay cracks or breaks, but one cannot be certain that it will hold: it should not be used for broken handles, for instance. A 'high-fire mender—mixed with slip from your own clay body' called Aztec (!) is listed by Baileys. Stress cracks will mend only temporarily.

For dry or biscuit pots certain high temperature cements are advertised, which, the makers claim, can be glazed over without showing. One type is called 'Alumide': the name is a clue to its content. 'Zircopax' (prepared zircon) with flint or quartz can be mixed with water to repair biscuit. Potclays sell a 'Magic Mender' for 'broken greenware or cracks in biscuit'. However if a pot is broken or cracked it will be unlikely to fire satisfactorily. (See also *stopping*, and *repairing pottery*.)

Mesh patterns

See *cloth pattern, lace*. In addition wire or other coarse mesh can be either impressed into the clay or a cast may be made and a raised-line impression derived from it.

Metakaolin

The layered form of clay is destroyed when heated between 500°C/932°F and 850°C/1562°F. Above 1050°C/1922°F *mullite* begins to form.

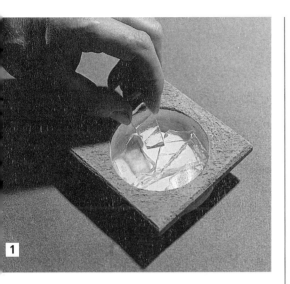

and *2* Broken pieces of window glass are placed on the glazed surface of a slab dish. After firing the glass has melted together and the pigment in the glaze has stained it. Not all types of glass or glaze are suitable—only trials will show which will work. (See devitrification.) Note the surface appears miraculously smooth despite the fierce crazing below.

Melting point

The point of change from a solid to a liquid phase. In some cases this takes place completely at a given temperature (and pressure) and without change in composition. This is known as congruent melting. Many pottery materials, however, go through mixed solid and liquid *phases*, i.e. they melt *incongruently*.

This behavior is of great service to the potter, allowing the development of *vitreous* stonewares and porcelains

Metal

A metallic element will generally unite with oxygen to form a base. Tin, titanium, zirconium, germanium, and aluminum are exceptions, forming *acidic* and *amphoteric* oxides.

Metal in the form of iron filings of various grades, small copper turnings, and so on can be beaten into the surface of a work. They will generally go black and spread out in a stoneware firing or be affected by any glaze laid over them, sometimes developing a green halo. (See also *brass*.)

The use of unfired metal strips and shapes as additions or inlays is a non-ceramic technique and, though used by several potters in an integrated style, is outside the scope of this book.

Metal release

The tendency of some heavy metals (high *atomic numbers*) to dissolve out of a glaze and into vinegar, fruit juices, or any strong alkali or acid. The most dangerous are lead (see *soluble lead*) and cadmium. *Copper* is also involved, especially in the presence of lead oxide. *Cadmium* is used mainly in orange and red enamels. Neither these nor cadmium glazes should be used on the inside of *tableware*, storage jars, or kitchenware. Some merchants are now rating their colored glazes and frits on a metal release scale, those with high potential danger to be used on decorative ware only. Associated more with earthenwares than stonewares. Barium carbonate is mentioned as suspect. One need not panic over possible metal release. If glazes have well-balanced formulas and are accurately fired, the great majority of pots would be less liable to be dangerous than, say, household bleaches. Tests for metal release are offered by some potters' merchants and by British Ceramic Research Ltd, Queens Road, Penkhull, Stoke-on-Trent, Staffordshire, UK. (See also below for test swab.)

One test has been given as: a 4% solution of acetic acid must not dissolve sufficient metals in 24 hours to color it. In some countries the tests are more stringent. Some pottery merchants (e.g. Potclays) offer this service. In the UK (1997) the compliance was for flatware 20 ppm (ppm = parts per million), hollow ware 7 ppm, storage vessels 2 ppm (Hamer). In the USA the revised compliance guide is more stringent and has been quoted (Georgies) as 3 ppm for flatware, 2ppm for small hollow ware, 1 ppm for hollow ware larger than 1.1 liters, 0.5 ppm for pitchers, (jugs) cups and mugs.

Axner list a 'Lead test swab' which can identify lead release of above 2 ppm, turning pink if positive.

Metaloid

An element with some metallic and some non-metallic characteristics. The *oxides* are *amphoteric* (Uvarov) though two metaloids which occur in glaze formulas, arsenic and antimony, are glass-formers and listed with the acidic oxides. The metaloids belong to the fifth group of the *periodic table*.

Metamorphic rock, mineral

A rock which has undergone transformation by natural agencies. *Igneous* or *sedimentary* rocks subjected to great heat and pressure are 'altered' and change their texture and appearance and sometimes their mineral composition. Limestone, for instance, re-crystallizes to form marble. Sillimanite is a metamorphic mineral.

Methane

A *hydrocarbon*, CH_4. The principal constituent of natural gas. (See *gas fuel*.)

Mica

A general term for a group of minerals composed of hydrated *silicates* of alumina, with other silicates, e.g. of the *alkalis*. The characteristic mineral of *schists*, and the glittering crystals or scales in granite. Some deposits will readily cleave into sheets. Feldspars are altered to kaolinite and mica in the formation of china clay. The shallow troughs which *levigate* the china clay are known as 'mica drags' and the 'white hills' of Cornish and other clay workings consist largely of mica which has been separated from the clay.

Biotite mica contains iron and magnesium and is sometimes present in feldspars and other ceramic minerals. Muscovite is white mica, ideal formula $H_2KAl_2(SiO_4)_3$ or K_2O. $3Al_2O_3$ $6SiO_2$. $2H_2O$ with fluorine sometimes given as an element. There may be wide variations from this formula. It can be used as a 'natural frit' in bodies, especially for ovenware, where it will strengthen the fabric against thermal shock. Muscovite mica will begin to lose water at c. 250°C/482°F and to decompose into *mullite* and liquid at 1050°C/1922°F. Ground mica is sometimes used to produce *mullite* in clays. Can be used in sawdust and raku pots (mica fragments can be scraped from some composition roofing tiles). The *lamellar* structure of mica has affinities with clay, though it is not plastic. This structure also makes mica difficult to grind. In the past the alkali fraction in clay has been attributed to feldspar in a *rational analysis* but it is now generally given to a mica percentage (*mica convention*) which leads to a re-assessment of the kaolinite content. Sheet mica is sometimes used as a heatproof window for furnaces and is a good electrical insulator.

Mica convention

In a *rational analysis* of clay the assumption, for many years, was that the bulk of the mineral could be described as *kaolinite, feldspar* and *quartz*. It is now considered that the alkali content can more accurately be discussed in terms of mica. The new computation alters the proportions of the other compounds. (See Cardew for details.)

Michigan slip-clay

A red fusible clay similar to *Albany slip.*

Micron, micrometer

One-millionth of a meter. Symbol p(m). A millionth may be written 10^{-6}.

Used in the discussion of light wavelengths, and very fine clay particle sizes. 1 micron = 10,000 ångström units.

Micropore

A very efficient heat insulating material for the outer skins of kilns. One $\frac{1}{2}$in/12.5mm is reputed to replace 3in/75mm of brick. (See also *insulation of heat.*)

Microwave

Generally associated with cooking, the technology has been used 'to combine microwave with radiant energy within a conventional kiln' (Drayton International). This is industrial and experimental (1999), but, who knows, may be developed to the point where it can have wider implications.

Mill

To grind finely, or, a machine for grinding materials to a powder. (See *ball mill, jar mill.*)

In CM 19/5 it was suggested that one could shake marbles and glaze in a glass jar to mill glaze materials. This sounds energetic and a little dangerous!

Mineral

In the process of the earth's cooling, and of its subsequent weathering, breaking down and re-combining, combinations of *elements* have formed with distinctive physical and chemical properties and, in the present environment, a degree of stability. In some crystal structures, ionic substitutions can occur causing variations in the detailed make-up of the mineral. Since the electron charges and the *atomic radii* must be similar to the displaced ions, the overall characteristics of the mineral remain within a certain range. *Rocks* consist of various minerals. Most minerals are of *inorganic* origin. The mineral is deemed to have an '*ideal' formula*, the actual material used will be the nearest approach in nature to this formula. Thus china clay or kaolin is often 98% kaolinite mineral. The principal rocks, ores and minerals of interest to potters are:

Alabaster. A pure form of micro-crystalline gypsum.
Albite feldspar. $Na_2Al_2O_3.6SiO_2$, 524. Igneous.
Amblygonite. Variable. Lithium, alumina, phosphorus, with a little silica.
Anorthite feldspar. $CaO.Al_2O_3.2SiO_2$, 278. Igneous.
Andalusite. $Al_2O_3.SiO_2$, 162.
Asbestos. Variable silicates of calcium, iron, and magnesia. Serpentine, amphibole.
Asbolite. Impure cobalt ore.
Barytes. Rock of barium sulfate, $BaSO_4$.
Basalt. Basic rock, high in iron. Volcanic.
Bauxite. Ore of aluminum. Residual.
Beidellite. Alumina-rich montmorillonite clay mineral.
Bentonite. Clay mineral of montmorillonite group.
Biotite. Mica mineral with iron and magnesium.
Borax. $Na_2O.2B_2O_3.10H_2O$, 381.5. Evaporate.
Boro-calcite $CaO.2B_2O_3.6H_2O$, 304.
Brucite. Ore of magnesia. $MgO.H_2O$.
Calcspar/Calcite Crystalline $CaCO_3$, 100. Deposit.
Carolina Stone. See *china stone.*
Cassiterite. Ore of tin, SnO_2.
Chalcopyrite. Ore of copper. $CuFeS_2$.
Chalk. Soft limestone. $CaCO_3$, 100. Deposit.
China Stone. $Na_2O.Al_2O_3.8SiO_2$, 644. Igneous.
Chromite. Ore of chrome. $FeO.Cr_2O_3$. Ultrabasic, meta-morphic.
Cobaltite. Ore of cobalt. $CoAsS$.
Colemanite, $2CaO.3B_2O_3.5H_2O$.
Copperas. Ferrous sulfate, $FeSO_4$.
Corundum. Crystalline, Al_2O_3. Igneous. Ultrabasic, or limestone rock.
Crocus Martis. Fe_2O_3, 160.
Cryolite. Na_3AlF_6, 210.
Cuprite. Ore of copper, Cu_2O.
Diaspore. Clay high in alumina.
Diatomite. Mainly SiO_2. Organic deposit.
Diopside. $CaO.MgO.2SiO_2$. Solid solution. Pyroxene, metamorphic.
Dolomite. $CaCO_3.MgCO_3$, 184.

Feldspar. See *albite, anorthite, orthoclase.*

Flint. Micro-crystalline SiO_2, 60. Boulder pebble in chalk.

Fluorspar. CaF_2, 78.

Galena. PbS, 239. Ore of lead.

Ganister. Fine-grain silica rock. Coal seams.

Garnet. Various, $RO.R_2O_3.3SiO_2$.

Gerstley Borate. See *colemanite.*

Gibbsite. $Al_2O_3.3H_2O$.

Granite. Variable; bases, alumina, silica, phosphorus, iron, titania, etc. Igneous, intrusive.

Gypsum. $CaSO_4.2H_2O$.

Halloysite. Clay mineral with a rolled plate structure.

Heavyspar. See *barytes.*

Hematite. Mineral of Fe_2O_3.

Hornblende. Silicates of calcium, magnesium, iron, and sodium. Amphibole, intermediate.

Illite. Micaceous clay mineral.

Ilmenite. $Fe_2O_3.TiO_2$, 152.

Ironstone. A hard iron ore.

Kaolinite. The ideal clay mineral, see *clays* as main dictionary entry. Igneous.

Kieselguhr. See *diatomite.*

Kyanite. $Al_2O_3.SiO_2$.

Lava. Basic rocks of variable composition.

Lepidolite. $(LiNaK)_2. (FOH)_2.Al_2O_3.2SiO_2$, 472.

Leucite, $K_2O.Al_2O_3.4SiO_2$. Feldspathoid, lavas.

Limestone. Rock of calcite, $CaCO_3$. Sedimentary.

Limonite. Ore of iron, $2Fe_2O_3.3H_2O$.

Magnesite. Mineral of $MgCO_3$, with some iron.

Magnetite. Magnetic iron ore, Fe_3O_4. A spinel.

Marble. Altered limestone.

Mica. Variable; hydrated silicates of alumina, with alkali silicates.

Monothermite. $0.2R_2O.Al_2O_3.SiO_2.1.5SiO_2$. Weathered Mica.

Mullite. $3Al_2O_3.2SiO_2$. Dissociation of kaolinite.

Muscovite Mica. $(NaK)_2O.3Al_2O_3.6SiO_2.2H_2O$. Alkaline, igneous.

Nepheline Syenite. $Na_2O.Al_2O_3.2SiO_2$, but variable with some potassium, Feldspathoid.

Ochre. Earthy iron oxide.

Orthoclase Feldspar. $K_2O.Al_2O_3.6SiO_2$, 556. Igneous.

Pegmatite. General granitic or feldspathic rocks. Sometimes a synonym for china stone.

Perlite. Fine-grain acidic laval rock. Rhyolite.

Petalite. $Li_2O.Al_2O_3.8SiO_2$, 612.

Petunze. Chinese equivalent of china stone.

Pitchblende. Ore of uranium.

Plagioclase. Feldspar series between albite and anorthite.

Pyrites. Metal sulfide minerals, e.g. FeS, CuS, CoS.

Pyrolusite. Ore of manganese, MnO_2.

Pyrophyllite. Clay family substance, $Al_2O_3.4SiO_2.H_2O$.

Quartzite. Rock of crystalline silica. SiO_2, 60.

Rutile. Crystalline titania, TiO_2. *Polymorphic.*

Salt. NaCl. Deposit.

Sand. Various coarse rock particles.

Sandstone. Rock of silica minerals, cemented with clay, lime and iron.

Shale. Lithified clay.

Sienna. An hydrated iron-manganese earth.

Sillimanite. $Al_2O_3.SiO_2$. A clay mineral. Metamorphic.

Smaltite. Ore of cobalt. $CoAs_2$.

Soapstone. '*Massive*' impure talc.

Spangles, Magnetic iron. Fe_3O_4.

Spodumene. $Li_2O.Al_2O_3.4SiO_2$, 372. Pyroxene, granitic.

Steatite. See *soapstone.*

Stibnite. Sb_2O_3. Ore of antimony. Replacement deposit.

Talc. $3MgO.4SiO_2.H_2O$, 379. Metamorphic magnesium-rich rocks.

Umber. A ferruginous earth. Hydrated.

Vermiculite. Biotite mica altered by hydrothermal solutions.

Volcanic Ash. Variable basic rocks, with iron.

Witherite. Rock of barium carbonate.

Wollastonite. $CaO.SiO_2$, 166.

Zincblende. Ore of zinc. ZnS.

Zircon. $ZnSiO_4$. Occurs as sands, etc.

See under individual minerals for information and use.

Mineral wool (block)

A fibrous material made by blowing steam through molten rocks, slag, or glass and used as comparatively low-temperature *heat insulation.*

The block is a material of compressed mineral wool (typically calcium silicate). Made in various sizes up to 3ft x 1ft/1m x 0.3m. A number of proprietary makes include: Caposil, Supertemp, Kipsulate, etc. The material is rather weak and friable, easily compressed locally, and very dusty in use (wear a mask), but is a very efficient insulator. $1\frac{1}{2}$in (38mm) of mineral wool block will replace 3in/76mm or more of standard insulating brick. Its low mass — a piece 1sq ft/930sq cm by 1in/25mm thick has an average weight of about 14lb/790g — enables kiln weight to be cut considerably. Maximum operating temperature of 900–1000°C/1652–1832°F confines its use to the outer skins of kilns. *Ceramic fiber* block is similar in appearance but has a higher operating temperature range.

Mineralogical constitution

The type and proportions of minerals present in a material, as distinct from its chemical constitution.

Mini-bars

Non-tapering pyrometric indicators which are smaller than standard cones but work in similar way except that they are laid horizontally across two supports, one at each end. The cone sags in the middle as it softens. Used especially for operating *kiln-sitters*. Pyro mini-bars are widely available. (See *Holdcroft Bar*.)

Minium

Red lead Pb_3O_4. (See *lead*.)

Mirror black

A name given to a type of fine black Chinese glaze. Probably derived from a mixture of cobalt and iron, or iron and manganese in a stoneware glaze. Has been obtained using iron alone in a laurel ash glaze. Can also be replicated to some degree with high percentages of manganese in an oxidized glaze, but test with care. (See also *black glaze*.)

Mishima

A delicate, often starry, form of inlay originating in Korea and widely practiced in Japan. Also called 'zogan'. The design, usually in fine lines, is *stamped* or *impressed* into clay at the *soft-leather* stage, and then filled with brushed-on slip (or even a glaze) which may or may not be scraped flat to give a sharp outline, or partially cleared to leave a 'swimming — ground streaked or clouded in white or gray'.

Mishima or slip inlay on a pot by Lex Dickson (Australia). The pattern is carved into the leather-hard clay and then brushed over with repeated layers of porcelain slip. When the inlay is just proud of the pot surface it is scraped back flat with a sharp tool. (Photo by Chris McLaren). See also illustrations at inlay.

Mitographic decal

Given in Dodd-Murfin as a *silk-screen* printed *transfer*.

Mixing clays

Most commercial bodies are combinations of clays, each chosen for a particular quality. These are rendered into slip, combined in recipe proportions, filter-pressed, and pugged. A similar routine but with the filter press replaced by weathering and drying in troughs can be practiced by the studio potter who has sufficient space and energy.

In the last few years many potters have bought dough mixers from old bakeries to mix clay powder and water to a plastic state. For most potters, however, it is a case of pugging already plastic bodies, or hand-layering and *wedging*. Cardew warns against wedging short clays into plastic ones, the whole mix tending to assume the lowest level of plasticity. He recommends a slop mix, at least for china clay.

It is possible to spread layers of dry clay onto a sheet of thick plastic in a wooden frame, slaking with water at each layer. The corners of the sheet are then folded in and the whole left to soak for a few days before *wedging* and kneading.

Mocha, *mocca*

If a coloring oxide is mixed with certain weak acids and a drop is applied to wet slip, it will travel by local deflocculation to form dendritic (tree or moss-like) patterns that fill with pigment and become permanent. The name has probably arisen from a resemblance to 'mocha stone', an Arabian quartz.

Today a few potters experiment with the technique. The deflocculating agent or 'tea' is most commonly brewed from tobacco. Andrews suggests $\frac{1}{2}$oz/15g black rolling tobacco in a pint of water to which is added a teaspoonful

'Wildacre' mochaware bottle and plate, by Carenza Hayhoe.

of red iron oxide. Harry Horlock Stringer offers one cigarette mashed in boiling water. The pigment must be finely ground and, together with the tea passed through a 120 or (better still) 200 mesh sieve before each use. Citric acid from orange or lemon is reputed to assist the pattern, while Storr-Britz recommends apple cider vinegar. For color, as well as oxides, underglaze black has been recommended.

Whatever the mixture, it is applied with a large brush or syringe as soon as the base slip has been poured or dipped. The pattern travels partly by gravity, and experiment is necessary as to the most useful angle for the piece. Rupert Andrews who expands on his methods in the article 'Mocha Magic' in CR69, achieves mysterious 'landscapes with trees' and utilizes the happy accident that a bluish color appears where the slip has been disturbed by the 'mocha tea' to suggest water and lakes, applying a rapid stroke of color around the base of a pot (held upside-down) and then a second stroke 'it is during these final strokes that the magic of mocha occurs — complete landscapes suddenly appear'. Robin Hopper flows irregular white slip onto his basalt bottles and induces mocha diffusions in a purely decorative way. The mechanical ease with which the patterns can be made to grow is, of course, a danger in itself.

Modeling

The sculptor models from the outside, generally applying clay to a solid core. The figure cannot be fired without the intermediary of a mold and cast (see *press mold*). In this book discussion is limited to techniques which allow for direct firing, e.g. modeling by *pinching, coiling, slab-building, throwing*, etc.

With some skill, practice, and ingenuity most forms can be constructed by these methods, although, in general, the pottery figure will be stylized, compact, and self-supporting. Clay is an amiable and versatile material but imposes its own limitations. Some of the most fundamental of these are:

1 It shrinks during drying and firing — if soft clay is applied to stiff clay, tensions and cracks will result.
2 Clay will not adhere to itself simply by being pressed together; moisture or slip must be used.
3 Air and water will expand on heating and can destroy the fabric if trapped in it.
4 Clay will become *pyroplastic* during firing.

An open, grogged clay, and a maximum wall thickness of ½in/12mm will help in all cases.

Simple models may be made from thumb pots and slabs. For a more involved slab figure, but one still within a student's capabilities, see Fournier CC. The superb coiling technique of Rosemary Wren can be studied with

advantage by all interested in building larger pieces. (See film 'Creatures in clay'.) All her figures are totally self-supporting both during building and firing. Inverted T shaped coils are used.

If a large piece has more than one support, e.g. the legs of an animal, it is advisable to biscuit and glaze fire on a flat slab made of the same body; the slab will therefore contract at the same rate as the figure. The slab should be bedded on alumina, as should any wide-based construction. Any horizontally extended parts of the model may need separate support in the kiln. Coil a hollow

A sculptural approach to animal modeling: a bear by Robert Fournier.

An impressive 'Bridge' by Brian Newman.

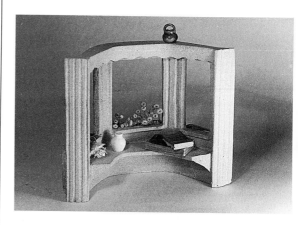

A 'standing window' by Sheila Fournier.

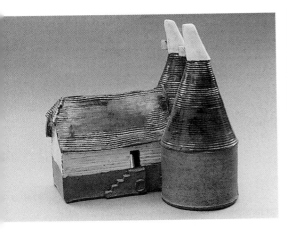

A slab-built oast house by Gordon Cramp.

A more stylized anteater by Rosemary Wren.

supporting cylinder from the same body. See at *armature* for crushed paper support.

Modeling clay

The so-called 'modeling clay' listed by many pottery merchants is, too often, a characterless white body with low plasticity and poor dry strength. A red or buff clay with good plasticity, opened with a fine grog, such as *T-material*, makes the best body for modeling.

Many attempts have been made to prepare a clay body which will have high dry strength without firing. (See *Newclay*, *unfired clay*.) These are not, of course, ceramic materials in the true sense. See also *paper clay*.

Modeling compound, unfired

There are several mixtures of clay with hardeners on the market, all fairly expensive, for semi-permanent models and the like. Newclay was one of the first; Darwi

(Cromartie) is another. (See also *unfired clay*.)

Modeling on surfaces

See *applied decoration, barbotine, boss, carved molds, cordon, embossing, frilled cordon, molded relief, rope decoration, seal,* and *sprigging*.

Modeling tool

The most useful clay modeling tool is a spatula-ended hardwood tool (see *spatula tool*). A large range of other shapes are available but many of them are too lumpy and insensitive for good work. Flexible steel palettes, are invaluable for working on large surfaces and built-up forms. 'Surform' tools and clay planes do a similar job. An ordinary penknife or a small fettling knife can be used as the clay hardens. Good metal tools are made in a variety of spatula and saw-tooth shapes. One can cut one's own tools from hardwood or even wooden meat skewers if nothing better is available, or from bamboo. Several splendid bamboo tools are now on the market. For hollowing-out a strong wire-ended tool is essential. A few familiar tools are more valuable than a wide range of expensive purchases.

Modulus, elasticity, rupture

A constant factor for converting units or indicating relationships between one system and another.

There are equations for arriving at the breaking point (the modulus of rupture) of a kiln shelf; these are essential to a manufacturer. (See Dodd/Murfin for details.)

The modulus of elasticity is the extent to which a material may be distorted under stress without failing. The industry calculates glaze-body relationships in these terms. For the average potter however, insufficient data is available to put these equations to practical use. (See also *conversion factor*.)

Mohs' scale

See *hardness scale*.

Moisture content

There is always some moisture in powdered minerals, though few of them suffer deterioration from damp. An appreciable or uneven moisture content can, however, cause error when weighing up a recipe, and one should keep all materials as dry as possible. If one of your materials is noticeably damp, dry off a weighed amount and note the loss in weight. The equivalent percentage can then be added to the *batch weight*.

Moisture crazing

Crazing due to the adsorption of water into the body after firing, causing it to swell very slightly. More likely in earthenware. Can take place days or weeks after firing. (See *crazing, adsorption.*)

Moisture expansion

See *adsorption, moisture crazing.*

Mold, mould

In its widest sense a mold is any former over or in which clay can be shaped. Molds such as one's own elbow, a sand-filled bag, or a stone, are dealt with under formers. More specifically a mold is a biscuit or *plaster of Paris* 'negative' of the shape required and is normally used for repetition work. Virtually all industrial pottery is made by means of *press molds* or *slip molds*. (See also *jigger and jolley.*)

Molded work will, inevitably, be more mechanical in appearance than hand-built or thrown pottery. The cast, however, can be treated merely as a starting point, to be worked on or beaten into a more original and creative shape. Of the types of mold used by craft potters the commonest is the dish mold, especially when decoration is the main interest. A square of cloth or canvas can be suspended from the corners to make an 'instant' mold. A rolling pin is a handy tool which can be utilized for molding or forming cylinders.

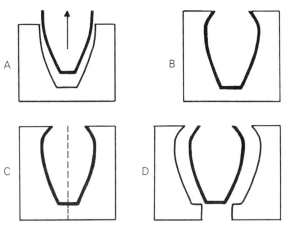

The principle of molded forms.
A The beaker shape can be lifted directly from a one-piece mold (as in jigger and jolley work).
B If the form has any shoulder or 'returning' shape, this will prevent its removal.
C and **D** Such a shape can be accommodated in a two-piece mold separated vertically as shown.

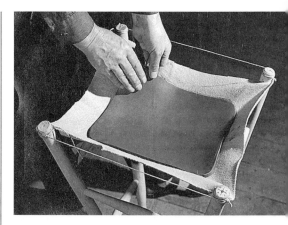

A very simple dish mold or former, using a square of cloth suspended from each leg of an inverted stool.

A lively and well-observed 'choir' of singers which look as if they might have been made from slab or pinchpots but, in fact, were pressed from cone-shaped molds and then varied by modeling, adding, and cutting away. By George Martin.

Of the true molds, the press mold is widely used (some of Leach's large square bottles, for instance) and is often combined with coiling or throwing, e.g. the neck of an oblong bottle. Slip molds are not very relevant to the craftsman, although again simple basic forms can be utilized as a base for further work, or in building larger constructions. They come into their own, however, for casting bone china and other very friable and delicate bodies.

The limitation of the mold is that it cannot deal with 'returning' forms unless it is split into sections. There is a limit to the number of pieces a mold can be divided into. Involved shapes are cast in sections in separate molds, the pieces being luted together. (See *hump molds, hollow molds, dish molds, slip molds, press molds, formers, plaster of Paris,* etc.)

Molecular formula

See *formula.*

Molecular weight

Abbreviated to m.w. The sum of the *atomic weights* of all the atoms which make up a molecule, or in the case of minerals, the whole *ideal formula*.

Examples:

Ferric oxide Fe_2O_3 = (56 x 2) + (16 x 3) = 112 + 48 = m.w. 160.

Dolomite $CaCO_3.MgCO_3$ = 40 + 12 + (16 x 3) + 24 + 12 + (16 x 3) = m.w. 184.

As mentioned under molecule, the term is used for convenience, and is not strictly accurate in cases where the first oxide or molecule mentioned in the formula is more or less than unity, an equivalent correction must be made before it can be used in glaze calculations. (See *equivalent weight*.)

Molecular weights of commonly used glaze materials:
(For molecular weights of *oxides* see under that heading.)

Albite feldspar	524	
Anorthite feldspar	278	
Barium carbonate	197.3	
Bone ash	310	(103)
Borax	381.5	
Boro-calcite	304	
China clay	258	
China stone	644	
Colemanite	412	(206)
Cristobalite	60	
Cryolite	210	(420)
Dolomite	184	
Flint	60	
Fluorspar	78	
Galena	239	
Ilmenite	152	
Lead bisilicate	343.5	
Lead monosilicate	283	
Lead sesquisilicate	313	
Lepidolite	472	
Litharge	223	
Lithium carbonate	74	
Muscovite mica	–	
Nepheline syenite	292	
Orthoclase	556	
Petalite	612	
Potassium carbonate	138	
Quartz	60	
Red lead	685	(228)
Sillimanite	162	
Sodium carbonate	106	
Spodumene	372	
Strontium carbonate	147.5	
Talc	379	(126)
White lead	775	(258)
Whiting	100	
Wollastonite	116	
Zircon	183	

Numbers in brackets indicate *equivalent weights* for glaze calculation.

Molecule

The smallest particle into which a substance can be divided while retaining the properties of the original substance. Molecules are built up of atoms united by electrical bonds. (See *atomic theory*.) Strictly speaking, only those atoms united in a covalent bond are true molecules; most salts and metallic *oxides* are *electrovalent* compounds and thus aggregates of *ions*. The true molecule is considered to exist in the gaseous state only. However, for convenience and simplicity, the term is applied (as in *molecular weight*, for instance) to any well defined combination of more than one atom. (See diagram at *covalent bond*.)

Molochite

A proprietary pre-fired china clay made by English China Clays, St Austell, UK *PCE* 1770°C/3218°F. Used as a refractory grog. Has some valuable qualities in bodies. The whiteness of Molochite makes it suitable for use in porcelain bodies which it also renders more refractory and slump resistant. Because it has been vitrified at great heat, the 'free' silica is combined with alumina to produce mullite and silica glass. Hamer warns that not all calcined china clays mentioned in catalogs are Molochite which is a registered product made only by English China Clays.

Supplied in various mesh sizes — sand-80s, 16–30s, etc. Molochite is listed by Whitfield and Sons, Cromartie, Potterycrafts, and others.

Molybdenum

MoO_3, 144. Very high melting point. **Toxic**.
Sometimes used in the industrial preparation of yellow stains and in glazes as a stabilizer.

Mono, monoxide

One, single. Used in chemistry to indicate one atom or molecule in a combination, e.g. CaO, one atom of calcium to one of oxygen; lead monosilicate $PbO.SiO_2$ has one molecule of lead oxide to one of silica.

Monothermite

A mineral, $0.2R_2O$, Al_2O_3, $3SiO_2$, $1.5 H_2O$, produced by the weathering of hydrated mica, and present in fireclays.

Montmorillonite

A group of minerals allied to kaolinite and included in the clay 'family'. They differ from kaolinite in being of a much finer grain, often containing magnesia, and having a slightly different cell structure (details in Cardew and Worrell). 'Small flat hexagonal crystals', Hamer. The name originates from its original discovery in Montmorillon in France.

The bonds between the layers are weaker, allowing more water to penetrate. The outer layers of electrons exhibit a negative charge which together with a less stable structure allows the substitution of *bases* (Ca, Mg, Na, Fe, especially) for some of the alumina.

The composition is therefore very variable. The weaker 'bonds' also mean that they sheer easily and this gives the material an exceptional kind of plasticity. However its very high shrinkage and the release of silica during firing preclude its use alone or in any great quantity in a pottery body. The usual form of the mineral used by potters is *bentonite*, and the proportion in a body or glaze 2–3%. There are montmorillonites with little or no plasticity, e.g. *fuller's earth*.

It is thought possible that most secondary clays contain some montmorillonite in their make-up. The mineral is usually the result of the decomposition of basic rocks such as *basalt*, rather than acidic *granite*.

Mop

A large round floppy brush without a point. Does not leave brushmarks to the same degree as do flat dusters and is thus suitable for laying on washes or large brushstrokes.

Mortar

Bricklaying mortar for kiln-building is usually a mixture of 10–30% fine grog with fireclay or china clay. A little soda silicate, about $\frac{1}{8}$ of a pint to 10lb of dry clay (or 0.07 liters to 4.5kg) may be added to give a degree of dry setting. The mortar is used in an almost liquid state and is spread thinly — 'buttered' — on. It is less a jointing material than a leveling bed.

Normal bricklayer's mortar is composed of lime and sharp sand. This may be used for exterior work exposed to the weather. Sand/cement is not generally recommended.

Grinding a teaspoonful of color in a mortar.

Cardew warns against the use of mortar in the foundations of a kiln.

Commercial heat resistant mortars are available, e.g. Sairset, which can also be used as a *kiln wash*.

Mortar and pestle

Mortars, thick-walled semi-circular bowls generally made of biscuit porcelain, and pestles of the same material on a wooden handle, are used together for grinding materials; however they are used much less frequently, now that most minerals are supplied in a finely ground form. For experimental quantities they are still useful, for grinding a rock sample, for instance. Do not overfill the mortar — a teaspoonful at a time will grind more efficiently than a larger quantity. All materials must first have been broken to at least sand-size with a hammer. For general workshop requirements a *ball* or *jar mill* can replace the mortar and pestle.

Mosaic

Small pieces of stone or ceramic fitted together to form an overall pattern or design. The traditional mosaic is flat, or with the pieces very slightly tilted to catch the light. Modern mosaic or wall-decoration includes the use of impressed, textured and three-dimensional effects.

Small tiles or 'tesserae' can be cut from slabs of clay and finished either separately or in blocks. In the latter case a fairly coarse (wide) cut is taken not quite through the clay, the tesserae being broken apart at a later stage. With care they can be glazed as a block. Mosaics can be built up from random pieces; from more formal units such as a square or triangle; or from pieces shaped to fit the design. The last involves drawing the design full scale on a sheet of thin paper and dividing it into conveniently shaped pieces which are numbered on the reverse side. The design is then laid on a slab of clay, the shapes and numbers traced through with a suitable tool. If too large to be conveniently handled as a whole it can be cut into sections, each laid on a slab of clay. The clay pieces are cut apart when at soft-leather stage, and trimmed. They must be glazed individually and reference can again be made to the original design as regards color. Glazed tesserae should be set on alumina for firing. The tedious work of glazing can be avoided by the use of vitrified *colored bodies. Egyptian paste* and *enamels* are other possibilities. The breaking of glazed slabs or tiles into pieces is not very satisfactory. A tile cutter could be used but this is also a long job.

It is difficult to dry large or long pieces of tesserae so that they remain flat. One system is to lay them on an absorbent material (e.g. kiln shelves or *Asbestolux*) and dry quickly on a hot surface such as the top of a firing kiln or a stove.

The pieces can be assembled in several ways:

1 As the Byzantine mosaics were set; piece by piece into a cement background, e.g. a lime mortar (or a retarded plaster of Paris could be used).

2 If the tesserae are of even thickness, or an uneven surface is acceptable, they can simply be glued onto a wooden base.

3 If the face needs to be quite flat, e.g. for a table top, the pieces must either be assembled face down, or a sheet of 'Contact' or other adhesive plastic laid over the glazed face and smoothed on. Sandwich the whole mosaic between two boards and turn it over. Level the back with a fairly liquid cement (no sand) or with a proprietary tile cement. Battens fastened alongside the mosaic can help in achieving a level. The whole can be adhered to a wooden base either with a bonding glue or even with a layer of Polyfilla or similar cement. The mosaic must be turned face-up before the cement has quite set (usually three or four hours

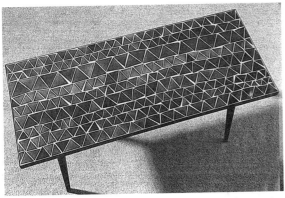

A mosaic table of earthenware triangles in blue and turquoise glazes, by Robert Fournier and Albert Shelly.

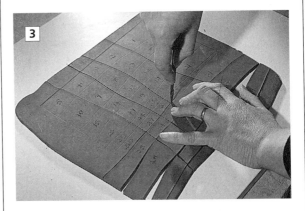

Transferring a design from a drawing to clay tesserae for building into a mosaic.

1 The design is made on tracing paper and each piece numbered.

2 The sheet of paper is reversed and laid onto a slab of clay, the shapes and the numbers traced through with a pointed (but not sharp) tool.

3 The numbers will now be on the back of the tesserae which, with the paper removed, can be cut apart with a knife.

later) so that the design can be cleaned off and grouted with a similar material. To grout, wipe over with a liquid mixture, working it into all the cracks, then wipe the tesserae clean with a rag. An edging, preferably of metal, is needed to finish off a table. This can either be made to size and dropped over the finished mosaic, screwed to the wooden base, or it can be made in angle iron and fitted over the back while the mosaic is reversed, and previous to the final grouting, Mosaics can also be built up on plastic clay by pressing pellets of colored body on to the dampened surface. This is very suitable for mosaic tiles in schools.

Mother of pearl luster

Bismuth and tin oxide lusters can give this iridescent effect. (See *lusters*.) Potterycrafts list a mother-of-pearl spray (600–800°C/1112–1472°F) for use on clear glazes.

Mud kiln

See *Leca granules*.

Mudstones

Some river deposits of dust and mud such as *Keuper marls* have formed clays.

Muffle, muffle kiln

In a kiln, an internal shell or box which protects pottery from the effect of flame or hot gases, these being directed between muffle and kiln wall. A saggar is a kind of muffle. Some gas kilns are semi-muffle, protected at the base and about halfway up the walls.

Muffle colors

A term applied to enamels fired in a muffle kiln.

Mug

See *beaker*.

Mulberry color

A pigment color obtained from a mixture of cobalt and manganese.

Muller

See *glass muller*.

Mullite

A compound of alumina and silica, $3Al_2O_3.2SiO_2$, m.p 1880°C/3416°F, which results from the dissociation o kaolinite at high temperatures. This leaves a proportion o free silica which is steadily converted into *cristobalite* up to 1660°C/3020°F. Some mullite begins to form at 1000°C 1832°F, and most of the alumina is in this form a 1340°C/2444°F. The crystals are needle-shaped and are believed to have a 'felting' effect, strengthening stoneware and porcelain bodies. Mica at stoneware temperatures produces mullite (Cardew). Can be added to clay bodies.

Mullite grog, 48 mesh and 100 mesh, is listed by PSH (Pottery Supply House).

Multiple brush

A Chinese brush with pegs which fit into a second and further brush handles. Various designs can be achieved with multiple brushes which a potter can construct. (See *brush*.)

Multi-wire clay cutter

See *harp, bow*.

Multi-zone control

Scutt Kilns offer a system with a thermocouple in various parts of their electric kilns, programmed to even out a firing.

Muscovite

A mica with the theoretical composition (Na_2K_2O). $3Al_2O_3. 6SiO_2. 2H_2O$. The form of mica considered to be a constituent of most clays. (See *mica*.)

Mushroom mold

A convex dish mold on a stem or stand, over which plates and dishes can be formed. (See *hump-mold*.)

Musical instruments

Many types of musical instruments can be made in ceramic. In CR123 Erik Mandaville investigates several of these. See *bell, drum, flute, ocarina, whistle*.

Naples yellow

A color derived from *antimonate of lead* with a little ferric iron for use at temperatures up to about 1090°C/1994°F. Use as a pigment, or add 5–10% to glazes.

Natrium

An element, symbol Na, see *sodium*. 'Washing soda' is a crystalline sodium carbonate; 'natron', a sesquicarbonate.

Natural gas

A very clean gas, mostly methane, as derived from wells or bore-holes in the earth's crust. (See *gas fuel*.)

Neck

The narrow terminating section, often more or less elongated, of a bottle-shaped pot. A long neck may be thrown separately, or thrown onto the shoulder of a pot from a thick coil. See film 'David Leach' (Films for Potters).

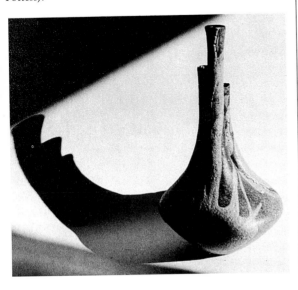

A triple-necked hand-built stoneware bottle with poured glaze. The necks were formed round a brush handle. By Robert Fournier.

A variety of necks applied to identical bodies, showing how the whole impression of the form is dependent on the type of neck.

Necklace

See *bead*.

Needle awl, *pricker*

'Pricker' is the American term. A fine awl for cutting clay. A simple type can be made by pushing a coarse needle through a cork, but this will snap off rather easily. Commercial awls are stronger and are set in a wooden handle. Use 'fine' grades for clay cutting, especially for the rims of thrown pots; thicker awls with a blunt point for less delicate work. The use of a dart has been suggested to avoid the dangerous loss of needles in clay.

Using a needle awl (pricker) to level the top rim of a thrown pot. Note the oblique angle which avoids rucking the clay (not to mention spearing the finger!), and the positions of the other fingers ready to whip away the ring of clay as soon as the cut is complete.

Negative expansion

Only one oxide, that of boron, expands on cooling, i.e. has a negative value for its coefficient of expansion. (See *coefficients of expansion*.)

NEMA receptacle guide

The National Electrical Manufacturers' Association guide to Canadian and USA plug receptacles (sockets).

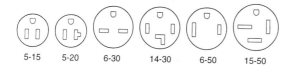

| 5-15 | 5-20 | 6-30 | 14-30 | 6-50 | 15-50 |

USA receptacle guide, courtesy Georgies catalog. The numbers refer to the recommended load in amperes.

Nepheline syenite

Nepheline, an igneous rock, is theoretically $Na_2O.Al_2O_3.2SiO_2$ but as it almost invariably contains some potash it may be written $K_2O.3Na_2O.4Al_2O_3.8SiO_2$, 1168, equivalent weight 292, m.p. 1200°C/2192°F. Syenite is a crystalline rock of feldspar and hornblende.

The natural material is variable in constitution but always high in alumina and soda when compared with feldspar. It usually contains some iron which can be extracted magnetically. Deposits in Canada and Norway.

It is an interesting material to use in glazes, making possible formulas which are difficult to convert with feldspar. It is also used in small quantities in porcelain bodies.

A typical analysis by weight:

Na_2O	8.1	Al_2O_3	24.9
CaO/Mgo	1.7	Fe_2O_3	0.1
SiO_2	56.3	K_2O	1.7

Compare with any *feldspar* percentage analysis. It differs from spar in tending to have a more defined *melting point* and at a lower temperature. In stoneware glazes it can be used empirically to replace some of the feldspar. 'May be used in clay bodies to reduce crazing — i.e. increases vitrification' (Georgies). Rarely used in earthenware but a recipe was given in CM 19/6 (Behrens):

Nepheline syenite	69
Frit (3134)	20
Whiting	10
Bentonite	1

Neriage, neritage

A form of decoration originating in Japan. Slabs of contrasting clays are laid one on another, cut into strips, and rolled or folded into a block. These are sliced end-on so that a whorl or other design of marbled color is obtained. The pieces are pressed into a mold side by side to form a continuous skin, often with subsequent additions and modifications. Saskia Koster (Netherlands) makes paper

The technique of neriage is not a new one as this bowl from Song China proves.

A startling and involved 'Lunar Bowl' in neriage technique by Dorothy Feibleman.

Spirals derived from the neriage technique — used as inlays. By Felicity Aylieff.

models in order to determine the planes of her architectural forms. The pieces need very slow drying. Many potters first fire the piece to biscuit and then work on the surface with wet-and-dry silicon carbide paper to give a smooth sheen.

Neriage has become very popular in the West. The many variations on the bowl shape are the most popular but involved and highly decorative forms are achieved by Dorothy Feibleman and others. The technique is very suitable for jewelry. See Fournier DPD for more details and illustrations. (See also *agate, rolled inlay*.)

Net

See *Internet*.

Network, *former, modifier*

A molecular three-dimensional pattern of linked atoms, a *lattice*. In glass this pattern has a certain underlying regularity of formation but is random in detail (*amorphous* or non-crystalline).

Only a few acidic oxides can initiate a glass network (see *glass-formers*); the chief of these is silica. On its own, silica needs a very high temperature to vitrify or develop a glassy nature, but the atomic pattern can be loosened, or modified by other oxides so that a fluid material is formed at a lower temperature — as low as 650°C/1202°F. The larger atoms intrude into the network and, themselves having weaker *electrical bonds*, lower the cohesion of the whole structure. Sodium and potassium have the ideal *ionic valency* and radii for this purpose. Calcium is interesting in that small quantities will modify a glass above about 1080°C/1976°F and yet the glaze (or the body, in the case of *bone china*) will tend to be stable and viscous. At higher temperatures and concentrations, however, this behavior may be reversed and 20% or more at 1290°C/2354°F can make a glaze very fluid.

Neutral atmosphere

A kiln atmosphere which is neither strongly oxidizing nor reducing. The flame uses all the available oxygen without forming carbon monoxide — a state of perfect combustion. An electric kiln is usually neutral although the combustion of impurities in body or glaze can cause a slightly reducing atmosphere in a tightly closed kiln.

Neutron

The electrically neutral particle in an atomic core. (See *atomic theory*.)

Newclay

A proprietary name for a clay containing nylon fibers which give it a degree of dry strength. For use in junior schools where it is not intended to fire the work into ceramic. Its principal use is in modeling. Hardeners can also be added to form cements as the clay dries. Supplied by Newclay Products Ltd. There are also other types of clay mixes which develop some physical strength without firing, sold by some of the larger suppliers.

Nextel

A proprietary name for mullite fibers.

Nichrome wire

A *resistance wire* suitable for temperatures up to 1100°C/2012°F, e.g. Kanthal Nikrothal wire, in electric kilns.

Nickel

A metallic element Ni, 59.
Black nickelous oxide NiO, 75, s.g. 6.7.
Green nickel carbonate NiCO₃.
Black nickelic oxide Ni₂O₃, 166. Also quoted as NiO₂. Black nickel. Decomposes into the monoxide at 600°C/1112°F.

A fairly refractory oxide, producing in oxidation muted browns, grays, and greens, of a not usually very exciting nature. Tends to be unstable at over about 1200°C/2192°F, 'causing a scum' (Hamer).

Between 1–3% is soluble or partially soluble in a soft glaze, the lower percentage tending to gray, the higher to brown, but with varying effect in different types of glaze; at its least attractive in *borax glazes*. It often contaminates cobalt to which it is a near neighbor in the periodic table. Will tend to increase glaze mattness. Nickel and zinc are reputed to give pinks and mauves in a barium glaze. Gives uncertain and sometimes unexpected colors in reduction: Rhodes mentions yellow and purple; blue has also been mentioned. The tendency towards blue in any type of glaze will be increased by the addition of zinc oxide. A formula quoted in Webb CNS is:

ZnO	0.33	SiO₂	2.5
PbO	0.32	N₂O	0.35
Al₂O₃	0.2	B₂O₃	0.2

Nickel with titanium in a feldspathic glaze has been known to produce yellow. Hamer mentions its use in *black* colors and Georgies blues. Lithium has been recommended for inclusion in nickel glazes. Nickel is most often used to 'quench' or modify other coloring oxides.

'Nichrome' is a nickel/chrome *resistance wire*.

Nitrogen

The second constituent (with oxygen) of pure air. It is inert and, in a firing, takes a great deal of energy (fuel) to heat up. It is important, therefore, only to admit sufficient air into a kiln to combine the oxygen and fuel into carbon dioxide; any excess is wasteful of energy. The Glendale Control leaflet states that one third of the input (natural gas is quoted) is 'wasted' in heating the nitrogen in the air intake. The weight of this nitrogen is quoted in tons! The use of an *oxygen/carbon sensor* could therefore save both fuel and firing time.

Non-ceramic bodies, surfaces, finishes

Outside the scope of this book but, nevertheless, used by some potters. So-called *cold colors* are paints, as are certain 'glaze finishes' (known as organic powder coatings), some of which are fairly permanent and need only a kitchen-oven temperature of about 200°C/392°F to 'fix'.

Wax and teak oil, buttermilk, house paints, acrylics and lacquer have been used on biscuit. More permanent have been metal rims and lids, and decorative and formal wire, wood, metal, and plastic additions to ceramic work. Gold leaf has been glued on. (See also at *gloss ware, polishing, porosity, unfired clay*.)

Non-vitreous, non-vitrified

A pottery body in which the glass phase is absent or has barely begun, e.g. soft earthenware or any porous biscuit. In the USA the official definition is a water *absorption* above 10% for pottery or 7% for tiles.

Notched rim

Indenting the rim, especially of cooking dishes, is not only decorative but also compresses and consolidates the edge. The work can be done with the finger, with a wooden or metal tool, or with a *roulette* which is quicker and gives a more regular pattern. (See also *coggle*.)

Ocarina

From the Italian for 'little goose'. An ovoid pottery wind-instrument, traditionally of porcelain but can be made from any pottery material. (For details of the mouthpiece, see *whistle*.) There should be eight fingerholes. To quote Scholes: 'the pitch is affected by the number of holes left open, i.e. if one hole is left open it does not much matter which, and so with more than one'. The range of the notes will rise as the clay shrinks in drying and firing and it is difficult to get a particular pitch. The notes are controlled by the size of holes not by their position which can be purely for comfort in use (Neil Ions CR90). CM19/2 also gives advice on making the instrument. The ocarina has a pleasant sound when properly used.

The whistle or ocarina in bird form has a long history (the original meaning of ocarina is 'little goose') and this is a charming modern variation by Neil Ions.

Ochre

A natural *hydrated* earthy *ferric oxide*, ideally, $Fe_2O_3.H_2O$, 178, but together with impurities and often some clay and sulfur. Very variable.

Yellow ochre contains hydrated iron oxide: red ochre anhydrous ferric oxide.

Yellow ochre can be calcined at 550–600°C/1022–1112°F to form red ochre, which is more stable and inert, or the red (terracotta) ochre can be purchased already prepared. Both forms can be used in slips, pigments, and glazes, though the yellow ochre sometimes has a *flocculating* effect which makes it difficult to use in any quantity in a glaze or slip batch. The raw ochre usually produces a yellower color than iron oxide, because of the bleaching action of calcium impurities, which effect, however, can be reversed at high temperatures and in reduction. Leach suggests using calcined ochre for celadon glazes. He also quotes Old Seto Yellow as containing 25–40% ochre, the glaze used thinly and oxidized. Emmanuel Cooper puts as much as 20% in his 'oil spot' glaze at 1260°C with nepheline 70% and alkaline frit 10%.

Ochre is commonly used as a reduction vehicle in *lusters*.

Ohm

Symbol Ω. A unit of electrical resistance, named after G. S. Ohm, a German physicist, (1787–1854).

Example: To obtain 30 amps at 240 volts in an electric kiln we need a wire resistance of 240 (E) ÷ 30 (I) = 8 (R) ohms. Element wire is rated at ohms per ft.

Thus if the wire you are using has a figure of 0.07 ohms per ft length then you will need 8 ÷ 0.07 = 114 ft.
Useful equations:

$$\frac{E}{I} \quad or \quad \frac{E^2}{P} \quad or \quad \frac{P}{I^2}$$

(E in volts, I in amperes, P in watts. For further clarification see *electrical symbols*.)

Oil, fuel, burner

Various grades of petroleum can be used in the firing of pottery, the more unrefined oils producing more smoke. A medium grade has been quoted at 135,000 *Btu* per gallon (3.3 mJ per liter).

Oil must be transformed from a liquid into a mist or vapor before it will burn efficiently. This can most simply be done by drip-feed onto a hot metal plate; more controllably by atomizing the oil by means of a jet of air at the burner. This involves the provision of air-pressurizing equipment. Rhodes K describes several types of burner. The domestic heating burner would be adequate for a 2cu ft/(0.06cu m) chamber but lacks control and would probably give too rapid a heat rise. The 'Swirlamiser' burner is reasonably priced and has had good reports. All oil kilns will burn more effectively when hot.

The advantages of oil over other fuels are its relative cheapness and the ease with which its temperature and atmosphere can be controlled. On the other hand it tends to be noisy and smoky, while the flame is not kind to kiln refractories. It is more suitable for high-fired pottery than for earthenware. (See also *drainoil, forced draft*.)

Oil-fired kiln

Oil is most efficient in medium and large kilns — 10cu ft/0.3cu m and upwards. Built on the site, they are often constructed by the potter. Some detailed instructions were given in CR16. Rhodes K deals quite extensively with oil kilns, as do several other books including Cardew, Leach, Olsen, etc.

Oil-fired kilns tend to be variable in performance and need a reasonably isolated site because of the noise and smoke—not to mention a 600 gallon tank some 12–16ft/3.5–5m above the ground (although pumped oil from a surface tank is also a possibility). A low, stable flame is difficult to maintain at the beginning of the firing and some potters practice pre-heating with *bottled gas*.

Oil spot glaze

An effect which occurs on the surface of a high iron reduced stoneware glaze. Sometimes crystalline formations can have a silvery appearance. Both Sutherland and Hamer suggest the use of *mafic* materials (containing iron, magnesia, and lime) and 'mudstones' such as *Keuper Marl* in a viscous glaze, taking care not to overfire. Albany slip has been mentioned used with ochre, spodumene, and feldspar. Also the use of two layers of glaze, the top layer being the more fluid, the under layer containing an excess of iron — up to 30%.

Once-fired pottery, glazing

Also known as green- or raw-glazed, or single fired pottery. A technique which bypasses the *biscuit* stage by glazing the raw clay and firing both together. There are hazards, especially when using the average commercially supplied body: collapse or blistering due to rapid absorption of liquid from the glaze; the scaling away of the glaze due to shrinkage differences; and the bubbling of the fired glaze. However, a majority of the world's ceramics have been once-fired and a number of modern potters have successfully overcome these difficulties, including Colin Pearson in stoneware, Lucie Rie in porcelain, and Alan Frewin in slipware.

The traditional once-fired earthenware glaze has a high lead content together with some plastic clay. A simple example (firing at 1100°C/2012°F) based on suggestions by Alan Frewin is given on the next page (suitable for decorative pottery, especially slipware, but see *soluble lead* if tableware is envisaged).

Lead sesquisilicate	58
Body clay	38
Whiting	4

Used on body of 45% red clay, 45% buff clay, and 10% grog.

It is also possible to adapt leadless and, of course, stoneware and porcelain glazes for once-fired ware. Some plastic clay (varying between 10% and 40%) is normally added to the glaze batch to allow for the necessary shrinkage. The glaze can be applied at the *leather-hard* stage, though some clays with a high dry strength and low absorption will take the glaze when quite dry. In some cases, however, glazing a bone-dry body can lead to the development of bubbles in the fabric (bloating) both before and during firing; thin walled pots being no less liable to trouble than thick ones. In spite of this, in his book, a valuable and enthusiastic guide to the technique, Parks recommends bone-dry clay and appears to have little trouble with it. If a bubble does develop his instructions are to press the blister flat from both sides.

Alan Graham (CR75) suggests a deflocculated glaze so that less water is taken up for a given thickness of glaze. Obviating the water absorption problems entirely, Dennis Parks dusts dry glaze or wood ash straight onto damp flattish surfaces or onto the shoulders of pots, etc. This can be most effective on a damp slip or siccative, but it must be remembered that dusting is always a health hazard and an effective mask is advisable.

Christopher Buras, in CR84, also ignores the possible blisters from water adsorption and glazes 'white bone-dry pots' quickly and thinly with the following glaze recipe. There is no magic about the body he uses — the well-tried Potclays St Thomas' Body (oxidizing).

Ball clay	10
Petalite	20
Potash feldspar	40
Quartz	10
Dolomite	10
Bentonite	5

He fires at 1250°C/2282°F in an electric kiln.

Almost any recipe can be adapted for glazing on unfired clay but experimentation will always be necessary to achieve a glaze which will match the shrinkage and other characteristics of the body you are using. To adapt a stoneware glaze one can start with a normal biscuit-glazing recipe and replace the china clay with ball clay, e.g. 50 feldspar, 20 whiting, 20 ball clay, 10 flint. A little bentonite will increase shrinkage if the glaze peels. Zinc oxide has a high drying shrinkage if it can be accommodated in the formula. (See *Bristol glaze*.)

According to Parks the clay can be adjusted for minimum absorption by a *pH value* as near neutral as possible.

A binder or added bentonite in glazes can help to avoid lifting off, especially when one is poured over another. Up to 12% of bentonite has been suggested, replacing either the ball clay or the feldspar in the recipe.

Isaac Button glazed inside and out at one go but his was a remarkable clay and, for the average potter, it is safer to glaze the inside and leave for an hour or so before tackling the outside. To accommodate the expansion Dennis Parks lightly sponges or sprays the unglazed area with water, especially the outsides or bases of bowls and large plates. Handles will dry before the body of the pot and should be protected or moistened. Spray equipment is useful for large structures. Glaze can also be brushed on though this tends to drag on dry clay and is easier on leather-hard surfaces.

The ware needs careful and thorough drying and a steady firing with plenty of ventilation to allow the easy escape of *hydrocarbons* from the body which the covering glaze will tend to inhibit. A burst pot can obviously cause widespread damage with the whole load needing to be unpacked and cleaned.

The firing cycle must combine the typical *graphs* of a *biscuit* and a *glaze* firing and it may therefore take a longer firing than either alone (see also *firing*). Interaction between body and glaze is greater than when the glazing is done on the biscuit. Some of the body surface will combine with the glaze to assist its maturity, especially in earthenware. Slips and engobes must be of adequate thickness or they will become transparent or disappear completely.

On-glaze

Color applied to a pre-fired ceramic, generally at a low temperature. (See *enamels*.) A very wide range of color is available at 700–900°C/1292–1652°F. It is a more explicit term than 'overglaze' which may also include *maiolica* painting. True on-glaze color adheres to the surface of a glaze but barely penetrates it. Color can also be brushed, sprayed, or otherwise applied to a fired glaze to give a more permanent and integrated effect than enamels though without their brightness and sharp outlines. (See also *ground-lay, overglaze,* and *tin-glaze*.)

Opacity, opacifiers

When light cannot pass through a glaze but is reflected back from its surface, the glaze is termed opaque. Opacity is caused either by reflective matter suspended in the glaze, or by an uneven (*matt*) surface (see also *translucent*). Most glazes will become transparent or nearly so if fired to a high enough temperature.

The principal opacifying agents operate by remaining as

uspended, white, undissolved particles distributed through a glaze, as minute bubbles, or in the case of zirconium and titanium as recrystallization during cooling (it follows that slow cooling when using these materials is useful, see also below). The main opacifying agents are the oxides of *tin*, *zirconium*, *titanium*, and *zinc*; the average addition to a *soft glaze* being 8–12%; rather less for stoneware. A degree of opacity can be caused by the formation of crystals on the surface, which can be stimulated by calcia and baria in quantities in excess of their requirement in the fluxing process. Chrome is an opacifying coloring oxide. Refractory oxides such as alumina can be increased in a glaze giving an opacity which is linked with a matt surface. Bubbles which have been unable to escape from an earthenware glaze (often inhibited by too thick a coating) may appear as uneven milky white patches. The formation of crystals to induce opacity is assisted by low alumina levels in the formula.

Opalescent

Applied to a semi-translucent, cloudy glaze showing iridescence. Like an opal. A high boron content can induce opalescence (Rhodes) and it is a quality sometimes found in reduced raku glazes. The so-called 'jun' glazes (relatively high in magnesia and low in alumina) show opalescence. Iridescence often results from raku reduction or smoking. (See *color*, *optical color*.)

Open body

A body with large pores. Usually contains grog. Normally applied to unfired clay mixtures. At stoneware temperatures an open body may *vitrify* but the surface texture will remain characteristically rough or coarse.

Very fine-grain clays need 'opening' with *fireclays*, *calcined china clay*, or *grog*. Grog is more efficient in assisting drying than the addition of *sand*. An open body will usually have a lower wet/dry shrinkage and greater standing strength, but also faster water *absorption*. A low-fired open body will have high resistance to *thermal shock*. Modeling clays are usually open to allow for possibly excessive wall thicknesses.

Optical color

Certain glazes without coloring oxides will nevertheless give an appearance of color, e.g. Jun. The effect arises from very fine particles which approximate to the wavelengths of light, e.g. around 0.5 *microns*. A very thin coating on a glaze can also produce color, like oil on water; bismuth mother-of-pearl luster is an example. The colors are frequently bluish. Cardew mentions the hypothesis of the suspension of one glass or glaze within another to explain *Jun* blues.

Optical decoration, effect

A term which has been coined to describe deliberate decorative or formal disorientating or illusory effects.

Optical pyrometer

Commonly the 'disappearing filament' type, where the temperature is measured by the comparison of two light sources: firstly the light from a lamp filament, which is adjustable and secondly the light radiated through the kiln spyhole. Both are viewed through a red filter which renders them monochromatic. The system takes advantage of the fact that the intensity of light at any one wavelength depends on the temperature of the 'hot body'. The brightness of the filament is adjusted until it matches that of the kiln when it will apparently disappear. The setting on a connected ammeter reads on a scale as a temperature. The device needs recalibrating at intervals. If your kiln has a small spyhole some sort of stand or tripod is essential. It has been found to produce somewhat subjective results.

Orange-peel glaze

A finely crinkled surface usually associated with *salt-glazes* and which will vary in texture according to the grain-size of the underlying body. A sprayed-on glaze will also sometimes develop this texture.

An extreme 'orange-peel' effect, resembling crawling, from soda-glazing. By Ruthanne Tudball.

Organic bond

A gum or starch added to a material or body to give *dry strength*. These fire away.

Organic chemistry

The chemistry of substances produced by living organisms as distinct from the inorganic chemistry of substances of mineral origin. More recently confined to the study of carbon compounds, excluding the metallic *carbonates* and the oxides and sulfides of carbon (Uvarov). The term is useful in a general sense but can be imprecise in particular instances, e.g. calcium carbonate deposits which are considered inorganic but are formed of the accumulation of myriads of the shells of once-living creatures.

Orthoclase

Potash feldspar $K_2O.Al_2O_3.6SiO_2$, 556. (See *feldspar*.)

Orton cones

American pyrometric cones. They are numbered in a similar way to Staffordshire and Seger cones but their temperature equivalents differ and there are complicated tables for speed of heat rise and size (length) of cone. As with all heat measuring devices, experience is a better guide than lists of temperature equivalents. (See also *cones*.)

The range for standard 63mm cones at a temperature rise of 150°C/302°F per hour is given in the chart.

It will be seen that the equivalents given in Rhodes are variations on the temperatures quoted by suppliers of the cones, especially in the 7–11 range. His glaze recipes presumably refer to his cone chart, e.g. cone 9, the glaze melting at around 1250°C/2282°F. Evan Rutherford offers his experience of Orton cones in CR86 and has found that Seger cone 8 more nearly equals Orton 9 which doesn't coincide with the above tables though it is nearest to column four. As they are all based on similar principles the rate of firing should not be a factor, but see first paragraph above. It is the results that you obtain from your particular kiln and methods of firing which are important. Trial firings are essential.

Oval shape

Oval dishes may, of course, be pressed in oval molds (see note below), or they may be derived from circular thrown bowls either by beating or by the following method. Cut a leaf-shaped sliver from the center of the base (which must be thrown with a reasonable and even thickness). Only

Orton Cones

Temperature at which the point of the cone has curved over level with its base. See temperature degree for Fahrenheit conversions.

Orton Cone No	Temp. °C	Nearest Seger	Temp. given in RCGP
020	635	021	
018	717	018	
016	792	015	
015	804	014	
013	852	012	
011	894	010	875
010	894	010	
09	923	09	930
08	955	08a	
07	984	06	974
06	999	05	
05	1046	03a	1030
04	1060	02	
03	1101	1	1080
02	1120	2	1095
01	1137	3	1110
1	1154	3a	
2	1162	4	1135
3	1168	4a	1145
4	1186	5a	1165
5	1196	6	
6	1222	6a	1190
7	1240	7a	1210
8	1263	8a	1225
9	1280	9	1250
10	1305	10	1260
11	1315	11	1285
12	1326	11	1310
13	1346	12	1350

about $3/16$in/5mm at the widest point need be removed. Make the cuts at an angle, both sides sloping the same way, damp the faces with slip and ease them together by pressure from each side of the dish. The work should be done at the *soft-leather* stage. Another method is to cut out two sections near opposite walls of the dish and to press the faces together again. These joins tend to be stronger than the center cut illustrated. Oval pots are usually pressed into shape; beating may destroy the surface quality. A third system employs a previously thrown sturdy wall and rim which is luted onto a thrown slab cut to the required shape.

To draw an oval; lay a sheet of paper on a drawing board or wooden surface. Fix two drawing pins at a distance from

A glaze-trailed oval oven dish by Ray Finch.

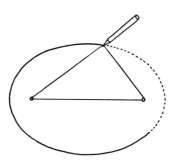

System of drawing an oval as described in text.

Forming an oval dish from a circular thrown one.

1 and *2* A narrow leaf shape is marked in and cut away at an oblique angle.

3 The faces of the slot are slipped and brought together by pressure on the walls of the pot, allowing the angled cuts to ride a little over one another so that a firm join can be smoothed over.

one another $1\frac{1}{8}$–$3\frac{7}{8}$in/30–100mm less than the breadth of size of oval that you require. Make a loop of string which, when held taut, from one pin, extends $\frac{5}{8}$–2in/15–50mm beyond the second pin. With the loop over both pins, hold the string taut with the point of a pencil and the oval can be drawn by moving the pencil round the loop of string. The larger the loop compared with the distance between the pins, the nearer the shape will approach a circle. (See diagram.)

Ovenware

There are a number of factors governing the efficiency of ceramic cooking vessels. Our chief concern is with the expansion and contraction which occurs at oven temperatures. A low-fired open body like that of African cooking pots, and some Mediterranean and European wares, can accommodate these strains within the fabric of the pot (see also *flame-proof ware*). At harder earthenware temperatures some cristobalite will form in the body. This helps to prevent crazing, an important factor in hygiene (though Cardew maintains that a case of food poisoning due to a crazed cooking vessel has still to be proved), but cristobalite also has an *inversion* within the oven range. A reasonably open-bodied earthenware dish fired below 1050°C/1922°F and with a low-expansion glaze (see *coefficients of expansion*) is, theoretically, the most likely to be successful. Against this is the fact that porous ware has low conductivity and heat applied to one point will not rapidly be dispersed through the fabric. Oven heat, however, is reasonably even; it is when taking the dish from the oven and putting it down on a metal or conductive surface that trouble may occur. This depends as much on the cook as on the potter.

A well-fired stoneware casserole has a good chance of resisting the thermal shocks of cooking, with the proviso above. Advice from various sources for increasing this resistance includes: a minimum of *free silica* in the body; the use of high alumina clays, such as high grade *fireclays*, which will help the development of *mullite* without a release of excessive silica; an *open* stoneware body, not quite *vitrified*, which may be less brittle than a glassy one; *mica* minerals and *zircon sand* have been mentioned as suitable additions to the body; the increase of thermal conductivity can be increased with *silicon carbide* (but this poses glazing problems); and the addition of sillimanite.

Finally, the form of the piece can help, a well rounded casserole approximating to the sphere being under less strain. A wide, flat base is not recommended for ovenware. (See the curved form illustrated under *flame-proof ware*.)

The glaze should, of course, be in slight *compression*. If lead is used, the glaze must be well-balanced in its formula and adequately fired. A low-solubility or a leadless glaze is advisable.

High magnesia bodies and glazes are mentioned by Behrens, and he gives recipes which include quite high proportions of *talc* and frit in both bodies and glazes. The use of *lithia* has also been suggested.

It has been suggested that a potter might be advised to take out product liability *insurance* to cover such possibilites as scalding from a defective pot.

Overalls

It is recommended that a potter's overall should be of terylene or some smooth material which will not retain dust, should not have pockets, lapels or any dust traps. (See also *dust, poisonous materials*.)

Over-firing

Over-firing means firing above the temperature which would obtain the desired result. Thus an overfired *opaque* glaze will go translucent; a *matt* glaze, shiny. The fluidity of the glaze is increased and with it the possibility of the glaze running onto the kiln shelves. *Volatilization* will lead to blistering and a thin 'starved' glaze. An over-fired glaze will always show a different color and appearance. Earthenware tin glazes will often stand considerable over firing without disastrous results. *Oxidized* stonewares are more liable to violent change in a short temperature range than are reduced ones. Very occasionally desirable characteristics may emerge but an overfired body will vitrify, probably bloat, distort and eventually melt and collapse. Prolonged soaking may have the same effect a higher temperature. Excessive over-firing will severely damage the kiln and kiln furniture. Elements should be used with a maximum temperature rating at least 50°C/122°F above the firing temperature. (See also *flashing, pyroplastic deformation*.)

An impressive heap of melted and vitrified pots and kiln furniture (see also pyroplastic deformation) from a grossly over-fired kiln which continued burning over a weekend, the 'automatic' controls failing to switch it off. (See fail-safe for means of avoiding such a calamity.)

Overglaze

Colors applied on top of the glaze. In its widest sense it includes *enamels*, though these are better described as *onglaze*. It is possible to paint onto a fired glaze with the pigment oxides or stain thickened with gum or fat oil, but overglaze color is more easily applied by the *maiolica* technique on the *raw glaze*.

A large dish by Robert Barron (Australia). Shino glaze with overglaze decoration.

Oxford clay

The raw material of many English bricks, e.g. the Peterborough Flettons (UK). Carbonaceous material burns in the brick during firing, which therefore requires a minimum of fuel.

Oxford spar

A feldspar from Maine, USA. More siliceous than English spar and approximating nearer to *china stone*. Mixed feldspars (potash and soda spars) could form an English near-equivalent.

Analysis by weight:

K₂O	7.9	Al₂O₃	17.0
Na₂O	3.2	Fe₂O₃	0.1
CaO	0.4	SiO₂	69.0

Oxidation, oxidize, oxydize

The combination of a metal or other element with oxygen to form an oxide. All pottery materials are used in the oxide form. Although one may refer to the metal as, for instance, in 'an iron glaze', it is the oxide that is always implied. The abbreviation occurs quite frequently in this book.

Heat is generated during the process of oxidation. The burning of fuel is the rapid oxidation of *carbon*, C into *carbon dioxide*, CO_2. Most elements oxidized during the cooling of the earth. Metals, etc. can be oxidized in a workshop or factory.

Oxygen is present in the atmosphere in molecules of two oxygen atoms which can receive transfer of electrons from another element according to its valency. Thus $2Mg + 2O$, $4K + 2O$, etc. are generally written MgO and K_2O respectively. Elements may have more than one oxide form, one of which will be more stable than the others.

Oxide

A compound of an *element* with oxygen. The combination may be in various ratios, e.g. 2:1 as in potash, 1:1 in lime, two ratios representing the first group of the *Seger formula* where the middle group of oxides is in 2:3 proportions; and the last group in 1:2 ratio. There are other, less common, ratios such as 3:4, e.g. magnetic iron Fe_3O_4.

Elements may combine in more than one ratio although one of these will be more stable and normally only one enters into combination in a glaze.

The suffix -a is often applied to the root name of the element to indicate the oxide. Thus, aluminum — alumina; titanium — titania; silicon — silica. The suffix -ic indicates the higher (most oxygen) ratio (the stable form) and -ous, the lower more unstable proportion. For instance: ferric — ferrous (iron); cupric — cuprous (copper); cobaltic — cobaltous.

Water is hydrogen in 2:1 combination with oxygen. It will be seen that oxides bear no obvious physical relationship to the elements which make them up. (See *compound*.) Carbonates are oxides in combination with CO_2. They are written not as $RO.CO_2$, but RCO_3 (R being the element in combination). Oxides in combination with one another form more elaborate compounds such as *minerals*. Each oxide used in pottery is discussed under the entry for each particular element. To save continual reference, however, the principal *oxides* are listed (see p.232) with their *molecular weights* or *equivalents*.

The term 'oxidation period' has also been used to indicate the range from 400–900°C/752–1652°F at which the carbonaceous matter burns away. (See *biscuit firing*, *black core*, *bloating*.)

See chart on following page.

Oxidized stoneware

Stoneware fired in a clear atmosphere with plenty of air. Electric kilns will normally have an oxidized or at least a *neutral atmosphere*. Many potters regard reduction as the apex of achievement in stonewares, but there is still a wide field to be explored in oxidation. In the latter the 'interest' must be integral to the glaze itself, and the potter's handling of it. Janet Leach, describing Hamada's Mashiko pottery, says that all 5000 pots in his eight-chamber climbing kiln were oxidized, except those in the first chamber.

In my experience, manganese and copper are more useful than iron as coloring oxides, but potters are deriving kaki and other iron stonewares from oxidized firings. (See also at *saturated glaze* and under *oxide* headings.) A recipe which gives pleasant black, deep red, and yellowish colors and which I have used on tableware for many years is:

Feldspar	51
Hardwood ash	32 (black, with carbon not fully burnt)
Flint	8
China clay	6
Bentonite	3
Red iron oxide	7.5
Synthetic iron oxide	7.5

If the glaze turns out to be dark or dead-looking, dilute with the plain glaze mixture (i.e. without the iron) until satisfactory. The type of ash will alter its behavior. Fired at

1230–1250°C/2246–2282°F in an electric kiln.

Ochre is another useful material in oxidation and 20% or more has been used in a glaze but it sometimes has an unwanted *flocculating* effect.

The maturing range of glazes seems to be shorter than in reduction, making careful and precise firing essential. The firing can be rapid — 7 to 8 hours. Up to 20% red clay can be included in the body. A *stepped firing graph*, i.e. soaking or even dropping the temperature at certain points in the firing (Japanese 'firechange') may be essential for certain effects.

Oxides

Oxide entering fusion	Molecular wt	Name	Materials commonly used to supply oxide
Al_2O_3	102	Alumina	Clay Minerals, Feldspars, Alumina Hydrate
B_2O_3	69.5	Boric Oxide (Boric Acid)	Borax, Colemanite, Frits
BaO	153.3	Baria	Carbonate, Barytes
CaO	57	Calcia, Lime	Whiting, Dolomite, Anorthite, Feldspar, Wollastonite, Wood and Bone Ash, Fluorspar, Colemanite
CoO	75	Cobalt Oxide	Black and Gray Oxides, Carbonate
Cr_2O_3	152	Chrome, Chromic Oxide	Green Oxide, Iron Chromate
CuO	79.5	Copper Oxide	Black Oxide, Carbonate, Red Oxide
Fe_2O_3	160	Iron Oxide, Ferric	Hematite, Red Ferric, Black Magnetite, Spangles, Ilmenite, Ochre, Sienna, Copperas, Red Clay, Synthetic Red Iron
K_2O	94	Potash	Orthoclase Feldspar, Pearlash (Carbonate), Nepheline, Stone, Wood Ash
Li_2O	30	Lithia	Oxide, Carbonate, Petalite, Spodumene, Amblygonite
MgO	40	Magnesia	Carbonate, Talc, Dolomite
MnO	71	Manganese Oxide	Dioxide, Carbonate
Na_2O	62	Soda	Albite Feldspar, Nepheline, Borax, Alkaline Frits, Salt, Carbonates, Silicates, China Stone
NiO	75	Nickel Oxide	Black or Green Nickel Oxide
(P_2O_5)	173	Phosphoric Oxide	Bone and Wood Ash
PbO	223	Lead Oxide	Litharge, Galena, Red and White Lead, Silicate Frits
SiO_2	60	Silica	Flint, Quartz, most Clay and Feldspathic Minerals, Talc Silicates, Frits, Lithium Minerals
SnO_2	151	Tin Oxide	Oxide
SrO	103.5	Strontia	Carbonate
TiO_2	80	Titania	Precipitated Oxide, Rutile
U_3O_8	842	Uranium Oxide	'Depleted' Oxide, Sodium Uranate
V_2O_5	182	Vanadium Oxide	Oxide, Ammonium Metavanadate
ZnO	81	Zinc Oxide	Oxide, Calcined Oxide
ZrO_2	123	Zirconia (Zircon)	Zirconium Oxide, Zircon (Silicate), various prepared forms to assist dispersion

Oxidizing fire

A clear fire with plenty of air intake, in which *oxides* remain unaltered and any elements, such as carbon, will find sufficient oxygen in which to oxidize freely. In a closed electric kiln organic matter may consume the oxygen early in the firing and give rise to a slightly *reducing* atmosphere. In a fuel-burning kiln sufficient *secondary air* must be admitted.

Earthenware, with the exceptions of *copper reds, lusters,* and some *raku,* is fired in a fully oxidizing atmosphere. (See also *stoneware glazes.*)

Oxygen

A gaseous element O, 16. An odorless invisible gas essential to life, and to combustion. The most abundant element in the earth's crust. Comprises about 21% of dry air. Present in the atmosphere as *molecules* of two oxygen *atoms.* Combines with *elements* to form *oxides.*

Oxygen /carbon sensor

An electronic instrument for the fast and accurate monitoring of kiln atmospheres in relation to the oxygen carbon balance, i.e. the proportions of oxygen, carbon dioxide and carbon monoxide. Fuel efficiency levels and the degree of reduction can thus be ascertained. Sensors can be obtained from Glendal Controls, Axner, and others. Effective for temperatures above 700°C/1292°F (red heat). (See also *nitrogen.*)

Oxygen formula

A system of calculating glaze formulas and recipes by means of comparing *cation* to oxygen ratios. It is explained in CR27 by Michael Gill. I asked John Anderson for his views on the system and he replied 'the article does not appear to make out any case for the use of the Oxygen Formula in a practical situation', and he goes on to advise that 'the Seger ... formula being directly expressed in terms of oxides — as, frequently, are compositions of minerals — would seem to make for easier conversion to a recipe.'

Packing kilns

An evenly and reasonably closely-packed kiln is not only economical but is also likely to fire better than a half empty one. Kilns and pots vary too widely to give more than a general guidance. In fuel burning kilns space must be allowed for the proper circulation of hot gases, and the pack or setting will control the behavior and efficiency of the firing. Keep the density as balanced as possible, especially in an electric kiln. Do not crowd closely packed shelves into one side of the kiln but try to disperse them.

Large kilns may be packed with a combination of *saggars* and *shelves.* In the biscuit fire, pots may be piled in *bungs*

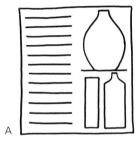

*Packing of a combination of large pots and close shelves in a kiln. In arrangement **A** the density is unbalanced and although **B** would still entail tall props it will better maintain an even temperature throughout the pack, especially in an electric kiln.*

When packing a top-loading kiln it is easy to see whether the pots are laterally separated but the height must be checked to avoid rims sticking to the underside of kiln shelves. This is most easily done by laying a strip of wood across the supports and ensuring that all rims lie below it.

(see *boxing*) but it must be remembered that clay has a degree of *pyroplasticity* at all firing temperatures and will warp under any uneven strain. An oval shape set in a round one may deform both. The rim of a jug is seldom flat and a thin tile bat should be inserted if pots are to be set on top. (See also under *biscuit firing*.)

In the gloss pack, glazed surfaces must not touch each other, although they can be set very close for high-fired stoneware, since the shrinkage during firing will further separate them. (See also *bat, bung, kiln furniture, prop*.)

In an electric kiln tall pots, especially slab pots, will incline towards the elements if packed too close to them, due to the greater shrinkage on that side.

Paddle, *paddling, paddled decoration, and anvil*

A beater or bat-shaped wooden tool (see *beater*) which can be used either for shaping or decorating pots, or for stirring glazes and slips. In America the term 'paddling' may be used for beating. Many primitive peoples used a paddle to thin a pot wall by beating it against a rounded surface (like a *darning head* and known as an anvil) held inside the pot.

Pots can be decorated by beating with carved, string-bound, or textured paddles.

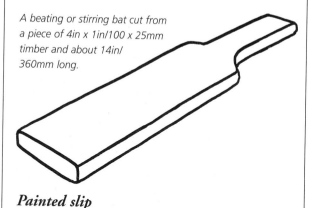

A beating or stirring bat cut from a piece of 4in x 1in/100 x 25mm timber and about 14in/ 360mm long.

Painted slip

See *brushed slip*.

Painting on pottery

Pots can be decorated with brushed color at any stage from wet clay to fired porcelain.
1 On the raw clay with *pigment oxides, slips,* or *underglaze* colors.
2 On *biscuit* with oxides or underglaze *stains* (but see *binder, hardening on, siccative*) or with specially formulated engobes.
3 On the unfired glaze with oxides or suitable glaze stains.

4 On the fired glaze with *enamels*.
All can be used on earthenware, stoneware, or porcelain, although the range of possible pigments decreases as the temperature rises. (For further discussion see *brushes, brushwork, calligraphic, maiolica, paper resist, wax resist* as well as the individual pigment oxides, etc.)

Pallet, *palette,* palette knife

The Oxford Dictionary defines a 'pallet' as 'a flat wood blade with handle used by potters'. A palette knife, however, is of flexible steel with a round-ended blade on a wooden handle, and is used for grinding and mixing colors in water or enamels in oil, working the knife from side to side on a glazed tile.

A steel palette is a thin, very flexible piece of sheet steel, usually kidney-shaped, a valuable tool. A wide variety are available from Kemper and other suppliers. (See *kidney tool*.)

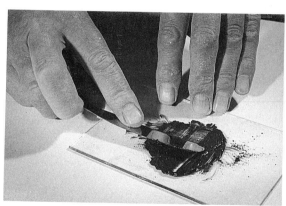

Using a palette knife for grinding and mixing colors on a tile. A sideways motion is used, raising the forward edge of the knife at each stroke to compress the color. Use a minimum of color at a time.

Pan mill

A primitive grinding mill in which hard stones (chert) are dragged over a paved area by rotating paddles. Used until recently in some English country potteries. More sophisticated mills use heavy metal rollers on a perforated metal floor, but the principle is the same. Smaller versions are available, or can be constructed by a potter. Now largely superseded by the *crusher mill*.

Paper clay

A mixture of shredded or pulped paper and clay (see also *fiber clay*) which can be very strong in its raw state and is used for masks and figures in India and Asia. In the West, however, the material is usually fired, burning out the paper and leaving traces of china clay (from the 'glazing' on the paper, though unglazed newsprint and similar papers are much easier to soak and pulp and are thus preferred) and a textural quality. A test for the suitabilty of the paper is if it tears easily then the fibers are shorter and better for paper clay.

Ewen Henderson (CR158) uses an industrial waste disposal unit to produce 'ghastly (smelly) gray stuff which I sieve out' (this, however, is not the experience of other paper clay users) and is mixed with all the clays he uses. Newsprint and wood pulp can be used with clay as a slip which is then dried sufficiently to use. Excess water can first be squeezed out using a cloth bag. Joseph Neville in CR153 suggests tearing up newsprint into small, rough squares, and immersing separate pieces in hot water with a little washing-up liquid. When soaked, roll balls of the paper onto a rough-surfaced paving slab, which will result in a grey pulp which is then mixed with the clay for use. Various types of fiber are commercially available — cardboard and newsprint; cellulose, and cotton. Nylon and polyester fibers, $\frac{1}{2}$in/12mm in length are reputed to assist dry strength, to decrease shrinkage, and even to increase plasticity according to Metrosales (GB) who recommend as little as 1 or 2g (0.04 or 0.07oz) of dry fiber to 1000g/35oz of soft clay, whereas the paper pulp can be used as strongly as 1:1, starting at 1 pulp to 4 parts thick clay slurry by volume. Most paper fibers are bio-degradable and so it is not recommended that wet mixture be stored for any great length of time. Paper clay is lighter and reputedly easier to work with than normal clay, useful when constructing large pieces, more brittle, however, as biscuit. Brian Gartside (CR150) says that paper clay has the ability to stick to itself no matter how dry or wet. It is often laid out on a plaster slab and used in this form to build vessels and constructions. It is resistant to warping. Some potters claim to be able to throw with it, others say that this cannot be done — probably depends on the type and proportion of paper used. Tucker's supply paper clay bodies (which they call P-Clay) but do not mention throwing; Axner, on the other hand, make a paper clay 'especially formulated for the wheel'.

Wet-to-dry shrinkage 6.5–7%. Surfaces can be smoothed with glass paper. One of the great advantages is that pieces can be repaired or added to when dry. Tuckers state that 'you may be able to repair bisque cracks with fresh P-Slip or P-Clay, or even build anew over the bisque (then) re-bisque'.

After biscuit firing (which will destroy the fibers, causing fumes, especially from an electric kiln, so ventilation is essential), glazing is as normal. Wear gloves or use a barrier cream when handling the material, especially potters with sensitive skin.

Paper for placing

See note at *placing sand.*

Paper kiln

A one-off type of firing using rolled-up 'doughnuts' of newpaper which are built to surround the pots and the whole thing set alight. Malcolm Smith (CR152) used about 55 newpapers for firing 5 or 6 test bowls; 1000°C/1832°F was reached and the firing took about 80 minutes.

For biscuited pots, after small bowls of copper and iron have been placed, tightly wrapped coils of paper can be 'woven' round the pots and set alight. Reduction reds and smoky effects can result. (David Metcalf CR149.)

Paper resist

A technique of decoration with characteristic bold, open patterns. As with all *resist* methods it is the background which is colored with slip or pigment, the design being reserved in the original surface color. Of especial value to the beginner or student who is usually more fluent with scissors than with a brush. The design can be altered and developed at will before its actual application to the dish or pot.

1 A thin paper design is adhered to the pot with a little water and a sponge.

2

3

2 The color is brushed with firm, broad strokes over clay and paper.

3 The paper peeled away to show the resisted design. (See other examples at counter change, resist.)

Method: paper resist can be practiced in association with *glaze on glaze* but is most useful on *soft-leather* or *leather-hard clay*. Cut or tear the design in a thin, fairly absorbent paper such as typing copy paper and apply it to the surface of the pot or dish with a little moisture. Sponge over the surface of the paper when finally in position, and work the edges gently but very firmly onto the clay, or use thicker paper and adhere with *latex*. Alternatively use stiffer paper and press the edges well into the soft clay, giving an almost molded appearance. Designs can be built up of a number of pieces of paper which may overlap. The coloring material should have been prepared previously and be ready to apply. As soon as any excess moisture has dried from the surface, brush your pigment on with broad, even strokes, spray color on, or flood the surface with slip, pouring gently to avoid floating the paper. Put aside until the surface has dried to leather-hard and then remove paper with a needle or fine knife, making sure that you have found all the pattern!

When designing for paper avoid large areas: they will look very blank on the finished piece. A large shape can be given interest by cutting smaller design elements within it. A simple but effective idea is to cut a single shape, a fish for instance, and then to slice it into several sections placing these a little apart. The result will be an 'exploded' shape broken up with lines of color. One can also mask off larger areas and use a second color. For resist on biscuit (color, vitreous slip, or glaze), self adhesive labels might be useful.

To soften the hard edge, paper can be torn instead of cut. This will introduce a greater element of freedom and lessen the danger of over-representational design.

Parallel wiring

Many pieces of electrical equipment can be taken from a *single phase* (2 wire) mains input. The number is limited only by the ability of the input wires to carry the load. To maintain full voltage, however, each must be wired directly to a line and neutral connection. (See diagrams under *series wiring*.)

Parian body

A favorite Victorian material for unglazed models, etc., comprising around 33% china clay to 66% feldspar, possibly with a little soft frit. A white, vitreous though not usually translucent semiporcelain. For the modern potter a white body, originated by Dorothy Feibleman and obtainable from Potterycrafts, approximates to it. It can be thrown, and fires at 1120°–1180°C/2048–2156°F. It will have a degree of translucency at the higher temperature.

Parts of a pot

Just as we use the word 'body' for the clay fabric of a pot so the pot is described in human terms: foot, belly, shoulder, neck. Leach also calls the termination of a pot the 'head' but this term is less common. The top edge is the 'rim'. A pot may also have a 'waist', e.g. a diabolo shape. 'A Potter's Portfolio' (Leach) includes an analysis of pottery form in these terms. The relationship between them is the art of pottery form. In general, these analyses are more easily applicable to the traditional full-bodied pot forms.

Paste

A term often used by archaeologists and historians to indicate a *body* mixture, especially the artificial, prepared mixtures used for the old *soft-paste* wares. To a potter it suggests a smooth body with low plasticity, e.g. porcelain or bone-china.

Pastry cutter

Circular metal cutters sold at large kitchen equipment shops. Invaluable for cutting circles and rings of clay from slabs. (See *coiling, slab pots*.) At one time the cutters were sold in sets of up to 16 sizes but these are difficult to find. Other shapes are available but these are usually too definitive to be of much use.

PCE

Abbreviation for *pyrometric cone equivalent.*

Pearl ash

Potassium carbonate, K_2CO_3.
Billington gives potassium oxide also as 'pearlash'. Present in wood ash. *Deliquescent* and *soluble.* Unsuitable for raw glaze but used in *frits.*

Pebble mill

A *ball mill* using flint pebbles.

Peeling of glaze

The lifting of glaze from a pot can be due to very low *thermal expansion* with consequent excessive *compression* strain, although this could better be described as *shivering*.

Glaze can also peel or flake away from the pot surface during drying, or early in the firing, and this is often caused by excessive shrinkage of the glaze (e.g. from a

A pinched pot form by Sheila Fournier glazed with an ash glaze which flocculated in the bin, causing excess shrinkage as it dried. The peeling has been used as a deliberate decorative effect in the well of the piece. Stoneware.

flocculated ash batch) or from too thick a coating. An over-plastic slip can peel and crack. Zinc and colemanite, as well as ash, can cause shrinkage. The use of *calcined* materials or the substitution of china clay for plastic clay will help. Glaze which has begun to peel in drying will *crawl* in the firing.

Pegmatite

Geologically the term is given a very wide connotation, from *granitic* minerals to nearly pure *quartz*, and branching into *lithia-micas* and the *syenite* group. Pottery books will, however, often use 'pegmatite' as a synonym for Cornish granite or *china stone* with a formula of RO (made up of soda, potash, and some lime and magnesia). Al_2O_3. 7.0–7.5 SiO_2. 'Feldspars are a common constituent of pegmatites' (Dodd/Murfin).

Pen

Various colors, gold, and silver enamel felt pens are available. Also refillable nib pens which allow the potter to draw in underglaze in a great variety of colors, or for work on fired glaze (Potclays, Tuckers, and others). A square-ended brush can give a calligraphic stroke similar to a lettering pen. Georgies and Axner also list a fountain-type pen with four assorted sized metal tips from 'fine' to 'bold', and a wax pen which lays down a $1/16$in continuous line.

Pencil

Underglaze colors are obtainable, made up into pencils or *crayons*. The name is also, rather misleadingly, given to a pointed sable brush, also listed as 'majolica pencils'.

An ordinary 'lead' (actually *graphite*) pencil line will act as a slight resist to delineate designs when flooding a dish with slip (Jane Searle CR130). Pencil marks will usually burn out but sometimes a faint mark is left on stoneware biscuit.

Percentage composition

The percentage by weight of the elements or oxides in a compound. (See also *analysis*.)

To derive percentage composition from a *formula*:

1 The percentage of elements in an oxide

$$\frac{Total\ atomic\ weight\ of\ the\ element}{molecular\ weight\ of\ compound} \times \frac{100}{1}$$

Example: the amount of oxygen in MnO_2

$$\frac{2 \times 16\ (atomic\ wt.\ of\ oxygen)}{87\ (molecular\ weight\ of\ MnO_2)} \times \frac{100}{1} = 37\%\ oxygen$$

Leaving 63% of manganese metal.

2 The percentage of an oxide in a compound, transposing molecular for atomic weights in the equation above

Example: the amount of calcia in whiting, $CaCO_3$

$$\frac{Molecular\ wt.\ calcia,\ 56}{Mol.\ wt.\ of\ calcium\ carbonate\ 100} \times \frac{100}{1} = 56\%\ calcia.$$

Some 44% of the recipe weight is the carbonate (CO_2) and will therefore be lost during firing.

The equation can be extended to work out the percentages of oxides in minerals.

Percentage recipes

A recipe can be listed as batch weights with a random total, or as parts of a hundred. It is much easier to compare recipes in the latter form.

Example: two batch weight recipes.

	A	B
China stone	74.0	128.4
China clay	116.1	185.7
Whiting	90.0	144.0
Quartz	105.0	168.0

If we bring each of these recipes to percentages, we find that they have the same proportions (to the nearest whole number: stone 20, clay 30, whiting 23, quartz 27). It is therefore worth bringing all batch weights to percentages both for easy comparison and also to get an immediate impression of the proportions, and thus the sort of glaze or body likely to result.

Method: Total the batch weights and divide each of the items in the recipe by this total, then multiply by 100.

i.e $\dfrac{Item}{Total\ batch\ weight} \times 100$

Example:

From the above batch **A** the total is 385. To work out the percentage of whiting:

90 divided by 385 = 0.23.   0.23 x 100 = 23.

Batch **B** totals 626.1. Thus 144 whiting divided by 626.1 x 100 = 23.

Periodic table

A table or chart (see following page) in which the elements are arranged in order of their *atomic numbers*, and grouped according to their electron configuration and *valencies*. As far as their behavior in ceramics is concerned the groupings are often appropriate. In Group IA (one electron in the outer shell) we find lithium, potassium and sodium vertically adjacent, as are the slightly less 'efficient' fluxes calcium, strontium and barium. However another important base — lead — is found in Group IVA with the glass-formers, silica and germanium. Many of the pigment colors are contained between numbers 23 and 29 and are called the *transitional* elements.

The table's practical value is limited but the information it contains can give some explanation and forecast of behavior. Hamer deals very fully with the table and its relevance to potters.

Perlite

A fine-grained acidic laval rock (*rhyolite* type), composed

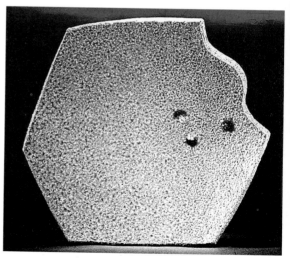

A saltglazed platter by William Hunt (USA) with 'substantial additions of expanded perlite, which leaves many small voids like soft brick, but with far more durability'.

of 70–75% silica; 12–14% alumina; and 6–8% alkalis. Swells when rapidly heated—'expanded perlite'. Used in the making of insulating bricks. Expanded perlite can be found in garden stores for use in potting soil. It burns out or melts (loses its expanded form) at about 1260°C. Can be used as a 'grog' at lower temperatures as in *raku*, helping to resist *thermal shock*, or to develop apertures and small craters at stoneware temperatures. (See William Hunt's article in CR70.)

Permeability

The rate at which one substance (a liquid or a gas) can pass through another. In pottery, the rate at which water will pass through a ceramic body. It gives some idea of the size of the pores as distinct from total pore volume, which is demonstrated by *porosity* tests. Scientific tests for permeability are beyond the potter's range but simple comparative trials can be made. For example one can test several similar-sized but differently fired containers by filling them with water, and sitting them in glazed saucers. The rate at which the saucers fill will be a rough comparative test of permeability.

Petalite

A mineral Li_2O, Al_2O_3, $8SiO_2$, 612.

A *fluxing* mineral with a rather high melting point and low *thermal expansion*. Sometimes referred to as a lithium feldspar. A *feldspathoid*. Can be used as a source of lithia in glazes and porcelain bodies. Should be pebble-ground. A sample analysis by weight:

Na_2O	1.1				
MgO	0.3	Al_2O_3	16	SiO_2	77.2
CaO	0.2				
Li_2O	4.3				

Related to *spodumene*, which has half the amount of silica in its formula. Lithium minerals are recommended by Cardew for *flameproof* bodies, using as much as 60% petalite to 40% plastic clay for very low thermal expansion. Listed by Potters Supply House.

A 1280°C/2336°F recipe from the late Katherine Pleydell Bouverie is:

Petalite	15.0	Feldspar	22.5
China clay	7.5	Quartz	11.5
Ash	22.5	Whiting	22.0

See also once-fired pottery for a 1250°C/2282°F recipe by Christopher Buras (CR84).

Petrology

The study of the rocks of the earth's crust as distinct from the earth as a whole (see *geology*).

The Periodic Table of the Elements

IA	IIA	IIB	IVB	VB	VIB	VIIB	VIII			IB	IIB	IIIA	IVA	VA	VIA	VIIA	0
1 H																	2 He
3 Li	4 Be											5 B	6 C	7 N	8 O	9 F	10 Ne
11 Na	12 Mg											13 Al	14 Si	15 P	16 S	17 Cl	18 Ar
19 K	20 Ca	21 Se	22 Ti	23 V	24 Cr	25 Mn	26 Fe	27 Co	28 Ni	29 Cu	30 Zn	31 Ga	32 Ge	33 As	34 Se	35 Br	36 Kr
37 Rb	38 Sr	39 Y	40 Zr	41 Nb	42 Mo	43 Tc	44 Ru	45 Rh	46 Pd	47 Ag	48 Cd	49 In	50 Sn	51 Sb	52 Te	53 I	54 Xe
55 Cs	56 Ba	57 La	72 Hf	73 Ta	74 W	75 Re	76 Os	77 Ir	78 Pt	79 Au	80 Hg	81 Tl	82 Pb	83 Bi	84 Po	85 At	86 Rn
87 Fr	88 Ra	89 Ac															
RARE EARTHS Lanthanides			58 Ce	59 Pr	60 Nd	61 Pm	62 Sm	63 Eu	64 Gd	65 Tb	66 Dy	67 Ho	68 Er	69 Tm	70 Yb	71 Lu	
ACTINIDE Series			90 Th	91 Pa	92 U	93 Np	94 Pu	95 Am	96 Cm	97 Bk	98 Cf	99 Es	100 Fm	101 Md	102 No	103 Lw	

Petunze

The Chinese equivalent of china stone or feldspar.

pH factor

Refers to the hydrogen *ion* concentration in a solution, denoting relative *acidity* or *alkalinity*. pH7 is neutral, i.e. pure water: lower numbers are increasingly acidic: the higher numbers alkaline. Used in testing casting slips. Caroline Wyman (see booklist) recommends slightly acidic water for 'the optimum plasticity of porcelain' which can be obtained by the addition of small amounts (she quotes 5 ounces to 100 pounds of dry clay) of *Epsom salts* or *vinegar*.

Phase diagrams

A diagram or graph showing changes in the physical state or composition of various mixtures of two materials at increasing temperatures. Shows *eutectics* and the degree of *vitrification* or glassy liquid likely to be present at a given temperature. The diagram for alumina and silica is important to potters, especially in the manufacture of refractories.

There follow two simplified diagrams based on McMurdie and Hall's Phase Diagrams for Ceramists.
1 Mixtures of potash and silica in the range between 60:40 and 10:90 K_2O/SiO_2, and between 700 and 1300°C/2372°F. There are two eutectic mixtures at 55:45 and 33:67.
2 Mixtures of calcium feldspar (anorthite) and silica. There is a eutectic at almost equal parts with solid

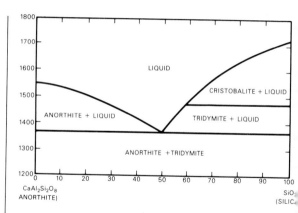

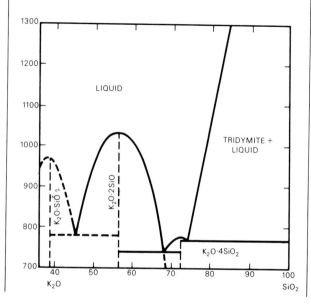

solutions either side. It can be seen that additions of quartz or flint to anorthite feldspar will lower its melting point.

Phase, electrical

A line of electricity supply. (See *single phase, three phase*.)

Phases of matter

Distinct physical states which include *states of matter* and also changes within solids and liquids. Thus alumina and silica compounds at high temperatures have phases where liquids are present within solids. Most phase changes occur at a definite temperature, but for ceramic materials they are very involved and the process is 'dynamic' or continuous with overlapping phases. One can discuss, for instance, 'glass phases' in a pottery body. (See also *phase diagrams*.)

Phosphorus

Element P. 31.
Pentoxide P_2O_5. 173.
One of the glass-forming elements (i.e. high *valency*, 5, and low *ionic radius*, 0.35 A). Wood ash for example usually contains 2–5%, and *amblygonite* larger concentrations. The element occurs only in the combined state in ceramics, the main source being bone ash, $Ca_3(PO_4)_2$, calcium phosphate. Small amounts of calcium phosphate are considered a help in Jun glazes. It probably has a subtle effect on glazes (and on bone china body) which is not fully understood. Although acting as a glass-former it 'does not enter the silica chain' (Hamer).

Photoceramic processes

A number of processes have been developed which allow the transfer of photographic or other images to pots without the intermediary of a *transfer* (decal). They are often quite complicated and can necessitate equipment such as a photographic darkroom. Books (Scott's 'Ceramics and Print' is recommended) and articles are available on the subject and some information is given in Fournier DPD. Photo systems can also be used to produce *silk screen* prints of images.

Photo-electric pyrometer

A heat measuring device in which the light given off by a 'hot body' in a kiln is measured and transformed into an electric current which will operate a pointer on a dial, similar to a photographic light-meter. Normally used only for high temperatures.

Phototrophy

A slight and short-lived deepening of color as seen in rutile/titanium glazes (totalling 15%, Hamer) when a cover, e.g. a cup in a saucer, is removed.

Pierced decoration

The cutting away of clay to produce decorative effects, as distinct from ventilation of candle and incense burners and the like, has arisen largely in 'sophisticated' societies and is used by modern potters on stoneware, or on porcelain to

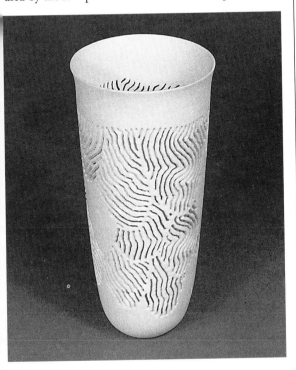

Delicate piercing of a porcelain cylinder.

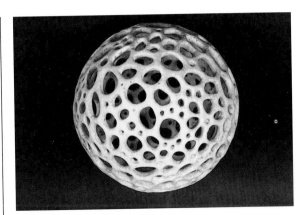

Holes cut into a sphere by Mary Rogers.

Pierced porcelain bowl by Angela Verdon.

enhance its translucency. Sand-blasting and dentist's drills have been used in addition to a fine knife, the favorite tool. The apertures can be rough edged and irregular, cut or, more rarely, punched through, or fine and controlled. Cracking during drying is more likely to arise from strains imposed during the work rather than from the piercing itself. (See also illustration of fine piercing at *bone china*.)

Pigment oxides

The various metals whose *oxides* provide *color* or *opacity* to glazes are dealt with in detail under their individual headings. Ordinary oil paints and other painting pigments will provide color in fired pottery only to the degree to which they contain these metals — all organic materials burning away.

Their number is few but there are many variations and combinations. It is somewhat misleading to give a tidy list of colors resulting from the use of the oxides. Cobalt, for instance, can confidently be quoted as providing a strong, stable blue, but it can also give viridian green with zinc, or even purple and red with magnesia under certain conditions.

It is well-known that a range of colors from red to blue can result from the use of iron, while copper can give apple-green, turquoise, purple, red, or copper luster. The final hue, the result of the absorption of certain wavelengths from white light, is dependent on the material in which it is dissolved or suspended and on the particular oxide or compound which has been formed in the glass.

The fired color will bear little resemblance to the raw oxide unless it is undissolved in a glaze, e.g. painted onto the biscuit when it will be largely unaltered from the unfired oxide. In this case copper and manganese, though of different qualities, will remain black, iron will lose its brightness but remain red-brown to black, and cobalt may develop a gray-blue.

The principal oxides are those of the metals:
1 The common coloring materials: copper, cobalt, chromium, manganese, iron, nickel antimony, and their variants such as ilmenite, ochre, rutile, etc.
2 The rare or precious metals: vanadium, cadmium, selenium, uranium, gold, silver, platinum.
3 The opacifiers: tin, zirconium, titanium, zinc.

To minimize the confusion when using oxides for painting, slightly different chemical forms can be used, e.g. the *carbonates* of copper or cobalt which, at least, are distinguishable from manganese!

Most carbonates are poisonous. The prepared colors listed in suppliers' catalogs are *fritted* mixtures of oxides with other ceramic materials. Chrome is often included to give stability to the darker colors and in reaction with tin to give pink. Oxides are stained to give an approximation to their fired color. The hues as listed may not be true for all glazes.

Temperature is another factor in the quality of color in general, the lowest temperatures produce the brightest colors, e.g. a bright red can be obtained from iron or chrome at below 900°C/1652°F. It is also true, however, that cobalt in stoneware can be pretty lurid, as can high-temperature reduced copper. Finally, the kiln atmosphere is crucial, whether *oxidizing* or *reducing*.

Reference books list theoretical maximum percentage proportions of pigments in glazes and slips. These are good guides to the relative coloring power of oxides but it is instructive to exceed the limits in test batches. In some cases, copper for instance, an excess will destroy the glaze surface, producing an ashy black, but very considerable proportions of iron or manganese can be used.

Some generally recommended maxima are: copper 3%, iron 12%, chromium 5%, nickel 3%, rutile 10%, ilmenite 5%, manganese 10%, iron chromate 3%, antimoniate of lead 5%, cobalt 2%, the opacifiers 10%. The impure and 'diluted' ochres, etc. can be as high as 25%.

There is no harm in trying combinations of any pigments. (See *color trials*, *line blends*, etc. Rhodes CGP

gives useful lists of mixtures.) The colors mentioned, however, are those which are likely to develop in a 'neutral' glaze the actual results may be different under your particular conditions. A few mixtures can generate *volatile* particles which will affect other glazes. Copper has this tendency and can stain right through a pot wall to show on the other side (See also *chrome-tin pink*.) Dolomite and zinc glazes may produce a similar mushroom pink reaction in stoneware (See also *color*, under the individual element headings, *colored glazes*, *enamels*, *maiolica*, *painting on pottery*, etc.)

Pin, saddle

A piece of kiln furniture, about 4in/100mm long and triangular in section (see diagram at *saddle*).

Pinch pot

Also known as thumb pots. Pressing one's thumb into a ball of clay and squeezing it up into a hollow shape is the most instinctive and intimate way of handling clay. It is often presented to the beginner as the first and not very important step towards making 'real' pots, but this is to seriously underestimate the technique. Not only can one's fancy run free but, with practice, quite large thin-walled shapes with subtle organic qualities can be achieved.

Simple pinched pots are especially suitable for sawdust, raku, and other primitive firings.

Method: As the clay will dry fairly rapidly during the process, moist plastic material should be used—normally a red clay. Grog may be added but if used in excess the necessary plasticity is lost. If cracks appear on the surface smooth them over immediately. To make a single pot roll the clay into a ball, the rounder the better for a symmetrical shape. Hold in one palm and start to press the thumb of the hand centrally into the lump, tuning with short movements as the thumb penetrates. When down to within $\frac{1}{4}$in/6mm or $\frac{1}{2}$in/12mm of the base grip the pot between the thumb

A pinched pot with a well-fitting lid by Rosemary Wren.

side and the fingers outside and begin to squeeze the walls
an even thickness, revolving the pot about ½in/12mm
tween each pinch. Do not try to thin the wall haphazardly;
ep up a steady and rhythmic series of movements. Work

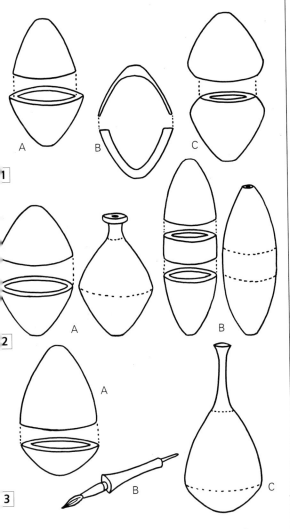

1

2

3

4

5

4 A pinch pot is formed by squeezing a ball of clay between the thumb inside and the fingers outside, steadily turning the piece after each 'pinch'. Outward spread is controlled by gripping the whole pot with the palm and fingers of the other hand. Larger shapes are possible using both hands (see handbuilding).

5 When two pinch pots have been joined together, rim to rim, the shapes can be perfected by rolling the 'egg' as shown. This is done before cutting any aperture. The pressure must be steady and gentle or the wall may split.

Assemblies and additions to the basic pinch pot shape.
*1 Three common faults which can occur when forming the sections of multiple pots: **A** The openings are of different sizes. **B** The walls are uneven and the top half too thin to secure an adequate join. **C** It is almost impossible to join walls which are inturned.*
*2 The second diagram offers some suggestions for double pinch pots. **A** An aperture can be cut after joining and shaping, and a neck modeled or coiled on. **B** A short cylinder or collar can be inserted to give a taller form.*
3 By varying the proportions of the parts high or low-bellied shapes can be obtained. A tall neck may be modeled round a paintbrush or suitable rod and luted on for a bottle form.

round and round in an ascending spiral towards the neck of the pot. If a shoulder is required on the finished shape, keep the mouth as small as possible.

Do not stand the pot on its base while soft; rest it on its rim or in a suitable hollow support. To control the spread of the shape hold it sideways in the palm and squeeze slightly round the circumference after each 'pinch'.

The pinch pot can be used as a unit or basis for future work. Examples are illustrated. Multiple pinch pots luted mouth to mouth, or with a 'collar' between, can be built up to quite respectable sizes. Oval balls of clay can be pinched into asymmetric forms. The finished pots can be *burnished*, or colored, slipped or glazed in the usual way.

For large bowls the initial pinching can be done with all the fingers inside the bowl, while a combination of pinching and stroking is used for the walls. (See illustration under *handbuilt* pots.)

Pinholing in glaze

In glazes pinholes often result from the escape of gas or air which has usually been trapped between particles in the raw glaze. A particularly aggravating fault, found most often in viscous stoneware glazes. According to most authorities, pinholes result from blisters or bubbling in a glaze which has not quite settled down. Recommended as precautions: a thinner glaze coating; a more fluid glaze; the avoidance of *over-firing*, a heat *soak* at melting temperature. Rhodes also mentions over-zealous *reduction* early in a firing as a contributory cause. Even 'perfectly' fired pieces, especially plates, can show pinholes. I have noticed that the holes are often quite deep, suggesting pits in the body over which the glaze refuses to flow, rather like paint over cracks in woodwork. In these cases they show no signs of a burst bubble. Clean clay and the careful smoothing of 'flatware' will help; you may well find the same glaze to be perfectly smooth on a vertical surface. Sulfur released from the clay (made very evident to the nose by some bodies) may also be a cause. Air trapped between particles of glaze powder is suggested by Dodd. Glaze which regularly pinholes is difficult to cure without adding more *flux* which will change its character. Try altering the clay body.

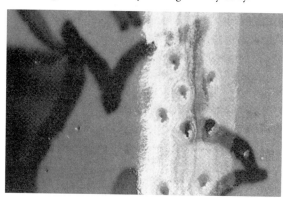

Pinholing in a glaze, caused by gases given off by the body bursting through the glaze.

Pink, rose

The somewhat unsympathetic *chrome-tin pink* is dealt with under that heading. A softer pink or rose color is derived from gold see *purple of Cassius*. Cobalt can give pinkish flushes in high-fired magnesia glazes; there is a zirconium/iron pink; pink crystals may form in dolomite/

rutile glazes, Cooper gives a recipe for a 'shocking pink' and rosy flushes can result from the use of tin glaze ove black slip (see *tin-over-slip*).

Pint weight

The weight of solid matter in a pint of slop glaze or slip Usually quoted in ounces: 26–28 being the average fo casting slips; 28–30 for glazes. (See *Brongniart's formula* Now largely superseded by kilograms per liter.

Pipe clay

A white clay of the type used in the manufacture o tobacco pipes and, in general, applied to any discovered pocket of white-firing, possibly *calcareous clay*. According to some authorities it is un-plastic and siliceous — often containing 50–70% silica (Hamer) — but Worral describes it as plastic and fusible. It is sometimes associated with fireclays, which may be why Leach uses the term in connection with a wide range of marls and fireclay, bu another explanation for this may be that 'pipe clay' is also applied to any clay made into drainage pipes.

Pitcher, pitchers

In the singular the word is applied to a large water jug, (in USA any jug). In the plural it applies to broken pots, generally biscuit, which may be crushed and used for *grog*. Electrical porcelain factories grind glazed pitchers to add to the body. (See also *jug*.)

Pit firing

A pit dug into the ground, $2\frac{1}{2}$ft (76cm) deep, and used as a kiln in a similar way to *sawdust firing*.

Placing

The setting of pots or sculptures in a kiln (see *kiln furniture*, *kiln packing*, *tile setter*, etc). Wads of clay are also said to be 'placed' between saggars for ventilation and stability. Hamer uses the word to mean the packing of pots in saggars, bedded in a fairly coarse sand (for earthenware), or alumina (for bone china); an industrial technique for high-fired biscuit. (See *bone china*.)

Placing sand

Fine white or 'silver' sand used for *setting* earthenware and high-fired biscuit, or it may be used under large pots or multi-based ceramics providing tiny 'rollers' over which

*method of 'placing' a
ece of pottery with
ore than one base or
g. It can be set on a
ab of the same clay as
e body of the piece
hich, in turn, is placed
n a generous layer
f sand or calcined
lumina to allow it to
hrink without splitting.
he arrangement can be carried through drying, biscuiting,
nd glaze fire with the same slab.*

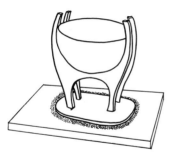

he piece can move as it shrinks. For most setting purposes,
owever, *alumina* is replacing sand. Some potters even use
everal thicknesses of glossy paper (the gloss is derived
rom clay) in electric kilns. These may be cut to the shape
f the base. Quite a lot of smoke will be generated.

Plagioclase

A series of feldspars between *albite* and *anorthite*, i.e. with
ariable amounts of soda and lime as the base oxides. The
mixtures occur because of the similarity in ionic radius of
he atoms of soda and calcium. Although the series is con-
inuous it is divided, for convenience, into half a dozen
mineral types including *andesite*. Listed in Cardew.

The two types of feldspar are considered to be 'melted'
into one another (see *solid solutions*).

Plane

A clay plane is similar to a woodworking plane but has a
somewhat larger aperture in front of the cutter. Alternatively the Surform type of plane can be used, with the

Using a Surform plane on a grogged surface.

advantage that blades of various sizes and curved shapes
can be bought. Clay particularly with grog, is highly abrasive and no metal edge will last long. If used with discretion the clay plane can be a valuable item of equipment,
especially for the hand-builder.

Planter

See *hanging planter*.

Plaster of Paris

A partially dehydrated gypsum known as a *demihydrate*
($CaSO_4.2H_2O$) which, when mixed with water, recom-
bines to form a soft porous stone. It has the quality, partly
by reason of a slight expansion during setting, of reproducing in great detail the shape and surface texture of any
material or object onto which it is poured and allowed to
set. It was known to the ancient Egyptians and to the
Greeks but its name derives from the fact that the original
modern material was prepared from deposits in the Mont-
martre district of Paris.

Plaster of Paris is made in various qualities, from a
coarse, yellow-pink builders' plaster to a very fine-grain
white 'dental' plaster. There is a special type supplied for
pottery molds. The so-called 'dental' plaster is quick-
setting and rather too close and hard for our purposes.
Plaster of Paris is prepared by roasting crushed gypsum
in a revolving retort to 120°C/248°F. Commercial pottery of all kinds is formed in or on plaster molds, the
shape being as much conditioned by the plaster as by the
clay. Its main use in a school or pottery will be for non-
circular dish molds, or in the form of slabs or bowls
which will absorb moisture from very wet clays. Pieces of
plaster in clay will cause it to split or bloat in the kiln. If
it is heated to 150°C/302°F or above it will become
'dead-burnt' — weak and powdery so do not put molds
to dry directly onto a hot kiln.

Method for mixing plaster. Once plaster has been stirred
into water it is difficult to add more without forming
lumps or even nodules of dry powder. Start, therefore,
with up to half a bowl of water, as required, and sprinkle
handfuls of plaster into it, without stirring, until the powder is heaped into 'islands' just above the surface. Leave
these to soak for a few minutes and then stir vigorously,
keeping the hand beneath the surface to avoid aeration. A
proportion of 2½–3lbs of plaster to 2 pints/1.25 kilograms
to 1 liter) of water will give about 80cu in/1000cu cm of a
reasonably hard mix.

Materials can be added to alter the performance during
setting: lime added to the plaster will lessen expansion;
dextrin, milk, vinegar, sodium carbonate, and size have

been mentioned as setting retardants and/or hardeners; warm water, salt and alum can accelerate setting but may also aerate. Molds should not contain additional materials.

Mixing plaster of Paris.

1 and *2* *It is sprinkled into a bowl of water until small islands stand above the surface, or the measured proportion of plaster is used up. Do not stir at all until all the plaster is in the water and allow it to soak for a minute or so.*
3 *Mix thoroughly by swinging the hand to and fro beneath the surface of the liquid.*

Plastic

Capable of being easily molded. (See *plasticity*.)

Plasticity

With reference to ceramic materials, especially clay, it the property which permits the shape to be altered b pressure and yet retain the given shape when the pressu is removed. The 'yield point' of a clay will vary with th type and with the amount of water present.

The sheet structure of clay is a possible explanatio of this behavior. Between each leaf or sheet of cla material (which is molecular thin) a layer of water wi lubricate movement relative to one another, while th electrical attraction is sufficient to hold the leaves i place when not under pressure. This simplified view has not been definitely proved and the movement ma be between larger particles. *Colloidal* gels from bacterial action have also been suggested as a contribu tory factor. Clay is unique in possessing true plasticit allied to dry strength. Shaw illustrates the distinctio between the flat plates of *kaolinite* and the curled o tube structure of *halloysite* which has otherwise simila constituents.

In common use the term is widened to include genera workability, but excess plasticity can render a clay unwork able. The *bentonites* (*montmorillonites*) cannot be used alone and, like the *ball clays*, are valued for their very plastic nature but are used as additions to a body rathe than as a working clay. Plasticity involves a high water con tent with fine grain and consequently high shrinkage and frequently, *fusibility*.

Clays may be arranged, as a general rule, in the following order of increasing plasticity: china clay, fireclay, stoneware clay, buff secondary clays, ball clay, red clay, montmoril lonite clay. (See also *aging*, *thixotropy*, *weathering*, etc.)

Plastics

A series of synthetic resinous or other 'organic' polymer ized substances shaped in a liquid state and allowed to set. They have low melting points. (See *polythene*.)

There are 'thermosetting' and 'thermoplastic' plastics, the second softening under mild heat, the first staying more rigid. The first type includes the polyurethanes, silicones, and epoxy resins; the second, polythene, poly styrene, etc. The first type is obviously more useful to the potter for storage, etc. where they may come into contact with warm conditions. For homemade *sieves* as described under that heading, the second type would be necessary.

Plate

Making handmade plates creates problems of throwing, warping, 'humping', and uneconomical packing in the kiln. Therefore they are not widely produced. Some potters jigger and jolley their plates but this is tantamount to failure on the part of a craft potter. With practice, care and the use of large circular throwing bats, it is not difficult to make plates on the wheel. The illustrations show some of the stages.

After centering (by the *annular* method) the block of clay should be pressed down to a wide, shallow block before actual throwing starts. Leave plenty of clay for the rim which should be firm and well-defined. Alternatively, a thick even coil can be laid round a thrown or rolled slab and thrown up to a rim. Avoid a ridge or hump just before the wall of the rim begins to rise, and also any suggestion of a dip in the middle. A slight rise is preferable towards the center — the cutting wire will tend to rise as the plate

is cut off. Use the wire with the wheel turning very slowly. Trimming with a pointed tool close to the wheelhead will help to keep the wire flat and low. Leave the plate on the bat until it is *soft-leather*. If adequately thrown it will need no turning but if a foot-ring is turned leave a second ring nearer the center to support it. At the hard-leather stage, plates can be inverted to dry on their rims.

Stages in throwing a plate.
1 The first spreading, down and outwards pressure using the palm or a sponge.
2 The rim is formed, taking care not to make a depression just inside the rim.
3 If felt necessary, the well and curve can be smoothed and adjusted with a metal kidney tool.
4 The angle between the bat or wheelhead and base is cut to a bevel.

5 Plates are most easily thrown on a circular bat and removed when somewhat stiffer. When turning, a second foot-ring nearer the center of the base, as shown in the photograph, will help to prevent slumping in the firing.

Ray Finch *once-fires* large plates to minimize *dunting*. In the biscuit fire the heat retention of the kiln shelf can cause trouble and some potters biscuit their plates on clay pellets to allow air under them. I have not found this necessary when using shelves up to 1in/25mm thick. Plates may also be glazed in the well only and fired boxed.

Plate setter

A piece of kiln furniture which allows for a number of plates to be packed one above another. Useful where *tableware* is a major item of a potter's production but are more often used in the industry where plates are identical in size. (See also *thimble*.)

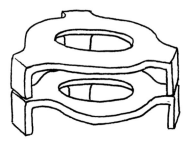

Plate setters, more space-consuming, more stable but less versatile than thimbles.

Plucked ware *The splendid German Bellarmines (Bartmannkrugers) were apparently piled against one another in the kiln. The resultant scars are very evident in this photograph.*

Platinum

Used as the salt, platinic chloride, to obtain silver enam for overglaze painting, bought as a liquid pigment. Pla inum and its alloy with rhodium are used in the therm couples of high temperature *pyrometers*.

Plucked ware

Scars caused by glazed ware touching the kiln wall, or i earthenware by supporting stilts, or each other durir firing. Very evident on old salt-glazed pots. See picture.

Plumbic, plumbago

Apertaining to lead. Note however that 'plumbago', th 'lead' in lead pencils, is, in fact, a graphite.

Plunge pots

A name given to the technique of making pots by pressing batten of wood into a block of clay. The walls can t thinned by stroking and easing the clay upwards against th wooden former, or by slicing away surplus clay with a wi or knife. See illustrations below and on next page.

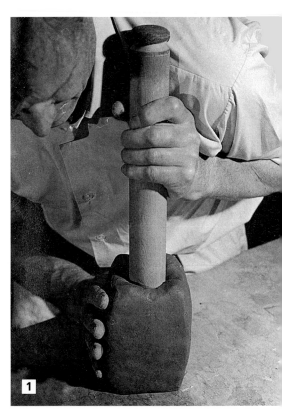

1

...orming a plunge pot.

Thrusting a rolling pin into a block of clay.
The clay is eased up along the roller to form a taller pot.
The wall is reduced to a reasonable thickness by cutting
...cets with a wire, these facets being normally integral to the
...rm of the piece.

...lutonic rocks, *intrusive rocks*

...neous rock orginating as molten magma, which has
...oled and hardened deep in the earth's crust. Including
...anite, *syenite* and *gabbro*. Generally *acidic* with high SiO_2
...ntent.

...ocket clay

...refractory, siliceous clay found in 'pockets' in limestone,
...Derbyshire in England.

...oise

...unit of *viscosity*. Occasionally quoted when discussing
...azes at the melting stage. The viscosity of water at
...°C/68°F is 0.010 poise, molten glass varies widely, of
...urse, but its viscosity is at least 5000 times as great.

...oisonous materials

...arked as 'toxic' where applicable at each main entry.
...uite apart from those used by the potter, many materials
...daily use would not be recommended for breathing
...or ingesting! Similarly, in the pottery, care should be

A carved-side plunge pot form by Leslie Pearson.

taken at all times. A few rules I have always carefully
adhered to are:
1 Not to eat, drink, or smoke in the workshop.
2 Not to raise dust when sweeping or cleaning up; wash
equipment, worktops, etc; rather than dry brushing. As far
as possible use all materials in a wet state.
3 When dealing with powdery materials, spraying, cutting
any form of kiln sheeting, brick, or rubbing down a dry
clay surface, wear at least a handkerchief round the nose
and mouth or a *mask* (very cheap from a pharmacist).
4 Ventilate the kiln room well during firing, especially
with electric kilns.

The prime villain among pottery materials is considered
to be lead oxide, with others not far behind. Be wary of
barium, antimony, dusty silica (flint), and most of the carbonates. *Manganese* has been mentioned as a hazard.

As mentioned, fumes from firing can be very noxious,
not to mention *carbon monoxide* and *natural gas* which are
heavier than air and can collect at ground level. Silica is
well-known for causing lung congestion and worse.
Poisons in the fired piece are more complex, sometimes
being released in use by the action of acids such as fruit

acids. (See *metal release*.)

Copper can cause trouble, especially in association with lead, if in an unbalanced (often a *matt*) glaze. Selenium and cadmium are suspect. A well-fired (not overfired) balanced glaze will usually be blameless. It is possible (and if lead is used on tableware, legally necessary) to have glazes tested for toxicity. (See *soluble lead*.) The longevity of many potters, however, does not suggest exposure to great danger. A degree of knowledge and care are all that is necessary.

Polycell

Although this is a standard wallpaper paste it has appeared in a few recipes as a binder or siccative.

Polishing clay

The actual application of furniture or other polish to pots after firing can have undesirable effects, especially if the pot is wetted. Use sparingly, if at all, on burnished pots (see also *burnishing, gloss ware, non-ceramic finishes*).

The Elers brothers were reputed to have polished their red stonewares on a lapidary's wheel as does Martin Smith today. Homoky and others achieve fine, eggshell-like surfaces on biscuit porcelain with fine-grade wet-and-dry emery or silicon carbide paper (see also *abrasive)*. Some faults in glazed ware can be polished using an electric drill and a very fine abrasive.

Polymorphic

Having more than one form, in the case of ceramic materials, crystalline form. *Rutile* is polymorphic — existing also as *anatase* and *brookite*.

Polythene, polyethylone

A synthetic material (the polymer of C_2H_4, if it interests you!), useful, cheap, and at once a bane and a blessing to potters. Because it is chemically inert it is suitable for glaze and slip containers, while in sheet form it has eased the potter's problem of keeping pots moist, doing away with the rotting rags and the usually inefficient damp-cupboard, not to mention the rusting biscuit tins of earlier days. On the other hand it has, more than any other material, been responsible for the rapid decline, almost to the point of extinction, of the traditional country potter throughout the world.

It is *thermoplastic*, i.e. will melt under heat and care must therefore be taken to keep it away from fire or the kiln. (See also *plastics*.)

Polyurethane block printing

A design is marked out on a polyurethane foam block and the areas not required for printing are burnt away with a soldering iron or hot wire. The resultant noxious fumes must be blown away by the use of a fan and, of course, an efficient mask worn. The technique is not recommended for enclosed areas of work!

The printing can be done on biscuit or on a raw, damp glaze.

Porcelain, body

In China the definition of porcelain (T'zu) is wider than generally accepted in the West; it could be any fine, pale body of primary clay with a distinctive ring when struck fired to *vitrification* but often too thick to show the translucency which we expect today. Essentially porcelain is kaolin and silica with a little flux, fired to vitrification point. This is 'true' of hard-paste porcelain and requires a high temperature in the region of 1350°C/2462°F. An increase or multiplication of the bases (or of the acids, boron or fluorine) can lower the melting point and it is possible that the Eastern kilns averaged no more than 1250–1300°C/2282–2372°F.

Richard Parkinson asserts that 1360°C/2480°F is needed to fully develop the 'felted mass of mullite needles bonded in a glassy cement' by which he defines true porcelain, and that the lower temperature mixtures such as David Leach's 1270°C/2318°F body, give a white stoneware. To a degree this is a matter of words and preferences. Certainly the bentonite porcelains lack the white purity of the harder types and one must learn to counter what Harry Davis calls their 'evil properties'. The color is better in reduction. The best of modern porcelain bodies throw pleasantly and thinly (although they are 'thirsty' and take up water very readily up to about 9in/22cm, and can also be used for pinching, modeling, and slab pots (although the joins tend to show up after firing, the edge of the clay taking on a slightly different color to the face; try mitered joints). Georgies advise 10–12 hour firings for their porcelain bodies.

The basic recipe for porcelain is 50% kaolin (china clay), 25% feldspar, 25% flint or quartz. See also *Seger's porcelain*. It is wise to leave the feldspar at 25% although this may be replaced in small part by nepheline: silica can be reduced to a 15% minimum. This leaves the clay. English kaolins lack plasticity, limiting the development of porcelains in England and frightening off studio potters. By swapping a proportion of kaolin for ball clay the throwing qualities are improved but the translucency diminished. Rhodes suggests up to 15% ball clay. 2–5% 'white' bentonite will make a body throwable but will increase shrinkage and impurities. Bentonite will also greatly increase *thixotropy*, apparently stiff or even leathery

A dramatic photograph by Ron Sloman (St. James Gallery, Bath, UK) emphasising the translucency of a porcelain bowl by Mary Rogers.

hard clay may soften suddenly and alarmingly under pressure or when turning. Practice can overcome the dangers here. More serious is the tendency to warp in drying and firing.

The amalgamation of the body ingredients needs to be thorough for complete fusion of the particles. Parkinson recommends a 300 screen lawn but this seems excessive — many particles would not pass through. For many potters the simple compounding of already finely ground materials, followed by efficient hand kneading and a week or so of 'resting', will suffice. (See *clay preparation*.) Two recipes:

1 David Leach

Grollegg china clay powder	53
Potash feldspar	25
Water-ground quartz	17
White bentonite	5

Firing to translucency 1250–1280°C/2282–2336°F. Substitute some quartz for china clay if *crazing* is persistent.

2 Parkinson (published in CR3)

EEC JM china clay	51
Potash feldspar	18
EEC BB ball clay	7
Fine (300 mesh) quartz	24

Firing 1320–1370°C/2408–2498°F.

Richard Parkinson also suggests that these high temperatures can be obtained in an electric silicon carbide element kiln.

A traditional commercial earthenware body, fired to 1280°C/2336°F or more, can also be used. This yields a low translucency 'proto-porcelain'. (See also *electrical porcelain*.) There are dolomite-based porcelains. The English industrial porcelain equivalent is *bone china*. Bernard Leach's recipe given in PQ1 is near to the 'earthenware' body type:

China clay	25
Black ball clay	33
Feldspar	30
Quartz	12

Joanna Constantinidis uses the Audrey Blackman Porcelain Body (obtainable from Valentine Clay Products, The Slip House, Birches Head Road, Hanley, Stoke-on-Trent, Staffordshire, UK) for her splendid reduced and fumed pots. Sculpture House list a 'Royal porcelain which at cone 5 (1205°C/2201°F) a thin porcelain becomes translucent — difficult to throw —'.

Porcelain glaze

Hard paste porcelain glazes have a very high silica equivalent. Parmelee quotes 7.0 SiO_2 with bases $0.3K_2O/0.7CaO$, for 1320°C/2408°F and even as much as 12.0 with $0.5K_2O/0.5CaO$ for a high-gloss glaze at the same temperature. These very nearly correspond to the Seger cone formulas. The alumina equivalents in the above examples are 0.8 and 1.3 respectively. At the other extreme, the low temperature bodies (1250–1270°C/2282–2318°F) may have glazes with as low as 2.0 parts silica. This proportion has been found in analyses of Chinese glazes, and also features in a formula given by Victor Margrie in CR2 for a barium semi-matt glaze.

K_2O	0.32	Al_2O_3	0.4	SiO_2	2.0
BaO	0.34	SnO_2	0.1		
CaO	0.34				

This has been translated into raw materials:

Potash feldspar	58.1	Barium carbonate	22.0
Whiting	11.1	Alumina hydrate	4.1
Tin oxide	4.7		

(See CR4 which also contains other recipes.)

Feldspar is the principal mineral in most porcelain glaze recipes. It will melt into a viscous glaze at cone 10 and over, and so needs only the modification of additional alumina, usually as china clay, with perhaps the diversification of the fluxes with lime or zinc. Magnesium can give a milky quality and a slightly subdued surface. Glazes for the lower-fired porcelains can be similar to those for stoneware.

A glaze suitable for use on the porcelain body developed by David Leach has been quoted as:

Feldspar	12	Dolomite	12
Quartz	22	China clay	14

Ball clay	9	Petalite	28
Bentonite	3		

My standard white stoneware glaze works quite well, although it may craze on some bodies. It fires at 1260°C/2300°F.

Feldspar	40	Nepheline	20
Whiting	15	China clay	10
Talc	10	Flint	5

Porosity

Used by potters in a general way to indicate both water *absorption* and permeability. More strictly defined as the proportion of pores, both open and sealed, compared with the total volume, and normally refers to the fired body of a ceramic. The open, connected pores allow water to seep into and through a pot, the closed pores simply increase heat insulation (and marginally decrease strength).

Earthenware biscuit is porous and must be covered with an unfractured (uncrazed) glaze in order to be rendered watertight. Porosity declines as molten materials fill the pores, i.e. with an increase in vitrification. There is no sudden change from one state to the other; stonewares are porous to a small degree. An increase in *fluxes*, such as a little red clay, will aid *vitrification*.

A rough test for porosity is to weigh a dry pot, immerse it in water for 12 hours and re-weigh; the difference being the weight of water absorbed.

It may sometimes be found that stoneware, as biscuit or with a crazed glaze, can let water through in time. Harry Fraser (CR142) warns that the base of a piece may not be as highly fired as the walls due to the cooling effect of the bats on which they stand. Soak or use supports or perforated bats.

John Temple (CR39) confidently asserts that porosity (and even small cracks) can be remedied by filling with strong tea and leaving overnight! For waterproofing glazed but crazed decorative pieces not to be used for eating or drinking or holding food of any sort, one can flood them with a liquid polyurethane (or there are special commercial equivalents in pottery suppliers' catalogs), pour out the surplus and leave to dry for several days, taking care not to allow a thick pool to form in the bottom of any curve. This of course, is something of a last resort and the customer must always be informed.

Portland cement

A limestone/clay mixture, which has been calcined in a kiln, and which hardens when mixed with water. It is not, however, refractory in the ceramic sense and should not be used as such. Special high-alumina cements are available which will stand higher temperatures. Cardew warns against using Portland cement in the bases of kilns. (See *cement, concrete*.)

Pot, potting

A vessel, generally rounded, for holding liquids or solids. The development of 'ceramic sculpture' has led to a blurring of the definition but if a hollow fired clay shape has any sort of hole near the top it may be considered to be a 'pot'! The word is also used as an adjective in place of 'pottery', and as a verb 'to pot' (see at *pottery*), i.e. to make pottery.

Pot gauge

A tool used to assist in the repetition throwing of pieces of a similar size and shape. It consists of one movable arm which is set with its point just clear of the rim of the pot, or with two arms the second of which indicates the widest point of the circumference.

In its simplest form the pot gauge can be merely a stick set in a wedge of clay; this is all that most of the old country potters would have used. Two modifications of the jointed arm type now in use by craft potters are recommended, a stiff rubber end to the pointer, and a means of swiveling the whole gauge to one side so that it does not inhibit *centering*. It is brought into position again when the pot is well under way. (See also *card measure*.)

Pot lift

A device for lifting pots from the wheel listed by Potters Supply House.

Potash

The common term for potassium oxide, as in 'lead-lime — potash glazes', etc.

Potassium, oxide, compounds

A metallic element K, 39.
Oxide K_2O, 94 Potash
Carbonate K_2CO_3, 138, Pearl ash
Di-chromate $K_2Cr_2O_7$
A base, strongly *alkaline*, and a powerful *flux* in glazes and bodies. Both the oxide and carbonate are *deliquescent* and *soluble* and can be used only in a *fritted* form. There are a number of 'natural frits' (minerals) containing potash, including: orthoclase feldspar, wood ash, nepheline syenite, china stone, and to a smaller degree, many other vitrifiable materials, e.g. clay. Potassium is frequently associated with sodium, so much so that the RO for some minerals may be

changing to orange and then to a dull yellow as the firing temperature rises. The addition of iron oxide can help to maintain the color at higher temperatures.

Potsherd

A broken piece of pottery. (See *pitchers*.)

Potter's plaster

See *plaster of Paris*.

Pottery

Fired clay objects. The term is narrower in its application than ceramics and is often used for the less sophisticated types of earthenware or, sometimes, for handmade ceramics in general. As its root 'pot' suggests, it is applied mainly to containers, though these may be asymmetric and purely decorative. May be used as an adjective as in 'pottery modeling', i.e. modeling carried out by means of recognized pottery techniques such as coiling.

Poured glaze

Pouring swathes of glaze across a plate or down the sides of a pot has long been a decorative technique. It was popular in the early days of studio pottery with Chaplet, Delaherche and others. The possibilities are many; from the simple pouring of glaze onto the shoulder of a pot, often over another glaze, to the more deliberate shaping of the run of glaze by judicious movement of the piece as the

1 The simplest form of pot gauge: a rod stuck into a wedge of clay.
2 Shows a more sophisticated form of pot gauge. Each arm is adjustable in length and vertical movement, and is fitted with a soft rubber end. To obviate the disadvantage that the gauge can inhibit movement and may be knocked out of true, the whole assemblage can be pivoted so that it can remain set but be swung out of the way. The use of a single screw in the base allows this movement.

written KNaO indicating a variable mixture.

Potash occurs in all but the simplest glazes and at all temperatures. Equivalents vary between 0.1 and 0.5 of the RO group. Its effect on the coloring oxides is more neutral than soda or zinc. Potassium nitrate replaced some of the lead oxide to produce the 'coral red' of Chinese enamels (Nigel Wood). The di-chromate (soluble and toxic) in a lead frit can give a red color at around 900°C/1652°F,

Decoration by poured and splashed glazes.
1 A large plate by Nigel Cox; the reduced copper on a white ground brilliantly controlled to produce a striking pattern.

2 A more managed pour on a handbuilt bottle by Robert Fournier. The pot was abruptly twisted to develop the design as the glaze flowed down. Odd, unwanted dribbles were wiped away.

pour flows down, as in the work of Janet Leach, myself, and others. The various thicknesses of glaze can often result in a variety of colors from a single glaze. (See *glaze thickness.*)

The shape of the surface will influence the result as will a quick sideways twist of the vessel as the liquid flows down. Very controlled designs can be achieved on dishes. Dry (matt) ash glazes are very suitable for pouring over the more rugged types of slab pots and constructions. Interesting if chancy effects can be obtained by pouring over a revolving pot, producing spiral and other effects. See Fournier DPD for illustrations of the great variety of poured glaze.

Powdering

Pigment can be blown or dusted as a dry powder onto a body or glaze to achieve a stippled or spotted effect. A fired glaze can first be brushed over with an oily or gummy medium. The technique is something of a health hazard as many of the pigments are toxic and none are good to breathe in! The use of a mask is therefore essential.

Power wheel

A potter's wheel driven by a motor. The simplest system for transmitting the power of an electric motor to a wheelhead is where a rubber or leather drive is brought into contact with the flywheel of a traditional kick wheel by foot pressure, springing back when the foot is removed. In a sophisticated version in general use in England, the drive wheel can be moved to any position from the center to the circumference of the flywheel, thereby controlling the speed of the wheelhead.

In the typical industrial wheel the speed is modified by two slightly convex cones which can be swiveled on their axes relative to one another. Other systems are the *expanding pulley*, and the variable speed motor (of which the Alsagar wheel is a good example). The latter is now available without any great loss of torque at lower speeds and is thus likely to supersede other methods which are generally

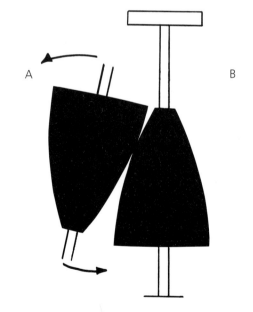

The double cone principle of transmitting power and varying the speed of the wheelhead. The left-hand cone is driven from a shaft or motor and is so mounted that it will swing in the direction of the arrows while remaining in contact with the second cone, to the shaft of which the wheelhead is attached. As the comparative diameters in contact vary, an infinitely graduated speed is transmitted to B from the fixed speed of cone A. In the diagram the speed of B would be near its maximum. (See also expanding pulley.)

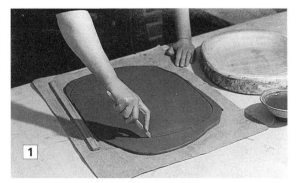

The simplest form of drive from a leather wheel attached to an electric motor onto the perimeter of a large flywheel. The motor unit is sprung so that it lifts from the flywheel when pressure on it is released, giving a degree of control.

noisier and lose power through friction. The motor has a slight whine which some potters may find unacceptable. The average commercial wheel can handle 10–25lbs/5–12 kilos of clay according to the strength of its construction. It is important to try various wheels before purchasing: if the potter and his wheel are not in 'sympathy' it is difficult to do good work.

Praseodymium, *oxides*

A metallic element Pr. 141.
Oxides Pr_2O_3, 330; PrO_2, 157.
One of the '*rare earths*' or 'lanthanides' group. Fulham Pottery quote a zircon/praseodymium yellow for use up to 1280°C/2336°F. Considered to be a more stable, rather weak (though Dodd calls it clean and bright) yellow than *vanadium*.

Pressed dish

Dishes formed by pressing sheets of clay into molds. (See *dishes*.)

Making a pressed dish. (See also hollow mold for illustrations of preliminary rolling.)
1 and 2 The clay slab is cut to the approximate shape of the mold, carefully lifted, supported with the hand as shown and dropped into a hollow mold (or it can simply be reversed into the mold from the rolling cloth).
3 and 4 The bulk of the surplus clay is cut away before sponging the slab snugly into the curve of the mold with gentle strokes from the center towards the perimeter.

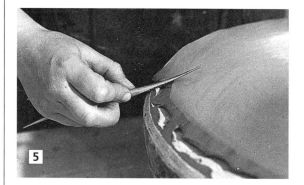

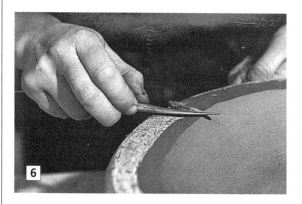

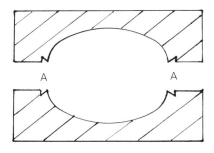

5 and *6* The edge is trimmed flat in two stages: the first by using a wooden spatula at a slight upward angle (use the outer edge of the mold as a guide) and cutting with sweeping movements towards the outer edge to avoid parting the clay from the mold. The final cut is made with the tool held level with the top face of the mold.

7 After a final smoothing of sharp corners, the dish is left to stiffen a little.

8 Cover with a board and invert with mold and board held tightly together. The mold can then be lifted away.

9 The outer edge of the dish may be sponged or planed.

Press mold

A mold in which the clay cast is formed from plastic clay, as distinct from a slip mold. The term can indicate a mold into which clay is pressed, as in dish molds, or a hollow mold, the sections of which are pressed together. It may be designed with an aperture large enough to put one's hand in, so as to press slabs or pellets of clay into a continuous skin around the inner wall.

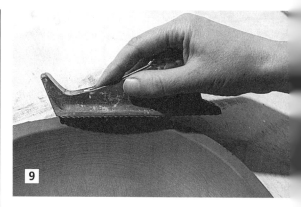

The clay form in the mold is left a little proud of the surface and is scored and slipped in order to make a sound join when the two halves are pressed together. It is inevitable that some wet clay will be squeezed outwards and to accommodate this a channel is cut all round the inner edge as shown in the section diagram. If this is omitted the two halves may not come completely together.

Other types may be taken apart, each section being dealt with separately, the edges scored and slipped, and the whole pressed together. A channel is cut to take the surplus clay as it is squeezed from the join, and which would otherwise prevent the parts making close contact. The handles for industrial tableware are often press molded.

Its advantages over the *slip mold* are: grogged and other mixed bodies can be used, the wall is generally firmer and thicker than a slip wall; pressed forms can be regarded simply as a basis for further work or as a unit in a construction; the cast piece can be deformed by pinching, beating, etc.

Squared bottles are often made in two-piece press molds; the neck is thrown seperately and luted on. *Jigger and jolley* work is a form of press-molding. (See also *dishes, molds*.)

Pricing

See *costing*.

Pricker

An American term for a *needle-awl*. Often simply a needle set in a cork. Professional varieties can be bought.

Primary air

Air which is mixed with fuel to promote initial combustion; that drawn into the gas or oil behind or at the burner, or through the grate to burn solid fuel. Air introduced subsequently into the flame or hot gases is *secondary air*. The control of air input promotes *oxidizing* or *reducing* atmospheres. An electric kiln does not need primary air.

Primary clay

A clay which has remained on the site where it was formed from the parent mineral — usually from granite via feldspar. The china clay of Cornwall is the classic example. Often called kaolin.

The term is also sometimes used as a synonym for *sedimentary clays*. Primary clays however are generally thought to have been formed by chemical action from below (by hot gases from the earth's core) whereas sedimentary clays are usually weathered minerals and may have been moved and re-deposited.

Primary phase

The first crystalline phase to appear when a liquid (glaze) is cooled (Dodd). (See also *phase diagrams*.)

Printer's type

Historically used for impressed lettering on tiles, dishes, and pots. Printer's type can also form patterns and abstract decoration by overlay and repetition.

Printing, ceramic

William Hall (CR158) describes his method of brushing slip onto an engraved plaster or cast slab, cleaning away the surface, a wall built around it, and a casting slip containing Molochite gently poured onto it. When at a leather-hard state the cast is pulled away with the image 'printed' onto it. He warns that this is a complex process.

Other forms of printing on pottery are too varied and complex to be dealt with in detail here, but Paul Scott's 'Ceramics and Print' gives detailed instructions. (See also *bat printing, cut brick, cut sponge, lithography, photoceramic processes, silk screen, sponge decoration,* and *stamping*.)

Prop

Refractory kiln furniture used for supporting shelves. Props may be in the form of blunt cones thrown from grogged fireclay, square columns, or units which will rest firmly one on another. There are a number of ingenious designs on the market, some of which are illustrated. Props may be cast, but slip-cast props will fail in high temperature and reduction and this is not always made clear in catalogs (check with supplier). HT insulating bricks can be cut with an old saw into suitable props for light loads. (See also *bit, crank*.)

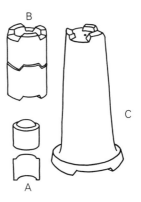

Interlocking props for kiln shelf supports.
A Domed and recessed
B Castellated
C Cast (not normally suitable for reduction firings. Check with supplier).

Propane

The third *hydrocarbon* of the paraffin series $CH_3CH_2CH_3$. Rhodes quotes a heat value of 2558 Btu per cu ft or 93,000 per gallon/21.56 mJ per liter. An equivalent electrical consumption to a gallon of propane is therefore around 27 kWh (perhaps 20 kWh of useful heat). More efficient than *natural gas* but less so than *butane*. (See also *bottled gas, burner*.)

Proton

The positively charged particle in the core of an atom. (See *atomic theory*.)

Protoporcelain

An early or transitional porcelain, usually applied to pre-Song Chinese ceramics. Cardew discusses the analysis of a protoporcelain glaze in terms of the Seger formula and finds silica equivalents as low as 2.0 parts (Cardew pp133–134). The barely translucent fabric obtained by firing a commercial earthenware body to vitrification has been termed protoporcelain.

Pug, pug mill

A machine composed of a metal barrel or cylinder tapered at one end, through which clay is forced by rotating blades in order to consolidate it into a firm column. Dodd makes a distinction between a pug and a pug mill, but this is not maintained in practice. The barrel can be vertical or horizontal, usually horizontal in smaller pugs. A vacuum chamber can be inserted halfway along the barrel to de-air the clay. The clay must be shredded as it enters the vacuum chamber. A pug mill can be constructed by a potter who is also something of an engineer. A de-airing pug has been developed by Harry Davis for studio potters to build. (Davis).

There are several machines on the market, usually with outlets of 2–3in/50–77mm and handling about 3cwt/153 kg an hour. A pug will only work with clay which is in reasonable condition. Very wet or dry clays must be soaked together before they are put through, otherwise the block of clay in the pug may begin to turn as a whole. The action of the blades is to propel the mass forwards as it cuts it up but, in practice, some pressure is often needed at the hopper to keep it moving. A pug mill is a useful but not essential item in a small workshop. If several bodies are used it will need cleaning at each change of use, a tedious process. Clays should be 'rested' after pugging.

Pulling a handle

A method of forming a pot handle by stroking and squeezing a 'tail' of clay (see illustrations under *handle*) The term is misleading as you will soon find if you try to stretch a piece of clay by pulling. The handle may be formed separately or from a tab of clay attached to the vessel.

Pumice

A volcanic acidic *laval* rock (*rhyolite* group) 'consisting largely of feldspar' (Brickell) composed of around 73% silica: 13% alumina; and various small amounts of iron and alkalis. Its texture is spongy, having many cavities caused by bubbles of gas trapped in rapid solidification. It is usually used as a mild abrasive in the form of powder or a block. As much as 40% has been used, finely ground, to give a clear glaze at stoneware temperatures. Has also been recommended as a *matting* agent in glazes.

Punch test

A rather rough and ready test for glaze-body fit. As described by Dodd: a $^1/_{16}$in/1.5mm center punch is placed on the glaze and hit hard enough to break the surface. If cracks radiate from the point of impact, the glaze is in *tension*; if a circular crack has formed it is in *compression*. Score highest marks for the latter!

Purple of cassius

A pigment composed of chlorides of gold and tin. The over-firing of gold enamel on a tin glaze will produce a pale version.

Purple stone

See *china stone*.

Purpling

'— Is liable to occur with *chrome-tin-pink* if the amount of alkali and borax is too high and the lime too low' (Dodd).

Putnam clay

A white, fairly plastic *primary* clay from Florida, USA.

Pyrites

Metal sulfide minerals.

Iron pyrites FeS$_2$.
Copper pyrites CuFeS$_2$, 'Fool's gold'.

The iron pyrites may occur as small nodules in clay, especially fireclay. Rigorously extracted by the industry, but the dark, slightly ashy spots which they develop on a reduced glaze are considered decorative by many craft potters. Larger nodules, however, can be unsightly in their effect. There are also tin pyrites and cobalt pyrites (*smaltite*).

Pyro mini-bars

See *mini-bars*.

Pyrolusite

An ore of manganese dioxide.

Pyrometer

A device for measuring high temperatures, as distinct from low temperature mercury thermometers. The commonest type consists of two parts. A fused, silica or sillimanite tube containing wires of dissimilar metals, the *thermocouple*. For high temperatures the wires must be made of platinum alloys and are therefore expensive; for soft glazes they may be of base metals, chromium, nickel, etc. It follows that you must not use a pyrometer for firings above those specified by the manufacturers. When the tube is inserted into the kiln a minute current of electricity is set up, proportional to the temperature. This is measured on the second part of the instrument, a galvanometer or a potentiometer, and transmitted to a dial calibrated in degrees of temperature, which may be analog (with a pointer) or digital (giving the actual temperature in figures). (See *controlling pyrometer*.)

The pyrometer will, of course, measure only temperature and not heat-work. Its main value is in indicating

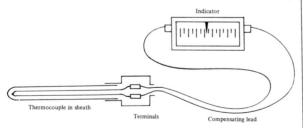

The pyrometer system. The thermocouple (enclosed in a refractory sheath) which generates an increasing microvolt charge as the heat increases and is connected to an indicator where the tiny current operates either an arm on a dial or an electronic temperature figure.

intermediate stages of firing; for the 'end point' *pyrometric cones* are very reliable. Pyrometers are very delicate instruments and are not infrequently damaged in transit or by other means. The calibration can be inaccurate and it is wise to check against cones. However, once the difference between a reading and a cone indication has been established it can usually be applied over the whole scale. Instruments are made with automatic switch-off or 'soak' mechanisms; these can be very useful but do not trust them absolutely. The electronic devices are reputed to be more reliable than the motorized ones.

Other forms of heat-gauging devices are the photoelectric pyrometer and the *optical* or disappearing filament type. The latter has the advantage of portability. The pyrometer is a very useful but not absolutely essential aid to firing and if economy is necessary there may be more urgent needs on which to spend money. (See also *automatic kiln control, thermocouple*.)

Pyrometric cone

Heat indicators in the form of sticks or elongated pyramids of ceramic materials which deforms at a given temperature. (See *cones, Holdcroft bars, Orton cones*.)

Pyrometric cone equivalent, PCE

The measurement of *refractoriness* of a clay or ceramic material obtained by firing a test of the material with cones. The cone number nearest the softening temperature of the test is the PCE of that material. Example: a high duty fireclay (USA) has a PCE of 33; cone 33 melts at 1730°C/3146°F.

Pyrophyllite, Pyrax

A clay-family substance with the formula Al$_2$O$_3$. 4SiO$_2$. H$_2$O. Used in some bodies, especially wall tiles, and naturally present in many clays. Helps 'craze resistance and thermal and moisture expansion resistance' (Georgies).

Pyroplastic Deformation

Long words to describe the warping or bending of ceramics as they 'soften' at high temperatures. Applied especially to the bending of *kiln shelves* under load. See also *over-firing* for illustration.

Pyroscope

A general term for *heat-work* recorders which operate by change of size or shape. (See *Buller's rings, cones, Holdcroft bars*.)

Quadrivalent

Having a *valency* of four, as silica, tin, etc. The oxides reading RO_2, the acidic oxides.

Quartz

A natural crystalline silica, SiO_2. Occurs as visible crystals (rock crystal) or as silica sand, *quartzite* or *ganister*, and in many clays.

Ground quartz is allegedly purer than *flint* and is preferred by many potters although the difference is difficult to detect in the fired body or glaze. Ceases to be stable at 870°C/1598°F but see *quartz inversion* and *silica* for further information.

Fused quartz is very resistant to chemical change and has a low thermal expansion; it is used for crucibles, etc.

Quartz inversion

A volume change in the crystal of silica due to a 'straightening out' during heating into a state of greater symmetry of the SiO_4 lattice. It occurs instantaneously at 573°C/1063°F — the increase in size being variously at between 0.45 and 1% linear expansion. On cooling the crystals revert to their previous squeezed or deformed state at the same temperature with a corresponding contraction. These changes are in addition to the normal *coefficient of expansion* of silica.

If the silica is heated beyond 1050°C/1922°F it begins to change into *cristobalite* which has its own inversion at a lower temperature. The forms of crystal are known as alpha (sub 573°C/1063°F) and beta quartz (above 573°C/1063°F). Flint is, of course, also affected in the same way. The inversion occurs only in 'free' silica and not in *silicates* (glasses) or in altered silica; cristobalite, *tridymite*, *mullite*, etc. which behave in different ways. More than about 25% of silica as crystals in a cooling body can shatter it, but smaller additions can give the contraction necessary to put a glaze into compression (see *crazing*). The inversion of flint is said to be less abrupt and taxing than that of quartz, because of its microcrystalline structure. The failure of a kiln at around the inversion point can lead to severe shattering of pottery, as also can slow cooling, especially from the top temperature to around 1050°C/1922°F in stonewares and porcelains which allows the formation of crystals of silica out of the melt.

Quartzite

A *metamorphic* rock, formed from quartz sandstone cemented by silica. The name is also applied to a pure silica rock.

Quicklime

Anhydrous lime, CaO. Unstable and is slaked with water to produce $Ca(OH)_2$. The stable $CaCO_3$ form is used in ceramics.

R

There is no element with the symbol R and so the letter is useful to denote any appropriate element of an oxide, as in the Seger formula $RO.R_2O_3.RO_2$.

Radiation, heat

The heat given off by a 'hot body'. Electric elements give radiant heat. In a fuel burning kiln, most of the work is done by hot gases, but radiation from the walls and from pot to pot plays an increasing role as the peak temperature is reached, leveling out the heat through the setting. This is one of the chief values of *soaking*.

Raku

A technique involving a rapid firing cycle, the pots being placed in and removed from the kiln at or near the optimum firing temperature. In Japan it was merely left to cool but in the West it is now usually *carbonized* or reduced. Most raku is low-fired but this is not invariable — some Japanese raku was stoneware.

It was raku that brought Bernard Leach into ceramics. Its Japanese symbol means 'enjoyment' — a 'conscious return to the direct and primitive treatment of clay' (Leach). Eastern raku was usually oxidized, often painted, and air cooled. Modern western techniques have developed along the lines of sawdust reduction and quenching in water.

Raku may be made in any style but, because of the thermal shock to which it is subjected, the typical piece has been fairly small, sturdy, often asymmetric in form, and hand-built. All these criteria, however, have been superseded in the late 20th century when the size and complexity of pieces was dramatically increased, partly due to the ceramic fiber revolution in kiln design. So wide in scope has the technique become that one of its progenitors in the West, Paul Soldner, has coined 'ukar' as an anti-raku joke title. Much modern raku is almost indistinguishable as such at first glance and many immensely skillful and sophisticated methods and finishes are employed.

Surfaces are often left smooth; the often remarkable richness of color and surface obtained from plain or painted glazes, and the contrast with the gray or black of the body in reduction, can be weakened rather than enhanced

by excessive texturing or modeling of the clay. *Neriage, inlay,* and other decorative techniques are also employed.

The reduction (often, more correctly, *carbonization*) is achieved by covering the pot when it is still red-hot with sawdust, peat or leaves. Variation will result from partial immersion. The firing chamber or saggar should be kept free of coke or fuel. Wally Keeler (CR1) states that, whatever the kiln atmosphere, pots will oxidize on removal. This has not been my experience: if coke falls into a saggar it is very difficult to get an oxidized glaze out of it. In Japan the system is sometimes reversed: the pots are carbonized in random patterns by biscuit firing in an open trough with charcoal dropped amongst them. The smoked pots are then covered with a clear glaze and cooled in air. Judith

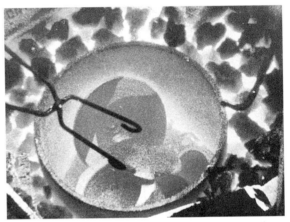

The act of removing a piece of glazed pottery from a simple raku coke kiln as described in the text and diagrams at brazier kiln. (From the film/video 'Raku, English Style', see Suppliers at end of the book.)

A raku pot by Paul Soldner (USA).

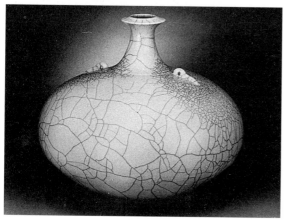

Two fine, large, superbly controlled coiled pots in raku. By David Roberts.

Fisher (CR69) presses leaves or paper shapes into the surface of the clay before dipping leaving an imprinted 'shadow' after firing.

Method: the body must be *open* and often *grogged* but need not be coarse-textured. It should have a high silica content with some 35–40% of alumina and 'at least 1% of

titanium oxide' (Tom Buck CR143). The inclusion of kyanite or Molochite is also mentioned. Buff clay is usual but red clay and mixtures can be tried. The pots are normally biscuit fired to about 900–1000°C/1652–1832°F in an ordinary kiln. Pots could be biscuited in the raku kiln, packing before firing starts, but this limits the pieces available for glazing; there should be sufficient available for a firing every 20 minutes or so for two or three hours. Once the kiln has reached cone 016 (Staffordshire) or 750–800°C/1382–1472°F, the lid or front is removed and completely dry, glazed pots which have previously stood on the kiln to get warm are quickly placed in the chamber with long tongs. They are loosely packed to allow for expansion but may be laid directly on one another. An inspection after about 20 minutes will show whether the glazes are shiny and fluid, and if this is the case, the pots are removed one by one with tongs and either laid in or covered over by sawdust, wood chips, straw, paper, or any organic substance to create the 'reduction' of body and colors, then plunged into cold water (use a metal not a plastic bowl!). When cool the glazes will need scrubbing with a nail brush to reveal their surfaces. The muffle is repacked as soon as one batch has been removed and the cycle recommences. See the films/ videos 'Raku English Style' for a complete session in detail, and 'Robin Welch' for raku firing with individual larger pieces.

The development of the lightweight top-hat kiln has widened the possibilities for raku firing but the excite-ment of removing pots with tongs from a red-hot kiln is less evident. Bruce Chivers has designed a raku-type fiber lined kiln, fired with propane gas, which will attain 1300–1450°C/2372–2642°F (1000°C/1832°F in 20 minutes!). See Suppliers.

Ian Byers' book 'Raku' is an excellent and wide ranging guide to the technique and there are others.

Raku glaze and pigment

Almost any glaze which will melt below 900°C/1652°F is suitable for the soft earthenware type of raku. Leach's white lead recipes are now taboo but low temperature *frits*, e.g. lead silicates or alkaline frits, can be used with a little clay to provide some alumina (5–15% clay). Frits may also be obtained which are complete in themselves, including borax and high-alkali melts. 2–5% of bentonite will assist suspension and glaze coating. These glazes will crystallize after a few weeks and it is advisable to dry them out after use. Alkaline (soda) frits develop exciting glaze colors especially from copper. The metallic copper, which is comparatively easy to obtain with reduction in sawdust, etc. is likely to be fugitive (fade or change) in time. David Roberts in CR160, suggests heavy reduction in the kiln before being covered with sawdust, while J. Parmenter takes the non-ceramic route and sprays on picture varnish.

Any coloring oxides can be used; 2% each of the oxides of cobalt, manganese, and iron for black; 5% of tin will opacify and can produce a mother-of-pearl sheen in reduction. Always glaze reasonably thickly. Areas or strips of unglazed body will give an attractive contrast but should not be overdone. Enamels and gold can be used for painting, in addition to the ordinary oxide pigments, and can contrast with the rough clay in a stimulating way.

Some typical raku recipes:

1 Soft alkaline frit 93, china clay 4, bentonite 3, copper oxide (for turquoise) 3.

2 Lead sesquisilicate 50, soft borax frit 50, china clay 2, bentonite 2.

3 A simple and unusual recipe from CM15/10 — Gerstley borate (colemanite) 80, feldspar 20. Harold MacWhinnie in CR104 lists seven raku glazes, all crackled and also using up to 80% gerstley borate with nepheline syenite and clay.

Most of the pigment oxides can be used on raku, as paints, in slips, or in the glazes. Copper is the most lively, giving green, red, luster, and any variation in between. In-glaze lusters can be used. Enamels are possible and Byers discusses fuming in the kiln itself for special and remarkable, if sometimes rather lurid, effects. Some special raku pigments have been suggested (in relatively oxidized conditions), e.g. for:

iron-red:	frit, iron oxide and yellow ochre
green:	frit and copper oxide
blue:	cobalt, a lead frit, and flint
white:	alkaline frit with china clay and zircon or tin oxide
yellow:	lead frit with a 3:1 mixture of ferric oxide and antimony

(See also *crackle*.)

Raku kiln

A raku kiln must satisfy the following conditions: it must reach 800°C/1472°F and, unless it is used for one special piece at a time, maintain that temperature for several hours, the chamber must be readily accessible and easily opened and closed with the kiln at full temperature; reasonably oxidizing conditions must prevail. There must be no danger (e.g. from shock in an electric kiln) when inserting metal tongs into the chamber.

One of the most popular and easily built is the *brazier kiln* (see for details of building). The Japanese type kiln, illustrated in Rhodes, Reigger and Leach resembles a Roman kiln, a long firemouth feeding into a circular chamber via a perforated hearth. Flame throwers, oil burners, acetylene burners, etc. have all been utilized by modern western potters. Wood and coke fuels are commonly

1 David Roberts lifting out one of his big pots from a top-hat kiln.
2 Plunging the pot into a bin for reduction. Note tongs adapted to hold pot inside the neck.

used. Electric raku poses problems. Firstly the kiln must be absolutely protected from damp or rain, but the pots must be reduced in the open if everybody is not to be choked and blackened; secondly the elements must be completely shrouded from any possible contact with the tongs; thirdly a complete *muffle* within the kiln is essential. CR1 describes one type and the illustration below shows another. In PQ36, John Chalke has advice and a series of

A special muffle or saggar, coil built in a well-grogged clay for use with a top-loading kiln to enable it to be used safely for raku firing. The first photo shows the saggar itself, the second in place in the kiln. The wide flanged rim gives space which prevents the elements over-heating. When firing, of course, the lid is lifted by means of a metal hook or tongs — not the finger as shown!

drawings for raku kilns. Reigger and Byers give a good coverage of kiln types, the latter concentrating on the latest lightweight oil drum and top-hat kilns using ceramic fiber. These can quickly be built by the potter, and are also supplied commercially, e.g. by Chivers (Vacuum formed fiber kiln) and Fordham Thermal Systems.

Rare earths

Actually these are neither very rare nor 'earths' (they are true metals); they are the elements numbers 57–71 in the *periodic table* and are known as *lanthanoids* and include *cerium* and *praseodynium*. A few are coming into use in ceramics, though mainly as prepared pigments. Praseodymium yellow will fire to 1300°C/2372°F. Others are used in optical glasses but may well become available to

potters.

Rasorite

Listed as B_2O_3 66.3, Na_2O 30.0, i.e. a form of borax.

Rational formula, analysis

The description of a material in terms of its oxides in a formula, or its minerals in an analysis. Thus feldspar can be written as $K_2.Al_2.SiO_{16}$ or, as its rational formula $K_2O: Al_2O_3: 6SiO_2$. From the latter one can associate the mineral with the *Seger formula* to arrive at some idea of its reaction in the fire. A rational or 'calculated' analysis will list the probable minerals present, and is used for rocks and clays. Cardew Appendix 10 gives the method for arriving at a calculated analysis from an *'ultimate'* or oxide one. Shaw considers rational formulas to be of little value to craft potters but the information is essential to build up an overall picture of the material and its behavior.

Raw clay

Green clay; unfired clay.

Raw glaze, glazing

A glaze in which none of the constituents are fritted. The term 'raw-glazing' is often confusingly applied to *once-fired ware*, where the term 'raw-clay glazing' would be more accurate.

Reactive slip, glazes

A fusible slip which will start to melt before the covering glaze and thus will 'burn' through it. Potclays issue a series for firing at around 1200°C/2192°F. Damion Keefe in CR156 deals with his own 'reactive' slips and glazes using titanium, together with high percentages of pigments in the slip, firing to 1200–1280°C/2192–2336°F in an electric kiln. Harry Horlock -Stringer was a pioneer in this field.

Glazes of different characteristics can be laid one over another to give broken surfaces and other reactions.

Receptacle, socket, electrical

See *NEMA* for USA and Canada. In the UK the 13 *ampere* socket is normally the maximum (although it is possible to conduct higher ratings through special sockets). Otherwise direct connection to the mains supply through a switch is needed. Check with your electricity supplier. (See *electric wiring to kiln, NEMA, socket.*)

Recipe

A list of materials, with proportional physical weights, which make up a specific slip, glaze, body, or color. Distinct from the *formula* which is expressed in theoretical atomic or molecular parts. *Percentage weights* are preferable to *batches* for comparing one weight with another.

Beginners in pottery are often hopeful that a good glaze recipe will solve their problems. However the recipe is only one (albeit a prime one) of the variables which affect the fired glaze. Others include the particular samples of raw materials used, the speed of firing, the glaze thickness, and the body on which it is put.

Trials and alterations may be necessary to arrive at a mixture which will suit your unique conditions. Some knowledge of the principles on which the recipe is based will prove invaluable: the first step towards preparing your own individual glazes. (See *chemistry of pottery*.)

Recipe-into-formula

A recipe will give some idea of the possible behavior of a glaze but the Seger formula will be more instructive and may be compared with those of known glazes.

The chart used for the computation is the reverse of that used in *formula-into-recipe* and, for simplicity, the formulas used are the *ideal* ones. The results are therefore approximate. Greater accuracy would demand an analysis of your particular samples, and would involve much more arithmetic although the principle still holds good. There are several variations on the system. (See also Cardew, Appendix 10.)

In the first column we list the recipe figures followed by the mineral or oxide they represent. This figure is then divided by the *molecular* (or unit) weight of the material; the resultant figure representing the unity figure in the formula, the alumina in clay for instance, or the potash in feldspar. This figure is entered in the appropriate column and multiplied in the others according to the formula ratio, e.g. clay, 1 alumina to 2 silica; feldspar, 1 alumina to 1 potash to 6 silica.

In the illustrative charts below the examples dealt with under formula-into-recipe are reversed.

To bring the figures to the Seger formula:
1 Total the bases.
2 Divide each of the totals in the base line by this figure.
3 Arrange as RO.R$_2$O$_3$.RO$_2$.

Recipe-into-formula Chart A (reverse of Formula into Recipe, chart A)

%	Material	Parts	–	Mol. Wt.	=	Mol. parts	PbO	Al$_2$O$_3$	SiO$_2$
70.5	Lead sesquisilicate	70.5	–	313	=	0.225	0.225		0.337
17.4	China clay	17.4	–	258	=	0.0675		0.0675	0.135
12.1	Flint	12.1	–	60	=	0.202			0.202
100.0		100.0		TOTALS			0.225	0.675	0.674
	Molecular equivalents						1.0	1.0	3.0

Recipe-into-formula Chart B (reverse of Formula into Recipe, chart B)

%	Material	Parts	–	Mol. Wt.	=	Mol. parts	K$_2$O	CaO	MgO	Al$_2$O$_3$	SiO$_2$	TiO$_2$
48.47	Feldspar	48.47	–	556	=	0.087	0.087			0.087	0.522	
14.53	Whiting	14.53	–	100	=	0.145		0.145				
5.34	Dolomite	5.34	–	0.029	=			0.029	0.029			
1.5	China clay	1.5	–	258	=	0.006				0.006	0.012	
25.52	Quartz	25.52	–	60	=	0.425					0.425	
4.64	Titania	4.64	–	80	=	0.058						0.058
100		100		TOTALS			0.087	0.174	0.029	0.093	0.959	0.058
	Molecular equivalents						0.3	0.6	0.1	0.32	3.3	0.2

Records, *workshop*

Some records, such as the total sales of work produced, are required by law and you will also need proof of expenditure to set against income from sales (see *costing*.) The extent of your additional records depends on your temperament and style of work. Kiln logs are useful and can save worry and spoilt firings. Tests and trials of materials and glazes will be a waste of time without adequate records. One's memory is fallible and one doubts it most when the unexpected occurs.

It is not practicable to record all the factors which influence a result but the mere note of recipe and temperature is not quite enough. The following data will enable a fair appraisal to be made.

1 A test number for identification; a running number with or without a prefix. Codes are apt to get muddled or forgotten.

2 Percentage recipe and the amount actually weighed. The batch can be divided into fluid measures to facilitate future additions, line blends, etc.

3 Type of test piece — cylinder, tile, etc. and whether fired flat or upright.

4 Body color and texture.

5 Glaze thickness; vital in the appearance of the glaze (the method of application is also a factor and should be noted).

6 Position in kiln.

7 Kiln and firing as *kiln log*.

For the recording of clay tests see under *clay testing*. Briefly the record should be of plasticity and workability; soluble materials; shrinkage; raw and fired colors; absorption; deformation and faults and the behavior of glaze on sample. Other useful records can be kept of weights of clay for reproduction items, with their size and shape. (See *card measure*.)

Red clay

An iron-bearing *secondary clay*. Includes brick clays. Although called 'red' clay its fired color is brown or terracotta. It is present in vast quantities and a great variety of qualities all over the earth's surface, 'typified by Etruria marls' (Dodd).

A potter needs a plastic but not sticky clay, fairly smooth and with a shrinkage within 12% plastic-to-fired. It should contain negligible 'free' impurities such as lime fragments and soluble alkalis.

The fine particle size adds to the plasticity but also lowers the *fluxing* temperature, and red clays are normally used only for earthenwares, notably slip-wares. In England the Etruria marls are well-known high-iron clays some of which, from the Staffordshire region, will stand up to 1260°C/2300°F in an oxidizing fire without serious

trouble. They are vitrified and 'self-glazed' at this temperature. In *reduction* red clays will generally fail or melt as the iron is turned to its fusible *ferrous* state.

Red clay may be added to other clays, and also to glazes to provide iron in an ultra-fine form. In stoneware glaze it also provides valuable fluxes, and up to 50% can be used. Adding 5–10% of a suitable red clay to a stoneware body can lessen the possibility of *shattering* during cooling in the kiln or afterwards. A body of 7 parts Potclays Buff Body to 1 part of their Staffs red clay in oxidation at 1230–1260°C/2246–2300°F gives the hardest, most unchippable body I have known for tableware and other purposes. Slip glazes are high-clay glazes or are composed mainly of very fusible clays such as *Albany clay*. Local red clays may be useful as pigments.

Red color and glaze

Reduced *copper reds* were, until recently, the only true reds available to the studio potter at 1100°C/2012°F or over. Red colors (often nearer purple or terracotta) are now becoming available in this range and also up to 1300°C/2372°F. Various red glazes appear in merchants' catalogs for lower temperature firing under careful conditions up to about 1050°C/1922°F. Most are opaque. The standard, slightly purplish red up to around 1140°C/2084°F is *chrome-tin pink*.

Selenium is a comparatively new oxide and with cadmium will give orange and red but the compound is difficult to stabilize and is subject to *volatilization*. Research is improving the performance of these frits. Chromium oxide at around 900°C/1652°F in a high-lead low-alumina glaze can produce red with 3% of chrome or 5% potassium bichromate. Until recently uranium has been unobtainable but is now appearing in some lists as 'spent' uranium. It is a source of orange-reds up to 1020°C/1868°F. A chrome-tin reaction will give pinks, as will zircon-iron compounds at higher stoneware temperatures (Dodd).

Iron reds rely on undissolved crystals of Fe_2O_3 which are difficult to maintain in the fired glaze.

Cardew recommends a pure nepheline in the batch with a high-alumina, low-calcium formula. Rhodes reverses this advice. In Cardew's type however the color is from an undissolved suspension within the glaze, while the latter is derived from precipitated surface crystals. The glazes need applying fairly thickly. Some of the formulas quoted in Cardew include:

K_2O	0.8	Al_2O_3	1.17	SiO_2	5.35
Na_2O	0.2	Fe_2O_3	0.05		

Difficult to transform into a recipe. The use of an alkaline frit may help.

A recipe suggested by Peter Smith, and which approaches the formula is:

| Nepheline syenite | 42% | Potash feldspar | 35% |
| Fremington red clay | 20% | China clay | 3% |

Another recipe for iron red appeared in CM37/20 (John Reeve) and an even simpler recipe is David Leach's nepheline syenite with ball clay or some red clays for a tomato red in reduction, applied thickly. The calcium content controls the ability of the glaze to dissolve the iron oxide. Potterycrafts make a high temperature iron/zirconium red; Ivo Mosley suggests adding as much as 60% to an underglaze slip.

Soaking and slow cooling (but see *dunting*) to 1000°C/1832°F are reputed to help. The aesthetic attraction of a bright red on craft ceramics is open to doubt even if it becomes easily available. Of course it is always possible to use enamels which exhibit a very fine range of reds. Geoffrey Whiting has produced a persimmon red at 1200°C/2192°F in an electric kiln by varying the temperature rise, a method known to the Japanese as 'fire change'. Details have not been published. Titanium is reputed to enhance the redness of iron in very fluid glazes. Damion Keefe in CR156 states that 'bone ash seems to be the key if you want reds and yellows — (and) another key ingredient is titanium' in both the slip and glaze. In CR127 Ingeborg Gose (Belgium) quotes a glaze: Gerstley borate 50, Georgia kaolin 30, flint 20, first fired to 1200–1260°C/2192–2300°F then refired to 1000°C/1832°F. (See also *ash glaze, copper reds, kaki glaze, reactive slips, oxidized stoneware glaze*, the last for a broken-red 1250°C/2282°F recipe.)

Red lead

Lead peroxide Pb_3O_4, 685 (equivalent weight 228). Also known as 'minium'. Poisonous. A strong *flux* in a glaze. Forbidden for use in most countries . Traditional slipware glazes used red lead and it figures in several of the older raku glaze recipes by Leach and others. Can be replaced by lead frits (silicates).

Red pigment

Similar considerations apply to red pigments as to red glazes: they are plentiful in the enamel range and below 1000°C/1832°F. Underglaze reds include the ubiquitous chrome-tin sometimes with vanadium. Above 1050°C/1922°F most compounds revert to brown, but there are prepared fritted colors from iron/vanadium and other compounds for use at stoneware temperatures. (See *red color and glaze*.)

Red slip, body

Like red clay this is brown rather than red and is normally a simple liquid red clay. Lighter colored slips and bodies

can be stained with iron oxides or with prepared body stains, often iron-based, to give red-browns, pinks, and 'coral' up to as high as 1280°C/2336°F. These need a white body to develop their color. The addition of 25% of iron oxide to red clay will give a more intense color. Up to 20% of rutile has also been used.

Reduction

The extraction of oxygen *atoms* from *oxides*. The most startling color changes in reduction are those of the iron and copper oxides. More subtle alterations take place in other oxides, in the glaze quality and in bodies. The reduced oxides are usually unstable and will revert to their 'higher' oxide unless protected from the air by dispersal in a glaze. Precipitated iron will re-oxidize (see *kaki*, and *red color and glaze*).

Reduction is generally considered to be the result of starving the fuel of oxygen during the firing, creating *carbon monoxide* and *hydrocarbon gases*. The first is a very poisonous gas and kiln rooms should be well ventilated. David Ketteridge (CR12) mentions reduction by hydrogen as it forms water with oxygen 'stolen' from the glaze oxides, e.g. $Fe_2O_3 + H_2 = 2FeO + H_2O$, or elemental carbon by a simple equation yielding the metal and CO. This contradicts several accepted theories including that of the negative role of smoke. Searle in PQ8 lists carbon monoxide, hydrogen, coal gas, incompletely burned oil, and finely divided carbon in luminous flames as the chief reducing agents. The wide variety of results from 'reduction' suggests that more consideration should be given to the fundamental chemistry. The CO/CO_2 and the H/H_2O ratios control the degree of reduction (together with elemental carbon) and it is possible to measure the atmosphere with instruments placed in the kiln or the chimney flues, now available to the studio potter, e.g. from Glendale (see *oxygen/carbon sensor*). The reduction in a kiln is normally sufficient to produce only the ferrous iron oxide, FeO, but copper oxide is easily reduced to the metal under certain conditions (see *luster*). The moisture given off by burning fuel helps to develop celadons. It has been noticed that a humid day is better for reduction than a dry one.

Reducing atmospheres are built up by the adjustment of *primary* and *secondary air* controls, judicious use of the *damper*, and sometimes the extraction of chimney bricks to cut down the draft. Reduction started before 800°C/1472°F may stain the glaze gray or black which subsequent firing will fail to burn away. During reduction the fuel is inadequately burned and the temperature may fall; reducing periods are therefore interspersed with clear-fire conditions. With wood or coal firing, each stoking tends to set up reducing conditions willy-nilly. Alternatively a semi-reducing atmosphere can be maintained from about 1000°C/1832°F so long as the temperature can be steadily increased.

Other cycles have been recommended: Ray Finch reduces for 55 minutes of every hour from 1000–1240°C/ 1832–2264°F but not sufficiently fiercely to prevent a steady rise in heat, then continuously until the peak temperature is reached, *soaking* for half an hour in oxidation. Some potters maintain a neutral atmosphere from 1050°C/1922°F with a reduction at the end; or give half an hour of reduction at 1000°C/1832°F, 1100°C/2012°F and 1200°C/2192°F. Shaw mentions reduction starting at top temperature and continuing during cooling to 800°C/1472°F.

The weather has its effect. I have found that a still, bright fine day is more conducive to success than a dull or windy one. It does not seem to matter whether or not one 'cleans' the kiln at the close with an oxidizing fire. When a kiln is reducing, flame may appear at cracks and spy-holes wherever the gases come into contact with free oxygen. Any sign of 'escape' should be ignited to reduce the danger from carbon monoxide. Beware gas burners 'blowing back' into the pipes: turn off and re-light if this happens.

Kiln furniture will be affected by reduction and it is advisable to check with the manufacturers that it is suitable. Cast props are very vulnerable. Shelves need to be thicker: ¾in/18mm for alumina or silliminite bats, slightly less for silicon carbide. Obviously a refractory body must be used for pots, often a ball clay strengthened with fireclay, china clay, and flint. Few red clays will stand up and all are more liable to fail during reduction than in oxidation. A proportion of red clay — usually about 5% though this varies widely — can aid vitrification and warm the body color, a darker body often giving improved glaze color. In glazes the red ferric iron is most commonly used: 2% or less for celadons; up to 12% for other effects (see *tenmoku*, *kaki*), black iron oxide, crocus martis, ochres, and other forms of iron have also been used with good results. Reduced iron may be the spinel $FeO.Fe_2O_3$ (the formula for 'magnetic' (*magnatite*) iron).

Reduction is a skill which can be learned only with practice in your particular kiln. A *kiln log* is essential. Copper reduction will take place at lower temperatures than iron: 600–800°C/1112–1472°F for producing copper-red *enamels* and *lusters*. It may be taken to the extreme of producing the metal by the same method as on-glaze painting and in *raku* firings. ½% of copper, or less, is added to a glaze for high temperature reds. See *copper red*. Cobalt is not altered; manganese may produce a gray, or green.

Peter Smith has kindly made available the following recipes for reduction glazes in a neutral atmosphere:

The simple gas-fired kiln, built by Steve Mills (Bath Pottery, UK) shown at top-hat kiln is frequently used for raku firing but also for cone 9 reduction firings (1280°C/2336°F); the atmosphere controlled by this equally uncomplicated vent in the lid, constructed of pieces of cut brick. Following a fast rise to top temperature, cooling is slower and accompanied by prolonged reduction.

Feldspar 72, Whiting 13, China clay 7, Flint 8, Calcium phosphate (bone ash) 5, Charcoal 8% of total, Ferric oxide 3% of total. Giving a green matt glaze.

Use animal charcoal if available as it contains calcium phosphate. This recipe gives a celadon type glaze without the calcium phosphate. Another recipe reads: Fremington red clay 28.2, Cornish stone 28.2, Whiting 21.1, Flint 7, Ball clay 14.1, Ochre 1.4 plus 10% of charcoal, coal-dust, or graphite. A celadon type glaze.

The above glaze is viscous but can be made shiny by the addition of 10% flint or quartz. The reducing agent should then be increased by 5–10%. Add extra iron for *tenmoku*.

Reduction in electric kilns

In an electric kiln reduction is usually a trial activity only, although the development of silicon carbide elements widens the scope as has already been mentioned. Porcelain has responded to small sticks of wood about 5in/125mm long and ¼in/6mm square inserted into the lower spyhole during the last half hour of firing, giving a gentle greeny-buff color to a $1\frac{1}{2}$% iron glaze at 1270°C/2318°F. Kanthal wire will stand reduction without damage (even regular reduction according to some potters). (See also *electric kiln, Kanthal.*)

Glazes can be reduced in a neutral atmosphere, e.g. in an electric kiln, by means of local reducing agents incorporated into the glaze batch itself. Soot, charcoal, animal charcoal, black *ash* and silicon carbide can be used, the last mentioned being the least effective. A fairly viscous glaze is needed to prevent re-oxidation. The more fluid the glaze the more reducing agent is needed. The amount will vary with the kiln as well as the glaze and experiments should be made with additions of between 10% and 20% to the batch. Copper and iron will respond to this type of reduction (Peter Smith). In electric kiln reduction, two outlets, one lower front and the other top back are advisable in order to direct the reducing agent right through the pack, with the top outlet controllable.

Stephen Coulsting reduces with gas in an electric kiln, heavily at 1050°C/1922°F and at intervals with decreasing strength to 1210°C/2210°F then continuing the firing to 1310°C/2390°F. He suggests a number of inlets, including the floor. Care must be taken not to introduce the gas at temperatures below 1000°C/1832°F in order to avoid minor explosions. He recommends butane as a rapid reduction agent, though propane and natural gas are possible. Details in CR88. The introduction of wood strips (red pine in the case of the Japanese Koheiji Miura) into an electric kiln from around 950°C/1742°F and continuously until the optimum temperature is reached (1250–1300°C/2282–2372°F) can give good blues and celadons from 2.5% of iron oxide (see illustrations in CR155).

Nitrogen piped into an electric kiln or, preferably, a closed saggar, can maintain an 'inert' atmosphere and, if iron is introduced into the glaze as black iron oxide, FeO, it will not reoxidize and a 'reduced' effect can be obtained. The system, however, would prove expensive. For checking the CO levels in any type of kiln there are meters which register the gas, normally used by garages to test exhaust gases; also Glendale and other suppliers sell an *oxygen sensor*. see also *ash*.

Re-firing

A second glaze firing for faulty ware is seldom successful. The glaze may change its whole character on re-fire, only very occasionally for the good. In all cases it is advisable to re-coat the pot with glaze, or to rub it well into crawling, etc. Use a thick glaze mixture, and warm the pot before re-dipping. Repeated re-firing may destroy the fabric of a pot.

Refractories

Heat-resisting materials used in those parts of the kiln which must stand high temperature and reduction without deforming or spoiling: bricks, tiles, shelves, supports, saggars, etc. The term is most often applied to the bricks. High grade *fireclays*, *high alumina* bodies, and *silicon carbide* are some common materials, as are *magnesite*, *sillimanite*, and *carbon* (in the absence of air). Special types are made from chrome ore, etc. The official rating of a refractory is a PCE of 18 or above. Ciment Fondu is a refractory cement for use up to 1320°C/2408°F. Some refractories are also designed to insulate — the lightweight bricks used in electric kilns for instance — others such as silicon carbide shelves to conduct heat.

Study of the alumina-silica *eutectic* will show why high alumina refractories are preferred. Even though a material whose make-up approaches the eutectic is way above our working temperatures, a certain degree of pyroplastic movement is always likely because of small amounts of impurities which lower the melting point. Refractories need a long *soaking* fire to develop a mat of *mullite* needles throughout the fabric. (See also *bricks, fireclay*, etc.)

Refractory coatings

In addition to the traditional washes of alumina and sodium silicate, silicon carbide, and other mixtures, a great deal of effectiveness is claimed for a spray-on coating, 'a proprietary (probably zirconia) formula' (Nils Lou), called ITC (International Technical Ceramics, Florida. Available from Scarva). This can be applied in one thin coat to any surface; brick, ceramic fiber, kiln furniture, shelves (supplied by Axner), even to kiln elements. 'The material functions as an isolator rather then an insulator' (Nils Lou). 'Furnascote', another zircon-based material (Metrosales) is recommended for all firings including salt-glazing for coating and repair of kiln linings.

Refractory materials

Applied to oxides or minerals which are heat-resistant in their own right or which tend to raise the firing temperature of a glaze. The *acidic* oxides are considered refractory, especially silica, tin oxide, titania, chrome, zirconia and antimony. Zinc and boron have ambiguous positions. Alumina in molecular proportions greater than 1–8 compared with silica has a refractory effect. Lime has a very high melting point (2615°C/4771°F) but acts as a base in high temperature glazes above 1200°C/2192°F. Barium has a similar role. (See also *refractories*.)

Refrasil

Proprietary name — Chemical & Insulating Company, Darlington, UK — for a fused silica fiber.

Regenerative principle

In kiln design: the use of heat given off by cooling ware to pre-heat other chambers. The climbing kiln is very efficient in utilizing heat. A regenerative brick kiln is illustrated in Rhodes K, p.53.

Release limits

The degree of metal release from glazes under the influence of acids, etc. registered in parts per million, ppm. (See *metal release* for details.)

Relief decoration

See *applied decoration, boss, carved molds, chatter, embossing, ribbing, roulette, seal, sprigging, studs, strip decoration, throwing rings, tube lining.*

Repairing pottery

For broken pots the most commonly used glue is Araldite. Equal amounts from two tubes are mixed on a wooden surface with a wooden tool. As the glue takes several hours to harden, some method must be found to hold the join tight together meanwhile. Adhesive tape, string, clamps, and rough 'molds' are possible depending on the size and shape of the piece. Other glues are available which harden much more quickly. If several breaks are involved it is better to do the job in two or more stages. For earthenware a less permanent and quicker drying glue is sufficient, but whichever is used wash, dry, and dust any loose pieces from the break before sticking. When the join comes together make absolutely certain that the faces are flush with one another; run your finger gently along the join to feel for any step. The glue must be used thinly and care should be taken not to let it set on the surface. Contact glues are less satisfactory as there is no second chance once the pieces are pressed together.

A good join will scarcely show but if the surface is broken then it will need filling with Polyfilla or something similar. The colors can be matched in water paint and touched in. For glazed ware the join can be carefully worked over with nail varnish using a fine brush. The riveting of pottery is now seldom practiced.

For cracks or pre-firing damage see *stopping* and *mending*. A remarkable claim is made by Susan Bennett in

Fournier PT that hairline cracks incurred after the glaze fire by careless handling may heal in a subsequent re-fire.

Repetition throwing

While many believe that the role of the craft potter lies in producing the one-off piece, the basis of much professional work is the repetition throwing of tableware, etc. It is a test of ability to control clay on the wheel, and each piece can still be given its due quota of care and attention.

A 'set' does not involve the absolute uniformity of the industrial product but rather a family resemblance and an identity of feeling and character. This is easier to achieve with a distinctive shape and color than with a simple, more anonymous form. There is more to matching pieces than mere design: the clay mix, the weight, the throwing method (movements and pressures) and the surface spirals are all fundamental to the result. Take care to control the base thickness and, of course, the finished size which can be checked with *calipers*, a card measure, or a pot gauge. Allow half a dozen trials before starting the actual group or run. Do not change your wheel or

Repetition throwing on the grand scale in Richard Batterham's workshop.

rowing position. Use clay balls of equal softness.

When turning and handling follow the same rules and o the whole group at one session, endeavoring to establsh a rhythm of work and movement. Practice each stage n your trial pieces and use the same tools throughout. 'ariations in the details of decoration can add interest roviding that a good match has been achieved in the arly stages.

There is great satisfaction, in addition to technical develpment, to be obtained from repetition throwing, which is ot so different from the creation of the 'one-off' piece as ome imagine.

Repetitive strain injury, RSI

The effects of continuous similar muscle movements, leadng to pain or a breakdown of the muscles involved. A ecent variation of this, most often affecting the wrist and ower arm, is known as Carpel Tunnel Syndrome nd has been the subject of much discussion. Rosemary Atencio's books on the subject give useful exercises to help elieve the condition. It is easy to tell potters to vary their work and movements and to have comfortable wheels and working surfaces, but this is the only sure way to avoid the condition, together with suitable exercise.

Residual clay

There is some disagreement on the use of this term. Many authorities use it as a synonym for primary clay. Cardew, however, links it with sedimentary clay; a clay that has been leached or weathered to remove impurities, e.g. fireclay.

Resist method, techniques

Resist techniques are essentially methods of obtaining a design with a colored background as opposed to a colored stroke on a plain background. The resist agent can be wax, latex, or paper or flat objects such as leaves. The material to be 'resisted' can be slip, pigment, or glaze. Paper is more suitable for slip. (See *airbrushing, latex resist, paper resist, wax resist.*) On a more mundane level wax can resist the glaze on foot rings and lid flanges when dipping pots. (See *wax.*)

A form of slip resist was quoted in CR171 by Jerry Caplan in which biscuit is coated with slip, cut through in sgraffito and given a raku firing with light reduction. When the slip is peeled away the design is left as a smoky black line.

For enamels and oil-based pigments a water-soluble gum, or a proprietary brand of resist is needed. The enamel

A square 'cat' plate by Chris Speyer, using cut paper and latex resist combined with brushed color.

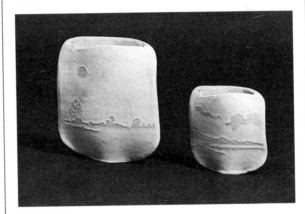

Delicately resisted glaze 'landscapes' on porcelain by Val Barry.

is then sprayed or painted on, covering the surface resist and then gently washed away from the resisted areas.

Resistance wire

All materials set up some resistance to the flow of electricity. This is measured in ohms. The wire for kiln elements (Kanthal, Nichrome, etc.) is made in various grades and thicknesses which offer greater or lesser resistance, as measured in ohms per foot run. The greater the length of any given wire the less current will flow, while an increase in diameter will increase current flow. (See also *electricity, electric kiln wiring, Kanthal, silicon carbide.*)

Retarder

Sodium citrate, borax, gelatine, alum, the use of lukewarm water for the mix, and keratin have been mentioned for adding to *plaster of Paris* to retard setting time.

Reverbratory kiln

A type of multichamber brick kiln where the heat is transferred from one chamber to the next, using it efficiently to pre-heat, fire, and control the cooling of the loads.

Rheology

The science of flow and deformation. These are crucial factors in the behavior of pottery materials under heat. Also applied to flow characteristics of plastic clay and casting slips.

Rhyolite

A medium or fine-grained glassy acidic rock in the granite bracket but containing less iron oxide.

Rib

A wooden or metal tool for smoothing or assisting in the throwing of a pot on the wheel (see figs **1** and **2**). So called because the older potters used a bone for this purpose. Ribs often have one flat and one curved edge and are made of a flat sheet of a rigid material. Isaac Button cut himself ribs from an old spade, but they may also be of wood — sycamore, box, obeche, bamboo, etc. They are normally used on the outside of a pot to minimize throwing ridges. Average size about 3 x 4in/75 x 100mm. A pliable *steel*

2 Using a bamboo rib during the latter stages of throwing for trimming the base of a pot on the wheel.

palette can sometimes be useful. A 'throwing stick' in the form of a wooden hook shape for use inside tall or narrow necked forms is listed by Potterycrafts (see illustration at *egote*).

Ribbing, rilling

Decorative relief ridges around pots, generally formed on the wheel during throwing, but also found on hand built ceramics.

Rilling indicates similarly placed indentations round pots, this time usually made with a tool during turning, when the clay is leather-hard.

Rice hulls

Rice husks burnt to an ash yield 96% and more of silica. Where they are plentiful (e.g. Italy) they may be used in the manufacture of insulating *refractories*.

Riddle

A coarse-mesh sieve. A garden riddle can be used for separating the larger particles from the finer ones when dealing with crushed rocks, wood ash, etc. A cook's nylon sieve is useful for the initial breaking up of weighed-up glaze materials (in water, of course).

Rigidiser

A liquid obtainable from some suppliers for hardening ceramic fiber.

Rim

The top edge of a pot or bowl.

1 The use of a rib in throwing a flowerpot; in this case it is merely an oblong piece of iron cut from an old spade.

The rim is more than a simple termination of the form it is the final accent and should have shape and character of its own. It should therefore be carefully considered in all cases; a weak rim can spoil a good piece. The rim can even become the focal point of interest as in this 'stepped' rim on a strongly formed bowl by Rachel Northam.

Cut and over-lapped rim by Martin Smith.

RO group

The symbol for the total of bases in a glaze formula, R indicating any suitable element and also covering the R_2 alkalis. The RO is kept at unity for easy comparison with the amphoterics and acids. (See *Seger formula*.)

Rock

The earth's crust is made up of minerals and rocks. Rocks are usually conglomerates of minerals and have no *ideal formula*. They are not necessarily hard; clay, to a *petrologist*, is soft rock. The minerals in a rock may be detectable with the unaided eye, e.g. the mica in granite. Rocks are graded according to their base/silica content into basic, intermediate, and acid rocks. The first are dark in color, 'heavy' or dense, and fine grained; volcanic *basalt* is characteristic. Acid rocks tend to be lighter in color, coarser grained and with a lower specific gravity. *Granite*, the mother rock of feldspar and kaolinite, is the commonest. The *syenites* (nepheline) are intermediate. One may liken the acid rocks to the body of a pot and the basic rocks to the glaze. A rough color guide to the iron content of a rock has been given as: less than 1.5%, a very pale blue; 1–1%, light green; 2–2.5%, olive green; 5–10%, black.

Rock wool

Proprietary name for a form of *mineral wool*.

Rolled inlay

A method of decoration in which a pattern or design is cut from thin slabs of colored clay, laid onto a clay sheet of a contrasting color, and pressed into the surface with a rolling pin. Coils can also be used in place of slabs though with rather less control. The technique was originated, as

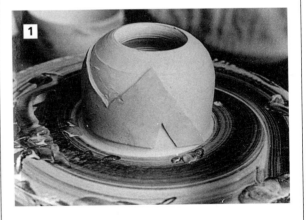

Jack Doherty with his thrown variation on rolled inlay: in this case the colored clay motifs are adhered with slip to a thick-walled, partly formed pot and then thrown into the main body of the piece.

1 and 2 In the first picture he is applying the inlays to a half-thrown pot; in the second photograph throwing is continued, and the wall made smooth and flat.

3 *Shows an early stage in the similar treatment of a bowl.*

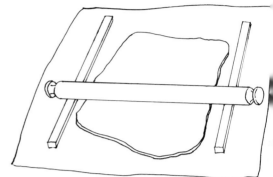

The use of laths of wood to control the thickness of a rolled slab means that one can adjust the thickness to suit the work in hand. It is also easier to roll with deeper laths to start the process and to replace them with thinner guides as the work proceeds.

far as I have been able to verify, by Sheila Fournier in an article in PQ10. Sabina Teuteberg rolls colored clay designs into slabs with a mechanical roller, transfers the decorated slabs to molds and forms her tablewares by jigger and jolley, details in CR100. (See also illustrations for a similar system of *thrown inlay*.)

Rolling clay

Rolled slabs of clay are needed for a number of techniques: dishes, slab pots, etc. and these are more likely to fire successfully if the slabs are made in a craftsmanlike way.

Use a dry cloth for rolling on: a fine hessian or some material which will stretch a little but not crease easily. It should have no knots or bad faults. Check that the cloth is laid on a surface which is smooth and free from grit or pieces of clay. Start with a well-wedged bubble-free block of clay beaten out to the general shape you require for the finished slab (e.g. a round block for a circular dish). Beat with the fist or palm to about ¾in/20mm thick. At this

stage, and at all future stages, give the clay and cloth an occasional quarter turn and also lift the slab from the cloth and let it down again to prevent it from working into the weave. If the clay really sticks to the cloth it cannot stretch any more. Using a good wooden rolling pin long enough for the work in hand, roll with a firm steady pressure and avoid thinning the edges. Turning the slab as mentioned above will help to maintain a level surface. Thickness can be gauged with the eye, or an edge cut through with a needle awl to show thickness.

Guide sticks can be used. These are strips of wood about 1in/25mm wide, as thick as the slab you require, and a little longer than the widest part of the slab. The sticks are used only in the latter stages of rolling. If bubbles appear these must be sliced through with a needle and not merely pricked. Make sure that your rolling pin is not warped. Door knobs or other circular pieces of wood on the ends of rolling pins can be used in place of sticks as slab thickness controls.

Clay or clay coils can be embellished with rope and other impressions by rolling them over meshed materials such as metal or coarse cloth, diagonally for rope patterns.

Today more potters are using mechanical rollers such as those supplied by Cromartie and other potters' merchants. These are fast and accurate but, like all mechanical devices, may eventually have their effect on the finished product. (See also *hollow mold*).

Rolling pin

A straight, wooden rolling pin at least 14–16in/355–450cm long is required for pottery. Do not leave the pin on a damp surface where it will warp — hang it up.

This kitchen utensil was often made in ceramic either as one piece or fitted with a wooden shaft and handles.

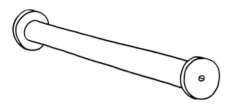

Door knobs or small wooden wheels can be attached to a rolling pin as shown to control clay slab thickness as an alternative to guide sticks.

Rolling pin pot

A rolling pin (or a cardboard cylinder) can be used as a mold or former for cylindrical pots. Wrap a sheet of paper round the roller and tape the edges. Roll out your slab in fairly damp clay and ease it round the cylinder. The joint can be pinched together forming a ribbed pattern, overlapped, or beveled and joined flat. The base may be luted on at the time of making or later when the pot is leatherhard (the base clay must be in a similar condition to the pot, of course). After an hour or so remove the rolling pin but leave the paper lining in the pot. The lining will have sufficient strength to hold the pot upright but will crease as the pot dries and shrinks; it can be removed as soon as the cylinder will stand unaided, or left in and fired away in the kiln.

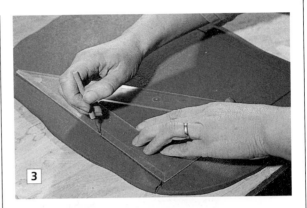

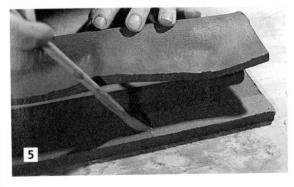

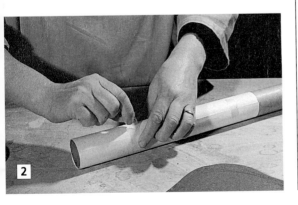

In fact this pot is being made round a card cylinder but the principle is the same as when using a rolling pin.
1 and 2 A sheet of paper is wrapped round the cylinder and fastened.
3 and 4 An oblong slab of clay is cut to the height of the pot, and the width measured by folding it over the cylinder.
5 and 6 The joint can be made in a variety of ways: overlapped; with slanting lapped cuts which can be worked into an invisible join; or, as shown here, the two ends slipped and fastened together in a pattern of pinches.
7 A base is cut to size and luted on.
8 Finally the card cylinder is removed, leaving the paper lining as a support until the pot is dry enough to stand on its own.

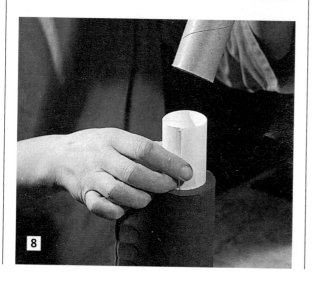

Rope decoration

Rope or *cord* can be used to impress clay, either by wrapping round a pot and beating it into the surface, or round a beater or paddle which is then used to impress the surface. The impressions can then be brushed over with a slip or pigment on a dryish brush. Rope can be plaited and used either to impress the clay directly or to roll it over.

An alternative use of rope is to soak it in salt water or other compound and fire, wrapped round a pot, in a saggar. (See *saggar firing*.)

Rotary sieve

Listed by Baileys, Potters Supply House, Potterycrafts. (See illustration at *sieve*.)

Roulette

A tool for producing a repeat decorative impressed pattern. See diagram for the most common type, but a suggestion in CR133 by Martin Cowley is a furniture castor which can be fitted with a handle, many of which can be carved or otherwise marked with a design. The technique is of great antiquity. A roulette is an engraved wheel or cylinder which, when rolled over clay, produces the pattern. It was much used by Roman potters. 'The edges of old English ovenware dishes were notched by this means' (Leach). In the film/video 'Isaac Button, country potter', Isaac Button is seen impressing the name of his pottery as a continuous band round flower-pots. Ladi Kwali rolled a carved roulette round the shoulder of her pots, combining it with free pattern (see also the film/video 'Ladi Kwali').

The most readily available roulette 'blank' is a piece of blackboard chalk, which can easily be carved with a simple pattern. Biscuit rollers can be mounted onto a wire handle or onto a forked twig with a piece of thick wire. Roulette wheels can be shaped for concave and convex surfaces.

A simple roulette wheel, which could be of pottery, plaster, or wood, and mounted on a wire or other form of axle so that it can be rolled over plastic clay to impress a repeat pattern or motif.

1 An engraved stick of chalk used as a roulette, rolled over a soft clay surface to produce a repeat pattern.
2 A large roulette wheel with address both advertises the Pottery (Isaac Button at Soil Hill, UK) and decorates the pot.

Rubber resist

Rubber can be used in a liquid form as a resist material (see *latex resist*).

Rubber stamp

Used industrially mainly as *marks* on the bases of ceramics, they can also be used decoratively to apply color either onto biscuit or glaze. Scott suggests making your own stamps by cutting a design with a scalpel knife into a soft pencil eraser. The motif is normally quite small as it is difficult to apply color from too large a stamp. See Thompson in booklist.

Run glaze

Apart from the unfortunate tendency for *crystalline glazes* in particular to run from the foot of a pot, glaze can be applied as a decorative element (see *poured glaze*).

Run slip

One of the slipware techniques (see figs **1**, **2** and **3**). The slip is trailed in blobs around one edge of a dish or on the shoulder of a pot, usually on a wet base-slip of a contrasting color. A shake will run the blots across the dish or down the sides of a pot, giving pleasant, liquid shapes. In a bowl, a sideways twist can give variety. Some practice is required and the shaking should be restrained. The comparative consistencies of the background and trailed slip will directly influence the resulting pattern.

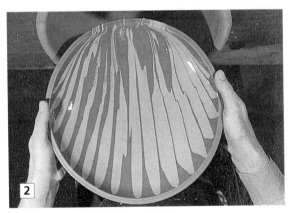

1 A leather-hard dish is flooded with slip and immediately trailed with blobs of contrasting color round one edge.
2 Without delay the dish is held vertically and the blobs given two or three sharp downward shakes. Triangular dishes are especially suitable but all shapes can be used.

3

3 A completed dish.

Rust

Hydrated iron oxide, $2Fe_2O_3, 3H_2O$.
Actual rust can be scaled from iron and used for decorative purposes; beating it into the surface of a piece, or adding to glazes and slips.

Rusticated slip

If thickish damp slip is patted with a paddle or the hand it can produce a broken surface similar to 'rusticated' concrete.

Rutile

One of the crystalline forms of titania. To a chemist rutile is synonymous with titania, TiO_2, but to a potter it indicates the impure iron-bearing ore of titanium, an accessory mineral of igneous rocks. Also occurs as ilmenite beach sands, $FeTiO_3$. Available in 'ceramic grade' and 'granular' the latter used as a specking agent (Georgies and others).

The distinctive mottled appearance of rutile in borax glazes has led to its use ad nauseam on commercial tiles, etc. The titanium content will opacify a glaze. Small amounts (1–3%) of rutile are useful in modifying other pigments in earthenware and stoneware glazes. In reduction, rutile may give a bluish glaze.

Saddle

An item of *kiln furniture*. A bar of refractory material used to support tiles, etc. during firing. In section it is a concave triangle. Supplied in sizes 1–11in/25–280mm long by $\frac{3}{8}$–$\frac{3}{4}$in/10–20mm across. A similar shape is called a 'pin'.

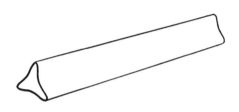

A saddle, used during firing to support tiles or wide-based pots which are not glazed beneath the foot. Most kiln furniture of this type (spurs, etc.) are suitable only up to the higher earthenware temperatures. Check with supplier.

Safety in the workshop

See *health hazard, poisonous materials, dust.*

Saffil

Proprietary name (ICI plc) for alumina/zirconia *ceramic fibers.*

Saggar, saggar firing

A clay (usually fireclay) box in which pottery is fired to protect the ware from flame and ash. Used in larger kilns as the unit of a *bung*. The box is made of well consolidated refractory clay with up to 50% graded grog. It can be coiled, slab built round a drum, formed on the wheel using soft clay and a rib, or by a combination of thumping and throwing. Industrial saggers may also be jolleyed or cast. Wall thicknesses average about $\frac{3}{4}$in/20mm. Saggars may be oval, circular, oblong, or square (but always with rounded corners). The industrial norm is a 17 x 23in/430 x 585mm oval but they come in all sizes and thicknesses of wall. For some purposes they have holes in the sides. With the coming of cleaner fuels, smaller kilns, and 'continuous' firing the use of the saggar has declined sharply and it is becoming difficult to purchase them.

The striking result of 'saggar firing' on a pot by John Leach. He stands a pot on a bed of sawdust in a saggar, then packs further sawdust around it, sometimes adding straw or even rolled newspaper. The level of the packed material controls the misty white line to some extent. The saggar is made as airtight as possible with a lid and wads, and the whole fired in a reduced stoneware kiln. The chamber temperature is around 1290°C/2354°F but the actual pot is insulated by the carbonized sawdust and, surprisingly, remains slightly porous; having been subjected to no more the 1100°C/2012°F at the most. Carbon, in the absence of air, is very refractory and is also one of nature's insulators.

Saggar clay, marl

A *refractory* mixture of clay and grog, the latter may be in proportions of 50% or more. The inclusion of grog from broken used saggars is useful. The 'dust' should be removed from the grog. The clay content is generally fireclay, but the inclusion of some vitrifiable clay will set up a liquid phase which will help the growth of *mullite* crystals. Sillimanite is a useful addition. Up to a point saggars will get stronger with firing. Cardew discusses the problems involved in making saggars pp 158–60. (See also *marl*.)

St Agnes fireclay

A source of fine fireclays (probably since pre-Roman times) in N Cornwall (W. J. Doble).

Sairset

A commercial name for an air-setting kiln cement or mortar for jointing bricks or facing walls.

Salt, expansion

Common salt is sodium chloride, NaCl, a colorless, soluble crystalline substance. It is believed to assist glaze suspension but its main use in ceramics is in the production of salt-glaze. The re-crystallization of salt, an irreversible expansion, in *salt pots* can cause trouble: a crazed earthenware glaze will allow dissolved salt to permeate the body and it may lift the glaze away.

A chemical salt is a compound: the reaction of an acid with a base, e.g. sodium sulfate, barium chloride, etc. A glaze may be considered as a salt, or as a salt into which additional material is dissolved. Salts are, in general, more stable than their separate constituents.

Salt and pepper pots

While these pose design problems and opportunities there is also a hazard in their use; the re-crystallization of salt, an irreversible expansion, can cause trouble: a crazed earthenware glaze will allow dissolved salt to permeate the body and it may lift the glaze away. It is advisable, therefore, to use a vitrified body or at least a craze-proof glaze. The former is the easiest option.

Slab-built salt, pepper and mustard pots by Sheila Fournier.

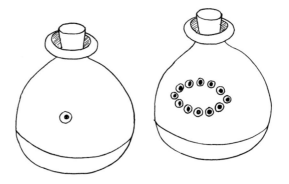

Bottle-shaped salt and pepper pots from Coxwold Pottery.

Salt-glaze

Stoneware ceramics, generally once-fired, with a glaze achieved by throwing common salt or rock salt onto the hot fuel, normally at around 1200°C/2192°F and upwards (but see note below). The NaCl decomposes into a variety of chlorine gases and sodium, the latter reacting with the silica of the clay to form a thin, slightly orange-peel textured glaze which is very hard and resistant to corrosion. The iron oxide in the clay leads to the formation of ferric chloride vapour. Developed in Germany, it went out of favor for tableware around 1760, its use since confined mainly to cheap jars, bottles, and drainage materials. Several craftsmen potters are now reviving the technique, which produces a very integrated and interestingly variable finish. The degree of glaze texture will depend on the grain size of the clay body. A fine, white stoneware body will show a correspondingly fine 'orange peel'; a porcelain will be even smoother.

A siliceous clay or a wash of silica slip has been recommended, although alumina is also needed. More complete glazes, or ash, can be applied, the salt being used as an additional flux. Borax additions will produce a thicker and more lustrous glaze but at the expense of the typical texture. Carbonates of copper, etc. thrown onto the fire have been reported to produce psychedelic color. Anne Shattock uses stains (Mason Stain Co. USA) in slips to produce colored salt glaze in a neutral atmosphere (CR95). Some Potterycraft stains are also suitable. Mary Rich uses lusters over her salt-glazed pieces.

A good deal of modern salt-glazed ware is decorated in subdued colors which, though attractive, can be somewhat at odds with the powerful surface/color textures of salt-glaze on stoneware. A milder color break in the glaze itself, e.g. on a finer-grained body, would help.

Most fuelled kilns (i.e. other than electric) which have a reasonable chimney to carry away the chlorine fumes, can be utilised for salt-glaze. The Wren family developed small coke and gas kilns to produce excellent salt-glaze. Hamada used the technique for several years. Once a kiln has been used for salt-glaze it cannot be used for feldspathic glaze firing, as the deposited salt will be released on to other glazes. All lid flanges, etc. should be washed with pure alumina or silica to minimize sticking. Be generous with alumina on shelves, tops of props, etc. The technique is hard on refractories but high-alumina shelves are reputed to stay reasonably free from glaze though Parks prefers silicon-carbide shelves with a thick coat of kiln wash. Firebricks are vulnerable, although the Wrens fired their gas kiln for salt-glaze some 90 times without serious damage. Rosemary Wren recommends slightly damp salt (table salt, rock salt, or 'water-softener' salt) at 1lb to every 3cu ft (5kg to 1cu m) of kiln space, applied in three doses, starting the highest temperature. The temperature will drop aft salting. Beware blow-back of steam when using damp sa Wear goggles. See also *fuming, soda glazing* — of whi salt-glaze is, of course, a variety.

Guy Sydenham (CR65) uses a seawater drip into t firemouth just behind the flames. Extra salt can be di solved in the water where necessary and he finds th kinder than solid salt to both pots and kiln. David Mill in CR85, explains low temperature salting 950–1000°C/1742–1832°F. He uses a vitreous sl (engobe) with copper carbonate, etc. as does Wally Keel (CR152 recipe —feldspar 60, china clay 40).

Bowls will become glazed all over by the salt b enclosed spaces such as mugs and bottles may need a th wash of a suitable glaze inside. Wally Keeler (CR77) h the simplest possible glaze for salting: equal parts feldsp and china clay, and also uses Phil Wood's recipe — corni stone 70, wollastonite 30, red iron oxide 8. Jane Haml fires her lids in a perforated saggar to avoid the unsight marks of fly ash settling on them during firing.

In 1991 the new Environmental Protection Act (Gre

Powerful salt-glaze faceted bottle by Phil Rogers.

...ushed and trailed slips with sponged oxides under salt-...aze. By Rosemary Cochrane.

...ively trailing on a rich brown salt-glaze, fired in the wood-...ired kiln shown at kiln, by Janet Mansfield (Australia).

...Britain) was enacted to control the emission of harmful ...olluting substances. This is not intended to affect small ...scale craft businesses but salt-glaze potters are advised to ...gain authorization, on the grounds that their level of pro-...duction is 'trivial', from HM Inspectorate of Pollution. ...Addresses and information from the Grants Officer, Crafts ...Council, 44a, Pentonville Road, London N1 9BY, UK.

Saltpetre

Potassium nitrate KNO_3. Soluble and normally used only in frits.

Sampling

Natural materials may vary slightly throughout a batch. A true sample must be made up from small amounts taken from various parts of a batch. A lengthier, rarely necessary system is to divide the batch into four, discarding two parts and remixing the rest, continuing the process until only a sample amount remains.

Sand

Coarse particles of rock, generally, but not always, impure silica. 'Sand size' is given as 0.6–2.0mm (70 mesh) (Georgies). Some sands contain heavy mineral impurities such as zircon, rutile, ilmenite. Seashore sand can contain large quantities of shell (calcia), basalt, and powdered shale.

The use of a pure silica sand as a *placing* material has largely given way to alumina. The grain shape varies and some sands are much more rounded than others. Some potters prefer smooth granules but sharper types are more likely to increase standing strength. Its addition to bodies will give 'bite' to throwing clays; will assist drying (though not as efficiently as grog); and decrease shrinkage. However it introduces '*free*' *silica* which may give trouble at the inversion point if used in large quantities. Builder's sand is supplied in sharp and 'soft' qualities, the former being washed sand. The impurities in builder's sand can add interest to a body. Beach sands are variable and will need washing to remove salt, etc; river sands are preferable. Zircon sand has been recommended for *saggars*, *refractories*, and for *ovenware*. Sand additions can lead to pitted glazes especially in oxidized stoneware.

Sand blasting

Sand used as an abrasive sprayed under pressure to achieve textural and other effects on biscuit or glazed pieces. An efficient extractor and the invariable use of a well-fitting *respirator* or *mask* is essential. 'Shadow' images can be obained with the use of masking materials. While a number of modern potters use the method, the initial equipment could be expensive. A separate room is required, the whole operation taking place in a closed box with a window and armholes connected to rubber gloves. The technique, therefore, is not one to adopt unless it becomes a major part of the work. Also the nozzles are quickly eroded by the sand. It can be used to pierce or 'carve' porcelain.

Sand size

Given as 0.6–2.0mm (70 mesh). Rocks or minerals must be broken to sand size before grinding in a mill or mortar.

Sandstone

A *sedimentary* rock of silica (quartz or sand) particles cemented with clay, lime, and iron oxides. White clays may be found in association with sandstone.

Sange de boeuf

A red in-glaze effect from reduced *copper*. A little tin oxide is reputed to help the color.

Satin matt glaze, *vellum glaze*

A name given in suppliers' catalogs to semi-matt glazes 'usually of the tin-zinc-titanium type' (Dodd). A recipe for a satin matt lead glaze (not for use on tableware) which includes zirconium, titanium, tin, and zinc is quoted by Fraser. See also *vellum glaze*.

Saturated glaze

A glaze with the maximum color content which it is capable of dissolving. Liquids can hold more material in solution at high temperatures than at lower ones; some metal or oxide may therefore be precipitated onto the surface of the glaze during cooling. Pigment/glaze-ratio varies with the oxide and, to a lesser extent, with the glaze formula. A lead glaze with 3% of copper can produce a metallic black but a glaze will still be shiny with 10% or more of manganese dioxide of which some stoneware glazes can dissolve as much as 25% in oxidation. In general, the more fluid the glaze the more color in solution it will accommodate.

A list of 'saturation points' is therefore misleading but as a comparative guide the following list may be useful. Average for soft clear glazes, color in solution:

cobalt	2%	copper	2.5%
nickel	4%	chrome	6%
lead antimoniate	8%	iron	10%
manganese	10%		

Some types of kaki are examples of supersaturated reduced stoneware glazes where the surplus iron has been precipitated onto the surface, to re-oxidize during cooling.

Saucer

Its design must always be considered in relation to the cup which is to be set on it. Saucers tend to flatten during firing and should be thrown with a slightly generous curve or lift. The foot-ring is placed outside the line of the 'well' both for stability and strength. Saucers are thrown either as short cylinders, the walls of which are then thrown outwards to the desired shape, or as a plate is thrown, the edge being shaped from a ring of clay after the well is forme[d]. The well must be flat or slightly dipped or the cup m[ay] spin. One can finish the well at the turning stage. Sauce[rs] can be turned with a foot-ring but this is time-consumi[ng] and they are often left as cut from the wheel, merely trim[m]ing the outer corner to a bevel.

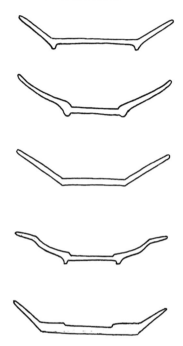

Sections through five types of saucer. Those with a wider we[ll] and shallower rim can double as a small plate.

Sawdust firing, decoration

The firing of pots in slow-burning sawdust is fun but as a[n] educational exercise may be misleading. The heat generate[d] is not often sufficient to turn clay into ceramic and th[e] pots will disintegrate in water. A low initial biscuit fire wi[ll] rectify this and the sawdust treatment will then be a[ ] mainly decorative one, subtle graduations of color result[t]ing from reduction and carbonization. With practice an[d] care, a measure of control can be exercised. In our so-calle[d] temperate climate the sun is rarely hot enough to avoid th[e] all too common mishap of *dunting* as the piece is expose[d] during the firing. An open body helps but also increase[s] the difficulties of burnishing. A rounded form with a[ ] sturdy rim is most likely to survive. The inclusion of san[d] or other silicas is not recommended, the firing always hovering round the *inversion-point*.

Resin from using pinewood 'sometimes produces beautiful blue and silver markings' (Judy Cunningham). A degree of control can be exercised by partially lifting the

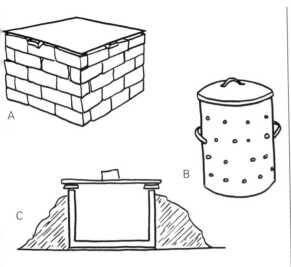

Three types of sawdust kiln.
A A simple, dry-built brick box with a sheet metal cover raised slightly on shards or brickbats. It burns reasonably well but the pots are liable to dunt.
B A dustbin perforated to allow air for combustion.
C A saggar or brick box insulated with soil, the lid is propped as in **A**.

piece from the burning sawdust as soon as it shows above the surface.

Method: A brick box is dry-built, usually about an 18in/450mm cube. Ventilation holes can be left between bricks but these increase the incidence of dunting. In some designs earth is banked round the kiln for insulation or a dustbin is pierced with holes and used instead of a brick box. Galvanized metal may give off poisonous fumes when heated and should be avoided. Whatever type of kiln is used, an outer bale wall or windbreak is useful. An easily removable and fireproof cover must be provided, set on three or four pieces of brick to allow air to enter. The box is filled with alternate layers of dry sawdust and pots until full, finishing with 3–5in/80–130mm of sawdust. It is ignited from the top and burns downwards; a sprinkling of paraffin (kerosene) on top will facilitate lighting. There is little point in 'topping up' with sawdust and if this is done there is the slight danger that the sawdust, given sufficient air, may ignite with a mildly explosive force. As the sawdust burns down pots will be exposed and settle down onto those beneath. Put the strongest ones at the bottom. As mentioned above, success is most likely on a hot, still day.

A purely decorative technique is to sprinkle sawdust onto the surface and set it alight which gives more control of the surface decoration. Siddig el Nigoumi simply burnt a piece of paper and held the pot over the flame to smoke-mark the surface.

Scales, weights

The most useful weighing balance for the small potter is a $\frac{1}{2}$oz–2lb/15–1000g 'sweet shop' scales. A 15lb/7kg set is also useful for weighing clay and larger glaze batches. The cheaper spring balances are rarely accurate enough, but dial scales working on a counterweight principle can be adequate for throwing clay lumps. Good quality beam scales are the most reliable but are fairly expensive (Axner list a reasonably priced model). There is also a torsion balance which is reputed to be very sensitive from 0.1g up to 2kg. 'Electronic' scales are becoming more common with digital reading: but they still rely on a mechanical system.

Gram weights are sold in sets from $\frac{1}{2}$g to 1kg, graded in such a way that all weights between can be measured. The set is 1 x 1kg, 1 x 500g, 2 x 200g, 1 x 100g, 1 x 50g, 1 x 25g, 2 x 10g, 1 x 5g, 2 x 2g, 1 x 1g, 1 x $\frac{1}{2}$g.

Scewback

A sloping-faced *brick* (see *springer*).

Schist

A coarse-grained metamorphic banded rock of mainly mica, quartz, and feldspar: 'weathered schists form good clays' (Brickell).

SCMC

Sodium carboxymethylcellulose. A glaze binder and an engobe deflocculator. (See also at *CMC*.)

Scraper

The ordinary triangular paint scraper with the sharp corners filed away provides the best scraper for cleaning tables, etc. A cook's rectangular plastic scraper is also excellent and is less likely to damage polythene bins, etc. The *steel palette* can also be brought into use and is the best tool for shaping and finishing hand-built pots. (See illustration under *former, handbuilding, surform.*)

Screen, printing

A wire mesh or perforated plate for sieving materials. The term is often applied to the coarser meshes. (See also *lawn, sieve, silk screen, vibratory sieve.*)

Screw stopper, lid

Not often made by potters but described some 450 years ago by Picolpasso and in our time by Cardew.

Scumming of clay

A white efflorescence which can mar the surface of fired terracotta. It is due to soluble basic salts, often calcium sulfate which has been brought to the surface by capillary attraction during drying, the crystals being crushed by the fingers while working on the clay. It is almost impossible to remove. If a salt-free clay cannot be found, the addition of 1–2% of *barium carbonate* will help. This however is a toxic material. Barium sulfide (barytes) can also be used. (See *efflorescence*.)

Sea-water magnesia

Of no practical use to potters but a fascinating entry in Dodd-Murfin concerns the extraction of large quantities of *magnesia* from sea-water in the USA (California) and England since 1935.

Seal, stamp

All potters, whether amateur or professional, should have their own stamp with which to identify their pots. A seal is usually about $\frac{1}{2}$in/12mm across and must be simple in design — initials, a monogram, or a cipher. More information (the name of the pottery for instance) can be shown on a *roulette* seal.

The design may be either in relief or recessed (intaglio). The former is useful for pots that have become rather dry but the latter is more impressive. If you have a steady hand

the seal can be cut directly into leather-hard clay; otherwise it is cut into a wood or plaster block from which cast can be taken. One can paint or scratch one's signature straight onto the pot—these are 'marks' rather than seals.

A seal used as an item of decoration on the porcelain box by Sheila Fournier.

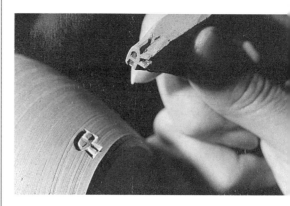

A seal cut in relief to give an intaglio impression (which can be inlaid with color, glaze or slip)

Geoffrey Whiting's pottery seal (A for Avoncroft Pottery) and his monogram on a coarser clay body.

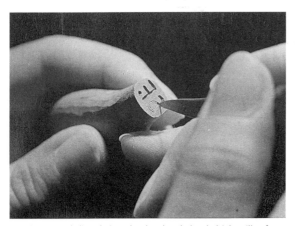

Cutting a seal directly into leather-hard clay (which will, of course, give raised initials in use).

stamp pressed onto a little pellet of clay gives a raised seal which is attractive and can be a decorative item on a plain pot. It also minimizes the risk of pushing the stamp right through a thin pot wall.

Seat earth

The material immediately beneath a coal seam, often fire-lay but sometimes silica rock (Dodd). 'The seat earth for vegetation' (Worrall), i.e. the vegetation which produced the coal.

Seaweed

Seaweed wrapped round a pot before firing can leave glossy imprints on biscuit. (See also *firecord*.)

Second

Given by Dodd as 'pottery ware with small not readily noticeable blemishes', a definition which some potters would be advised to study (see also *lump*).

Secondary air

The air supply allowed into the kiln to assist the combustion of the fuel beyond the actual source of the flame, i.e. to *oxidize* any unburned carbon or gases given off by the fuel. Manipulation of secondary air can control kiln atmosphere. Secondary air will be more efficient if it is pre-heated. Kiln design should take this into account, directing it through a hot zone before it enters the chamber.

Secondary clay

A clay which has been transported from the site of its formation by water, wind, or glacial action. The clay is thus ground and levigated to a fine particle size which increases its plasticity but, inevitably, it picks up impurities in the process. Some may be very pure (e.g. English ball clays) but most are fusible and fire to a terracotta color. In some cases (fireclays for example) the impurities have been leached out again later, the clays becoming more refractory.

Sedimentary clay, secondary clay

Sometimes confused with *primary clay*, these are very variable in character and origin. The common factor is that they have been deposited in depressions in the earth's crust (lake basins, etc.) and most of them have been formed by the decomposition of feldspar. They are weathered clays often containing micas, hydrated iron oxide, lime, '*free*' *silica*, etc. English *ball clays* probably have their origin in a *primary clay* which has been washed away and re-deposited as a fine-grain but reasonably iron-free sedimentary material.

Sedimentation

Although all solid particles will eventually settle in a liquid in which they have been suspended, the heavier and larger ones will settle first. Thus the finer particles carried by rivers tend to travel the furthest, finally coming to rest in estuaries or lake basins, forming reasonably pure clay beds. Sedimentation is used to separate heavier minerals from lighter, e.g. mica from china clay. (See also *levigation*.)

Seger cone

A *pyroscopic* device in the form of an elongated pyramid of ceramic material graded and numbered to 'squat' at a given temperature. These mixtures, the first to be devised, represent a logical series of steps originated by Hermann Seger, a 19th-century German ceramic chemist. (See *Seger formula*.) Modifications have been made for the lower temperatures but the principle on which the series is based still holds.

The RO group is made up of $0.3 K_2O. 0.7 CaO$, while the alumina is kept at one-tenth of the equivalent of the silica. A No. 6 cone is: $RO. 0.6R_2O_3. 6.0RO_2$; a No. 9 in the ratio $1:0.9: 9.0$. The silica ratio will be seen to be higher than that used in stoneware glazes but some porcelain glazes have similar formulas. (See *cones* for a list of cone numbers and equivalent temperatures.)

Seger formula

Originated by the German chemist Hermann Seger more than a century ago, this is still one of the standard procedures for representing a glaze formula and, although according to Hamer 'his name has been dropped from use', is used in this dictionary because of its comparative simplicity. The system lists oxides as comparative molecular equivalents in three groups: *basic, amphoteric,* and *acidic,* written $RO.R_2O_3.RO_2$, R denoting any appropriate element. The RO group also includes R_2O oxides, e.g. potash, and the sum of all the basic oxides is taken as unity — 1.0 equivalent. In this way the other constituents can be directly and immediately compared. The R_2O_3 is represented by alumina; ferric oxide may also be included. When we come to the acid group certain ambiguities creep in. The principal acid and the foundation of all ceramics, SiO_2 fulfills the role, as do TiO_2, SnO_2, etc. but boric acid, antimony, and others have *amphoteric* type formulas (B_2O_3 etc.) and are still listed with silica. The symbol RO_2 is therefore not to be taken literally but as including all the *glass-formers*.

The placing of B_2O_3 continues to be questioned since it acts more like a base or flux and falsifies the silica proportion (see *leadless glazes, glaze formula*, and under the oxides of individual elements).

Seger rules

Hermann Seger's rules for dealing with *crazing* and *peeling* of glaze.

For crazing adjust body thus:
1 Decrease clay content
2 Increase flint
3 Replace some clay with kaolin (china clay)
4 Raise biscuit fire
5 Decrease feldspar
(1 and 5 refer more specifically to industrial bodies.)

For crazing adjust glaze thus:
1 Increase silica base ratio
2 Replace some SiO_2 with B_2O_3
3 Replace high molecular weight bases with low weight ones.
For peeling, reverse these adjustments.

Seger's porcelain

Given in Dodd as a body introduced by Seger with a recipe of 30–35% kaolin (china clay), 30% feldspar, and 35–40% quartz, biscuited at 'a low temperature' and gloss fired at cone 9.

Selenium

A non-metallic element Se, 79. 'Resembling sulfur in its chemical properties . . . occurs as selenides of metals' (Uvarov). A *metalloid*.

Used in combination with cadmium, as sulfides, to produce low temperature orange and red glazes and enamels. Can be toxic and there is some doubt about its use on tableware. Quick cooling helps to retain color. Normally only available as a complete fritted glaze. A quoted frit is: soda ash 15.0, *saltpetre* 2.0, cryolite 6.0, fluorspar 14, borax 29.0, sand 34.0, with 3% selenium.
At the present time the firing temperature of selenium reds is around 960°–1020°C/1760–1868°F. (See *red color, glazes*.)

Self-hardening clay

See *air-setting clay, unfired clay*.

Self slip

According to Dodd/Murfin this is an archaeological term for a wet-smoothed surface layer on a clay vessel.

Semi-muffle

A muffle in a kiln which does not completely protect the ware. In effect a bag wall on each side.

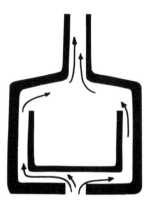

A semi-muffle kiln.
The example shown
is an updraft type
but can be adapted
to downdraft. Many
gas kilns are of this
type.

Semi-conductor

A material with a limited power of conducting electricity, eg. *silicon carbide* kiln elements. 'Most ceramics become semi-conducting at high temperatures' (Dodd).

Semi-porcelain

According to the Brussels Nomenclature it has: 'The commercial appearance of porcelain without being really opaque like earthenware or truly translucent like porcelain. These products may be slightly translucent in the thinner parts such as the bottoms of cups (and) . . . can be distinguished . . . because the fracture is rough-grained, dull, and non-vitrified . . . a fracture clings to the tongue'. Some studio porcelains come into this category.

Umqua White (listed by Georgies) is a smooth, plastic semi-porcelain which 'blushes to a warm apricot color in a wood or gas fire'.

Series wiring

A number of resistances wired one to another. This reduces the voltage to each one and the total resistance will be the sum of all the resistances in the circuit. Thus two similar

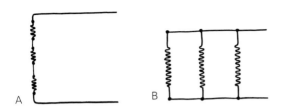

A *Three resistances connected in series, e.g. may represent three kiln elements but all wired one to another so that they 'share' the voltage, the resistance being the sum of all three.*
B *The same equipment wired in parallel, i.e. each at full voltage.*

lamps in series will reduce the power by a factor of the square of half the voltage — in other words you will get a very dim light! The various kiln elements in a circuit are wired in series and so must be calculated as if they were one unbroken length, but the various circuits are wound in *parallel*. Series/parallel switching is used for slow/medium/fast kiln controls. (See *heat control*.)

Serigraphy

A term used by Scott, see *silk screen printing*.

Sesquioxide, *silicate*

'Sesqui' is strictly 1.5 ($1\frac{1}{2}$), but in molecular formulas this is expressed as the whole number relationship 2–3. Thus, among the commonest of these are alumina — Al_2O_3 and lead sesquisilicate — the relationship is 2 molecules of lead oxide to 3 molecules of silica, $2PbO. 3SiO_2$.

Setter

Supporting refractories for pots during firing which closely follow the contours of the ware, or separate it from the shelf (see *placing*). Dishes can be set on sand or alumina in the biscuit firing (as is *bone china biscuit*). (See also *kiln furniture, tile setters*.)

Setting, *density*

A *kiln* pack, including *shelves* and *furniture*.
Setting density will influence kiln behavior, a full kiln generally firing better than a half empty one (see *radiation*). However, problems of heat transfer can arise from too solid a pack — of very close tiles for instance. The professional potter will arrange his work with the kiln setting in mind so that the space can be fully utilized, yet allowing for variety. (See *packing kilns*.) Setting density can be recorded in terms of weight; the number of pieces, the

market value, or, at least described in general terms as 'very full', 'loose pack', etc. which will be of some help in assessing *firing graphs* and the practical results.

Settling of glaze

The settling of solid material in slips and glazes, often to form a hard cake on the bottom of the container, is a perennial headache for the potter. Frits are especially prone to settling. Attempts to stir up a hard, settled glaze are often a hopeless task and the only way to deal with it effectively is to pour off all the liquid. The cake of glaze will then usually come away quite cleanly and can be cut and broken up with the hands and reworked little by little into the liquid.

The suspension of glazes depends on several factors (see *flocculant, suspender, suspension*).

s.g.

Abbreviation for *specific gravity*.

Sgraffito, *sgrafiato*

Decoration in which slip or other coating is scratched or cut away to reveal the clay body beneath. A variety of tools can be used: the fingers for very wet slip (also called 'finger combing'), a stiff brush, a knife, or more traditionally, a bamboo or cane tool cut to a flat end resembling a very broad pen nib. The condition and thickness of the slip at the time the design is cut will also affect the result. Glaze and pigment, as well as slips, will respond to sgraffito treatment. Sgraffito through glaze is necessarily treated in

Eric Mellon at work on one of his decorated bowls, using a sharp metal tool. He often combines sgraffito with brushwork. (See a fired example of his work at underglaze.)

The typical sgraffito cut through soft, though not liquid slip with a chisel-ended cane tool.

Two sgraffito cylinders by Mick Casson (photo by Eileen Lewenstein).

a broad and simple way; at the other extreme, through pigment, designs can be worked out in very fine lines.

Designs are too varied to discuss in a short article. Compare, for instance, a Leach bottle with a decorated Greek amphora for extremes of sgraffito styles. The line should be fluid and yet taut, rapidly executed and, once cut, left alone. Backgrounds can be cut away leaving textured areas which will throw more solid shapes into relief. Do not

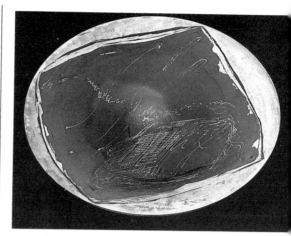

An excellent example of fine-line sgraffito on a bowl by Greg Daly (Australia). It was glazed with cobalt/copper glazes, fired in oxidation to 1280°C/2336°F and then decorated with resin luster.

become carried away by the fascination of the work and do not forget the vital correlation between the decoration and the form of the piece, which is as important for dishes and bowls as for pots. The alternative term 'sgrafiato' is sometimes used for designs in which the background is cut away, as opposed to linear pattern. James Tower's combination of resist and sgraffito between a light and a dark glaze proves how the simplest of techniques can result in successful and subtle work. (See also *combing, finger combing, wax resist.*)

Shale

As the water was squeezed out of clay in geological time by strata movements, pressure and heat, it hardened or 'lithified' into mudstone and shale. Slate is a further, metamorphosed stage. *Fireclays* are often shaley and need grinding for use.

Shattering

The break-up of the pot fabric after glaze firing, happily a rare phenomenon. It is almost always due to an excess of fine, 'free' silica in crystalline form and to the shock of its inversion. This not only strains the body itself but can also put a glaze into a state of such extreme compression that it splits the body. Associated with *peeling* (see also *Seger rules, crazing, quartz inversion*). A large dish glazed on one side only is at especial risk, a thick glaze coating more dangerous than a thin one. Glass, melted in a ceramic piece as a decorative effect, can break the piece through excessive contraction and tension.

To cure compression-shattering use less flint or quartz in

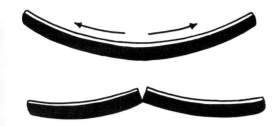

A glaze in high compression on the top face of a dish can exert sufficient outward thrust to break or shatter the body.

the body and/or higher contraction bases in the glaze and/or increase body fluxes to form silicates, which do not 'invert'. Cool rapidly from top temperature to about 950°C/1742°F in order to minimize crystal formation. Geoffrey Whiting found that 5% of a red clay cured bad shattering. A clay with a high incidence of the trouble may be best discarded. (See also *shivering*.)

Shavings

Clay shavings from turning or scraping, beaten into a damp pot surface, can produce a somewhat 'rustic' textured surface. Eileen Lewenstein combines shavings with coarse wood ash, sand, and gravel (though the last of these should be used with care as they may explode in firing).

Shelf, kiln

See *bat, kiln shelves*.

Shell-stone

Given by Dodd as a Cornish china stone with 'too much iron (as brown mica) for use as a flux in pottery glazes'. But it sounds as if it may have some potential for way-out finishes!

Shivering

The action of glaze breaking away from the body, especially on rims and edges. It is usually suffering from over-*compression* associated with a poorly developed *interface*. The treatment generally recommended is as for *shattering* or *peeling*. The replacement of some of the feldspar with nepheline syenite or china clay with ball clay may help, especially with ash glazes. Rim crawling is a similar complaint, the glaze lifting away from the body at a sintering stage. It is difficult to cure (see *crawling*).

Slip can also 'shiver', especially a white slip on a red body, and this is most often caused by unequal slip/body shrinkage. Add more plastic clay to the slip, a fusible ball

clay for instance. If shivering happens during drying, apply the slip to rather stiffer clay, or apply it more thinly. Slip shivering during the cooling of the kiln may be associated with quartz or cristobalite inversions and can be helped by the addition of about 5% of flint.

Short circuit

See *circuit, fuse*.

Short clay

Clay with poor plasticity or workability, also known as 'lean' clay. Large-grain, pure clays are short; ball clays are *fat* or plastic. Most bodies contain both types. Bentonite 2–3% in a short body will impart some of the qualities of plasticity. Shortness can result from *overwedging* or *pugging*, or from too small a water content.

A few days' rest in a damp atmosphere will restore a normally plastic clay, and a month or two may help a short one.

Shoulder

The upper part of a pot where it turns in towards the neck or rim. It is the most eye-catching area of a pot and generally takes the most important part of the decoration.

Shrinkage of clay

Clay progressively decreases in length and volume during both drying and firing though the rate of decrease is not constant over the whole cycle (see below). Firing shrinkage is non-reversible, and is not to be confused with heat expansion and contraction (*coefficient of expansion*) which all materials undergo during heating and cooling, or with silica *inversions*.

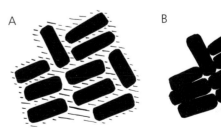

A In the plastic clay the plates are held apart by layers of water. As the water evaporates the particles come closer together.
B The interstices can still hold some water and the diagram can represent either leather-hard or dry clay. Hence the comparatively low shrinkage between leather-hard and dry clay.

Showing the shrinkage of slab pots, all made to a similar size, at various stages from clay to fired pot. From left to right: wet plastic clay; leather-hard clay; dry clay; biscuit; stoneware. It is obvious that the greatest shrinkage occurs between the first two and between the last two. From dry to biscuit it is minimal. (See text.)

There are two phases. First, wet to dry shrinkage caused by the evaporation of films of water of plasticity from between the particles of clay. This varies with the fineness of grain; a red surface clay or a bentonite may shrink too much to be any use at all. English ball clays have a high wet/dry shrinkage. The maximum for a useful body should not exceed 10%. The shrinkage is reduced by the addition of flint, sand, or grog. (See *clay tests* for shrinkage test.)

Second, firing. There is little or no shrinkage from leather-hard clay to a low biscuit, in fact there may even be a slight expansion. However, as soon as glasses begin to form in the body through heat reaction between basic impurities and silica, the unmelted particles pack closer together and an overall lessening in volume occurs, continuing at an increasing rate to complete vitrification.

Some approximate shrinkage rates:

Etruria and brick clays—*wet to fired to 1000°C* average 12%
Fireclays—*dry to fired*   average 3%
China clay—*Low wet to dry shrinkage:*
    If fired up to 1300°C   12%
Ball clays *wet to dry*   up to 12%
(For the effects of 'shrinkage' in glazes see *crazing, glaze-body fit*.)

Shuttle kiln

An interesting type described in Dodd; a kiln with floor rails and doors at each end. One or two stacked 'cars' are pushed into the kiln and fired. When cool, further cars are pushed into the kiln displacing the fired ones. A cross between an intermittent and a continuous kiln. Suitable for large output potteries.

Siderite

A ferrous carbonate $FeCO_3$. Ironstone. Sometimes an impurity in clay. Could be used as a glaze colorant.

Sienna

A hydrated iron-manganese ochrous earth. Similar to *umber* but with less MnO. May need to be calcined, when it is called 'burnt sienna'. (See also *ochre*.)

Sieve

Regular mesh or perforations which will control the grain size of a material which is passed through the sieve. Made of metal, metal wire or nylon.

Useful sieves (screens or lawns) for potters are ½in/12mm garden sieves for removing the worst roughage from ash, stony clays, etc; 8 or 16 mesh cooking sieves usually of nylon, which can be used for the first breaking down of a slip or glaze batch and for grog; 60 to 100 phosphor-bronze lawns for slips and stoneware glazes; 100 or 120 for earthenware glazes; and 200 mesh for colors. The number indicates the wires per linear inch (see *lawns*). In practice some slightly larger particles will pass through because of unevennesses in the weave (which may be forced apart by clumsy usage) and oblong particles which slip through endways. Grog is graded by sieve range.

Use only a brush for working material through a sieve, not tools or fingers! A hand-operated rotary sieve (see diagram) is listed by Potters Supply House (USA) and Potterycrafts (UK), with 40–200 mesh replacement screens. The most accurate grading of material is probably given by a *vibratory sieve*, but this sort of precision is rarely required in craft work.

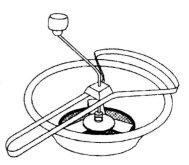

A simple hand rotary sieve ('Talisman', obtainable from a number of suppliers).

Sieve, use of

It is easier, and quicker in the long run, to use more than one sieve size when preparing a slip or glaze, working from coarse mesh to fine. For slips and glazes made up from commercially supplied materials sieving is more a question of breaking down loose aggregates rather than separating particle sizes. Use a 'cooking' sieve of nylon for the first break-down and then the appropriate lawn for the resultant slurry (see *lawn, sieve*). Sieve a glaze at least twice through the finest sieve if it is to be used immediately, to

Using a sieve, deeper rim uppermost (the number of students who instinctively used a sieve with the shallow section uppermost always surprised me), and supported on two sticks over a bowl, the glaze worked gently but firmly through with a nylon washing-up brush.

assist the intimate mingling of particles. A newly made-up slip will improve if left to rest for a day or so, and is then thoroughly restirred.

Slips should ideally be sieved every time they are used but this can be confined to the amount required. Glaze will need resieving every so often anyhow, bits of pot, grit, and other rubbish will fall into it. It is advisable to pour the glaze from its container to ensure that a 'cake' does not form on the bottom which will alter the constituents of the remaining mixture.

In persuading the mixture to pass through the lawn use an appropriate brush — never a rigid tool or your fingers — and do not work it too hard. Use plenty of water — it can always be poured from the settled mixture later. A thick sludge will form a coating on the lawn and never pass through. The ideal is to use little or no direct force and in this respect the *vibratory* sieve may not be a complete luxury; a rotary sieve (see diagram at *sieve*) is cheaper. If slips or high-clay glazes are forced thickly through a sieve they will only re-unite on the other side and the result will be nearly as lumpy as the original. More water, as mentioned above, will make easier work, more effective screening and prolong the life of the sieve which, with care, should last many years.

Sieve frame

Lawns must be mounted on frames. These are usually circular and vary in size from 3in/75mm to 12 or 14in/300 or 350mm wooden or polypropylene frames. The standard frame is about 4in/100mm high and is designed to be used with the deeper wall upwards so that it will hold the maximum quantity of liquid (many students use sieves

upside down). A good average diameter for a frame is 8 in/200mm. Wooden (ashwood) frames inevitably overlap at the joins and are difficult to clean completely and it is advisable to keep one sieve for each major class of work: for transparent glaze, white opaque, and colored for example. The more recently developed plastic frames in which the lawn can easily be replaced should be an improvement.

As mentioned at *lawn*, it is possible to fuse lawns onto plastic frames (of the right type, see *plastics*) on round plastic boxes with the bottom cut out, or from pipes, with a soldering iron or by heating the lawn on a stove top. This, when successful, forms a neat and waterproof junction.

Silica

Silicon dioxide SiO_2, 60, m.p. 1610–1713°C/2930–3115°F. Normally oxides are discussed under the element but silica is such a fundamental material in ceramics that an exception is made for it. All ceramics are based on silica both in the body and glaze, except for a few specialized industrial products. Many sands are mainly silica. It is the principal glass-forming oxide.

Used as a white powder, it is derived from calcined and ground *flints* or ground quartz. Its place in the Seger formula is with the acidic oxides (though its refractory character may be modified if it is introduced in too finely ground a form). It is more often used to produce *silicates* than on its own (see *fused silica*). Crystalline silica has an *inversion point* at 573°C/1063°F, changing from alpha to beta forms with a linear expansion of about 1% (given variously at 0.45–1.0), with an equivalent contraction on cooling. It ceases to be stable at around 870°C/1598°F and will begin to convert to *cristobalite* from 1050°C/1922°F.

However most of the silica in a glaze, and to a lesser extent in the body, will unite with bases to form silicates, in which case the reverse beta to alpha inversion does not occur. Silica also combines with alumina and these have a *eutectic* at 1595°C/2903°F (see also *phase diagrams*) and form *mullite* and *corundum* at different temperatures according to their respective proportions.

Silica is a glass forming-compound and, in contrast to *boron*, needs around 3–1 equivalents compared to the bases (see *Seger formula*)–less does not make the glaze more fusible. For a full and exhaustive discussion of the nature and uses of silica in bodies and glazes the reader is referred to the article in Hamer PDMT.

Silica refractory

A silica brick or other material containing 90% or more silica and a PCE (i.e. deforms like a pyrometric cone) of not less than 1500°C/2732°F.

They are resistant to deformation under load but, as might be expected, are subject to *thermal shock* in the *inversion* ranges. Potters' *refractories* are therefore more usually aluminous.

Silicate

A compound of a base or bases with silica, that is, a salt. Many pottery minerals and all clay and glazes are silicates, many of them complex. In its simplest form a silicate may be written $RSiO_3$ or $RO.SiO_2$, the 'R' indicating the other element involved, but there are also other combinations. Clay includes combined water in its formula and is thus a 'hydrated aluminum silicate'. The frit, lead monosilicate, is one part lead oxide to one part silica, $PbSiO_3$ or $PbO.SiO_2$.

Siliceous

Rich in silica: often in a 'free' or separate crystalline form. Applied to refractories and sometimes to ball clay.

Silicon

A non-metallic element Si, 28, Oxide SiO_2, 60. (See under *silica* for general information.)

Silicon carbide

SiC, 40, s.g. 3.2. Low thermal expansion, 5.0 (see *coefficient of expansion*). Made by fusing coke and sand. 'Ground to 450-600 mesh' Axner.

Silicon carbide's excellent thermal shock resistance, refractoriness, and *thermal conductivity* make it a useful material, mixed with clay and fired, for kiln shelves. It is also a conductor of electricity, a property which has been utilized as silicon carbide heating elements. *Silicon carbide shelves*, however, because of the way they are manufactured are not a great hazard in electric kilns.

It has been used in a powdered form as a glaze ingredient to produce 'crater' glazes (it bubbles with the release of the carbon), in speckled red copper glazes as a local reducing agent (to be effective the kiln must be sealed during the last part of the firing and during cooling), and by Lucie Rie in a blue-gray slip with iron and cobalt. Hamer recommends the addition of around 1% of tin oxide as a 'stabilizer' in silicon carbide glazes.

Silicon carbide fibers are also used 'in fiber-reinforced composites'.

Silicon carbide elements

Kiln *elements* in the form of straight hollow rods. Middle range diameter just over $\frac{1}{2}$in/14–18mm. The performance of these elements has been greatly improved since their introduction in the 1930s. They no longer need an expensive transformer, which once cost more than the kiln. Crystal growth within the rod increases its resistance to the passage of electric current by about 10% every thousand hours, the kiln consequently taking longer to fire. An ingenious system has been invented by Peter Taylor by which the wiring, on three phases and neutral, can be modified to compensate almost indefinitely for this loss by increasing the voltage through each element from 60 through to 120 volts.

The rods are self-supporting, the working area producing the bulk of the heat. The ends, which must be $\frac{1}{2}$in/12mm longer than the kiln wall thickness, are designed to offer less electrical resistance. Connections are made with braid and clips. The use of modern refractory insulators can reduce the wall thickness to six inches or

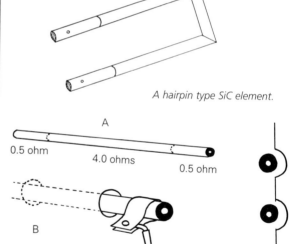

A hairpin type SiC element.

A single silicon carbide element.
A *The ends which pierce the kiln wall are rated at only 0.5 ohms (compared with 4.5 ohms in the working portion) in order to save current and prevent overheating in the enclosed space.*
B *Shows the end of a bar through the kiln wall. The hole diameter must be at least 1.25 that of the rod. The braid and clip connector is shown diagrammatically.*
C *The bar is self-supporting from the points where it enters the wall. The kiln face is grooved so that the bars need not stand out too far into the kiln chamber. Care must be taken to protect bars when packing the kiln. See Fournier EKB for more advice on the use of SiC rods.*

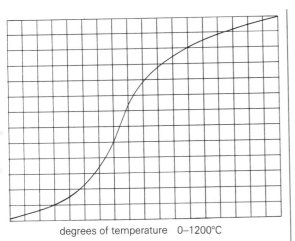

degrees of temperature   0–1200°C

Approximate heating curve for silicon carbide elements from cold to 1200°C/2190°F.

less. The cost of these elements is greater than that of equivalent wire ones, but they should have a very long life and are less affected by reduction. They are fairly brittle and need the protection of a board against the possibility of damage when packing the kiln. Details of a silicon carbide kiln were given in CR17, and in Fournier EKB. (See also at *truck kiln*.) Richard Parkinson suggests that temperatures as high as 1380°C/2516°F, should be possible using silicon carbide elements!

Notes on silicon carbide elements:
Wiring systems for resistance alteration compensation (by kind permission of Peter Taylor).
Using 12 elements or multiples of 12; three phase supply:
A 3 series of 4 in star connection. 60 volts per element.
B 4 series of 3 in star connection. 80 volts per element.
C 3 series of 4 in delta connection. 100 volts each across phases.
D 6 series of 2 in star connection. 120 volts per element.
Change when firing time has increased by 25%, e.g. from eight to ten hours. Average resistance increase 10% per thousand hours. See diagram at *star and delta*.

No support is needed if the correct size is used for the length of span.
Up to 32 in – 14 mm diameter.
Up to 39 in – 16 mm diameter.
Up to 50 in – 18 mm diameter.

Silicon carbide shelves

More conductive of heat than normal shelves, though initially more expensive they are very resistant to firing and may outlast clay shelves. Although silicon carbide is also a conductor of electricity (see *silicon carbide elements*) the method of manufacture into shelves obviates this risk. They are very hard, almost impossible to cut with the tools a potter is likely to have.

They are resistant to pots sticking to them during firing although a *bat wash* is also often used. Have been recommended for *salt-glazing.*

Silicone

A series of organic compounds of hydrocarbons with silica (R_2SiO), some of which will stand temperatures up to 300°C/572°F. Used as sealers and water-repellents, they have been mentioned as a last-ditch method of waterproofing the bases of leaking or scratchy pots.

Silicosis

A disease caused by fine silica dust inhaled over a long period. The dust cannot be eliminated from the lungs and so builds up to a solid substance. The studio potter is not at special risk unless he is in the habit of sandpapering dry clay. Reasonable hygiene and cleanliness are essential, working as far as possible with liquid or damp materials especially in handling glazes, ash, etc. Alumina can replace silica for *setting* — for spreading on kiln shelves, etc.

Silk screen printing

A decoration technique, especially useful for tiles. A stretched piece of silk or other fine mesh material is marked with a design and those areas not required to be colored are varnished or otherwise made *impermeable.* The 'screen' is then laid flat on a tile and color (generally an enamel, but possibly other pigments) is brushed through or pressed through with a squeegee roller.

Sillimanite

A brown or gray metamorphic mineral Al_2SiO_5 ($Al_2O_3.SiO_2$). A highly refractory material (melting point around 1900°C/3452°F) found as a type of fireclay. Its heat resistance and high *thermal conductivity* makes it valuable for *kiln furniture.* Chief sources S. Africa and India. There is a sillimanite zone in N. Scotland. *Kyanite* and *andalusite* are similar in composition but have different properties. It is also made into bricks suitable for *bag walls.*

Silver

A metallic element Ag. 108.
A clear yellow is derived from silver salts for temperatures

up to 1000°C/1832°F. Copper and silver and silver compounds will give orange-red to yellow *lusters*. Silver colored enamel is made from platinum, silver can be used but will tarnish. Silver sulfide with ochre can be used for *luster*, with reduction near top temperature of 700–800°C/1292–1472°F and during cooling. Silver enamel felt pens are available (Potclays). Silver as a metal has been used with ceramics as *inlay*.

Silver marking

Silver or any relatively soft metal cutlery can leave a smear mark on glaze which is slightly pitted.

Sindanyo

A proprietary type of very hard and durable asbestos sheet. It has a special use for throwing bats. Expensive but almost everlasting and unmarked even by steel turning tools. Suppliers not known but Bath Potters' Supplies provide throwing bats 'from exterior grade MDF (known as Medex)'.

Single-fired ware

See *once-fired ware*.

Single phase supply

The normal household *electricity* supply, conducted through a live and a neutral wire. Usually in Great Britain, 60 amps, with 30 amps the maximum for any

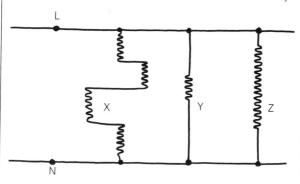

A single phase supply. Between the line (L) and neutral (N) various items of equipment can be connected so long as the total load does not exceed the strength of the mains input wires to conduct without overheating. In the diagram X might represent a 5kW kiln; Y a 200 watt lamp; and Z a 2kW electric fire. If all were on together the total load would be 7.2 kW on the input wires (which would be too great a load on the normal 13 ampere British household socket/receptacle).

one piece of equipment, e.g. a 7 kW kiln of about 3cu ft. However, some electricity authorities are now allowing 40 amps or more on a reasonably new line and it is worth contacting your local electricity authority for advice. Single phase motors are dearer and marginally less efficient than *three phase* — the alternative form of supply.

Sintering

An intermediate stage in the firing of a ceramic, either glaze or body, where the liquid phase has not yet begun but 'solid state reactions or intercrystallization' (Dodd) or the beginning of a reaction between two solids has fused the material causing a decrease in porosity and an increase in strength. The sintering temperature of a material is called the Tamman temperature, being between 0.55 and 0.6 of the *K. temperature* of fusion (Cardew). If the melting point is 1500°C/2732°F, then the material will sinter at about 0.6 of the K. temperature, in this case 1773 (1500+273; see *absolute temperature*).

Thus, 1773 x 0.6 = 1064°K (or 790°C/1454°F).

A certain expansion takes place in clays up to sintering temperature.

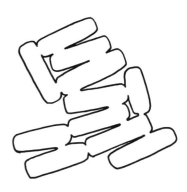

Sintered particles of clay or other material. The points of contact have fused together giving a stronger fabric but with very little shrinkage between dry clay and low-fired biscuit. In practice the particles would have begun to assume a more spherical shape.

Size

A preparation, usually soft-soap, for use on plaster molds. For lithograph decoration the size used is generally boiled linseed oil.

Skipping

Sometimes used to indicate the peeling or shivering of glaze or slip on the rims of pots or bowls.

Sky firing

A term, sometimes used by potters in the USA for the burning of small pieces of wood at the top of an updraught kiln to increase the draft (Dodd).

Slab cutter

Where a number of slabs of equal thickness are required it is sometimes useful to use a *harp*. In the example illustrated (from Bailey) various thicknesses of slab can be cut.

An adjustable slab cutter; the cylinder can be slid up and down the uprights to give various clay thicknesses. Suitable for comparatively small slabs; anything over about a foot wide would need individual rolling or a slab roller.

Slab pot, *modeling*

Pots built up from slabs of clay can be very diverse in form and character. They may have the sharp clean lines which result from cutting the pieces from leather-hard clay, or the more squashy, rounded forms of plastic clay building.

Leather-hard slabs are cut with a fine bladed knife held quite vertically, scored at the edges and luted together with slip made from the body clay. Press down well with a wooden spatula. The surfaces can be decorated before or after assembly by *impressing, beating, applied decoration*, etc. or by *wax resist, brushwork* or *poured glaze*. Several pourings of thin ash glazes will give an attractive and appropriate finish.

The proportions of a slab pot are all-important. Rules cannot be laid down but a rectangular plan tends to be of more interest than a square one. The clay is usually fairly well grogged for stoneware, but there is a wide field in earthenware. If the technique is used for open containers, the rim needs to be strengthened with an additional strip forming an inward or outward angle in order to counteract the almost inevitable warping. Cylindrical slab pots are described under rolling pin pots. The inside corners of larger slab pots will need reinforcement with thin clay coils worked well into the angle.

Slab pots make good lamp bases. Large composite pots can be built up from smaller ones. Curved surfaces can be partially dried over a former before assembly. Slab modeling is too varied a technique to be adequately covered in a dictionary; many primers deal with it. John Maltby has raised the simple slab into an art form with his ear-ringed 'kings', 'queens', and birds.

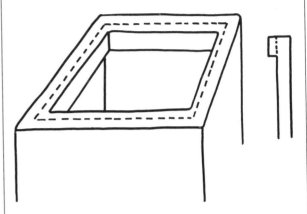

As mentioned in the text, straight lengths of wall in a slab pot tend to warp during drying and firing and may be strengthened by the addition of a strip attached at right angles to the wall as shown.

Building a slab bottle.
1 The sizes of the various pieces having been worked out (remember to allow for extra wall thicknesses at top and base, for instance), cut the sections from a soft-leather slab of clay, keeping the cutting tool; awl, spatula, or knife, quite upright.
2 The neck aperture can be made with a pastry cutter.
3 All joints are moistened, using slip or slurry (made from the body clay or it will show as a different color).
4 to *6* The first pieces are put together and the inside joins are sealed and cleaned off with a square-ended tool. Some potters work a thin coil into the angle.

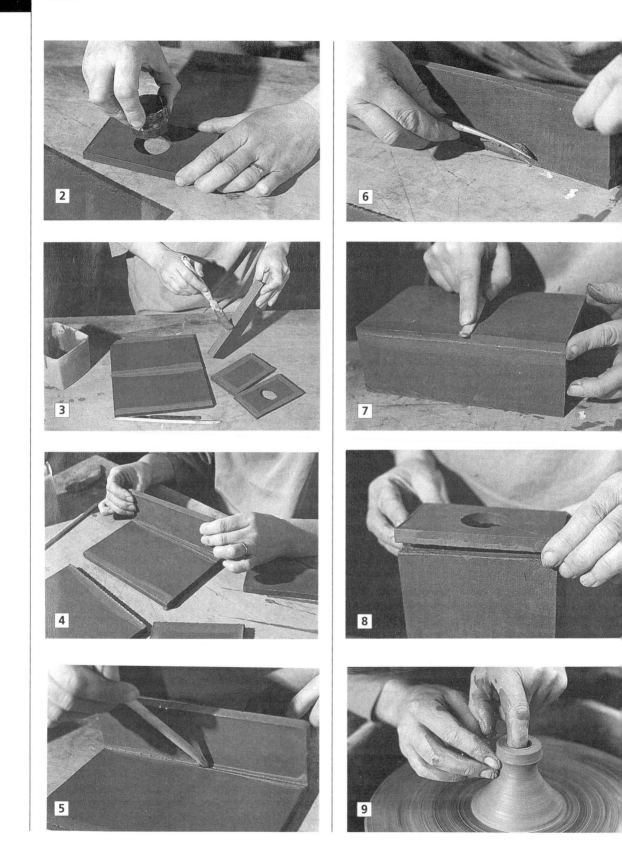

10

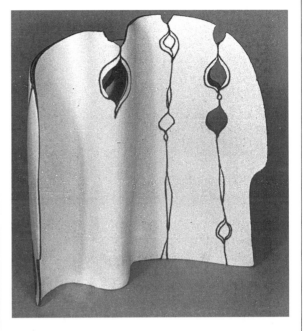

Slab-built construction in porcelain (a risky venture), which is also a pot, the back being a steady curve. By Sheila Fournier.

11

Two possible finishes for the necks of slab pots, using circular cutters. Both have the effect of keeping the walls rigid.

7 When the open box stage is complete the joins are further pressed together with a firm stroking action.
8 The top and base are applied to the walls. The base can be set inside the pot, if desired, when only three walls have been joined together. The top and base can be treated in various ways: the top can be left open if the walls are sturdy, or fitted with a narrow flange; a true slab neck can be made; or a thrown neck can be added. Other finishes will occur to you. Similarly, a slightly recessed foot, either circular or oblong will give a certain lightness to the pot if this is desired.
9 and **10** Show a thrown neck luted on when half-dry.
11 Corners may be left sharp, beveled, or rounded.
12 For curved slab shapes a biscuit former is useful.

12

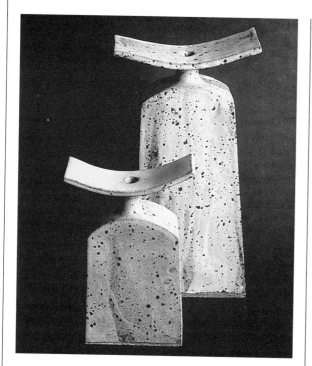

Slab bottles by Michael Hardy.

An unusual slab-built dish by John Maltby.

A king and queen by John Maltby.

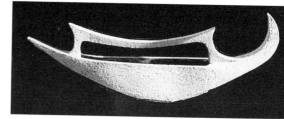

A slab-built sculptural stoneware boat by Sheila Fournier.

Made in the early 1970s this is still one of the most powerful slab pots ever constructed. By Ian Auld.

Slab roller

Mechanical slab rollers are available but are something of a luxury and take up space unless large scale or large production work is envisaged. The great advantage is that various sizes of slab can be rolled, up to around 3in (7.5cm) thick and 24–36in (60–90cm) wide. Several suppliers list them, and a number of potters are very enthusiastic about them.

Slag

The product of the reaction between *fluxing* materials, e.g. ash, and a *refractory* kiln lining. Also applied to a non-metallic fusion which floats on metal during its extraction, or to any encrusting, semi-molten material — 'our slip-ware body . . . would turn to slag at 1300°C/2372°F' (Leach PB). (See also *basic slag*).

Slake

Apart from the pint after a long day's potting, to 'slake' also indicates the disintegration of clay and other materials in water. This will occur most readily with clay when it is bone dry and broken up into at least pebble-sized pieces.

Slant mill

A type of ball mill which does not revolve but is inclined and rotates around a central axis. Less power is reputed to be used.

Slick

The movement of a metal blade over clay tends to bring water and fine particles — a 'slick' — to the surface. It sometimes causes lamination in pugged clay.

Slide-off transfer, decal

See *decal*.

Slip

Any clay or body mixed with water to a smooth creamy consistency. Originally used to provide a thin coating of the then rare light-firing clays over a red body, but has also been used worldwide for decoration (see *feathering*, *hakeme*, *run slip*, *sgraffito*, *trailing*, etc.).

The term 'slip' is generally reserved for liquid 'natural' clays or bodies used for decorative pottery. Those which contain significant proportions of non-clay materials are known as 'engobes'. *Slip casting* is an exception. (See various colors of slip, e.g. *black slip*, *blue slip*, *green slip* and for technical notes *engobes*, *slip making*, *slip recipe*, etc.)

Slip-casting

The making of pottery in *plaster* molds using liquid body or slip. The mold is filled with slip; the absorption of the plaster causes a thin wall of clay to be deposited on the inner surface. Surplus slip is then poured off and the cast

A quick way of making the occasional slip, when joining slab pots, for instance. A piece of almost dry clay is rubbed over a Surform as in illustration, into a saucer or bowl of water where it will quickly become saturated.

A method of flooding a plate, dish, or bowl. An adequate amount of slip is poured into a dish which is immediately tipped slightly and revolved, spreading the slip just up to the rim. The movement is almost complete in the picture. Surplus slip is poured out as neatly as possible with only the gentlest shake of the dish. Do not use too thick a slip.

is left to dry and shrink away from the mold, when it can be removed (see *molds*). *Casting slip* is made up of a clay with up to 75% of china clay, stone and flint. Nevertheless it is still too viscous to be used for casting and must be *deflocculated*.

A perfect cast is not easily obtainable. In addition the seam line left by the mold join is almost impossible to eradicate; even if trimmed quite flat it is liable to rise again during firing. A possible cure is to biscuit the piece to a low temperature and then to refettle seam lines at this stage. Some of the faults which may occur are dealt with in the table issued by the British Ceramic Research Association

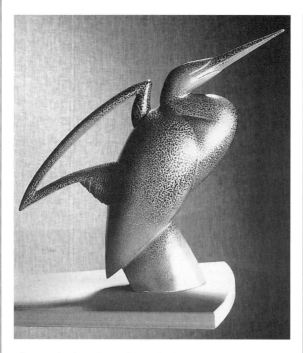

Slip-cast 'bird jug' by Anthony Theakston.

(see under *casting slip*). When drying molds beware of overheating which can destroy the plaster (see *plaster of Paris*) and fasten the mold parts together with the slip hole on one side. Detailed instructions for slip casting for the craft potter were given in CR9 by William Hall. Cromartie advertise a slip-casting machine which will maintain the slip in condition and fill and drain molds, large and small! See Sasha Wardell's book for information.

Slip decoration

Slip may be used as a complete or partial covering on a pot or dish. A '*bib*' can be dipped, or contrasting colors poured over. Other techniques include *brushed slip*, *feathering*, *hakeme*, *marbling*, *resist*, *run-slip*, *sgraffito*, *sponging*, and *trailing*, and they are dealt with under those headings.

Anthony Phillips (CR124) illustrates the use of combining brushing, sponging, and sgraffito to build up his complex decoration, see *sponging*.

Slip decoration at its best is very direct and free. Essentially an earthenware technique, it can also be used on stonewares, often using special *engobes*.

Slip gauge

An instrument for measuring the consistency of slip or glaze. (For details see *hydrometer*.)

Slip glaze

A slip derived from a very fusible clay which will melt to a hard glossy surface at stoneware temperatures. *Albany clay* is commonly quoted, also *Alberta clay* and *Fremington clay*.

One can make up a slip glaze using 50% or more of a suitable red clay with other glaze ingredients. The difficulties lie not in the actual melting of the glaze, but in countering the effects of *high shrinkage* during drying and sintering stages. Dolomite, feldspar, colemanite or a frit will lessen shrinkage and increase *fusibility*. Additions of iron rutile, or spodumene (Rhodes) will alter its behavior. Two simple slip recipes by Andrew Holden are mentioned in CR45.
1 Ball clay, 50; Whiting, 50 — for a 'bright yellow'.
2 CY ball clay 50; Potash feldspar 50 — a 'rich orange red' Stoneware fired.

Any red or surface clay may have the necessary qualities to make a glaze, and experiments with local materials are always worthwhile. Slip glazes are useful for oxidizing conditions, though not so variable as in reduction. They will always be dark brown, red-brown if you are lucky, or black. It is possible that tenmoku and other dark-colored Oriental glazes were slip. If a slip glaze shows bubbles or blisters a slightly higher or longer firing may help.

Slip making

For plain colors, the clay is broken into small pieces and soaked in water. When well saturated, the slurry is

A press-molded plate with painted slips and sgraffito, by Kim Walker.

brushed through a coarse sieve and then through a 60 mesh. Brush lightly with plenty of water.

If pigments are to be added, the ingredients must be weighed dry. The clay must therefore be used as a powdered body, or thoroughly dried and broken into small pieces. The appropriate proportion of pigment oxide is ground separately and passed through a 200 lawn. The liquid color can be added to the clay at the slurry stage before all is passed through a 60 or 80 mesh two or more times. Newly made slips should be 'rested' for a few days before use.

Slip painting

See *brushed slip, engobe, slip,* and illustration with technical details at engobe.

Slip recipe

The following are the simplest recipes for slips for trailing, etc. (all dry weights) but there are countless more intricate ones.

White or buff slip 100% buff clay (throwing clay)
Red slip 100% red clay
Black slip 100% red clay + 9% manganese dioxide. Cobalt oxide 0.5% can be added for a blacker slip
Blue slip 100% buff clay + 0.5–1.5% cobalt oxide
Green slip 100% buff clay + 1.25% chrome and 1.25% copper oxide

(See also under slip headings, i.e. *black slip* etc.)

Slips made from 'found' clays (see *clay winning*) can sometimes give interesting results under glazes. Cooper (CR160) gives a number of recipes for such slips, incorporating feldspar, nepheline syenite, crocus martis, ochre, and other materials for use under an oxidized stoneware glaze. Patient experimentation is required!

If slip *crazes* or *shivers* (peels or flakes) see under these headings for possible remedies. Stoneware slips are generally iron slips, variation being obtained by reduction. (See also under *casting slip, engobes.*)

1 Filling a soft rubber bag type slip trailer. A funnel in the mouth of the bag is filled with slip which will probably need 'milking' in by gripping the top of the neck and sliding the fingers downwards. This is repeated until the bag is almost full. It is not always easy to introduce the funnel into the bag: damping the inside will help but the outside must be dry in order to maintain a grip.

2 A more involved slip trailer designed by Peter Smith, the flow controlled at the mouthpiece.

Slip trailer, tracer

These vary considerably in shape, but are all designed to direct a controlled stream of slip onto a surface.
1 The commonest type is a soft rubber bag with a glass or plastic nozzle. The bag is filled with a funnel.
2 Stiff rubber bulb containers have the advantage that slip can be drawn in by suction, but the control is not so

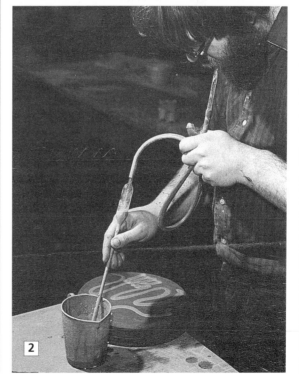

A triple-spouted trailer was used on this 18th-century dish. Such a trailer could be constructed from a flattened pottery form (two joined pinch pots would be suitable) with a hole in the top over which the thumb or a finger could be conveniently placed to control the flow of slip, and three smaller holes cut in the end to take the trailing spouts, either built-in or inserted. Quills would probably have been used originally. Similar multi-trailers, slab-built, were made with sections to separate different colored slips.

delicate as with the first type.

3 A rigid container with a direct outlet — sometimes a quill. A pottery tracer can be made which fits snugly into the palm. It will have two holes: one is for the quill or nozzle, and the thumb fits over the other to control the entry of air and thus the outflow of slip. Two or more streams of slip have been used.

4 A rigid container with a rubber tube. Slip can be forced out of the nozzle by blowing down the tube. A baby's bottle is a possible container.

5 Cloth icing bags. These tend to drip after some use.

6 Paper containers, wrapped over like a sweet bag. Used by Odney Pottery, who published details in PQ2. These are made of waxed paper or soft plastic. A segment of a circle is held point downwards and wrapped over the hand. Fastened with a pin or dab of clay.

7 A cup or container with one or more holes in the base. This method needs free, sure and rapid movement. Hamada used a ladle with a hole for trailing slip and glaze.

8 For decorative drops of slip an eye dropper can be used.

Slip trailing

A decorative technique. (See *trailing*.)

Lettering reponds well to slip trailing and here we see John Pollex at work, completing the border with cross-hatching.

Slipware

See *brushed slip, feathering, hakame, marbling, run slip, sgraffito, slip decoration, trailing.*

Slop glaze

A suspension of glaze materials in water; a glaze ready for use, in fact.

Slop weight

The weight of solid material in a slip or glaze, measured in ounces per pint. Industrial pottery materials are measured and combined as slop weights. (See *pint weight* and *Brongniart's formula*.)

Slumping

The collapse of a pot in the kiln due to *pyroplastic deformation*, i.e. in a semi-molten state. Impure clays and porcelains will slump if over-fired, as a result of the high degree of glass formation in the fabric. (See *over-firing*.)

Slurry

A thick, half-mixed slip, or a rough, wet, sandy mixture used for *clamming*, etc.

Smalt

A fused mixture of cobalt, silica and a flux. A sort of cobalt frit, or glass, sometimes used as a pigment or for staining.

Smectite

Old name for *halloysite*.

Smock

See *overall.*

Smoke

Unburnt particles of fuel, mainly carbon, caused by insufficient air in the combustion chamber of a kiln. Smoke coming from the chimney is a sign of wasted fuel (as well as being antisocial and perhaps illegal), but in the firing chamber elemental carbon assists reduction.

Smoked ware

A body or glaze discolored by a smoky reduction fire. The black body of raku and sawdust firings is a mixture of reduction and smoking or carbonization. Early reduction, below about 900°C/1652°F, can stain pots with carbon which will not burn out. Celadons are rather liable to smoking.

Soaking, heat

Maintaining a glaze or body in a kiln at a certain temperature, generally at the maturing point. Many potters believe that a soaking period is essential to the maturity of a glaze. A slower firing from about 1000°C/1832°F will have similar results. A kiln graph, with its steadily flattening rocket-like curve, will show that many kilns slow down considerably after 1200°C/2192°F and give a soaking effect with little deliberate control.

Time must be allowed for the glaze in its fluid state to release gases, and for the resultant bubbles to smooth out, but an excessively long firing can set up secondary reactions which aggravate the trouble. The act of reduction will slow down or reverse the temperature rise, and this 'stepped' firing may be crucial to the development of some iron colors (see *kaki*).

Most *earthenware glazes* benefit from a soak of about 20

minutes, but remember that the glaze is fluid and may be slowly running down the pot. A *controlling pyrometer* is needed to soak an electric kiln efficiently. A degree of soaking can be achieved by switching on and off at intervals of one or two minutes. Use a second cone, one number above the optimum temperature to ensure that the kiln does not get too hot. Alternatively one can set the 'medium' control if the kiln is wired in this way; this will retard the cooling rate.

Stoneware is more subtle in its reactions, and it is difficult to lay down rules. Oxidized glazes are often very susceptible to even ten degrees of over- or underfiring and a soak can be a mixed blessing. Very fast firings in a test kiln have produced more exciting and silky-surfaced glazes than have the same recipes in larger, slower kilns. Triple cones are useful for soaking without a pyrometer, the higher number warning if the optimum temperature is being exceeded.

Soapstone

Or *steatite*. An impure, 'massive' form of talc. Frequently used in 'soft paste' recipes. Now used in electroceramics and in *cordierite* bodies. Available from Georgies for carving.

Socket, electrical, receptacle

In the UK the 13 *ampere* socket is normally the maximum (although it is possible to conduct higher ratings through special sockets). The equipment is protected by the appropriate fuse (2–13 amperes) in the plug. Otherwise direct connection to the mains supply through a switch is needed. Check with your Electricity Supplier. (See *electric wiring to kiln,* and for America, *NEMA, receptacle.*)

Soda

Refers (in pottery) to sodium oxide Na_2O. Used to describe glazes which contain sodium oxide, e.g. lead and soda glaze. Pure forms soluble but contained in many minerals. (See *sodium.*)

Soda ash

Anhydrous sodium carbonate Na_2CO_3, 106.
Hygroscopic and soluble. Used in alkaline frits, also as a deflocculant for casting slips. Ann Hirondelle (Washington, USA) quotes a soda ash glaze for cone 7–8 in reduction:

| Silica | 55 | Soda ash | 30 |
| Plastic kaolin | 15 | Nepheline syenite | 10 |

which, with a variety of pigments gives attractive broken glazes. She does not say how she copes with the solubility of the soda ash but stresses the use of 'cold water only'.

Soda firing

A method of glazing similar to salt-glazing but with its own qualities (and difficulties!). It is considered more environmentally friendly than salt-glazing. Sodium carbonate and bicarbonate with, sometimes, potassium and lithium carbonates, or borax (Ruthanne Tudball CR128 uses sodium bicarbonate with about 10% borax) are introduced into the kiln during firing. Another method is to soak the biscuit in sodium carbonate, dry, and then fire. This can be done in an electric kiln but care must be taken to ventilate the fumes. Gerhild Tschachler-Nagy (CR138) 'salt vapor' glazes at around 1000°C/1832°F in a wood-firing kiln and wraps her pots in salted straw or metal wire, or in rags steeped in solutions of metal salts to achieve striking individual results. Other potters, however, fire to stoneware temperatures of around 1260°C/2300°F. (See also *Egyptian paste*, *salt-glazing*, and see booklist for Ruthanne Tudball's 'Soda Glazing' book.)

Soda ash in a mixture with calcium and water will crystalize into a solid mixture for introduction to the kiln — Gail Nichols (Australia) CR161.

Soda glaze

Soda alone can produce a glass with silica, and this may be so 'soft' that it will dissolve in water (see *water-glass*). The turquoise soda and copper glaze was used by the ancient Egyptians and though considered to be unstable has lasted for three thousand and more years! (See also *copper*, *turquoise*, *Egyptian paste*.)

A majority of glazes contain some soda which must be introduced as a frit, the raw compounds being soluble, or as a *mineral* (see *sodium*). The molecular equivalent of soda is usually kept at a maximum of 0.3, on account of its high thermal expansion. High-soda glazes will nearly always craze. Soda is inextricably mixed with potash in many minerals, so that the symbol NaKO may occur denoting random proportions. Piccolpasso mentions the calcining of wine lees (the sediment that forms during fermentation) with sand to produce a soda silicate for *maiolica* glazes (marzacotto). Pigments will give brighter colors in soda-glazes. See also *soda firing* and illustration at *facet*, and for more information, Ruthanne Tudball 'Soda Glazing'.

Soda, washing

Hydrated, or hydroxide of, sodium carbonate $Na_2CO_3.10H_2O$. Crystalline.

Sodium, oxide, compounds

A metallic element Na. 23. (Natrium). Oxide Na_2O, 62.

'Soda'. Other compounds are listed below.

An *alkali*. A large *atomic radius* similar to potassium with which it is often found in combination giving rise to the compound symbol KNaO. A very powerful flux (network modifier) with silica. All soda glasses need some lime or alumina to prevent their becoming soluble in water. Very high *coefficient of expansion* (37.0).

All simple compounds of soda are soluble and must be used as *frits*, or as 'natural' frits, e.g. the *feldspathic* minerals. Small amounts of soda figure in the analyses of most clays and of many other pottery materials. The high thermal expansion leads to the crazing of glazes, and the molecular equivalent is normally kept to within 0.3 parts. Brightens most colors, turning copper turquoise if in a high concentration. The hexameta phosphate is used in *terra sigillata*.

Sodium compounds and minerals used in ceramics:
Sodium antimoniate, Na_2O, a source of *antimony*.
Sodium bicarbonate $NaHCO_3$, 84.
Sodium borate (bi-borate) $Na_2O.2B_2O_3.10H_2O$, 381.5.
Sodium carbonate Na_2CO_3, 106. *Soda ash*.
    Listed by PSH.
Sodium carboxymethylcellulose. See *CMC*. A glaze binder.
Sodium chloride NaCI, 58. Common table *salt*.
Sodium hexa-metaphosphate. See *Calgon*.
Sodium silicate, $Na_2O.SiO_2$, but in practice variable.
    See also water-glass below. A *deflocculant* and used in *air-setting cement*.
Sodium tannate. Unstable. An efficient *deflocculant*. Prepared from NaOH and tannic acid.
Sodium uranate (see *uranium*).
Washing soda $Na_2CO_3.10H_2O$, 286. Caustic soda, the hydroxide NaOH, 40.
Water-glass, i.e. a glass which will dissolve in water. Na_2O_2-$3.5SiO_2$. A *deflocculant*. Used also in *airsetting cements*.

Chief soda minerals:
Albite feldspar $Na_2O.Al_2O_3.6SiO_2$, 524.
    Also some soda in nominally orthoclase feldspar.
China stone Na_2O (or NaKO).$Al_2O_3.8SiO_2$, 644.
Nepheline syenite R2O ($0.75Na_2O$. $0.25K_2O$). Al_2O_3, $2SiO_2$, 182.
All are variable within certain limits.

Soft glaze

A glaze which matures at around 1150°C/2102°F or below, and usually including in its formula lead or boron. Earthenware (and bone china) are covered with a 'soft' glaze. The erm is comparative in the sense that the glaze can be scratched with a steel knife. The converse term 'hard glaze' is not, however, in general use.

Soft-leather stage

Used in this book to indicate clay slightly damper than leather-hard — that is, at the point where it has stiffened but can still be deformed manually without breakage.

Soft paste

A general term for all the experimental and glassy bodies which were developed in Europe from the time of the Medicis to the end of the 18th century, in an attempt to imitate oriental porcelain. The factories of St Cloud, Bow and Chelsea, etc. used soft paste. The material was immensely difficult to handle and fire, having little plasticity and a rapid and very fluid glass phase at maturity. Soapstone, bone ash, alkalis, tin, oxides, white clays, are among the ingredients mentioned. Firing temperatures around 1100°C/2012°F, but variable. The very soft glaze with which they were covered took *enamels* very well. The bone ash/china clay mixture finally triumphed in England around 1800 (by Spode), and continues to hold its own against hard paste porcelain. (See *bone china*.) Some porcelain bodies in current use among craft potters hover between soft paste and true hard paste. A soft paste for low-fired (1020°C/1868°F or less) beads and jewelry can be made up from roughly equal parts of ball clay and frit. Fire on a bed of alumina. *Boron phosphate* has been used in low-firing porcelain bodies becoming 'translucent porcelain' at 1000°C/1832°F.

Soft soap

A potash soap which remains in a liquid or jellified state. Used to lubricate the surfaces of plaster molds, to prevent plaster casts sticking, e.g. when reproducing dish molds. (See also *molds*.)

Software

See *computer programs*.

Solar firing

A long way from the sun-dried bricks of early times is the elaborate 'solar kiln' described in CR59 by Zelijko Kujundzic — elaborate, that is, except for the 'kiln chamber' itself which was a 3lb coffee can! A large, circular parabolic reflector concentrated the sun's rays onto the can which contained a small pot surrounded by ceramic wool, the narrow beam being directed through a hole in the top directly into the pot itself. The main problem was keeping the reflector aligned exactly to the sun. Temperatures of 1060–1260°C/1940–2300°F were attained.

Fun, but a lot of time and energy for a small result and it is obvious that much more technical work needs to be done before it becomes a viable technique.

Solenoid

A circuit which becomes a magnet when electric current is passed through it. Used to open and close valves, etc. and in control mechanisms for kilns.

Solid solution

Materials dissolved one into another at high temperatures, reverting to a homogeneous solid mixture on cooling.

Soluble, solubility, solution

A soluble material is one which will dissolve in a liquid to form a solution, an intimate combination but without chemical change, e.g. sugar in water. Materials which are soluble will crystallize out of solution and are not suitable for raw glaze batches. Pouring the water from the top of such a glaze will also pour away dissolved materials, altering the constitution of the glaze. There may be slightly soluble elements in any mineral or material, and it is always a wise precaution to retain the poured-off water for re-use if necessary. Dusting of soluble glaze materials onto wet clay (even immediately after throwing) with a garden 'puffer' has been suggested (CM18/2) — it is necessary to wear a mask during this process — but the usual method of using them is in the form of frits. The alkalis and boron are soluble in all their simple compounds, even colemanite is slightly soluble.

Glaze is a super-cooled liquid and we can therefore refer to certain materials and oxides as being soluble in a glaze, e.g. most of the *pigment oxides* will, up to a certain concentration, yield transparent color. The acidic oxides are mainly insoluble. Tin, for instance, will remain little changed in suspension rendering the glaze opaque. Glaze will also form compounds, one of which will dissolve in the other (see *solid solutions*). Liquids, including glazes, will hold only certain proportions in solution, the excess remaining in its original form or being rejected (precipitated). Hot liquids will hold more than cold ones; certain oxides may therefore come out of solution as the glaze cools, especially if this takes place slowly. Iron may do this in stoneware (see *red color* in glaze). Using 3% or more of copper and 12% or more of manganese will have the same effect, the degree of precipitation varying with the *fluidity* of the glaze. In an 'under-fired matt' or a high-base stoneware glaze the oxide may not dissolve at all: copper, for instance, giving gray instead of green.

Soluble materials (soluble in water) used in pottery:
Boric oxide. Most boron minerals including borax and calcined borax to a lesser degree.
Colemanite is slightly soluble.
Soda. Most silicates and carbonates of soda, salt (sodium chloride), borax.
Potash oxide and carbonate, pearl ash. In soluble form in many ashes.
Frits. Very soft frits may partly dissolve, to re-crystallize after a few days.

Soluble alkali

Plant ashes contain soluble and caustic alkalis. These may crystallize; invade the fabric of the biscuit; cause flocculation of the batch with attendant cracking of the glaze coating; and make it impossible to pour liquid from the batch without altering its behavior. Ash is therefore usually 'washed'. (For method see *ash preparation*.)

Soluble lead

Lead and lead oxides are soluble in the bloodstream, where they act as cumulative poisons. The lead in a fired glaze, unless it is very stable, may also be 'dissolved' by the action of strong acids, such as those in certain fruits and vinegar, and by fermentation.

Raw lead compounds are forbidden by law in all but a few situations, and their use in manufactured materials is controlled. The potter working on his own may use them but not his employee. In Britain all lead, (or cadmium) glazes on any tableware must conform to British Standard BS4860, and all potters using them should have their work tested regularly and obtain certificates to that effect. Fritted lead silicates are powdered glass, which (in spite of detective fiction!) is much safer in use. The frits must be made to certain standards of solubility (not more than 5% must dissolve in a standard hydrochloric acid test). Those that pass this test are labeled low sol. or LS frits. Monosilicate is too 'soft' to satisfy the regulations; sesquisilicate and bisilicate are usually satisfactory but the latter is recommended. Suggested starting recipe:
   Bisilicate 65, China clay 25, Whiting 10
The dangers to the potter can be minimized by common sense and hygiene; the fired product presents a more involved problem. Shaw states that 'lead glazes are brilliant, highly craze resistant and, if properly fritted, are absolutely safe in use'. He gives the rule that the bases plus alumina must equal at least 2.0 parts of silica in the molecular formula (see *Thorpe's ratio*).

Copper will increase lead solubility; indeed, Harry Fraser warns against the use of copper even with leadless glazes if there are also plumbic glazes in the same kiln.

Of other commonly used oxides:

Boric acid	increases solubility
Alkalis	increases solubility
Alumina	decreases solubility
Silica	decreases solubility
Lime	decreases solubility
Zinc	decreases solubility (but see below)
Barium	decreases solubility
Zircon	decreases solubility

There is, however, some doubt about the role of zinc oxide.

At high temperatures, lead is *volatile* and may be inhaled from a kiln. Do not open the kiln door when ware is very hot. It can also be deposited as a thin skin on leadless glazes, rendering them dangerous in use.

A test for the presence of lead not completely involved in the melt has been described in various magazines (Tactile, New Zealand Potter, CR): Two ounces of vinegar are left in the test pot for 12 hours. The vinegar is then poured into a glass and 2oz of fresh vinegar poured into a second glass. One-eighth of a teaspoon of liver of sulfur is mixed with 2oz of hot water, and two teaspoonsful are added to each glass. If the test vinegar is tinged tan or brown compared with the fresh batch, then heavy metal is present. Axner list a 'lead test swab' which can identify lead release of above 2 ppm, turning pink if positive.

(See also further notes at *lead, metal release*.) Some potters' suppliers (e.g. Potclays, UK) offer a testing service.

Soluble salts

Sulfates and carbonates of calcium, magnesium, and sodium are present in some clays and may 'migrate' to the surface, especially when they are much handled in modeling. They are most apparent on red clays (see *scumming* for remedy). *Egyptian paste* relies on this phenomenon to develop its glaze. *Filter pressing* tends to eliminate salts. Soluble alkalis are also a feature of ash (see *ash preparation*).

Solution

See *soluble*.

Solution color

Colors derived from metal oxides dissolved in a molten glaze, having the same hue by transmitted and reflected light, which includes most of the colored ceramic glazes.

Soot, sooting

'Black deposit from imperfect combustion of carbonaceous matter' (Chambers Concise Dictionary). Can be used as a reducing agent but other, less messy materials are generally preferred. Sooting is sometimes used to describe the early reduction staining (see *carbon, reduction*).

Sorting, tool

'Sorting' is the removal of the sharp points of glaze left by stilts, etc. after glaze firing. A sorting tool is a type of cold chisel with a tungsten carbide or other very hard edge. To use it, hold the pot firmly in one hand and bring the tool down sharply and square onto the pot just behind the snag to be removed, so that the tool catches the snag as near to its base as possible. Repeat with short, sharp movements, working into and under the blemish. With skill the sharpness of the blemish will sheer off after very few jabs.

Souring

The bacterial effect of the *aging* of clay to improve plasticity and other qualities.

Spalling

The breaking away of flakes or larger pieces from the faces and corners of refractory *hot-face bricks* in the kiln. *Thermal shock, crystalline inversion*, inadequate expansion allowances called 'pinching' (Dodd) (see *bricklaying*), and slag formation are among the causes. Free silica should be minimal in the refractory fabric.

Sudden heating or cooling will alter the *expansion* of the face of the brick compared with its back, and can cause deep spalling.

Spangles

Iron spangles, magnetic ferroso-ferric iron Fe_3O_4, 233. Magnetite. A coarse black iron oxide used to produce speckling in bodies and glazes.

Spar

Feldspar and allied minerals are often referred to as 'spars'.

Spathic iron

Ferrous carbonate, $FeCO_3$. Used in pigments (Dodd).

Spatter brush

See diagram at *brush*.

Spatterware

White or colored glaze spattered over another.

Spatula tool

A tool with a flattened, curved and rounded end. It can be of wood or metal and is a most useful tool for potters. Strangely absent in its simple double-ended form from many suppliers' lists.

A wooden spatula tool, one of the most useful in the potter's collection.

Specific gravity

The ratio of the mass of a material to that of an equal mass of water at 40°C/104°F. A specific gravity (s.g.) figure of less than one will therefore indicate that the material is 'lighter' than water (i.e. will float). The s.g. of clays and most common ceramic minerals averages 2.6; feldspars slightly less, and quartz a little more at 2.65. This is useful when using *Brongniart's formula*. The mass or weight of a material divided by its volume will give its density. The equation must be either in lbs/pints or kg/liters. The figure obtained is divided by the s.g. of pure water, but since this is 1.0 the density and s.g. are the same.

The s.g. value will also control the settling speed of pottery materials in water. Lead compounds (s.g. around 11), will drop quickly and such glazes must be stirred repeatedly. The high s.g. of zircon sand limits its use in refractories, saggars etc., for which it would be otherwise very suitable; high concentrations make these too heavy.

Specific heat

The heat required to raise a unit of a substance through

one degree. (See *British thermal units, calorie, joule*.) 'The mean specific heat of most traditional ceramics lies between 0.23–0.28 (20–1000°C/68–1832°F)' Dodd.

Speckled slips, *glazes*

Iron spangles, dried pulverized low-fired colored clays, and 1% each of ilmenite and vanadium pentoxide have been quoted as giving speckles in or under a glaze. Spots of pigment under a glaze can give a vague type of speckle. (See also *bleed-through*.)

Spinel

A mineral built up into regular *crystals* from a *bivalent* and a *trivalent* (tervalent) metal. The general composition is $MO.R_2O_3$, where M equals magnesium, ferrous oxide, manganese, zinc, cobalt or nickel; and R equals ferric oxide, chromium or aluminum. The typical mineral is magnesium aluminate, $MgO.Al_2O_3$. Magnetic iron oxide $FeO.Fe_2O_3$ is a spinel, and cobalt also forms spinels. They are considered to be the most stable form of oxides.

Spinner

A plate or saucer which has sagged or warped in the center of its base so that it will not sit firmly, i.e. it can be spun round. This may be caused by careless turning or may develop while drying. Test before packing in the kiln and, if necessary, flatten with a pad of glass paper (can also be used on soft biscuit).

Spiral wedging

See *wedging*.

Split form

Broken and split form is essentially a modern phenomenon and makes gentle mockery of established shapes and approaches. (See also illustration at *copper-manganese gold*.)

Spodumene

A lithium mineral $Li_2O.Al_2O_3.4SiO_2$, 372. Similar to *petalite* which has eight molecules of SiO_2, and is likewise sometimes referred to as a lithium feldspar.

Undergoes an irreversible expansion from alpha to beta forms at 900°C/1652°F. Used in bodies where a low thermal expansion is required. Cardew discusses the compounding of an artificial spodumene body or the use of spodumene rock (60%, 60–200 mesh) with plastic clay for flame-proof bodies. A very simple glaze recipe using 54.5% spodumene to

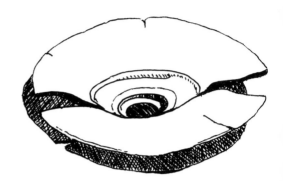

A double-layer, split-rimmed, handbuilt bowl form by Ruth Duckworth. The breaks are carefully considered and the final form has its logic, a feature missing from much of this type of pottery.

45.5% talc is given by Behrens in CM20/3. (See also *lithium*). Brian Dewsbury uses up to 20% of spodumene in stoneware electric kiln firings. Obtainable in UK from Cromartie, Axner in the USA, Coastal Ceramics NZ, and others.

Sponge

Various synthetic sponges are now made, but none can equal a fine-grain natural sponge for sensitivity and working qualities. The ideal type is the 'elephant's ear' Turkey sponge, about 2½in/65mm across. Natural sponges are becoming rarer and more expensive. If you can visit a supplier to choose your own, so much the better. The 'grain' should lie all in one direction with no holes or tears. Once found, a good sponge is worth treasuring; wash it after use and avoid highly abrasive surfaces.

Synthetic bath-sponges with large holes are best for swabbing and cleaning. The type which dries stiff can more easily be cut to shape and used for throwing, but most of them become loaded with clay, which is difficult to wash out.

Sponge stick

A natural or polyester fiber sponge fastened to the end of a dowel or stick, and used for absorbing surplus water from pots during throwing. A small natural sponge stretched tightly over the end of a ½ or ¾in by ¼in (say 15 x 7mm) stick can be used as a *throwing stick*.

Sponged decoration

The sponging on of color to represent foliage, etc. has been practiced for a long time. Using a sponge, natural or artificial, to apply color, glazes, and slips is a useful technique for the potter. It is one of the few ways of getting an

Sponged decoration on a plate by Emma Bridgewater.

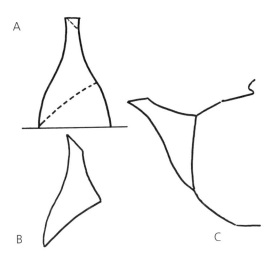

A *The shape of a thrown teapot spout which, when cut along the dotted line **B** and attached to the body of the pot as **C** forms a spout with a single curve above and a double curve below.*

overall area of color, and an encouragement to free decoration. See Scott for some imaginative applications of the technique. Anthony Phillips (CR123 and 124) uses cut sponge shapes with slips, laying one color over or beside another to build up 'a more mysterious decoration'. An earthenware glaze eats away some of the finer layers and creates a feeling of translucency. Normally a pigment — oxide or prepared color — is mixed with water for application. The design is generally built up from smaller motifs, perhaps overlaying to develop more involved patterns.

Scott describes and illustrates sponge printing with luster.

Historically the root of the sponge was used, from which designs can be cut with a fine knife. Artificial sponges, however, can be cut or burned with a hot rod into quite large motifs for sponging onto pottery but this is only recommended in the open air, or with the use of an efficient exhaust system (and a mask of course), as dangerous noxious fumes are given off in the process.

Spout

A tapering tube which conducts and controls the flow of liquid from a tea or coffee pot, etc. It is useful to bear the definition in mind, especially with regard to 'control', when designing a spout. The object of the taper is to build up a pressure or weight of liquid so that it issues in a steady, arching stream. A large and clumsy spout will not do this efficiently. Nor will it pour well if the grid behind the spout will not allow more water to pass through it than can issue from the narrowest part of the spout.

Spouts are usually thrown, leaving sufficient extra clay top and bottom for trimming. The form can be straight-sided, concave, or slightly bottle-shaped. Trim the large end to fit the pot at the correct angle, about 45° to the vertical, and ensure that the other end is at least level with the lid flange, if not higher. If the lower part of the spout is too thick it can be trimmed inside with a knife. Mark the outline on the pot and drill grid holes before scoring, slipping, and luting it on. Trimming the small end presents problems. Clay has what Cardew calls 'memory', that is, it will continue to twist during firing in the direction of the throwing strain. This means that the spout may be pointing

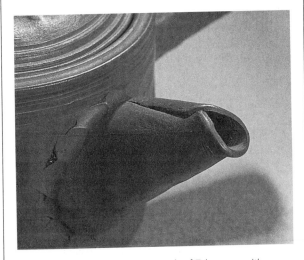

A modern Japanese teapot by Futoh of Tokoname with an unusual slab spout.

9

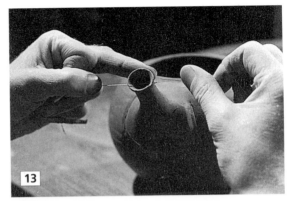

13

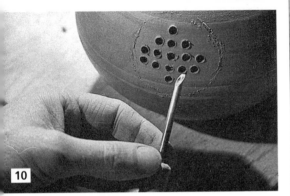

10

14

11

Michael Casson applying a spout immediately after throwing.

1–4 Showing stages in the throwing with the last picture especially important, all trace of slip on the surface being removed with a rib so that it is dry enough to handle.

5 and 6 The spout is removed from the block of clay on which it was thrown and cut through to the appropriate angle with a wire.

7 and 8 The top of the base aperture is eased upwards with the finger, and the spout pressed onto the pot just firmly enough to make a mark.

9–12 Within this line the grid is cut through, the spout placed in position, and fastened on with a few careful but free-moving strokes.

13 The end of the spout is now cut. To allow for the twist ('unwinding') which often occurs during firing, the wire is held sloping slightly downwards to the left when facing the pot, as in the picture.

14 The last picture shows the spout, completed only a few minutes after throwing.

12

sideways after firing if it has been trimmed horizontally. Slower, 'easy' throwing will help. Allowance can be made when trimming by facing the spout away from you and cutting it to slope slightly to the right and point a little to the left. Some potters avoid the difficulty by leaving the end of the spout as a right-angle, but the form needs to be very carefully worked out if this is not to look blunt and unfinished.

Spouts have been *press molded* and applied to thrown pots, but not with conspicuous success. Thrown spouts are usually applied at soft-leather stage, but Michael Casson and others lute them on almost immediately after throwing. This demands great skill but at its best can be very fresh and integrated in its effect. A spout may be 'pulled' (see also *handles*) into a curve when half-dry. The very tip of the spout should be reasonably sharp, and its pouring qualities will be enhanced by a slight downwards curve (see *lip*).

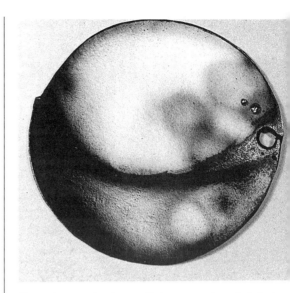

Pigments sprayed onto a matt stoneware glaze. By Robert Fournier.

A salt-glaze coffee pot with a bold 'bridge spout'. By Ruthanne Tudball.

Spraying, *spray gun, booth*

The application of glaze or color by rendering it to a fine mist under pressure. It is often done with a spray-gun similar to those used for paint, or a simple hand-operated spray gun. The granular nature of ceramic suspensions will clog some types, especially the cheaper electric drill sprayers. Compressed carbon dioxide cylinders are available for small scale work. For more than experimental work a booth is essential both to restrict the spread of colors and glazes which can quickly invade every corner, and

more importantly, the lungs of the potter.

This involves an air-pressure pump and pressure tank. is noisy and dangerous, and a spray-booth with an exhau fan is strongly advised. The cost of equipment, with booth, is considerable. An even more sophisticated 'wat back' booth is listed by Axner (USA), Metrosales and Ba Pottery (UK) in which a curtain of water at the back tra the glaze spray and washes it down into a tank. Spraying practiced in the industry, but has less value in the sma workshop. A mask should *always* be worn. A 'Lo-Tec' sprayer, available from Bath Pottery Supplies (UK) consis of a tapered blowpipe and a blown spray is supplied k Coastal Ceramics (NZ). Sprayed glaze is liable to uneve thickness and to pin-holing. Although small amounts glaze can be used, there is considerable waste. Spraying useful for once-fired wares, especially large plates ar bulky pieces. Color can be sprayed onto resist or, from finely controlled jet — 'drawn' on the dish or pot. It is di ficult to avoid a mechanical, commercial appearance. Th use of resists and stencils will help to give sharper outin to a design. A number of professional potters are, howev er, experimenting with sprayed decoration.

Sprig

A bas-relief or medallion made in a small press mold an stuck with slip onto a pottery surface. Typified by 18t century bi-colored sprigging, salt-glazed bellarmir masks, and in the industry by Wedgwood's cameos. Th craft potter can still devise new and entertaining uses fe the sprig.

simple sprig mold with casts.

he sprig mold can be cut either directly into clay and
en biscuit fired, the design can be cut into a slab of plas-
r (this is recommended by Jerry Harper in CR157 for
ttering which is then in relief on the final sprig), or the
rig can be modeled separately and cast in plaster.
emember, if the design is cut directly into the clay and
scuited, a cast will be reversed.

To make a sprig for application to a piece of ceramic,
ork plastic clay firmly into the mold with a flat tool and
atten the back, removing any surplus clay with a tool or
harp. It can then be removed from the mold by pressing
damp metal spatula or palette knife onto the back and
ting sharply. Position the sprig on the damped surface of
pot (Philip Wood CR160) uses a clay lump to support
e sprig, and press gently with a wooden tool in the hol-
ws of the design. Alternatively a damped or lightly slip-
ated sprig can be applied directly from the mold onto
e surface of the piece. This method can leave an impres-
n of the edge of the mold, framing the sprig. Do not
tempt too large a sprig; it is easier to build up from
aller units.

The technique can be used as a starting point for further
ork which may alter or partially obliterate the original
sign.

pringer

r scewback. A brick with one sloping face from which an
ch can be 'sprung' when building a kiln. (See *brick,
icklaying*.)

pun color

addition to simple *banding*, larger areas or whole sur-
ces can be covered with a loaded brush on a spinning
ate, bowl, or pot. It is impossible to achieve an absolute-
even coating but this limitation can be turned to advan-
ge. The spiral nature of the brushstroke is inevitable but
is, again, is a decorative aspect of the technique. Usually

applied to a damp surface; bubbles or bare patches can
result from spinning onto a dry surface.

Spur

A small piece of kiln furniture with one point up and three
down. For use at earthenware temperatures only.

Square liner

Long slender brushes with the end cut square. For lining
with the whole length of the brush. Can also be used to
develop a calligraphic character.

Squatting

A term used to indicate a less severe but still usually disastrous form of *slumping*.

Stable, stability

A stable glaze has a well-balanced formula, is adequately
fired and will not react easily to acid or other corrosion. An
excess of bases or coloring oxides may render a glaze unstable. Stability is always desirable, but especially so in lead
glazes (see *lead solubility* and *metal release*). Adherence to
the generally recommended ratios of the *Seger formula* will
assist in computing stable glazes. (See *Thorpe's ratio.*) Materials can be added to a recipe to render lead, for instance,
less likely to be dissolved from the glaze. Titanium and calcium are used in small quantities in lead frits.

The physical stability of a pot is also a virtue. Tall shapes
with very small bases are seldom good pot forms. The
strengthening of a narrow-walled pot with a metal rod is
an acceptance of failure. An uneven base is aggravating,
and all pots and bowls should be tested before firing. A
slightly hollow or concave base may be achieved during
making or turning by tapping with the finger when soft-
leather. A wobbly base can be flattened by holding the pot
hard down on to a wetted wheelhead or whirler, which is
then revolved. Dry pots can be sandpapered in the same
way. See *abrasive*.

Stack throwing

Term sometimes used to describe several small pieces
of pottery thrown from one large block of clay. The top
surface clay should be well compressed after cutting off
each piece so as to minimize the chance of cracking
because of excessive wetness remaining from the previous
throwing.

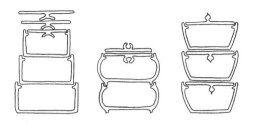

Possible stacking methods for lidded pots or casseroles.

1 Throwing from a cone of clay—stack throwing—in this case a small glaze test bowl.
2 A method of cutting off with a needle awl held slightly sloping upwards towards the center of the base giving a slight recess (if you are clever!).

Stacking pots, *bowls*

Designing pots which will sit comfortably on one another is an important aspect of domestic ware which can greatly add to the comfort of customers with small kitchens. The diagrams give some ideas on this subject but there are many more solutions to the problem of stacking pots which the inventive potter can think up. (See also *kiln packing.*)

Rounded forms tend to slide about when stacked and can be unsteady and difficult to pick up.

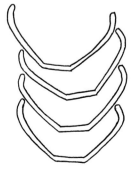

Staffordshire cone

A range of *pyrometric cones.* Most numbers correspon within 10°C/50°F to Seger cones. Graded in 10°C/50° steps above 08 (940°C/1724°F) up to 11 (1320°C 2408°F), except 1200–1215°C/2192–2219°F and 1215 1230°C/2219–2246°F. The numbers are prefixed by H. nought (zero) in front of any number indicates a tempera ture below 1100°C/2012°F. (See under *cones* for list.)

Stain

A term widely used in pottery, but without a specifi meaning. It can indicate an organic *identifying stain* (used industrially for different bodies, especially porcelain), o any oxide or prepared pigment used for coloring bodies slips or glazes. The term might with advantage be restrict ed to fritted, prepared colors, in which sense it is generally used in merchant's catalogs. Prepared stains, most of which can be used in clay bodies, glazes, or decoration are sold by most suppliers, some formulated for stoneware or porce lain firings. Many will stand temperatures up to 1300°C/2372°F including the reds.

Industrial stains more often than not contain chromium and/or zinc, both of which can affect and be affected by the glaze while many of the red-purple colors need calcium (6.7–8.4% for Mason stains whose lists also usefully spec ify the make-up of each color).

For high temperature bright colors for slips, Ivo Mosley (CR86) reduces his colors from 850°C/1562°F to within 100°C/212°F of his top temperature to maintain their brilliance but he warns that some high temperature stains will be less successful than others. However, most prepared stains are intended for oxidized firings and the color may be very different in reduction.

Stained clay

Most clays are 'stained' in the sense that they usually con tain iron or manganese oxides in various degrees but the erm is normally used to indicate the deliberate addition of metal oxides to pale clays. The addition of oxides to clays will alter their behavior in the kiln to some degree, e.g. manganese will lower the melting point. Barium additions were used by Wedgwood to increase the brightness of his stained bodies but these are insufficiently plastic for general studio use. Stained bodies are widely used in modeling. Commercially prepared body stains are available. (See at agate, colored body, inlay, neriage, slip, and stain.)

Stamp, stamping

An embossed or intaglio stamp can be used to build up a pattern on clay. Impressing is a type of stamping but the term can also indicate the printing of color onto the surface without involving impression. Sponge 'root', cut into patterns, has been used for stamping designs onto pottery. Some potters' 'marks' are rubber-stamped with pottery pigment. (See also mark, seal, sponged decoration.)

Standard black

A color derived from 4% each of cobalt, manganese, and iron oxides but also given (Dodd) as 30% cobalt oxide, 56% ferric oxide, 48% chrome oxide, 8% nickel oxide, and 31% alumina. (See also black glazes.)

Stannic

Applied to a tin compound or a glaze containing tin. From 'stannum', the international name for tin, hence its symbol Sn. More exactly 'stannic' indicates quadrivalent tin oxide, SnO_2 as distinct from the 'stannous' bivalent SnO.

Star and delta wiring

Systems for wiring three-phase equipment. See diagram.

States of matter

The three most distinct states of matter are the gaseous, the liquid and the solid. No chemical change takes place between these states, but only the physical 'loosening' of the bonds between the molecules. Energy, usually heat, is involved in the changes.

Steatite

The massive form or rock of talc. Soapstone. One of the softest rocks. Can be carved into pot and other forms and is still known as 'pot-stone'. Also used as 'French chalk'.

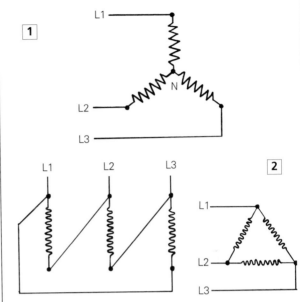

1 Star wiring for a three-phase kiln, each line connected back to a common neutral. This will give full mains voltage on each phase or circuit. (See also three phase.)
2 Delta wiring for three phases. Element circuits are connected across phases to give 415 volts from a 240 volt supply. The neutral is not employed in this system.

Steel palette

A very thin, flexible, sheet-steel tool, rectangular or kidney-shaped. Made in two thicknesses and several sizes, averaging 5in/127mm across. Invaluable for scraping and smoothing plastic clay, especially for handbuilding. Can be used as a throwing rib or, occasionally, for turning.

Steger's crazing test

See crazing.

Stencil

Allied to resist, a stencil is a piece of shaped card, paper or other material laid onto a surface so as to control a design. It has apertures cut in it, through which color, slip, or glaze is applied; it can be used as a resist shape, producing a blank shape on a background of color; or to divide a surface into two areas. The comparative rigidity of stencils, and the difficulty with isolated parts, confines their effect to simple shapes and masses, often as a foundation for other decoration. Sponging or dabbing the color will give sharper outlines than will brushing, alternatively pigment can be sprayed on. Shallow dishes and tiles present no problems, but stencilling is more difficult on a pot

Brushing color across a paper stencil on a dish.

Stiff paper shapes, one cut from the other, have been held against this dish and sprayed over. The occasional 'leaks' of color under the edge of the stencil help to soften the otherwise hard lines. By Sheila Fournier.

although Jane Cox (CR168) achieves sharp and complex designs using stencilled slip on a variety of forms. Leach used a stencil to divide his 'mountain' dish designs. (See also *cut paper resist, paper resist.*)

Stepped graph

A variation on the steady rise in temperature of a kiln graph which shows periods of heat maintenance or even a fall, associated usually with *reduction* or *soaking*.

Stibium

See *antimony*.

Sticking-up

The assembly of parts of a model, teapot, or similar construction, either at the *leather-hard* or a softer stage. An industrial term.

Stiff glaze

An expression denoting a *refractory* glaze which does not easily run, often with high alumina or opacifier content.

Stilt

An item of *kiln furniture*. It is made in a bewildering variety of designs but fundamentally consists of three or four arms radiating from a center, with vertical points, generally at the end of each arm though on some models a number of points can be accommodated. Glazed pieces are supported on appropriately sized stilts, the points about $1/4$in/ 6mm in from the edge of the base. The point adheres to the glaze and breaks away when the stilt is removed. Stilts are therefore expendable, though they may last three or four uses. There are also bar stilts, the points set in a straight line. Originally designed for the industry with its thin, fritted glazes, a stilt can become firmly welded into thick or carelessly applied glaze. Glaze the base sparingly, therefore, or wipe some of the glaze away. Do not jam the points into a foot-ring or extend them beyond the ring. Long rods are also made for specialist placing. *Spurs* may be used in place of stilts for large dishes. Remember also that the pot will shrink, but the stilt will not. Remove stilts with a *sorting tool*.

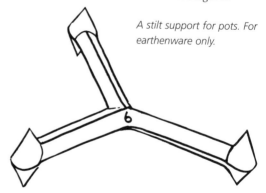

A stilt support for pots. For earthenware only.

Sizes are available from 1–4in/25–100mm point to point. 'Egg stilts' are triangular in plan, with a hole in the center. Stilts are for use in earthenware firings only, and will fail in stoneware.

Stoichiometric

When the constituents of a material exactly correspond to

formula. Rarely happens in nature but a close similarity is usually sufficient in ceramic compounds. Tests, however, when using a new batch of material, e.g. feldspar, are advisable.

Stones

Some small stones or stone chips will explode on firing, so beware and test in a saggar or small kiln. Others will stay whole or alter, or will disintegrate.

Stoneware

According to the Brussels Nomenclature — 'impermeable, and hard enough to resist scratching with a steel point… more opaque [than porcelain] and normally only partly vitrified'. Stoneware is distinguished from earthenware by:
1 Its higher firing-temperature. The generally accepted minimum is 1200°C/2192°F, and the range is 1200–1350°C/2192–2462°F. Bodies with artificially lowered vitrification points have been marketed.
2 Its degree of vitrification. A *porosity* of not more than 5%. The higher fired stonewares will also be *impermeable*. The surface has a close and glassy appearance but may be rough to the touch.
3 A well developed reaction zone across the *interface*, giving greater integration and subtlety of glaze.
4 Low iron content in the body. Red clay will not form a true stoneware, though it may be added to a *refractory* body.
5 Does not need either lead or boron in its glaze, although the latter is sometimes used in small quantities.
6 Jun glazes and celadons in reduction.

In spite of stoneware's apparent advantages over earthenware, the qualities of the two types of ceramics are so different that neither has an inherent superiority.

Stoneware body

A naturally fusible but reasonably iron-free plastic clay is the basis for a stoneware body. Many fireclays and other sedimentary clays may be suitable as the major constituent. Sources of 'stoneware' clay are reported in the USA in Colorado, Wyoming and New Jersey (*Jordon clay*).

Most stoneware bodies are mixtures of a number of materials each chosen for their particular qualities.
1 For plasticity: ball clays and red clays, up to 40% of the first and 20% of the second.
2 For fusibility: natural fusibility from the ball and red clays. Additional non-plastic fluxes such as feldspar, stone, (5–15%), or 5% of talc have been mentioned.
3 Refractoriness and low shrinkage: china clay, quartz or

flint (15–20%), sand, grog (ideally the body biscuit), or aluminous fireclay.
4 For color: red clay, or 5–10% of ochre (Leach).
5 Texture: grog, sand, coarse fireclay up to 25%.

Ilmenite in the body will cause glaze speckle. The materials should be blunged to a slip for maximum efficiency.

Many potters buy a prepared plastic body which when bought is often too smooth and characterless, but which can be modified as above. (Cardew warns against wedging china clay into a plastic body.) Others buy dry powdered materials and work them together in a *dough mixer*.

Stoneware clay

A general name for plastic, refractory, *secondary* clays which are not as fine-grained as *ball clays* or as deepseated as *fireclays*. In Germany and the USA., and in other parts of the world, grades of clay can be found which will fire to 1300°C/2372°F with few if any modifications. They have no massive commercial use and are therefore more difficult to obtain than kaolins and fireclays.

Stoneware glaze

A range of glazes firing between 1200°C/2192°F and 1350°C/2462°F, with the great majority in the midway range, 1260–1310°C/2300–2390°F. The two oxides which feature so prominently in soft glazes (lead and boron) have little or no place in stonewares, which are generally based on feldspars or wood ash.

The average formula for a stoneware glaze is 1.0 RO, 0.35Al$_2$O$_3$. 3.5SiO$_2$, but there are numerous combinations outside this ratio, e.g. above 1300°C/2372°F the silica ratio can rise sharply, while formulas with only 2.0 parts of silica have been reported in analyses of Chinese glazes. At temperatures of 1250°C/2282°F plus it is difficult not to produce a glaze of some kind by mixing two or three ceramic minerals. The classic starting point is 40 parts feldspar, 30 flint, 20 whiting, 10 clay; but in other recipes the feldspar is much more dominant, e.g. 70 feldspar, 13 flint, 10 whiting, 7 china clay.

Try line blends or biaxial mixtures of nepheline syenite, talc, barium, china stone, with other more exotic minerals such as petalite or basalt, also with red clay and, of course, ash. It is useful to be able to translate any interesting result back to a glaze formula (see *recipe-into-formula*). The effects of the various oxides and minerals are discussed under their headings. (See also *oxidation* and *reduction*.)

Iron is the principal coloring oxide in reduced stoneware glazes, which seem to have a wider firing-range without violent character changes than do oxidized glazes. In the latter the range is wider but the effects, in general, are not so subtle. Manganese and copper have a place, the latter in *matt* glazes to prevent *volatilization*. Cobalt needs to be well 'quenched' with iron, red clay, etc. if it is not to be strident.

Stopper

Ceramic stoppers are rarely airtight. The old bungs were often wound with straw. A tapered stopper in a similarly formed bottle neck helps, but corks or flanged plastic stoppers are usually used. It is, perhaps, easier to start with available cork sizes and throw the pots to fit them rather than the other way round. Cardew, in 'Pioneer Pottery', describes an ingenious tool he made for cutting screw threads on bottle necks and stoppers.

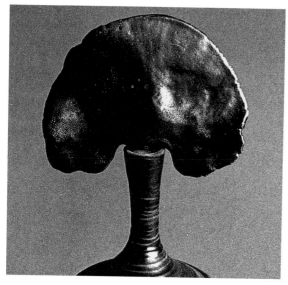

A decorative, tree-like stopper on a bottle by Mary Rich. Note slightly conical neck form.

Stopping

Mixtures for filling cracks in biscuit ware. Merchants list 'red', 'white' and 'stoneware' stopping — generally composed of china clay, flint and a little flux. If a biscuit pot has cracked, this suggests strain which may cause further damage in the glaze fire, and the piece is better discarded. With modeling there is more justification for attempted repair. The stopping called Alumide, its makers claim, can be glazed over.

Storage of clay

Clay improves with aging, and facilities for storing clay in a damp atmosphere are very desirable. For large quantities,

some sort of clay 'cellar' with non-absorbent walls, a tiled floor, no ventilation and a close-fitting door is ideal, but for most craft potters something more modest is called for. The polythene bags in which plastic clay is often delivered provide storage, if unpunctured, for many months. Similarly, plastic sacks, bin-liners and the like can be utilized for mixed and wedged batches, which should be rested for at least a day or two before use. Damp the interior of the bags with a sponge to avoid dry flakes of clay.

Clay bins present problems: drying layers of clay on the sides; the decomposition of zinc on galvanized surfaces and the difficulty of extracting clay from a pressed-down mass. If clay has been pugged, try to keep the rolls separate so that they can be more easily lifted out; sheets of stiffish polythene between layers help. Pug your clay fairly soft. A full bin is more efficient than a half empty one. Asbestos substitute tanks need filling with water first to saturate them. Plastic bins keep clay damp, but are easily damaged by scrapers. They will also melt easily, and can crack in frost.

Strap handle

See *bail handle*.

Straw ash

A highly refractory ash, usually containing up to 75–80% silica. An exception is 'bean straw ash' (Leach).

Strontium, oxide

A metallic element Sr, 87.5.
Oxide SrO, 103.5. Strontia.
Carbonate $SrCO_3$, 147.5.

An *alkaline earth*. A slightly soluble, non-poisonous but expensive carbonate used as a glaze flux. Similar to calcium and barium which it can replace, though 'you definitely want to test it. Also there is often a color loss' (Georgies). Strontium glazes should be low in lime, however, if crystallization is not required. Parmalee states that good earthenware glazes (firing at *c.*1090°C/1994°F and upwards) can be had by replacing some other bases with strontia, and that colors also benefit. The oxide provides a long firing-range and is very craze-resistant. There are no common strontia-bearing minerals. Strontium earthenware glazes are reported to be widely used in Russia, the oxide replacing lead.

Studio potter

An artist-craftsman working alone, or with very few assis-ants, who takes part in all the ceramic processes so that the final piece has his or her individual stamp or character. It is not a very satisfactory term, and others have been suggested: craftsman potter; artist potter; workshop potter; hand potter; non-industrial potter; ceramicist, etc. As the industry becomes more and more remote from its craft origins, perhaps simply 'potter' will soon be sufficient.

Stupid

An old term for a wad-mill!

Styrofoam

A dense form of polythene which has been carved and used as a model for casting large and involved forms, a method used by Felicity Aylieff (CR165).

Sucking

Lead oxide and some other oxides are liable to volatilization and deposits on the walls of kilns and saggars. Isaac Button's kiln had a thick coat of lead glaze from this effect. It is done deliberately, of course, in *vapor glazing*.

Sulfide, sulfate

Many elements will form a salt or binary compound with sulfur. Its release during firing, however, can have ill-effects on glazes, and the form is rarely used. Galena is a sulfide of lead PbS, barytes $BaSO_4$ a sulfate of barium (contains oxygen) which liberates sulfur dioxide during firing. Plaster of Paris is a calcium sulphate $CaSO_4$ $(\frac{1}{2}H_2O)$. *Cadmium sulfide* is a pigment. (See also *sulfuring*.)

Sulfur

An element S, 32.
Combines with metals to form binary compounds, sulfides.
    Sulfur may be present in clays, especially fireclays, and in some concentrations in yellow ochre. Its presence is made obvious when firing an electric kiln! Mentioned in the 'Dictionary of Science' as 'essential to life', but it is not good for the lungs for all that!

Sulfuring

The dulling of a glaze surface through attack by sulfur. Parmalee discusses the effects at length pp308–11. Sulfur as sulfites — salts of sulfurous oxide SO_2 — will burn away, but those of SO_3, sulfuric oxide, are resistant to change by heat. Early ventilation is therefore necessary to clear fumes

from the kiln, especially in soft-glaze firings. At higher temperatures a *reducing* atmosphere is more likely to drive out the sulfur in sulfates.
    Leadless glazes and those with a high calcium or barium content appear to be at greatest risk from sulfur gas. The sulfur gases liberated by some clays in an electric kiln are a nuisance, or worse. Ensure good ventilation.

Sump oil

See *drainoil*.

Superpax

A trade name for *zirconium silicate* (Georgies).

Supersaturated glaze

A glaze with more coloring oxide than it can dissolve, the surplus being precipitated on cooling. (See *saturated glaze*.)

Surface combustion

Fuel burns more readily as gases and on contact with hot surfaces. This will be obvious to anyone who has tried to start a drip-feed kiln from cold. Kiln design should take this into account; the heating of *secondary air* is important.

Surface tension

An effect, resembling that of a stretched elastic skin, seen at the boundary or surface of any liquid. For instance, when gently pouring liquid from the surface of a glaze it will pile up on the rim before bursting through and running off. Glaze, in its liquid state, has a high surface tension value — some 200–300 as compared with 74 for water. This will be seen from the globules of glaze which hang at the foot of an over-fired or over-glazed pot. Crawling in its final stages is influenced by surface tension, the glaze failing to 'wet' the surface. The surface tension of the glaze is greater than gravity which would otherwise spread it over the surface. Cracks in the glaze coating, the primary cause of crawling, increase the surface area and thus the tension. Dust under the surface will have a similar effect. Zinc and magnesium are reputed to lower the surface tension.

Surform tools

A proprietary name for a very useful form of rasp or plane which can be used to shave clay surfaces at the leather-hard or drier state. Can be obtained as a plane or as a foot-long rasp. Particularly useful for slab pots. See *slip, tool*.

Suspender, floatative

A glaze or slip additive which will help to retard settling and aid suspension. This can be by physical means, using gums (tragacanth, dextrin, arable), size, bentonite or ball clay, or by the electrical or molecular effect of salt, deflocculants or ammonia. All have intrinsic disadvantages. Other *organic* materials (Parmelee also includes quince pips and blood!) can be used but will decompose if glaze is kept for long periods and need the further addition of *formalin*. Deflocculants thin the mixture; salt introduces unwanted soluble ingredients. Dodd mentions calcium chloride to prevent settling — about 0.02%. Epsom salts have been mentioned, as has *Macaloid*.

Suspension

All insoluble materials stirred up in a liquid will eventually sink to the bottom again. Fine particles will remain suspended in the liquid longer than coarse ones; those with a low *specific gravity* will remain longer than those with a high one. A lead frit will thus have the worst of both worlds. *Colloidal* particles will remain longest in suspension, hence the use of bentonite. Suspension does not of course refer to *soluble* materials. Some glazes will stay in suspension for a longer period if the container is tightly sealed. See also *CMC*.

Glaze becomes liquid during firing. Certain oxides, generally *acidic* oxides, will fail to dissolve but will remain in suspension in a fundamentally unaltered state. These are the opacifiers, notably tin and zircon.

Sweeping compounds

These are dust absorbent materials which are strewn on to floor before sweeping. Obtainable form various sources (Axner, etc). A sprinkling of water is not as effective but better than nothing.

Swirlamiser

A very efficient oil and gas burner (Autocombustions, Telford).

Syenite

See *nepheline syenite*.

T°

Symbol for degrees of temperature.

Tableware

A general term for pottery directly concerned with the serving of food and drink. (See *plate, cup, saucer, teapot,* etc.)

Tailings

The portion of a material which will not pass through a particular screen, for instance, coloring oxide in a 200 sieve. The tailings go back into the *mortar* for further grinding, (or more often in practice, down the sink! But see *waste disposal* for a warning).

Talc

A mineral, a hydrated magnesium silicate $3MgO.4SiO_2.H_2O$, 379 (convenient equivalent weight 126). Low *coefficient of expansion* (2.0).

The chief mineral of soapstone and steatite. Used as an insoluble form of magnesia in glazes. Dolomite is now more commonly used for this purpose. Typical analysis by weight:

MgO	32.0	Al$_2$O$_3$	7.0
CaO	3.0	Fe$_2$O$_3$	1.5

Small amounts, 2% in the batch or up to 0.3 of the RO, will act as a flux; more than this will tend to make the glaze more viscous, but can impart a pleasant sheen to the surface. Lowers the thermal expansion (see *cordierite*). It affects some colors—iron goes brown, cobalt a less intense blue. Can be mixed with cobalt when this oxide is used as a pigment.

Talc has a fine, powdery nature and is difficult to mix with water in a glaze batch, floating on the top and blowing away in the slightest breeze. It is advisable to mix it well with the other dry ingredients, and to slowly add the water to the batch.

Tamman temperature

The *sintering* point or temperature range.

Tank gas

See *bottled gas*.

Tannin, tannate

An organic compound derived from trees and plants. Sodium tannate can be used as a *deflocculant*.

Teapot

Like the jug in the hands of Alison Britton, the humble teapot has become a jumping off place for riotous imagination and has suffered many transmogrifications and indignities over the last ten years: multi-spouted, deformed, pornographic, Victorian kitsch, (the variations are endless); forms which are beyond the scope of a practical dictionary.

A good teapot is difficult to make but, when successful, few things can give a potter more satisfaction. One of our most distinguished potters, Geoffrey Whiting, gave this advice in PQ 7: 'A teapot needs to be fairly broad and certainly stable. Throw as thinly as possible, and keep the opening as small as is compatible with easy filling and cleaning. Throw the spout on a fairly thick base, which should be wide enough to allow a grid, the holes of which have a slightly greater cross-sectional area than that of the narrow end of the spout. Make the knob on the lid something worth getting hold of, and vent the lid with a generous $\frac{1}{10}$in/2mm hole.'

It is vital to trim the spout so that it is higher than, or at least level with, the top of the teapot (see also *spouts*). Punch plenty of grid or strainer holes, each about $\frac{1}{8}$in/3mm across, and leave the ragged edges inside the pot severely alone until quite dry, when they can be

A compact, multi-faceted teapot with paneled glaze and brushwork decoration. By John Maltby.

An attractive example of the modern 'fun' teapot which had almost overtaken the practical type in the 1980s, harking back, in a sense, to Victorian styles.

chipped away without blocking the holes. Hole cutters with semi-circular hollow blades are widely available and can give a cleaner cut if used on just leather-hard clay. Mark and score the spout position and attach with slip. Geoffrey Whiting prefers a spout which grows 'smoothly out of the body of the pot and makes a continuous unbroken line with it', but other teapots show more articulation between spout and pot.

The handle is very important. It must be efficient and comfortable, with room for three fingers on a medium pot and four on a large one. Its form and the area of void its loop encloses must balance the spout and the lid. Always attach the handle after the spout, and with the completed lid in place. 'You [may] find that, to form a comfortable efficient hold, the handle looks wrong on the pot... in which case you may have to redesign the whole thing. This

Still among the best teapots ever made is the classic form by the late Geoffrey Whiting. If there is any criticism, the knob could have been a little bolder to match the strength of the rest of the form.

sort of difficulty is implicit in the nature of design and craftsmanship and it is no good being afraid of it. Pencil sketches will help but do not allow yourself to become a slave to paper designs. They militate against the freedom and spontaneity the thrown shape should always have.'

Arched-over handles can be of cane or clay. They must be high enough for comfortable removal of the lid. The lugs of a cane handle should be sturdy; a good deal of weight depends on them. (See also *cane handles, glazing, handles, knobs, lids, spouts*.)

Temmoku

See *tenmoku*.

Temperature color

The optical effect of rising heat (in the absence of light) is a change from black to blue-white, through reds, oranges and yellows. It is difficult to give names to these 'colors' which will make them recognizable when peering through a kiln spyhole. Green gives a color chart, but the light reflected from an illustration is different in kind from the radiant heat color. With these reservations in mind, the following table may have some use.

Seger cone	Degrees	Color
022	600°C/1112°F	dull red
015	800°C/1472°F	red
010	1000°C/1832°F	cherry red, between red and orange
1	1100°C/2012°F	orange
5	1180°C/2156°F	light orange
7	1230°C/2246°F	pale yellow
10	1300°C/2372°F	yellow-white
12	1350°C/2462°F	white tending to blue

The intensity of heatlight, in fact, produces color effect.

Temperature control

See *heat control*.

Temperature degree

Heat produces internal activity in matter: 'hotness' or temperature is a measure of the kinetic energy of the molecules of which the matter is composed. Heat can lead to fundamental alteration and rearrangement in the basic atomic structure. Certain reactions (e.g. oxidation) in themselves produce heat. Temperature is one factor in *heatwork*.

The degree of heat is indicated by a constant scale. Those in common use are based on the interval between

Temperature conversion tables — Centigrade (Celsius), Fahrenheit, and Kelvin.

C	F	K	C	F	K
−273	−477	0	1000	1832	1273
−18	0	255	1050	1922	1323
0	32	273	1080	1976	1353
10	50	283	1100	2012	1373
50	122	323	1120	2048	1393
100	212	373	1140	2084	1413
120	248	393	1150	2102	1423
200	392	473	1180	2156	1453
225	437	498	1200	2192	1473
250	482	523	1220	2238	1493
300	572	573	1230	2246	1503
350	662	623	1240	2264	1513
400	752	673	1250	2282	1523
450	842	723	1260	2300	1533
500	932	773	1275	2318	1548
550	1022	823	1280	2336	1553
573	1063	846	1285	2345	1558
600	1112	873	1300	2373	1573
660	1220	933	1310	2390	1583
700	1292	973	1325	2417	1598
750	1382	1023	1335	2435	1608
800	1472	1073	1350	2462	1623
870	1598	1143	1380	2516	1653
900	1652	1173	1400	2552	1673
950	1742	1223	1450	2642	1723

the freezing- and boiling-points of water. The Centigrade or Celsius scale divides this interval into 100 degrees and commences at freezing point, 0°. The freezing point in the Fahrenheit scale is 32°, and the interval is divided into 180 degrees, giving 212°F, as the boiling point. Conversion cannot therefore be made directly except by memory. The arithmetic is:

Centigrade into Fahrenheit — divide by 5, multiply by 9, add 32 to total.

Fahrenheit into Centigrade — subtract 32, divide remainder by 9, multiply by 5.

Tempering clay

Adding water to clay powder, or distributing it more intimately. This can be done with a *paddle* and bin, with a *dough mixer*, or, really professionally, by *blunging* and *filter pressing*. See also *mixing clays*. In the historical sense, the word 'tempering' is often used to indicate the addition of non-clay materials to a body; for instance, shell, grit, grog, sand, etc.

Template

In general, a template is any guide or mold shaped to the outline of a piece of work. In pottery it is generally confined to describing a sheet of card, metal, or other stiff material cut to the profile of a pot, plate, bowl, or mold and used as a guide to scrape or model the clay surface to the desired curve (see *jigger and jolley, hollow mold*). It can also be applied to card or *paper resist* used in decoration where these are held against the piece rather than adhered to it, as with *stencil*.

Temporary kiln

The spate, in recent years, of large 'sculptural' ceramics has given rise to firing problems. When pieces are too heavy or too awkward to be packed into a standing kiln, simple drybuilt kiln structures have been erected round them and the whole fired in situ. Firing is generally by oil, carried out through strategically placed burner apertures. More than one burner is needed. A simple updraft kiln might be easier to fire. (See also diagrams in Rhodes K.) Raku and sawdust kilns are also generally temporary structures, erected and taken down in a few minutes. A more traditional structure erected as a temporary kiln can be very instructive with regard to kiln design and performance. (See also *raku kiln, top-hat kiln*.)

Like all kilns of this type their weight and complexity for the same degree of insulation, has been considerably reduced by the development of *ceramic fiber*.

Tenmoku, temmoku

The Japanese name for very dark colored reduced iron stonewares of early Chinese types, including 'hare's fur', 'oil spot' and other effects on a near-black glaze, which can also break to an iron-red.

Quoted percentages of iron in the batch vary widely: 4.5–5% with slow cooling (Cardew); 10% burnt sienna, or a slip glaze of the Albany variety (Rhodes); up to 12% (Leach); a precise 7.6% from Dodd, who also gives this recipe: feldspar 50, whiting 10.9, magnesite 2.3, kaolin 5.9, quartz 23.0. Margaret Gebhard (CR88) suggests the following recipe for a once-fired (raw-clay glazed) 1240°C/2264°F, (soaked for 25 minutes), electric kiln oxidized firing: potassium feldspar 40, nepheline 15, whiting 10, red clay 35, with an additional 2.5% red iron oxide and 1% spangles.

It obviously depends upon the type of glaze, usually a fairly fluid one, and on how much iron it will dissolve. A supersaturated glaze will tend to break with lighter browns. (See also *black glazes, red glazes, iron*, etc.). Shaw mentions manganese, chromium, and cobalt, and Dodd lists *magnesite*, in connection with tenmoku glazes.

Tensile strength

The resistance a material exhibits to being torn apart by tension or pulling. The tensile strength of glazes and bodies is important, one or the other usually being in a state of tension. Soft glazes are reputed to be more 'elastic' or resistant than stonewares, but it is easier to get a stoneware glaze into *compression*. (See *crazing, shattering*.)

Tension

A state of tensile or 'pulling' strain. Glazes under tension will *craze*.

Terra rosa

Listed by Dodd/Murfin as a red hematite glaze pigment.

Terra sigillata

A reddish-brown, slightly glossy surface found especially on Roman pottery. Probably a very fine (*colloidal*) red slip.

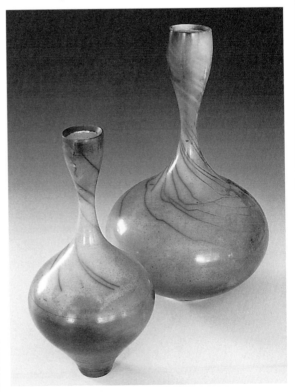

Two terra sigillata bottle forms by Duncan Ayscough.

Potash additions (including wine lees) have also been mentioned. For the modern potter Behrens suggests: clay 40, water 100, soda ash 4. Allow the slip to settle, pour water from the surface and use only the top one-third or so — the finest grain (see *suspension*). Colors in the form of carbonates and also zinc or titanium can be added before sedimentation. Parks mentions the proprietary water softener Calgon or sodium hydroxide, around 1 to 200 parts, but sodium hexameta phosphate is preferred. The fine particles can be further improved by milling.

Fiona Salazar sprays her basic slip onto pots, burnishes them, then adds decoration, using several coats of stained ball clay slips brushed on, followed by a final reburnishing (CR107). Her slip recipe is: 3500 centiliters water; 1500 grams ball clay; 7.5 grams sodium hexameta phosphate (SHP), see *calgon*. The sodium is ground before adding to the slip. After 48 hours water is syphoned off and the top layer of fine clay particles used. Duncan Ross (CR129) uses some red clay in his bodies, fires in saggars with sawdust after a preliminary biscuit fire to 1000°C/1832°F; uses masking tape as a resist between slips; and controls carbon penetration by varying the thickness of the slips. He finishes with a light coating of paraffin-based wax.

Remarkable effects are obtained by saggar-firing terra sigillata coated pots which have been either sprayed with glazes and colorants or packed with sawdust, salt, copper carbonate, etc.

Terracotta

Literally 'cooked earth', the term most commonly indicates unglazed red clay modeling or architectural ceramic. It is also applied to the color of fired red clay. Rhodes CGP equates terracotta with a low-grade open *fireclay*, but this would not be a widely understood meaning. Cardew describes a terracotta wood-firing kiln for temperatures up to 950°C/1742°F.

Tertiary air

An infrequently used term for a supply of pre-heated air to the chimney of a kiln to assist combustion of smoke and to minimize pollution. The chimney can be large enough to accommodate pots for biscuit firing, it will then act like an updraught kiln.

Tessha

A Japanese glaze of the tenmoku family but more metallic and breaking to iron reds. The standard 4:3:2:1 glaze (see *stoneware glaze*) with the addition of 26% quartz and 13% Fe_2O_3, in reduction, is given for tessha. The firing schedule

will radically affect the glaze. Quick cooling to 900°C, 1652°F is recommended.

Test kiln

The value of very small trial kilns is limited. By their nature they fire and cool more quickly than a production kiln and this, with other factors, will give misleading results. They are more useful in earthenware, the results approximating more closely to those from larger kilns than in stoneware. However, they can give a general impression at various temperatures and can reveal gross errors in glaze mixes before a full pack is spoiled. Tests are always more valid, when worked in with the general run of production in normal kilns.

Electric test kilns can be built quite cheaply and quickly, although the limited element lengths will necessitate a thinner gauge wire than is normal for high temperatures. 90ft./27m of 17 swg, producing 2.5 kW, can generally be housed in a test kiln.

Test-piece

See *draw trial, glaze trial, temperature indicator*.

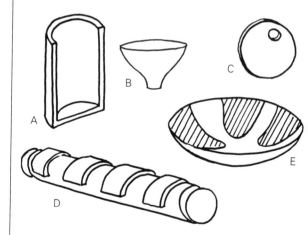

Test pieces for glaze, etc.

A A thrown cylinder can be cut in two as shown or, if wider, into four or six segments. Each will give an upright inside and outside surface, simulating a pot.

B A small bowl, thrown on a stack.

C A ring with a hole in it is useful for hanging on a board or for stringing together.

D Strips of clay can be dried over a rolling pin so that each piece will stand on a curved edge.

E A shallow dish from the center of which several glaze tests may be poured, keeping a series together for reference and comparison. It is instructive if the tests overlap.

Texas talc

'A good clay body, having round rather than platey particle shape. Fires white' (Georgies).

Texture

The same root as 'textile'. The 'Oxford English Dictionary' gives 'an arrangement of threads'. In general usage the term indicates fine markings or irregularities of the surface, or the degree of smoothness of the surface, as apparent to sight and touch.

With the increase in handbuilding and the decline in brushwork and pattern-making, texture is often the main interest provided by the surface. Sand or grog is either beaten into the surface or exposed by working it over; coarse metal oxides (e.g. ilmenite) or even fragments of metal (e.g. copper filings) produce varied texture on a surface. More consciously controlled markings are made with hacksaws, fine combs, etc. or by beating with engraved or string-bound bats, etc. (See also *beaten patterns, impressed decoration, stones.*)

Christopher Selwood (Chisholm Institute of Technology,

Strong texture achieved by rolling soft clay onto a ridged surface, the slabs further manipulated into this striking standing form by Peter Wright.

Strong clay and glaze textures on a slab dish in raku by Robert Fournier.

Victoria, Australia) suggests adding organic materials — sawdust, crushed coke, etc. either singly or together, or inorganic materials including silicon carbide, pumice, basalt, or scoria (the slag from metal workings), or laval deposits, to give physical texture to clays, or color breaks and speckle to the overlaying glaze. Deliberate *crawling* and *crater glaze* could be seen as a type of texture. A lightly textured ash glaze on a porcelain bowl by Sheila Fournier is illustrated at *glaze*.

Therm, thermal unit

A unit of quantity of heat equivalent to 100,000 British thermal units or 29.3 units of *electricity*. Around 100cu ft of *natural gas* are needed to produce a therm; one gallon/4.55 liters of propane; or $^3/_4$ gallon/3.4 liters of *fuel oil*.

A 'therm' unit is used by gas companies to price their product based on the calorific value of a cubic foot of gas; 200 feet cubed of town gas or 100 feet cubed of natural gas produce one therm. (See *gas fuel*.)

Even the best-designed kiln will not utilize all the heat produced, and the 'useful therm' is reckoned at about two-thirds of the 'true therm'. Electricity is direct conversion and there is almost no loss. One gas therm is therefore equated with about 20 kWh. In joule units one therm equals 105 mJ.

Thermal conductivity

The rate at which heat passes through a material. High conductivity is required in kiln furniture, a low rate in kiln walls. Materials with low conductivity are 'insulators'. The variation between common ceramic materials can be startling, e.g. silicon carbide is given a factor of 120, while a white porous insulating brick may be as low as 0.8. The factor is arrived at by computing the Btus per square foot of face area per hour per degree Fahrenheit per inch of thickness, written Btu/ft.^{2}/h/°F/in. Other measurements

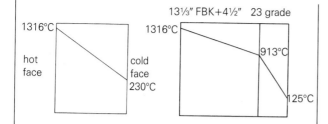

The conductivity and heat storage of firebricks.
1 13½in firebrick. Heat storage 51, 500 Btu/ft² Conduction loss 1450 Btu/ft²
2 13½in firebrick + 4½in 23 grade HTI brick. Heat storage 78,050 Btu/ft² Conduction loss 540 Btu/ft.²

can replace certain items, such as square meters for square feet, or °C for °F, but it is the comparative figures derived from any one factor which are of practical interest. The diagram for conductivity through a brick shows a section through the thickness (through the kiln wall); the *hot-face* temperature is marked on one side by dividing the upright into degrees (like a graph). The outer face is similarly divided and the temperature indicated is that which is maintained when the brick has reached full heat storage. The flatter or more horizontal the line, the more complete is the thermal conductivity and the poorer are the insulating qualities.

Two bricks of different constitution are often used in a kiln, the inner one chosen for strength and physical heat resistance, the outer one for low thermal conductivity. It will be seen that, as the hot-face temperature rises, the initial heat input into the kiln will go to warm the brick itself (*heat storage*); when this is complete the outer temperature will rise in direct relationship with the inner one. At a certain temperature the radiation (which increases with the difference between the outer face and the ambient temperatures) will equal input into the kiln, and the chamber temperature will become static. (See also *heat loss*.)

Air, except when in free movement (*convection*), is a poor conductor of heat. The inclusion of pores in a material will therefore lower its rating, and it follows that dense, heavy materials have a much higher conductivity factor than lightweight 'open' ones. (See also *heat*.)

Thermal expansion

The expansion which all materials undergo when heated, and which is normally reversed on cooling. (See *coefficients of expansion*.) Not to be confused with inversions, or with the structural changes which occur in a clay body and are not reversible (see *shrinkage*).

Thermal shock

Bodies and glazes as a whole, or some oxides within them undergo changes in volume during firing, some of which are reversible on cooling. If expansions and contraction cannot be accommodated within the structure, then damage will occur. The *inversions* of quartz and cristobalite will cause thermal shock. The latter, which spans cooking temperatures, is the more important in ovenwares. Quartz inversion is instantaneous and can damage a high-silica ceramic in the kiln. Alumina rather than silica refractories are therefore preferred. Limit '*free*' *quartz* or flint additions to bodies to 20%, and cool reasonably slowly over the 600–150°C/1112–302°F range. Rapid cooling of a glaze can cause shock and *crazing*, especially if it is high in alkalis.

As well as firing stress, pottery is liable to thermal shock in use, as when taken from an oven and placed on a cold surface. For discussion of this hazard see *flame-proof ovenware*.

Thermocouple

The activating part of a pyrometer. Two wires of dissimilar alloys are fused together at one end. For temperatures below 1100°C/2012°F the alloys are usually Chromel and Alumel, but above 1100°C/2012°F pure platinum is used with an alloy of platinum and rhodium. The fused junction is protected by an aluminous porcelain, mullite, or a similar refractory sheath and inserted into the kiln, protruding about 1in/25mm beyond the hot-face. The ends of the wires outside the kiln are connected by special compensating cable to the pyrometer indicator, so completing the circuit. As the wire junction gets hot a small voltage (only a few millivolts) is generated which is measured by the indicator and moves a pointer across a dial calibrated in degrees of temperature. The length of the connecting cable will affect the reading so do not shorten or lengthen these wires once the pyrometer is installed. Ensure as far as possible that the terminals do not get too hot, or the indicator either too warm or cold. See *pyrometer* and in Fournier for more detailed information.

Thermotrophy

Most potters will have noticed that the colors of glazes when opening a kiln while the contents are still just too hot to touch show some rather startling variations; white glazes appear creamy-gray and the quality of reds and browns is altered. Some glazes, especially those containing titania will again alter color if subsequently heated, a phenomenon which can surprise a cook when withdrawing a dish from a hot oven. This change of color at comparatively low tempertures is known as thermotrophy, and reverts to the original color on cooling. An associated effect is that of *phototrophy* which is activated by light (or the lack of it) rather than heat.

Thimble

An item of kiln furniture, now more rarely listed by merchants. One thimble fits into another, and each has a short horizontal arm. Three piles, set into bases, provide support for similar sized plates or tiles. Used for earthenware only. *Cranks*, *plate setters*, and *tile setters* are other constructions listed in suppliers' catalogs for supporting a number of similar sized pieces.

Thixotropy

A factor of *plasticity*. A clay body 'softens' momentarily under pressure (e.g. of the fingers when throwing) and solidifies again when released. It controls standing strength. The *lamellar* structure of clay with strong electrical bonds between the layers seems to hold the key to this behavior but other explanations have been suggested, e.g. 'house of cards' or 'scaffold' structures. In general scientific terms, thixotropy indicates an increase in *viscosity* with the passage of time, as in thixotropic paints.

Excess *electrolyte* can produce thixotropy in slips, causing them to 'set', becoming fluid only when stirred. (See also the converse of thixotropy at *dilatancy*.)

Thorpe's ratio

An equation controlling the base (especially lead/silica ratio) in a glaze. A simplified version given by Kenneth Shaw in CR11 (after Mellor) to help computation of safe lead glazes (*low solubility*) reads:

$$\frac{RO + R_2O + Al_2O_3}{RO_2 \ (mainly \ SiO_2)} = \text{a maximum of } 0.5$$

Examples:

Formula 1. 0.8 PbO
0.2 K_2O 2.5 Al_2O_3 2.0 SiO_2
gives $\frac{0.8 + 0.2 + 0.25}{2.0} = \frac{1.25}{2.0} = 0.625$

Formula 2. 0.8 PbO 0.3 Al_2O_3 3.0 SiO_2 0.2 K_2O
gives $\frac{1.3}{3.0} = 0.43$

Formula 1 is in excess of the maximum and is therefore likely to be outside the allowed solubility limits; Formula 2 is a better figure.

This is to be taken as one guide only in working out glazes: the alumina/silica ratio and other factors must also be considered. (See *glaze*, *Seger formula*, etc.)

Three phase supply

An electrical mains input through three lines or 'live' wires and one neutral. A high load can be equally distributed over the lines, each supplying a third of the required wattage, or they can be connected in such a way (line to line) to increase the voltage. This enables the electricity company to balance its supply and also reduces the cable size necessary for each phase. The normal domestic supply is on one live and neutral only — single phase — and this may be limited to a total load of about 60 amps. For wiring diagrams on three phase supply see *star* and *delta*.

Kilns of over 4cu ft/0.11cu m capacity will need more than one phase. Sometimes a two phase supply may be installed. The cost depends on the distance from the mains cables to the meter position and to your kiln. In England it appears to be fairly arbitrary and negotiable. (See *electric kiln, element* etc.)

Electric motors are marginally cheaper and more efficient on three phases. Some authorities will allow up to 70 kW on one phase, especially where three phase is not available.

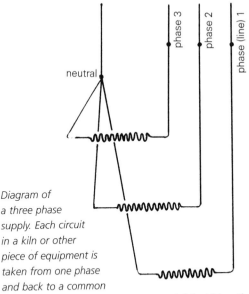

Diagram of a three phase supply. Each circuit in a kiln or other piece of equipment is taken from one phase and back to a common neutral. (See also single phase, star and delta.) More than one piece of equipment (resistance) can, of course, be taken from each phase but these must be in parallel, i.e. each taken from a mains line to obtain full voltage.

Throwing

The hand forming of hollow shapes on a revolving wheel head. Various techniques of coiling, pinching, and molding preceded throwing, probably assisted by a 'slow wheel' or turntable and the precise date of its inception is unknown but there is evidence of throwing some 30 centuries BC. The changeover from built to wheel pots seems to correspond with a change from women to men potters.

Throwing, when treated in a direct and spontaneous way, gives a distinctive quality to pottery, offers a wide range of shapes, and allows for infinite subtle variations. It is the hallmark of the individual potter and the general public is coming to appreciate its qualities. It can never recover a prime position in pottery which, industrially, is the place of the *mold* and the *jigger and jolley*, but it is likely to maintain an honorable and distinctive place. A thrown pot is often distinguished by the spiral groove, especially on the inside, and which can be strongly marked or only just perceptible.

It is an extremely personal technique and one cannot dogmatize on method. The following is an outline of the principles. The clay is well kneaded and formed into a ball or blunt cone with a rounded base, which is brought sharply down onto a damp but not wet wheelhead with sufficient force to drive any air from under the base and to attach it firmly to the wheel. It is then 'centered' — for details see *centering* and *coning*. At all stages the surface of the clay is moistened (lubricated), but not saturated, with water or slip. Some potters throw almost dry. For the actual throwing, the thumb (or fingers for a very large pot) is pressed steadily into the clay precisely on its vertical axis until it is $\frac{1}{4}$in/6mm or so (more for bowls which are to be turned) from the surface of the wheelhead. The rest of the hand is cupped round the clay during this process, and the whole gently supported by the left hand. The thumb is then thrust at right-angles to the first movement, parallel to the wheelhead, supporting the clay with the fingers outside until thumb and fingers are within about $\frac{1}{2}$in/12mm of one another. The right hand is now raised slowly while gripping the revolving wedge of clay which is squeezed and allowed to flow between thumb and fingers resulting in a thick-walled cylinder. The thinning and raising of the wall is continued using both hands, the middle finger of the left hand (supported by the others) replacing the thumb inside, and the crooked forefinger of the right hand exerting the outside pressure. Shape can be introduced by increasing the pressure inside or out, by raising the inner finger slightly above the outer (for concave profile) or vice versa for convex shapes. It must always be remembered that clay can be worked only by squeezing it between two surfaces — it will not stretch. This holds good for any pottery technique. Widening a pot on the wheel by means of pressure on the inside only will cause it to split or slump.

More complete instructions are to be found in

Isaac Button throwing a large flowerpot.

1 to *3* Opening out, using both thumbs inside and squeezing the clay up to the fingers outside and into a thick collar which is gripped and lifted with a slight change in position, the little finger crooked over to exercise control over the rim. Note that the extra thickness required for the finished rim is already apparent in illustration.
4 The hands are in the usual position for thinning the wall, the knuckle outside and the straight fingers inside.
5 The still slightly narrow pot is brought up higher than the guide stick so that, when brought out to full width, it is the correct height as at *6*. The outside has been smoothed with a rib.

Colbeck but personal tuition and continual practice are essential. (See also *bowl, cutting off, jug, lids, pot lift, turning,* etc.)

Throwing gauge

See *pot gauge.*

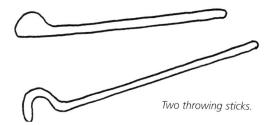

Two throwing sticks.

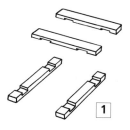

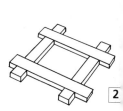

1 The halved joints of a tile frame.
2 The frame assembled. See at 3 in text methods of making tiles. It helps if two people cooperate with this type of tile frame, one holding, one pulling. Alternatively the frame can be held steady by two nails in a board, spaced to hold the outer arms.

Throwing stick

Called an *'egote'* in Japan where they are much used. Shaped wooden sticks used as interior *ribs* when throwing, especially narrow-mouthed vessel. The more usual Western method is to pull up a wider pot and throw the shoulder inwards. (See the film/video 'Isaac Button, Country Potter'.) Sometimes a stick with a sponge on the end is used.

Thrown inlay

See *rolled inlay*.

Thumb pot

See *pinch pot*.

Tile

The industrial tile, usually 4 x 4in/100 x 100mm or 6 x 6in/150 x 150mm is power-pressed from a barely damp powdered body in a die or metal mold. This minimizes shrinkage and warping (the latter being the main obstacle to making tiles from plastic clay) but it also tends to destroy any subtlety in the finished ceramic. Thicker tiles may also be extruded from between rollers. A number of potters use industrial tiles as surfaces to be decorated with brushwork, trailed glaze, etc.

There is an account of pre-industrial tile-making in Berendsen. Roughly cut rolled tiles were piled up to 'yearn' (even out their moisture content) before a final rolling and cutting using an iron-edged template. They were fired in pairs, upright, bedded in 'wads'. Throughout the history of the tile there has been a steady diminution in thickness from around $^3/_4$in/20mm to $^1/_4$in/6mm. The average thickness of a handmade tile is $^3/_8$in/10mm.

Methods of making tiles:

1 Slabs can be rolled out freehand or with the use of guide sticks: the tiles cut leather-hard with a fine knife using a square template.
2 A block of clay cut into appropriately sized slabs with a multi-wire 'harp' and then treated as above.

3 Wooden frames or plaster molds: a two-piece mold with a separate base needed for the latter. Clay is beaten into the frame with the palm of the hand and the surplus is scraped off with a ruler, wetting the clay for the final smoothing movement. Turn the frame 45° between each pull. Lay the frame on a square of paper before commencement to avoid the clay sticking to the table.
4 Metal tile cutters, with ejection plates, can be purchased. Usually made for 4in/100mm squares or circular tiles. The tile is cut from a rolled-out slab.

Methods of drying tiles:

1 Tiles can be dried in the open, turning them over frequently to correct warping.
2 Between absorbent bats, such as asbestos sheets or several thicknesses of newspaper.
3 Leach suggests that tiles cut from a large sheet of clay

Part of a large tile panel 'The back of the Moon' by Maggie Angus Berkowitz. White glazes were trailed and brushed on, fired, and then a dark blue transparent glaze poured over the figure. A silicon carbide glaze was used on the 'Moon'.

3 Cutting a tile with the aid of a card template.
4 and **5** Two stages in the use of a tile cutter.

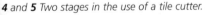

Two porcelain tiles with painted underglaze, by Paul Scott.

should be not quite separated so that they hold each other flat.

4 Smaller or thinner tiles can be dried very rapidly on a hot surface such as a kitchen range, or the top of a hot kiln. Lay them on a kiln shelf.

Tiles can be biscuited in piles of five or, preferably, in a *tile setter*. They are glazed by skimming over the surface of a well-stirred glaze (see diagram at p.150); or they can be sprayed.

Tile work has always included other shapes than square, and has often had relief treatment. There is a greater variety today than ever before, in shape, size, and finish. On the walls of our rather dim modern buildings they can add a touch of gaiety and interest, but their use is seldom really understood or fully exploited, and there is a wide open field for the potter to explore, including three-dimensional decoration and surfaces. (See also *mosaic*.)

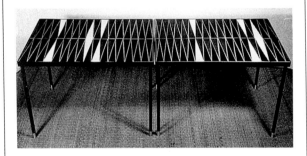

Tile-mosaic tables by Albert Shelly and Robert Fournier.
(See note in article on mosaic for the system of keeping these long triangles of clay flat while drying.)

Tile setter

Systems for holding tiles apart during firing.

A slide-in tile setter.

Setters with turned down 'legs'; these restrict the size; in another type the tiles are fired on edge.

Timer

A one-hour or five-hour cooking timer is an invaluable aid when firing. In a classroom, or when engrossed in other work it is easy to forget the passage of time. The warning ring has saved many a pot from disaster!

Tin, oxide

A metallic element Sn (stannum), 118.5.
Stannic oxide SnO_2, 151. s.g. 6.7.

A useful opacifier at all temperatures, with unique qualities which cannot be matched by zircon, etc. It is acidic and refractory, and does not dissolve to any great extent in a glaze up to about 1200°C/2192°F but remains suspended as a white powder. It has a tendency to cause crawling.

Its principal use is in *soft glazes* for *maiolica* painting or colored glazes (the latter often rather misleadingly called 'tin enamels' or 'maiolica glaze' in suppliers' catalogs and by historians). Tin gives a pleasant texture, and a soft clear color from oxides. Make additions of 9–10% in a lead silicate glaze; 3–5% in stonewares. Beware *chrome-tin pink* reaction (see also *tin glaze*). A little tin oxide is reputed to assist *copper reds*.

Tin ash

Tin *calcined* with lead, used as a more fusible white *pigment* than tin oxide alone. The early maiolica potters used mixtures varying between 2:1 and 4:1 lead/tin, calcined and ground as one of the ingredients of their glazes.

Tin glaze

Any glaze which owes its *opacity* to tin oxide. An adequate glaze coating is needed to achieve opacity but not so thick as to crack and subsequently crawl. Calcined clay, or the use of tin ash is reputed to help prevent crawling in a soft glaze. (See *tin* for percentage additions.)

Ideally a tin glaze will include around 0.5 RO equivalents of lead oxide. The tin will increase the viscosity of glaze, which is an asset in *maiolica*, helping to prevent the running of colors. High-lead glazes with 15% or more of tin will break red on the edges of red clay pots. Michael Casson's early and immensely attractive work used this technique. Alan Caiger-Smith in PQ 35 states that 'a glaze deriving… alumina and silica from stone or feldspar is likely to have richer color-carrying properties than one dependent on china clay'. Much other useful information is to be found in this article and in his book Caiger-Smith TG. Tin can also be used in a stoneware glaze although its opacifying effect diminishes at high temperatures.

Tin glaze over slip

A useful and versatile technique for earthenware. A lead glaze with 10% of tin oxide is used over slips which have rather more than the normal pigment content, e.g. black slip with 15% MnO_2, or blue slip with 2% CoO. The slip is used as a vehicle for dispersing the oxide evenly over the

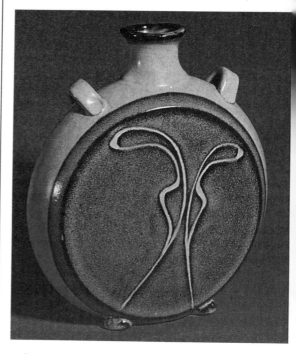

A flask by Robert Fournier, built from two shallow thrown bowls and decorated with sgraffito through black slip covered with a tin glaze (10% in an earthenware glaze). Note the dark line on the edges of the form and the cuts where the manganese has broken through giving emphasis to both. The manganese in the slip can also, sometimes, give an attractive rosy tint.

urface of a dish or pot — a difficult feat by brushing or ny other method. The iron in red clay will produce only faint gray if any color at all; the chrome in green slip will ave little effect but the copper will give a watery green. We are, therefore, largely limited to blue and black slips ut a great variety of shades will result from varying thicknesses of glaze and with practice this can be used to great dvantage. The technique is used in combination with *graffito*, *paper resist*, and other *resist techniques*.

Strangely, a lower tin concentration in the glaze does not necessarily lead to stronger color from the slip, the effect being watery and much less striking than with the full maiolica type glaze. The color will also be directly affected by the firing temperature and degree of soaking. A slightly higher firing or a marginally softer glaze than that normally used for maiolica painting will give improved results. Do not glaze too thickly. (See also illustration at *button*.)

Tin-vanadium yellow

Around 85% of tin oxide with vanadium (as ammonium meta-vanadate) and, often, a little titania, will give a yellow pigment.

Titania

Oxide of titanium TiO_2.

Titanium, oxide, compounds

A metallic element Ti, 48.
Titanic oxide (titanium dioxide) titania, TiO_2, 80, m.p. 1850°C/3362°F.
Sesquioxode Ti_2O_3, 144, c.o.e. around 16.

Precipitated titania is white but the rutile and anatase forms are brown. It will tend to produce a cream color when used as an opacifier when 'it dissolves almost completely in the glaze and recrystallizes on cooling' (Royle). Very small proportions can be used to stabilize lead and coloring oxides (up to 1%) especially in frits. The iron-bearing form produces *rutile* mottle (ad nauseum on commercial tiles, etc.) and is used with pigments. It is an agent in *crystalline glazes*. Tends to give yellows with chromium. In some Bristol glazes titania can turn iron green according to Parmalee who quotes 0.1 of titania to 0.9 of iron. In reduction, various colors from blue to red have been reported. *Rutile*, though strictly a form of titania, is used to describe the iron-bearing mineral.

T material

A plastic, refractory grogged clay containing *Molochite*.

Obtainable from Potterycrafts, Potclays and Fulham Pottery. It was a favorite clay of Hans Coper, and is ideal for modeling and pottery which requires some 'tooth' or a light surface texture. It is expensive — several times the price of stoneware clay but many think its virtues outweigh its cost. A ball clay, china clay, and *Molochite* mixture has been suggested for an approximation. Potclays also issue a similar and somewhat cheaper 'Y' material. An approximation by Sally Robinson (CR167) reads: plastic ball clay 40, china clay 15, feldspar 6, flint 6, Molochite 30 (mesh 33).

It has been used as a slip (Gabrielle Koch CR144) on her burnished pots, colored with commercial body stains.

Toki

According to Dodd, a Japanese name for a high-fired earthenware of the composition: 70% clay; 10% pegmatite; 20% grog.

Tongs

Tongs are required for raku. Now usually listed by merchants, or can be made from flat or round iron rod. Rod will be more efficient if beaten flat at the hinge. About 3ft/1m long, they should open 5 or 6in/125–150mm at the working end. They must be light and easy to use; wooden handles will help grip and insulation. A distinction is made in Japan between the shape of the gripping ends for red and black raku (see Sanders). A more elaborate type are 'accordion' tongs. Kemper Manufacturing Co. California, among others, supply a range of raku tongs.

Typical raku tongs made from two $^1/_4$ x $^3/_4$in/5 x 20mm metal strips. The jaws are twisted at right angles to the handles. The whole can be about 3ft/1m long. Wooden handles at the 'cold' ends will insulate and give a better grip.

Tongue test

If the tip of the tongue is touched against a biscuit pot one can get an idea of its porosity by the extent to which the tongue sticks to the pot momentarily. The more porous the biscuit the more it will adhere. If the surface feels slippery and the patch stays wet or absorbs only slowly, the biscuit is partly vitrified and will take up very little glaze when dipped.

Tools

There are as many tools as there are potters, and suppliers' catalogs show a bewildering variety but one can list half a dozen or so essential ones. Some of these are shown in the photograph; these and others are discussed under *beater, bow, chamois, cutting wire, handle cutter, harp, kidney tool, knife, modeling tool, needle awl (pricker), palette, plane, scraper, spatula, sponge, sponge stick, turning tool,* etc.

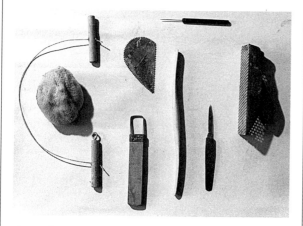

Some of the essential tools of the potter, all quite cheap and simple: a nylon or metal wire on wooden handles; a natural sponge; a scraper; a hoop turning or scooping tool; a wooden spatula; a fine needle awl; a small knife; and a Surform plane.

Top-hat kiln

A type of kiln in which the muffle is lowered over the piece to be fired instead of the ceramic being inserted into it. Modern lightweight ceramic fibers have made the top-hat kiln more practical for the studio potter and it is often used for raku and other rapid firings. The muffle is either lifted off manually (using gloves) by means of handles, or it is suspended from a counterweighted pivoted arm which makes control easier and safer, but involves more construction and a more permanent site.

In the industry the tophat type of kiln has long been employed in firing large electrical ceramics such as power-station insulators.

Gas is the usual fuel for potters' top-hat kilns but it is possible to use other methods of heating.

Steve Mills, of Bath Pottery Supplies UK has doubts about the safety of the top-hat kiln and cites scorched trousers and, even more dangerous, the redhot pack toppling over when the 'lid' is lifted off. He prefers a horizontally split kiln, with the lift-off section being rather less than half the total height. This leaves the pack intact though still easily removed, and the pots suffer less thermal

David Roberts' top-hat kiln showing lifting gear and counterweight for raising the upper section. See also at raku for illustration of this kiln in action.

Steve Mills with his safety first variation on the top-hat design (more of a flat-hat kiln in this case!) constructed from a paint drum lined with ceramic fiber blanket. (See text and also ceramic fiber.)

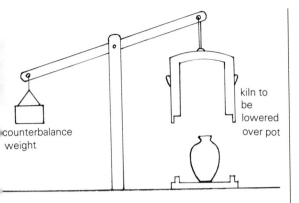

The system for a 'top-hat' kiln which is too heavy to be lifted directly from the pot by hand. The kiln and its base are drawn in section to show a flange on the base and an overlap in the kiln wall which will hold it in place when lowered over the pack.

shock, although I feel that this can lead to other dangers such as bending over a red-hot kiln to remove pots. Like David Roberts he utilizes a simple paint or oil drum lined with ceramic wool. See also *ceramic fiber* for details of the cheap and simple fastening he uses. Axner list a raku kiln with a built-in raiser, leaving about six inches of wall in the lower section.

Top-loading kiln

While many pottery kilns open in the front, an increasing number are packed from above. Both types have advantages. Top loaders, usually electric kilns (though raku is often top loaded), are easier for the potter to build, and they can be heated all round. Pots can be tightly packed laterally. When firing, the top is at a convenient level for the supervision of drying pots and it can also provide an extra working surface in a small workshop. The height is limited by the potter's ability easily to reach to the floor of the chamber, the width by the available roofing bats which support the top bricks or slabs. The maximum capacity is therefore in the region of 12cu ft/0.34cu m, e.g. 2ft/60cm high x 2 ft/60cm deep x 3ft/90cm wide, although the width is not so crucial. As with all types of electric kiln a safety switch, which operates when the door is opened, is advisable.

Full details of top-loader construction is given in Fournier EKP. Many commercial models are available, most of them hexagonal or round in plan. (See also *electric kilns, packing kilns.*)

Torn paper resist

See *paper resist.*

Toseki

A *china stone* from Japan.

Tourmaline

An *accessory mineral* to *granite*. An alumino-borosilicate.

Towing

The industrial term for the act of smoothing the outer edges of plates, etc. on the wheel, traditionally with 'tow' but also with glasspaper or scrapers.

Town gas

Gas fuel produced from coal at a gas-works. It is now almost obsolete in Great Britain. (See *gas.*)

Tragacanth

See *gum.*

Trail and feather

Slip-trailed lines and dots which are feathered through, generally at right angles. The decoration is done on a flat slab of clay, the plate or dish being formed over a hump-mold when the surface is partly dry. (See also *feathering, trailing.*)

Trailer, tracer

See *slip-trailer.*

Trailing

Decorating by means of slip or glaze extruded through a nozzle onto the surface of a piece of pottery. A similar technique to cake-icing but with a more fluid material.

The trailing may be done straight onto the body clay, as was practiced in the 17th century notably on the fine 'Toft' and other large platters. 'Dry' trailing is linear in character — masses may be filled in with washes of brushed slip.

Trailing onto a wet-slip surface allows a more flowing style. The design can be trailed onto a flat slab of clay, the dish being formed when the surface has dried somewhat. The clay can be eased into a *hollow dish mold* from the edges of the slab, or made over a *hump-mold.* The back must be kept damp with sheets of damp newspaper or the clay will crack. Alternatively the dish can be made first, covered

Temmoku glaze over red clay trailing. Fired at 1280°C. By Wayne Hathaway. See also illustration at dotting.

with slip when stiff enough to handle, and the design applied immediately. This is easier as far as making the dish goes but more difficult in the actual trailing. Drop the dish back into the mold as a support when trailing.

Contrasting slips can be spooned into roughly sponged-off areas on the surface of the dish to give some solidity to the background. *Finger combing* can be combined with trailing. The consistency of the slip will affect the style of the design — the thinner the slip the faster and freer will be the trailing movement. A very thick slip will give lumpy results, physically and aesthetically! A sure and unhesitating movement is called for, the design growing as much from the immediate behavior of the slip as from premeditated ideas. A sharp blow on the worktable, or lifting the corner of the mold a fraction and letting it drop again, will spread and unify the trailed line with the background. Trailing on pots is possible but difficult, the face to be worked is generally held nearly horizontal. (See also *dotting, feathering, glaze trailing, slip, slip-trailers,* etc.) Mary Wondrausch (CR164) quotes a recipe for her slipware glaze: lead sequisilicate 75, china clay 18, flint 6, iron oxide 1, for a '*honey*' glaze firing at 1060°C/1940°F. Spots of slip trailed onto the lines are known as *dotting* or *jeweling*.

Transfer, decal

Designs, printed onto special paper backgrounds (see also at *covercoat* for more details), which can be applied to biscuit or glazed ware, the paper peeling or soaking away (see *decal, lithographic transfers, lithography, photoceramic processes*).

They are fundamentally an industrial technique and have lesser place in craft pottery although *silk screen* printed transfers have been used effectively on tiles and potter have used the decal imaginatively. There are firms which will make transfers to your design for repeated pieces o as a repeat element in a pattern, e.g. Pamela Norto Ceramics.

Transfer pen

Supplied by Potclays to be used on special paper to trace design and to transfer it onto a pot surface.

Transitional element

The elements nos. 23–29 in the *periodic table* together with some of the *rare earths*. These elements form coloring oxides.

Translucent

Transmitting light, but not *transparent*. Objects between the translucent object and the light source will be seen through it as shadows. It is one of the properties of porcelains and occasionally of thin stoneware. The term is also applied to semi-transparent soft glazes with 3–6% tin or titanium oxide, and other glazes, cooled slowly to promote crystallization. (See also *lithophane, porcelain*.)

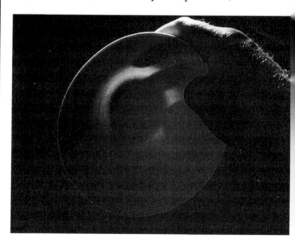

The translucency of a porcelain bowl by Lucie Rie. Oxidized fired in an electric kiln. (See also porcelain.)

Transparent

Transmitting light without diffusion so that objects behind the transparent material can be plainly seen. A majority of glazes, if taken up to full fusion, will be transparent or nearly so. Transparency is a characteristic of glass. Lessened or destroyed by *opacifiers*, and by underfiring, by the development of *crystals* during slow cooling, by trapped bubbles, and by the opalescent effect of mixed glasses within the melt. Also, of course, by coloring oxides, especially the *acidic* or refractory ones. The ratio of 0.1 Al_2O_3:1.0 SiO_2 should be maintained for transparency in glazes.

Tri-axial blending

Or ternary system. A diagrammatic method of studying the effects of the various mixtures possible with three materials or colors. (See *line blends* for two materials.) Four variables would require the construction of a pyramid. The triangle used has 100% of each material at the corners. Halfway down each side indicates, therefore, 50% of each of the materials denoted at the extremities of that line, and pro rata at any point along the line. In fig. **B** point 2 is at the center of the triangle. The lines which intersect at this point cut the sides at 33%. An off-center point 3 in fig. **C** makes this clearer and 3 would indicate a mixture of 75% of X, 15% of Y, and 10% of Z.

A line drawn within the triangle represents any mixture at any point on the line. It might be labeled 1250°C/2282°F, meaning that all the mixtures within that range would melt at that temperature. An area marked within the triangle would similarly indicate all the possible combinations within the area. For instance, it might show all the mixtures of three materials which would be craze-free,

those outside the area being liable to crazing. See fig. **D**. Tri-axial diagrams are also used for phase diagrams. In CR97 and 99, tri-axial blending is dealt with in detail.

In CR142 John Veg Mitchell suggests the use of tri-axial graphs for recording recipes for comparison.

Tri calcium phosphate

$Ca_3(PO_4)_2$.
Similar to *boneash*. A source of phosphate in low and high-fired glazes.

Tridymite

A *primary phase* of silica, probably with a disordered crystal lattice and with several inversions between 170°C/338°F and 870°C/1598°F. Stable up to 1470°C/2678°F. It seems likely, however, that the involved make-up of plastic bodies may often prevent the formation of tridymite although it has been used with cristobalite to mitigate the latter's sudden contraction (or expansion) at 226°C/439°F.

Trimming

Used in America for *turning*.

Trip switch, ELCB

(ELCB stands for Earth Leakage Circuit Breaker.)
A type of electrical mains switch, usually installed by the supply company, which will cut the current as soon as it detects any earth leakage. If, when one tries to switch the current on again, it persists in 'tripping' this indicates a continuing fault or short circuit which must be detected before supply can be resumed. A thunderstorm, a surge of current, or a fault on a neighbor's installation can all trip the switch off, in which case it can merely be reset. There is usually a switch for each main group of circuits, and a special one would be installed for a kiln. Many electrical gadgets now have circuit-breakers incorporated.

Trivalent, tervalent

Elements which combine with three atoms of hydrogen. The oxides (since oxygen is bivalent) are written R_2O_3, e.g. alumina, ferric iron, boric oxide.

Truck kiln, trolley kiln

A kiln from which the loading area (usually the floor and front wall or 'door') can be inserted and withdrawn before and after firing. The packing can then be done in the open

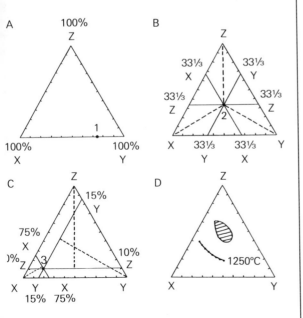

A–D Four tri-axial diagrams, see text.

An electric truck kiln heated by silicon carbide rods.
1 The very clean and simple interior. The brick wall facing the camera is attached to the trolley and not to the chamber.
2 One of the trolley packs being wheeled out after firing. The trolley is a double one with a brick wall between the packs so that the other half, in this picture, would be following into the chamber, loaded with unfired ware.
Photographs courtesy of Labbeat. (See also illustration at kiln.)

but must be fairly sturdily packed so that it will not be disturbed as it is wheeled back into the kiln shell.

True porosity

The sum of open and closed or sealed pores in a fired body.

Tube lining

A Victorian term and technique developed from the Spanish *cuenca* and *cuerda seca*, and having parallels in early Staffordshire and other slipwares. Thickish lines of slip (or a stiff glaze, see below) are trailed onto a plate or pot, building up enclosed areas which can later be filled with slip, color, or colored glazes.

A variation is to glaze the whole piece white and then paint within the spaces. Margery Clinton (CR159) quotes an unusual tube line recipe for use on earthenware: potash feldspar 60, ball clay 10, alumina hydrate 10, lead bisilicate 20, gum arabic 2.

The main outline on a tile panel by Maggie Berkowitz is tube-lined to keep it visible when glaze and oxides were added. (See also at tile.)

Tungsten

A metallic element W (Wolfram), 184.
Trioxide WO_3, a yellow, insoluble powder, m.p. 1473°C/2683°F. Could be used for high temperature yellow pigment, possibly with molybdenum (Billington). Also used in very hard steel alloys.

Tunnel kiln

A kiln in which ware is transported through a hot zone in

he middle of a long tunnel. The firing is a continuous process. The nearest a studio potter can approach the tunnel kiln is with a kiln with doors back and front, the ware being packed on trolleys and wheeled in. This is still, however, an intermittent firing. (See diagram at *continuous kiln*.)

Turning, decoration

The trimming of a thrown pot on the wheel. This can be done immediately after throwing but more generally when *leather-hard*. Excessive turning will destroy the lively effect of throwing. However very *short* bodies such as porcelains are sometimes thrown thickly and turned to a thin wall. It is obvious that the Chinese practiced a good deal of turning. The little industrial ware still thrown is turned on a horizontal lathe like a piece of wood, the short body making very high turning speeds possible.

Jugs, bottles, and most pots can be trimmed as the final action of throwing; alternatively they can be turned at a drier stage but still right way up, re-adhering them to the wheel head with a little water. If a flat base is given a sharp tap with the fingers to make it slightly concave, the pot will have more stability.

If a foot-ring is required the piece must be inverted. For tall pots a hollow *chuck*, or a *cup head* and a wad of clay can be used. A solid chuck is generally used for bowls or squatter shapes. Bowls and many pots can be adhered to the wheel head simply by moistening the rim. A 'grabber pad' is listed by Axner which 'because of the no-skid properties — you will not need to adhere your pottery with wads of clay'. More complicated 'grips' are available which hold the bowl or pot in place on the wheelhead but are not strictly necessary. The clay should be leather-hard, the parings coming away crisply like wood shavings. If it is too soft it will stick to the tool. If too hard the work will be slow and tedious. See also *chatter* for the method of dealing with the corrugations which sometimes develop when turning; also *plates*, *knob*.

Rings can be cut in the wall during turning, as decorative elements sometimes deeply cut, or to emphasise form. Alternatively, on a thickly thrown pot, the wall can be cut away to leave ridges or rings. Spiral turning marks are effective on lids, while those on the inner foot rings of David Leach's pots exhibit an almost voluptuous character. Turned decoration is integral to the piece and has wide potential. (See also *foot-ring*.)

Turning the foot-ring on a bowl.
1 The rough flange left from cutting-off is removed by a vertical cut followed by an upward-sloping cut from the outside, both with a pointed triangular tool, giving true surfaces for further work.
2 The outer wall of the ring is turned with a square tool.

Turning in the industry. On the rare occasions when the wheel is still used bodies are thrown relatively thickly and turned on a fast horizontal lathe.

Supporting small-necked pots for turning.
A (In section) a thrown, diabolo-shaped supporting chuck in leather-hard clay adhered to the wheelhead with a little slip. B A cup head used in turning a smaller pot centered and held in place with a coil of clay. Note in A that the pot drops in as far as it will go but does not touch the bottom of the chuck, while in B the pot is set firmly down before the coil is applied.

Turning tool

The only essential feature of a turning tool is a short, firm cutting edge which can be held at a right-angle to the rotating pot. The actual design varies widely. The standard tool is made from a 7 x ½ or ¾in/180 x 12 or 20mm iron strip. A 1in/25mm length at one end is bent to 90° and cut either to the shape of a rectangle, a triangle, a rounded end or a 'leaf' shape. A V-shaped nick cut away at the angle makes for cleaner working. The cutting end of the tool is then beveled to a sharp edge all round. Loop tools are also made, using a thinner steel strip and a wooden handle, and there are other designs. Each potter will recommend the type to which he has become accustomed.

Clay is abrasive and tools need regular sharpening. They should not, however, be honed to a knife edge, which is as liable to *chatter* as is a very blunt one. A slight burr seems to help. A *steel palette* can be used for turning a large plain area. A bamboo tool is a pleasant tool to use for trimming the foot of a pot immediately after throwing.

3 and 4 The inner face of the ring is incised, and the interior cut away with a square tool, working from the center outwards. Leave the foot-ring a little wider than finally required to allow for accidents.
5 The curve of the bowl is perfected, the ring cut down to its final size, and the outer edge beveled. The bevel gives a pleasant line of shadow beneath the bowl and also prevents chipping.

The four shapes most useful for turning tools. (See also hoop tool under tools, and another useful type at electric kiln.)

Turquoise glaze, *color*

Generally derived from copper oxide. For the purest color, soft glaze must be virtually free from alumina while soda must predominate in the RO. Such a glaze lacks stability (pure soda-silicates are soluble in water) and is very liable to *crazing*. A recipe of one part sodium silicate to one part quartz with 0.5% copper carbonate would make a turquoise frit, but in practice small additions of alumina or lime would have to be made. Published formulas include equal parts of CaO and Na_2O with no alumina and 2.6 SiO_2, 0.6 B_2O; and more involved glazes which include small proportions of alumina, lime and zinc. A *frit* is always needed for this type of glaze. (See also *Egyptian paste*.) Any type of turquoise frit will work better on a *siliceous* body or slip. The Egyptian bodies are reported to consist of up to 90% silica by analysis.

Turquoise stoneware glazes are rare but can be developed from formulas high in calcium and barium, using dolomite to also introduce some magnesium. None of the rules governing soft glaze turquoise colors seem to apply. Use about 2% copper carbonate. A quoted glaze is nepheline syenite 56, barium carbonate 25, ball clay 6, flint 7, copper carbonate 3. It is my experience that the color in stoneware which varies between black and a rich blue-green largely according to the thickness of the glaze coating, is very dependent on a precise firing temperature as well as on the thickness of glaze. It is always variable.

Small amounts of vanadium and zircon are reputed to produce turquoise in an alkaline glaze.

A turquoise-to-blue stoneware glaze I have used for many years is:

Feldspar	52
China clay	10
Dolomite	19
Barium carbonate	19

with 0.8% copper oxide; 0.95% copper carbonate.

Some variation is possible in these percentages, and with the firing temperature which can be between 1220°C/2228°F and 1250°C/2282°F. Not really suitable for tableware as it is likely to be attacked by strong fruit acids, etc. Will give a variety of colors if one layer of glaze is poured over another. The inclusion of *lepidolite* into the glaze recipe (up to 45% according to one source) for a stoneware turquoise has been suggested.

Twaddle degrees

Symbol °Tw. A system for denoting the specific gravity of a liquid.

°Tw = (s.g −1) x 200.

Used for solutions of sodium silicate in casting slips.

Two piece throwing

Large pots may be thrown in two or more sections (the method is also useful when working with porcelain or other short bodies). A neck can be thrown from a coil or squat cylinder stuck to a half dry base. It is possible to build up very large forms section by section, throwing from a fresh coil as each previous one stiffens. Shrinkage of the last thrown section must be taken into account. Leach shows a considerable outward bulge immediately above the join in his diagram in 'A Potter's Book'.

Alternatively the two sections of a pot may each be shaped on the wheel, luted together when stiff enough, and the join worked together on the wheel, perhaps with a throwing stick inside. The rims to be joined must be broad and fairly flat and, of course, of similar diameters. (See also *amphora*.)

Type

See *printer's type*.

Types of pottery

Firing temperatures and categories of pottery (see *temperature degree* for Fahrenheit conversions:

Temp. (°C)	Type
700–800	Enamel colors
	Raku
800–1000	Soft earthenware
	Building bricks (Flettons, etc.)
950–1150	Soft paste porcelains
1000–1140	Range of most craft earthenwares
1150–1200	Hard earthenware (industrial)
1160–1180	Bristol glazed ware
1200–1250	Bone china (biscuit firing temperature)
1220–1320	Stonewares
	Salt glaze
1255–1275	Low-temperature porcelain
1320–1350	Porcelain
1350–1430	Hard paste porcelain

U

μ

Pronounced mu. The symbol for a micron or 0.001 of a millimeter (one-millionth of a meter). Many clay particles are less than 0.5 microns in size.

Ulexite

A mineral containing the oxides of calcium, boron, and sodium. $Na_2. 2CaO. 5B_2O_3$. See *Gerstley Borate*.

Ultimate analysis

The chemical breakdown of a material into its constituent oxides (see *analysis, rational formula*). Also called an 'element analysis'.

Ultimate formula

The arrangement of atomic symbols as the total numbers present in the formula, e.g. $Al_2Si_2H_4O_8$, as distinct from the *rational* or oxide formula $Al_2O_3\ 2SiO_2, 2H_2O$.

Ultrox extra

A *zircon* (listed by Potters Supply House).

Umber

A natural *ferruginous* earth or *hydrated* iron oxide with some manganese oxide. Allied to *ochre* and *sienna*. Calcined as *burnt umber*.

Under-firing

Under-fired biscuit will be very porous and breakable. The word will have a different meaning in terms of temperature for different materials. In general the more fluxes and impurities there are in the clay, the lower will be its optimum firing temperature. For stoneware, biscuiting is simply a method of making it possible to dip the pots into glaze without disintegration, but for earthenware other factors are involved and a very low-fired biscuit is not recommended. (See *crazing, cristobalite*.)

Badly under-fired glazes will be opaque, with rough matt surfaces and probably with a quite different color to the mature glaze. Slightly under-fired tin glazes are liable to *crawl*.

Underglaze, chalk, crayon, pen, pencil

See under individual headings.

Underglaze color, painting

Pigments applied to the raw clay or biscuit and covered with a glaze. When used on biscuit they must either be fixed in a *hardening-on* firing, or a gum or other binding material must be mixed with the color. The latter will tend to influence glaze take-up. The binder generally used for stoneware underglaze painting is simply a little clay. Underglaze colors are limited to those oxides, mixtures, or prepared *fritted* pigments which will withstand the temperature of the glaze which is to be put over them.

If simple oxides are used on raw clay it may be found that some color is still loose after the biscuit firing. This must be washed off under a tap and the pot thoroughly dried before glazing. A little *flux* — a frit, china stone, etc. — mixed with the oxides will help them to adhere, especially cobalt which often fails to *sinter*, and will help to prevent glaze crawling on loose pigment. An addition of a plastic clay, as mentioned above, will at least prevent the color from blurring when dipped in glaze.

Christine Rainbird (CR120) suggests protecting underglaze painting on biscuit with two coats of hairspray to

Underglaze painting on stoneware, covered with a transparent ash glaze. By Eric Mellon.

void smudging when handling or packing in the kiln.

Most pigment oxides yield transparent color (chrome is an exception). Opacity can be increased by the addition of tin, *zinc* (but beware of its effect on some oxides, notably iron), zirconium, or china clay and flint. (See also *pigments*, and under the individual metals.) Commercially prepared underglaze colors are fritted compounds with various 'fillers', flint, clay, etc. and opacifiers which may include *chrome* (see for effects with tin) for the darker colors. Leadless or low lead glazes are usually recommended. In the workshop, a *jar mill* is useful for preparing underglaze colors.

The character of the glaze used over pigments will affect them and there is an optimum thickness of application for all colors. The oxides, especially copper, need careful handling. Practice and experience are needed to get the best from them. Reward issue 'one strike' concentrated underglaze colors; useful for fine line work. Underglaze pens are available (Axner, and others).

Unfired clay, bricks, coatings, painting

Clay will not become a ceramic until it has been subjected to a temperature of at least 550°C/1022°F. A cooking oven (max. *c.* 275°C/527°F) is obviously insufficient, as is sun heat. Some clays, however, dry very hard, perhaps because of a particular grain structure or the presence of cementing materials.

A great number of the houses in the Mediterranean countries and elsewhere were built of unfired bricks or slabs reinforced with straw and chaff, sometimes called *adobe.*

Several attempts have been made to produce a material with the plastic advantages of clay but which will not easily break on drying, using fibers of nylon, etc. to form a sort of felting throughout the body, or the addition of resins as setting cements (see *Newclay*). Cernit (Georgies) bakes in an oven at 215°C/419°F. Materials described as 'air-hardening clays' and given names such as Airset, Marblex, Mexican Pottery Clay, Roma Plasteline, *Coldclay*, etc. are widely available.

In place of glazes there are finishes on the market which can be heated in a cooking oven to around 200°C/392°F to a fairly permanent state. These are obviously more suitable for decorative pieces and in junior school work. Unfired decoration has a long history and acrylics and paints have been used on modern pottery, though what these pieces will look like in a few years' time is a moot point! (See also *cold color.*)

Units of electricity

The units of immediate interest to potters are discussed under *volt, ampere, watt, ohm.*

The 'unit' on which the pricing of electricity supply is based is one kilowatt-hour, symbol kWh, the amount consumed by a 1000 watt appliance (e.g. a single bar electric fire) in an hour. The same fire would consume 5 kWh in 5 hours; if rated at 1.5 kWh then it would consume 7.5 kWh in 5 hours, and so on. To estimate the cost of firing an electric kiln: kilowatt rating x hours of firing x cost per unit, thus a 6 kWh kiln x 10 hours firing x 8p/12 cents per unit = £4.80/$7.20 per firing.

The sum is slightly complicated by the fact that the kiln may not be running at full all the time, or there may be a standing charge in addition to the unit cost, but a little common sense can allow for these. Estimate one-third the rating if you have a 'slow' setting and two-thirds for a 'medium'.

Unity formula

Applied to the Seger arrangement for glaze formulas, where the first group of bases (broadly, the fluxes) add up to one: e.g. soda 0.2; calcia 0.5; potash 0.3; total 1.0. This allows instant comparison with the 'amphoteric' and 'acid' figures (groups two and three), and an appraisal of the probable fusibility or refractoriness of the glaze. (See *formula, formula into recipe, Seger,* etc.)

Updraft kiln

The simplest form of true kiln: a fire beneath the floor, the hot gases and flame rising through the ware to a chimney or vent at the top. The heating tends to be uneven — hot at the base — and a great deal of heat is wasted.

Nevertheless it was the type in use for thousands of years and is still fired. Interesting variations are found; in Cyprus a perforated hollow dome is built inside the kiln, and the pots stacked in the space between it and the outer wall. A wood fire is burnt inside the dome which is reached by a low tunnel. There is no chimney — merely vents in the

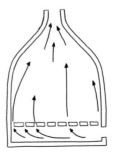

In an updraft kiln the flame and hot gases travel through a perforated floor and up among the pots to a short chimney or simple vent.

top. Sometimes bottomless pots are stuck over holes in the upper part of the kiln, often pointing downwards. The form of the kiln itself acts as a chimney. In updraft gas kilns a semi-muffle may be used, or the jets injected horizontally through separate flues, greatly extending the life of the floor refractories. (See many illustrations of updraft kilns in Rhodes K.)

Uranium, oxides, compounds

A metallic element U, 238.
Oxide UO_2, 270.
Sodium uranate $Na_2.2UO_3. nH_2O$.
'Depleted' oxide U_3O_8, s.g.7.3.

The *radioactive* potentialities of uranium are well known and it has not been available since 1944. However, the depleted oxide is now appearing in the catalogs, albeit still expensive. With regard to its radioactivity British Nuclear Fuels states that the natural mineral is not dangerous and the depleted variety even less so, but great care must be taken with its use, as with all toxic materials. Harry Fraser, of Potclays, however, is categoric in banning its use (CR146). The following information must be considered in the light of these contrary opinions.

The use of uranium as a pigment oxide is generally limited to *soft glazes*, giving reds and oranges up to about 940°C/1724°F and turning to a cool yellow at higher temperatures. A high-lead glaze is recommended, with a little tin oxide. Boric oxide and whiting are to be avoided.

At stoneware temperatures Leach gives a recipe for Kawai's yellow which used 2% uranium oxide in the traditional 4:3:2:1 recipe (see *stoneware glaze*) with an additional 15% of feldspar. Uranium is liable to turn gray or black above 1260°C/2300°F.

Vacuum cleaner

If a vacuum cleaner is used to deal with dust in a pottery it can be dangerous in itself if the filters are not sufficient to deal with the finest particles as is sometimes the case. The very fineness of the dust which is not trapped by the machine renders it even more dangerous to health. A cleaner with an efficiency of 99% or more is required. Metrosales list such cleaners but they are, naturally, expensive. A cheaper alternative is to vent the cleaner into the open air through the wall of the pottery (Clive Davies in CR171). Alternatively use a dust inhibitor such as plain water or one of the *sweeping compounds* available. (See *dust, poisonous materials*.)

Vacuum filter

An idea developed by Harry Davis. The usual method of squeezing the water from slip is reversed, a semi-vacuum being used to draw it out. No heavy machinery is required and the equipment is neither bulky nor costly. See his book 'The Potter's Alternative'. A similar system has been developed in the USA.

Vacuum hand

A suction holder for *glazing* pots. Needs a vacuum pump to operate. Listed by Axner and others.

Vacuum pug-mill

See *de-airing clay*.

Valency

The way in which atoms combine. The inert gases contain 8 *electrons* in their outer shell (helium has 2) and other atoms with different configurations aspire to this stable state, borrowing or sharing electrons with neighboring atoms. Shared electrons take part in covalent bonds.

The transfer of electrons results in an unbalanced electrical charge on the nucleus (electrons being negatively charged) and the formation of ions (see also *electrovalent*). Chemical action, the formation of compounds and new materials, is the result of one or other of these bonds or a combination of them.

The ratio in which atoms combine is thus in terms of simple whole numbers, and the valency is the number of hydrogen atoms with which an atom or an element will combine (or which it will replace). A compound or molecule must balance these numbers if it is to be stable. Thus tin has a valency of 4; oxygen 2 (as in H_2O) and they combine in the ratio which will balance them — bring them both up to 4 — i.e. two oxygen atoms with valency 2=4, one tin atom with valency 4=4 or one tin (Sn) to two oxygen (O) written SnO_2. Many elements can be made to combine in different ratios i.e. have more than one valency, but there is often a single stable combination, or oxide, e.g. TiO_2, Al_2O_3. The transitonal elements in particular occur in nature in more than one combination, e.g. iron as Fe_2O_3 and Fe_3O_4.

1

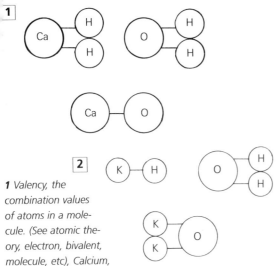

2

*1 Valency, the combination values of atoms in a molecule. (See atomic theory, electron, bivalent, molecule, etc), Calcium, Ca, will combine with two hydrogen H, atoms and is thus bivalent. Oxygen, O, is also bivalent and the two can therefore combine in the ratio of one to one, giving the oxide CaO.
2 Potassium, K (Kalium), is monovalent (will combine with one hydrogen atom) and thus two of its atoms must be present to balance the bivalency of oxygen, giving the oxide K_2O.*

Van der Waals forces

Weak electrostatic forces between atoms or molecules. (See *atomic theory*.)

Vanadium

A metallic element V, 51. Pentoxide V_2O_5, 182 m.p. 685°C/1265°F. Ammonium metavanadate $NH_4 VO_3$, 117.

A fairly rare mineral found in bauxitic clays and also recovered from fuel oil soot. Only the pentoxide is now listed by suppliers. The pentoxide, however, is water soluble and can penetrate the skin — wear gloves. John Chalke has mentioned that his glaze stirring sticks assume a yellowish green color when using vanadium! Vanadium is used in proportions of 5–10% to produce a yellow color; rather weak in a clear glaze but stronger in combination with titania and tin oxide (see *tin-vanadium yellow*).

Zirconium-vanadium blues have been quoted and are available in prepared form (as is also the yellow stain), the blues being suggested as a substitute for copper in lead glazes in order to avoid the latter's tendency to increase *lead solubility*. Similar high temperature stains are also available. Gray colors with tin have been mentioned. The metavanadate is reported to be refractory to 1300°C/2372°F, and to be unaffected by reduction, though Behrens mentions blue from reduced vanadium. The pentoxide can be used in oxidized firings.

Vapor-glazing

This form of usually partial glazing or coloring uses *volatiles* (materials which become gaseous on heating)

An altered thrown form, vapor-glazed in a saggar by Joanna Constantinidis. A monochrome print does not do justice to the subtlety of the silvery and other nuances of the surface color.

which will attack or become attached to a pot surface altering its color, texture, or degree of shine. Salt-glaze is a form of vapor-glazing, but the term is normally restricted to the use of volatiles (usually contained in a small bowl) and enclosed with the ceramic in a sealed saggar. During the firing the vapor causes flashing or color changes to the surfaces. The technique is slightly hit-or-miss but can produce fascinating and striking results. Joanna Constantinidis has been very successful in this field. (See also *flashing* and *volatile* for materials which can be used.)

Vellum glaze

A merchants' term for an opaque glaze with a dulled or satiny sheen. Often achieved by means of various combinations of oxides of tin, zinc, and titanium in the glaze recipe. Magnesia may also help to promote a silkier surface.

Ventilation

Ventilation to the outside air is desirable under many potting situations and essential where dangerous fumes or gases, especially *carbon monoxide*, are likely to be present (see *poisonous materials*). Skutt and other suppliers list venting systems which are fairly easy to install.

There are several types of kiln ventilator on the market (perhaps the best ventilation comes from an open window in the kiln room but this is not always a practical proposition). The simplest of these is a ducted hood (like an

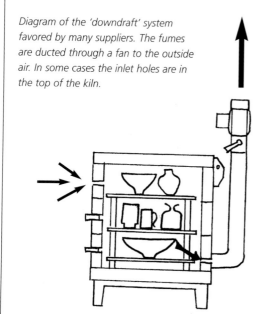

Diagram of the 'downdraft' system favored by many suppliers. The fumes are ducted through a fan to the outside air. In some cases the inlet holes are in the top of the kiln.

ordinary oven hood) which is suspended over the kiln or counterweights so that it can be raised and lowered. Others draw air in from the top of the kiln and vent it from the bottom via a window or through the studio wall. This is bound to lead to some loss of heat (though the suppliers optimistically urge that it also helps to balance the heat distribution). (See also *dust, fumes*.)

Venturi burner

An inspirating gas burner with a constricted flow just beyond the point where the gas exits. This increases the speed of the gas flow and draws air in from behind. The principle was formulated by the Italian scientist Venturi. (See Rhodes K. for illustrations.)

Vermiculite

An expanded (exfoliated) mica. From South Carolina and Montana, USA. Fairly refractory. Main use as a heat insulator for temperatures up to $1000°C/1832°F$. Has also been mentioned as a type of grog for lightweight brick and, finely ground, for other bodies.

Vibratory mill

Upright ball mills for grinding frits and other materials are now standard in the industry. They do not revolve but are vibrated at very high speed and the time taken to reduce sand size or even $3/4$ inch material to powder is dramatically reduced. They have not yet appeared widely on the studio potters' market although Fraser illustrates an Op-po mill which grinds $3/4$ inch to 'the desired fineness' in a few minutes!

Vibratory sieve

A sieve or lawn which is shaken rapidly in a lateral direction by an eccentric drive on an electric motor. Marketed by various suppliers. Something of a luxury for most potters but the action gives a more even particle separation and is kinder to the lawn than is brushing through. (See *sieve, use of*.) Chris Aston, in CR96, describes the building of a vibratory mechanism employing weights bolted to a revolving spindle.

Videos

Demonstration of the various aspects of potting on tape or disc for display on television. Partly because they are comparatively easy and cheap to make, compared with film, there are too many to be included in this book. Axner list some 44 videos, The Potters Shop (MA) some 60 or more, and they are widely advertised and available. 'Studio Potter Network' video reviews by Richard Aerni (see booklist) is a useful book. A list of UK videos on craft and design is available from the Crafts Council, 44a Pentonville Road, London N1 9BY.

Vinegar

Contains 3–6% acetic acid. It has a *deflocculating* effect on clay and can be used to repair dry pots or modeling (so long as the damage is not a result of strain). Work the vinegar with a brush onto both surfaces and press them together. It has been successful with large coiled pots but must not be used for handles. Odors from the kiln are similar to fried fish shops during firing!

Rada suggests grinding luster colors in a mixture of vinegar with gum arabic; they can then be thinned with water. Vinegar will also slow down the setting of plaster of Paris.

Vingerling clay

Vingerling BV, B.O. Box 70, NL-2 850 Ab Haastrecht, Katrien Van Lerberghe, Bruges. (CR166). Listed by Potterycrafts. A terracotta clay recommended for sculptural pieces with 30% grog and a white clay which can be thrown or cast. Firing to 1040–1080°C/1904–1976°F. There is also a smooth white stoneware, and a 'C' material with molochite (Potterycrafts). John Maltby uses a grogged white Vingerling clay.

Viscosity

Resistance to flow offered by a liquid, due to internal frictions. A very fluid glaze would run from a pot at peak temperature (and sometimes does!) but the presence of alumina increases viscosity, distinguishing glaze from glass. Viscosity also prevents glaze from soaking too readily into the body of a pot, and inhibits crystal growth. The unit of viscosity is the *poise*.

Magnesia increases viscosity, as will zircon and tin oxide. The alkalis have the opposite effect and are vigorous in promoting *fluidity*. Lime has an ambiguous role. It will increase viscosity at low temperatures and, in certain proportions, in stoneware. The point of maximum fluidity will vary from 15–35% at 1250°C/2282°F and over. Celadon needs high viscosity (Cardew).

Water decreases in viscosity as it is heated to a factor of 3 between 0°C/32°F and 40°C/104°F, hence the greater efficiency of hot water in various processes. It is known that the temperature of the water affects clay during throwing.

Vitreous

Glassy, or containing glassy materials. Vitreous bodies will have low *porosity*. 'Vitreous' slip or *engobe* is one with a high base content and is fired to fusion point. Vitreous silica, or *fused silica*, has been heated to translucency (see also *thermocouple*). Any pottery body or associated mineral will become vitreous if heated sufficiently.

Vitreous silica

Fused, glassy silica from either sand or quartz.

Vitreous slip, engobe

Slips compounded with fluxing oxides can be used on stoneware and porcelain to produce slightly glossy colors on biscuit or to affect the color of overlaying glazes. Geoffrey Eastop (CR121) mixes clay and whiting, modifying the result with borax frits. In place of the calcium he has also tried wood ash. His experiments with colors make interesting reading.

Vitrify, vitrification

To assume the nature of a glass (glaze) or to form glassy melts within a fabric which flow into the pores and allow the particles to become more closely packed. It involves the breaking down of crystalline structures. A vitrified body will be non-porous and impermeable, although in pottery this is rarely completely achieved (see *porosity*).

Vitrification — the progressive fusion or glassification of a clay — is accompanied by shrinkage and leads eventually to deformation and collapse. The temperatures at which it occurs will vary with the *fusibility* of the clay (the number and type of fluxes) and the alumina content. The 'vitrification range' is the temperature interval between the initial glass formation (beginning of shrinkage) and eventual deformation. The first figure is around 850°C/1562°F for plastic clay, and deformation varies between 1030°C/1886°F for a very impure red clay to 1450°C/2642°F for the most refractory kaolin porcelains. Aluminous fireclays will have an even greater range.

Porcelain is a mixture which will vitrify to *translucency* without collapse.

Volatile, volatilization

In ceramics the terms refer to those materials which pass into vapor with increasing temperature; water, of course, will turn to steam at 100°C/212°F but above red heat chlorine and carbon compounds release gases at around 700°C/1292°F; sulfur and fluorine at 1000°C/1832°F. Copper will begin to volatilize at 1000°C/1832°F and increasingly at 1200°C/2192°F and can stain neighboring pieces, especially in reduction, or can be seen to stain right through a body. The fluorine from fluorspar can cause glaze pitting. Lead will volatilize increasingly with temperature, slowly coating kiln walls and furniture if used with regularity, as will other bases, zinc and soda. Volatilized lead in a high-fired closed electric kiln can be a health hazard when unpacked. Volatilized sodium from salt is the basis of salt-glazing, but potters can also produce many remarkable and attractive effects on bodies and glazes by enclosing volatiles (the sulfates, nitrates and chlorides of metals) in a saggar with pots, known as *vapor glazing*.

The term is also used to denote the removal by heat of CO_2 and other components of a glaze batch but this is better described as decomposition or dissociation.

The remarkable deposits of volatalized lead on the wall of a country potter's kiln.

Volcanic ash

Volcanic lava frequently produces basic rocks which can eventually decompose into clay of the *montmorillonite* type. The typical volcanic rock is basalt, which can be used for dark colored stoneware glazes.

'Volcanic ash' is available cheaply in the USA and has been quoted as roughly equivalent to 70% feldspar, 30% flint. It is probably more fusible than this sounds for it is also said that 25% volcanic ash with 75% red clay will vitrify at earthenware temperatures. It can be combined with Gerstley borate as a glaze.

A sample of volcanic ash has been analyzed (parts by weight).

MgO	0.35	CaO	1.0
Na_2O	3.	K_2O	4.5
Al_2O_3	13.0	Fe_2O_3	3.0
SiO_2	73.0	Cl_2	0.03
H_2O	1.5		

Around 10% is suggested as a secondary flux, while as much as 50% has been used for a clear, fluid glaze.

Volcanic glazes

See *crater glazes*.

Volclay

A proprietary sodium *bentonite* (Wyoming).

Voltage

Symbol E (electromotive force, or e.m.f.). The force which carries one ampere of current against one ohm of resistance. The unit is the volt, symbol V.

Useful equation:

$$E = I \times R, \text{ or } \frac{P}{I} \text{ or square root of } P \times R$$

(I, current in amperes; R, resistance in ohms; P, power in watts.)

Until 1994 the standard was an average 240 volts in Great Britain. From 1995 a change to a 230 volt supply (plus/minus 6%) to conform to the European Council figure, was introduced in an apparently haphazard way. If your kiln, therefore, appears to be struggling to reach top temperature, this may be a reason. In the USA 'the most common voltages are 208 and 240. Many people think they have 220 volt power because most appliances are designed to run on either voltage and are labeled 220' (Skutt Kilns). It is therefore important to determine which voltage you are on when ordering or building a kiln.

Voltage drop

If more than a certain amount of current is taken from an electrical supply, the 'pressure' or voltage will drop and all appliances will become less efficient, e.g. lights will dim, kilns take longer to fire. Power is proportional to the square of the voltage, and for a voltage drop of up to about 20% the loss of power will be approximately double the percentage, e.g. from 240 V to 220 V is an 8.3% voltage drop but 16% less power is produced if the resistance remains constant. See discussion in Fournier EPK.

industry beds bone china in alumina (its high fire is its biscuit fire) but the craft potter must design self-supporting ceramics. (See *kiln furniture*.)

Badly placed stilts and spurs causing warping due to unsupported weight.

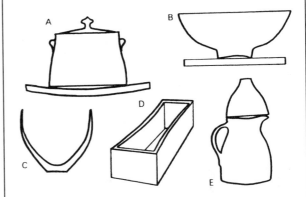

Some other common causes of warping during firing.
A *Bent kiln shelves.* **B** *Uneven foot-rings or bases.*
C *Very thin rims.* **D** *Long unsupported sides (see slab pots for possible remedy).* **E** *The boxing of uneven or dissimilar pieces.*

Washing ash

To remove *soluble alkalis*. Steep the ash in plenty of water and stir well. When the solid matter has settled, pour off the clear liquid. Refill with clean water and repeat the process. Three washings are usually sufficient. At the first wash the liquid may be sufficiently caustic to harm the hands, so wear gloves. (See also *ash*.)

Waste glaze disposal

1 Amalagamate your glazes and try to alter or add to them to make them usable. Not often an alternative as mixed glazes tend to result in a sludgy color. But try.
2 Let them dry. A solid is easier to dispose of than liquids.
3 Put them into an old bowl and biscuit them.
4 Call your Local Council.

Pouring them down the drain simply moves the problem on, puts toxic chemicals into the water supply, and is illegal.

Wad, wad mill, dod box

The 'wad' is a coil or extruded column of clay used for coiling or other modeling, and, using fireclay, for placing, and separating saggars, etc.

A wad box or wad mill is a simple hand-operated screw plunger enclosed in a cylinder with a die at the aperture and is used to extrude plastic clay in coils or wads. Can be utilized for coiling. Some catalogs suggest that it is a sort of pug-mill, which it is not.

See *extrusion* for larger scale work. Various small extruders are sold, e.g. the Kemper Klay Gun, which forces clay by means of a plunger through shaped dies in the manner of cake icers.

Warping

Deformation which can take place at any stage in the making of a pot. Few fired pieces escape totally—try spinning a commercial saucer on the wheel. Warping will be aggravated by:

During making and drying	High wet/dry shrinkage
	Uneven clay walls
	Very thin rims
	Poor wedging
	Unsupported weight, including open slab boxes
	The joining of clay of different consistencies
	Unlevel bases or foot rings
	Uneven drying
	Plastic 'memory' (see *clay memory*)
During the biscuit fire	Close proximity to kiln wall
	Unsupported weight
	The boxing of pots on jugs
	'Bungs' too high
	Bent kiln shelves
During the glaze fire	Unsupported weight
	Bent kiln shelves
	Overfiring
	Inefficient stilt support (earthenware)
	Molded dishes which are too flat or thin

Pots which are deformed during drying may revert even if the fault has been corrected in time, see *clay memory*. Wooden cones are useful for rounding out cups, etc. An extreme case of unsupported weight is the handle of a porcelain cup pulling it out of true during firing. The

Waste heat drying

Very little use is made of the heat generated by kilns. It is worth planning your pottery so that heat liberated during cooling has some work to do, either as space heating or to dry pots. *Top-loading kilns* are very useful in this respect. Fans and ducts can distribute heat: more simply it can be directed through a gap to an upper floor. Kiln exhaust gases can first be directed beneath a drying cabinet before reaching the chimney. See film/video 'Isaac Button, country potter'.

Waster

A piece of pottery spoiled, generally in the firing, beyond use and thrown away. Wasters, however, because of their profusion at kiln sites, have yielded valuable information for archeologists.

Water

The 'oxide' of hydrogen, H_2O, 18.

The normal water supply contains impurities and these can, to some extent, affect the behavior of clay and glazes. Water impurities can be considered as a contributory cause of *crawling* after a pot has been sponged with very 'hard' (high calcium) water, and the *pH* of the water can affect glazes and slips; alkalis deflocculate, acids have the opposite effect. Though the amounts in tap water are not usually strongly operative, they may explain some variations in the behavior of slops.

Water in pottery can exist in a number of forms:
1 In its familiar liquid state, mixed with clay to promote plasticity or in excess of this to produce slip. This water is drawn or driven off at temperatures up to 100°C/212°F (see *drying*).
2 As *adsorbed* water, not obvious as a liquid and more tenacious in its hold and can only be completely dispersed by heating to 120–200°C/248–392°F.
3 The H_2O which is built into the molecular structure of clay, sometimes known as 'combined water'. This needs considerable heat (500°C/932°F plus) before it will separate as vapor, with fundamental and irreversible changes in the fabric.

Other *hydrated* minerals may lose their H_2O at different temperatures, plaster of Paris for instance at a much lower heat. Water decreases in viscosity as it is heated and hot water will have a different effect from cold on many materials including clay, as will the pH factor. (See also *absorption, adsorption, hydration, pH factor*.)

Water-glass

Sodium silicate $Na_2O.SiO_2$, with grade from 1.2 to 1:3.5 soda/silica ratio. Used as a deflocculant and in air-setting cement. Soluble in water. (See also *mending*.)

Water of plasticity

The water content of clay in the range between soft plastic and leather-hard. Clays vary in the percentage of water needed to attain plasticity, the average being about 40% of the dry weight.

Water smoking

The evolving of vapor at temperatures beyond 100°C/212°F. 'Bone dry' clay will still contain *adsorbed* and mechanically held water which will continue to vaporize up to 250°C/482°F, in *bentonite* type clays especially. Care must be exercised throughout this range. The term probably arose because the steam and smouldering organic matter combine in a steamy smoke.

Watt

Electrical unit of power (P): the rate of working in a circuit where electromotive force is one volt and the intensity of current is one ampere. Symbol W. Named after James Watt.

Useful equation:
$$P = \frac{E^2}{R}, \text{ or } E \times I \text{ or } I^2 \times R$$
(E in volts, I in amperes, R in ohms.)

The load or power of a kiln or other electric appliance is stated in watts, as in a 60 watt electric lamp. Multiples of 1000 watts are called kilowatts or kW, e.g. a 4.5 kW kiln — 4500 watts.

Wax

Used in a fluid form for *wax resist* decoration or resisting glaze when glazing. Candle wax melted on its own is not satisfactory since it sets hard before it can be properly applied. Mixtures of paraffin wax, or candle with paraffin are very inflammable. Equal parts of candle and a thin oil makes a very usable mixture, kept warm over an electric or gas ring in a double saucepan or old fashioned glue-pot.

There are several proprietary cold wax emulsions and resist materials on the market. They are generally less workable and some must be left to dry and have poorer 'resist' qualities. Axner's wax resist liquid is reputed to dry more quickly, with dipped glaze 'falling away cleanly' (Robert Tetu). While these are geneanrally water-soluble and brushes can therefore easily be cleaned after use, they may become clogged up over time and Susan Bennett

CR165) suggests cleaning with gasoline/petrol, (great care must be taken to keep it in a container away from the studio, however, using only a little at a time). A liquid *latex* resist is now sold which can be removed from the surface at any time and one can envisage interesting decorative possibilities. Very low temperature paraffin waxes are also available.

Wax can be applied by using sticks of candle like crayons (see *wax resist*). Georgies list a wax pen which lays down a $^1/_{16}$ inch continuous line and Tucker's a series of colored waxes in felt-tipped pens.

Do not leave your brush in the wax: it may burn during heating or may develop a permanent bend. On the other hand do not attempt to clean it with water — this will destroy the hairs. Stroke the hairs flat and leave to set either hanging or lying flat. Take care not to drip the wax where it is not required—it is difficult to remove. Turpentine removes a certain amount, but absorption is still affected. Badly waxed biscuit pots may need refiring to remove the wax.

Wax emulsion

A water/wax emulsion which can be painted onto pottery (biscuit or glaze) as a resist. It has the advantage that brushes can be washed out in water. It takes a little time to dry. There are a number of proprietary brands.

Wax resist

For decoration. Wax designs are applied to a pottery surface in order to repel liquid pigments, thin slips, or glazes. The wax is usually applied as free brushwork, but a design can also be drawn with a wax crayon or piece of candle. Wax resist pens for fine lines are listed by Bailey and others. The work can be done at various stages:
1 On the raw clay, generally when leather-hard. The wax design is applied and color or slip is spun on or laid over the whole surface with a brush, or poured or dipped. The waxed parts will be left in reserve against a painted background. The wax rarely repels the overlaid color completely and the small blobs and dots of color within the resisted areas give the technique its attractive and distinctive character. The wax can be cut through, sgraffito fashion, and then brushed over with pigment. Resist on stoneware can be cut through to the biscuit or used between glazes. The wax itself can be pigment stained which affords new possibilities of subtle colors and finishes.
2 A reserved biscuit design will result from waxing on the raw clay for once-fired pottery, or on the biscuit before glazing.
3 The unfired glaze surface can be waxed and painted as on the raw clay or covered with a second glaze coat of

contrasting type for *glaze-over-glaze* techniques.

A more mundane but extremely useful and time-saving application of wax resist is to coat bases, foot-rings, lid flanges, and all those parts of a pot which are to be free of glaze. The whole piece can then be dipped or poured. A heavy *whirler* or banding wheel is essential for the efficient waxing of thrown pieces. (See illustration under *glazing*.)

1 Wax has been painted onto a plate and the first band of pigment applied.
2 and *3* The color is laid on at different strengths to give added variety to the pattern.

351

Wax resist combined with glaze-trailing and other techniques on a dish by David Frith.

Calligraphic wax brushstrokes on a spun luster dish by Alan Caiger-Smith.

Weald clay

A variable brick clay from SE England.

Weathering of clay

Exposure to rain, sun, and frost will improve the working qualities of most clays, breaking them down and oxidizing pyrites and other metals, leaching out soluble alkalis, and by the development of an intimate and uniform water content. Long weathering, over geological time, has probably been a major factor in the plasticity of clay. The minimum useful period for weathering, usually in outside troughs with some protection from excessive rainfall and dirt, is a year.

Weathering is a different process to *aging* or resting but they all assist workability.

Web, www, world wide web

See *world wide web*.

Wedging, mixing, & kneading clay

Originally 'wedging' referred to the cutting of two wedge shapes from a block of clay and banging one down on the other. It is now loosely applied to the whole process of the hand mixing of clays and working them into a consistent bubble-free mass. There are two stages in mixing clays of different types or consistencies:

1 Layering. The clays are cut into thin slabs which are slapped down alternately on one another. If grog is being added it can be spread between the layers. Harder and soft conditions of the same clay can be alternated. The whole pile is then cut vertically; one half lifted and brought smartly down on the other, taking care that the layering remains horizontal. Repeat until the layers have merged.

Mixing and wedging clay.

1 and *2* Blocks of clay (light and dark, hard and soft, etc.) are sliced into layers about $1/2$in/12mm thick and slapped down alternately one upon another.

3 and *4* The mass is cut through vertically and the blocks are again combined, bringing one smartly down on the other while taking care to keep the layers horizontal — this is crucial

5–7 The block is compressed, recut, and the process continued until the layers merge together.

8 Mixing is almost complete.

9–11 The final mixing is generally done by kneading, using one of two allied methods. For up to 7lb/3kg of clay the 'bull's-head' method is suitable, so-called because the typical overlapping layers resemble an animal's head as shown in illustration 9 The main block is lifted towards the potter and then forced down and back with the pressure of the palms, the hands enclosing the sides and exerting a certain inwards pressure which prevents undue sideways spread. The base of the block must grip the bench surface so that the whole mass is spread over itself as it is forced away from the potter's body. Keep the arms fairly straight and use your body weight to exert pressure which will be less tiring than working from the elbows (do not use too high a bench). A pellet of colored clay placed on the forehead of the 'bull' should travel downwards and finally disappear under the base as the work continues.

12–15 Attempt to show stages in spiral wedging. The basic movement is not very different from the above but the pressure is applied to one corner of a large mass forming a spiral shell shape as the work proceeds. The clay is lifted, rolled a little forwards, gripped and thrust down and away. In the last picture the spiral is finally being worked into a suitably compact shape by slapping and rolling it on the bench.

The mass of clay is cut into balls of around 3lb/
.53kg. These are kneaded either by the forward and
nwards thrust of the 'bull's head' method or by the spiral
method which allows for somewhat larger blocks of clay.

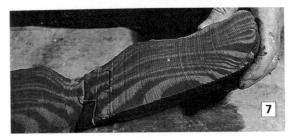

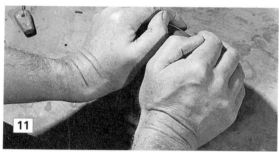

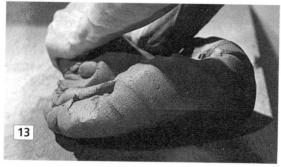

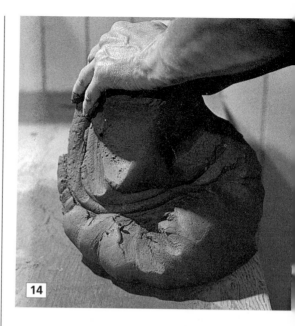

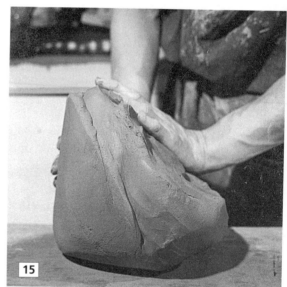

Wedgwood pyrometer

A sytem of heat measurement devised by Josiah Wedgwood and now forming the basis for *Buller's rings*.

Weighing of materials

When weighing out large amounts of glaze materials it is usually necessary to split the weight into thousand gram lots. In order not to lose track of the amount weighed it is useful to tip them into separate heaps (in a large bowl) hich may overlay at the base but remain recognizably separate and can be counted. This is in addition to noting each batch in a notebook.

Very small batches of 300g/10½oz and under for the total glaze batch are notoriously liable to inaccuracy giving misleading results, and are of limited value as trials.

Wet clay, slip decoration

The slip generated during throwing can be manipulated on the wheel to provide decorative ridges and textures, or thick slip can be applied with a loaded brush on surfaces to develop swirls and ridges of varying thickness and shapes.

Wet firing

A rather controversial system of drying clay during the actual firing. CR1 gives particulars. The method resembles that of raku in some respects. The newly thrown, wet pot is inserted into the red-hot kiln. Cooling by rapid evaporation, the principle of refrigeration, may be the factor at work. Even as described by an enthusiast the technique seems hedged about by provisions, exceptions, and uncertainties, such as the danger of a minor explosion. It sounds fun as an exercise but does not seem to have been generally accepted as a technique.

Little has been heard of the system since this article was written for the first edition of this book.

Wheel, throwing

A potter's wheel is, essentially, a flat circular slab of wood, metal or stone so mounted as to revolve on a vertical axis. There is generally a heavy flywheel which stores energy and ensures a steady and even movement. It probably evolved from a slow wheel (whirler) used for coiling, etc. In the Far East a stick is inserted into a hole in the rim of the wheelhead which is spun round by this means and then withdrawn, the throwing being done before the impetus is lost. The European wheel has a wide stone flywheel which is spun by the sole of the foot on its surface. Manually powered wheels using pulleys and ropes featured in the 18th-century factories. The traditional English wheel is the cranked wheel described under *kickwheel*.

Wheels are now usually powered by a self-contained electric motor. See *power-wheel*.

The design of a wheel can make or break a potter. Stand-up wheels which are operated by a bar are definitely not recommended for a professional potter who spends any great amount of time throwing — the standing leg is liable to be damaged. A seated wheel is also liable to generate back pains if the wheelhead is in a poor position (usually too low). A wheel therefore needs either to be adjustable or to be designed for a particular potter. A multi-level wheelhead is listed by Georgies.

Wheel bat

A circular bat which can be removed from the wheelhead complete with the thrown pot. Useful when making plates, large pots, shallow bowls, and for repetition throwing.

They can be made of wood, fiber board, plaster, or mineral wool sheet (see *ejector head* for plaster type), or more recently in injection molded plastic and Masonite which are very hard-wearing though possibly their lack of absorbency may be a disadvantage. Bath Potters Supplies list a throwing bat made of 'exterior type MDF (known as Medex)'. Wood is 'sympathetic' to the touch and has good clay-release properties but can warp or soften in use. Waterproof plys are available. Potter's Mates supply 11in/300mm bats and special wheelheads. Of the asbestos type materials Asbestolux is easily shaped but is too absorbent and needs partial sealing, for example with a polyurethane varnish, to make it usable: alternatives include E flex — Eternit UK Ltd. 01763 260421, and Masterclad; Cape Boards 01895 237111 (CR172). Sindanyo bats are expensive but very hard and durable. Bats can be fastened to the wheel by means of two short lengths of metal rod set into the wheelhead, one in the center and one about 2½in/70mm from it. The bats are drilled to fit over these 'pins', the outer one can be a fairly loose fit. Alternatively they can be adhered to the wheelhead by a ring or thin slab of clay. (See illustration at *bat*.)

Whirler

A hand operated turntable also called a *banding wheel* although this term has a narrower application. Used for decoration, waxing, or glazing and for modeling and hand-building. There are many types and designs: in some the base will fall away if the whirler is lifted by the head: these are dangerous and should be avoided especially in schools. The head may be of aluminum or cast iron — the latter gives greater stability and momentum. You should choose as heavy a model as you can handle. Weights vary from 4–36lb/2–15kg — 15lb/6.5kg is a useful average.

The term is also sometimes used to describe a *spinner*.

Whistle

Richard Dunning in PQ13 gave full instructions for making clay whistles. A pinched or hollowed out pear shape is formed as shown in diagram **1**. The 'whistle stick', a

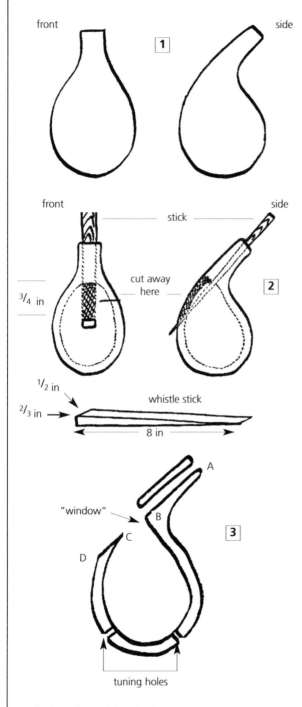

front

1

side

front

stick

side

2

3/4 in

cut away here

1/2 in

2/3 in

whistle stick

8 in

"window"

A

B

3

C

D

tuning holes

1 The basic form of the whistle.

2 The 'whistle stick' is thrust through the mouthpiece (see text for explanation). A small wedge is now cut away from where the stick emerges back to the beginning of the system.

3 Points A –D should lie in a straight line and point C should have a sharp edge. Tuning holes are suggested but these should be placed where they are most readily accessible to the fingers.

tapered piece of wood 8 inches long, ½in/12mm wide, an ⅔in/16mm deep at the wide end is thrust through th mouthpiece and out at the top of the bulb at a point n more than ¾in/19mm from its junction with the stem. small wedge or 'window' is now cut away from the poir where the stick emerges back to the beginning of the ster or mouthpiece. The stick is very carefully withdrawn (se diagram **2**). Ascertain that the points A –D (in diagram ? lie in a straight line while point C should present a shar edge. From point B to point C should be abou ½in/12mm.

The whistle can now be tried — it is often helpful t 'tongue' the breath, as when playing a recorder. If it does no produce a clear note the aperture is probably at fault an careful trimming may put it right. The one error which car not be put right easily is too wide an aperture, due to mis calculating in the first place the angle of the stem to th body; too much air escapes. It is better to start again. Tur ing holes are made, when the whistle has stiffened, with th handle of a paintbrush (see diagram **3**). Each successive hol gives a note of higher pitch. Make sure that your fingers ca easily reach the tuning holes. Straight pipes (flutes) are pos sible, even double pipes as made by Neil Ions, see CR9 where he describes an alternative system of forming th mouthpiece. (See also *ocarina*, and illustration at *flute*.) Th Whistle Press issue a book and video on whistle-making.

White, glaze, body, slip, pigment

Tin oxide will give the purest and best quality whit opaque earthenware glaze. Zircon is also efficient bu harder and shinier. Use 8–12% of either in a soft glaz Titania will opacify but tend to produce a cream. Zin and Bristol type glazes can be very white. Stonewar glazes are often naturally white and opaque: barium zinc, and lime can assist, the last, perhaps, in the form o bone-ash.

A white body will always be a 'short' one. China cla and flint are used to whiten bodies in the industry, an John Solly uses 50:50 ball clay and china clay for a whit slip. Small quantities of cobalt are sometimes added t impart a certain spurious whiteness. Porcelain is normall very pale in color and will have a whiter appearance i fired in reduction, the iron traces being bluish instead o cream. White engobes are mixtures with very little bal clay and various fillers — see recipes in Rhodes CGP. *Tin ash* may be used as a white pigment or tin oxide mixe with a little frit.

White lead

'Basic' lead carbonate 2PbCO₃.Pb(OH)₂, 775. Convenien

quivalent weight 258 (see also under *lead*).

Poisonous. A very active flux in soft glazes. Gives a lear transparent glaze for slipware or, opacified with tin xide, for use with maiolica painting. Formerly the stan-ard material for lead-lime-potash glazes. Now forbidden or use as a material in most countries. May be replaced y frits (silicates of lead).

Whiting

inely ground cretaceous chalk, practically pure — 97% — $CaCO_3$. (See *calcium carbonate*.) Decomposes to *cal-ium oxide* at 825°C. The most commonly used glaze naterial for the introduction of 'lime' into bodies and glazes.

Wicket

The door of a kiln. Usually bricked up for firing.

Winged form

An extension of 'handles' on either side of a pot form, orig-inating in Spain and used to great effect by Colin Pearson and others.

Wire

See *bow, cutting wire, electric kiln wiring, element, harp, resistance wire.*

Witherite

A comparatively rare rock of almost pure barium carbon-ate. It is, however, **toxic** (Cardew) and should be treated with care.

Witness cones

A term sometimes used to indicate sets of three *cones* (warming, firing and guard) for visual temperature check or control.

Wollastonite

Calcium metasilicate $CaO.SiO_2$, 116. m.p. 1540°C.
There are natural and synthetic forms with thermal expan-sions of 11 and 6 respectively. Listed by Potters Supply House, Coastal Ceramics, NZ, and others. Sometimes used as a part substitute for feldspar in low temperature vitreous bodies. Can be used as a source of calcium in glazes. Wollastonite with barium and about 20% of clay is used for the very strong bodies of electrical porcelain. Whiting and flint mixtures give a cheaper equivalent. David Eeles has rendered his stoneware glazes free from opacifying bubbles by replacing whiting (with its release of carbon dioxide) by wollastonite which has no such loss on ignition. Also occurs in *salt-glaze* recipes.

Wood ash, glazes

See *ash, ash glazes.*

Wood firing

Wood firing, at its best, gives a quality to both earthen-ware and stoneware which is unmatched by other fuels. It entails long and continuous work both in the preparation and firing. It is a fuel of comparatively low specific gravi-ty and a great volume of material is required to fire a kiln: 42 cords of wood (about 580cu ft) were used by Michael Cardew to fire his large 100cu ft kiln to stoneware. The calorific value is less than half that of oil. The Chinese potters are said to have been largely responsible for vast tracts of desert through their rapid destruction of the forests. (This role is now taken over by newsprint, although a more conscious effort is made to replace the trees.) Nevertheless, wood of the right type, condition, and size is not easy to obtain and comparatively few pot-ters rely on it as their only or principal fuel. It is more often used as a boost towards the end of a firing, fed through subsidiary fireholes. Its long clear flame makes it an ideal fuel in many ways, especially for stoneware.

Leach specifies dry pine 3–8in/75–200mm in diameter and 2ft–2ft 6in/600–750mm long. At the height of the firing up to 12 such logs are burned every four minutes. Common deal cut-offs from timber yards can be used but are likely to come in small and odd-shaped pieces which makes the use of the semi-automatic grate impossible and thus increases the time taken up in stoking and surveil-lance. Advice on wood firing can be found in Leach, Cardew, and Rhodes K.

In a survey by Coll Minogue and Robert Sanderson for Great Britain it was found that sizes ranged from 8 to 800cu ft with an average 30cu ft. Temperatures ranged from 1040–1350°C/1904–2462°F. There has also been a marked increase in the number and size of kilns in the USA and Australia.

Workability

'An evasive synonym for plasticity' (Dodd). Nevertheless the word sums up the various qualities which a potter requires in his clay: plasticity, standing strength, low water absorption, together with the less tangible qualities of 'feel' and texture.

Working surface

The working surface for potting should be slightly porous, so that clay comes away cleanly, but not so porous as to dry it too rapidly. Nothing fulfills these requirements as well as a sound wooden bench, preferably, though not necessarily, a hardwood. Education authorities often provide plastic surfaces on which it is impossible to *wedge* or work with damp clay with any comfort. They are not even particularly easy to clean and they damage easily with metal scrapers.

World wide web

A part of the *Internet* with wide-ranging information provided by other users. There is not, at the time of this book going to press, a great deal of practical information available but this should rapidly increase as more potters supply material. The 'Ceramicsweb' site (USA) has good information and links to other web sites of interest to potters. Its address is 'http://art.sdsu.edu/ceramicsweb/'. It is accompanied, however, by the warning that 'no guarantees of accuracy can be made for any of the information presented here. All information has been provided voluntarily by a number of ceramists. Use at your own risk'. Ceramic Review (UK) has a web site: http://www.ceramic-review.co.uk. Tony Hansen (Canada) has pages of technical information on http://digitalfire.com. There are many others. Most suppliers now have a web site.

Yellow, *glaze, pigment*

The sources of yellow color in ceramics are antimony, uranium, vanadium, iron and cadmium, and the compounds zircon/praseodymium and chrome/titania have been mentioned. An ochre yellow stoneware glaze quoted is: a red firing clay 55; limestone 26.25; quartz 18.75.

Uranium will give a cool yellow at medium temperature and is mentioned in a stoneware recipe in Leach. Antimony must be *fritted* with lead and used in a high-lead soft glaze for its best color (see *lead antimonite*). Vanadium is used as the pentoxide or as ammonium metavanadate for high temperatures — to 1280°C/2336°F. (See *Vanadium*.) Cadmium is used only at low temperatures and is even then difficult to stabilize. Iron yellows are cream or brown-yellows. See under the various materials mentioned for percentages in a glaze, etc. and *antimonite of lead* for use on maiolica.

Nigel Wood tells us that the fine Imperial Yellow of Qing China was derived from 3.5% ferric oxide in a lead/silicate base.

Yellow ochre

See *ochre*.

Ying ch'ing

Translated as 'shadow blue' or 'sky blue', the term is used to cover a large family of pale blue-green reduced iron glazes from the East, usually on engraved porcelain. The term is now in some disfavor among ceramic historians but remains a convenient description for similar glazes used by craft potters today.

David Leach's recipe gives a close approximation using 1% of iron oxide in reduction to about 1255°C/2291°F.

25 Feldspar, 25 Whiting, 25 China clay, 25 Quartz.

Zaffre

An impure cobalt arsenate, or a roasted mixture of cobalt re and sand. Now largely obsolete as a pigment, but it ounds as if it might yield a more attractive color than the resent vivid cobalt blues.

Zettlitz kaolin

A Czechoslovakian kaolin, high in alumina.

Zinc, oxide

A metallic element Zn, 65.
Oxide ZnO, 81, c.o.e. 6.5, s.g. 5.6.

In small quantities, up to 2%, it acts as a flux in many glazes and increases craze resistance. Larger additions tend to opacify and promote a matt surface. Used in both earthenware and stonewares. The Bristol glaze was an attempt to replace lead with zinc. The $ZnO.Al_2O_3.SiO_2$ eutectic is high at 1360°C/2480°F but the inclusion of other bases will lower this figure. Zinc has a balancing effect in glazes. The oxide reduces easily to the metal and it is not, therefore, recommended for reduction glazes (Cardew).

The raw material has a high shrinkage which gives trouble in a glaze on biscuit, though it is advantageous on once-fired ware. Shrinkage is reduced if the ZnO is calcined. An example stoneware formula:

    0.4 KNaO
    0.3 CaO   0.6 Al_2O_3   3.5 SiO_2
    0.3 ZnO

Zinc has a strong effect on pigments: poor color with iron, brighter with copper (sometimes a pink!), brown with chrome, with cobalt mauve or even an intense green have been obtained — these reactions all in oxidation. A versatile oxide but somewhat unpredictable and must be handled with care. With regard to the fumes given off during firing, these are no hazard with reasonable ventilation. See also *crystalline glazes* where it can form crystals of two molecules of zinc oxide to one of silica.

Zinc zirconium silicate

$ZnZrSiO_2$.
'An opacifier giving brilliance to glazes. Usually mixed with other zirconium products' (Georgies).

Zircon

See *zirconium*.

Zirconium, oxide, silicate

A metallic element Zr, 91. Oxide ZrO_2, 123, zirconia, m.p. 2700°C. Silicate $ZrO_2.SiO_2$. The spinel $ZrO_2.SiO_2.Al_2O_3.ZnO$.

The oxide has an *inversion* of about 2.5 % at 1200°C/ 2192°F. (See also *calcium zirconium silicate* and *magnesium zirconium silicate*.)

Zircon sands occur abundantly in Australia. They are very refractory.

The spinel is 'a synthetic silicate which has excellent color stabilizing abilities often combined with other zirconium opacifiers. Extends the firing range of a glaze and aids in preserving a bright finish' (Georgies). Zircon is used in *oven proof* bodies and as a glaze opacifier. A very refractory material called Furnascote Novit, used as a wash-coat of 1–2mm to protect the kiln linings from the effects of heat, is zircon based and is available in many parts of the world including Great Britain and the USA.

In glazes it operates mainly by recrystallization during cooling. The first 3% of zircon will dissolve in a glaze and not recrystallize (Derek Royle CR32). For opacity, use glazes low in alkalis, higher in lime and alumina. Zircon can replace some or all of the tin oxide, giving a harder, shinier, more scratch-resistant surface. Less favorable reactions with pigments which are, however, very stable in a zircon glaze over a wide range of temperatures. The zircon needs to be well mixed with the batch either by grinding or very thorough stirring if it is not to show white specks. Special coated zircon is made to assist dispersion. Up to 12% is required in a soft glaze for opacity, but up to 30% can be added to promote crystalline and broken color effects in a soft glaze. Zircon has a low *thermal expansion* and will increase craze resistance, at the same time making a glaze more viscous. A trade name for a prepared zircon is Zircopax. There is a zirconium-iron pink which fires up to 1280°C/2336°F and a zircon-vanadium blue in an alkaline glaze. Used in the manufacture of *refractories*, e.g. platinum melting crucibles, sparking plugs, etc. Can be used as a bat wash and kiln wash: 10 parts zircon to one part clay.

Zircopax

A trade name for *zirconium silicate*.

Suppliers mentioned in the dictionary

Acme Marls Ltd.
Clough Street, Hanley, Stoke-on-Trent, Staffordshire, England.
Tel: 01782 577757. Fax: 01782 575368.
Kiln shelves and refractories.

Alpha Insulations
10 Water Street, Newcastle, Staffordshire, England, ST5 1HP.
Tel: 01782 711155. Fax: 01782 712510.

Aremco Products Inc.
PO Box 429, Ossining, NY 10562, USA.

Axner Company Inc.
490 Kane Ct., Oviedo FL 32765, P.O. Box 621484, Oviedo FL 32762, USA.
Tel: (800) 843 7057.
Fax: (407) 365 2600. E-mail: axner@attmail.com
Web sites: www.axner.com
(and for books) www.ceramicssoftware.com

Bailey Pottery Equipment Corp.
PO Box 1577, Kingston, NY 12402, USA.
Tel: (800) 431 6067. Fax: (914) 339 5530.

W. G. Ball Ltd.
Longton Mill, Anchor Road, Longton, Stoke-on-Trent, Staffordshire, England, ST3 1JW.
Tel: 01782 313956/312286
Frits, etc.

Bath Pottery Supplies
2 Dorset Close, Bath, BA2 3RF, England.
Tel: 01225 337046. Fax: 01225 462712.
E-mail: sales@bathpotters.demon.co.uk
Web site: http://www.@bathpotters.demon.co.uk
General supplies (and new ideas!).

Briar Wheels & Supplies Ltd.
Whitsbury Road, Fordingbridge, Hants, England, SP6 1NQ.
Tel: 01425-652991. Fax: 01425-656188.
E-mail: sales@briarwheels.demon.co.uk

Ceramatech Ltd.
Units 16 & 17, Frontier Works, 33 Queen Street, London, England, N17 8JA.
Tel: 020 8885 4492

Bruce Chivers
The School House, Dunsford, Exeter, Devon, England, EX6 7DD.
Vacuum formed fiber kiln.

Coastal Ceramics
124 Rimu Road, Paraparaaumu, 84377 Pram, New Zealand.
Tel: 0 4 298 4377. Fax: 0 4 297 3107.

**Contemporary Ceramics
(formerly the Craftsman Potters Shop)**
7 Marshall Street, London, England, W1V 1LP.
Tel: 020 7437 7605
Books and some tools.

Cromartie Kilns Ltd.
Park Hall Road, Longton Stoke-on-Trent, Staffordshire, England, ST3 5AY.
Tel: 01782 313947. Fax: 01782 599723
Kilns, equipment & materials.

W J Doble Pottery Clays
Newdowns Sand & Clay Pits, St. Agnes, Cornwall, England, TR5 0ST.
Tel: 01872 552979. Fax: 01872 552433.
Clays, Molochite, ceramic fiber.

Dragon Ceramex
Dept CV, 5 Normis Park, Congresbury, Bristol, England, BS49 5HB.
Tel/Fax 01934 833409.
Hand-operated extruders (bulleys).

Fordham Thermal Systems
Studlands Park Industrial Estate, Newmarket, Cambridgeshire, England.
Ceramic fiber modules, gas kiln kits.

Georgies Ceramic & Clay Company
756 NE Lombard Portland, OR 97211
Tel: 800 999 2529 or 503 283 1353
Web site: http://www.georgies.com

Glendale Controls
10 Derwent Crescent, Whitehall, Kidsgrove, Stoke-on-Trent, Staffs, England.
Tel: 01782 774261
Oxygen/carbon Sensor.

Hansen, Tony
34 Upland Drive S.E, Medicine Mat, Alta T1A 3N7.
Web site: http://digitalfire.com.

Kanthal Ltd.
Festival Way, Stoke-on-Trent, ST1 5SG, Staffordshire,
England. Tel: 01782 224800.
Fax: 01782 224820.

Kemper Enterprises Inc.
13595, 12th Street, PO Box 696, Chino,
CA 91710, USA.
Hand-crafted tools, doll supplies, accessories.

Kilns & Furnaces Ltd.
Keele Street, Tunstall, Stoke-on-Trent, Staffordshire,
England, ST6 5 AS.
Electric kilns.

Laser Kilns Ltd.
Unit C9, Angel Road Works, Advent Wry, London,
England, N18 3AH.
Tel: 020 8803 1016. Fax: 020 8807 2888.
Kilns, slab rollers and equipment.

Metrosales
Unit 3, 46 Mill Place, Kingston-on-Thames, Surrey,
KT1 2RL
Tel. 0181 546 1108. E-mail: sales@metrosales.co.uk
*Equipment, vacuum cleaners, health and safety
equipment and advice.*

Morganite Thermal Ceramics Ltd.
Norton, Worcester, England, WR5 2PU.
Tel: 0905 76300. Fax: 0905 763007.
Kaowool ceramic wool.

Pamela Moreton Ceramics
226 Holt Road, Cromer, NR27 9JW, England.
Tel/fax: 01263 512629.
Decals, Transfers.

Potclays Ltd.
Brickkiln Lane, Etruria, Stoke-on-Trent, Staffs, England.
Tel: 01782 219816. Fax: 01782 286506.
General suppliers.

Potters Connection Ltd.
Dept C, Longton Mill, Anchor Road, Longton, Stoke-
on-Trent, Staffordshire, England, ST3 1JW.
Tel. 0178 598729.
Materials, tools, kilns.

Potters' Mate
Malcolm Headley-Saw, Cust Hall, Toppesfield, Nr.
Halstead, Essex, England, CO9 4EB.
Tel: 01787 237704. Fax: 01787 238444.
Lotus wheelhead system, and other equipment.

The Potters Shop
31, Thorpe Road, Needham Heights, MA. 02494, USA.
Tel: 781 449 7687. Fax: 781 449 9098.
E-mail: sbranfpots@aol.com
All the books on craft ceramics, and tools.

Potterycrafts Ltd.
Campbell Road, Stoke-on-Trent, Staffs, ST4 4ET.
England.
Tel: (Head Office) 01782 745000 Fax: 01782 746000.
E-mail: sales@potterycrafts.co.uk
Web site http://www.potterycrafts.co.uk
General supplies, including the Feibleman Parian body.

Pottery Supply House Ltd. (PSH)
1120 Speers Road, Oakville, Ontario, L6L 2X4. Canada.
Tel: (905) 827 1129. Fax: (905) 827 1129.
Web site: www.pshcanada.com
Supplies & kilns.

Scarva Pottery Supplies
Unit 20, Scarva Road, Banbridge, Co. Down.
Northern Ireland, BT32 3QD.
Tel: 018206 69699. Fax: 018206 69700.
E-mail: vicky@scarvapottery.demon.co.uk
Clays, ITC, materials.

Skutt Kilns
6441 SE Johnson Creek Boulevard, Portland,
OR 97206 9594. USA.
Tel: (503) 774 6000
Electric kilns and equipment.

The Whistle Press
128 Pumping Station Road, Petal, MS 304685 USA.

Tucker's Pottery Supplies Inc.
15 West Pearce Street, Richmond Hill, Ontario, Canada
L4B 1H6.
Tel: (905) 889 7705 Fax: (905) 889 7707
North America Toll Free (Free phone): 800 304 6185
E-mail: tuckers@passport.ca
Web site: http://www.tuckerspottery.com

Books mentioned in the Dictionary

AUTHOR and CODE LETTERS (code letters given where there is more than one book by the same author)

Aerni Aerni, R. *Studio Potter Network* — video reviews (Box 70, Goffstown, NH 03045, USA. Tel. 603-774-3582, Fax 603-774-6313)

Alfred Alfred, R. *Refractories in the Electrical Industries*. Electricity Council,

Berendsen Berendsen, A. *Tiles, a general history*. Faber & Faber, London, 1967.

Billington Billington, D. *The Technique of Pottery*. London, Batsford, 1962.

Brickell Brickell, B. *A New Zealand Potter's Dictionary*. Reed Methuen, 1985.

Byers Byers, I. *Raku*. Batsford, London, 1990.

Caiger-Smith LP Caiger-Smith, A. *Lustre Pottery*. Faber & Faber, London and Boston, 1985.

Caiger-Smith TG Caiger-Smith, A. *Tinglaze Pottery*. Faber & Faber, London, 1973.

Carlton-Ball Carlton Ball. *Making Pottery without a Wheel*. Van Nostrand Reinhold, New York and London, 1965.

Cardew Cardew, M. *Pioneer Pottery*. Longmans, Harlow, 1969.

CCC *Chamber Concise 20th Century Dictionary*.

Chandler Chandler, M. *Ceramics in the Modern World*. Aldus, London, 1968.

Clark PPC Clark, K. *Practical Pottery and Ceramics*. Studio Vista, London, 1964.

Clark PM Clark, K. *The Potter's Manual*. Macdonald, London, 1983.

CM (Periodical) *Ceramics Monthly*. Columbus, Ohio, U.S.A.

Colbeck Colbeck, J. *Pottery, the Technique of Throwing*. Batsford, London, 1969.

Colson Colson, F. *Kiln Building with Space-Age Materials*. Von Nostrand Reinhold, 1975.

Cooper Cooper, E & Lewenstein, E (Eds.) *Clay and Glazes*. Ceramic Review Books, Craftsmen Potters Association of Great Britain, 1988.

CR (Periodical) *Ceramic Review*. Craft Potters Association of Great Britain, London.

Davis Davis, H. *The Potter's Alternative*. Methuen. (Australia). 1987; Chilton (U.S.A.), 1990.

Dodd Dodd, A.E. *Dictionary of Ceramics*. Newnes-Butterworth, 1964.

Dodd/Murfin Dodd, A.E. & Murfin, D. *Dictionary of Ceramics. 3rd Ed*. The Institute of Materials. 1993.

Flight Flight, G. *Ceramics Manual*. Collins, London, 1990.

Fournier CC Fournier, R. *Ceramic Creations*. Sterling, New York, 1972.

Fournier DPF Fournier, R. *Illustrated Dictionary of Pottery Form*. Van Nostrand Reinhold, New York, 1981.

Fournier DPD Fournier, R. *Illustrated Dictionary of Pottery Decoration*. Prentice Hall Press, New York, 1986.

Fournier EKP Fournier, R. *Electric Kiln Construction for Potters*. Van Nostrand Reinhold, New York, 1976.

Fournier PT (Ed). Fournier, R. *Potters Tips*. Ceramic Review, Craft Potters Association of Great Britain, 1990.

Fraser Fraser, H. *Glazes for the Craft Potter*. Pitman/Watson-Guptill, London/New York, 1973.

Green Green, D. *Experimenting with Pottery*. Faber & Faber, London, 1971.

Hamer C Hamer, F & J. *Clays*. Pitman/Watson-Guptill, London/New York, 1977.

Hamer PDMT Hamer, F & J. *Potter's Dictionary of Materials and Techniques*. 1st, 2nd, & 3rd, Editions. A & C, Black/Watson-Guptill, London and New York, 4th Edition A & C Black, London University of Pennsylvania Press, Philadelphi 1997.

Holderness Holderness, A. *Inorganic and Physical Chemistry*. Heinemann Educational, London, 1963.

Leach Leach, B. *A Potter's Book*. Faber & Faber, London, 1945.

NZP (Periodical) *New Zealand Potter*, Box 147, Albany, New Zealand.

Parks Parks, D. *A Potter's Guide to Raw Glazing and Oil Firing*. Pitman, London, 1980.

Parmalee Parmalee, C. *Ceramic Glazes,* 2nd (revised) edition. Industrial Publications Inc., Chicago, 1951.

Pogue Pogue, D. *Macs for Dummies*. IDG Books. 1996.

PQ (Periodical) *Pottery Quarterly*. Tring, Hertfordshire.

Rhodes SP Rhodes, D. *Stoneware and Porcelain*. Pitman, London, 1960.

Rhodes CGP Rhodes, D. *Clay and Glazes for the Potter*. Pitman, London, 1969; second edition, Chilton (U.S.A.), 1973.

Rhodes K Rhodes, D. *Kilns: Construction and Operation*. Pitman, London, 1969; second edition, Chilton (U.S.A.), 1981.

Riegger Riegger, H. *Raku Art and Technique*. Studio Vista, London, 1970.

Sanders Sanders, H. *World of Japanese Ceramics*. Kodansha International Ltd, Tokyo/Palo Alto, California, 1969.

Shaw Shaw, K. *Science for Craft potters and Enamellers*. David & Charles, Newton Abbot, 1972.

Scott Scott, P. *Ceramics and Print*. A & C Black, London. 1994.

SOED *Shorter Oxford English Dictionary*. Clarendon Press. Oxford, 1977.

Sutherland Sutherland, R. *Glazes from Natural Sources*. Batsford, 1987.

T (Periodical), *Tactile*. Canada.

Thompson Thompson, G. L. *Rubber Stamps and How to Make Them*. Cannongate Publishing Ltd., 1982.

Tudball Tudball, R. *Soda Glazing*. A & C Black, London/University of Pennsylvania Press, Philadelphia, 1995.

Uvarov Uvarov, E. (Ed). *Dictionary of Science*. Penguin, 1969.

Wardell Wardell, S. *Slipcasting*. A &C Black. 1998.

Webb Webb. *Cobalt, Nickel and Selenium*. Mond Nickel Company.

Wikey Wikey, M. *Calibrating and Calculating the Electric Kiln*. Marshall Craft, California, 1974.

Worrall Worrall, W. *Clays: their Nature, Origin and Natural Growth*. Applied Science Publishers, London, 1986.

Wyman Wyman, C. *Porcelain*. B. T. Batsford Ltd., London. 1994.

Yates/Fournier Yates-Owen, E. & Fournier, R. *British Studio Potters' Marks*. A & C Black, London. 1999.